D0578340

Concise Dictionary of British Literary Biography
Volume Seven

Writers After World War II, 1945-1960

Concise Dictionary of British Literary Biography
Volume Seven

Writers After World War II, 1945-1960

A Bruccoli Clark Layman Book
Gale Research Inc.
Detroit, London

Printed in the United States of America

Published simultaneously in the United Kingdom
by Gale Research International Limited
(An affiliated company of Gale Research Inc.)

The paper used in this publication meets the minimum requirements
of American National Standard for Information Sciences—Permanence
Paper for Printed Library Materials, ANSI Z39.48-1984. ∞™

Contents of Volume 7

Authors Included in This Series

Volume 1
Writers of the Middle Ages and Renaissance
Before 1660

Francis Bacon

Francis Beaumont & John Fletcher

Beowulf

Thomas Campion

Geoffrey Chaucer

Thomas Dekker

John Donne

John Ford

George Herbert

Ben Jonson

Sir Thomas Malory

Christopher Marlowe

Sir Walter Ralegh

William Shakespeare

Sir Philip Sidney

Edmund Spenser

Izaak Walton

John Webster

Volume 2
Writers of the Restoration and Eighteenth Century,
1660-1789

Joseph Addison

James Boswell

John Bunyan

William Congreve

Daniel Defoe

John Dryden

Henry Fielding

Oliver Goldsmith

Thomas Gray

Samuel Johnson

Andrew Marvell

John Milton

Samuel Pepys

Alexander Pope

Samuel Richardson

Richard Brinsley Sheridan

Tobias Smollett

Richard Steele

Laurence Sterne

Jonathan Swift

William Wycherley

Volume 3
Writers of the Romantic Period, 1789-1832

Volume 4
Victorian Writers, 1832-1890

Volume 5
Late Victorian and Edwardian Writers, 1890-1914

Volume 6
Modern Writers, 1914-1945

Volume 8
Contemporary Writers, 1960-Present

Plan of the Work

The eight-volume *Concise Dictionary of British Literary Biography* was developed in response to requests from school and college teachers and librarians, and from small- to medium-sized public libraries, for a compilation of entries from the standard *Dictionary of Literary Biography* chosen to meet their needs and their budgets. The *DLB*, which comprises more than one hundred volumes as of the end of 1991, is moving steadily toward its goal of providing a history of literature in all languages developed through the biographies of writers. Basic as the *DLB* is, many librarians have expressed the need for a less comprehensive reference work which in other respects retains the merits of the *DLB*. The *Concise DBLB* provides this resource.

The *Concise* series was planned by an eight-member advisory board, consisting primarily of secondary-school educators, who developed a method of organization and presentation for selected *DLB* entries suitable for high-school and beginning college students. Their preliminary plan was circulated to some five thousand school librarians and English teachers, who were asked to respond to the organization of the series. Those responses were incorporated into the plan described here.

Uses for the Concise DBLB

Students are the primary audience for the *Concise DBLB*. The stated purpose of the standard *DLB* is to make our literary heritage more accessible. *Concise DBLB* has the same goal and seeks a wider audience. What the author wrote; what the facts of his or her life are; a description of his or her literary works; a discussion of the critical response to his or her works; and a bibliography of critical works to be consulted for further information: these are the elements of a *Concise DBLB* entry.

The first step in the planning process for this series, after identifying the audience, was to contemplate its uses. The advisory board acknowledged that the integrity of *Concise DBLB* as a reference book is crucial to its utility. The *Concise DBLB* adheres to the scholarly standards established by the parent series; the *Concise DBLB* is a ready-reference source of established value, providing reliable biographical and bibliographical information.

It is anticipated that this series will not be confined to uses within the library. Just as the *DLB* has been a tool for stimulating students' literary interests in the college classroom—for comparative studies of authors, for example, and, through its ample illustrations, as a means of invigorating literary study—the *Concise DBLB* is a primary resource for high-school and junior-college educators.

Organization

The advisory board further determined that entries from the standard *DLB* should be presented complete—without abridgment. The board's feeling was that the utility of the *DLB* format has been proven, and that only minimal changes should be made.

The advisory board further decided that the organization of the *Concise DBLB* should be chronological to emphasize the historical development of British literature. Each volume is devoted to a single historical period and includes the most significant literary figures from all genres who were active during that time.

The eight period volumes of the *Concise DBLB* are: *Writers of the Middle Ages and Renaissance Before 1660; Writers of the Restoration and Eighteenth Century, 1660-1789; Writers of the Romantic Period, 1789-1832; Victorian Writers, 1832-1890; Late Victorian and Edwardian Writers, 1890-1914; Modern Writers, 1914-1945; Writers After World War II, 1945-1960; Contemporary Writers, 1960-Present.*

Form of Entry

The form of entry in the *Concise DBLB* is substantially the same as in the standard series. Entries have been updated and, where necessary, corrected.

It is anticipated that users of this series will find it useful to consult the standard *DLB* for information about those writers omitted from the *Concise DBLB* whose significance to contemporary readers may have faded but whose contribution to our cultural heritage remains meaningful.

Comments about the series and suggestions for its improvement are earnestly invited.

A Note to Students

The purpose of the *Concise DBLB* is to enrich the study of British literature. Besides being inherently interesting, biographies of writers provide a basic understanding of the various ways writers react in their works to the circumstances of their lives, the events of their times, and the cultures that envelop them.

Concise DBLB entries start with the most important facts about writers: what they wrote. We strongly recommend that you also start there. The chronological listing of an author's works is an outline for the examination of his or her career achievements. The biography that follows sets the stage for the presentation of the works. Each of the author's important works and the most respected critical evaluations of them are discussed in *Concise DBLB*. If you require more information about the author or fuller critical studies of the author's works, the references section at the end of the entry will guide you.

Illustrations are an integral element of *Concise DBLB* entries. Photographs of the author are reminders that literature is the product of a writer's imagination; facsimiles of the author's working drafts are the best evidence available for understanding the act of composition—the author in the process of refining his or her work and acting as self-editor; dust jackets and advertisements demonstrate how literature comes to us through the marketplace, which sometimes serves to alter our perceptions of the works.

Literary study is a complex and immensely rewarding endeavor. Our goal is to provide you with the information you need to make that experience as rich as possible.

Acknowledgments

This book was produced by Bruccoli Clark Layman, Inc. Karen L. Rood is senior editor for the *Dictionary of Literary Biography* series. David Marshall James was the in-house editor.

Production coordinator is James W. Hipp. Projects manager is Charles D. Brower. Photography editors are Edward Scott and Timothy C. Lundy. Permissions editor is Jean W. Ross. Layout and graphics supervisor is Penney L. Haughton. Copyediting supervisor is Bill Adams. Typesetting supervisor is Kathleen M. Flanagan. Systems manager is George F. Dodge. The production staff includes Rowena Betts, Teresa Chaney, Miriam E. Clark, Patricia Coate, Gail Crouch, Margaret McGinty Cureton, Mary Scott Dye, Sarah A. Estes, Robert Fowler, Cynthia Hallman, Ellen McCracken, Kathy Lawler Merlette, John Myrick, Pamela D. Norton, Cathy J. Reese, Laurrè Sinckler-Reeder, Maxine K. Smalls, Teri C. Sperry, and Betsy L. Weinberg.

Walter W. Ross and Henry Cunningham did library research. They were assisted by the following librarians at the Thomas Cooper Library of the University of South Carolina: Jens Holley and the interlibrary-loan staff; reference librarians Gwen Baxter, Daniel Boice, Faye Chadwell, Jo Cottingham, Cathy Eckman, Rhonda Felder, Gary Geer, Jackie Kinder, Laurie Preston, Jean Rhyne, Carol Tobin, Virginia Weathers, and Connie Widney; circulation-department head Thomas Marcil; and acquisitions-searching supervisor David Haggard.

Concise Dictionary of British Literary Biography
Volume Seven

Writers After World War II, 1945-1960

Concise Dictionary of
British Literary Biography

Kingsley Amis

(16 April 1922 -   )

This entry was written by Arthur Waldhorn (City College of New York) for
DLB 15: British Novelists, 1930-1959: Part One.

See also the Amis entries in DLB 27: Poets of Great
Britain and Ireland, 1945-1960 *and* DLB 100:
Modern British Essayists: Second Series.

BOOKS: *Bright November: Poems* (London: For-
    tune Press, 1947);
A Frame of Mind: Eighteen Poems (Reading, U.K.:
    School of Art, University of Reading, 1953);
Lucky Jim: A Novel (London: Gollancz, 1954; Gar-
    den City, N.Y.: Doubleday, 1954);
Kingsley Amis: Poems (Oxford: Fantasy Press,
    1954);
That Uncertain Feeling: A Novel (London: Gol-
    lancz, 1955; New York: Harcourt, Brace,
    1956);
A Case of Samples: Poems 1946-1956 (London:
    Gollancz, 1956; New York: Harcourt, Brace,
    1957);
Socialism and the Intellectuals (London: Fabian Soci-
    ety, 1957);
I Like It Here: A Novel (London: Gollancz, 1958;
    New York: Harcourt, Brace, 1958);
Take a Girl Like You (London: Gollancz, 1960;
    New York: Harcourt, Brace & World, 1961);
New Maps of Hell: A Survey of Science Fiction (New
    York: Harcourt, Brace & World, 1960; Lon-
    don: Gollancz, 1961);
The Evans Country (Oxford: Fantasy Press, 1962);
My Enemy's Enemy (London: Gollancz, 1962; New
    York: Harcourt, Brace & World, 1963);
One Fat Englishman: A Novel (London: Gollancz,

Kingsley Amis, 1970

1963; New York: Harcourt, Brace & World,
1964);

3

The Egyptologists: A Novel, by Amis and Robert Conquest (London: Cape, 1965; New York: Random House, 1966);

The James Bond Dossier (London: Cape, 1965; New York: New American Library, 1965);

The Book of Bond; Or Every Man His Own 007, as Lt.-Col. William ("Bill") Tanner (London: Cape, 1965; New York: Viking, 1965);

The Anti-Death League: A Novel (London: Gollancz, 1966; New York: Harcourt, Brace & World, 1966);

A Look Round the Estate: Poems 1957-1967 (London: Cape, 1967; New York: Harcourt, Brace & World, 1968);

Colonel Sun: A James Bond Adventure, as Robert Markham (London: Cape, 1968; New York: Harper & Row, 1968);

Lucky Jim's Politics (London: Conservative Political Centre, 1968);

I Want It Now (London: Cape, 1968; New York: Harcourt, Brace & World, 1969);

The Green Man (London: Cape, 1969; New York: Harcourt, Brace & World, 1970);

What Became of Jane Austen? and Other Questions (London: Cape, 1970; New York: Harcourt Brace Jovanovich, 1971);

Girl, 20 (London: Cape, 1971; New York: Harcourt Brace Jovanovich, 1972);

Dear Illusion (London: Covent Garden Press, 1972);

On Drink (London: Cape, 1972; New York: Harcourt Brace Jovanovich, 1973);

The Riverside Villas Murder (London: Cape, 1973; New York: Harcourt Brace Jovanovich, 1973);

Ending Up (London: Cape, 1974; New York: Harcourt Brace Jovanovich, 1974);

Rudyard Kipling and His World (London: Thames & Hudson, 1975; New York: Scribners, 1975);

The Alteration (London: Cape, 1976; New York: Viking, 1977);

Jake's Thing (London: Hutchinson, 1978; New York: Viking, 1979);

The Darkwater Hall Mystery (Edinburgh: Tragara Press, 1978);

Collected Poems 1944-1979 (London: Hutchinson, 1979; New York: Viking, 1980);

An Arts Policy? (London: Centre for Policy Studies, 1979);

Collected Short Stories (London: Hutchinson, 1980);

Russian Hide-and-Seek: A Melodrama (London: Hutchinson, 1980);

Every Day Drinking (London: Hutchinson, 1983);

Stanley and the Women (London: Hutchinson, 1984; New York: Summit, 1985);

How's Your Glass? (London: Weidenfeld & Nicolson, 1984);

The Old Devils (London: Hutchinson, 1986; New York: Summit, 1987);

Difficulties with Girls (London: Hutchinson, 1988; New York: Summit, 1988);

The Folks That Live on the Hill (London: Hutchinson, 1990; New York: Summit, 1990);

Memoirs (London: Hutchinson, 1991; New York: Summit, 1991).

Collections: *A Kingsley Amis Omnibus* (London: Hutchinson, 1987);

The Amis Anthology, edited by Amis (London: Hutchinson, 1988);

The Amis Collection: Selected Nonfiction, 1954-1990, introduction by John McDermott (London: Hutchinson, 1990).

OTHER: *Oxford Poetry, 1949,* edited by Amis and James Michie (Oxford: Blackwell, 1949);

Oscar Wilde: Poems and Essays, second edition, edited by Amis (London: Collins Classics, 1956);

"You That Love England; or, Limey, Stay Home," in *New World Writing,* edited by Stewart Richardson and Corlies M. Smith (Philadelphia: Lippincott, 1960), pp. 135-145;

Samuel Butler, *Erewhon, or Over the Range,* edited by Amis (New York: Signet Classic, 1961);

Spectrum: A Science Fiction Anthology, volumes 1-5, edited by Amis and Robert Conquest (London: Gollancz, 1961-1966; New York: Harcourt, Brace, 1962-1967);

"Communication and the Victorian Poet," in *British Victorian Literature: Recent Revaluations,* edited by S. K. Kumar (New York: New York University Press, 1969), pp. 39-52;

"Pernicious Participation," in *The Black Papers on Education* (London: Davis & Poynter, 1971), pp. 170-173;

"A Short Educational Dictionary," in *The Black Papers on Education* (London: Davis & Poynter, 1971), pp. 215-223;

Selected Stories of G. K. Chesterton, edited by Amis (London: Faber, 1972);

Tennyson, Selected by Kingsley Amis, edited by Amis (Harmondsworth, U.K.: Penguin, 1973);

"I.L.E.A. Confidential," by Amis and Conquest, in *Black Paper 1975: The Fight for Education,* edited by C. B. Cox and Rhodes Boyson (London: Dent, 1975), pp. 60-61;

Arthur Hutchings, *Mozart: The Man, the Music*, introduction by Amis (London: Schirmer, 1976);

Harold's Years: Impressions from the "New Statesman" and the "Spectator," edited by Amis (London: Quartet, 1977);

The New Oxford Book of Light Verse, edited, with an introduction, by Amis (London: Oxford University Press, 1978); republished as *The New Oxford Book of English Light Verse* (New York: Oxford University Press, 1978);

The Faber Popular Reciter, edited by Amis (London: Faber & Faber, 1978);

"Getting It Wrong," in *The State of the Language*, edited by Leonard Michaels and Christopher Ricks (Berkeley: University of California Press, 1980), pp. 24-33;

The Golden Age of Science Fiction, edited by Amis (London: Hutchinson, 1981);

"Oxford and After," in *Larkin at Sixty*, edited by Anthony Thwaite (London: Faber, 1982), pp. 23-30.

SELECTED PERIODICAL PUBLICATIONS—
UNCOLLECTED: "At the Jazz Band Ball," *Spectator*, 197 (28 September 1956): 409-411;

"Anglo-Saxon Platitudes," *Spectator*, 198 (5 April 1957): 285;

"Good, Brave Causes?," *Listener*, 65 (22 June 1961): 1087, 1092;

"What's Left for Patriotism?," *Observer*, 20 January 1963, p. 21;

"More Will Mean Worse," *Times* (London), 2 January 1967, p. 11; reprinted in *PMLA*, 82 (June 1967): 3;

"Involvement: Writers Reply," *London Magazine*, new series 5 (August 1968): 7;

"Real and Made-up People," *Times Literary Supplement*, 27 July 1973, pp. 847-848;

"Why Poetry?," *Observer Colour Magazine*, 30 September 1973, p. 7;

"The Art of the Impossible," *Times Literary Supplement*, 5 June 1981, p. 627;

"How I Lived in a Very Big House and Found God," *Times Literary Supplement*, 20 November 1981, p. 1352.

More than thirty-five years after the turbulence attending the publication of his overwhelmingly popular first novel, *Lucky Jim* (1954), Kingsley Amis remains a controversial figure in English letters. Many find him an affable and entertaining novelist whose heroes are engagingly antic mimes. Behind the mild lunacy and benign irreverence, others discern in Amis's fiction a profound concern with serious moral problems. Fellow novelists such as Anthony Burgess, Anthony Powell, V. S. Pritchett, and C. P. Snow have praised him. He has been lauded by critics as the successor to the satiric genius of Evelyn Waugh; as a dissenting realist in the tradition of Daniel Defoe and Henry Fielding; as a diverting wit like P. G. Wodehouse or Peter DeVries; and even paradoxically labeled an "antiliberal, antigenteel, antimoralist . . . Left Conservative," like Norman Mailer.

Amis's antagonists demonstrate similar vigor, articulateness, and excess. Writing in the Christmas 1955 issue of the London *Sunday Times*, Somerset Maugham described Jim Dixon, the young academic hero of *Lucky Jim* (which had, ironically, just won the Somerset Maugham Award for fiction), and his ilk as "white collar proletariat" who "do not go to the university to acquire culture, but to get a job, and when they have got one, scamp it. . . . They are mean, malicious, envious. . . . Charity, kindliness, generosity are .qualities which they hold in contempt. They are scum." In 1970 Q. D. Leavis accused Amis of targeting as "the consistent objects of [his] animus" the "only bastions against barbarism: the university lecturer, the librarian, the grammar school master, the learned societies, the social worker. . . ." In 1978, twenty-four years and fifteen novels later, after *Lucky Jim* had been translated into nine languages and gained further popularity as a movie, Amis's novel *Jake's Thing* (1978) caused at least one critic to find himself "virtually retching at its sheer awfulness . . . cynicism . . . plaintive self-pity and puzzled misogyny."

More pertinent than the often immoderate zeal manifested in the controversy are its underlying causes. To some extent, they take root in Amis's lower-middle-class origins. As Amis says in "A Memoir of My Father," "Not only were my environment and upbringing insular almost to a fault . . . it was also fiercely non-crazy." An only child, Amis was born in London on 16 April 1922 and enjoyed a comfortable but bland relationship with his Baptist, Conservative, lower-middle-class parents, William Robert and Rosa Lucas Amis. Recalling his father, an office worker, as "the most English human being I have ever known," Amis adds that boredom rather than hostility was his chief response to his father's company.

School was more rewarding, first at Norbury College, where at the age of eleven he had his first story, "The Sacred Rhino of Uganda," published in the school magazine, and then at the City of London School, where he remained until 1941 as a scholarship student. Amis writes enthusiastically about his years at this excellent day school, recalling the broad range of social strata from which its students were drawn and its humane spirit of tolerance: "I have never in my life known a community where factions of any kind were less in evidence, where differences of class, upbringing, income group and religion counted for so little." Academic standards were high, and Amis, specializing first in classics, then in English, maintained a level that earned him a scholarship to St. John's College, Oxford.

Amis completed a year of reading English literature at St. John's before being commissioned as an officer in the Royal Signal Corps in 1942. During that first year at Oxford, he made friends with Philip Larkin, John Wain, and Elizabeth Jennings, all, like himself, middle-class, literary, and able students. Writing about those years in the preface to his novel *Jill* (1946), Larkin cites as Amis's shining distinction a "genius for imaginative mimicry" (a talent Amis says he inherited from his father). "He used it," Larkin writes, "as the quickest way of convincing you that something was horrible or boring or absurd." Whatever the topic (Amis was at that time intensely political and pro-Soviet, and edited the bulletin of the University Labour Club) Amis was usually, says Larkin, "the target of delighted laughter and violent abuse in the same evening and from the same people."

Amis served three years in the army (in France, Belgium, and West Germany), having been commissioned because, he says, "an Oxford man was likely to be enough of a 'gentleman' to do all right as an officer." Late in 1945, at the age of twenty-three, he returned to St. Johns where he earned a first-class degree in 1947 but failed to win a research degree when his thesis ("Poets and their Public, 1850-1900") was rejected. Within a year thereafter, Amis had written a novel, which remains unpublished, and a collection of poems, published as *Bright November* (1947); married Hilary A. Bardwell (in 1948); and taken a post as lecturer in English at the University College of Swansea in Wales.

During the next half-dozen years, Amis labored to clarify his roles as teacher, husband, father (two of his three children were born during this time), and writer. His traditionally structured, colloquial, and wittily antiromantic poems

began to appear in anthologies, and he occasionally read on Wain's distinguished BBC poetry program, "First Reading." A collection of his poems, *A Frame of Mind* (1953), helped to associate him in the public mind with Larkin, Wain, Jennings, and Robert Conquest as part of a concerted dissent from tradition known as "The Movement," a label whose validity each of them denied. But although Amis has continued to write and to edit collections of poetry—his *Collected Poems 1944-1979* was published in 1979, and he has edited *Tennyson* (1973) and *The New Oxford Book of English Light Verse* (1978)—his most significant work is his prose fiction. Also during these years, his first major work, *Lucky Jim*, was taking shape.

The germ of the novel was a brief encounter with faculty in the Senior Common Room at the university of Leicester, where Amis had gone to visit Larkin in 1946. "Christ," Amis recalls saying, "someone ought to do something about that lot." In 1951 he began "to do something," finished the manuscript a year later, and saw it published at the outset of 1954. The critical furor that greeted *Lucky Jim* was not an isolated phenomenon. Within a brief span during the mid 1950s, a cluster of works spread shock waves across the nondescript English cultural plain. Wain's *Hurry on Down* (1953), Iris Murdoch's *Under the Net* (1954), John Osborne's *Look Back in Anger* (1956), John Braine's *Room at the Top* (1958), and Alan Sillitoe's *Saturday Night and Sunday Morning* (1958), along with *Lucky Jim*, spurred critics to seek a convenient descriptive tag. "Angry Young Men" was the most popular, but none of those labeled willingly accepted the epithet.

What linked these writers, establishing a loose consortium, was less their anger (though all could pout and rage) than a shared class origin (lower or middle class, but not upper) and unsettled social and cultural values. They suffered the benefits of the post-World War II welfare state without grace or gratitude. Although the Labour party government made possible their attendance at Oxford or Cambridge, they resisted what they identified as an obligation to embrace—in the name of culture and progress—what Richard Hoggart called the "shiny barbarism" of the middle class.

Lucky Jim became their archetypal anti-hero. Jim Dixon's experience dramatizes the conflict between the lower-middle-class drive to invade a higher social stratum and the resultant guilt and self-contempt for abandoning one's own class. A lower-middle-class youth who yearns

by the author of 'Lucky Jim'

THAT UNCERTAIN FEELING

Kingsley Amis' new novel

Dust jacket for Amis's 1955 novel, about a Welsh librarian who resolves "to keep trying not to be immoral"

nihilistic, anti-intellectual egotists, others delighted in the novel, as much for its inspired comedy as for its social, moral, and cultural implications. *Lucky Jim* is a funny novel. When it was written Amis observed, "I had something serious to say. But I also thought the poor old reader had had a pretty thin time of it recently, with so many dead serious writers around, and that he could do with something funny." Sometimes a lout and a boor, Jim is always entertaining, his mimicry hilarious, his slapstick debacles uproarious. Amis's relaxed but precise vernacular prose, shrewdly located understatement, and devastating characterization uphold the comic spirit.

By the time laughter subsides and the reader must assess Jim, Amis has already endowed him with a cheerful, winning candor about his own limitations that inspires sympathy more than censure. For all his buffoonery, self-indulgence, and self-interest, Jim emerges fundamentally, if vaguely, decent, one of the "nice" rather than the "nasty" people between whom he is careful to discriminate. Contrasted with the fakes and powermongers who surround and threaten to destroy him, Jim deserves to survive. Still enterprising and opportunistic, he has rejected the role of toady. If he is scarcely a model for morally superior humanity, at least he is assuredly not inferior to the "nasty" creatures about him.

Few of Jim's fictional successors are as "nice" as he. John Lewis, the young Welsh librarian who narrates *That Uncertain Feeling* (1955), also faces the social and sexual temptations of provincial life. He yields (to an upper-class woman whose husband aids his career); despises himself (for betraying his wife and his own value system); and seeks redemption (by rejecting two further advances, one sexual, the other vocational). Confronted with the conflict between his desire to succeed and his desire to be moral, Lewis resolves "to keep trying not to be immoral, and then to keep trying might turn into a habit."

That Uncertain Feeling is another funny book, but the delights of its comedy are dulled by grotesque and implausible scenes and, above all, by the fundamental unpleasantness of its lecherous, vulgar, sometimes cruel protagonist. Amis's sharp, unsympathetic portrait of Lewis might be said to hone the cutting edge of satire if only one could rest assured that Amis views him askance. Instead, Amis sentimentally invites his reader to shrug off Lewis's flaws and to toler-

for the economic security academic tenure affords, Jim earns a degree in an area he neither likes nor understands. By luck, he gets a job as a junior lecturer in history at a provincial university. But it is ill luck, for not only does he detest the medieval history he teaches but he despises the cultural pretensions of his colleagues with whom he must curry favor, such as the Welches: the pompous senior professor, his wife, and their "artistic" sons. "One theme of *Lucky Jim* was getting good things wrong," Amis explained in an interview. "Culture's good, but not the way the Welches did it. Education is good . . . but it is self-defeating if it isn't done properly." He fails as an academic, but, with another dollop of luck (better this time), he gets a superior job outside the academy and, as a kind of added bonus (or revenge), wins from Bertrand Welch a young woman of superior social class.

While some readers, including Maugham, condemned the breed of Lucky Jims as whining,

ate him sympathetically for at least one more go-round.

I Like It Here (1958), one of Amis's weakest novels, was, the author confessed in a 1974 interview, "written in too much haste." The setting is Portugal, where Amis had gone in 1955 on the money from his Somerset Maugham Award. Its plot is ambiguous and clumsy, its characterizations superficial. The hero's dilemma is much the same as in the previous novels. Garnet Bowen is a journalist assured a large fee if he can prove or disprove the authenticity of a manuscript ascribed to an author who may no longer be alive. As Amis puts it for Bowen: "To decide whether, and if so how far, self-interest conflicted with decency meant using his conscience as a precision instrument." But Amis attends only casually to the comic possibilities latent in the moral issue, squandering laughter in a rather crude philistine assault on travel abroad.

In the same year as the publication of *I Like It Here*, however, Amis made a more extensive journey. On leave from Swansea for a year, he arrived in the United States as a visiting fellow in creative writing at Princeton University. At Princeton he delivered the Christian Gauss Seminars in Criticism, later published as *New Maps of Hell: A Survey of Science Fiction* (1960). During the next five years, pursuing an interest in science fiction developed as a boy, Amis, aided by Robert Conquest, edited *Spectrum*, a series of anthologies of science fiction. Science fiction is but one among several forms of popular culture with which Amis has become identified. In 1968, for example, he wrote (as Robert Markham) *Colonel Sun*, a mildly engaging continuation of the James Bond saga. He has reviewed films for *Esquire*, jazz for the *Observer*, and discussed wines and liquors for London's *Penthouse* magazine (a complete guide, *On Drink*, was published in 1972).

All of these interests are related to Amis's fiction. His fundamentally conservative sense of experience is reflected in the populist anti-intellectualism and moral consciousness that infuse most of his fictional heroes. They disdain cultural humbug and settle willingly for good drink, pretty girls, and crisp jazz (pre-World War II rhythms only). Their morality is similarly demotic. In *The James Bond Dossier* (1965), Amis's defense of the famous secret agent might readily apply to most of his early heroes. Readers ought not complain, Amis argues, about Ian Fleming's lack of profundity or that Bond wins out "only by virtue of being lucky and brave and—com-

Dust jacket for Amis's 1958 novel, which was, he said, *"written in too much haste"*

paratively—righteous." Amis, too, has apparently never required of himself or of his characters more precise coordinates for conscience.

Jenny Bunn is a case in point. A decorative but decorous twenty-year-old working-class schoolmistress, Jenny occupies the moral center of *Take a Girl Like You* (1960). One of Amis's favorite characters, Jenny has reminded critics of Henry Fielding's *Amelia* and Samuel Richardson's *Clarissa* in her stubborn defense of her chastity. Her chief assailant is the charming but amoral Patrick Standish, a university classics instructor whose tactical cunning as a seducer is usually matchless. With Jenny, however, his campaign reaches a sordid climax—he takes her while she is drunk, defenseless, and almost unconscious.

Humorous and entertaining, the conflict between the lovers is also a serious exploration of shifts in the moral landscape of the new generation. Amis has said that Jenny is a better person than Standish, but that she suffers from an inherited "moral imperative . . . without being temperamentally on the side of it." Nevertheless, Jenny's "old Bible-class ideas" compel admiration. To what extent her winning Patrick at last represents a triumph is arguable. Asked during an interview whether Patrick would change, Amis replied, "He'll marry her and bugger off."

Compared with Roger Micheldene, the over-stuffed satyr of *One Fat Englishman* (1963), Patrick Standish seems gentle and meek. For the first time, Amis's protagonist is incontestably and unabatedly repulsive: "Of the seven deadly sins, Roger considered himself qualified in gluttony, sloth, and lust but distinguished in anger." Unlike those earlier characters, who are socially insecure and culturally ambivalent, Micheldene is an assured, Oxford-accented snob with refined tastes in food, cigars, and snuffboxes, and limitless distastes—for Jews, Blacks, Americans, Protestants, parents, and even God (a Catholic, Micheldene frequently prays but always to rebuke God).

Also for the first time, Amis's setting is the United States, more particularly, the campus of Budweiser College in Pennsylvania, which Micheldene is visiting briefly. Claiming to be on a quest for usable manuscripts for his publishing firm, and planning to give an occasional lecture, in fact, he hopes to renew his affair with an ex-mistress, wife of a visiting lecturer at Budweiser. The stage is set for a heavily larded anti-American romp.

Instead, Micheldene is inexorably diminished and finally demolished. An unsuccessful pass at a "Yank college girl" gains him an unamorous bite deep into his shoulder. A gifted undergraduate novelist, a Jew whom Micheldene despises and whose novel he rejects, steals his lecture notes and his mistress. Disaster hounds Micheldene to the end, his voyage home doomed when he is claimed by an Anglophilic American bore as an ideal shipboard companion. As the ship eases from the pier, Micheldene begins to cry, suddenly aware that he really loved his mistress. A moment later, dry-eyed and contained, he contemplates—without, however, much enthusiasm—possible shipboard conquests: "Better a bastard than a bloody fool. . . ."

During an interview in 1974, Amis admitted that "Roger is a bastard . . . and he understands it and yet he can't be different. . . . So yes, I sympathize with him . . . without condoning anything he does." Not all readers will accede to Amis's plea for pity for Micheldene, but many more are likely to agree that *One Fat Englishman* is among Amis's funniest and most effectively crafted novels, and to agree as well that its comedy is serious and undertakes, as a reviewer for the *Times Literary Supplement* writes, to locate "the roots of human misery."

Some of the characters in *One Fat Englishman* may have been partially based on some of the people Amis knew at Princeton in 1958; certainly, Amis has remarked, his colleagues there fretfully and successfully decoded identities. While still at work on the novel, Amis left Swansea in 1961 to become a fellow at Peterhouse College, Cambridge, where he taught for the next two years. Except for a visiting professorship at Vanderbilt University in 1967-1968, his position at Peterhouse was his last teaching post. In his essay "No More Parades" and in various interviews, Amis states his dislike for the narrow, boring formality of social life at Cambridge, the inaccessibility of its tutors, and the pervasive lowering of its academic standards. He determined to abandon teaching, however, because of his devotion to it. The competing demands upon time and energy made by classroom and writing had become intolerable. Since Amis acknowledges becoming uneasy when away from his typewriter for more than two or three days, he had, he says, little choice.

Despite his freedom from the lecture hall, Amis produced little of significance for the next few years. Apart from *My Enemy's Enemy* (1962), a collection of short stories, an edited anthology of science fiction, and *The James Bond Dossier*, his only substantial work was *The Egyptologists* (1965), a novel written in collaboration with Robert Conquest, who provided the original draft, most of the characters, and much of the dialogue. Critical response was almost wholly negative. Amis credits himself with devising the plot, a tedious, overwrought comedy about a pseudoscholarly society of Egyptologists whose members use their seminar rooms for amorous rendezvous, frequently with one another's wives.

In 1966, a year after his second marriage, to the novelist Elizabeth Jane Howard, Amis plunged into new fictional territory with the publication of *The Anti-Death League*. "It's my favorite of my own books," Amis says, "partly because of being more ambitious than anything before. . . ." An amalgam of psychological spy thriller, tender love story, and novel of ideas, *The Anti-Death League* is among the least comic of Amis's novels. A few madcap characters animate the proceedings: a lunatic psychoanalyst who denies the validity of all protestations of heterosexuality; a charming nymphomaniac who prefers to present herself as "polyandrous"; and a witty army captain who is unashamedly a drunk and a homosexual. But the pervasive mood of the novel is dour.

Reduced to its simplest terms, *The Anti-Death League* is about human and cosmic evil. The main embodiment of the many forces of human evil is Operation Apollo, a grotesque scientific, military, and political plot to inflict plague upon Chinese Communists. The unique malevolent force of cosmic evil is God Himself, and an army chaplain observes: "To believe at all deeply in the Christian God, in any sort of benevolent deity, is a disgrace to human decency and intelligence." Together, God and Operation Apollo, cancerous forces Amis metaphorically describes as the "lethal node," assure death.

Arrayed against the alliance of death and destruction are the "Human Beings Anonymous" who constitute the Anti-Death League. The young soldier-hero, James Churchill, is at first in passive accord with the justifications for Operation Apollo, but gradually, he rebels. Unfortunately, his revolt against the army and God yields no clear philosophical resolution. Operation Apollo is abandoned more by accident than by design. The nuclear destruction of an ancient priory damages the image but not the power of God, who retaliates by gratuitously destroying the chaplain's dog and threatening the death of Churchill's fiancée, Catherine, from breast cancer. To confuse matters further, Catherine insists, while awaiting the report of her biopsy, that "if bad things can go together, so can good things." Amis's ambiguity is inexplicable, unsettling, and exasperating. Other problems beset the novel. Multiple plot lines clog the narrative flow. The love affair seems a calculated and ineffectual imitation of the death-afflicted lovers in Ernest Hemingway's *A Farewell to Arms*. Churchill is too narrowly dimensioned to sustain the complexities of the existential burdens of theology and politics. Even though *The Anti-Death League* falters beneath its own weight, and is, as one reader has observed, "too timid to engage the problems it raises," its intensity and high seriousness merit attention.

One of its critics suggested that the novel represented "a valediction to the world of Lucky Jim." For a short time, at least, the observation seemed valid, particularly insofar as Amis's shifting sense of reality was reflected in the changes in his political stance. Amis began applying Lucky Jim's distinctions of "nice" and "nasty" to political standards rather than cultural, social, or moral ones. Amis leaves no doubt about who the nasties are. Despite a teenage flirtation with communism, Amis notes that by 1946 he was at least neutral. "Hungary," he adds, "turned me into a violent anti-Communist." Amis discerned no contradiction between advocating the use of chemical warfare against a Communist enemy in the novel and his insistence that Operation Apollo symbolized the incarnation of evil.

But even though Amis had avowedly abandoned the "Lefties," as he calls them, and embraced the "Righties" by the mid 1960s, he had, in fact, little distance to travel. His earliest post-Oxford expression about politics came in 1957 with the publication of *Socialism and the Intellectuals*, a pamphlet based upon a lecture he delivered to the Fabian Society. In it, he traces his progress from "callow Marxism" to unenthusiastic support of the Labour party. The great causes—struggles against fascism and mass unemployment—are no more, Amis wrote, and politics in the welfare state breeds apathy and boredom. To identify with the working class is a "mug's game . . . why, some of them are actually better off than we are ourselves. . . ." Yet worse are the political "romantics" who, like George Orwell and W. H. Auden, "become inflamed by interests and causes that are not one's own, that are outside oneself."

By 1976 Amis's conservatism seemed well established. In a short pictorial biography, *Rudyard Kipling and His World* (1975), Amis acknowledges Kipling's racism and imperialism. But Amis argues that these are not the cruel attributes of a state-centered totalitarian government; rather, they are inevitable and defensible adjuncts of a strong, paternalistic, leader-centered authoritarian government that bears the weight of the "white man's burden." Predictably, Amis also supported the U.S. role in Vietnam in the essay "Why Lucky Jim Turned Right," published shortly after *The Anti-Death League* and included in *Lucky Jim's Politics* (1968) and *What Became of Jane Austen?* (1970). There, as in *Socialism and the Intellectuals*, he mocks the hypocrisy of leftist orthodoxy and damns the failures of Labour (especially its extending university privilege to academically unqualified students). Above all, Amis deplores the failure of politics to improve the human condition. Romantic aspirations have become inoperable in a real world: "All you can reasonably hope for is keeping things going . . . an injustice righted here, an opportunity extended there. This is not a very romantic sounding programme. In fact, it is not a programme at all. I like that." Amis bestows "grudging toleration" upon the Conservative party because it is "the party of non-politics."

Ronnie Appleyard, the hero of *I Want It Now* (1968), is apolitical, but he is, at the outset of the novel, certainly among those who prefer self-interest to public interest. A hedonistic, power-hungry television personality, Ronnie is determined to invade and to settle in the domain of the very rich. The moral reverberations of that invasion sound throughout this slight novel, a meager echo of earlier work. The hero wins the madcap heiress just as she loses her inheritance. Undismayed, he accepts her and prides himself on his diminished venality: "I was a shit when I met you," he confesses. "I still am in a lot of ways. But because of you I've had to give up trying to be a dedicated, full-time shit. I couldn't make it, hadn't the strength of character. . . ."

The Green Man (1969), a more successful novel, is an absorbing ghost story at once funny and grim. As in *The Anti-Death League*, a spirit of evil informs the environment. The ghost of a murderous seventeenth-century parson is roused by the actions of Maurice Allington, the middle-aged proprietor of The Green Man, a pub where the parson once lived. The depraved ghost senses a kindred spirit in Allington, mistaking his drunkenness and lechery for satanism. Actually, Allington is not at all diabolic; rather, he is an older version of the familiar Amis hero. He is no less naughty and no less the victim of humiliation and vexation than his predecessors in Amis's fiction. He arranges an orgy, for example, only to find himself a nonparticipatory observer as his wife and mistress delight in one another (and at last go off together).

Yet a forbidding pall hovers over the fun. A spectral young man, who may be God, appears from nowhere to discuss death and divine power with Allington. Urbane but frightening, the otherworldly being confides that divinity lacks foreknowledge and must set harsh limits to humanity's exercise of free will. In time, he predicts, Allington will learn to appreciate the virtues of death. Alone as the novel ends—having rejected a satanic ghost and been rejected by wife and mistress—Allington contemplates death as the only way to free himself of body and mind and from his own "ruthlessness and sentimentality and ineffective, insincere, impracticable notions of behaving better. . . ." For all its apparent concern with profoundly religious matters, *The*

Green Man has little theological significance, merely reaffirming Amis's doubts about divine beneficence (ironic since Amis insists he is a "non-militant unbeliever"). *The Green Man* is fundamentally a lively, readable ghost story encumbered with ambiguities that enhance the tone rather than clarify the plot or amplify its meaning. But then, as one reviewer noted, "when you've got a good ghost going, you shouldn't mix it up with hocus-pocus."

Amis's first two novels of the 1970s are disappointingly trivial. The better of them, *Girl, 20* (1971), exploits Amis's growing distaste for the "trendy Lefty." His exemplar is Sir Roy Vandervane, a middle-aged symphonic conductor who tries to delay senescence by comporting himself like a sexual as well as a "cultural frontiersman." He adopts all the postures of the youthful pop culture—long hair, slurred speech, capricious dress, musical fads—and shares them with his ultimate and youngest mistress, Sylvia Meera, the mindless but sexually inventive creature of the novel's title. Neither reason nor morality deters Sir Roy from his passion. Though he admits his affair with Sylvia is indefensible, he adds, "You can't imagine how it makes me look forward to each day. . . ." Even as Amis savages the excesses of youth and age, he creates affection and respect for Sir Roy in his foolish and futile quest.

Amis retreats to the 1930s and suburban London for his first detective story, *The Riverside Villas Murder* (1973). Slow-moving, mannered, the plot lumbers uncertainly toward its denouement. The subplot is more satisfying, a nostalgic evocation of adolescence in which the fourteen-year-old son of the prime suspect resolves his relationship with his father and manages as well to achieve—with an older neighbor—his sexual initiation.

In an interview with Clive James on the occasion of the publication of *Ending Up* in 1974, Amis cited as the donnée for the novel his household at Hadley Common, near High Barnet, where "we've got a species of commune going, with relations and people living in . . . the idea occurred, what would this sort of arrangement be like if one had a pack of characters who were all about twenty years older." The five inhabitants of the ramshackle Tupennyhapenny Cottage are all beyond seventy; they are also miserable, loveless, and unlovable.

Familiarity with his characters seems gradually to have bred in Amis contempt where once

Kingsley Amis

he had compassion. Bernard Bastable deserves little sympathy. Malevolently witty and actively malevolent, Bastable is, Amis says, "the most unpleasant of my leading characters." A cashiered army officer, Bastable resourcefully humiliates everyone, most particularly his erstwhile adjutant and lover, Shorty. What diminishes the comic force of *Ending Up*—and several of its set scenes are mercilessly funny—is that the other characters make poor targets for satire. Shorty is a harmless drunk and a reasonably efficient gardener and handyman. Bastable's sister Adela, the selfless housekeeper for the curious ménage, is gentle, unattractive, and unloved. Her kittenish friend, the widowed Marigold, grasps at frayed fabric from her past as her memory slips away. George, an ex-professor paralyzed by a stroke, must also endure the mortification of circumlocution necessitated by nominal aphasia (an inability to recall nouns).

Each of these pitiable creatures is the victim of physical frailty rather than social or moral foibles. Age is not a legitimate deterrent to satire. The folly of an aging grotesque is not exempt. Even the repugnant grotesquerie of dying may warrant laughter, however macabre or austere. But in the noblest satire, whether savage or gentle, some glimmer of affection for blighted humanity shines through the dark vision. Amis sends forth no such light. He wounds each of these already damaged creatures with detached savagery, displaying their agony in a grimly hilarious Christmas party scene and disposing of them altogether in a bizarre and grisly ending. In *Ending Up* the vision is black and misanthropic.

Nor is the view more pleasant in *The Alteration* (1976), Amis's first attempt at writing in the "alternate worlds" subgenre of science fiction. England in 1976 is much altered in Amis's novel, lacking airplanes and autos and belonging to a unified Christian world in which the Reformation has never occurred. A Yorkshireman is Pope, Jean-Paul Sartre is a Jesuit theologian, A. J. Ayer is a professor of dogmatic theology, and Heinrich Himmler and Lavrenti Beria are papal envoys.

A drastic alteration threatens Hubert Anvil, the ten-year-old hero. Anvil is a boy soprano of extraordinary talent whose fame reaches Rome, where a decision is made to castrate him in order to preserve his pure voice for church music. The machinations of the ensuing plot are clever but tortuous. The moral and psychological issues raised are staggering, among them the relationship between art and life, the conflict between religious and human values, and the limits to freedom of will. The resolution is ironic, bitter, and devastating, and the presence of evil (here the tyranny of the Church) is more marked than in *The Anti-Death League* or *The Green Man*. Amis the parodist is still present, and the novel has moments of good, if rather obvious, fun (the overdrawn clergymen and the built-in comic effects incidental to an alternate world). But *The Alteration* (for which Amis won the John W. Campbell Award) must be read as Amis's most serious fiction to date, as a novel in which, as one of its critics has written, "Tyranny and fate conspire, each in its own way, to thwart the impulse to live."

On a less lofty plane, Amis's novel *Jake's Thing* is also sobering beneath its comedy. In *The Alteration*, young Hubert's imminent castration precludes sexual experience. At sixty, Jake Richardson recognizes that his lifelong sexual vigor has suddenly flagged. Neither boy nor man enjoys a happy end, though Jake's may be less painful. An Oxford lecturer in early Mediterranean history, much like an older Lucky Jim, Jake lives lazily and well but no longer lecherously. The ability to perform is not Jake's problem; lack of desire is. No one arouses him, neither his third wife (young but overweight) nor the other women who occasionally drift in and out of his bed. Jake's quest for revitalization leads him into attempting modes of sexual therapy depressingly familiar in contemporary society. A Harley Street psychiatrist (half-Irish, half-Austrian, and wholly ignorant of such cultural phenomena as the *Titanic*, T. S. Eliot, James Bond, and the Taj Mahal) rejects Jake's denial of guilt and shame about sex and sets him to several therapeutic tasks. Among Jake's restorative chores are the reading of pornographic magazines while wired to an ingenious machine that computes his level of arousal; a regi-

men of nongenital caressing sessions with his wife; group-therapy workshops (once more shared with his wife); and an all-out weekend workshop intended "to release checks on emotion and to improve insight."

Nothing succeeds. Jake dismisses his therapist, saying, "What makes you think that what's deep down is more important than what's up top?" His wife leaves with her best friend's husband, leaving for Jake her best friend, whom he detests. When, finally, his family physician suggests a simple pharmaceutical cure—raising the level of his testosterone—Jake poises on the threshold of rejuvenation. He pauses for "a quick run-through of women in his mind," then tells the doctor, "No thanks." Unregenerately antifeminist, Jake opts for misogyny rather than virility and for an Olympian (or cynical) indifference rather than the travail of commitment to another human being.

Amis's three books on boozing, *On Drink* (1972), *Every Day Drinking* (1983), and *How's Your Glass?* (1984), are short, facetious, light in tone, and meant for a popular audience. They all grew out of Amis's fondness for wine and spirits—and out of the column on drink that he produced every month, beginning in 1972 and continuing through the 1970s, for *Penthouse*. Such a column is the stuff of which Jim Dixon's dreams were made—but it no doubt helped form the general impression in the 1970s that Amis was no longer a serious artist, or at least no longer one of central importance. Amis also wrote many jazz and movie reviews in the 1950s and 1960s.

If his opinions and his stature have changed over the decades, Amis is still highly readable. In recent years, he is becoming recognized as a persistent and persisting figure on the English literary scene: he was made an honorary fellow of St. John's College, Oxford, in 1976; in 1981 he was named a commander, Order of the British Empire (C.B.E.); in 1986 his novel *The Old Devils* was awarded the prestigious Booker Prize; and he was knighted in 1990.

Interviews:

W. J. Weatherby, "Mr. Sellers and Mr. Amis: A Conversation Reported by W. J. Weatherby," *Guardian Weekly*, 84 (4 May 1961): 12;

Pat Williams, "My Kind of Comedy," *Twentieth Century*, 1970 (July 1961): 46-50;

John Silverlight, "Profile: Kingsley Amis," *Observer*, 14 January 1962, p. 13; reprinted as "Kingsley Amis: The Writer, The Symbol,"

New York Herald Tribune Book Review, 21 January 1962, p. 6;

Harry Fieldhouse, "Penthouse Interview: Kingsley Amis," *Penthouse*, 2 (October 1970): 35-39, 42;

James Gindin, "Kingsley Amis," in *Contemporary Novelists*, edited by James Vinson (New York: St. Martin's Press, 1972), pp. 44-48;

Pauline Peters, "Two on an Island," *Sunday Times Magazine* (London), 3 February 1974, pp. 64-66;

Peter Firchow, "Kingsley Amis," in his *The Writer's Place: Interviews on the Literary Situation in Contemporary England* (Minneapolis: University of Minnesota Press, 1974), pp. 15-38;

Clive James, "Kingsley Amis," *New Review*, 1 (July 1974): 21-28;

Melvyn Bragg, "Kingsley Amis Looks Back," *Listener*, 20 February 1975, pp. 240-241;

Michael Barber, "The Art of Fiction—LIX: Kingsley Amis," *Paris Review*, 16 (Winter 1975): 39-72;

Dale Salwak, "An Interview with Kingsley Amis," *Contemporary Literature*, 16 (Winter 1975): 1-18;

Auberon Waugh, "Amis: A Singular Man," *Sunday Telegraph Magazine*, 17 September 1978, pp. 33-36;

Jean W. Ross, "Interview With Kingsley Amis," in *Contemporary Authors*, new revision series 8, edited by Ann Evory and Linda Metzger (Detroit: Gale, 1983), pp. 32-34.

Bibliographies:

Rubin Rabinovitz, "Kingsley Amis Bibliography," in his *The Reaction against Experiment in the English Novel, 1950-60* (New York & London: Columbia University Press, 1967), pp. 174-178;

Jack Benoit Cohn, *Kingsley Amis: A Checklist* (Kent, Ohio: Kent State University Press, 1976);

Dale Salwak, *Kingsley Amis: A Reference Guide* (Boston: G. K. Hall, 1978).

References:

Walter Allen, *Tradition and Dream: The English and American Novel from the Twenties to Our Time* (London: Phoenix House, 1964; New York: Dutton, 1964), pp. 278-282;

Kenneth Allsop, *The Angry Decade: A Survey of the Cultural Revolt of the Nineteen-fifties*, second edition (London: Owen, 1964), pp. 51-66;

Bernard Bergonzi, "Kingsley Amis," in his *The Situation of the Novel* (London: Macmillan, 1970), pp. 161-174;

Brigid Brophy, *Don't Ever Forget: Collected Views and Reviews* (New York: Holt, 1966), pp. 217-222;

Anthony Burgess, "A Sort of Rebel," in his *The Novel Now: A Student's Guide to Contemporary Fiction* (New York: Norton, 1967), pp. 141-144;

Philip Gardner, *Kingsley Amis* (Boston: Twayne, 1981);

James Gindin, *Postwar British Fiction: New Accents and Attitudes* (Los Angeles & Berkeley: University of California Press, 1962), pp. 34-50;

Philip Larkin, Introduction to his *Jill: A Novel*, second edition (London: Faber, 1964; New York: St. Martin's Press, 1964), pp. 11-19; reprinted in his *Required Writing: Miscellaneous Pieces 1955-1982* (London: Faber, 1983), pp. 17-26;

David Lodge, "The Modern, The Contemporary, and the Importance of Being Amis," *Critical Quarterly*, 5 (Winter 1963): 340-354; reprinted in his *Language of Fiction: Essays in Criticism and Verbal Analysis of the English Novel* (London: Routledge & Kegan Paul, 1966; New York: Columbia University Press, 1966), pp. 243-267;

Lodge, "The Novelist at the Crossroads," in his *The Novelist at the Crossroads and Other Essays on Fiction and Criticism* (New York: Cornell University Press, 1969), p. 20;

Somerset Maugham, "Books of the Year—I," *Sunday Times*, 25 December 1955, p. 4;

Neil McEwan, "Kingsley Amis," in his *The Survival of the Novel: British Fiction in the Later Twentieth Century* (London: Macmillan, 1981), pp. 78-97;

Blake Morrison, *The Movement: English Poetry and Fiction of the 1950s* (London: Oxford University Press, 1980);

William Van O'Connor, "Kingsley Amis: That Uncertain Feeling," in his *The New University Wits and the End of Modernism* (Carbondale: Southern Illinois University Press, 1963), pp. 75-102;

Rubin Rabinovitz, "Kingsley Amis," in his *The Reaction against Experiment in the English Novel, 1950-60* (New York & London: Columbia University Press, 1967), pp. 38-63.

Papers:

The Harry Ransom Humanities Research Center

at the University of Texas, Austin, possesses some of Amis's letters, working materials for many of his novels (notably the manuscript, typescript, and notes for *Lucky Jim*), and the typescript of *The James Bond Dossier*. Manuscripts of several early poems are in the Lockwood Memorial Library, State University of New York at Buffalo.

Samuel Beckett
(13 April 1906 - 22 December 1989)

This entry was updated by Deirdre Bair from her entries in DLB 13: British Dramatists Since World War II: Part One *and* DLB 15: British Novelists, 1930-1959: Part One.

See also the Beckett entry in DLB Yearbook: 1990.

BOOKS: *Whoroscope* (Paris: Hours Press, 1930);
Proust (London: Chatto & Windus, 1931; New York: Grove, 1957);
More Pricks Than Kicks (London: Chatto & Windus, 1934);
Echo's Bones and Other Precipitates (Paris: Europa Press, 1935);
Murphy (London: Routledge, 1938; New York: Grove, 1957); French translation by Beckett (Paris: Bordas, 1947);
Molloy (Paris: Editions de Minuit, 1951); English translation by Beckett and Patrick Bowles (Paris: Olympia Press, 1955; New York: Grove, 1955; London: Calder & Boyars, 1966);
Malone meurt (Paris: Editions de Minuit, 1951); published in English as *Malone Dies*, translation by Beckett (New York: Grove, 1956; London: Calder, 1958);
En attendant Godot (Paris: Editions de Minuit, 1952); published in English as *Waiting for Godot*, translation by Beckett (New York: Grove, 1954; London: Faber & Faber, 1956);
L'Innommable (Paris: Editions de Minuit, 1953); published in English as *The Unnamable*, translation by Beckett (New York: Grove, 1958; London: Calder & Boyars, 1975);
Watt (Paris: Olympia Press, 1953; New York: Grove, 1959; London: Calder, 1963); French translation by Beckett, Ludovic Janvier, and Agnes Janvier (Paris: Editions de Minuit, 1968);

Samuel Beckett (photograph by Zoë Dominic)

Nouvelles et Textes pour rien (Paris: Editions de Minuit, 1955); published in English as *Stories & Texts for Nothing*, translation by Beckett (New York: Grove, 1967);
Fin de partie, suivi de Acte sans paroles [I] (Paris: Editions de Minuit, 1957); published in English as *Endgame, Followed by Act Without Words* [I],

15

translation by Beckett (New York: Grove, 1958; London: Faber & Faber, 1958);

All That Fall (New York: Grove, 1957; London: Faber & Faber, 1957); published in French as *Tous ceux qui tombent*, translation by Beckett and Robert Pinget (Paris: Editions de Minuit, 1957);

From an Abandoned Work (London: Faber & Faber, 1958); published in French as *D'un ouvrage abandonné*, translation by Beckett and Ludovic Janvier (Paris: Editions de Minuit, 1967);

Waiting for Godot, All That Fall, Endgame, From An Abandoned Work, Krapp's Last Tape, and Embers (London: Faber & Faber, 1959);

La Dernière Bande, suivi de Cendres, French versions of *Krapp's Last Tape* and *Embers*, translation by Beckett and Pierre Leyris (Paris: Editions de Minuit, 1960);

Krapp's Last Tape and Other Dramatic Pieces (New York: Grove, 1960)—includes *Krapp's Last Tape, All That Fall, Embers, Act Without Words I*, and *Act Without Words II*;

Comment c'est (Paris: Editions de Minuit, 1961); published in English as *How It Is*, translation by Beckett (New York: Grove, 1964; London: Calder, 1964);

Happy Days (New York: Grove, 1961; London: Faber & Faber, 1962); published in French as *Oh les beaux jours*, translation by Beckett (Paris: Editions de Minuit, 1963);

Poems in English (London: Calder, 1961; New York: Grove, 1963);

Play and Two Short Pieces for Radio (London: Faber & Faber, 1964)—includes *Play, Words and Music*, and *Cascando*;

Imagination morte imaginez (Paris: Editions de Minuit, 1965); published in English as *Imagination Dead Imagine*, translation by Beckett (London: Calder & Boyars, 1965);

Assez (Paris: Editions de Minuit, 1966);

Bing (Paris: Editions de Minuit, 1966);

Comédie et actes divers, French translations by Beckett (Paris: Editions de Minuit, 1966)—includes *Comédie, Va et vient (Come and Go), Parole et Music (Words and Music), Dis Joe (Eh Joe), and Acte sans paroles II (Act Without Words II)*;

Eh Joe and Other Writings (London: Faber & Faber, 1967)—includes *Eh Joe, Act Without Words II*, and *Film*;

Come and Go (London: Calder & Boyars, 1967);

No's Knife: Collected Shorter Prose 1945-1966 (London: Calder & Boyars, 1967);

Poèmes (Paris: Editions de Minuit, 1968);

Cascando and Other Short Dramatic Pieces (New York: Grove, 1969)—includes *Cascando, Words and Music, Eh Joe, Play, Come and Go*, and *Film*;

Sans (Paris: Editions de Minuit, 1969); published in English as *Lessness*, translation by Beckett (London: Calder & Boyars, 1970);

Le Dépeupleur (Paris: Editions de Minuit, 1970); published in English as *The Lost Ones*, translation by Beckett (London: Calder & Boyars, 1972; New York: Grove, 1972);

Mercier et Camier (Paris: Editions de Minuit, 1970); published in English as *Mercier and Camier*, translation by Beckett (London: Calder & Boyars, 1974; New York: Grove, 1975);

Premier amour (Paris: Editions de Minuit, 1970); published in English as *First Love*, translation by Beckett (London: Calder & Boyars, 1973);

Breath and Other Shorts (London: Faber & Faber, 1972)—includes *Breath, Come and Go, Act Without Words I, Act Without Words II*, and *From an Abandoned Work*;

Film, suivi de Souffle, translation by Beckett (Paris: Editions de Minuit, 1972);

Not I (London: Faber & Faber, 1973);

First Love and Other Shorts (New York: Grove, 1974)—includes *First Love, From an Abandoned Work, Enough, Imagination Dead Imagine, Ping, Not I*, and *Breath*;

Oh les beaux jours, suivi de Pas moi, translation by Beckett (Paris: Editions de Minuit, 1975);

I Can't Go On, I'll Go On: A Selection from Samuel Beckett's Work, edited by Richard W. Seaver (New York: Grove, 1976);

That Time (London: Faber & Faber, 1976);

Fizzles (New York: Grove, 1976);

Foirade: Fizzles, bilingual edition, with French translations by Beckett (London & New York: Petersburg / Paris: Fequet & Baudier, 1976);

Footfalls (London: Faber & Faber, 1976);

Ends and Odds (New York: Grove, 1976)—includes *Not I, That Time, Footfalls, Ghost Trio, Theatre I, Theatre II, Radio I*, and *Radio II*;

Pour finir encore et autres foirades, translation by Beckett (Paris: Editions de Minuit, 1976);

Companie (Paris: Editions de Minuit, 1979); published in English as *Company*, translation by Beckett (New York: Grove, 1980);

Rockaby and Other Short Pieces (New York: Grove, 1981)—includes *Rockaby, Ohio Impromptu, All Strange Away*, and *A Piece of Monologue*;

Three Plays by Samuel Beckett: What Where, Catastrophe, Ohio Impromptu (New York: Grove, 1983);
Westward Ho (New York: Grove, 1983);
Stirrings Still (London: John Calder, 1988; New York: Blue Moon, 1988).
Collections: *The Collected Works of Samuel Beckett*, 19 volumes (New York: Grove, 1971);
Collected Poems 1930-1978 (London: John Calder, 1984);
Collected Shorter Prose (London: John Calder, 1984);
Collected Shorter Plays of Samuel Beckett (New York: Grove, 1984).

PLAY PRODUCTIONS: *Le Kid*, parody of Corneille's *Le Cid*, Dublin, French Group of the Modern Language Society of Trinity College, 1931;
En attendant Godot, Paris, Theatre de Babylone, 5 January 1953; produced in English as *Waiting for Godot*, London, Arts Theatre Club (transferred 12 September 1955 to Criterion Theatre), 3 August 1955; Miami, Coconut Grove Playhouse, 3 January 1956; New York, John Golden Theatre, 19 April 1956, 59 performances;
Fin de partie, produced with *Acte sans paroles I*, London, Royal Court Theatre, 3 April 1957; Paris, Studio des Champs Elysées, 26 April 1957; produced in English as *Endgame*, New York, Cherry Lane Theatre, 28 January 1958, 104; produced with *Krapp's Last Tape*, London, Royal Court Theatre, 28 October 1958;
Acte sans paroles I, produced with *Fin de partie*, London, Royal Court Theatre, 3 April 1957; Paris, Studio des Champs Elysées, 27 April 1957;
Krapp's Last Tape, produced with *Endgame*, London, Royal Court Theatre, 28 October 1958; produced in French as *La Dernière Bande*, translation by Beckett and Pierre Leyris, Paris, Théâtre Recamier, 22 March 1960; produced again as *Krapp's Last Tape*, New York, Provincetown Playhouse, 14 January 1960, 582;
Acte sans paroles II, London, Institute of Contemporary Arts, 25 January 1960;
Happy Days, New York, Cherry Lane Theatre, 17 September 1961, 29; London, Royal Court Theatre, 1 November 1962; produced in French as *Oh les beaux jours*, Paris, Odéon-Théâtre de France, 29 October 1963;

Spiel, translated into German by Elmar Tophoven, Ulm-Donau, Germany, Ulmer Theater, 14 June 1963; produced in English as *Play*, New York, Cherry Lane Theatre, 4 January 1964; London, Old Vic Theatre, 7 April 1964; produced in French as *Comédie*, Paris, Pavillon de Marsan, 14 June 1964;
Va et vient, Berlin, Schiller Theater, 14 January 1966; Paris, Odéon-Théâtre de France, 28 February 1966; produced in English as *Come and Go*, Dublin, Peacock Theatre, 28 February 1968;
Breath, Oxford, Oxford Playhouse, 8 March 1970;
Not I, New York, Lincoln Center, 7 December 1972; London, Royal Court Theatre, 16 January 1973; produced in French as *Pas Moi*, Paris, D'Orsay Petite Salle, 3 April 1975;
The Lost Ones, New York, Theatre for the New City, 7 April 1975;
That Time, London, Royal Court Theatre, 20 May 1976;
Footfalls, London, Royal Court Theatre, 20 May 1976;
A Piece of Monologue, New York, La Mama Experimental Theatre Club, 14 December 1979, 7;
Texts for Nothing, New York, Public Theatre, 24 February 1981;
Rockaby, Buffalo, State University of New York at Buffalo, 8 April 1981; Paris, Centre Georges Pompidou, 14 October 1981;
Ohio Impromptu, Columbus, Ohio State University, 7 May 1981, 2.

MOTION PICTURE: *Film*, screenplay by Beckett, New York Film Festival, 1965.

TELEVISION: *Eh Joe*, BBC, 1966; broadcast in French as *Dis Joe*, Official Radio Television Français, 1968.

RADIO: *All That Fall*, BBC Third Programme, 1957; broadcast in French as *Tous ceux qui tombent*, translation by Beckett and Robert Pinget, Official Radio Television Français, 1959;
From an Abandoned Work, BBC Third Programme, 1957;
Embers, BBC Third Programme, 1959; broadcast in French as *Cendres*, Official Radio Television Français, 1966;
Words and Music, BBC Third Programme, 1962;
Cascando, Official Radio Television Français, 1963; BBC Third Programme, 1964;

Lessness, BBC Third Programme, 1971;
Radio II, BBC Third Programme, 1976;
Ghost Trio, BBC, 1976.

Samuel Beckett, whose play *Waiting for Godot* has influenced several generations of contemporary playwrights throughout the world, was a dramatist who considered himself a much better novelist. He thought of his plays as diversions undertaken at times when work on his fiction brought him to a creative impasse, but since *Waiting for Godot* was first performed (as *En attendant Godot*) in Paris on 5 January 1953, the greater part of his literary career resulted in some form of writing for the theater.

An Irishman who lived in Paris since 1938, Beckett wrote in French and was a one-time follower of the other great Irish writer in exile, James Joyce. He has been lumped loosely at various times with groups ranging from the French *nouveau roman* to the existentialists, and his plays place him in the center of the theater of the absurd, one of the major movements in modern drama since the end of World War II. He has been labeled Proustian, Joycean, Sartrean, Jungian, and even a Christian writer, but while he does exhibit characteristics of each, it would be reductive to limit him to any single one. In his later years, both his drama and fiction took an intensely personal turn, and critics who had viewed Beckett as a disinterested theoretician, impersonal philosopher of negation, or abstract mathematician obsessed by permutation and combination began to recognize the extensive biographical underpinnings which are the foundation of his theoretical musings. Katharine Worth writes that "Beckett can only be surely placed as a man of many facets, the writer above all who has sensed the deep movements of the modern imagination and found spellbinding images to express them."

Samuel Barclay Beckett was born in the Stillorgan district of Dublin on Good Friday, 13 April 1906, a date to which he imparted significance in some of his dramatic writings and a date which had an almost mystical significance to him in his personal life. Both the Christian belief in Good Friday as the date of the death of Christ and the attendant theory that one of the two thieves who was to have been crucified with him was saved while the other was damned are ideas which Beckett used in various forms throughout his writings. Also, he sometimes used the date and place of his birth as a possible explanation of

his introspective personality. His parents were comfortably situated members of the Anglo-Irish professional class, descendants of Huguenots who had fled from France to Ireland in the late seventeenth century to avoid religious persecution. In Ireland, Beckett's ancestors found the freedom to practice their successful professions in the linen trade. William Frank Beckett, Jr., Samuel Beckett's father, was a robust man and jovial sportsman who had no affinity for intellectual endeavor and who left school at the age of fifteen to build a significant reputation and sizable fortune in the exacting profession of quantity surveying (the business of estimating from architects' drawings the amount of material necessary to construct a building). Beckett's mother was born Mary Jones Roe in Leixlip, county Kildare, and her father listed his profession as "gentleman," meaning that he lived off the income of his family's milling business and had no profession of his own. Mary Roe Beckett, called May, was strong-willed and independent, and, at a time when young women of good family were not expected to work, she trained as a nurse and worked in a Dublin hospital before her marriage. Of the two parents, she was the more rigid and demanding, and her role in Beckett's life has led to conflicting and mostly troubled representations of her in his writings.

The Beckett sons grew up in the architect-designed house commissioned by Bill Beckett and named by his wife Cooldrinagh, after her family home in Leixlip. Beckett followed his brother (Frank Edward, born 26 July 1902) to schools throughout his education: first to Miss Ida Elsner's Academy in Stillorgan, then to Earlsfort House School in Dublin, and in 1919, when he was thirteen, to the Portora Royal School in Enniskillen, County Fermanagh, in Northern Ireland. Both boys were excellent athletes, and by the end of his first term, Samuel Beckett had won a place on the varsity cricket team. It was the beginning of his lifelong interest in the sport, and he held the distinction of being the only Nobel Prize winner to be listed in *Wisden*, the cricketer's annual. He also boxed and swam and was one of the leaders of his class. Despite his apparent success at games and his popularity with classmates, Beckett had grown into an aloof young man, reserved in bearing and unwilling to take an easy pleasure in the activities of his school.

It was taken for granted that he would follow his brother to Trinity College, Dublin, and he entered in 1923, telling his tutor, Dr. Arthur

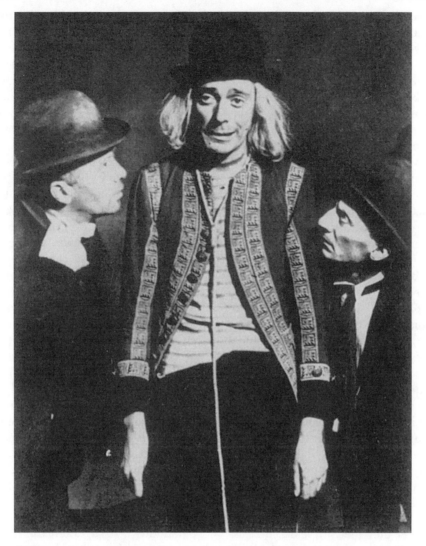

*Pierre Latour, Jean Martin, and Lucien Raimbourg in the Paris 1953 first production
of* En Attendant Godot (Waiting for Godot)

Aston Luce, that he wanted to study law and become a chartered accountant so that he could enter the family firm. His first two years were academically dismal, but he discovered modern languages in his third year and became the star pupil of Dr. Thomas B. Rudmose-Brown, Trinity's professor of French, an authority on Jean Racine and Pierre Corneille and one of the first to introduce contemporary French poetry to Ireland. Beckett's grades improved so dramatically that at the end of his third year he won the coveted Foundation Scholarship in Modern Languages, and he spent the summer of 1926, before his senior year at Trinity, in France.

Beckett received his B.A. degree from Trinity College on 8 December 1927, standing first in his class in modern languages. He received the large gold medal given for outstanding scholarship and an award of fifty pounds toward his expenses at the Ecole Normale Supérieure in Paris, where he had been named to the post of exchange *lecteur* for the years 1928-1930. Since Beckett's appointment did not begin until October 1928, he spent the first nine months of that year teaching in Campbell College, a secondary school in Belfast.

On his way to Paris, he traveled first to Germany to visit his father's sister, who had moved to Kassel with her husband. William and Frances (Cissie) Beckett Sinclair were artists and writers living with their five children a casual sort of bohemian life quite different from the elegant formality of Cooldrinagh. Beckett was quite taken with the Sinclair family, and, for the few remaining years that they lived in Kassel, he visited them frequently. He became fond of his cousin Peggy, and it is generally believed that she was the original for the green-eyed heroines who occur in his writing.

In Paris, Beckett made two friendships which were to have enormous importance in his life. The first was with the English *lecteur* whom he was to replace at Ecole Normale Supérieure, Thomas McGreevy, an Irishman who was also a graduate of Trinity College, but who, unlike Beckett, was a Catholic from a poor family in the west of Ireland. McGreevy—outgoing, witty, and brash—knew the other Irishmen in Paris, and he took Beckett to meet James Joyce.

The bond between Beckett and Joyce was a curious one, on Beckett's part forged at first because of great respect for Joyce's writing and then out of complex and still not completely understood psychological attitudes. Joyce became for Beckett both a surrogate father and a model of artistic integrity. Joyce's eyesight was very bad, and Beckett soon became the most eager and willing of all his young Irish helpers, tracking down obscure references, collecting arcane information, taking dictation when Joyce could not see to write, and even running errands for the Joyce family. Beckett marveled at Joyce's ability to write every day despite the trials of his personal life or the pain of his eyes, and later in his life Beckett would speak of the "moral effect" Joyce had on him, making him "realize artistic integrity."

Very soon after they met, Joyce asked Beckett to contribute an essay to the volume which became *Our Exagmination Round His Factification for Incamination of Work in Progress*, published by Sylvia Beach's Shakespeare and Company in 1929. Beckett's essay, "Dante...Bruno.Vico..Joyce," was his first published writing, one which shows his unbounded admiration for Joyce but which also demonstrates his ability to manipulate language, extract the essence of a writer's thought, and then use it to elucidate a critical theory.

By the start of his second year in Paris he had begun to explore philosophy, reading parts of Arthur Schopenhauer and all of René Descartes. He was expected to return to Trinity College with a thesis on the poet and novelist Pierre-Jean Jouve, but instead his interest in Descartes led him to the Belgian philosopher Arnold Geulincx. Geulincx's theory—that the thinking man must realize that the only area in which he can achieve total independence is his own mind, and therefore he should strive to control his own mental state rather than the exterior world—had a lasting effect upon Beckett's literary thinking. Geulincx's dictum, *Ubi nihil vales, ibi nihil velis* ("Where you are worth nothing, there you should want nothing"), became a central thesis in Beckett's novel *Murphy* (1938; French version, 1947) and has been expressed many times in his plays.

But Beckett's major interest at this time was poetry, possibly because of the influence of McGreevy and also because of the other, better-known poets he was meeting in Paris. Besides Richard Aldington, there were Ezra Pound (whom Beckett met only once and briefly), the Irish poets Brian Coffey, Denis Devlin, and George Reavey, and the American poet and translator Samuel Putnam, who was then editing *The European Caravan* (1931), an anthology of writings by French, Spanish, English, and Irish writers. Beckett prepared translations and reviews for several of the small literary magazines that proliferated in Paris at this time, but the culmination of these two years was his first separately published book, *Whoroscope* (1930), which he wrote in one night, 15 June, and which won the Hours Press competition sponsored by Aldington and Nancy Cunard, the owner of the press.

Ostensibly, the subject of entries in the competition was time, but time is present in Beckett's poem primarily in the title, a pun on the Greek word *horo* ("hour") that alludes to Descartes's superstitious refusal to tell the date of his birth so that no astrologer could use it to create his horoscope and thus predict the date of his death. It follows closely the life of Descartes written by Adrien Baillet and is more a prose monologue than a poem. It is strongly influenced by Joyce and the symbolist poets, and is filled with overtones of what John Fletcher identifies as Beckett's future themes, especially his preoccupation with the revolting.

Whoroscope led to Beckett's third published work, the essay *Proust* (1931), a study of *A la recherche du temps perdu* commissioned by London publisher Chatto and Windus for its Dolphin series probably because Aldington and McGreevy were friends of the editor, Charles Prentice, and had brought *Whoroscope* to his attention.

Beckett wrote the essay in the summer of 1930 in Paris. It shows his critical mind at its finest, and it also shows how much his writing was influenced by Proust's multilayered fiction. The essay is generally believed to be Beckett's first attempt to form a literary credo of his own. His literary thought is seen in its formative phase, when the ideas, such as habit and memory, that shape his mature writings were still some twenty years in his future.

Beckett was pleased to have the commission because he had not written the thesis on Jouve, and since he would soon return to Trinity College, it made his homecoming easier. As he had suspected two years earlier at Campbell College and had confirmed now that he was back, he was temperamentally unsuited to the profession of teaching. He disliked academic research, was ill at ease in the classroom, and was increasingly unhappy about his restrictive life in Dublin after the personal freedom he had enjoyed in Paris.

By November 1931 he had become seriously depressed and was unable to leave the bed in his darkened room. His parents consulted physicians, who decided that only a change of scene was needed, and so it was agreed that he should go to the Sinclairs in Kassel. He went there when the term ended in December and, shortly after his arrival, wired his resignation.

His depression persisted, but it was not as serious as it had been in Dublin. He stayed in Kassel for the first six months of 1932, trying to decide what to do. He was afraid to return to Paris because he had had a painful break with Joyce over his daughter, Lucia. She was then in the early stages of severe schizophrenia and had imagined herself in love with Beckett, who did not reciprocate. For real or imagined slights, Joyce refused to see Beckett, and Beckett's regard for Joyce was such that he felt he could not even try to live in the same city.

Beckett recovered enough to realize that he could not stay on in Kassel doing nothing. So he saved the small allowance that came to him from home each month until he had enough to make several exploratory trips to Paris, where he avoided Joyce. Beckett discovered that he was able to place the few stories, poems, reviews, and miscellaneous pieces he had written in the little magazines even though payment was nonexistent. He realized that he needed to earn money if he wanted to live in Paris and set to work to complete a collection of short stories to accompany the ones he had already written, thinking to offer them all to Chatto and Windus. He also thought he could supplement his writing with translation. By late May 1932 he was domiciled in a Paris hotel. He began to write what became the unpublished novel "Dream of Fair to Middling

Roger Blin in the first production of Fin de partie (Endgame)

Women," portions of which he used later in the collection of short stories *More Pricks Than Kicks* (1934). He finished the novel in a few weeks only to discover that it was too long for magazines, unsuited to serialization, of little interest to French publishers, and impossible to publish in English because it contained material that would be objectionable to the censors.

This brief stay in Paris came to an unforeseen close: the president of the Third Republic, Paul Doumer, was assassinated, and the French police were deporting all aliens who did not have valid papers. This included Beckett, who rushed to Edward Titus, publisher of the little magazine *This Quarter*, and offered to translate Arthur Rimbaud's *Le Bateau Ivre* for enough money to live in London while he hunted a publisher for the novel. Titus paid him enough money for passage to London but not enough to live there, so Beckett was forced to return to Dublin to face his family's disapproval. Thus began several years of unhappiness and misunderstanding while Beckett lived at home on a small allowance doled out by his parents, they unhappy because he would not find an occupation and he unable to write the commercially successful works he needed in order to leave.

Beckett was rewriting stories and trying to amass enough poetry for George Reavey (now in London where he had founded the Europa Press and begun acting as Beckett's informal literary agent) when his father died on 26 June 1933 from a second massive heart attack after an illness of one week. Six months later, following a second and even more severe mental breakdown, Beckett left Dublin for London. His mother had agreed to subsidize him for six months so that he could begin psychoanalysis and establish himself as a writer. Thus he began two years with Dr. W. R. Bion, later an authority on group psychology, but then practicing at the Tavistock Clinic.

Beckett had known for many years that he was not happy in the comfortable world of his parents or the achievement-oriented world of his Dublin peers. This was an era when many artists and writers, especially those he knew in Paris, were strongly influenced by Sigmund Freud and Carl Jung, and many of them had already been in analysis. Beckett had read Freud in a haphazard manner and was familiar with Jung's essay "Psychology and Poetry," which had been published in *transition* in 1930. Still, the idea of psychoanalysis for himself would probably not have entered his mind had it not been for the crippling instances of physical and mental debilitation he had suffered since his father's death.

Just as he was beginning psychoanalysis, the publication of several of his works made him think he could combine analysis with living and working in London. There were nineteen translations of prose and poetry for *Negro Anthology* (1934), edited by Nancy Cunard; an acrostic poem, "Home Olga," written for Joyce's birthday in 1932, appeared in the American magazine *Contempo* in February 1934; his collection of ten short stories, *More Pricks Than Kicks*, appeared in May 1934.

The stories in *More Pricks Than Kicks* received some critical attention but did not sell, and Beckett was forced by economic necessity to write reviews, criticism, and literary journalism. He was not successful at any of these, and since he had not been able to write fiction while in analysis, he decided to accept George Reavey's offer to publish a collection of poems. In order to subsidize the book, *Echo's Bones and Other Precipitates* (a requirement, as Reavey had no money for authors other than what they earned in royalties

once they had paid for the printing costs), Beckett was forced to return to Cooldrinagh, where he remained from August through September 1934. His mother was determined that his stay should be permanent, but he was just as determined to leave. In September he found a room in the World's End district of London, which became the setting for the novel *Murphy*. For the next three years Beckett found himself dabbling in poetry, writing an occasional book review, and trying to get on with *Murphy*, coping through false starts and hopeless stalls.

His analysis dragged on, and he chafed at the lack of positive results. If there was any one thing about it that could be considered positive, it was Bion's insistence that Beckett attend the third of a series of lectures given by Jung in October 1935 which have come to be known as the Tavistock Lectures. Jung's thesis was that the unity of consciousness is an illusion, and when the unknown number of complex or fragmentary personalities in each person is gradually channeled into a fascination with the unconscious, the increase of energy in that section of the mind grows so strong that the person "sinks into the unconscious altogether and becomes completely victimized by it. He is the victim of a new autonomous activity that does not start from his ego but starts from the dark sphere." This is an idea which has enormous resonance in Beckett's mature writings.

In the meantime, his mother's insistence that he return to live in the family home created a period of hostile uncertainty which was characterized by excessive peregrination. Beckett went back and forth between London and Dublin, each time returning to London in a state of rage, anxiety, or frustration at his inability to be what his mother wanted and his unwillingness to live in Dublin permanently. He was miserable in London, a city he described many years later as one he hated then. In November 1935 *Echo's Bones* was published. By December he was well along with *Murphy* and decided that the writing was progressing so smoothly that it did not matter where he lived, as he could finish it anywhere, and he went back to Dublin. Actually, his financial situation was so bleak that he had no other choice.

He abruptly ended the analysis, over Bion's concerned objections that it was incomplete. As his doctor predicted, Beckett's personal life in Dublin soon became intolerable. Very shortly, he had another breakdown of sorts, this time resulting in prolonged inactivity, physical dissolution and dishevelment, excessive drinking, and wandering around Dublin. He concluded that if he did not write his way out of Dublin, he would be there forever.

While *Murphy* was being refused in London by publisher after publisher, Beckett spent his time in Dublin reading, in his own word, "wildly." From Johann Wolfgang von Goethe to Franz Grillparzer to Giovanni Battista Guarini, he finally settled into a single-minded concentration upon the life and work of Samuel Johnson. He began to collect information about Johnson in the same manner as he had studied Descartes, filling page after page in a large three-ring notebook with miscellaneous facts and quotations. Quite possibly this exercise was a means to keep his mind off *Murphy*, which had recently been refused by the twenty-fifth publisher to see it, but also it represented a means to engage in a form of agreeable activity that counterbalanced his unpleasant circumstances.

During this time, Beckett began to be seen on the fringes of various dramatic groups in Dublin. He saw productions by the Dramiks, a local group which included playwright Denis Johnston and which performed German expressionist plays and, to a lesser extent, contemporary French drama. He went to performances by the Drama League, the real center of theatrical activity in Dublin, run by Mrs. William Butler Yeats and Lennox Robinson and with a company of actors who also performed at the Abbey Theatre and the Gate Theatre. He also mingled with the amateur Dun Laoghaire Theatre Group, which brought a high level of enthusiasm to performances of contemporary plays. Still, Beckett's involvement was peripheral: he was simply going about Dublin trying to find a group of young intellectuals which would be as congenial as his friends in Paris, and it just happened that the people he saw in Dublin were engaged in the theater. He was not a serious student of drama, nor was he eager to become actively involved in productions by any of these groups. In fact, his interest in the movies, first developed during his student days at Trinity College, was even more marked during this period, and he went more often to movies than to the theater.

Nevertheless, something convinced Beckett that he must turn all the material he had collected about Dr. Johnson into a play, and by early summer 1936 he was calling it his "Johnson Fantasy." He claimed to have the entire play outlined in his head and that he only needed to commit it to paper. His original idea was to write a long four-act play to be called "Human Wishes," after Johnson's poem "The Vanity of Human Wishes." He intended the play to concentrate on the mature Johnson's relationship with Hester Thrale and the obsessive, unspoken love Johnson felt for her. Each act was to be devoted to one of the four years between the death of her husband, Henry Thrale, and Mrs. Thrale's marriage to Italian music master Gabriel Piozzi, after which the enraged Johnson swore that he would never hear her name mentioned again.

Beckett wrote a ten-page scene of the play, but the rest of the material remains unwritten and the notes are unedited. His work was halted by the realization that he could not accurately capture the eighteenth-century English language as Johnson and his contemporaries spoke it. A way around this problem seemed to lie in having Johnson speak only those words found in James Boswell's account of his life, but that approach proved too complicated to work out for the other characters. Beckett also found it impossible to remove from the work his own twentieth-century sensitivities, which he felt veering from gentle irony to open sarcasm, and despite his struggle, he could not remove aspects of himself from the personalities he created for the characters in the drama. Finally, the four-act play would have required at various times a divided stage, many changes of scenery, elaborate stage directions, and even a live cat who would have had to perform on cue and then move off and on the stage according to Beckett's direction. All this proved insurmountable, and the burgeoning playwright was defeated. However mismatched Beckett and his medium were at this time, there are many instances, such as the brevity of the lines, the one-line exchanges of dialogue, the all-important directions (especially "silence"), that hint of the synthesis to come in his later writings for the stage. Beckett thought so little of this first attempt at dramatic writing that he did not mention it to Raymond Federman and John Fletcher, his official bibliographers, and when an American scholar asked him for the manuscript as well as the notebook containing the information he had collected, he was glad to give it all away.

At the time he was concentrating his energies on the "Johnson Fantasy," his personal situation had deteriorated to the point where he felt he was better off living somewhere else in poverty than remaining in Ireland. His only refuge seemed to be reading Schopenhauer, whose phi-

Hume Cronyn in the 1972 Royal Court Theatre revival of Krapp's Last Tape

losophy later became one of the important foundations of his novels and plays. By the last week in October 1937 he had gone to Paris. Soon after, Beckett received news that *Murphy* was finally accepted for publication by Routledge, the forty-second publisher who had seen it.

A celebrated but brief affair with American heiress Peggy Guggenheim marked the beginning of 1938. Around this time, Beckett was stabbed by a stranger while walking home late one night. He was hospitalized for a serious wound that penetrated his lung and just missed his heart, but his recovery was without complications. Shortly after he was released from the hospital he began a relationship with Suzanne Deschevaux-Dumesnil, a French pianist with whom he began a live-in relationship, and whom he married on 25 March 1961 in England for the same legal reasons that Joyce had married Nora Barnacle after they had lived together as man and wife for many years.

As 1938 progressed, he became once again integrated into the expatriate literary life of Paris and planned to write articles and reviews. Jack Kahane, owner of the Obelisk Press, asked him to translate Marquis de Sade's *Les Cent-vingt Jours*

de Sodom, but Beckett refused because he preferred to let *Murphy* provide him with a literary reputation and because he did not want to be associated with what he considered pornography. Beckett spent the rest of the year trying to translate *Murphy* into French with Alfred Péron. From early 1938 until the outbreak of war in 1939, he wrote short pieces to augment his income, as well as twelve untitled poems which were not published until 1946 as a cycle in *Les Temps Modernes.* Despite this brief flurry of literary journalism and the other publications, the decade of the 1930s is best characterized by the personal upheaval of Beckett's life rather than by a consistent development of literary activity.

Beckett tried to write during the early years of World War II, but all around him friends were disappearing, and he decided that he could not remain in Paris and be as uninvolved as his Irish citizenship required. He officially abandoned his neutrality by the end of October 1940, when he became a member of one of the earliest French Resistance groups. By August 1942 his group had been infiltrated and betrayed, and he and Suzanne Deschevaux-Dumesnil left their apartment as if they were going for a walk and

*Beckett rehearsing Billie Whitelaw at the Royal Court Theatre. The author claims to have heard
her voice speaking the woman's roles as he wrote* Not I.

never went back. For the next two months they
moved from one safe place to another until they
were smuggled across German lines into Unoccu-
pied France. In 1945, when the war ended and
Beckett returned to Paris, he received the Croix
de Guerre and the Médaille de la Résistance.

Beckett spent the years 1942-1945 in southeast France in Roussillon, Vaucluse, hiding from
the Germans and writing the novel *Watt*, probably the least appealing of all his fictions and the
one that has drawn the scantiest critical appraisal.
When the war ended, he took it to George
Reavey, who was unable to place it, and the book
languished for the next nine years as Beckett
turned to other things. It was finally published in
1953, not because of the sudden fame of *Waiting
for Godot*, but because a group of young people
who formed the editorial board of *Merlin* magazine liked it. Beckett always maintained that *Watt*
has its place in his canon and is an important
bridge from the prewar to the postwar writings,
but critics have neglected it until recently.

The first two years after the war ended
were filled with the same sort of unsettled movement that had characterized Beckett's life in the

1930s. There were trips back and forth to
Dublin. He sought writing assignments and even
attempted to take private pupils for English language lessons while he was preparing a French
translation of *Murphy* and working on his first original novel in French, *Mercier et Camier* (written in
1945 but unpublished until 1970), for expected
publication by the publishing house of Bordas.
Bordas declined to publish both books, and with
their financial situation in crisis and the feeling
of helplessness at not being able to organize his
prose into something publishable and profitable,
his wife, a gifted seamstress, became instrumental in their support, and Beckett turned once
again to drama as a means of escape from the realities of his life.

In 1972 Beckett spoke of how he came to
write "Eleuthéria," his first complete play: "I
turned to writing plays to relieve myself of the
awful depression the prose led me into. Life
at that time was too demanding, too terrible,
and I thought theater would be a diversion."
"Eleuthéria" is Beckett's longest and most complex dramatic writing, with three acts, seventeen
characters, and three sets. Like "Human Wishes,"

it also uses a divided stage (during acts 1 and 2) and requires rigorously executed spotlighting to focus the audience's attention upon the action. The title is the Greek word for freedom, and the plot mainly concerns the efforts of a young man called Victor Krap to free himself from the constraints of his bourgeois family. Half of the divided set is the overcluttered living room of the Krap family, and the other half is the shabby and spare hotel room in which Victor has gone to live. Beckett meant the set to symbolize two ways of life: Victor's family's exaggerated sense of propriety and his inactivity and indecisiveness amid squalor. The action takes place on three successive winter afternoons, and most of act 1 is on the half of the stage comprising the family living room, while act 2 is in Victor's room, and the third act has Victor's room filling the stage, while his family's living room is entirely absent.

Besides the length of the play and the complication of the set, the play is also atypical of Beckett's other plays in that there are none of the detailed instructions or precise directions that make directorial license or acting interpretation utterly impossible in his later works. Here, Beckett writes only that the text concerns the principal action of the play and that any marginal action is the concern of the actor. Still, there are hints of the mature playwright: Beckett's characters in "Eleuthéria" have names such as Krap, Piouk ("puke"), Skunk, and Meck ("Mec" is French for pimp); Victor's father has difficulty with urination as does Vladimir in *Waiting for Godot*, and, to a lesser extent, Krapp of *Krapp's Last Tape* (1958); Victor's conversations in the second act are similar to those between the boy and Vladimir in *Waiting for Godot*; the boredom of the female characters and the tenor of their conversation is strikingly similar to that in *Play* (1964; produced in German as *Spiel* the previous year). Indeed, the central character of the play, Victor Krap, is a man on a bed in a room, and there is comment throughout that this is a play within a play, as at one point a cry comes from the audience demanding to know who is the author of this play, with the response given as "Becquet," a French variant of Beckett's name. Both situations are characteristic of the rest of Beckett's canon.

Although Beckett often allowed other plays that he feels are not worthy of production to be published years after he actually wrote them, and even though he sent "Eleuthéria" to producers at the same time he sent *Waiting for Godot*, he remained firm in his resolve that it would never be published to insure that it would never be performed.

"Eleuthéria" followed the aborted *Mercier et Camier* and "Quatre Nouvelles" just as *Waiting for Godot* followed the novels *Molloy* and *Malone meurt* (1951; published in English as *Malone Dies*, 1956). Beckett began a pattern of creation at this time that he followed throughout his life: when he could not write fiction for whatever reason, when he was blocked or, in his own words, "at an impasse," he turned from the rigors of that form to what he considered the more accessible form of drama. For example, *Molloy* and *Malone Dies* were to be a continuation of the fictional heroes begun with Murphy, Watt, and the others, and their tales were to be a continuation and a development of the earlier ones. The development, as he envisioned it, would make unnecessary the various fictional techniques of distancing that he had first used in *Murphy* and *Watt*. With the two later novels, Beckett used for the first time a first-person narrator and allowed his characters, all perhaps variants of the same character and containing variants of Beckett himself, to confront the reader without the description or detail the third-person narrator had previously required. Authorial commentary necessitated by third-person narration ranged from sarcastic involvement to apathetic unconcern, but with the fictional "I" Beckett created beings of no fixed abode, discernible universe, or specific time. They involve the reader in what are often harrowing personal journeys through the desperate spirals of their existence.

Malone Dies was supposed to be the last "of the series" that began with *Murphy* and continued through *Watt*, *Mercier et Camier*, and *Molloy*. As he finished this work that had been so satisfyingly autobiographical during its creation but so devastating to reread when finished, he was once again a victim of the periodic blocks that threatened to disrupt his writing. A brief holiday did nothing to dispel his inability to work. Though the impetus to write was there, continuation of the fiction was impossible. At first as an exercise, then with increasing absorption, he began to write the play that made him famous and changed the nature of drama in the last half of the twentieth century, *Waiting for Godot*.

He wrote it quickly, from 9 October 1948 to 29 January 1949, and the writing became "a marvelous liberating diversion." Because Beckett's earlier attempts at writing drama left him with no real experience at writing for the stage, it now became a game to move the characters and plot the speeches of this play. "Eleuthéria" had gotten out of control with its elaborate setting and large number of characters, so in *Waiting for Godot* Beckett began by giving the framework of the play the same attention as he would have given to a game of chess. This play was much simpler than his earlier work: it contained two acts in which two men, Vladimir and Estragon, both down-and-out, wait for someone named Godot who is supposed to keep an appointment with them. They are joined by a man and his servant, Pozzo and Lucky, who stay with them briefly, then continue on their unspecified way. A boy comes at the end of the first act to tell Vladimir and Estragon that Mr. Godot will not come that day, but most surely the next. A tree which has been bare of leaves is the only setting, and a moon rises to signify that day has ended and night has come as the first act ends. In the second act, the tree miraculously sprouts a few leaves, but nothing else has changed for Vladimir and Estragon. Pozzo and Lucky return and then leave; the boy comes again and repeats the same information. Vladimir and Estragon are disappointed and consider suicide but agree that they have done the best they could—they have kept their appointment. They speak of leaving but do not. The moon comes up again, and the curtain falls as the two men stand silently facing the audience in attitudes of solemn dignity, displaying both resignation and dejection.

Beckett refined the play several times before he sent it to producers, but almost three years passed before it would be performed. During this period Beckett gave up hope many times, but his wife, acting as his agent, persisted and took the manuscript to various producers until she came to Roger Blin, the play's first director. Even then arranging for production was difficult—money had to be raised, theaters they had hoped to use became unavailable, and actors came and went. Nonetheless, Beckett's meeting with Blin was a fortunate one, for although Beckett had firmly in his mind the idea of what he wanted the play to represent, Blin's acute theatrical vision was responsible for much that brought the drama to life. Blin had already had a long career in the French theater as actor, producer, and director, and he was able to bring technical knowledge as well as artistic vision to Beckett's play. In fact, it was Blin who was responsible for the costumes the four characters wore as well as for much of the decor and a great deal of the

stage business in the first production. Beckett wanted to present a circus/vaudeville atmosphere in which his characters would speak in language much as anyone engaged in conversation would use. This marked a striking departure from the formal language, both eloquent and resonant, which was dominant in French theater at that time. The play retains the impersonal aspects of Beckett's fiction—characters with no past, no future, and very little present; no concern for the realities of life, such as occupation, abode, and relationships; and deliberate unconcern for the subject matter of ordinary discourse. But it also incorporated, just as the fiction did, much from Beckett's own life. His characters sing a German round song that first appeared in a letter Beckett wrote to a friend several years earlier; there are conversations that his friends and family felt were directly transposed from those that Beckett had with his wife in the presence of family and friends; and the line from Saint Augustine concerning one of the thieves being saved and the other damned was found in Beckett's correspondence as early as 1935 and had come to be one that Beckett used routinely for situations he defined as "either/or."

Beckett returned to fiction after completing *Waiting for Godot* and wrote *L'Innommable* (1953), which became the third work in a novel trilogy with *Molloy* and *Malone Dies* and which was translated into English as *The Unnamable* (1958). Finally, all the circumstances became propitious for the production of *Waiting for Godot* on 5 January 1953. *Le tout Paris* came to see this play in which, to use Vivien Mercier's words, "nothing happens twice." Critical attitudes toward the play were positive from the premiere, when Sylvain Zegel wrote in the very first review that "The audience understood this much: Paris had just recognized in Samuel Beckett one of today's best playwrights." Armand Salacrou wrote, "An author has appeared who has taken us by the hand to lead us into his universe." More than a decade later, Martin Esslin described the "*succes de scandale*" the play had become: "Was it not an outrage that people could be asked to come and see a play that could not be anything but a hoax, a play in which nothing whatever happened! People went to see the play just to be able to see that scandalous impertinence with their own eyes and to be in a position to say at the next party that they had actually been the victims of that outrage." At the age of forty-seven, Beckett suddenly found himself an overnight sensation.

Still, it was not until 1955 that the play was translated by Beckett and performed in England, where in 1955 it won the *Evening Standard* Drama Award for most controversial play, and not until the next year that the first American production was staged. Disastrously advertised as the "laugh sensation of two continents," it closed almost as soon as it opened at the Coconut Grove Playhouse in Miami. Since then the play has been performed, written about, analyzed, and categorized in numerous languages and according to many points of view. It has been called a parable of Christian salvation, an illustration of Schopenhauer's metaphysics, an exercise in the meaninglessness of existentialism, an allegory of French resistance to German occupation or the English occupation of Ireland, and so many other meanings that a sizable catalogue could be compiled of them with very little effort, and it has spawned a host of lesser plays written in direct imitation. Beckett expressed surprise over the effect this play had on world drama, generally dismissing the work as a diversion or exercise, and even in several instances calling it a "bad" play, although he never elaborated upon this remark. Nevertheless, it was the one manuscript he retained in his possession and adamantly refused to sell or give away.

His next full-length play, *Fin de partie* (1957; produced as *Endgame*, 1958), was one of his two favorite writings (the other was *Malone Dies*). Unlike *Waiting for Godot*, which was written through accidental circumstances, *Fin de partie* was deliberately conceived as a conscious intellectual exercise in which Beckett hoped to draw upon whatever he had learned of theatrical technique from his involvement with the several productions of the earlier play. *Fin de partie* marked the beginning of his preoccupation with dramatic exactitude and is replete with adverbial admonitions for anything the actor or director might wish to do. Once again Beckett chose a couple, Hamm and Clov, as the focus of the drama. Clov is perhaps younger, and some of his behavior makes him seem at times a servant, but at other times he is independent and distanced. To one side of the stage are Hamm's parents, Nagg and Nell, who live in two trash cans side by side simply because Beckett could think of no other dramatic device that would let them speak their lines on cue and then disappear from the audience's view as swiftly as he wanted.

The governing metaphor of the play is a chess game. Assisting with a 1967 Berlin produc-

tion, Beckett said, "Hamm is a king in this chess game lost from the start. From the start, he knows he is making loud senseless moves. That he will make no progress at all with the gaff. Now at the last he makes a few senseless moves as only a bad player would. A good one would have given up long ago. He is only trying to delay the inevitable end. Each of his gestures is one of the last useless moves which puts off the end. He's a bad player." Beckett has also stated that there "are no accidents in this play," and that, as with *Waiting for Godot*, "everything is based on analogy and repetition." Although, as with the earlier play, many interpretations have been attached to it, Beckett insists that one of the most important speeches in the play and one that should govern the entire performance is "nothing is funnier than unhappiness."

In a letter to his American director, Alan Schneider, Beckett made a strong objection to those who wanted elucidation of mysteries of interpretation that he said he had not made and insisted, "Hamm as stated, and Clov as stated. . . ." However, this play remains fertile exegetical ground for scholars and theatergoers alike, and they are all probably correct to insist on a more subtle and complex interpretation than Beckett seemed at times to have wanted. It moved Harold Hobson, writing in 1973, to comment: "In recent years there has been some danger of Mr. Beckett being sentimentalized. Self-defensively we are driven to persuade ourselves that his plays are not really filled with terror and horror, but are, at bottom, jolly good fun. Well, they are not jolly good fun. They are amongst the most frightening prophecies of, and longing for, doom ever written."

Both these plays were written first in French, just as "Eleuthéria" had been, and one of the ironies that surrounds much of Beckett's dramatic writings concerns the first production of *Fin de partie*. No theater owner in Paris wanted to risk losing money by renting the theater to Beckett and Blin for the second play, despite the dramatic stir caused by *Waiting for Godot*. Beckett regretfully withdrew it from French consideration and began to translate it for production at the Royal Court Theatre in London, then under the artistic direction of George Devine. Beckett was unable to complete it as quickly or as well as he wanted. When the date for rehearsal drew near and Beckett was still not finished, Devine agreed that since he could not present an English

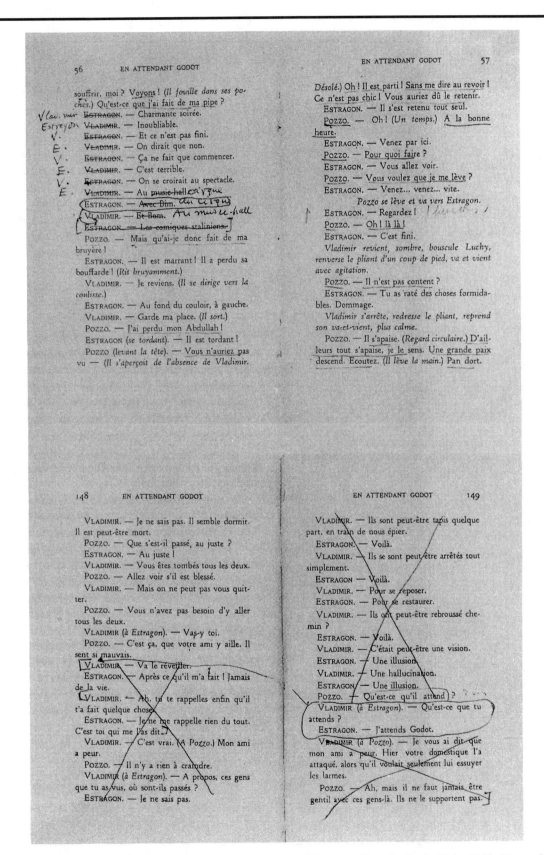

Pages from Beckett's working rehearsal copy for the first performance of **En Attendant Godot** *in Paris, 1953. Many of Beckett's revisions, some shown here, were incorporated into the second published edition of the play, which is the standard text (Sotheby's auction catalogue, 13 December 1990).*

Endgame, he would invite the French company to London to perform *Fin de partie*.

Thus, the French play received its world premiere in England and so outraged French patriotism that the management of the Studio des Champs Elysées Theatre, attracted by the commotion and hoping to profit from it, agreed to mount the play. Both productions of *Fin de partie* were accompanied by the mime *Acte sans paroles I* (1957; produced as *Act Without Words I*, 1957), written to round out the evening because *Fin de partie* was deemed too short for production without a companion piece.

Beckett never liked this combination and wanted to substitute another short play instead of the mime. Thus he began to write *Krapp's Last Tape* (produced in French as *Le Dernière Bande*, 1960), which became too long for his original intention and which marked a new development in his dramatic writing. His first postwar play written in English, it deals with biographical information much more gently than the three novels that preceded it. The emotion in this play is recollected in a tranquillity of sorts, as an old, exhausted Krapp sits in his room and listens to his tapes. Krapp's reflections include a summer day on the shores of the Baltic, where Beckett went with his Sinclair cousins, and the green-eyed girl in the boat whom he loves is generally assumed to be Peggy Sinclair. A character named Fanny, one of Beckett's aunt's nicknames, may represent Cissie Sinclair, and the woman who sings songs in the evening is probably a variant of the English-woman who hid during the war in the same village as Beckett. These, of course, are only some of the most obvious examples and do not capture the sensitivity of the use Beckett makes of them.

Dublin journalist Alec Reid has described the play as "total theatre," saying, "It is not the words, the movements, the sights severally which produce the impact; it is the new experience, evoked through their combination on stage. This process involving eye, ear, intellect, emotion, all at once, we shall call total theatre."

Beckett claimed that he had never seen a tape recorder before he wrote this play, but that it seemed a good way to allow a man to recapture his memories. It is quite likely that Beckett wrote the play in English because he was so taken by the voice of the English actor Patrick Magee. Beckett said that when he heard the lines he had written spoken inside his head, it was as if Magee's voice had been speaking them. Years later when he first heard the actress Billie

Whitelaw, who was a member of a 1964 Royal Court production of *Play*, he said that it was her voice he heard speaking his woman's roles when he wrote *Not I* (1972; produced in French as *Pas Moi*, 1975).

Although it is difficult to make any statement regarding the exact chronology of Beckett's dramatic writing, it is generally believed that the latest two-act play he wrote was *Happy Days*, completed sometime in 1961 and given its first performance in New York shortly after. The work was produced in French as *Oh les beaux jours* in 1963. It was deliberately written first in English to accomplish several things that had become important to Beckett. He was sensitive to the fact that none of his plays had been instant commercial successes, and he wanted public acclaim to go along with the critical approval that was building with each new production. Two subjects had also become important to Beckett to express dramatically, namely the Catholic church and the British government, both from the Ireland of his youth. He knew subjects such as these would suffer if expressed in French, so he wrote in English. However, many of the long passages denouncing Church domination of the Irish and what he considered to be British misrule were excised by Beckett from the final manuscript.

Happy Days is the story of a woman named Winnie, buried in sand up to her waist in the first act. She amuses herself with possessions, occasionally calling to her husband, Willie, who lives behind her mound and spends his time reading the newspaper and looking at a postcard. A bell governs Winnie's waking and sleeping, and she passes the time between the harsh clangs, which signify the beginning and end of her day, by talking. Occasionally she breaks down, but always she regains her composure. In the second act, she is buried to her neck and cannot even turn to her possessions for respite but must wile away the hours by inventing stories. Willie appears toward the end of this act, "dressed to kill," as Beckett writes, and tries to crawl up the mound. The ending is ambiguous as Willie's hand is outstretched toward Winnie, but also toward "Brownie," the little revolver she had amused herself with in the first act. She sings the waltz from Franz Lehár's *The Merry Widow*, and the curtain falls on this unsettling note. Ruth White won an Obie Award for her New York performance as Winnie despite Walter Kerr's objection to the play. *Happy Days* did not achieve the commercial success Beckett

/ ... imagine!   **1.4**

MOUTH: ... realized ... words were coming/... words were
(contd)   coming/ ... a voice she did not recognize ... at
              first ... so long since it had sounded ... then finally
              had to admit ... could be none other ... than her
              own ... certain vowel sounds ... she had never
              heard ... elsewhere ... so that people would stare
              ... the rare occasions ... once or twice a year ...
              always winter some strange reason ... stare at her
              uncomprehending ... and now this stream ...
              steady stream ... she who had never ... on the
              contrary ... practically speechless ... all her
              days ... how she survived! ... even shopping ...
out shopping... busy shopping centre ... supermart ... just handed
              in the list ... with the bag ... old black shopping
stand!   bag ... then ~~stood~~ there waiting ... any length of
              time ... middle of the throng ... motionless ...
              staring into space ... mouth half open as usual ...
              till it was back in her hand ... the bag back in her
              hand ... then pay and go ... not as much as goodbye
              ... how she survived! ... 'and now this stream ...
              not catching the half of it ... not the quarter ... no
              idea ... what she was saying ... imagine! ... no
! /   idea what she was saying/ ... till she began trying
              to ... delude herself ... it was not hers at all ...
              not her voice at all ... and/would have/no doubt/ ...
              vital she should ... was on the point ... after long
              efforts ... when suddenly she felt ... gradually ~~felt~~ *She*
              felt ... her lips moving ... imagine! ... her lips
              moving/ ... as of course till then she had not ...
              and not alone the lips ... the cheeks ... the jaws
              ... the whole face ... all those - ... what? ...
              the tongue? ... yes ... the tongue in the mouth
              ... all those contortions without which ... no speech
              possible ... and yet — in the ordinary way ... not
              felt at all ... so intent one is ... on what one is
              saying ... the whole being ... hanging on its words
              ... so that not only she had ... had she ... not only
... oh long after/ had she ... to give up ... admit hers alone ... her
              voice alone ... but this other awful thought/... sudden
              flash ... ~~oh long after!~~ even more awful if
... imagine!/ possible ... that feeling was coming back/... feeling
              ~~was~~ coming back! ... starting at the top/... then
              working down ... the whole machine ... but no ...
              spared that ... the mouth alone ... so far ... ha!
              ... so far ... then thinking ... oh long after/ ...
              sudden flash ... it can't go on ... all this ... all
              that ... steady stream ... straining to hear ... make
              something of it ... and her own thoughts ... make
w /   something of them ... all - ... What? ... the buzzing?

Page from Beckett's proofs, with corrections for Not I *(1973). Beckett made significant corrections, revisions, and deletions at the proof stage (Carlton Lake,* No Symbols Where None Intended, *1984).*

had wanted, but public reaction was generally favorable.

By the time he finished *Happy Days* Beckett was moving freely between writing in French or English. At first he agreed with Herbert Blau's statement that by writing in French he had been able to achieve the right "weakening" effect, that is, to rid his language of any affectation so that content and language were united in a simplicity of form that often belied the complexity of the statement he made. He moved from language to language with the same ease that he wrote mimes, radio plays, dramatic monologues, or whatever else he was inspired to try at the time.

In the same year that *Happy Days* was produced, Beckett had published *Comment c'est* (1961; published in English as *How It Is*, 1964), an elliptical text divided into three sections in which a speaker crawls through the mud dragging his few possessions with him in a sack pressed to his naked belly. It continues Beckett's preoccupations with identity and his obsession with words and things—both natural objects and phenomena. The nameless narrator might just as well have been an addendum to *The Unnamable* as he is a prefiguration of future writings, such as *Assez* (Enough, 1966), *Sans* (1969; published in English as *Lessness*, 1970), and *Le Dépeupleur* (1970; published in English as *The Lost Ones*, 1972).

The brevity of this prose also signaled the beginning of brevity in Beckett's plays as well. *Breath* (1970) is 120 words and lasts thirty-five seconds; *Not I* should be played in no more than sixteen minutes; and *That Time* (1976) should last between twenty-four and thirty minutes. Beckett continued to write fiction with *Fizzles* (1976), which Paul Gray called "slight to the point of frippery."

There has been much speculation as to Beckett's intention in these ever-diminishing writings. Opinions range from the purely psychological—once his fictional voices became integrated, all of his tellers of tales became unified to the point where the tale no longer needed to be told and so it decreased—to the literary—having perfected his artistic vision, Beckett no longer needed long-winded narrators who rambled on interminably because he could make all his fictional points with a precision so sharp as to leave audiences and readers breathless with the end, which comes so abruptly soon after the beginning.

In the mid 1970s, however, Beckett surprised publishers and scholars alike by announcing that he was hard at work on another novel which marked a complete departure from his previously published work. He said this one was to be a "romance," a novel of three hundred to four hundred pages written in the traditional manner and which would tell the story of himself and his wife. Instead, he produced in 1979 *Companie* (published as *Company* in 1980), just sixty-three pages long, strongly autobiographical, and resembling *Comment c'est* in style.

All this speculation only compounds the mystery of Beckett's vision and the chronology of the writing. Beckett surrounded his work with secrecy, privacy, and the occasional tantalizing clue as to a work's provenance and literary history. Many works which he called "trunk manuscripts" were suddenly given for publication with Beckett unable to remember how or when he came to write them, or even if they might or might not be variants of other works. He never knew when his creative impulses would grow fallow, and he refused to discuss his writing or his intention. His work became a Chinese box puzzle which continues to fascinate readers and theatergoers alike.

The years from 1965 to his death in 1989 were marked by Beckett's almost constant presence in a theater where his work was in production even though he still maintained that fiction was his most important writing. He acquired an increasing sense of self-confidence as the years passed, and the early dependence on Roger Blin in France and George Devine in London gave way to a sure sense of command of his material. Public acceptance of his work gave him the freedom to insist upon it being presented as he had written and envisioned it, and he soon grew independent enough to insist upon full charge of many productions. He who had been so insecure and unhappy about meeting people that he had had his wife take his first plays to producers became so confident that he stopped being only an adviser or spectator and became if not the director in name, certainly in spirit.

The years of his collaboration with Devine at the Royal Court were felicitous. Besides Blin, Beckett worked with varying degrees of satisfaction with Jean Louis Barrault and Madeleine Renaud in France. In 1964 he made his only visit to the United States to be present for the filming of *Film*, his only known writing for the cinema. *Film* won several awards, including the Prix Filmcritice (1965) and the Tours Film Prize

(1966). He was uncomfortable in New York despite his high regard for Alan Schneider, who usually directed American performances of Beckett's plays, and Barney Rosset, his publisher at Grove Press.

It was in Germany that he seemed most at home in the theater. He worked on an almost annual basis with the Schiller Theater in Berlin and went with the same frequency to Stuttgart, to assist or direct productions for radio and television. He directed the Schiller Theater actors in the definitive German production of *Waiting for Godot* in 1977 and again in 1978 and allowed the company to tour in London and in Brooklyn the following year. In 1979 he directed a festival of his work at the Royal Court Theatre and later made several more trips to Germany and London for recordings of radio plays. He even began to write dramatic pieces on request. In 1979 David Warrilow performed *A Piece of Monologue* in New York, and in 1981 Beckett wrote a short piece called *Ohio Impromptu* for presentation at a symposium at Ohio State University in honor of his seventy-fifth birthday.

Although all his plays have attracted respectable audiences, Beckett has become well known more because of *Waiting for Godot* than any of his other works. *Waiting for Godot* has been published in numerous languages and in so many editions that Beckett lost count. Editions of all the other plays combined do not come close to this achievement. With his novels, total sales in France are less than fifty thousand copies, and the figure is not much higher in all English-language editions.

Beckett lived quietly in Paris in the apartment he bought in the early 1960s and the small house in the country just east of Paris that he called "The house that *Godot* built." He kept to a schedule that would defeat most younger men, writing, translating, collaborating, and overseeing productions, and still finding time for an extensive social life. The rumor that he became a recluse skulking about the back alleys of Paris was one he particularly wanted to lay to rest.

A year prior to his death, Beckett was moved to a nursing home after falling in his apartment. When Suzanne died on 17 July 1989, Beckett left the nursing home to attend her funeral. He lived his last year in a sparsely furnished room with a television, on which he watched tennis and soccer. He kept a few books, including his boyhood copy of Dante's *Divine Comedy* in Italian. Beckett's last work to be published in his life-time was a short prose piece, *Stirrings Still* (1988), a meditation on aging.

It is probably not an exaggeration to say that his involvement with the theater was responsible in great part for his prolific output during the years between 1960 and 1980. All this activity requiring his involvement with people also led to a kind of personal harmony that had hitherto eluded him.

In 1969 Beckett received the Nobel Prize, an honor for which he did not actively campaign but one which he did not (as Jean-Paul Sartre had done) refuse. He had been nominated as early as 1957 by Maurice Nadeau and then by a succession of American professors who championed him. He seemed effectively out of consideration when Erik Wahlund, drama critic of *Svenska Dagbladet*, wrote that Beckett had written only a "single first-rank work," *Waiting for Godot*, and that none of his other writings had ever approached its depth of thought or structure. Thus, there was genuine surprise when the prize was given to Beckett for "a body of work that, in new forms of fiction and the theatre, has transmuted the destitution of modern man into his exaltation." This comment is probably the most accurate description of Beckett's writing, as in its succinctness it takes into account his prose, his plays, his achievement, his life.

Bibliographies:

Raymond Federman and John Fletcher, *Samuel Beckett: His Work and His Critics* (Berkeley: University of California Press, 1970);

Robin J. Davis, *Samuel Beckett: Checklist and Index of his Published Works* (Stirling, Scotland: The Compiler, 1979).

Biography:

Deirdre Bair, *Samuel Beckett: A Biography* (New York: Harcourt Brace Jovanovich, 1978; revised edition, New York: Summit, 1990).

References:

Cathleen Culotta Andonian, *Samuel Beckett: A Reference Guide* (Boston: G. K. Hall, 1989);

Linda Ben-Zvi, *Samuel Beckett* (Boston: Twayne, 1986);

Harold Bloom, ed., *Samuel Beckett: Modern Critical Views* (New York: Chelsea, 1985);

Enoch Brater, ed., *Beckett at 80/Beckett in Context* (New York: Oxford University Press, 1986);

Bell Gale Chevigny, ed., *Twentieth Century Interpretations of Endgame: A Collection of Critical Es-*

says (Englewood Cliffs, N.J.: Prentice-Hall, 1969);

Ruby Cohn, *Back to Beckett* (Princeton: Princeton University Press, 1973);

Cohn, "A Checklist of Beckett Criticism," *Perspective*, 11 (Autumn 1959): 193-196;

Cohn, *Samuel Beckett: The Comic Gamut* (New Brunswick, N.J.: Rutgers University Press, 1962);

Cohn, ed., *Samuel Beckett: A Collection of Critical Essays* (New York: McGraw-Hill, 1975);

Cohn, ed., *Waiting for Godot: A Casebook* (London: Macmillan, 1987);

Steven Connor, *Samuel Beckett: Repetition, Theory, and Text* (London: Blackwell, 1988);

Thomas J. Cousineau, *Waiting for Godot: Form in Movement* (Boston: Twayne, 1990);

Colin Duckworth, *Angels of Darkness: Dramatic Effect in Samuel Beckett With Special Reference to Eugene Ionesco* (New York: Barnes & Noble, 1972);

John Fletcher, *The Novels of Samuel Beckett*, second edition (New York: Barnes & Noble, 1970);

John Fletcher and Beryl S. Fletcher, *A Student's Guide to the Plays of Samuel Beckett*, revised edition (London: Faber & Faber, 1985);

John Fletcher and John Spurling, *Beckett: A Study of His Plays* (New York: Hill & Wang, 1972);

Melvin J. Friedman, ed., *Samuel Beckett Now: Critical Approaches to His Novels, Poetry, and Plays* (Chicago: University of Chicago Press, 1970);

S. E. Gontarski, *The Intent of Undoing in Samuel Beckett's Dramatic Texts* (Bloomington: Indiana University Press, 1985);

Gontarski, ed., *On Beckett: Essays and Criticism* (New York: Grove Press, 1986);

Lawrence Graver and Raymond Federman, eds., *Samuel Beckett: The Critical Heritage* (London & Boston: Routledge, 1979);

Charles R. Lyons, *Samuel Beckett* (New York: Grove Press, 1984);

Pierre Mélèse, *Beckett* (Paris: Seghers, 1966);

Vivien Mercier, *Beckett / Beckett: The Truth of Contradiction* (New York: Oxford University Press, 1977);

Kristen Morrison, *Canters and Chronicles: The Use of Narrative in the Plays of Samuel Beckett and Harold Pinter* (Chicago: University of Chicago Press, 1983);

Alan Schneider, *Entrances: An American Director's Journey* (New York: Viking, 1986);

Bert O. States, *The Shape of Paradox: An Essay on Waiting for Godot* (Berkeley: University of California Press, 1978);

Eugene Webb, *The Plays of Samuel Beckett* (Seattle: University of Washington Press, 1972);

Katharine Worth, *Revolutions in Modern English Drama* (London: G. Bell, 1972);

Worth, ed., *Beckett the Shape Changer: A Symposium* (London: Routledge, 1975).

Papers:

Portions of Beckett's papers are housed in the Harry A. Ransom Humanities Research Center, University of Texas, Austin; Baker Library of Dartmouth College; Ohio State University Libraries, Columbus; Beinecke Library of Yale University; and in private collections in the United States and Canada. In England, there is a Samuel Beckett Archive at the University of Reading. A few partial manuscripts are in Trinity College, Dublin.

Brendan Behan
(9 February 1923 - 20 March 1964)

This entry was updated by Patrick A. McCarthy (University of Miami) from his entry in
DLB 13: British Dramatists Since World War II: Part One.

BOOKS: *The Quare Fellow* (London: Methuen, 1956; New York: Grove, 1957);

Borstal Boy (London: Hutchinson, 1958; New York: Knopf, 1959);

An Giall (Dublin: An Chomhairle Náisiúnta Drámaíochta, 1958?); translated and revised as *The Hostage* (London: Methuen, 1958; New York: Grove, 1959);

Brendan Behan's Island: An Irish Sketchbook (New York: Bernard Geis, 1962; London: Hutchinson, 1962);

Hold Your Hour and Have Another (London: Hutchinson, 1963; Boston: Little, Brown, 1964);

The Scarperer (Garden City, N.Y.: Doubleday, 1964; London: Hutchinson, 1966);

Brendan Behan's New York (New York: Bernard Geis, 1964; London: Hutchinson, 1964);

Confessions of an Irish Rebel (New York: Bernard Geis, 1965; London: Hutchinson, 1965);

Moving Out and A Garden Party: Two Plays, edited by Robert Hogan (Dixon, Cal.: Proscenium Press, 1967);

Richard's Cork Leg (London: Eyre Methuen, 1973; New York: Grove, 1974);

The Complete Plays (New York: Grove, 1978; London: Eyre Methuen, 1978);

Poems and Stories (Dublin: Liffey Press, 1978).

PLAY PRODUCTIONS: *The Quare Fellow*, Dublin, Pike Theatre Club, 19 November 1954; Theatre Workshop version, Stratford, London, Theatre Royal, 24 May 1956;

The Big House, Dublin, Pike Theatre Club, 6 May 1958;

The New House, Dublin, Pike Theatre Club, 6 May 1958;

An Giall, Dublin, An Damer, June 1958; translated and revised as *The Hostage*, Stratford, London, Theatre Royal, 14 October 1958;

Richard's Cork Leg, Dublin, Peacock Theatre, 14 March 1972.

RADIO: *Moving Out*, Radio Eireann, 1952;
A Garden Party, Radio Eireann, 1952;

Brendan Behan (photograph by Ida Kar)

The Big House, BBC Radio Third Programme, 1957.

PERIODICAL PUBLICATION: *The Big House*, *Evergreen Review*, 5 (September-October 1961): 40-63.

Brendan Behan was the most important new Irish dramatist of the 1950s. Writing without the support of the theatrical establishment (the Abbey Theatre rejected his early efforts), Behan developed an original style that combined bawdy humor, genuine pathos, and social insight.

If he had a model for his role as dramatist, it was probably Sean O'Casey, whom Behan admired both as a playwright and as an opponent of censorship. The major influence on his plays, however, was Joan Littlewood's Theatre Workshop, which emphasized improvisational effects, songs, and contemporary allusions that are supposed to make the play more immediately relevant to an audience. Unfortunately, Behan's dependence on these methods led to such loose structuring of his plays that in his unfinished play, *Richard's Cork Leg* (1972), songs and joke sequences are substituted for the development of plot, character, and theme. Disappointed at his inability to repeat the success of *The Quare Fellow* (1954) and *The Hostage* (1958), Behan retreated more and more often into alcoholic binges until his death in March 1964.

It is evident from his plays and other writings that one of the major factors in Behan's life was his involvement with the Irish Republican cause. He inherited his Republican sympathies from his intensely patriotic working-class family: when Brendan was born on 9 February 1923 in Dublin, his father, Stephen Behan, a housepainter, labor leader, and soldier, was serving a jail term for IRA activities during the Irish civil war; his mother, Kathleen Kearney Behan, boasted of her ability to sing rebel songs; his uncle, Peadar Kearney, wrote the Irish national anthem; and at the age of seventy-seven, his stepgrandmother was arrested and sentenced to three years in an English prison for terrorist activities. Educated from 1928 to 1937 at Irish Catholic schools and employed as an apprentice housepainter from 1937 until 1939, Behan himself was imprisoned in 1939 when he was arrested in Liverpool for possession of explosives. After serving two years in a Borstal institution (an English reform school), Behan returned to Dublin but was soon involved in a drunken shootout with police that led to a sentence of fourteen years in prison. His sentence was commuted in 1946, but Behan remained at liberty only a few months before being arrested in Manchester, where he had gone to help an Irish prisoner escape. The four-month sentence he served for this adventure was his last major term of imprisonment for Republican activities, but in 1948 he was sentenced to a month in jail for being drunk and disorderly. In the remaining sixteen years of his life he would serve many more such terms for drunkenness, not only in Ireland but in several other countries as well.

One of Behan's favorite books was Irish revolutionist and journalist John Mitchel's *Jail Journal* (1856). That book, and other accounts of prison experiences, might have suggested to Behan the idea for his finest nondramatic work, *Borstal Boy* (1958), a sensitive, often ironic description of his two years in reform school. The four years he spent in Irish prisons may have had an even greater effect on his career, for it was during this time that Behan had his first significant article published, wrote his first play, "The Landlady" (based on the life of his eccentric paternal grandmother), and determined to make his way as a writer. While he was in Dublin's Mountjoy Jail he knew Bernard Kirwan, who was hanged for the murder of his own brother, and in 1946 Behan began work on a play about Kirwan's execution, which he called "The Twisting of Another Rope." Eight years later, after the play was rejected by the Abbey Theatre, he rewrote it and, at the suggestion of director Alan Simpson, who wanted to save space in newspaper advertisements, retitled it *The Quare Fellow*.

During the years between the initial conception that led to *The Quare Fellow* and the first performance of the play in Dublin in 1954, Behan was involved in a variety of occupations: painting houses in Dublin, soliciting customers for prostitutes in Paris, writing a column for the *Irish Press*, singing songs for a radio program. The broadcasting experience proved important in 1952 when Micheál Ó hAodha asked Behan to write a series of comedy shows for Radio Eireann. Behan wrote only two radio plays, *Moving Out* (1952) and *A Garden Party* (1952), for this series, but these short domestic comedies (later combined into a stage version, *The New House*, produced in 1958 and included in *Best Short Plays of the World Theatre 1958-1967*) showed that Behan had considerable talent in characterization and in developing comic situations. A later radio play, *The Big House* (1957), was less successful, although its satiric treatment of the conflict between the Anglo-Irish and Irish peasant classes is often very funny.

While these apprentice works are interesting, Behan's reputation as a dramatist rests on his two major plays, *The Quare Fellow* and *The Hostage*. *The Quare Fellow* is particularly impressive for its development of the audience's sympathy for a character who is never seen on stage: the "quare fellow" or condemned man who is scheduled to be "topped" in the morning for killing his brother. The *raisonneur* of the play is the

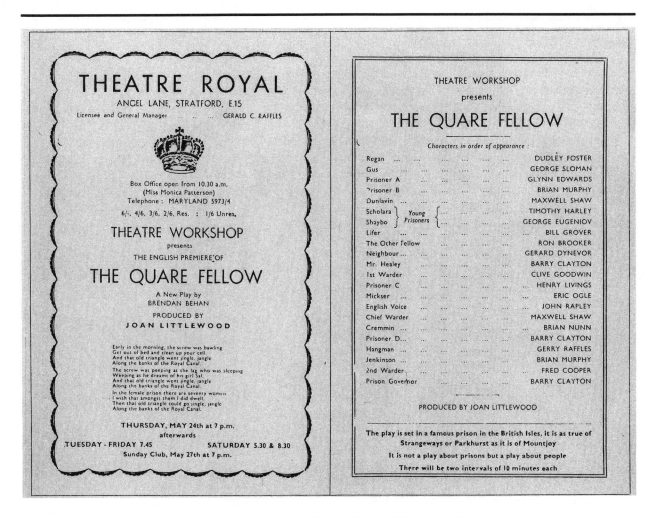

Program cover and cast list for the first production of Behan's work in London

prison guard, Regan, a sensitive man who despises hangings and sees past the hypocrisy of the judicial system but nevertheless considers his work "a soft job . . . between hangings," when he is not forced to see himself as part of the brutal prison system. Regan is a man caught between his conscience and his "duty" to keep order and to make preparations for hangings, but other representatives of the system are viewed less sympathetically. The governor of the prison is concerned only with appearances and formalities: he objects to jokes about hanging but not to the death sentence itself. The other warders are generally concerned only with advancing their careers while doing as little work as possible, and some of the prisoners are less interested in the fate of the quare fellow than in getting a cigarette or a drink or in maintaining their status within the prison's pecking order. The major exception is Prisoner C, a Gaelic-speaking youth from Kerry, whose honesty and innocence stand in contrast to

the hardened attitude of the English executioner and most of the Irish prisoners.

It is tempting to view *The Quare Fellow* simply as a protest against capital punishment, but Behan never confined any of his plays to so narrow a target. Actually, the death penalty is seen in the play mainly as the most obvious example of the brutality built into a system that punishes men for the very brutality that the system engenders. Behan's relentless attacks on the absurdity of the penal system, and the larger social system that it represents, are effective because the play's black humor builds in the audience a sense of horror even as the audience laughs at joke after joke. In *The Quare Fellow* one can observe what was to become the main technique of *The Hostage*: the revelation of serious thematic concerns through such apparently trivial elements as jokes and songs. In this respect, Behan bears at least a passing resemblance to such dramatists as Samuel Beckett and Bertolt Brecht.

Warden Regan—Dudley Foster   *Neighbour*—Gerard Dynevor
Dunlavin—Maxwell Shaw

Cartoon by Ronald Searle that appeared in the 8 January 1956 issue of Punch

If the years 1954-1958 were the most productive of Behan's career, part of the credit for his success during this period may undoubtedly be attributed to his 1955 marriage to painter Beatrice ffrench-Salkeld, an understanding and long-suffering woman who recognized her husband's weaknesses and tried to help him. Despite several arrests for public drunkenness, Behan accomplished a great deal during these years. In 1956 *The Quare Fellow* was presented in London by Joan Littlewood's Theatre Workshop. Meanwhile, Behan worked on *Borstal Boy*, which was published in 1958, and on a Gaelic play, *An Giall*, which was first produced in Dublin in June 1958. Reserving the right to "translate" the play into English, he actually introduced new characters, dialogue, songs, and dances; other material was added by Theatre Workshop during rehearsals for the 1958 London production. The result was *The Hostage*, a controversial play that is often deemed inferior to *An Giall* but is nonetheless a successful amalgam of farce and social commentary.

Behan had begun to see that the political aims of the Irish Republican Army might conflict at times with fundamental human values. As an artist, he was bound to portray the conflict of values, not merely to act as a propagandist for the IRA. *The Hostage*, which is about the kidnapping and execution of a British soldier by the IRA, reflects this new complexity in Behan's attitude toward the IRA. Pat, who comes as close as anyone to being Behan's spokesman in the play, is a cynical critic of the Republican cause, yet he joyfully sings a song in celebration of a victory over the British troops, the Black and Tans. The IRA is constantly depicted as a group of demented revolutionaries—like the Marx Brothers with guns and explosives—yet throughout the play Behan emphasizes the justice of Irish complaints against Britain. Small wonder that on one of his trips to America, Behan said that the IRA was un-

A scene from the 1958 London production of The Hostage

certain "whether to accept a charity performance of *The Hostage* or bomb the theatre."

Always uncertain of his talent, unable to cope with his success, Behan was soon to turn into a caricature of himself. For instance, he was barred from participating in the 1961 St. Patrick's Day parade in New York City because parade sponsors felt he gave the Irish a bad image. The legend of Behan the drunk was in fact superseding the reputation of the playwright. He was not to find freedom from the public image of himself that he created, nor was he able to marshal the creative energies necessary for another play on the level of *The Quare Fellow* or *The Hostage*. His final theatrical effort was *Richard's Cork Leg* (originally written in Gaelic under the title "La Breagh San Reilg," or "A Fine Day in the Graveyard"), which, like the books *Brendan Behan's Island* (1962), *Brendan Behan's New York* (1964), and *Confessions of an Irish Rebel* (1965), was composed largely by dictation into a tape recorder. That method of composition was unfortunate because it resulted in rambling works that resemble pub talk more than professional writing. *Richard's Cork Leg* has several flashes of brilliant dialogue; Behan's use of Irish speech had long been an arresting feature of his plays, as various critics have

noted. But this final play as a whole is a failure. Like Dylan Thomas and Malcolm Lowry, Behan spent his last few years haunted by creative triumphs that he was never to repeat.

Although he only wrote two notable plays, even that achievement entitles Behan to a place of some significance in the modern Irish theater. At a time when the only substantial Irish playwrights were émigrés O'Casey and Beckett, Behan helped to revitalize the theater in Ireland, largely by producing two plays that have more than a parochial interest, and by using realistic speech in combination with Brechtian music-hall effects. His public rebelliousness, combined with the consistently antiestablishment tone of his plays, has earned him comparison with John Osborne. Other critics have seen a relationship between Behan's method and the absurdist plays of Jean Genet, Eugène Ionesco, and Beckett. However, Behan might best be compared to John Millington Synge and O'Casey, who experimented boldly, offended Irish nationalists with their irreverence, and gave Ireland plays that later generations were to recognize as masterpieces. When Behan died in March 1964, only a few months after the birth of his daughter Blanaid, his outrageous public image made it diffi-

Brendan Behan in London, 1959

cult for the public to view him as more than a self-destructive exhibitionist. He was certainly that, but as the awards for *The Hostage* (the Obie Award and the Paris Festival Award, both 1958, and the French Critics' Award, 1962) and the inclusion of both *The Hostage* and *The Quare Fellow* in *Drury's Guide to Best Plays* indicate, he was also a talented dramatist. Behan's iconoclastic interpretation of the modern Irish scene, related in the tough language of the Dublin slums yet informed by a warm human vision, represents a substantial addition to the modern Irish theater.

Biographies:

Dominic Behan, *My Brother Brendan* (London: Leslie Frewin, 1965);

Rae Jeffs, *Brendan Behan, Man and Showman* (London: Hutchinson, 1966);

Sean McCann, ed., *The World of Brendan Behan* (New York: Twayne, 1966);

Ulick O'Connor, *Brendan* (Englewood Cliffs, N.J.: Prentice-Hall, 1970);

Seamus de Burca, *Brendan Behan: A Memoir* (Newark, Del.: Proscenium Press, 1971);

Beatrice Behan, Des Hickey, and Gus Smith, *My Life with Brendan* (London: Leslie Frewin, 1973);

Peter Arthurs, *With Brendan Behan: A Personal Memoir* (New York: St. Martin's Press, 1981).

References:

Ted E. Boyle, *Brendan Behan* (New York: Twayne, 1969);

Anthony Burgess, "The Writer as Drunk," in his *Urgent Copy: Literary Studies* (New York: Norton, 1968);

Bert Cardullo, "*The Hostage* Reconsidered," *Eire-Ireland*, 20 (Summer 1985): 139-143;

Peter René Gerdes, *The Major Works of Brendan Behan* (Bern: Herbert Lang, 1973);

Brendan Gill, "The Borstal Boy in New York," *Grand Street*, 8 (Summer 1989): 106-115;

Howard Goorney, *The Theatre Workshop Story* (New York & London: Eyre Methuen, 1981), pp. 110-116, 155-157;

Johan Hendricks, "The 'Theatre of Fun': In Defence of Brendan Behan's *The Hostage*," *Anglo-Irish Studies*, 3 (1977): 85-95;

Patrick Colm Hogan, "Class Heroism in *The Quare Fellow*," *Etudes Irlandaises*, 8 (December 1983): 139-144;

Colbert Kearney, *The Writings of Brendan Behan* (New York: St. Martin's Press, 1977);

Benedict Kiely, "That Old Triangle: A Memory of Brendan Behan," *Hollins Critic*, 2 (February 1965): 1-12;

Johannes Kleinstuck, "Brendan Behan's 'The Hostage,'" *Essays and Studies by Members of the English Association*, 24 (1971): 69-83;

Desmond Maxwell, "Brendan Behan's Theatre," in *Irish Writers and the Theatre*, edited by Masaru Sekine (Totowa, N.J.: Barnes & Noble, 1986), pp. 87-102;

Patrick A. McCarthy, "Triviality and Dramatic Achievement in Two Plays by Brendan Behan," *Modern British Literature*, 3 (Fall 1978): 113-121;

Sean McMahon, "The Quare Fellow," *Eire-Ireland*, 4 (Winter 1969): 143-157;

E. H. Mikhail, *Brendan Behan: An Annotated Bibliography of Criticism* (Totowa, N.J.: Barnes & Noble, 1980);

Mikhail, ed., *The Art of Brendan Behan* (Totowa, N.J.: Barnes & Noble, 1979);

Mikhail, ed., *Brendan Behan: Interviews and Recollections*, 2 volumes (Totowa, N.J.: Barnes & Noble, 1982);

Raymond J. Porter, *Brendan Behan* (New York: Columbia University Press, 1973);

Alan Simpson, *Beckett and Behan and a Theatre in Dublin* (London: Routledge & Kegan Paul, 1962);

Richard Wall, "*An Giall* and *The Hostage* Compared," *Modern Drama*, 18 (1975): 165-172;

Wall, "The Stage History and Reception of Brendan Behan's *An Giall*," in *Literary Interrelations: Ireland, England and the World*, volume 1: *Reception and Translation*, edited by Wolfgang Zach and Heinz Kosok (Tübingen: Narr, 1987), pp. 123-129;

Gordon M. Wickstrom, "The Heroic Dimension in Brendan Behan's *The Hostage*," *Educational Theatre Journal*, 22 (1970): 406-411;

Walentyna Witoszek, "The Funeral Comedy of Brendan Behan," *Etudes Irlandaises*, 11 (December 1986): 83-91.

John Betjeman

(28 August 1906 - 19 May 1984)

*This entry was written by John Clarke (University College, London) for
DLB 20: British Poets, 1914-1945.*

See also the Betjeman entry in DLB Yearbook: 1984.

SELECTED BOOKS: *Mount Zion* (London: James Press, 1931);

Ghastly Good Taste: a depressing story of the rise and fall of English architecture (London: Chapman & Hall, 1933; New York: St. Martin's Press, 1971);

Continual Dew: A Little Book of Bourgeois Verse (London: Murray, 1937);

An Oxford University Chest (London: Miles, 1938);

Antiquarian Prejudice (London: Hogarth Press, 1939);

Old Lights for New Chancels (London: Murray, 1940);

Vintage London (London: Collins, 1942);

English Cities and Small Towns (London: Collins, 1943);

John Piper (Harmondsworth, U.K.: Penguin, 1944);

New Bats in Old Belfries (London: Murray, 1945);

Slick But Not Streamlined: Poems & Short Pieces, selected and introduced by W. H. Auden (Garden City, N.Y.: Doubleday, 1947);

Selected Poems (London: Murray, 1948);

The English Scene (London: Cambridge University Press, 1951);

First and Last Loves (London: Murray, 1952; New York: Musson, 1952);

A Few Late Chrysanthemums (London: Murray, 1954);

Poems in the Porch (London: S.P.C.K., 1954);

The English Town in the Last Hundred Years (Cambridge: Cambridge University Press, 1956);

Collected Poems (London: Murray, 1958; Boston: Houghton Mifflin, 1959; enlarged edition, London: Murray, 1962; enlarged again, London: Murray, 1970; Boston: Houghton Mifflin, 1971);

Summoned By Bells (London: Murray, 1960; Boston: Houghton Mifflin, 1960);

Ground Plan to Skyline, as Richard M. Farren (London: Newman Neame Take Home Books, 1960);

A Ring of Bells (London: Murray, 1962; Boston: Houghton Mifflin, 1963);

The City of London Churches (London: Pitkin Pictorials, 1965);

High and Low (London: Murray, 1966; Boston: Houghton Mifflin, 1967);

A Pictorial History of English Architecture (London: Murray, 1972; New York: Macmillan, 1972);

John Betjeman

London's Historic Railway Stations (London: Murray, 1972);

A Nip in the Air (London: Murray, 1975; New York: Norton, 1976);

Church Poems (London: Pan, 1983).

Collections: *The Best of Betjeman*, selected by John Guest (London: Murray, 1978);

Uncollected Poems (London: Murray, 1983).

RECORDINGS: *The Poems of John Betjeman: The Golden Treasury of John Betjeman*, Spoken Arts 710, 819, volumes 1 and 2;

Summoned By Bells, Argo PLP 1069.

OTHER: *Devon: Shell Guide*, edited by Betjeman (London: Architectural Press, 1936);

Shropshire: A Shell Guide, edited by Betjeman and John Piper (London: Faber & Faber, 1951);

Collins' Guide to English Parish Churches, edited, with an introduction, by Betjeman (London: Collins, 1958); republished as *An American's Guide to English Parish Churches* (New York: McDowell, 1959);

A Hundred Sonnets by Charles Tennyson Turner, selected, with an introduction, by Betjeman

and Sir Charles Tennyson (London: Hart-Davis, 1960);

Cornwall: A Shell Guide, edited by Betjeman (London: Faber & Faber, 1964);

Victorian and Edwardian London from Old Photographs, edited, with introduction and commentaries, by Betjeman (London: Batsford, 1969);

Victorian and Edwardian Oxford from Old Photographs, edited by Betjeman and David Vaisey (London: Batsford, 1971);

Victorian and Edwardian Brighton from Old Photographs, edited by Betjeman and J. S. Grey (London: Batsford, 1972).

SELECTED PERIODICAL PUBLICATIONS—
UNCOLLECTED: "Lord Mount Prospect," *London Mercury*, 21 (December 1929): 113-121;

"The Death of Modernism," *Architectural Review*, 70 (December 1931): 161;

"Victorian Architecture," *World Review*, new series 23 (January 1951): 46-52;

"John Betjeman Replies," *Spectator*, 193 (8 October 1954): 441;

"City and Suburban," *Spectator*, 193 (15 October 1954) - 200 (10 January 1958);

"A Century of English Architecture," *Spectator*, 209 (24 August 1962): 252-254;

"A Tribute to Wystan Auden," in "Five," by Robert Lowell and others, *Shenandoah*, 18 (Winter 1967): 45-57.

John Betjeman was a unique figure in twentieth-century English poetry, enjoying a degree of fame and success unequaled by any poet since George Gordon, Lord Byron. His *Collected Poems* of 1958 reputedly sold more than one hundred thousand copies, and they are read by millions of people who normally never read poetry, and he became a household name through his many appearances on television panels and on programs about architecture. He was also quintessentially English, a pillar of the so-called establishment and the friend of royalty (Princess Margaret's affection for his poetry is well known), and during a long and diverse career, he accumulated several honorary doctorates, was made a commander, Order of the British Empire, and received a knighthood before being created the Poet Laureate in 1972.

Despite such public recognition (or perhaps partly because of it) Betjeman's stature as a poet has remained singularly hard to assess. Some critics have maintained that he is a poet of mediocre

John Betjeman, circa 1933

talents, a competent versifier whose adroit exploitation of the television medium in its early years enabled him to carve out for himself a reputation he does not deserve. The appearance of his poetry in Sunday newspaper supplements and the like, together with the popular image he cultivated as what Derek Stanford called "the sort of poet you expect to read about in a woman's magazine under the drier," has also aroused the distrust of purists. Others accord him a place in a central poetic tradition that would also probably include Alfred, Lord Tennyson, Thomas Hardy, and Rudyard Kipling. Less controversial is the widespread recognition that Betjeman's contribution to the appreciation of nineteenth-century English architecture—through books and broadcasts—has been deeply significant. Some have even described Betjeman as an architect manqué, though he preferred to be considered primarily a poet. It would be careless, however, to try to distinguish too sharply between the two roles: Betjeman's poetry and his architectural and topographical writings often share not only a similar

subject matter, but can be seen to form a coherent body of attitudes to English society and so continually comment upon each other. Most important for an understanding of Betjeman's artistic importance is a knowledge of the facts of his early life. Few other poets so openly recognized, or unashamedly described, the formative experiences of their childhood.

John Betjeman was born in London in 1906, the only child of Ernest Betjeman, a prosperous manufacturer of Dutch origin. The discreet opulence of the North London suburbs in which Betjeman spent his childhood is captured most memorably in a stanza from his poem "St. Saviour's, Aberdeen Park, Highbury, London, N." (1948):

> These were the streets my parents knew when they
>   loved and won—
>   The brougham that crunched the gravel, the
>   laurel-girt paths that wind,
> Geranium-beds for the lawn, Venetian blinds for
> the sun,
>   A separate tradesman's entrance, straw in the
>   mews behind,
> Just in the four-mile radius where hackney
>   carriages run,
>   Solid Italianate houses for the solid commercial
>   mind.

Betjeman's obsession with class, visible throughout all his poetry, derived in part from his early intuitions of the subtle snobbery permeating this polite childhood environment; while the terror of death, equally important to his poetry, was instilled in him at an early age by a Calvinistic nursery maid ("Hating to think of sphere succeeding sphere / Into eternity and God's Dread Will / I caught her terror then. I have it still.") The same nursery maid's alleged cruelty to Betjeman ("Lock'd into cupboards, left alone all day") may have been the origin of the deep sensitivity to pain and the fear of loneliness which are almost obsessive qualities in his later poetry.

This early sense of loneliness was to increase during Betjeman's adolescence, when his realization that he could not continue in the family business slowly estranged him from his father. "For myself," he wrote, "I knew as soon as I could read and write / That I must be a poet." At his preparatory school in Highgate, London, one of his teachers was the newly arrived T. S. Eliot, to whom the precocious schoolboy presented his first poetic attempts: "I bound my verse into a book / 'The Best of Betjeman' and

Evelyn Waugh and Betjeman, circa 1935

rized in some of his poems. At Oxford, Betjeman became part of the fashionable undergraduate set that was to provide material for the early novels of Evelyn Waugh, whose long friendship with Betjeman dated from this time. As an undergraduate Betjeman maintained his indifference to sport ("I still don't know where the playing fields are . . .") and cultivated instead a deliberate aestheticism. An early photograph shows him in dreamy contemplation under a pseudo-Gothic archway, and the poem "The Arrest of Oscar Wilde at the Cadogan Hotel," written at Oxford, reflects this pose in a similar manner.

Betjeman was as responsible as anyone for creating the popular image of this Oxford generation as one of rich mindlessness, notably through poems such as "The 'Varsity Students' Rag" (written while he was at Oxford):

> But that's nothing to the rag we had at the college
>   the other night;
> We'd gallons and gallons of cider—and I got fright-
>   fully tight.
> And then we smash'd up ev'rything, and what was
>   the funniest part
> We smashed some rotten old pictures which were
>   priceless works of art.

Perhaps unsurprisingly, Betjeman left Oxford having failed to receive a degree. After a short spell of teaching at Heddon Court School in Barnet, Hertfordshire (where, typically, he obtained the job by masquerading as an expert on cricket), he became in 1931 the assistant editor of the *Architectural Review*, a post which brought him into contact with leading architects and historians of architecture: "In my own unpleasant occupation of architectural journalism I am continually meeting architects," he wrote. Nineteen thirty-one also saw the publication of Betjeman's first book of poems, *Mount Zion*.

The spirit in which this book was conceived is suggested by Betjeman's description of it as a "precious, hyper-sophisticated book" and by the dedication of it to Mrs. Arthur Dugdale, mistress of Sezincote, an English country house to which Oxford's most fashionable undergraduates were frequently invited. Although *Mount Zion* smacks of affectation—not least in its highly ornate binding and blue leaves—it contains embryonic themes and preoccupations that recur throughout Betjeman's poetic oeuvre.

Notable among these are an interest in topography, particularly that of English suburbia ("Croydon," "Camberley"); nineteenth-century

handed it / To one who, I was told, liked poetry— / The American master, Mr. Eliot." Betjeman did not record Eliot's opinion.

From 1917 to 1920 John Betjeman attended the Dragon School, Oxford, where, under the influence of a teacher, Gerald Haynes, he first developed an interest in architecture. In 1920 Betjeman left this school for Marlborough public school in Wiltshire, where the fear of being bullied added to feelings of vulnerability and isolation in an already oversensitive mind.

After the "Doom! Shivering doom!" of Marlborough, Betjeman went up to Magdalen College, Oxford, in 1925. Here his poetic talents and already remarkable knowledge of English architecture earned him the admiration of the scholar C. M. Bowra, while his neglect of academic work— "While we ate Virginia hams, / Contemporaries passed exams"—earned the scorn of his tutor, C. S. Lewis, whom Betjeman later sati-

architecture; religion ("Hymn," "The Wykeham-ist"); and death ("Death in Leamington"), several of these elements often being present within a single poem, such as "For Nineteenth-Century Burials." Most obvious in *Mount Zion*, however, is Betjeman's early talent for comic verse and gentle satire, at its most extreme in "The 'Varsity Students' Rag," but creeping into virtually every other poem in the volume. "Prolonged solemnity is not in his nature," a friend of Betjeman's once remarked; the comment is certainly applicable to *Mount Zion*.

In 1933 Betjeman left his post on the *Architectural Review* and began to edit the Shell series of topographical guides to Britain. In the same year he married Penelope, daughter of Sir Philip (later Lord) Chetwode, Commander-in-Chief, India. Of his relationship with her daughter, Lady Chetwode is said to have retorted, "We ask people like that to our houses but we don't marry them." In the following year Betjeman became the film critic for William Maxwell Aitken, Lord Beaverbrook's *Evening Standard*. He was sacked within a year for writing overenthusiastic reviews, but there survives an anecdote from this time which typifies the humor and eccentricity for which he became well known. As Derek Stanford reports, "On one occasion, he had been asked to interview the star Myrna Loy. 'I took her out to lunch' he recollects, and asked her would she mind if he wrote that she 'was very interested in English Perpendicular' [an architectural style]. 'Not at all' replied Miss Loy, whereupon Mr. Betjeman duly reported his little witticism."

Betjeman's second volume of verse, *Continual Dew*, appeared in 1937. Its subtitle—*A Little Book of Bourgeois Verse*—pinpointed the emergence of what was to become a favorite poetic subject: the upper-middle-class milieu of the English home counties. In "Love in a Valley" he portrays this milieu with a characteristic blend of irony and affection:

> Deep down the drive go the cushioned rhododendrons,
> Deep down, sand deep, drives the heather root,
> Deep the spliced timber barked around the summer-house,
> Light lies the tennis-court, plantain underfoot.
> What a winter welcome to what a Surrey homestead!
> Oh! the metal lantern and white enamelled door!
> Oh! the spread of orange from the gas-fire on the carpet!

Betjeman at work in his flat, 1951

> Oh! the tiny patter, sandalled footsteps on the floor!

The complexity of tone apparent in a poem such as "Love in a Valley" was not recognized by the first readers of *Continual Dew*. As with Betjeman's first volume, a disproportionate degree of attention was given to his comic and light verse, of which "Slough," appearing first in *Continual Dew* and since highly anthologized, was the most notorious: "Come friendly bombs, and fall on Slough / It isn't fit for humans now / There isn't grass to graze a cow." Betjeman's desire to be taken seriously as a poet frequently suffered through the popularity of poems in this mode at the expense of his more serious endeavors. Referring specifically to "Slough" and the earlier "The 'Varsity Students' Rag," he later complained that "they now seem to me merely comic verse and competent magazine writing, topical and tiresome." Although *Continual Dew* shows only limited improvement on *Mount Zion*, one poem in it indicates the stirrings of a far maturer poetic vision. In "Death of King George V," inspired by the newspaper headline "New King Arrives in Capital By Air," Betjeman crystallized in a potent image the troubled sense of a passing era which the tone of post-war England was to confirm: "Old men who never cheated, never doubted, / Communicated monthly, sit and stare / At the new suburb stretched beyond the runway / Where a young man lands hatless from the air." Betjeman's doubt about modernity—with its implied disrespect for tradition, its faith in material progress and the kind of landscape and people produced by it—was to become overt pessimism in future volumes of verse.

During World War II Betjeman continued to work largely in the media, serving variously in the Admiralty, as the United Kingdom press attaché to Dublin, as a broadcaster with the BBC (1943), and in the books department of the British Council (1944-1946). The war period also saw the publication of *Old Lights for New Chancels* in 1940, followed by a further collection of poems, *New Bats in Old Belfries*, in 1945. Although both these volumes were well received and sold well, in the mid 1940s Betjeman was still better known as a writer of books on topography and architecture than as a poet, and he had already made a reputation for himself as an expert on (and champion of) the Victorian Gothic revival in architecture.

His first book on architecture, *Ghastly Good Taste: a depressing story of the rise and fall of English architecture*, appeared in 1933, when Betjeman was still at the *Architectural Review*. It was followed by *An Oxford University Chest* in 1938, and *Antiquarian Prejudice* (1939), which contained the early expression of what was to become a familiar argument: "Architecture has a wider meaning than that which is commonly given to it. For architecture means not a house, or a single building or a church . . . but your surroundings; not a town or a street, but our whole over-populated island. It is concerned with where we eat, work, sleep, play, congregate, escape. It is our background, alas, often too permanent."

Betjeman's fascination with the relationship between people and surroundings—the social history of architecture—forms the basis of all of his topographical writings, from *Vintage London* (1942) to *English Cities and Small Towns* (1943), the popularity of which was eclipsed only by *First and Last Loves* (1952), perhaps the most representative of his prose writings. A list of some of its chapter headings indicates the nature and variety of its author's topographical interests: "Aberdeen Granite," "Leeds—A City of Contrasts," "London Railway Stations," "Nonconformist Architecture."

The title itself—*First and Last Loves*—is indicative of Betjeman's approach to his subject: invariably enthusiastic, partisan, celebrating the places he likes, excoriating the things he detests. In *First and Last Loves* appeared a description of a Cornish church which has become a famous example of Betjeman's idiosyncratic style: "Saint Endellion! Saint Endellion! The name is like a ring of bells . . . on the top of the hill was the old church of St. Endellion. It looked, and still looks, just like a hare. The ears are the pinnacles of the tower and the rest of the hare, the church, crouches among wind-slashed firs." A reviewer of *First and Last Loves* wrote, "Any industrious fool with a good reference library can docket and classify a work of art, but to transmit it as an experience shared is an infinitely rare gift." This "gift" was invaluable in Betjeman's increasing popularity as a television broadcaster following World War II, a period which witnessed his influence in changing the British public's attitude to the Victorian achievement in the visual arts. Despite this activity, Betjeman always insisted that he was a poet first and foremost, even claiming that his topographical works were merely a means of gaining the financial freedom that allowed him to pursue poetry.

The publication of *Old Lights for New Chancels* seemed to justify Betjeman's insistence that serious attention be paid to his poetry. The poems that make up this collection show a marked advance in metrical subtlety and a more profound treatment of familiar themes, rather than any radical departure from his earlier poems. Indeed, Betjeman was never an experimental poet, differing from most of his contemporaries by remaining immune—even in the 1920s—to the pressures of modernism. Philip Larkin wrote that for Betjeman "there has been no symbolism, no objective correlative, no T. S. Eliot or Ezra Pound, no rediscovery of myth or language as gesture, no *Seven Types* or *Some Versions*. . . ." Instead, Betjeman preferred to create within the limitation of pre-existing metrical forms, particularly those of nineteenth-century poets, some of whom remain quite obscure. Betjeman described his selection and adoption of these poetic models in an unpretentious manner: "I am a traditionalist in metre and have made few experiments. The rhythms of Tennyson, [George] Crabbe, [Robert Stephen] Hawker, [Ernest Christopher] Dowson, Hardy, James Elroy Flecker, [Thomas] Moore and Hymns Ancient and Modern are generally buzzing about in my brain, and I choose one from

BAKER STREET STATION BUFFET

8th December 1952

Early electric! with what radiant hope
  Men shaped this many-branched electrolier
And curl'd the flex around the iron rope
  And let the dazzling vacuum globes hang clear,
And then with hearts the rich contrivance fill'd
Of copper, beaten by the Bromsgrove Guild.

Early electric! sit you down and see,
  'Mid this fine woodwork, these enduring tiles
The stained glass windmill & a pot of tea,
  sepia Metroland & its electric miles;
And visualise, far down the shining lines
Your parents' homestead set in murmuring pines.

Smoothly from Harrow, passing Preston Road,
  They saw the last green fields and misty sky,
At Neasden watch'd a workman's train unload
  Then, with the morning villas sliding by,
They felt so sure on their electric trip
That youth a progress were in partnership.

And all day long in murky London Wall
  The thought of Ruislip kept him warm inside
In Farringdon, that lunch hour, at a stall,
  He bought a potted plant of London Pride;
While she, adrift in sales at shoppers' heaven
Bought your first baby shoes at D. H. Evans.

Early electric! maybe even here
  They met that evening at six fifteen
Below the hearts of this electrolier
  And caught the first non-stop to Willesden Green
Then on and out through rural Rayner's Lane
To Autumn-scented Middlesex again.

Cancer has kill'd him. Heart is killing her
  The trees are down, an Odeon flashes fire
Where once the wind made murmur in the fir
  While "they would for their children's good conspire."
Of all those loves and hopes on hurrying feet
Thou art the worn memorial, Baker Street.

A late draft for the poem published in 1953 as "The Metropolitan Railway Station"
(Sotheby's auction catalogue, sale number 5998, 30 April & 1 May 1990)

John Betjeman, 1955

these which seems to me to suit the theme."
Betjeman's affection for the nineteenth century is
common both to his topographical writings and
his poetry, where it is revealed not only stylistically in pastiche, parody, or straightforward adoption of a particular stanza form, but in subject matter too. There is, in Betjeman's poetry, a high
incidence of narrative or anecdotal poems in
nineteenth-century settings. The whole tenor of
Betjeman's imagination has even been described
as Victorian: his fondness for the quaint and the
grotesque, his wistful piety, and his unabashed sentimentality.

In *Old Lights for New Chancels* and *New Bats
in Old Belfries* there emerged for the first time a lyrical poetry of a power and delicacy which surprised its early readers. In "Trebetherick" Betjeman discovers in memories of his childhood a
previously untapped source of inspiration. The
poem is one of several based on memories of holidays on the Cornish coast: "But when a storm
was at its height, / And feathery slate was black
in rain, / And tamarisks were hung with light /
And golden sand was brown again, / Spring tide
and blizzard would unite / And sea came flood-
ing up the lane." "Trebetherick" ushered in Betjeman's poetic maturity, achieved in those poems
which directly express personal experience. In another fine poem, "Ireland with Emily," he draws

again on memories of undergraduate holidays
spent in a country whose melancholy beauty
("Stony hills poured over space") never ceased to
fascinate him.

As had been the case with earlier volumes,
it was the lighter verse in *Old Lights for New Chancels* which was to receive the most attention, and
the emergence of the "Betjeman heroine" received particular notice. Beginning with "Pam,
you great big mountainous sports girl / Whizzing
them over the net with the strength of five," this
rather fearsome, asexual heroine reappeared in
New Bats in Old Belfries as Myfanwy, "Ringleader,
tom-boy and chum to the weak," before reaching
its apotheosis (also in *New Bats in Old Belfries*) in
"Miss J. Hunter Dunn, Miss J. Hunter Dunn /
Furnish'd and burnish'd by Aldershot sun, /
What strenuous singles we played after tea, /
We in the tournament—you against me." When
asked whether he really found this kind of
woman attractive, Betjeman admitted that, yes,
he did like such "great dominating creatures,"
and added characteristically, "Anyone who has
been to a Public School is a masochist."

Old Lights for New Chancels also contains a
preface in which Betjeman describes some of his
poetic interests: "I love suburbs and gaslights
and Pont St. and Gothic Revival Churches and
mineral railways, provincial towns and garden
cities." The importance of topography to Betjeman's poetry is reflected even by the number
of his poems which take their titles from the
names of places. But as W. H. Auden wrote in
his introduction to *Slick But Not Streamlined*
(1947), "Wild or unhumanized nature holds no
charms for the average topophile because it is lacking in history." Betjeman delights in describing
places and buildings not for their intrinsic value
but for their human associations. Starting with
the premise that architecture is the outward and
visible manifestation of a society's spiritual condition, the body of Betjeman's prose and poetry
from the 1940s onward reiterates the conviction
that happiness is difficult to achieve in a world
growing uglier. In the early poem "Death of
King George V," Betjeman registered an uncertain response to a new era; this attitude was
replaced by a more articulate criticism of the
spiritlessness and physical ugliness of postwar English society. His early satire on town planners, bureaucrats, speculators, and their victims was essentially comic, and his portraits of modern living,
in such poems as "Slough," too crude and extravagant: "In labour-saving homes, with care / Their

wives frizz out peroxide hair / And dry it in synthetic air / And paint their nails."

Such lightly worn attitudes were absorbed into a more comprehensive crusade against certain kinds of environmental change and their effects on society. Some commentators, including John Press, have for this reason placed Betjeman "in the direct line of descent from . . . [John] Ruskin and [William] Morris, whose love of the arts was linked with their desire for the regeneration of society." Others have been less impressed with Betjeman's aesthetic conservatism. His reputation has frequently suffered through what has been sometimes regarded as a lack of awareness of and sympathy with the life-style of the masses. It is true that Betjeman's professed disgust with much of modernity is sometimes indistinguishable from a rather unspecific, aristocratic disgust of the ordinary people who have to live in it. His appeal to the English people, in a 1951 lecture, to raise their eyes "from the privet hedge to the hills," is not free from condescension, and in his poetry he is often at pains to dissociate himself from what poet Alfred Alvarez has called the "post-war Welfare State Englishman: shabby . . . poor . . . underfed, underpaid, overtaxed, hopeless." One can see in Betjeman's descriptions of working-class and lower-middle-class people the influence of T. S. Eliot's *The Waste Land* (1922).

Both critics and devotees of Betjeman would find some truth in Larkin's descriptions of him as one who is "insular and regressive, against the dominant trends of today"; one who proclaims "a benevolent class system the best of all political worlds." Although Larkin writes partly in approval, others have been more critical, and Betjeman, in his journalism and his poetry alike, defended himself against criticism of this kind. He declared his attitude to modernity as one of reluctant acceptance ("Dear old, bloody old England / Of telegraph poles and tin"), while his deepened religious faith forced him to recognize his kinship with those whom he would have formerly satirized: "Our Creator is with us yet, / To be worshipped by you and the woman / Of the slacks and the cigarette." His proverbial nausea at contemporary suburban life is at least ambiguous: "I see no harm in trying to describe overbuilt Surrey in verse. But when I do so I am not being satirical but topographical." Affection and mockery are usually combined in Betjeman's finest poems about suburban living.

The 1950s and onward saw little reduction in Betjeman's output. In the fields of

Betjeman wearing Henry James's morning clothes (photograph by Hans Beacham)

architecture and topography he wrote prolifically, establishing his reputation internationally as a historian of English—especially nineteenth-century—architecture. A further collection of poems, with the rather premature title of *A Few Late Chrysanthemums*, appeared in 1954 and reinforced growing convictions that Betjeman had to be regarded as a serious artist. Four years later appeared the best-selling *Collected Poems*, following a year of regular BBC broadcasts. It was typical of Betjeman's style that *Collected Poems* was introduced not by a fellow poet or by a critic, but by a member of the English aristocracy. (The critic Bernard Bergonzi later described this introduction as "inept and unnecessary.") After 1958 two more collections of poetry appeared, *High and Low* (1966) and *A Nip in the Air* (1975), as well as the blank-verse autobiographical poem *Summoned By Bells* (1960), a modest account of the poet's life from first memories until his departure from Oxford in 1928. Since large sections of *Summoned*

By Bells merely seemed to repeat—and in a more pedestrian fashion—material already made familiar through the *Collected Poems*, it received only a quiet reception at its publication. But as an account of the growth of a disturbingly self-conscious mind ("Deep, dark and pitiful I saw myself / In my mind's mirror"), it sheds light on the introspective qualities of Betjeman's later poetry.

This introspection first became evident in *A Few Late Chrysanthemums*. Early readers were struck by its predominant gloominess. The fear of death, always present in Betjeman's work, becomes a major obsession in poems such as "The Cottage Hospital," in which the poet pictures his own death: "And say shall I groan in dying / as I twist the sweaty sheet? / Or gasp for breath uncrying / as I feel my senses drown'd?"

Similar to these are poems expressing the loss and displacement felt by a generation which has been discarded by the march of "progress." "The Metropolitan Railway Station" is typical: "Cancer has killed him. Heart is killing her. / The trees are down. An Odeon flashes fire / Where stood their villa by the murmuring fir / When 'they would for their children's good conspire.'" In such poems Betjeman's affinities to Larkin can be discerned. The two poets admired in each other's writing the properties they held in common: a traditionalism in form dictated by the need for simple, direct expression; an instinctive conservatism which struggles to accept contemporaneity; and a pervasive spiritual questioning. Betjeman's own tenaciously held Anglicanism offered little to ameliorate the deep pessimism that characterizes *A Few Late Chrysanthemums*. In an important article, "John Betjeman Replies," which appeared in the *Spectator* (October 1954), Betjeman accounts for the pervasive gloominess of this volume of poems. Speaking first of his earlier verse, he admits that "in those days my purest pleasure was the exploration of suburbs and provincial towns, and my impurest pleasure the pursuit of the brawny athletic girl," and goes on to add that "fear of death (a manifestation of the lack of faith I deeply desire) remorse and a sense of man's short time on earth and an impatience with so-called 'progress' did inform many of the poems in my latest volume." He then describes quite candidly the inadequacy of his religious faith: "the only practical way to face the dreaded lonely journey into Eternity seems to me the Christian one. I therefore try to believe that Christ was God, made man and gives Eternal Life, and that I may be confirmed in this belief by the sacra-

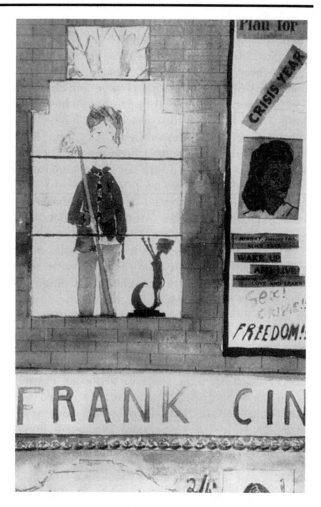

Crisis Year, watercolor by Betjeman

ments and by prayer." Betjeman was a Christian because he had no choice, finding faith easier to wear in public (in 1952 he was appointed governor of the Oxford Anglican Study Centre, Pusey House) than in private, and easiest to accept in its outward forms: "Eternity Contained In Time and coloured glass." Betjeman's later poetry reiterates this struggle to believe.

How is Betjeman's achievement to be judged? Despite his immense popular following and the scholarly respect paid to his prose writings, Betjeman's poetic stature has remained for a long time in doubt. The personality of the man looms so large (he liked to order champagne by the tankards; he owned, and wore, clothing that once belonged to Henry James) that criticism of his poetry has been partisan or of a limited and ad hoc nature. Although his work has been praised at different times by writers as diverse as Edmund Wilson and W. H. Auden (who dedicated *The Age of Anxiety* to Betjeman), most critics would concur that he is a poet of considerable importance who has yet narrowly failed to reach the front rank of modern English poetry.

The reasons for this failure include the limitations of his peculiarly English sensibility. In 1947 Larkin felt forced to write, almost apologetically, that "His poetry, with its wealth of local allusion and local sentiment, its high-pitched titter, does shut a door in the face of American or European visitors," adding that it is a "Special, English thing."

The more serious consequence of such insularity is reflected in the frequent criticism that Betjeman's poetic sympathy is either restricted to the experience of the class to which he belongs, or is exclusively personal. Certainly, it is true of his later poems about death that they are usually expressions of Betjeman's fear of his own death, or the deaths of close friends, and that they lack any universal application, just as his poems on the loss of innocence refer exclusively to John Betjeman's loss of innocence.

Again, his poetic response to World War II was also of this wholly personal nature: the elegies he wrote to friends killed in war are quite untroubled by the wider moral problems most poets encountered in trying to frame a response to an evil whose enormity disabled poetry's attempt to be sincere. John Press wrote in 1974 that Betjeman "does not, for all his variety and keenness of social observation, give us a powerful and comprehensive vision of society, or a sustained argument about the nature of man," a sentiment echoed by Bernard Bergonzi, who distrusted the unintellectual temper of Betjeman's writing: "One can only regret the association of so much cleverness with so little real intelligence." Bergonzi also criticized the sentimentality of Betjeman's religious faith (as expressed in his poetry) and his inability to defend it from any clear intellectual position. Indeed, Betjeman's poetry is often deliberately unintellectual, and he differed from most modern poets by eschewing doctrine, adopting no aesthetic, joining no movement, and making no excessive claims for the importance of his art. But it would be incorrect to conceive of him as one who created for himself a large popular audience at the expense of a poetry which fails to engage life at its deepest level. Auden argued that we should not associate Betjeman's frequent lack of earnestness with triviality. It *could* be said of his poems about the sea that their theme of human impermanence measured against the vastness and endurability of nature is only tentatively sug-

Sir John Betjeman, 1971

gested before Betjeman switches into a lighter mood. But it may be that his unwillingness to explore such ideas is deliberate, and that his humor provides a necessary bulwark against "a nature already prone to bouts of depression," and thus against what might be the natural conclusion to such poetic explorations.

More sophisticated biographical criticism, such as Press's, has gone on to suggest that the topographical accuracy and precision of period detail evident in Betjeman's poetry is born of this same need to allay restlessness and to stabilize an excessively gloomy imagination. In this need he has been compared to Tennyson, whose influence on Betjeman's poetry is considerable. Future attempts to evaluate Betjeman's importance as a writer are likely to find such psychologically oriented approaches among the most rewarding. Betjeman's position within the mainstream of

English poetry yet remains to be ascertained, though it will be related to the value placed on the reaction against modernism. After his important self-explanatory article in 1954 Betjeman offered few further insights into himself. His personal life became a mystery even as his public esteem led him to be regarded as much a part of English heritage as that which he defended in his poetry and prose.

Betjeman welcomed the honors lavished on him, including a knighthood and the Poet Laureateship. He relished the fun and glitter of fashionable society, valued the friendship of Princess Margaret, responded gladly to the command of Prince Charles that he should write a poem for his investiture as Prince of Wales, derived pleasure from staying in the splendid houses of the aristocracy. But his deepest loyalties were to friends of all classes and to poetry. He received on his seventy-fifth birthday a beautifully bound and printed book of poems written for him by some of the best living poets, a dozen of whom arrived at his house to present him with the unexpected gift.

He died on 19 May 1984 at his home in Trebetherick, Cornwall, where he spent so many holidays in boyhood and where he lies buried in the village churchyard not far from the sea that was for him the most potent symbol of eternity.

Bibliography:

Margaret L. Stapleton, *Sir John Betjeman: A Bibliography of Writings By and About Him* (Metuchen, N.J.: Scarecrow Press, 1974).

Biographies:

Patrick Taylor Martin, *John Betjeman: His Life and Work* (London: Allen Lane, 1983);

Bevis Hillier, *John Betjeman: A Life in Pictures* (London: Herbert Press, 1984);

Hillier, *Young Betjeman* (London: Murray, 1988).

References:

W. H. Auden, Introduction to Betjeman's *Slick But Not Streamlined* (Garden City, N.Y.: Doubleday, 1947);

Bernard Bergonzi, "Culture and Mr. Betjeman," *Twentieth Century*, 165 (February 1959):

130-137; (May 1959): 520;

Earl of Birkenhead, Introduction to Betjeman's *Collected Poems* (London: Murray, 1958; Boston: Houghton Mifflin, 1959);

C. M. Bowra, *Memories 1898-1939* (Cambridge, Mass.: Harvard University Press, 1967), pp. 165-172;

Jocelyn Brooke, *Ronald Firbank and John Betjeman* (London: Longmans, Green, 1962);

Frank Delaney, *Betjeman Country* (London: Hodder & Stoughton, 1983);

Pennie Denton, ed., *Betjeman's London* (London: Penguin, 1988);

Tim Devlin, "Sir John Betjeman, the new Poet Laureate," *Times* (London), 11 October 1972, p. 16;

John Hollander, "John Betjeman: Almost Uniquely Qualified," *New York Times*, 11 October 1972, p. 18;

Frank Kermode, "Henry Miller and John Betjeman," in his *Puzzles & Epiphanies* (New York: Chilmark Press, 1962), pp. 140-154;

Philip Larkin, "The Blending of Betjeman," *Spectator*, 205 (2 December 1960): 913;

Larkin, Introduction to Betjeman's *Collected Poems* (Boston: Houghton Mifflin, 1971);

John Press, *John Betjeman* (Harlow: Longman, 1974);

Bill Ruddick, " 'Some ruin-bibber, randy for antique': Philip Larkin's Response to the Poetry of John Betjeman," *Critical Quarterly*, 28 (Winter 1986): 63-70;

John Sparrow, "The Poetry of John Betjeman," in his *Independent Essays* (London: Faber & Faber, 1963), pp. 166-179;

Stephen Spender, "Poetry for Poetry's Sake and Poetry beyond Poetry," *Horizon* (London), 13 April 1946, pp. 221-238;

Derek Stanford, *John Betjeman: A Study* (London: Spearman, 1961);

John Wain, "Four Observer Pieces: John Betjeman," in his *Essays on Literature and Ideas* (London: Macmillan, 1963; New York: St. Martin's Press, 1963), pp. 168-171.

Papers:

The library of the University of Victoria, British Columbia, holds the major collection of Betjeman's papers.

Elizabeth Bowen

(7 June 1899 - 22 February 1973)

This entry was written by Janet E. Dunleavy (University of Wisconsin-Milwaukee) for
DLB 15: British Novelists, 1930-1959: Part One.

SELECTED BOOKS: *Encounters: Stories* (London: Sidgwick & Jackson, 1923; New York: Boni & Liveright, 1923);

Ann Lee's and Other Stories (London: Sidgwick & Jackson, 1926; New York: Boni & Liveright, 1926);

The Hotel (London: Constable, 1927; New York: Dial, 1928);

The Last September (London: Constable, 1929; New York: Dial, 1929);

Joining Charles and Other Stories (London: Constable, 1929; New York: Dial, 1929);

Friends and Relations (London: Constable, 1931; New York: Dial, 1931);

To the North (London: Gollancz, 1932; New York: Knopf, 1933);

The Cat Jumps and Other Stories (London: Gollancz, 1934);

The House in Paris (London: Gollancz, 1935; New York: Knopf, 1936);

The Death of the Heart (London: Gollancz, 1938; New York: Knopf, 1939);

Look At All Those Roses: Short Stories (London: Gollancz, 1941; New York: Knopf, 1941);

Bowen's Court (London: Longmans, Green, 1942; New York: Knopf, 1942);

English Novelists (London: Collins, 1942; New York: Hastings House, 1942);

Seven Winters (Dublin: Cuala, 1942); republished as *Seven Winters: Memories of a Dublin Childhood* (London & New York: Longmans, Green, 1943);

The Demon Lover and Other Stories (London: Cape, 1945); republished as *Ivy Gripped the Steps* (New York: Knopf, 1946);

Anthony Trollope: A New Judgement (London, New York & Toronto: Oxford University Press, 1946);

Why Do I Write? An Exchange of Views Between Elizabeth Bowen, Graham Greene, and V. S. Pritchett (London: Marshall, 1948; Folcroft, Pa.: Folcroft, 1969);

The Heat of the Day (London: Cape, 1949; New York: Knopf, 1949);

Collected Impressions (London: Longmans, Green, 1950; New York: Knopf, 1950);

The Shelbourne: A Centre of Dublin Life for More Than a Century (London: Harrap, 1951); republished as *The Shelbourne Hotel* (New York: Knopf, 1951);

A World of Love (London: Cape, 1955; New York: Knopf, 1955);

A Time in Rome (London & Toronto: Longmans, Green, 1960; New York: Knopf, 1960);

Afterthought: Pieces about Writing (London: Longmans, Green, 1962);

Seven Winters: Memories of a Dublin Childhood and Afterthought: Pieces about Writing (New York: Knopf, 1962);

The Little Girls (London: Cape, 1964; New York: Knopf, 1964);

Eva Trout, or Changing Scenes (New York: Knopf, 1968; London: Cape, 1969);

Pictures and Conversations (New York: Knopf, 1975).

Between 1923, when her first volume of short stories, *Encounters*, appeared, and 1975, when her last volume of memoirs, *Pictures and Conversations*, was published posthumously, Elizabeth Bowen produced a new book almost every year, her longest lapse being the five-year period between *A World of Love* (1955) and *A Time in Rome* (1960). Four of her books were republished short stories from earlier collections; the rest—twenty-five in all—are comprised of autobiographical and critical writings and histories as well as the prose fiction for which she is best known. In addition to these works in book form, Elizabeth Bowen regularly wrote reviews and articles for periodicals such as the *New Statesman and Nation*, the *Tatler*, the *Spectator*, *Cornhill Magazine*, the *Saturday Review of Literature*, *New Republic*, the *New York Times Magazine*, and *Harper's*, and in the late 1950s she became associate editor of the *London Magazine*, which had published her earlier critical essays. She frequently appeared on radio and television, especially after the end of World War II,

and her lectures and reading engagements often took her far from Dublin and London literary circles, in which she was most at home, to North America and continental Europe. Among her contemporaries she was widely regarded and honored as an author of major reputation. When she died in 1973, there was no question of the place she had earned in the annals of literature. Since her death her achievements have continued to receive praise by critics who have reassessed her work and by publishers who continue to make her books available to each new generation of readers.

Bowen was born in Dublin, Ireland, on 7 June 1899 to parents whose privileged social class still derived both wealth and social position from its English heritage and record of ancestral service in high military and government office in Ireland and England. Her father was Henry Charles Cole Bowen of Bowen's Court in County Cork, a direct descendant of Lieutenant Colonel Henry Bowen, who had received his eight-hundred-acre estate in 1653 as a reward for service in Oliver Cromwell's campaign against the Irish. The Bowens had come to Ireland from Wales before the seventeenth century—the family name originally was apOwen. From Cromwell's time until the winter of 1959-1960, when Elizabeth sold Bowen's Court, County Cork had been the Bowen family seat. Elizabeth's mother was Florence Colley of Mount Temple in Clontarf, a northern suburb of Dublin. A Colley ancestor, Walter Cowley, had served as solicitor general and surveyor general of Ireland in the sixteenth century. Through the Colleys, Elizabeth was related also to Arthur Wellesley, Duke of Wellington (1769-1852), the British general and statesman who dfeated Napoleon at Waterloo and served (1828-1830) as British prime minister.

Although Henry Cole Bowen was one of a family of eight and Florence Colley was one of a family of ten, Elizabeth was an only child. Her aunts and uncles, however, provided her with an ever-increasing number of older and younger cousins with whom she visited frequently, often for extended periods of time. As a result, all the cousins were very much at home with one another and with the aunts and uncles who served as parental surrogates. According to her biographer, Victoria Glendinning, the size and closeness of the two families became a matter of particular significance early in Elizabeth Bowen's life when, first because of the serious illness of her father, and then because of the death of her mother, a "committee of aunts" was formed to supervise her upbringing.

During her first five or six years, however, as Bowen reminisced in *Seven Winters* (1942), she enjoyed a normal Anglo-Irish childhood with her parents. Most of each year was spent in Dublin, where her father was first a barrister in private practice, then an official of the Land Commission; during the summer the family moved to Cork, the subject of another Bowen book, *Bowen's Court* (1942), which combines reminiscences with family history. By the time she was seven, this pattern of life had changed: Henry Cole Bowen, whose mental health had been precarious for more than a year, was hospitalized. On the advice of her doctors, Florence Colley Bowen took her daughter to England where there was, according to Glendinning, "a network of Anglo-Irish relatives" to look after them. For the next five years home was a series of rented villas on the Kent coast where Audrey Fiennes, a cousin close in age to Elizabeth, often spent her holidays; their escapades and those Bowen shared with a neighboring child were later woven into *The Little Girls* (1964). Meanwhile, Henry Cole Bowen recovered gradually. By the time Elizabeth was twelve he was making frequent visits to Hythe, the village in Kent where his wife and daughter were then living, and they in turn spent the summer of 1912 at Bowen's Court. Plans for a permanent return to Ireland and to the former pattern of family life were dashed, however, by the discovery that Florence Colley

Dust jacket for Bowen's fifth novel, which shows the influence of her friend Virginia Woolf

Bowen had developed cancer. Her death in September 1912 was a severe blow to Elizabeth, around whom the network of relatives closed once again. She was sent to live during the school year with one of her mother's unmarried sisters, who kept house for an unmarried brother in Hertfordshire, where Elizabeth was enrolled as a day student at Harpenden Hall; during the summers she returned to Ireland to Bowen's Court where she was looked after by her father and one of his sisters.

In 1914 Elizabeth Bowen was sent from the day school in Hertfordshire to continue her education at Downe House, a boarding school in Kent that had been established in the former home of Charles Darwin. In August of that year England entered the conflict that became World War I, but that fact had no immediate impact on Bowen's life. Insulated from the world as only a fifteen-year-old in Anglo-Irish Big House society could be, she was not aware that this conflict was the first of four major events that were to change entirely the world into which she had been born. The next event was the Easter Rising of 1916, during which Padraic Pearse read the Proclamation of the Irish Republic from the steps of the post office in Dublin, then led his fellow revolutionaries to martyrdom. Retaliatory measures adopted by England attracted world attention and polarized sympathies in Ireland. The Bowens were affected when Captain John Bowen-Colthurst was implicated in the death of Francis Sheehy Skeffington, a well-known pacifist. Although Henry Cole Bowen refused to become involved personally, referring his cousin Georgina, Bowen-Colthurst's mother, to others when she sought his help, Sheehy Skeffington's name became a rallying point for the Republican cause, and Bowen-Colthurst, denounced by Irish and Anglo-Irish alike, became a symbol of bigotry and oppression.

The third event that changed Bowen's world was the Anglo-Irish War (1919-1921), known in Ireland as the War of Independence. A Home Rule Bill providing for legislative independence for Ireland had been passed by Parliament on the eve of World War I but had not been implemented. Following the Easter Rising, the British military presence in Ireland had become more visible, increasing fears among supporters of Home Rule that it never would become law. In the general election of 1918 candidates in Ireland committed themselves either to continued union with Great Britain or to Home Rule: Home Rulers, adopting *Sinn Fein* ("Ourselves") as their slogan, vowed that, if elected, they would not sit in the British Parliament but would set up an independent legislature for Ireland. The *Sinn Fein* party won overwhelmingly; true to their word, its candidates established the first Dail (Irish Parliament) in Dublin, which England refused to recognize. Supporters of the Dail in turn refused to submit any longer to English rule. The inevitable armed conflict that followed pitted soldiers of the Irish Republican army, many of them trained by the British army during the war, against British soldiers garrisoned in Ireland and an auxiliary military force known as the "Black and Tans" (from the combination of the black uniform of the Royal Irish Constabulary and the tan uniform of the regular British army worn by its members).

For the most part the Anglo-Irish were Unionists; Big Houses therefore became targets for Republican attacks, especially in reprisal for violence committed by the Black and Tans. How-

ever, the Anglo-Irish also enjoyed the protection of the British army, and if they were sometimes in danger, the conflict also brought them a new crop of young officers to be entertained in Big Houses like "Danielstown" of Bowen's *The Last September* (1929). The treaty that ended the Anglo-Irish War confirmed the division of Ireland into Northern Ireland, a British province, and the Irish Free State. It also signaled the fourth event that changed Bowen's world: the Irish Civil War (1921-1923). This time the conflict was internal, between pro-Treaty and Republican forces, but it was nonetheless violent and bitter. Again Big Houses were burned (or captured and used as military command posts) while their owners, no longer protected by the British army, fled to Dublin's comparative safety or to England. Although Bowen's Court was occupied, it escaped serious damage. Henry Cole Bowen's neighbors were less fortunate. By 1923 many of the Big Houses to which Elizabeth had been invited for teas and dances and tennis parties as a young girl had been destroyed or abandoned.

Between 1914 and 1923—years drawn upon for the novel *Friends and Relations* (1931), set in England, as well as for *The Last September*—Elizabeth Bowen grew up. If war had seemed remote to her in 1914, in 1917, when she completed her studies at Downe House and returned to Dublin to work in a hospital for shell-shocked soldiers, it became very real. World War I ended in 1918, and immediately thereafter she returned to England to study at the London County Council School of Art, from which she withdrew after two terms. As a child she always had enjoyed drawing and painting, but as a young woman she was disappointed in what she saw as her limited ability. (All her life, however, she continued to have, in her own opinion, a "painter's sensitivity" that was evident in her literary work.) Meanwhile, in September 1918, her father had remarried. His second wife, Mary Gwynn, was the sister of Stephen Gwynn, a published author from whom Bowen obtained some advice about writing. Uncomfortable without a specific goal before her (she later confessed that what she feared most was "a life to let"), she next took a course in journalism, possibly at his suggestion. During this time a brief engagement to a lieutenant in the British army was all that came of an early romance: the "committee of aunts" disapproved of the match. Wintering with an aunt and cousins in Bordighera in 1921, she stored away memories of what she saw in the Italian resort as well as what she felt, having sent back her engagement ring; these memories were later drawn upon for several early short stories and for her first novel, *The Hotel* (1927). Two events of 1923 concluded this restless, unsettled period and set the course of her future life: *Encounters*, her first published volume of short stories, received a favorable reception, and on 4 August she married Alan Charles Cameron, an Oxford graduate six years her senior who had been befriended by her cousin Audrey Fiennes and Aunt Gertrude four years earlier, when he was recuperating from injuries suffered in World War I.

At the time of their marriage, Alan Cameron was assistant secretary for education in Northamptonshire, and the couple began their life together in Kingsthorpe, Northampton. In 1925, when he was appointed secretary for education for the city of Oxford, they moved to Old Headington, where Bowen found herself in a social circle that included such men as Lord David Cecil, C. M. Bowra, and other leading figures of the Oxford community. Earlier, the former headmistress of Downe House, Olive Willis, had introduced her to novelist Rose Macaulay, who had taken the young writer under her wing, providing introductions to editors, publishers, literary agents, and other people of influence. The intellectual atmosphere of Oxford was conducive to her continued development. A second volume of stories was published in 1926, and by 1929 it had been followed in turn by her first two novels and a third volume of short stories.

In 1930, at the death of her father, Elizabeth Bowen became the first woman to inherit Bowen's Court. She and her husband often stayed in the house during holidays, following the pattern that had been established in her childhood, but they continued to live in England, where he was employed. Two more novels published in 1931 and 1932 and a fourth volume of short stories published in 1934 further enhanced her literary reputation and introduced her to an ever-widening circle of literary acquaintances. By the early 1930s she had become a frequent visitor in Bloomsbury and a friend of Virginia Woolf; by 1935—the year in which her fifth novel, *The House in Paris*, was published—Alan Cameron had taken a job with the BBC, Elizabeth Bowen had begun to review regularly for the *Tatler*, and the couple had moved from Oxford to London, to a house they purchased in Clarence Terrace, Regent's Park.

In 1937 Bowen was elected to the Irish Academy of Letters. The next year a sixth novel, *The Death of the Heart*, appeared, and it became commonplace for reviewers to praise Bowen's technical skill and to compare her work to that of Virginia Woolf, E. M. Forster, Henry James, and Jane Austen. Each new book was given a full critical reception in the *Times Literary Supplement*, the *New York Times Book Review*, and other leading newspapers and periodicals on both sides of the Atlantic. Judgments ranking her work became fixed: in the next ten years the titles cited as evidence of her "best" work were *The Last September*, *The House in Paris*, and *The Death of the Heart*. In 1948 Bowen was made a Commander of the British Empire, and in 1949 she was awarded an honorary Doctor of Letters by Trinity College, Dublin. During the same year *The Heat of the Day* was added to the list of her major works. Soon after Bowen received these awards, Alan Cameron—who had remained physically weakened by his war injuries—became seriously ill. The Camerons moved from London to Bowen's Court in 1952, and in the same year Alan Cameron died.

For nearly eight years after the death of her husband, Bowen continued to make her home at Bowen's Court, where she completed *A World of Love* (1955) and often was visited by distinguished literary friends (some have published their recollections of her during this period). Her earlier work continued to attract critical attention: among those who discussed her in book-length studies of twentieth-century literature published between 1940 and 1960 were Walter Allen, Louise Bogan, David Daiches, William Frierson, Benedict Kiely, Sean O'Faolain, A. L. Rowse, L. A. G. Strong, and William York Tindall. Many more wrote articles about her work. In 1957 she was awarded a Doctor of Letters by Oxford University, an event that may have influenced her decision in 1959 to sell the Bowen estate and return to Old Headington, where she had spent the early years of her marriage and her career. She did not remain there long, however; in 1964 *The Little Girls*, a novel set in Kent, where she had lived with her mother during her father's illness, was published, and the following year she moved back to Hythe, where her mother had died. There she wrote *Eva Trout* (1968), her last novel, for which she received the James Tait Black Memorial Prize in 1970. During the last four years of her life Bowen was in declining health, suffering from repeated bouts of respiratory illness. In

Part I   Ch: I   Draft (I)

That morning's ice, no more than a brittle film, had cracked and now floated in segments. These slid together or, parting, left channels of dark lake water, down which swans in slow indignation swam. A mist had a sort of suspended grey breath made the air unclear; the trees soared frigidly up. ~~the sky~~ Charged with cold, the sky was lightless, ~~but~~ ~~though furnished~~ by the descending of an unseen sun. Inside its ~~quality~~ of vibration, Regent's Park had a hush that seemed immense. ~~The~~ swans on the lake, the ~~extending~~ ~~stucco~~ ~~terraces~~ ~~long path~~ facades of the terraces took an ~~unreal~~ glimmer, as though the cold were light.

On a footbridge linking an island to the mainland stood a man and youngish woman, leaning on the rail. Their unconcious stillness made them appear lovers; their ~~inside~~ elbows, however, were six inches apart. They were rivetted not to each other but to what she said, and a little to the scene. Their breath hung on the air over the water, their faces were whipped into a rude red. They were so well wrapped up that they ~~perhaps~~ looked like chessmen, inflexible and ~~sexless~~ sexless; inside their castles of clothing, his overcoat and her fur coat, their bodies generated a steady warmth. They could only see the cold. ~~distinct~~

Page from a draft of The Death of the Heart *(Sotheby's auction catalogue, 12 December 1961)*

1972 she learned that she had lung cancer, from which she died on 22 February 1973, less than four months before her seventy-fourth birthday. To an interviewer who had asked her how she felt about aging, during one of her last television appearances, she had replied, "I think the main thing . . . is to keep the show on the road." To the end she kept the show on the road, leaving little unfinished, according to Spencer Curtis Brown, whom Bowen charged with responsibility for arranging publication of *Pictures and Conversations* (1975), the work she had in progress when she died.

Critics often have referred to Elizabeth Bowen, both during her lifetime and after, as a social realist, but her work belongs in fact to the kind of twentieth-century fiction usually labeled psychological realism or literary impressionism. She herself declared that, for her, a novel is a prose statement of a poetic truth. She also acknowledged that the sources of her poetic truths are to be found in experiences she transformed— hence another of her descriptions of her prose fiction, "transformed biography." By this she meant that she took experiences out of her own life and used them in the lives of her fictional characters— characters who are not the author and cannot be identified as such, although in their fictional lives they are given a portion of the author's life history to share. Whatever Bowen believed about real life, fictional life, as she created it, has both pattern and purpose. The pattern may be studied in her mythic metaphors that establish character; in the rhythm of echoic events through which these characters learn to anticipate the future and understand the past; in symbols that link apparently disparate passages; and in the progress of fictional characters through concentric circles of fictional existence, from the purely personal, through the parochial, to the pansophic.

Bowen's first attempts to construct models of existence in her imagination were shared by her cousin Audrey Fiennes, the companion of her childhood who continued to be a close friend and confidante throughout the author's life. As children Elizabeth and Audrey created stories about imaginary families. In intervals between visits Elizabeth probed these imagined characters more deeply and shaped incidents involving them by herself. As an adolescent she continued to make up stories for the amusement of herself and her friends. She was a member of a group of young girls at Harpenden Hall who invented

dramas involving mysterious events, witchcraft, and occultism. These storytelling experiences, enhanced by the habits of observation that she sharpened as an art student, constituted her apprenticeship in literary art.

Elizabeth Bowen's first novel, *The Hotel*, focused on themes introduced in the two volumes of short stories, *Encounters* and *Ann Lee's and Other Stories*, that preceded it. Its central character, Sydney Warren, is an unsophisticated and inexperienced young woman in her early twenties who is wintering at a resort hotel in northern Italy. During the winter Sydney has a series of encounters through which she learns a little about men, a little more about other women, and quite a lot about herself. The novel has been compared with Jane Austen's *Emma* (1816), to which it bears some resemblance in character and development. Its setting and structure are reminiscent of E. M. Forster's *A Room with a View* (1908). It invites comparison also with Virginia Woolf's *The Voyage Out* (1915), which, like *The Hotel*, is an account of the experiences of an unsophisticated young woman at a resort hotel favored by English visitors in a foreign country. In both novels the central character is introduced to two men, one destined to become her fiancé, and has a close relationship with an older woman who serves as a kind of mentor. Echoes of Joseph Conrad's *The Secret Sharer* (1910) also may be found in Sydney's initial lack of a sense of self, misconstrued by others as aloofness and coldness, which is altered at the end of the novel as a result of a series of incidents that help her form a more integrated personality. Whither this personality will take her is a question left for the reader to contemplate.

Sydney has interrupted her studies to come to Italy as companion to her ailing cousin. Her family is not eager for her to return to school, for continual study seems to them to be a very curious occupation for a young woman. Her visit to Italy soon provides a host of new experiences. There she is befriended by Mrs. Kerr, an experienced older woman, and the Lawrence sisters, especially the less inhibited Veronica Lawrence, a young woman engaged to be married. Veronica's histrionics amuse Sydney—she even allows herself a few mocking rejoinders—but she is not drawn into the social games played by the Lawrence sisters. She is engaged briefly to the Reverend James Milton, not because she loves him, but because she wants to love him, to fill the emptiness left by her realization that Mrs. Kerr has taken her up as an amusement, not as a serious friend. "The whole past," she remarks wryly to Reverend Milton, ". . . may be one enormous abeyance." In Italy the season for English visitors is coming to a close. Sydney's future also is in abeyance. What will become of her? The question left unanswered suggests that beneath the surface social satire noted by most critics, *The Hotel* has a deeper, more philosophic tale to tell.

Bowen's second novel, *The Last September*, published two years after *The Hotel*, also concerns the growth and development of a young woman, Lois Farquar. The setting is Ireland—the author acknowledged that "Danielstown," the Big House in which Lois lived, was modeled on Bowen's Court, and that she, as she was at nineteen, was the model for the central character. However, she also stated unequivocally, in her 1952 preface to the Knopf edition, that the novel was not autobiographical. Nor could Elizabeth Bowen be Lois, for as the novel opens the fictional character is depicted as living one of those "unlived lives" that gave Elizabeth Bowen "the horrors." Indeed, Lois's engagement to Gerald Lesworth, a young British officer garrisoned in Ireland during the Anglo-Irish War, results less from passionate attachment than from her desire to escape the world of Danielstown, which she finds stultifying at best and uncongenial at worst. Her uncle, Sir Richard Naylor, like many of his Big House neighbors, has decided to ignore the war that has brought the Black and Tans and Irish rebels into open conflict just beyond the walls of his estate. He chooses to talk instead of whether it is time to get in the apples. His wife shares his ability to shut out what she does not wish to admit into her life, so there are luncheons and tennis parties at Danielstown and visitors are welcomed there, while just a few miles from the main house, patrols are ambushed, houses are burned, a rebel trembles in fear of his life in an old mill, and Gerald is killed. Eventually not even the Naylors can ignore the conflict: Danielstown itself is burned. As the world Lois sought to escape is taken from her—first because reality penetrates her protected and carefully nurtured consciousness, changing her perceptions of what is and what should be, and then because death and destruction change the actual physical circumstances of her life—she comes of age.

The Last September is a more artistically constructed novel than *The Hotel*, partly because its author probes Lois's consciousness with greater sophistication than she demonstrated in describing

Sydney Warren of the earlier book, and partly because it weaves two stories—one of personal lives, the other of a country's troubles—into a more textured work of fiction. Through juxtaposition, each story of *The Last September* becomes a commentary on the other. Moreover, the author's use of a narrative persona who is at first detached and then seems drawn into the story unwillingly, despite the fact that the tale is told in retrospect, offers a more interesting range of perspectives. *Friends and Relations* (1931), Bowen's third novel, again draws its characters from country estates where affluent inhabitants are insulated from the troubles of those who do not have the protection of money, manners, and tradition. In *Friends and Relations*, however, the luncheons, dinner parties, and weddings take place in English, not Irish, houses; the people are Georgian ladies and gentlemen rather than Anglo-Irish landed gentry. No threat of violence or arson provides a contrapuntal theme, as in *The Last September*. Yet the society into which Janet Studdart is born is not unlike that of Lois Farquar. It is similar in many respects to that of Sydney Warren.

Given these similarities of setting and character, readers of Elizabeth Bowen's early fiction no doubt expected that her third novel again would describe the initiation of an upper-class young woman into a less restrictive, more egalitarian postwar society, but *Friends and Relations* tells another tale. For the most part Sydney Warren and Lois Farquar acquired awareness and understanding from observation rather than from direct experience. To be sure, Sydney had been given little choice but to revise her emotional attachments, a difficult thing to do, and Lois's world literally went up in flames. But neither was forced to endure the pain of being directly responsible for the event or sequence of events that changed the course of her life. With Janet Studdart, Bowen introduced another kind of central character—a young woman who does not have to be taught about sexuality, but whose problems result from her being all too aware of it, a woman who is called upon to make significant choices not just for herself but for others.

As *Friends and Relations* opens, Laurel Studdart is preparing to marry Edward Tilney, with whom Laurel's sister, Janet, also is in love. Janet conceals her feelings from everyone except an *enfant terrible*, Theodora Thirdman, whose role in the novel seems both superfluous and inappropriate, serving only the inartistic purpose of conveying information to the reader through a

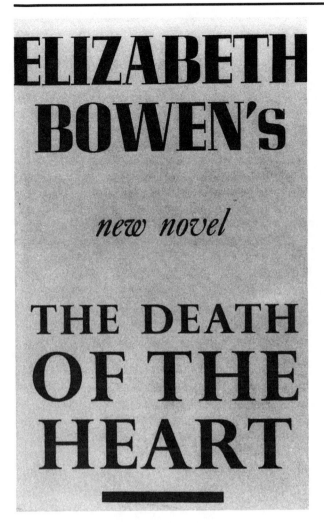

Dust jacket for Bowen's sixth novel, considered by many critics to be her most notable literary achievement

character dangerously close to caricature. Janet takes secret satisfaction in the knowledge that Edward's mother, Lady Elfrida, actually prefers her to Laurel. Six weeks after Laurel's wedding Janet announces her own engagement to Rodney Meggatt of Batts Abbey, whom she has known but a few short weeks. The news upsets Edward: Rodney's uncle, Considine Meggatt, had been his mother's lover when he was a child, and the affair that caused his parents to separate very likely had been a factor also in the death of his father. Laurel pretends to be unaware of the Meggatt family history—actually, she knows everything—and eventually the marriage takes place, despite Edward's objections. Ten years later the old wounds open again when Janet, who has an "unnatural sense of the natural," invites Edward's mother, Lady Elfrida, to Batts Abbey while Considine is there and the children of Laurel

and Edward are visiting. Edward arrives to save his children from exposure to what he regards as a corrupt environment, but while he is at Batts Abbey he confesses that through the years he has felt irresistibly drawn to Janet, and she acknowledges her feelings for him. Shaken, Janet goes to London, determined to exorcise her demons by talking things over with Laurel; her determination quickly crumbles when she finds that her sister is not at home, and she has lunch and a long talk with Edward instead. Later, Edward comes to her hotel room, and they teeter on the brink of an adulterous relationship. In an irony that strains the reader's willing suspension of disbelief, it is Edward who tries to persuade Janet that they might "comfort" each other, Janet who resists. As a result of Janet's moral restraint in the face of temptation, history just barely does not repeat itself in the Tilney family.

If Janet Studdart of *Friends and Relations* stops short of an extramarital liaison that she perceives to be harmful to herself and to those to whom she owes a debt of loyalty if not love, Emmeline of *To the North* (1932) does not. Emmeline, often called "angel" by the narrative persona as well as by other characters in the novel, is nearsighted in more ways than one and naive rather than angelic. She allows herself to be seduced by Markie, a man whose physical appearance and character identify him as reptilian. Markie's preliminary advances are made in a garden, where Emmeline's innocence is emphasized, reinforcing the developing metaphor of Eve tempted by the serpent. In the background Cecilia, Emmeline's widowed sister-in-law, and Julian, whom Cecilia is about to marry, provide a more wholesome example of safe and true (if unexciting) love. As their affair progresses, Markie begins to tire of Emmeline, and soon he resumes a relationship with Daisy, a former mistress. Unaware of their estrangement, Cecilia and Julian invite Emmeline and Markie to dinner. On the way home from Cecilia's, in the driver's seat with Markie beside her, Emmeline crashes her car, killing them both.

In addition to its obviously mythic substructure constructed from elements of the Eve and the serpent story, *To the North* carries other overly obvious symbolic messages: Emmeline and Markie are almost always in motion, traveling by car, train, or boat, in what appears to be the author's attempt to present the instability of the modern world and the transience of modern life; the diction of the narrative persona is extravagant, melodramatic—Jacobean, in the words of one critic. It is a curious novel for Elizabeth Bowen to have produced three years after publication of *The Last September*, in which she had exhibited truly professional control over the novelist's craft; it seems a further decline after *Friends and Relations*, which also did not match the achievement of her second novel. In character and development *To the North* appears to represent a working of themes found in *Joining Charles and Other Stories* (1929), the volume of short stories that followed *The Last September*. *The Cat Jumps and Other Stories* (1934), the volume of short stories that followed *To the North*, reveals an additional reworking of these themes. But for readers and critics who might have wondered in 1932 if Elizabeth Bowen's talents were waning, three years after *To the North*, in 1935, she produced a novel equal to, if not better than, *The Last September*: *The House in Paris*.

In structure *The House in Paris* is similar to *Friends and Relations* (that is, it contains three parts, with a ten-year passage of time between past and present); it is also similar to Virginia Woolf's *To the Lighthouse* (1927), especially in the integration of its separate parts. Its use of clock time to counterpoint psychological time and its repetition of phrases to effect transitions also are reminiscent of techniques used by Virginia Woolf.

The pivotal character of the novel is Karen Michaelis, who, like Lois Farquar of *The Last September*, wants to escape a family environment devoid of intellectual depth or sincere emotional attachment. Not that she is capable of either intellectual depth or sincere emotional attachment herself: in her "life to let" she has the bloodless, matter-of-fact attitude toward marriage of Sydney Warren and Lois Farquar. Nevertheless, she does not resist becoming engaged when, according to social convention, an appropriately respectable man of her social class, Ray Forrestier, proposes at the appropriate time. He departs to fulfill a diplomatic assignment; with time to reflect during a visit to her aging Aunt Violet in Cork, she realizes that her engagement has not brought her closer to freedom but has fixed her future with more certainty than ever. Back in London, Karen meets a friend, Naomi Fisher, who is accompanied by her fiancé, Max Ebhart, a man to whom Karen had felt strongly attracted five years before, in Paris, when they met in the Fisher home. Less in control of herself than Janet Studdart (and more inclined to upset her

Dust jacket for Bowen's seventh novel, her first in eleven years

well-ordered life), Karen allows herself to become drawn into an affair that leaves her pregnant and alone, for on his return to Paris, Max commits suicide. The child born of this union, Leopold, is sent to Rome to live with a childless couple; Ray returns and marries Karen, fully aware of the affair and the birth of Leopold, and knowing that Karen never has been able to accept the child. Nine years later a meeting between Leopold and Karen is arranged. It is to take place in the Fishers' house in Paris, where Karen and Max first met and where he committed suicide. There Naomi, unmarried, still lives with her mother. On the same day the house is also to be a stopover for another child in transit: eleven-year-old Henrietta Mountjoy comes to the Fisher home to spend a day between trains en route to visit her grandmother, a friend of the Fishers.

The two children are the central characters of the first part of the book. They meet and talk about their lives with a frankness and clarity of perception that none of the adults can bring to the situation. Leopold is revealed as high-strung and nervous; Henrietta is calm and wise beyond her years, a child like Henry James's Maisie of *What Maisie Knew* (1897) or Thomas Hardy's Father Time of *Jude the Obscure* (1895), who has learned to understand adults without embarrassing them by revealing her understanding. By midday it is clear that Karen will not come as expected; Ray arrives to explain Karen's absence. After meeting and talking with Leopold, Ray decides to take the child home with him; henceforth, Leopold will live with Ray and Karen.

The technical achievements of *The House in Paris* are its compression of time and the characterization of the children. They spend half a day together, anticipating Karen's arrival, before Leopold is given the distressing news that his mother is not coming. The second part of the novel returns through time—not as flashback but as disembodied memory—to the year in which Karen and Ray were engaged, Karen and Max had their affair, and Leopold was conceived. In the world of the novel the year of ten years ago is an envelope of existence, separate from the present. The present returns in the third part with the same phrase that has ended the first part of the novel. Less than half a day remains. Ray arrives, and he and Leopold leave the dark and narrow house in Paris (as dark and narrow as the moments of life that have been lived there) to go out just at the time of evening when Paris becomes, in truth, a City of Lights.

The Death of the Heart, Elizabeth Bowen's sixth novel, was published in 1938. To many Bowen critics it represents the pinnacle of her achievement as a writer of fiction. Its narrative mode incorporates an expertly handled range of viewpoints which evoke a multiplicity of responses to a single event or situation. Thomas and Anna Quayne, two of the main characters of the novel, talk not to, but at each other, in the manner of long-married people accustomed to living side by side while remaining uninvolved in each other's life: their dialogue would suit a comedy of manners. Yet the unfulfilled desires of their inner lives, revealed by a perceptive and understanding narrator, give them a softness and poignancy that the reader otherwise might not expect. Into their lives comes another central character, Portia, the child born to the second wife of

Thomas Quayne's father. Portia's mother and father have died, and the teenage girl has been sent to stay for a time with the Quaynes. Thomas and Anna have no children of their own and are not child-oriented, but they accept the arrangement as tolerable because it is to be temporary. Fortunately for Portia, the Quaynes have a housekeeper, Matchett, who is more capable than Thomas or Anna of reaching out to the child, mothering her, and making her feel at home. Matchett's view of Portia's parents and the Quaynes is both instructive to the child and bolstering. Matchett's perspective and sense of values help dispel the child's fear and awe of the relatives with whom she has been sent to live. While acknowledging the Quaynes's human foibles, she is able to assure Portia of their basic humanity. In her homely wisdom, often succinctly expressed, the Quaynes are people who do the right thing but not necessarily the good thing.

Portia's presence in the Quayne household is felt not only by Thomas, Anna, and Matchett but also by three men, unrelated to the family, who are frequent visitors: St. Quentin Martin, a novelist, to whom Anna confides the contents of Portia's diary, which she secretly is reading and which reveals Portia's feelings about the Quaynes and their friends; Eddie, a young man who likes to dramatize his own emotions but does not wish to be responsible for those he evokes in others, least of all Portia; and Major Brutt, who knows Anna as others do not, because he was a friend of the man with whom Anna was in love before she married Thomas. Within the novel each character reflects on the others; through her diary, Portia records her impressions of them all.

Because he is the only member of this circle close to her in age, Portia quickly fastens on Eddie as the one eligible for a romantic attachment. Eddie is not unreceptive; indeed, he enjoys playing the role as long as he can be sure that it is not serious or confining. The Quaynes go off on a holiday to Capri, and Portia is sent to an English seaside town to stay with the family of Anna's former governess, Mrs. Heccomb. Eddie allows Portia's letters to persuade him to visit her, but instead of fulfilling her romantic expectations with the kind of attention she desires, he flirts with Mrs. Heccomb's daughter, Daphne. When Portia protests, Eddie reminds her of the limits both of their relationship and of her claim on him. The Quaynes return from their holiday, and Portia is brought back from the Heccombs', only to face another betrayal. St. Quentin reveals that Anna has been reading Portia's diary. Believing that Anna also has been sharing the contents of her diary with Eddie, and that they both have been laughing at her, Portia leaves the Quaynes. She goes first to Eddie, to convince him to let her live with him. He refuses, and she next runs to Major Brutt, crying that she is homeless, and asks him to marry her. "A 1914-1918 model," in the words of the narrator, the astonished Major Brutt insists on telephoning the Quaynes. Having learned from Matchett what is best calculated to move them, Portia asks the Major to tell the Quaynes that they must do the "right thing." At first this message is received with consternation, for the Quaynes are not sure what the "right thing" is in such a situation. In discussing the possibilities, they each come closer to thinking about Portia and her feelings than ever before. Eventually Matchett is instructed to bring Portia home.

The three sections of *The Death of the Heart* are titled "The World," "The Flesh," and "The Devil." Employing a technique reminiscent of that used by James Joyce in *Ulysses* (1922), Elizabeth Bowen reinforces these titles through the diction of each section. Thus in "The World," objective views of each character are presented, and Portia learns Matchett's wisdom; in "The Flesh," the language is that of sensory perception; in "The Devil," the emphasis is on manipulation and betrayal. Throughout the novel, dialogue is used not only to dramatize interaction (or lack of it) but to reveal character and to provide essential background information. When Portia, for example, complains about Eddie's flirting with Daphne, he protests that he was just feeling "matey." To Anna—who was responsible for introducing him into the Quayne circle and instrumental in his finding employment with Thomas—he presents another self and uses different diction. One narrative persona, aloof and philosophical, comments on each character's words and behavior. A more intimately involved narrative persona sees inside each character, past silliness, brusqueness, and pomposity, to the essential humanity of each. Inserted passages from Portia's diary contrast the perceptual level of the young girl (whose resemblance to Henry James's Maisie of *What Maisie Knew* has been noted by William Heath, among others) with the impression she tries to convey and the opinions others have of her.

The Heat of the Day (1949), Bowen's last major novel, was published eleven years after *The Death of the Heart*. Between them, Bowen pro-

duced two new collections of short stories, a selection of previously published short stories, a radio play, a critical study of the novel, two volumes of memoirs and family history, and a play (*Castle Anna*, coauthored with John Perry and produced in 1948, although never published). She also continued to write, of course, the reviews and critical articles that appeared regularly in various periodicals. The eleven-year gap, therefore, was not empty; Bowen had not hit what writers sometimes refer to as a "dry" period following the achievement of *The House in Paris* and *The Death of the Heart*. It was, however, a time of change and development, for *The Heat of the Day* is written from a perspective very different from that which the author might have chosen for her story in 1938. By 1949 World War II was over—the second world war in her lifetime and the fourth war to shatter her personal world. Her perspective on wartime London, the setting of the novel, reflected that fact.

Bowen intended *The Heat of the Day* to be a retrospective novel. In the center she set a love story: Stella Rodney, a woman in her forties, has a son, Roderick, by a former marriage. Her husband had left her for his nurse on his return from World War I and had died shortly after their divorce. Stella has a lover, Robert Kelway, who (like Stella) is employed in secret government business. Harrison, an associate, tries to blackmail Stella by offering to conceal the fact that Kelway is passing documents to the enemy if she will become his mistress. Stella tells Kelway what Harrison has said about him; he of course denies everything, but shortly before the end of the novel he admits that Harrison's accusations are true. Soon after this confession he slips or jumps to his death. Trying to understand Kelway, Stella reviews what she knows of his family, which seems cold and rigid to her, and of his political ideas, which reject nationalism and suggest that he has deluded himself into believing the Nazi destruction to be somehow cleansing. She also reviews her own life in "the heat of the day"—that is, in the danger of wartime London, where air raids are almost constant and the threat of death is always present. (The phrase also recalls the song from Shakespeare's *Cymbeline* that echoes in Clarissa's mind throughout Virginia Woolf's *Mrs. Dalloway* [1925]. Clarissa's world is also one in which death must be faced, and Septimus Smith, whom Woolf pairs with Clarissa, although the two never meet, commits suicide.) For Stella, the threat of death increases her sensitivity and heightens her awareness of what is important and unimportant. Thus, she is able to accept Kelway's treason and death and refuse Harrison's advances without bitterness. The story of these three individuals is interwoven with historical fact; the technique of the novel appears to have been adapted from *Bowen's Court* (1942), the family history in which Bowen had woven together public record and personal recollection. Applied to fiction, it is a successful technique, and *The Heat of the Day* deserves the critical attention it received when it was published and the praise of Bowen critics who have reassessed her work in recent years.

Although Bowen wrote three more novels before she died, none matched the achievement of *The Last September, The House in Paris, The Death of the Heart*, and *The Heat of the Day*. *A World of Love* is the story of a group of women, known and unknown, who have loved and been loved by Guy, an Irishman from a small Irish country estate who had joined the British army and had died in France. In outline, it is the same story Bowen employed for *Castle Anna*. Even in death Guy continues to exert a strong influence on these women and on a young woman of the next generation as well. The latter, Jane Danby, is the daughter of Lilia, the Englishwoman who had been engaged to Guy. Antonia, Guy's cousin, also had been in love with him, and had inherited his estate, Montefort. There she installed, as tenants, Lilia and Fred Danby, an illegitimate cousin, whose marriage she arranged. There they all live with the pernicious, destructive memory of Guy. When Jane finds and reads Guy's letters, she, too, becomes infatuated with him.

A World of Love is a loosely constructed fiction in which both the power and failure of illusion appear to be connecting threads. Its characters are not so finely drawn as in Bowen's better-known novels. *The Little Girls*, also regarded by critics as less effective than her four major works, is by contrast better structured and therefore a more interesting psychological study. It reunites three women in their sixties who had been "best friends" when they were eleven-year-old students at Saint Agatha's school in Kent. At that time they had buried in the school garden a coffer containing a note and personal objects. Now one of the three, Dinah Delacroix (Dicey), insists that they dig it up, although the garden is now part of someone else's property. First, Dinah must reestablish contact with the other two, Clare Burkin-Jones (Mumbo) and Sheila Artworth (Sheikie), for since their schooldays their three lives have been very different. Notices placed in English newspapers bring the three together once again. The coffer is located; it is empty. The discovery has a devastating effect on Dinah, to everyone's surprise. The responses to the empty coffer on the part of each of the women reveal hidden aspects of their personalities. These responses are directly related to what each hid in the coffer so many years ago. As these objects are not named until the end of the novel, *The Little Girls* is a suspense story as well as a psychological study.

Eva Trout, Elizabeth Bowen's last novel, presents her most unconventional fictional character, one that has puzzled even the most loyal of her critics. On her twenty-fourth birthday Eva inherits a fortune that she already has decided to use to acquire the good things in life: a home, a baby, and a husband. This is the order she has established; therefore, the home comes first. The child comes next, and to find Jeremy (he is not her natural child), Eva goes to Chicago. Jeremy turns out to be a deaf mute, and for some years Eva spends her time and money seeking help for him, ultimately sending him to France, to be trained by a doctor who has specialized in the education of deaf mutes. Eventually she turns to the matter of a father for Jeremy, and she settles on Henry Dancey, a young man twelve years her junior whom she knew as one of the children of the local rector when she lived in Worcestershire, before she came into her inheritance. He is a reluctant bridegroom: first he declines her proposal, then he agrees to accompany her to Victoria Station as if he were going to marry her. Finally, at Victoria Station he concedes that he will marry her, for they have been friends for a long time, and he is fond of her. Jeremy returns from France to join Eva's friends in seeing the about-to-be-married couple off at Victoria Station. With him he has a gun, found in his mother's stored luggage, which he thinks is a toy. He rushes toward her, pointing the gun, and pulls the trigger. Eva is killed instantly.

In 1969 newspaper reviewers were unwilling to be unkind to the seventy-year-old author whose place in literature had been assured by her past achievements: they found *Eva Trout* "curious" and confessed to "mounting incredulity," but they also were willing to allow Bowen her playful moment, if that was what pleased her. Mary Lavin, among others, herself a writer and a longtime admirer of Bowen's work, believed that

Dust jacket for Bowen's last novel, published five years before her death

Bowen's extended career had earned her that consideration.

Eva Trout, then, is not likely to receive an esteemed place in Elizabeth Bowen's canon. Although not the best examples of her fiction, *Friends and Relations*, *To the North*, and *A World of Love* reveal the development of her literary art. *The Hotel* is assured continued critical attention not only because it was Bowen's first novel, but also because it reveals its antecedents, suggesting the influences to which she responded. *The Little Girls* deservedly is singled out for its deft handling of psychological portraits. But Bowen's reputation as a major English novelist rests, as most critics agree, on the achievement represented by *The Last September*, *The House in Paris*, *The Death of the Heart*, and *The Heat of the Day*. She is also acclaimed for her short fiction, which deserves mention even in a discussion of her novels, for many of her short stories are related to her novels as sketches in character, setting, or technique, or as studies of a theme.

Bibliography:

J'nan M. Sellery, *Elizabeth Bowen: A Descriptive Bibliography* (Austin: Texas University Press, 1977).

Biographies:

Victoria Glendinning, *Elizabeth Bowen: Portrait of A Writer* (London: Weidenfeld & Nicolson, 1977);

Patricia Craig, *Elizabeth Bowen* (Harmondsworth, U.K.: Penguin, 1986; New York: Viking, 1986);

Phyllis Lassner, *Elizabeth Bowen* (Savage, Md.: Barnes & Noble, 1989).

References:

Alan E. Austin, *Elizabeth Bowen* (New York: Twayne, 1971);

Harriet Blodgett, *Patterns of Reality: Elizabeth Bowen's Novels* (The Hague: Mouton, 1975);

Harold Bloom, ed., *Elizabeth Bowen* (New York: Chelsea House, 1987);

Jocelyn Brooke, *Elizabeth Bowen* (London: Longmans, Green, 1952);

David Daiches, "The Novels of Elizabeth Bowen," *English Journal*, 38 (June 1949): 305-313;

James Hall, "The Giant Located: Elizabeth Bowen," in his *The Lunatic Giant in the Drawing Room: The British and American Novel Since 1930* (Bloomington: Indiana University Press, 1968);

William Heath, *Elizabeth Bowen: An Introduction to Her Novels* (Madison: University of Wisconsin Press, 1961);

Frederick Karl, "The World of Elizabeth Bowen," in his *The Contemporary English Novel* (New York: Farrar, Straus & Cudahy, 1962);

Edwin J. Kenny, *Elizabeth Bowen* (Lewisburg, Pa.: Bucknell University Press, 1975);

Hermione Lee, *Elizabeth Bowen: An Estimation* (London: Vision Press, 1981; Totowa, N.J.: Barnes & Noble, 1981);

Sean O'Faolain, "Elizabeth Bowen: Romance Does Not Pay," in his *The Vanishing Hero: Studies in Novelists of the Twenties* (London: Eyre & Spottiswoode, 1956).

Papers:

Elizabeth Bowen's manuscripts, as well as letters to and from Bowen, are in the Harry Ransom Humanities Research Center, University of Texas, Austin; letters written by Bowen are also in the Berg Collection of the New York Public Library.

John Braine

(13 April 1922 - 28 October 1986)

This entry was updated by Judy Simons (Sheffield City Polytechnic) from her entry in
DLB 15: British Novelists, 1930-1959: Part One.

See also the Braine entry in DLB Yearbook: 1986.

BOOKS: *Room at the Top* (London: Eyre & Spottiswoode, 1957; Boston: Houghton Mifflin, 1957);

The Vodi (London: Eyre & Spottiswoode, 1959); republished as *From the Hand of the Hunter* (Boston: Houghton Mifflin, 1960);

Life at the Top (London: Eyre & Spottiswoode, 1962; Boston: Houghton Mifflin, 1962);

The Jealous God (London: Eyre & Spottiswoode, 1964; Boston: Houghton Mifflin, 1965);

The Crying Game (London: Eyre & Spottiswoode, 1968; Boston: Houghton Mifflin, 1968);

Stay With Me Till Morning (London: Eyre & Spottiswoode, 1970); republished as *The View from Tower Hill* (New York: Coward-McCann, 1971);

The Queen of a Distant Country (London: Methuen, 1972; New York: Coward-McCann & Geoghegan, 1973);

Writing a Novel (London: Eyre Methuen, 1974; New York: McGraw-Hill, 1975);

The Pious Agent (London: Eyre Methuen, 1975; New York: Atheneum, 1976);

Waiting for Sheila (London: Eyre Methuen, 1976; New York: Methuen, 1976);

Finger of Fire (London: Eyre Methuen, 1977);

J. B. Priestley (London: Weidenfeld & Nicolson, 1978; New York: Barnes & Noble, 1979);

One and Last Love (London: Eyre Methuen, 1981);

These Golden Days (London: Eyre Methuen, 1985);

Two of Us (London: Magna Print Books, 1987).

MOTION PICTURES: *Room at the Top*, screenplay by Braine, Remus, 1958;

Life at the Top, screenplay by Braine, Remus, 1965.

TELEVISION SCRIPTS: *Man at the Top*, Thames Television, 1970, 1972;

Waiting for Sheila, Yorkshire Television, 1977;

Queen of a Distant Country, Yorkshire Television, 1978;

John Braine

Stay With Me Till Morning, Yorkshire Television, 1981.

John Braine was one of the most prominent of the British novelists who in the 1950s earned the title of Angry Young Men, a phrase with which Braine's name is inevitably associated. Together with contemporaries, such as Kingsley Amis and John Wain, he asserted an ethic of individualism and of rebellious, amoral youth, which fitted perfectly into the new cultural and social viewpoints of a changing and often discontented postwar Britain. Braine was in the forefront of the wave of populist writers who, with a contempt for avant-garde fictional devices, rejected notions of artistic elitism and of the refined sensibilities and unique moral position of the writer. Adopting the defiant stance of the naif-artist, he relied on traditional forms and techniques, above all strong narrative direction and satiric social observation, to create an accessible and deliberately nonspecialist vision. He presented a forceful, often inarticulate hero, a product of the British welfare state, who is striving to define a moral position in a system of unjustly acquired authority and bourgeois values. Braine's work consistently

developed and explored certain major themes: class consciousness, the concept of success, and the nature of a provincial perspective, all of which characterized his first outstanding success, *Room at the Top* (1957).

John Gerard Braine was born in Bradford, Yorkshire, on 13 April 1922. His mother, Katherine Joseph Henry, came from an Irish Catholic family, and Braine's Catholicism, with its attendant problems of conscience, pervades much of his writing. His father, Fred Braine, was a sewage-works supervisor for the local council, and John enjoyed a happy and secure, if not affluent, childhood, imbuing him with the ideals of family stability and parental responsibility which are extolled with some sentimentality in his novels. His early work consistently presents family ties as binding and the family unit as the one reliable source of affection his heroes recognize.

In 1933 Braine won a scholarship to Saint Bedes Grammar School, which he left five years later without taking his school certificate examinations. He subsequently studied for these at the age of twenty-one by correspondence course. From 1938 until 1940 he had a variety of temporary jobs, working as an assistant in a furniture store, a secondhand bookshop, a pharmaceutical laboratory, and as a progress chaser in a piston-ring factory, before settling, in 1940, to the career structure of the public library service. Apart from a year of military service in the Royal Navy in 1942-1943, which he had to cut short because of illness, he worked from 1940 to 1948 as an assistant in Bingley Public Library. In 1947 he attended Leeds School of Librarianship, passed his librarianship examinations at the fourth attempt, and was consequently promoted to chief assistant in the Bingley Library, where he stayed for three more years.

However, in 1951 he gave up his secure job to become a free-lance writer. Encouraged by a modest success with articles published in *Lilliput, Tribune,* and the *New Statesman,* he went to London with a meager capital of £150 to try to earn his living, but his provincial upbringing and attitudes made him unhappy there. With no university degree and no other formal qualifications, his idealism was almost totally destroyed by the experience of what seemed to him to be an alien culture, and the conflict between provincial and metropolitan perceptions became a recurrent theme in his fiction. When his mother died in a road accident in 1951, he returned to Yorkshire, where he became ill, feeling, as he describes it, "a sense of

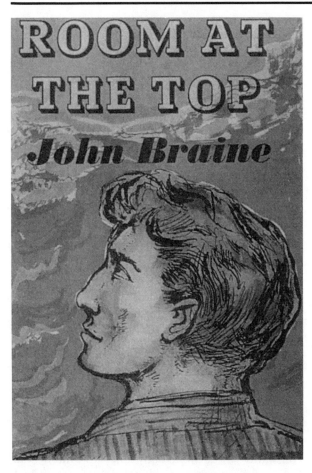

Dust jacket for Braine's first novel, about a man who wants to escape his lower-class background and to acquire the power and status of the affluent

something being physically broken." Tuberculosis was diagnosed, and he spent the following eighteen months in a hospital. It was at this emotional and physical nadir that he began to write his first novel, with the thought that "it wouldn't really matter if I died after it had been finished; what was important was that it should be known that I had been alive." For the next two years Braine stayed in Yorkshire, miserable and frustrated, working on his novel and writing occasional articles for the local newspapers. In September 1954 he began work as chief librarian with Northumberland County Library, and the following year, shortly before his marriage to Helen Patricia Wood, he completed the book that he had been struggling to finish for the past three years.

Braine's determination for recognition dominates his first novel, *Room at the Top,* which was rejected by four publishers before reaching the British market, where it received immediate public acclaim. This popularity was perhaps in part due to the sexual vigor of the hero and the unaccus-

tomed explicitness with which Braine described his exploits. The novel sold thirty-five thousand copies in the first year and was serialized in the *Daily Express,* an unheard-of achievement for a new writer. The book's astonishing success forms a comment on the unsophisticated nature of the society that received it with such adulation, a society clearly ready for social change, which found in the book a perfect expression of its postwar radicalism. Subsequent critical opinion has tended to judge the novel in the context of its decade, when, as Malcolm Bradbury has remarked, "fiction became the voice for times when new social groups and classes were seeking articulacy."

Although Braine has denied any autobiographical resemblances, the central character of his book, Joe Lampton, is an obvious projection of his author's aspirations. In the first flush of postpublication notoriety, Braine stated flamboyantly, "What I want to do is to drive through Bradford in a Rolls Royce with two naked women on either side of me covered in jewels." Such a statement can only have served to encourage the public's identification between the author and the hero, who is determined to discard his working-class background and to acquire the power of the affluent bourgeoisie. The desperation with which Joe covets the wealth and women of the moneyed clique in the northern industrial town gave a solidity of dimension to the previously unvoiced enmity of class warfare of that time. Braine's definition of status in terms of specific material possessions enabled him to communicate exact social levels in the provincial milieu of his novel and to visualize his hero as a distinct product of contemporary circumstance.

Joe's single-minded ambition for hypergamy is temporarily deflected by a passionate love affair with an older woman, whom finally he callously abandons in favor of a marriage which will provide the social entrée for which he longs. Braine's establishment of the clash between love and money, feeling and reason, in the central section of the book centers around Joe's attempt to juggle his relationships with two women—his mistress and his future wife—against a background of opportunism and social pressure. When he succumbs to the temptations of materialism and makes an advantageous marriage to the daughter of a local magnate (the girl who had originally seemed to him to symbolize female desirability), his father-in-law takes him into the family firm, and Joe gains the trappings of the power he has so ruthlessly pursued. His mistress, Alice, dies a particularly gruesome death in a "suicidal" road accident, a death detailed with the vivid realism that was to become Braine's trademark. Joe's success contains a bitter awareness of the personal exploitation such success involves, together with a realization of the sacrifice of his emotional and moral conscience. While Braine's moral imperative indicts Joe for his loss of integrity and, in particular, the society that exonerates him from guilt, the novel's tone conveys the absolute importance of material and social achievement to one whose origins exclude him from it; an ironic ambivalence results.

It was, however, the concept of the "angry" hero and his individualist ethic which captured the public imagination and caused sales to boom. Braine's ability to embody a shared fantasy in a realistic dimension contained the irresistible combination of fable and truth which has attracted readers ever since the publication of Samuel Richardson's *Pamela* in 1740. While the critical reception was mixed, most reviewers realized the potential impact of the novel in terms of its distinctly contemporary vision. The *Times Literary Supplement* commented that "an extraordinary vitality pulses through *Room at the Top*," and the *Atlantic Monthly* similarly credited its "capacity to project with passionate sharpness the hungers of youth." Braine's commitment to his hero's aggressive challenge to the establishment seemed to represent the insistence of youth to be heard. There was an urgency about the tone of the novel which overcame, by its stridency, the often crude and sometimes clichéd characterization and plot mechanics. The *Times* noted that "this latter day [Arnold Bennett's] *Card*'s progress is a grimmer, more intense affair than [Bennett's hero] Denry Machin's was," and in 1958, reviewing the previous decade, Kenneth Allsopp found the book impressive because "few books have revealed so explicitly the actual shape and shimmer of the fantasy life longings of a Joe Lampton, and certainly no-one until John Braine has described the exact kind of urges operating within the postwar specimen." In a perceptive essay on the period, G. K. Hunter identified Joe Lampton as a hero functioning within the framework established by "D. H. Lawrence's opposition of the irrational, the instinctive, the tender as against the poised, the conceptual, the correct, of knowing how to feel as against knowing how to behave." Kenneth Young in the *Sunday Times* had also noted similarities with Lawrence, "but there is no question of influence; Mr. Braine and Lawrence start from the

same point and naturally proceed to a similar effect." In retrospect, critics have continued to see the work as an accurate reflector of the contemporary cultural climate, its appeal to latent anxieties about the morality of affluence at the heart of its success, as Stuart Laing has convincingly argued.

Braine took obvious pride in his self-created role as bluff, working-class Northerner, with a native innocence, an honesty of insight, and an accompanying bluntness of expression. He fit neatly into Leslie Fiedler's definition of the young British writer who, "when he is boorish, rather than well-behaved, rudely angry rather than ironically amused, when he is philistine rather than arty—even when he merely writes badly, can feel that he is performing a service for literature, liberating it from the tyranny of a taste based on a world of wealth and leisure which has become quite unreal." Such a stance as Braine represented was naturally unpopular with intellectuals. John Bayley in the *Spectator* found Joe Lampton's "wide-eyed coarseness" unappealing. He preferred, with like-minded critics, to commend Braine's evident gifts for social observation and the clarity of his hero's perceptions about the life he both desired and found repellent. Braine's claims to artistic seriousness have been constantly undermined by the anti-intellectual image he cultivated at this time, an image which was augmented by the popular success of the film versions of *Room at the Top* and, later, *Life at the Top* (1962). In their presentation of glamour, ambition, and sex in highly emotive and stereotypic terms without the complex ironic undertones of the books, both the films and his television series, *Man at the Top*, captured an uncritical audience.

None of Braine's subsequent work had the impact of that first novel, and, as part of his campaign to demystify literature, much of it deliberately catered to an undiscriminating market. *The Vodi* (1959), nonetheless, reveals much sensitivity in its compassionate study of a hero as obsessed with the nature of failure as Joe Lampton was obsessed with success. A patient in a tuberculosis hospital, Dick Corvey broods on his childhood fantasy of a hostile and vindictive organization determined to destroy him, the Vodi, a nightmarish metaphor of social injustice. Clearly based on Braine's own hospital experiences, the novel's action provides an insight into a patient's perception of illness as part of a sinister system which threatens his ambitions and his opportunities. Dick's feelings of defeatism, fostered by the oppressive regimen of the ward, are ultimately lifted by his love affair with Nurse Mallaton, who responds to his desire and restores his self-confidence. When Dick is discharged from the sanatorium at the end of the novel, his future remains unclear. He returns to his family, his only genuine source of affection, and determines to fight the malevolent forces of existence, come what may. "Because he was young, he could only go forward, he couldn't go back."

The conditions for a psychological study of isolation are beautifully drawn in Braine's fabulist construction of the two worlds of subjective and objective experience. The flashback technique of narration extends the concept of dualistic experience, but the potential established by the central situation is never fully developed, and critics, who noticed analogies with Thomas Mann's *Magic Mountain* (1924), were disappointed by Braine's constant emphasis on realistic environmental detail. Those who, like Frederick Karl, felt that "the trivial details of the narrative diminish the theme," were, however, balanced by the appreciation evident in Cal Hines's recognition that "it has a solidity of scene and character that is always impressive. Few writers today can have a firmer grasp of milieu."

Braine's anger, modified in the more modulated tone of *The Vodi*, is as sharp as ever in his acute awareness of the values that determine worldly achievement. In his concern with success he ironically presents Dick as a character whose consciousness of failure produces in him the will to survive and a moral insight, as opposed to Joe Lampton's success, which is a pointer of moral inadequacy. Anthony Burgess recognized Braine's efforts to define success as a highly personal concept and identified the basically unheroic aspects of Braine's heroes as endemic to their conception; the characters share a modesty of protest, a helplessness in the face of larger social powers or pressures, and a fundamental inefficiency. Unfortunately, in *The Vodi* these qualities lacked the magnetism which had contributed to Joe Lampton's triumph, and in *Life at the Top* Braine returned to the original formula of his first novel, with a sequel to Joe's story, a bitter analysis of the price of worldly success.

In his third novel, Braine presents Joe's inner conflict between the restrictive sterility of his married state and his impulse to escape. Accurate evidential detail is used as an incisive tool to expose the emptiness of a life crammed with the artifacts of affluence. Braine reveals the spiritual

wasteland of a man who has exchanged the values of his own class for the superficial temptations of prosperity, and implicit here, as in much of his early work, is the apotheosis of working-class innocence and integrity. Joe has become trapped by the circumstances he has created. His fundamental dynamic is channeled into the acquisition of women and wealth, but his necessarily nonactive role denudes the novel of much of the power which had characterized *Room at the Top*. Several critics commented on the portrayal of Joe's bewilderment as essentially passive, and some took this as a sign of Braine's corresponding lack of vehemence. As Michael Ratcliffe noted, however, the book's reliance on implicit as opposed to direct moral statement is a reflection both of Braine's increasing maturity and of the uncertainties in the cultural climate of the early 1960s. In noting the melancholy which suffuses the novel, he commented on Braine's extreme sensitivity as a reflector of his times.

Life at the Top is flawed in its simplistic identification of sophistication with corruption. Braine's use of children as images of innocence sentimentalizes the basically complex issue with which he is at heart concerned: the confrontation with compromise that is forced on social man. In Joe's return to his family responsibilities at the end of the novel and in his renouncing forever any chance of personal fulfillment, critics felt that Braine was abandoning any genuine exploration of the notions of social freedom he had only tentatively begun to consider. Martin Price, writing in the *Yale Review,* was one who felt that "the whole issue of Joe Lampton's passivity, of the control that is exercised over him by the life he tries to leave, is too easily resolved by his choosing what he cannot escape." Although the novel's ending can be seen in this light, it can also be interpreted more subtly as failing to provide a positive direction, because it intends to suggest Joe's fundamental inability to protect his children from the world of false values which he has encountered and which they will inevitably encounter.

Braine recognized the constraints imposed by his adherence to the Joe Lampton formula, and in *The Jealous God* (1964) he broke away from them to produce an absorbing study of the tensions inherent in a Catholic conscience. The clash between an inbred asceticism and the temptations of the flesh is an important underlying theme in his novels, and here it is given a sharper focus by the introduction of the Catholic

71

John Braine three years after the success of his first novel

perspective. In retrospect, the portrayal of thirty-year-old Vincent Dungarvin as a sexual innocent seems curiously dated, and the description of his amorous initiation almost prurient in effect. In the context of the period, however, it was seen as "a powerful moral tale" and as "a religious tract for the times." The conflict between the intellectual and the sensual life, between the passive and active modes, is confined within the single central character, externalized as a conflict between the vocation of the priesthood and the profound acknowledgment of sexual love.

Again, it is Braine's realism in his evocation of the restrictive home life, with pretensions but no real access to social superiority, that gives the book much of its power. His analysis of the problems adherent to class strictures, which have always been a feature of British fiction, places Braine firmly in the tradition of Lawrence and George Orwell, who, in this century, were the most notable exponents of these problems. The

pressures of environment and the moral problems these pressures produce are starkly revealed in Braine's terrifying creation of Vincent's repressive mother, who infuses him with guilt and inhibits his potential for development. Despite the positive technical attributes and the imaginatively realized moral situation, the novel was criticized for its pedestrian, even monotonous, format. The review in the *Times Literary Supplement* was typical and perhaps accurate in its assessment of what appeared to be Braine's artistic watershed: "try as he might to explore new ground, his hero's predicament remains essentially just what it has been ever since *Room at the Top*—how to achieve the bigger and better satisfactions of *l'homme moyen sensuel* without paying the price of a bad conscience and social ostracism."

It did, in fact, take Braine some time to escape the mold he had formed for himself, and his next two books, *The Crying Game* (1968) and *Stay With Me Till Morning* (1970), show a disap-

pointing lack of desire to extend his artistic hori-
zons either through theme or technique. During
this period, Braine's work began to show evidence of an emphatic change in his political attitudes. From the original antiestablishment stance
of *Room at the Top,* it became clear that he was moving toward the Right in endorsing the values he
had once condemned. His criticism was now lev-
eled at liberal or, as he termed it, "progressive"
thinking, which he saw as undermining the basic
stability on which society depended.

Intended as a piece of prophetic pessimism
and set "shortly in the future," *The Crying Game*
depicts a provincial journalist working on Fleet
Street who is drawn into the swinging London of
the 1960s and who successfully conveys the culture shock the parochial consciousness receives
when faced with metropolitan mores. More significant than this aspect of the novel, however, is the
reversal of Braine's approach to Socialist values, a
reversal greeted with repugnance by the critics.
"Surely this crude novel is the melancholy climax
of the Angry Young Man phenomenon," wrote
the reviewer in the *Times Literary Supplement,*
bitterly deploring "all that mindless moaning
against the upper classes now directed against
the so-called 'liberal establishment.'" Braine personally attributed his change of heart to the British income-tax system, which deprived him of substantial profits from his earlier best-sellers. The
novel follows the progress of the reactionary Catholic journalist Frank Batcombe through the decadent society he encounters when he moves in
with his cousin Adam, a public relations man.
The plot concerns Frank's pursuit of a story
about a Socialist cabinet minister who is involved
in sexual scandal, but this is secondary to the
descriptions of the permissive society of which
Adam is a part: glamorous, materialistic, sexually
liberated, and amoral. At first fascinated but ultimately disgusted by this life of opportunism,
Frank returns to the faithful Catholic girl who
has waited patiently for him to recover a sense of
order.

Both this book and *Stay With Me Till Morning,* a story of disillusioned middle-aged, middle-
class adultery in a northern town, reinforce values of conformity and conservatism. Set once
more in Braine's native Yorkshire, *Stay With Me
Till Morning* shows a hero, Clive Lendrick, who is
trapped in a prosperous suburb populated by in-
dustrialists and their bored wives. His wife takes
a youthful lover, and in retaliation Clive drifts
into love affairs, none of which are ultimately con-

soling. Temporarily he abandons his family to
live with a younger woman in an artistic milieu,
but he suffers a heart attack and returns to his
wife and children, the only stability his life can provide, however unsatisfactory.

It was at this time too that Braine moved
away from his northern environment and set up
home in what was known as the stockbroker belt
of Surrey, a place where he had once claimed he
could never feel comfortable. He joined the Conservative Association, electioneered on its behalf,
and made provocative reactionary public statements in the press and on television. In 1967 he
had said "Goodbye To The Left" in a pamphlet
written with that title for the Monday Club, the extreme right wing of the British Conservative
party, and subsequently he agitated for the restoration of hanging and championed corporal punishment. In 1975 the *New Statesman* quoted his
views that trade unions wish "to lay the country
open to communist invasion" and that foreign
aid "is a waste of time and money." He completed his defection with the slogan, "Down with
Oxfam!" He acquired a public reputation for
being as vehement a spokesman for the Right as
he had once been a ferocious champion of the
new Left, but the propagandist elements in his
work hampered any sense of serious artistic perspective. "His progress as a writer has been curiously static." "His trademarks are as clear as ever,
and his themes as confined." "There is absolutely
no selection in his work." "His characters likewise
function like robots." Such statements were typical of the critical reception given to his writing at
this time.

Undaunted, Braine continued to produce
novels at a steady rate. Although he always dis-
claimed authority as a theorist, during these
years he had been formulating the literary philosophies which tacitly formed the basis for all his writing, and positive evidence of these is revealed in
The Queen of a Distant Country (1972), a delicately
evoked portrait of a successful writer returning
to the scenes of his youth and exploring the nature of his artistic origins. The novel signals a
new direction in Braine's work. Best-selling novelist Tom Metfield remembers the older woman
who encouraged him when he was a struggling
young writer. With her advice, he developed his
natural talents for accurate observation and vivid
description, and made good use of the material
available to him, his home environment of the
northern industrial town and its inhabitants.
Urged on by nostalgia, he pays a visit to Mi-

John Braine, age forty

It was only with his next novel, *Waiting for Sheila* (1976), that he reasserted his absolute control of the medium in which he was assured. *Waiting for Sheila* is one of Braine's most impressive achievements. Breaking with the chronological structure adopted for most of his fiction, he returns in this confessional novel to the flashback technique of *The Vodi*. His middle-aged hero remembers, painfully and haltingly, significant incidents in his childhood and early manhood which affected his sexual development and contributed to the impotence which has always haunted him. The sexual dimension, while the central subject of the book, is presented without the sensationalism that vulgarized some of Braine's earlier work and evolves into a pregnant metaphor for experience.

Braine extends his psychological insights in this sensitive and acute rendering of a sense of failure in a man who epitomizes material success. The portrayal of a dichotomy between the worlds of genuine and false achievement explores the basic notions underlying such a concept. Braine's uncompromising attitude does not permit him to force an unnatural resolution. He is in total control of his form and allows the novel to end only when the hero has fully relived the Freudian horrors of his past. The book is a natural sequel to *Room at the Top*, but the completion had taken Braine nearly twenty years to realize.

Besides two spy stories, *The Pious Agent* (1975) and *Finger of Fire* (1977), Braine produced a biography of Yorkshire writer J. B. Priestley (1978) and another novel. Although he admitted to being unhappy with the nonfictional mode, Braine recognized in Priestley the Yorkshireman's qualities of tenacity, loyalty, and a belief in the enduring value of personal relationships which characterize his own work. His penultimate novel, *One and Last Love* (1981), is a book which he described as being "quite simply a love story, with a happy beginning and a happy ending, committed to the proposition that men and women have a great deal to give one another." In this and in *These Golden Days* (1985), Braine adopted the persona of Tim Harnforth, a Yorkshire novelist exiled in London, a character who, according to Braine, was the most accurate self-portrait he had ever drawn. In late middle age, Tim escapes the stale, unsatisfactory marriage he has drifted into to find love and happiness with Vivien, a sophisticated metropolitan journalist, in Hamp-

randa, his literary mentor, and discovers that she has become a Communist, holding court to the liberated youth of the 1970s, a breed that Tom despises. The depiction of the foundations of Tom Metfield's literary career illuminates Braine's artistic position in the outspoken defense of realism it contains. The novel's technique becomes its subject as Braine inquires into the relationship between fictional and actual experience in a book whose hero's development so closely resembles the author's. The first-person narrative is sensitively used to create a lyrical, subjective authenticity. Autobiographical and fictive elements are interwoven to form a model illustration of the thesis postulated: that the imaginative reconstruction of true experiences contains its own communicative power.

Adverse criticism of the book attacked the banality of its intellectual argument while admitting its undeniable conviction, and, when Braine attempted to present his ideas in nonfictional form in *Writing a Novel* (1974), he failed precisely on these conceptual grounds. He was essentially a storyteller who depended on artistic distance and his imaginative ability to create meaning. His manual on fictional skills, with its efforts at simplifying the mystique of literary production, merely re-

stead, Braine's own ultimate home. The realism, the precision, and the honesty of presentation in these last two books carried all the conviction of his first. Braine was aware by this stage that time for him was running out, and although in the past he had always felt the need to be economical with his material, as he put it, he now wanted, nearly thirty years after *Room at the Top,* to let himself go.

When John Braine died on 28 October 1986, he was one of the most widely read authors in Britain, among the twenty who received the maximum five-thousand-pound Public Lending Right share, an allocation based on the demands of library borrowers—a fact that gave the ex-librarian much pleasure. As a writer he remained totally without pretension, aware that he was atypical of general directions in British fiction in the 1980s, but continuing, by virtue of his determined anti-intellectualism, to proclaim a nonconformist stance.

In some ways it is ironic that he will be best remembered for *Room at the Top,* a novel whose impassioned attack on materialism he no longer supported, but whose gesture of protest he defended to the end and whose fundamental message of true experience he always upheld. In a consciously literary milieu, he was curiously out of step, intensely professional in his attitude toward writing, and contemptuous of the safe and overcivilized academic backgrounds of many of his literary contemporaries, whom he saw as removed from the pressures of modern life and, consequently, limited in the truth they could convey.

Braine's work remains of central academic interest to critics whose main concern is with the social context of literature, and no study of fiction of the 1950s can afford to ignore his earlier books. He saw his main achievement as having established the validity of subject introduced in *Room at the Top* and sustained in later books, and the affirmation of the importance of the individual life irrespective of class or setting. In destroying the false distinction that had previously been drawn between "serious" and "regional" novels, he felt he made a significant contribution to the mainstream of English fiction. Unpretentious in his approach to writing, he continued to assert his close identification with the provincial consciousness, and a strong sense of human sympathy pervades his work. The basis of his artistic credo can be provided by Ernest Hemingway, whose statement on the writer's role Braine took as epitomizing his own literary manifesto: "From

things that have happened and from things as they exist and from all things that you know and all those you cannot know, you make something through your invention that is not a representation but a whole new thing, truer than anything true and alive, and you make it alive, and if you make it well enough, you give it immortality. That is why you write and for no other reason that you know of."

References:

Kenneth Allsopp, *The Angry Decade: a Survey of the Cultural Revolt of the Nineteen-Fifties* (London: Owen, 1958);

Claude Alrayac, "Inside John Braine's Outsider," *Caliban,* 8 (1971): 113-138;

A. Alvarez, "Braine at the Top," *New Statesman* (5 October 1962): 458;

Phyllis Bentley, "Yorkshire and the Novelist," in *Essays by Divers Hands. Being the Transactions of the Royal Society of Literature,* volume 33, edited by Richard Church (London & New York: Oxford University Press, 1965), pp. 151-155;

Vincent F. Blehl, "Look Back in Anger," *America,* 103 (16 April 1960);

"The Boy from Bingley," *New Statesman* (21 March 1975): 368-369;

Anthony Burgess, *The Novel Now* (London: Faber & Faber, 1967), pp. 140-152;

A. C. Capey, "Post-war English Fiction," *Use of English,* 20 (Summer 1969): 20-24;

David Daiches, ed., *Britain and the Commonwealth* (Harmondsworth, U.K.: Penguin, 1971);

G. S. Fraser, *The Modern Writer and His World* (Harmondsworth, U.K.: Penguin, 1964), pp. 160-187;

John Gibbon, "Some Thoughts on the State of the Novel," *Quarterly Review* (January 1962): 50-52;

James Girdin, *Postwar British Fiction: New Accents and Attitudes* (Berkeley: University of California Press, 1962);

Frank Hilton, "Britain's New Class," *Encounter,* 10 (February 1962): 62-63;

Cal Hines, "John Braine," *Wilson Library Bulletin* (November 1963): 297;

John D. Hurrell, "Class and Conscience in John Braine and Kingsley Amis," *Critique,* 2 (Spring-Summer 1958): 40-42;

Linda Kuehl, "The Poor, the Power Structure, and the Polemicist," *Commonweal,* 90 (15 May 1962): 269;

Stuart Laing, "Making and Breaking the Novel Tradition," in *The Theory of Reading*, edited by Frank Gloversmith (Brighton, U.K.: Harvester, 1984);

Laing, "The Morality of Affluence," in *Popular Fiction and Social Change*, edited by Christopher Pawling (London: Macmillan, 1984);

Alice E. Lasater, "The Breakdown in Communication in the Twentieth Century Novel," *Southern Quarterly*, 12 (October 1973): 1-14;

J. W. Lee, *John Braine* (New York: Twayne, 1968);

Doris Lessing, "The Small Personal Voice," in *Declaration*, edited by Tom Maschler (New York: Dutton, 1958), p. 197;

David Lodge, "The Modern, The Contemporary and the Importance of Being Amis," *Critical Quarterly*, 5 (Winter 1963): 337-339;

John Montgomery, "Young? Angry? Typical?," *Books and Bookmen*, 11 (December 1965): 88-89;

W. van O'Connor, "Two Types of Heroes in Post-War British Fiction," *PMLA* (March 1962): 169-170;

Valerie Pitt, *The Writer and the Modern World; A Study in Literature and Dogma* (London: Society for Promoting Christian Knowledge, 1966);

Rubin Rabinowitz, *The Reaction Against Experiment in the English Novel 1950-1960* (New York: Columbia University Press, 1967);

Michael Ratcliffe, *The Novel Today* (London: Longmans, Green, 1968);

Kenneth Richardson, ed., *Twentieth Century Writing* (London: Newnes, 1969);

Dale Salwak, *Interviews with Britain's Angry Young Men* (London: Borgo Press, 1984);

Stephen Shapiro, "The Ambivalent Animal: Man in the Contemporary British and American Novel," *Centennial Review*, 12 (Winter 1968): 15-16;

Derek Stanford, "Beatniks and Angry Young Men," *Meanjin* (17 December 1958): 417-418;

Randall Stevenson, *The British Novel Since the Thirties: An Introduction* (London: Batsford, 1986);

Fraser Stokes, "Current British Fiction," *English Record* (16 February 1960): 7-12;

Robert Weaver, "England's Angry Young Men," *Queens Quarterly*, 65 (Summer 1958): 183-194;

Colin Wilson, *The Craft of the Novel* (London: Gollancz, 1975);

Mas'ud Zavarzadeh, "Anti-intellectualism in the Post-war British Novel: Anatomy of a Metaphor," *Ball State University Forum*, 12 (Autumn 1971): 68-73.

Lawrence Durrell

(27 February 1912 - 7 November 1990)

This entry was updated by Michael H. Begnal (Pennsylvania State University) from his entry in
DLB 15: British Novelists, 1930-1959: Part One.

See also the Durrell entries in DLB 27: Poets of Great Britain and Ireland, 1945-1960 *and* DLB Yearbook: 1990.

BOOKS: *Pied Piper of Lovers* (London: Cassell, 1935);

Panic Spring: A Romance, as Charles Norden (London: Faber & Faber, 1937);

The Black Book: An Agon (Paris: Obelisk Press, 1938; New York: Dutton, 1960);

A Private Country (London: Faber & Faber, 1943);

Prospero's Cell: A Guide to the Landscape and Manners of the Island of Corcyra (London: Faber & Faber, 1945); republished with *Reflections on a Marine Venus* (New York: Dutton, 1960);

Cities, Plains and People (London: Faber & Faber, 1946);

Cefalû: A Novel (London: Editions Poetry London, 1947); republished as *The Dark Labyrinth* (London: Ace, 1957; New York: Dutton, 1962);

On Seeming to Presume (London: Faber & Faber, 1948);

Sappho: A Play in Verse (London: Faber & Faber, 1950; New York: Dutton, 1958);

Key to Modern Poetry (London: Peter Nevill, 1952);

Reflections on a Marine Venus: A Companion to the Landscape of Rhodes (London: Faber & Faber, 1953); republished with *Prospero's Cell* (New York: Dutton, 1960);

The Tree of Idleness And Other Poems (London: Faber & Faber, 1955);

Selected Poems (London: Faber & Faber, 1956; New York: Grove, 1956);

Bitter Lemons (London: Faber & Faber, 1957; New York: Dutton, 1958);

Esprit de Corps: Sketches from Diplomatic Life (London: Faber & Faber, 1957; New York: Dutton, 1968);

Justine: A Novel (London: Faber & Faber, 1957; New York: Dutton, 1957);

White Eagles Over Serbia (London: Faber & Faber, 1957; New York: Criterion, 1957);

Larry Durrell

Balthazar: A Novel (London: Faber & Faber, 1958; New York: Dutton, 1958);

Mountolive: A Novel (London: Faber & Faber, 1958; New York: Dutton, 1958);

Stiff Upper Lip: Life Among the Diplomats (London: Faber & Faber, 1958; New York: Dutton, 1961);

Clea: A Novel (London: Faber & Faber, 1960; New York: Dutton, 1960);

Collected Poems (London: Faber & Faber, 1960);

The Poetry of Lawrence Durrell (New York: Dutton, 1962);

*The Alexandria Quartet: Justine, Balthazar, Mount-
    olive, Clea* (London: Faber & Faber, 1962;
    New York: Dutton, 1962);

An Irish Faustus: A Morality in Nine Scenes (Lon-
    don: Faber & Faber, 1963; New. York:
    Dutton, 1964);

Acte: A Play (London: Faber & Faber, 1964; New
    York: Dutton, 1965);

Sauve Qui Peut (London: Faber & Faber, 1966;
    New York: Dutton, 1967);

The Ikons and Other Poems (London: Faber &
    Faber, 1966; New York: Dutton, 1967);

Tunc: A Novel (London: Faber & Faber, 1968;
    New York: Dutton, 1968); republished with
    Nunquam: A Novel as *The Revolt of Aphrodite*
    (London: Faber & Faber, 1974);

Spirit of Place: Letters and Essays on Travel, edited
    by Alan G. Thomas (London: Faber &
    Faber, 1969; New York: Dutton, 1969);

Nunquam: A Novel (London: Faber & Faber, 1970;
    New York: Dutton, 1970); republished with
    Tunc: A Novel as *The Revolt of Aphrodite* (Lon-
    don: Faber & Faber, 1974);

Le Grand Suppositoire: Entretiens Avec Marc Alyn
    (Paris: Pierre Belfond, 1972); translated by
    Francine Barker as *The Big Supposer: A Dia-
    logue with Marc Alyn* (London: Abelard-
    Schuman, 1973; New York: Grove, 1975);

Vega and Other Poems (London: Faber & Faber,
    1973; Woodstock, N.Y.: The Overlook
    Press, 1973);

The Revolt of Aphrodite (London: Faber & Faber,
    1974);

Monsieur, or the Prince of Darkness (London: Faber
    & Faber, 1974; New York: Viking, 1975);

The Best of Antrobus (London: Faber & Faber,
    1974);

Sicilian Carousel (London: Faber & Faber, 1977;
    New York: Viking, 1977);

The Greek Islands (London: Faber & Faber, 1978);

Livia, or Buried Alive (London: Faber & Faber,
    1978; New York: Viking, 1979);

Collected Poems, 1931-1974, edited by James A.
    Brigham (London: Faber & Faber, 1980;
    New York: Viking, 1980);

A Smile In The Mind's Eye (London: Wildwood
    House, 1980; New York: Universe, 1982);

Constance, or Solitary Practices (London: Faber &
    Faber, 1982; New York: Viking, 1982);

Sebastian, or Ruling Passions (London: Faber &
    Faber, 1983; New York: Viking, 1983);

Quinx, or The Ripper's Tale (London: Faber &
    Faber, 1985; New York: Viking, 1985);

Antrobus Complete (London: Faber & Faber, 1985);

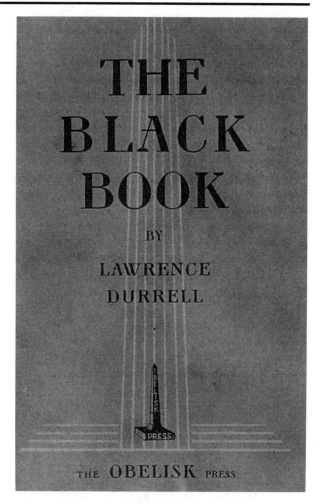

*Front wrapper for Durrell's third novel, published in Paris
to avoid British censorship*

Caesar's Vast Ghost: Aspects of Provence (London:
    Faber & Faber, 1990).

TRANSLATIONS: George Seferis, *The King of
    Asine, and other poems*, translated by Bernard
    Spencer, Nanos Valaoritis, and Durrell (Lon-
    don: Lehmann, 1948);

Emmanuel Royidis, *The Curious History of Pope Joan*,
    translated by Durrell (London: Deutsch,
    1960; New York: Dutton, 1961).

A follower in the footsteps of D. H. Lawrence and James Joyce, Lawrence Durrell explored in his novels the quintessential concerns
of the twentieth century: space, time, consciousness, sexuality, and identity. Equally at home in
all the genres of literature, he employed fiction
to continue the structural experiments and investi-
gations of the literary generation which preceded
him, while at the same time producing a body of

work that is lusty, vital, and affective. Durrell was a writer, a philosopher, and an experiencer who scorned the sterility of contemporary existence, which he called "the English death." He was concerned with the inner spaces of the psyche, with the few levels of the human being's encounter with another which he could call valuable, and with the realities of physical experience. Without doubt a maverick within the artistic establishment, Durrell was at the same time a paradox: an exile who often wrote about England and Englishmen; an acclaimer of Henry Miller who wrote an adventure tale for adolescents; a journalist who called for the destruction of the very structure which, for a very long time, supported him. He was a truly interesting thinker bounded by a world which he felt was regimented, programmed, and predictable.

Lawrence Durrell was born in Julundur, India, on 27 February 1912 to Anglo-Irish parents who had never seen England. His father was an engineer who worked on the construction of the Darjeeling railroad line which skirts the Himalayas, and his family had been resident in India for three generations. Durrell attended the College of St. Joseph in Darjeeling, and at the age of eleven he was sent to Britain to continue his education at St. Edmund's School in Canterbury. This move was the first great change in his life, but his father's attempt to groom him as a member of the British ruling class did not succeed. After secondary school, according to Durrell's own account, he purposely failed the entrance examinations for Oxford four times, a conscious rebellion against his father; he became instead a jazz pianist at a London nightclub called The Blue Peter while aspiring to be a writer. He educated himself thereafter. After marrying the artist Nancy Myers, Durrell gave up his odd jobs and began to work at the job of becoming a novelist.

Certainly his discovery of the works of Henry Miller had a tremendous effect on his writing, and Durrell initiated a correspondence which was to continue until Miller's death in 1980. In 1938, after censorship problems had complicated its British Isles publication, Durrell's *The Black Book* appeared from Obelisk Press in Paris, and he became what he called a "serious" writer. The novel established Durrell's reputation and drew lavish praise from Miller: "You've crossed the equator. Your commercial career is finished. From now on you're an outlaw, and I congratulate you with all the breath in my body. I seriously think that you truly are 'the first English-

man!'" The success of the novel, in terms of fame rather than in number of copies sold, instilled in Durrell the confidence that he was on the right track artistically, and took him out from under the shadow of Miller's influence as well.

In form, *The Black Book* is the diary of one Herbert "Death" Gregory, Esquire, which is found, presented, and commented upon by a narrator who calls himself Lawrence Lucifer. Though the novel has no plot in a conventional sense, it chronicles the day-to-day existences of the denizens of the Hotel Regina, a motley crew of miserable and emotionally perverted loners. Durrell himself called it "a savage charcoal sketch of spiritual and sexual etiolation." Among the characters are Lobo, the Peruvian student who meditates on "tweed Englishwomen who wear padlocks between their legs," and the disconsolate homosexual Tarquin, who is in love with Clare, the black dancing master. Gregory emerges as the spokesman for "the English death." Spiritually crippled, unable to love, Gregory is involved in an affair with the prostitute Gracie in which neither can understand or please the other. Gracie is crude and uneducated, while Gregory calls himself "the average Englishman. . . . I carry my virginity and my self-satisfaction on a string round my neck." The two eventually marry, for no discernible reason, and the squalor of their lives continues until Gracie's death from consumption. Gregory feels no grief or bereavement whatsoever, and he goes off to escape from life by marrying the widowed barmaid Kate, "the most ordinary person I could find." In her sterility, she will ease him into his own. As his farewell, dying into an English life, Gregory writes his last will and testament, including this bequest to himself: "I offer only the crooked grin of the toad, and a colored cap to clothe my nakedness."

The sterile wasteland of British society is all too evident here, but strangely enough *The Black Book* is not simply concerned with this sterility alone. Like Lawrence Durrell, Lawrence Lucifer is a novelist living on Corfu; he has sifted through Gregory's memoirs in an attempt to understand and exorcize his English heritage. Out of this chaos, things have begun to fall into place, and the artist, in his Christ-like struggle, has begun to emerge: "I am beginning my agony in the garden and there are too many words, and too many things to put into words. In the fantastic proscenium of the ego, when I begin my soliloquy, I shall not choose as Gregory chose." Lucifer has received a surfeit of "the English death"

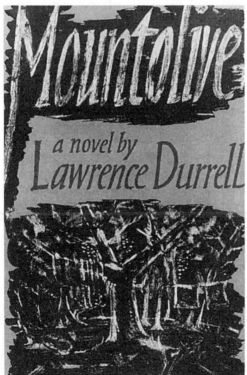

Dust jackets for The Alexandria Quartet

and can now regurgitate it. Like Darley in Durrell's later work, *The Alexandria Quartet* (1962), the artist both Durrell and Lucifer wish themselves to be must pass through a catharsis in order to achieve emotional regeneration. Lucifer lies dormant in the end, thinking of Greece, the sea, the woman in bed beside him, watching "the eyelashes of God moving, delicate as talc." Despite the nullity of Death Gregory, *The Black Book* ends on a note of brooding and impending promise, a refutation of sterility and a hope for a new life rooted in both art and the physical.

It is his explorations into the identity and character of the artist that lie at the center of Durrell's development as a writer, his definition of himself; it is a definition that is sometimes obscured for the reader by the paradoxes of his canon. If there is the serious novelist of *The Black Book*, there is also the Durrell who wrote the light romance *Pied Piper of Lovers*, published in 1935, and *White Eagles Over Serbia*, an adventure story that appeared in 1957. There is the Durrell who wrote the thriller *Panic Spring* in 1937 (under the pseudonym Charles Norden, a character in Henry Miller's *Tropic of Cancer*, 1934) as well as the Durrell who wrote a social satire à la Aldous Huxley, *Cefalû*, in 1947, republished as *The Dark Labyrinth* (1957). If the paradox of Durrell's character as an artist is to be resolved, perhaps Durrell himself did it best in an apologetic note to Miller in 1958: "I had to pay for the baby's shoes somehow," and, "All this is very perplexing to my fans who don't know whether I am P. G. Wodehouse or James Joyce or what the hell." But it would seem that an earlier explanation to Miller for using the Norden pseudonym brings us closer to the truth: Durrell says that Norden "is a double I need—not for money or any of the fake reasons I'm always giving—but simply for a contact with the human world. I am so alone really that I'm a bit scared of going crazy. Norden would keep me in touch with the commonplace world which will never understand my personal struggle."

Durrell's art is inextricably intertwined with his own existence, and *The Alexandria Quartet*—*Justine* (1957), *Balthazar* (1958), *Mountolive* (1958), and *Clea* (1960)—probably his most important work, is an individual, personal investigation as much as it is an artistic one. For Durrell, certainty lies in multiplicity, and, like a Prospero in his cell, he strives to hold all the strands together. Nineteen years passed between the publication of *The Black Book* and *Justine*, and, in the in-

terim, like Lawrence Lucifer, Lawrence Durrell refined his life through art and his art through life.

One pragmatic reason for the long artistic hiatus, though Durrell did publish many less serious pieces during this time, was the chaos and uncertainty which engulfed his existence. He became worried about the problem of supporting a family, and managed to obtain a position with the British Council even though he had not received a university degree. With so many Englishmen in the armed forces, it was probably not a difficult thing to arrange. In 1939 he accepted a teaching appointment at the British Institute in Athens, but the onset of World War II and the constant shifting of the battle lines forced him on to Crete and eventually to Egypt. From 1941 to 1944, Durrell was the British foreign press officer in Cairo, before assuming the duties of press attaché in Alexandria. During this period his marriage dissolved; his wife and daughter returned to England; and Durrell ended up as the British public information officer on the Greek island of Rhodes. It was at this point that things began to calm down a bit for him; he married Eve Cohen in 1947 and began the first drafts of *The Alexandria Quartet*. Durrell's ability to cloak himself in the Establishment seems to have provided him the stability and contact with normality which he needed in order to write. It is little short of amazing that he managed to publish the wealth of poetry, drama, and travel impressions which he did during the period from 1940 to 1947. After lecturing in Argentina and Yugoslavia for the British Council between 1947 and 1949, he settled on Cyprus and began work in earnest on *Justine*.

As Durrell describes it, "It took me years to evolve *Justine*, because I was having to work on so many different levels at once; history, landscape (which had to be fairly *strange* to symbolize our civilization), the weft of occultism and finally the novel about the actual process of writing."

Durrell's long-deserved success as a novelist came with *Justine*, which captured the imaginations of a vast readership with its exotic imagery and sensuality. But the reader, perhaps warned in a prefacing statement by Durrell that this was "the first of a series," was soon plunged into the labyrinth of perception which constitutes *The Alexandria Quartet*. In *Balthazar*, Durrell conceives of his four-volume novel as based in form upon the theory of relativity, the first three volumes to be deployed spatially while the final volume represents time. Thus the first three parts are not re-

Lawrence Durrell

lated as sequels, but are designated "siblings," and are to be superimposed, one upon another, to expand the idea of an ultimately unknowable objective reality. The writer Darley's view of his affair with Justine in the first novel, for example, is displaced in the second novel by his Alexandrian friend Balthazar's information that Darley was used only as a decoy by Justine so that she could hide her affair with the novelist Pursewarden from her husband Nessim. The omniscient narrator of the third novel, *Mountolive*, informs us that Nessim and Justine are plotting to run arms and ammunition in support of an emerging Palestine, later to be Israel, and that her affairs are simply a smoke screen to hide their machinations from the British and Egyptian authorities. What is important here is not what *actually* happened, since that, to Durrell, is irrelevant history. The essence of truth lies in its individual perception by a myriad of characters, each striving and struggling for some sort of self-perception. Certainty is an impossibility, but any sort of unity can only be found in multiplicity.

As the reader progresses through *The Alexandria Quartet*, he is faced with a growing number of questions. Is Balthazar a sage or a fool? Who murders Nessim's brother, Narouz? Does Purse-

warden commit suicide because he has compromised Nessim and Mountolive, the British ambassador, or does he do it because he wishes to free his sister, Liza, from their incestuous affair? Are Justine and Nessim patriots or traitors? Is Pursewarden a great novelist or a maundering drunkard? Durrell has a marvelous ability to create plot as well as aesthetics. But one cannot approach *The Alexandria Quartet* as one would a mystery novel. One of its basic themes is perception, and Durrell is working with the notion that perception is occult, Gnostic, based on nothing concrete. The historical or the scientific method cannot operate here, since we have no definite facts to work with, and opening any one of these hollow dolls will only reveal another one nestled inside it. Truth is relative, and, as Darley wonders: "Perhaps then the destruction of my private Alexandria was necessary . . . perhaps buried in all this there lies the germ and substance of a truth— time's usufruct—which, if I can accommodate it, will carry me a little further in what is really a search for my proper self." The outer world is as inscrutable, and maybe as unchanging, as the Alexandrian sights and smells which Durrell describes in such lush detail and color. The apprehension of experience is finally important, not as an aid to knowing another, but only as an entrance into the self. As Pursewarden phrases it, "every interpretation of reality is based upon a unique position. Two paces east or west and the whole picture is changed."

In a succinct definition of his intention in the *Quartet*, Durrell called its central direction an investigation of modern love, but modern love in the novel seems not always what it is commonly supposed to be. Love in the *Quartet* is certainly sensual, but it is also transitory, often one-sided, and succumbs quite often to treachery, ennui, or simply the passage of time. Sometimes the relationships are so complicated and interwoven that it becomes difficult to keep them in order, and Durrell's fascination with incest is presented in the novels in several ways: Darley lives with the dancer Melissa, has an affair with Justine, and finally is involved with Clea. Justine, married to Nessim, has affairs with Clea, Darley, and Pursewarden. Nessim fathers a child by Melissa. Mountolive, after an early affair with Leila, the mother of Nessim and Narouz, lives with Liza, who has had a child by her brother, Pursewarden. Narouz is in love with Clea. Sex is cheap, but expectations of a lasting relationship are only illusions. Continuing the theme he introduced in *The Black Book*, Durrell depicts love in a modern context as a situation in which rarely can either partner understand or communicate with the other. Pleasure is momentary, and sooner or later every love is thrown back upon itself. Some at least can survive, but no one escapes unscathed. Mountolive is swarmed under in a brothel of child prostitutes; Balthazar is publicly humiliated by a Greek actor; and the transvestite policeman Scobie is beaten to death by a gang of sailors. Modern man and woman are ultimately alone, at the mercy of their desires and a swiftly changing reality in which nothing really is as it seems. No one is exempt from passion, yet almost all are denied any fulfillment. Durrell, despite the influence of D. H. Lawrence on his thinking, paints a rather shoddy picture of love as the saving grace for the modern predicament, until we are returned to Darley.

After *Clea* was published in 1960, Lawrence Durrell moved to the south of France and married the novelist Claude-Marie Vincendon in 1961. The capstone volume of the series attempts to put events into perspective through time, and it also places Darley back in the center of the stage. With Darley's patient evaluation of what has gone before and what is transpiring between

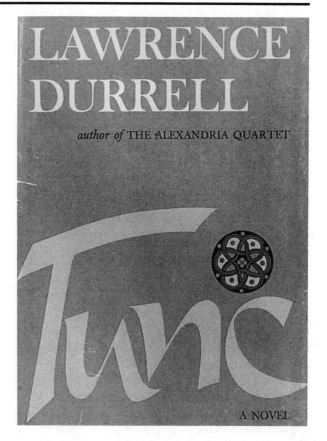

Dust jacket for the American edition of the first novel in the two-volume work The Revolt of Aphrodite

Clea and himself comes the emergence of another central theme: the maturation of the artist. His first attempt at writing about his experiences a failure, Darley has come into possession of Pursewarden's notebook, in which Darley finds himself designated the pompous "Brother Ass." Among the records of Pursewarden's struggles within his own psyche, Darley begins to find the illuminations which he can turn to his own benefit: "The sexual and the creative energy go hand in hand. They convert into one another—the solar sexual and the lunar spiritual holding an eternal dialogue." Despite the fact that the love of Darley and Clea slowly erodes, and that the relationship is severed after Clea loses her right hand in a swimming accident and Darley returns to Europe, the novel holds out hope that they will meet again. Despite her mechanical hand, Clea begins to paint the most important pictures of her career. Even more important, Darley, like Lawrence Lucifer in *The Black Book*, has learned something from his experiences and begins to write again. His artistic resurrection is founded upon insights such as these: "Blind as a mole, I had been digging about in the graveyard of relative fact piling up data, more information, and completely missing the mythopoeic reference which underlies fact. I had called this searching for truth!"

Darley's first view of Clea in this final novel is of her sitting at the same café table at which he had often sat with Melissa. A new and meaningful love with Clea has taken the place of a previous relationship into which he could not enter fully. Darley has pierced the curtain between illusion and reality, and has found the means to transform the solitary state of love into art. "If two or more explanations of a single human action are as good as each other then what does action mean but an illusion—a gesture made against the misty backcloth of a reality made palpable by the delusive nature of human division merely?" Once again Durrell is defining the lonely path the artist must take through experience to put it all into artistic perspective, and here appears the central and unifying thread of *The Alexandria Quartet*. If action means little, then thought and insight and love are essential to the aesthetic process. *The Alexandria Quartet* is a vast tapestry of love and intrigue, these facets fascinating in themselves alone, but Durrell is also treating the artistic consciousness and its reaction to a world which more and more limits the possibility of one human being reaching out and touching another in any meaningful way.

He continues these explorations with *The Revolt of Aphrodite* (1974): *Tunc* (1968) and *Nunquam* (1970). The titles for this double-decker novel come from Petronius's *Satyricon*, in which a Roman character compares a fertile and spiritual past with a present filled with people who are only concerned with profit. Petronius's line, *"aut tunc aut nunquam,"* means "then or never." In describing his new work, Durrell said: "In the Quartet I tried to see people as a function of place. . . . Now . . . I am attempting to set my people against a backcloth of an idea of culture as something generic," and, "in the culture sense it's always now or never."

Tunc is narrated by the inventor Felix Charlock, who works on memory and recording devices and who is dictating his impressions and his history into his Dactyl recording machine. Felix has gotten involved with the Firm, a vast enterprise run by the brothers Julian and Jocas Merlin that controls almost all international business and even has managed to purchase the Parthenon. Realizing that the Firm has been slowly but surely

turning him into a robot, Charlock has escaped to Athens after compiling everything he knows about the Firm into a gigantic computer named Abel, but the agents of the Firm are hot on his heels to recapture him. As Julian has warned: "The Firm is self-subsisting now, rolling down its appointed path with a momentum which neither you nor I can alter. Of course he that is not with it is against it, and so on."

Like Darley in the *Quartet*, Felix Charlock is a Sherlock, a detective sifting through his past for the key to where things all went wrong. The variety of his acquaintances is rich and strange: Julian, whose face is never seen; Caradoc, the architect who delivers a drunken masterpiece of a speech on architecture and humanity in the ruins of the Parthenon; Mrs. Henniker, who manages a bizarre brothel named the Blue Danube. But Charlock's life is defined by the two women he has loved, opposites of one another: Iolanthe, the prostitute who later becomes a film star, and Benedicta Merlin, the sister of Julian and Jocas, whom he marries. It is Iolanthe, speaking as she is dying of cancer caused by an injection of paraffin into her breasts, who tells him: "only the free man can really be loved by a woman," and his marriage to Benedicta is a disaster. Felix is certainly not free. After a too brief period of love and passion during which his wife becomes pregnant, she leaves him alone for years at a time. In our last view of her, she is standing naked in a mirrored hall in their country house, muttering the Lord's Prayer and blasting away at her multiple images with a shotgun. Julian is satanic, a vampire, but we come to see that the Firm merely tempts—man is not attacked by monsters, but instead he traps himself and gives up his own freedom. With his characteristic authorial sleight of hand, Durrell reverts to an omniscient point of view for the last pages of *Tunc*. Charlock's son, Mark, admits to Julian that the computer Abel has been booby-trapped; Julian and Benedicta seem to be in league, erstwhile incestuous lovers; a shot rings out upstairs. The reader has no choice but to proceed on to *Nunquam*.

Once again Felix resumes his narration, but we should remember an aphorism from *Tunc*: "human life is an anthology of states; chronological progression is an illusion." Something has gone wrong. Awakening in the Paulhaus sanatorium, Felix remembers a blow on the head, or was it an operation? Felix is no longer Charlock, and a contented patient has replaced a dissatisfied detective. Throughout his career as a novelist,

Henry Miller, Alfred Perlès, and Lawrence Durrell, 1959; drawing by Eve Miller

Durrell was an experimenter with narrative point of view, and in *Nunquam* the insightful voice of *Tunc* is replaced by a blandness and acceptance which much resembles that of Dowell in Ford Madox Ford's *The Good Soldier* (1915), a novel which Durrell much admired. With little explanation, other than the statement that Mark's death has reunited them, Benedicta, balanced and loving, is nursing her husband back to health, and Felix is once more devoted to the Firm. Julian reappears, no longer sinister and faceless, and defines the Firm in words that Felix finds acceptable: "the very terms under which it operates reflect the basic predispositions of the culture of which it is only an offshoot . . . they can't escape reflecting the firm, just as the firm can't help reflecting the corpus of what, for want of a better word, we must call our civilization." Thus *Nunquam* is in essence presenting an update of

what, in *The Black Book*, Durrell called "the English Death."

Though he is impotent, Julian has fallen in love with Iolanthe, and her death has shattered him. Here begins the greatest creative triumph the Firm has yet attempted: the construction of a new Iolanthe, so perfect in every detail that even she will not know that she is a dummy. What Julian desires is "a neo-Aphrodite—one who cannot eat, excrete, or make love," and Felix and his assistant Marchant begin work in their laboratory, located next door to the Firm's embalming department. The experiment proves to be a total success, perhaps too much so, since Iolanthe, like any human, demands freedom and finally escapes from the Firm's clutches. Ironically enough, the plastic Aphrodite achieves the freedom that the human being cannot—she can control her own actions—but even this is to be perverted. A Frankenstein monster, a Jack the Ripper in reverse, Iolanthe, though she is incapable of becoming aroused, becomes a common prostitute who murders the men she seduces, and the new Aphrodite cannot be caught as she blends into the underworld of slums and brothels. She is not to be seen again until the members of the Firm gather in St. Paul's Cathedral in London, a kind of sanatorium like the Paulhaus, for the funeral of Jocas Merlin, dead from cancer. In his struggle to recapture her, Julian, who has chased Iolanthe to the heights of the cathedral, topples from the Whispering Gallery to the floor below, still clutching the Iolanthe who is finally his, and Felix ascends to the directorship of the Firm. Felix, in a gesture of beginning afresh, plans to burn all of the Firm's multinational, industrial contracts, "so it will be either/or once again; it will be now or never," but the obvious implication of the novel's conclusion is that nothing will change. It is never. In his joy at his new importance, Felix ends with a statement the implications of which unfortunately he does not truly understand: "we have been dancing, dancing in complete happiness and accord. And we will keep on this way, dancing and dancing, even though Rome burn." The culture which Lawrence Durrell celebrated in *The Alexandria Quartet* seems to have sold itself out cheaply when we arrive at *The Revolt of Aphrodite.*

For a time Durrell concentrated on his poetry and verse drama, much of which was to see print in the *Collected Poems* of 1980, but in 1974 he returned to the novel with the publication of *Monsieur, or The Prince of Darkness.* After the untimely death of Claude-Marie Vincendon in 1967, Durrell married Ghislaine de Boissons in 1973 and continued to live and work in the south of France. His wandering days were over. By this time, his reputation as a novelist, especially in Europe, had attained almost monumental proportions, and he was called by many the greatest living prose writer. The sales of all his works increased at a steady pace.

Durrell's artist-magician tricks and twists are more evident than ever in *Monsieur.* We are treated to the reminiscences of Bruce Drexel, involved in a ménage à trois with Piers de Nogaret and his sister, Sylvie, summoned back to Avignon by the news of the death of Piers. All three have become involved with Gnosticism in varying degrees through the influence of the Egyptian Akkad, a mystic sect, and one mystery only serves to generate another. Are the Gnostics in-

volved with ritual murder, and why was Piers's head severed from his corpse? Why has Sylvie gone mad? Before we have gone very far, however, we learn that all of this is the narrative of a novel being written by one Robin Sutcliffe, who describes the work as "an unholy trinity of romantics, a love sandwich with the perplexed and thick-thewed Bruce making the filling." The links between art and reality are less than clear-cut, since, as Bruce later says, "the resulting manuscript is indeed something of a puzzle, for almost before he [Rob] could get the book started his 'characters,' that is to say Piers, Toby, Sylvie and myself, started to look over his shoulder, so to speak, and talk for themselves." Robin's wife Pia, the sister of Bruce, has run off with a Negro lesbian, Trash, and over all hangs the Gnostic concept that Satan has usurped Christ's throne once and for all, and will reign forever. Rob scorns another novelist named Bloshford, never seen, and in the final section of *Monsieur,* Durrell reveals startlingly that all of the preceding narrative is yet another novel being written by Aubrey Blanford. "Soon he [Blanford] would have done with the book, done with the masks under which he had so successfully disguised his weaknesses and disappointments and misadventures." But where does one "novel" stop and another begin? The title *Monsieur* is applied to the novel by Blanford, while *The Prince of Darkness* is the appellation given it by Sutcliffe, and behind all of this is the novelist Lawrence Durrell.

Livia, or Buried Alive (1978) seems simultaneously to clarify and to confuse the issues raised in *Monsieur.* Blanford, along with holding conversations on the telephone with the imaginary Sutcliffe, begins a history of his own youth and complications. The time is now the period between the two world wars, and young Blanford spends his summers in Avignon with the new set of characters from the de Nogaret family, Livia, Constance, and their brother, Hilary. As is usual with Durrell, exotic characters and situations abound, along with continuing speculations about the Order of the Templars and their struggle against the Devil. But the upshot is that Blanford marries Livia, only to find that she is a lesbian with a Negro lover named Thrush. Once more, Durrell has stacked level upon level. A comment made by Blanford may help to assuage some of the doubt and uncertainty caused by these two novels: "squinting round the curves of futurity I saw something like a quincunx of novels set out

Lawrence Durrell

in a good classical order. Five Q novels written in a highly elliptical style invented for the occasion."

With *Constance, or Solitary Practices* (1982), Durrell plunges his characters into the chaos of World War II with intricate twists and turns of the narrative. Blanford, a conscientious objector, has gone off to Egypt as a private secretary, where he will be crippled in an artillery accident. Livia disappears, only to resurface in Berlin as a high-ranking Nazi official, while Constance emerges as a major figure in her own right. A student of Sigmund Freud and psychoanalysis in Vienna, she becomes embroiled in an affair with the Gnostic Sebastian Affad, and the two explore the mysteries of the orgasm. In an interview from this period, Durrell attempted to explain what he was doing: "I was intending to go over five books this time, which sounds pretty ambitious at my age, and I was going to do a telescopic form, what the French call *gigogne*." A striking feature of *Constance* is that though clearly the set of characters that includes Sylvie, Piers, Sutcliffe, and Drexel exists as the fictional creation of Aubrey Blanford, they are free to intermingle with their "real" counterparts: Constance, Hilary, Livia, and Blanford. The conventional lines between fiction and reality have dissolved

completely. Even characters from *The Alexandria Quartet* make brief appearances. As Robin Sutcliffe defines the situation, this is "a book full of spare parts of other books, of characters left over from other lives, all circulating in each other's bloodstreams. . . . I dream of such a book, full of not completely discrete characters, of ancestors and descendants all mixed up."

Durrell completes what has come to be called *The Avignon Quintet* with *Sebastian, or Ruling Passions* (1983) and *Quinx, or The Ripper's Tale* (1985). The war is now over, and Constance's existence is thrown into confusion with the suicide of her sister Livia and Affad's murder by a deranged mental patient named Mnemidis. Yet the characters are united again by the search for the lost treasure of the Knights Templar, said to be buried somewhere beneath the city of Avignon. Constance has taken up with Aubrey Blanford, destined to become the love of her life, and all come together for one last magnificent expedition in the south of France. However, just at the moment of revelation at the conclusion of *Quinx*, Durrell ends abruptly, refusing to provide his reader with conventional narrational closure, and forcing the reader back upon him- or herself. What is important to Durrell is not what will happen to characters who are, after all, fictional, but instead how these entities have come to stand for basic and essential male and female principles. Blanford's explanation of his own work might service for Durrell: "The old stable outlines of the dear old linear novel have been sidestepped in favour of soft focus palimpsest which enables the actors to turn into each other, to melt into each other's life space if they wish. Everything and everyone comes closer and closer together, moving towards the one." *The Avignon Quintet* is certain to challenge readers for generations to come, and it stands as a major contribution to the evolving art of the novel.

In all this lies the great interest and the great importance of Durrell as a modern novelist. He never ceased to explore the possibilities of fiction as a literary form, always pushing at the boundaries of what could and could not be done, always expecting that his readership would bear with him as he pursued his explorations. His efforts were rewarded with the Duff Cooper Memorial Prize for *Bitter Lemons* in 1957, the *Prix du Meilleur Livre Etranger* for *Justine* and *Balthazar* in 1959, and the James Tait Black Memorial Prize for fiction for *Monsieur, or the Prince of Darkness* in 1975. All of his novels are spiritual journeys of one kind or another, testing the possibilities of love and sexuality, attacking what he saw as the modern linkage of excrement, money, and materialism. Ultimately, he celebrated the refusal of the human spirit to give in. Despite the pessimism that often surfaces in his work, Durrell was a humanist who offered up art as the saving grace. He consistently matured and evolved as a novelist, never content to rest on what he had achieved, and he was always ready to shout out against dullness and sterility. An artist who melded the romanticism of D. H. Lawrence with the classicism of James Joyce, Lawrence Durrell was a twentieth-century writer who consistently maintained the profession and the appellation of novelist.

Letters:

Art and Outrage. A Correspondence about Henry Miller between Alfred Perlès and Lawrence Durrell (London: Putnam, 1959; New York: Dutton, 1961);

Lawrence Durrell and Henry Miller: A Private Correspondence, edited by George Wickes (New York: Dutton, 1963; London: Faber & Faber, 1963);

Literary Lifelines: The Richard Aldington-Lawrence Durrell Correspondence, edited by Ian S. MacNiven and Harry T. Moore (London: Faber & Faber, 1981; New York: Viking, 1981);

The Durrell-Miller Letters, 1935-80, edited by MacNiven (London: Faber & Faber, 1988; New York: New Directions, 1988);

Lawrence Durrell: Letters to Jean Fanchette, 1958-1963 (Paris: Two Cities, 1988).

References:
Michael H. Begnal, ed., *On Miracle Ground: Essays on the Fiction of Lawrence Durrell* (Lewisburg, Pa.: Bucknell University Press, 1990);

G. S. Fraser, *Lawrence Durrell: A Study* (New York: Dutton, 1973);

Alan W. Friedman, *Lawrence Durrell and The Alexandria Quartet* (Norman: University of Oklahoma Press, 1970);

Friedman, ed., *Critical Essays on Lawrence Durrell* (Boston: G. K. Hall, 1987);

Tiger Tim Hawkins, *Eve: The Common Muse of Henry Miller and Lawrence Durrell* (San Francisco: Ahab, 1963);

Frank L. Kersnowski, *Into the Labyrinth: Essays on the Art of Lawrence Durrell* (Ann Arbor: UMI Research Press, 1989);

Harry T. Moore, ed., *The World of Lawrence Durrell* (Carbondale: Southern Illinois University Press, 1962);

Jane L. Pinchin, *Alexandria Still: Forster, Durrell, Cavafy* (Princeton: Princeton University Press, 1977);

John Unterecker, *Lawrence Durrell* (New York: Columbia University Press, 1964);

Susan Vander Closter, *Joyce Cary and Lawrence Durrell: A Reference Guide* (Boston: G. K. Hall, 1985);

John A. Weigel, *Lawrence Durrell* (New York: Twayne, 1965).

Papers:
Many of Durrell's papers are in the Morris Library of Southern Illinois University. Others are in the libraries of the University of California, Los Angeles, and the University of Southern California.

Ian Fleming

(28 May 1908 - 12 August 1964)

This entry was written by Joan DelFattore (University of Delaware) for
DLB 87: British Mystery and Thriller Writers Since 1940.

BOOKS: *Casino Royale* (London: Cape, 1953; New York: Macmillan, 1954); republished as *You Asked for It* (New York: Popular Library, 1955);

Live and Let Die (London: Cape, 1954; New York: Macmillan, 1955);

Moonraker (London: Cape, 1955; New York: Macmillan, 1955); republished as *Too Hot to Handle* (New York: Permabooks, 1957);

Diamonds Are Forever (London: Cape, 1956; New York: Macmillan, 1956);

From Russia, with Love (London: Cape, 1957; New York: Macmillan, 1957);

The Diamond Smugglers (London: Cape, 1957; New York: Macmillan, 1958);

Dr. No (London: Cape, 1958); republished as *Doctor No* (New York: Macmillan, 1958);

Goldfinger (London: Cape, 1959; New York: Macmillan, 1959);

For Your Eyes Only: Five Secret Occasions in the Life of James Bond (London: Cape, 1960); republished as *For Your Eyes Only: Five Secret Exploits of James Bond* (New York: Viking, 1960);

Thunderball (London: Cape, 1961; New York: Viking, 1961);

The Spy Who Loved Me (London: Cape, 1962; New York: Viking, 1962);

On Her Majesty's Secret Service (London: Cape, 1963; New York: New American Library, 1963);

Thrilling Cities (London: Cape, 1963; New York: New American Library, 1964);

You Only Live Twice (London: Cape, 1964; New York: New American Library, 1964);

Chitty-Chitty-Bang-Bang (3 volumes, London: Cape, 1964-1965; 1 volume, New York: Random House, 1964);

The Man with the Golden Gun (London: Cape, 1965; New York: New American Library, 1965);

Octopussy, and The Living Daylights (London: Cape, 1966); republished as *Octopussy* (New York: New American Library, 1966).

Portrait of Ian Fleming by Amherst Villiers used as the frontispiece to a 1963 limited edition of On Her Majesty's Secret Service

MOTION PICTURE: *Thunderball,* screenplay by Fleming, Kevin McClory, and Jack Whittingham, United Artists, 1965.

OTHER: Herbert O. Yardley, *The Education of a Poker Player,* introduction by Fleming (London: Cape, 1959), pp. 7-9;

Hugh Edwards, *All Night at Mr. Stanyhurst's,* introduction by Fleming (London: Cape, 1963), pp. vii-xx;

"The Property of a Lady," in *The Ivory Hammer: The Year at Sotheby's,* by Frank Davis and others (London: Longmans, Green, 1963; New York: Holt, 1964);

"Introducing Jamaica," in *Ian Fleming Introduces Jamaica*, edited by Morris Cargill (London: Deutsch, 1965; New York: Hawthorn Books, 1966).

SELECTED PERIODICAL PUBLICATIONS—
UNCOLLECTED: "Raymond Chandler," *London Magazine* (December 1959): 43-54;

"James Bond's Hardware," *Sunday Times* (London), 18 November 1962, pp. 18-22.

Ian Fleming was the creator of James Bond, the most popular hero of espionage fiction in the late 1950s and the 1960s. Bond, whose name still suggests a certain type of spy-hero—sophisticated, sexy, glamorously dangerous—is particularly well known because of the James Bond film series, which exaggerates the guns-gadgets-and-girls aspect of Fleming's original stories.

Ian Lancaster Fleming, the second son of Valentine Fleming and Evelyn Beatrice Ste. Croix Rose, was born in the elegant and expensive London district of Mayfair. His birth certificate describes his father's occupation as "of independent means"; his paternal grandfather, who had founded the prosperous London banking firm of Robert Fleming and Company, was a multimillionaire. Fleming's mother's family claimed descent from John of Gaunt, fourth son of King Edward III and founder of the royal house of Lancaster—hence Fleming's middle name.

Fleming was nine years old when his father, who was then a major in the Oxfordshire Hussars, was killed by a German shell at Gillemont Farm in Picardy, France. Valentine Fleming's will left his entire estate to his wife in such a way that she could, if she wished, disinherit any of their sons, and during her lifetime she had absolute control over all of the income from her late husband's fortune. As a result, Ian Fleming, who survived his mother by less than a month, coveted but never enjoyed the luxury of inherited wealth. Throughout his life he associated with wealthy and class-conscious people, in part because of family connections but largely by choice. Perhaps because he had less money and less leisure than many of his friends, he made a point of stressing quality, exclusiveness, and singularity in clothing, food, wine, and recreational activities. James Bond's much-discussed snobbery and his somewhat eccentric epicureanism derive primarily from this source.

Fleming's formal education began when, at the age of eight, he was sent to Durnford School on the Isle of Purbeck, near Corfe Castle. Its headmaster, Tom Pellatt, placed great emphasis on the cult of physical toughness, which was to become an important part of Fleming's self-image and a primary characteristic of his fictional hero. The boys at Durnford School bathed naked in a cold natural pool every morning, ate large quantities of unpalatable food, bullied one another, played rough games, and roamed freely around the countryside. Academic work was not stressed, and Fleming was, in any case, uninterested in it.

After five years at Durnford, Fleming was sent to Eton, where he continued to do mediocre academic work. His performance at team sports, which were an important part of life at Eton, was uneven because of his erratic and unsocial behavior and because his desire to display ruggedness and courage gave his play a kamikaze quality which was sometimes breathtaking but often ineffective. However, he consistently excelled in field sports such as racing and hurdling, and in 1925, at the age of sixteen, he won almost every event in the school competition: the 220-yard, quarter-mile, half-mile, and mile races; the hurdles; the long jump; throwing the cricket ball; and the steeplechase. In 1925 and again in 1926 he was Victor Ludorum (Champion of the Games).

Despite his athletic accomplishments Fleming's personal eccentricities brought him into conflict with his housemaster, E. V. Slater, who was old-fashioned in his ideas and abrupt in his manner. Slater was annoyed by Fleming's use of strongly scented hair oil and by his habit of eating late breakfasts at a local inn. At a time when British schoolboys were expected to be keen, lively, and straightforward, Fleming affected to be bored, languid, and Byronesque. Finally he enraged Slater by keeping a car, which was forbidden, and a mistress, which was insupportable. Mrs. Fleming was persuaded to remove him from Eton a term early to send him to study with a colonel who specialized in helping boys to "cram" for the Sandhurst entrance examination.

Mrs. Fleming's decision to send Fleming to the Royal Military College (now the Royal Military Academy) at Sandhurst rather than to Oxford was based partly on his academic mediocrity and partly on his evident need for discipline. She was anxious to see all of her sons settled in respectable positions in life, and she thought that a prestigious regiment would be the best place for him. After passing the entrance examination credit-

Telegrams : " Guinpen, Piccy, London."
Telephone : Regent 9996.
Mayfair 6215

78 GROSVENOR STREET
72 CONDUIT STREET, LONDON, W.1.

18th June. 1935.

Ian Fleming Esq.,
118, Cheyne Walk,
    CHELSEA.   S. W. 3.

To Elkin Mathews Ltd.
Booksellers

Directors : A. W. Evans, Hon. R. E. Gathorne-Hardy, H. V. Marrot, P. H. Muir, Camilla Koenigswald,
The Earl of Cranbrook   NET

EINSTEIN	Uber einen der Erzeugung u. Verwandlung.	5	5	-				
"	Einheitliche Feldtheorie.		10	-				
"	Riemann-geometrie mit aufrechterhalting.		10	-				
"	Einheitliche Feldtheorie v. Gravitation.		18	-				
"	Allgemeine Relativitatstheorie.		18	-				
"	Zur einheitlichen Feldtheorie.		10	-				
"	Neue Moglichkeit f. eine einheitliche Feldtheorie.		10	-				
"	Ather u. Relativitatstheorie.		18	-				
"	Die Grundlage der allgemeinen Relativitatstheorie.	1	5	-				
		11	4	-				
	Less 10%	1	2	5	10	1	7	
CLIMATE:	Vol. lll. Oct. 1901. No. 9.	1	10	-				
ANGELL:	The Great Illusion	1	10	-				
ANSTEY:	Vica Versa	3	10	-				
PLIMSOLL:	Our Seaman	1	10	-				
RUSSELL:	The Atlantic Telegraph	2	-	-				
JANE:	All the World's Airships	4	-	-				
CONDITIONS:	of Peace	5	-	-				
KIPLING:	Rewards and Fairies	1	10	-				
"	Barrack-room Ballads	1	10	-				
ELIOT:	The Waste Land	4	10	-				
MACKENZIE:	Extraordinary Women	1	1	-				
"	Vestal Fire		12	6				
BATESON:	Mendel's Principles of Heredity	1	5	-				
CURIE:	Theses.	8	10	-				
"	Recherches	1	5	-				
GRAY:	The Early Treatment of War Wounds		3	6				
RONTGEN:	Eine neue art von Strahlen	2	-	-				
EHRKICH & HATA:	Experimental Chemotherapy of Spirilloses.		4	6				
MOORE:	Omnibuses & Cabs		16	-				
ACCUM:	Practical Treatise on Gas-light	1	10	-				
LETTER:	to a Menber of Parliament from W. Murdock	1	10	-				
PITMAN:	Dhonography	2	-	-				
STRACHEY	Eminent Victorians	3	-	-				
GOEBEL:	Friedrich Koenig	1	15	-	52	2	6	
					£ 62	4	1	

Invoice for books purchased by Fleming for his western civilization collection (Lilly Library, Indiana University)

Goldeneye, Fleming's home in Oracabessa, Jamaica, where he wrote his novels

ably, Fleming was enrolled as a gentleman cadet. Predictably, he responded well to the physical training and poorly to the discipline. He was finally caught climbing over the Sandhurst wall after an evening with a girl in Camberley and was severely disciplined. He decided that army life was not congenial to him and declined to take up his commission.

During the summer before his entrance into Sandhurst, Fleming had visited the Tennerhof, an experimental educational community located in Kitzbühel, in the Austrian Alps. The Tennerhof was run by Ernan and Phyllis Forbes-Dennis, who attempted to put into practice the psychological theories of Alfred Adler in dealing with troubled young adults. They also provided a sophisticated and challenging academic program. After leaving Sandhurst, Fleming returned to the Tennerhof for a year. There he dramatized himself as a romantic young Englishman who, having quarreled with his commanding officer over a point of honor and given up a promising military career, was in terrible disgrace with his wealthy and influential family. His looks, charm, and reputation made him a favorite with the Austrian girls; in fact, his amorous affairs almost led to his expulsion from the Tennerhof, where the conservative Forbes-Dennises were appalled to learn of his behavior. After a tearful scene of repentance, however, he was allowed to remain.

At the Tennerhof, Fleming became an avid mountain climber and skier, partly for the sake of the exercise and partly because he loved danger and tests of endurance. He also succeeded in setting for himself an academic goal which stretched his abilities and thereby held his interest: preparing for the Foreign Office examination. Phyllis Forbes-Dennis, who wrote fiction

under her maiden name, Phyllis Bottome, also encouraged Fleming to develop his skills as a creative writer. The only extant Fleming story from this period, "Death on Two Occasions," has never been published.

After a year at the Tennerhof, Fleming went to Munich to live with a German family and to attend lectures at the University of Munich. His German improved, and he began to study Russian. From Munich, Fleming went to Geneva, where he studied at the University of Geneva and improved his French. In 1931 he was one of sixty-two candidates who sat for the ten-day Foreign Office examination. He claimed, later in life, that he had ranked seventh in a year when there were only five vacancies; in fact, there were three vacancies, and Fleming ranked twenty-fifth.

While he was at the University of Geneva, Fleming became engaged to a French-Swiss girl named Monrique de Mestral. However, Fleming's mother felt that the girl was not a suitable match for her son, and, since Fleming's failure to qualify for a position in the Foreign Office had left him without the means to support a wife, the engagement was broken. Family influence and his own appearance and bearing helped Fleming to secure a position at Reuters news agency, but because he was being trained he received only a nominal salary of three hundred pounds a year. This meant, of course, that Fleming was forced to live with his mother in her Chelsea home. After the independence that he had enjoyed abroad, Fleming found this a difficult adjustment to make, and his lifelong determination to acquire enough money to live as he liked became stronger.

The highlight of Fleming's brief career (1931 to 1933) at Reuters was his assignment to cover the Moscow trial of six British engineers, em-

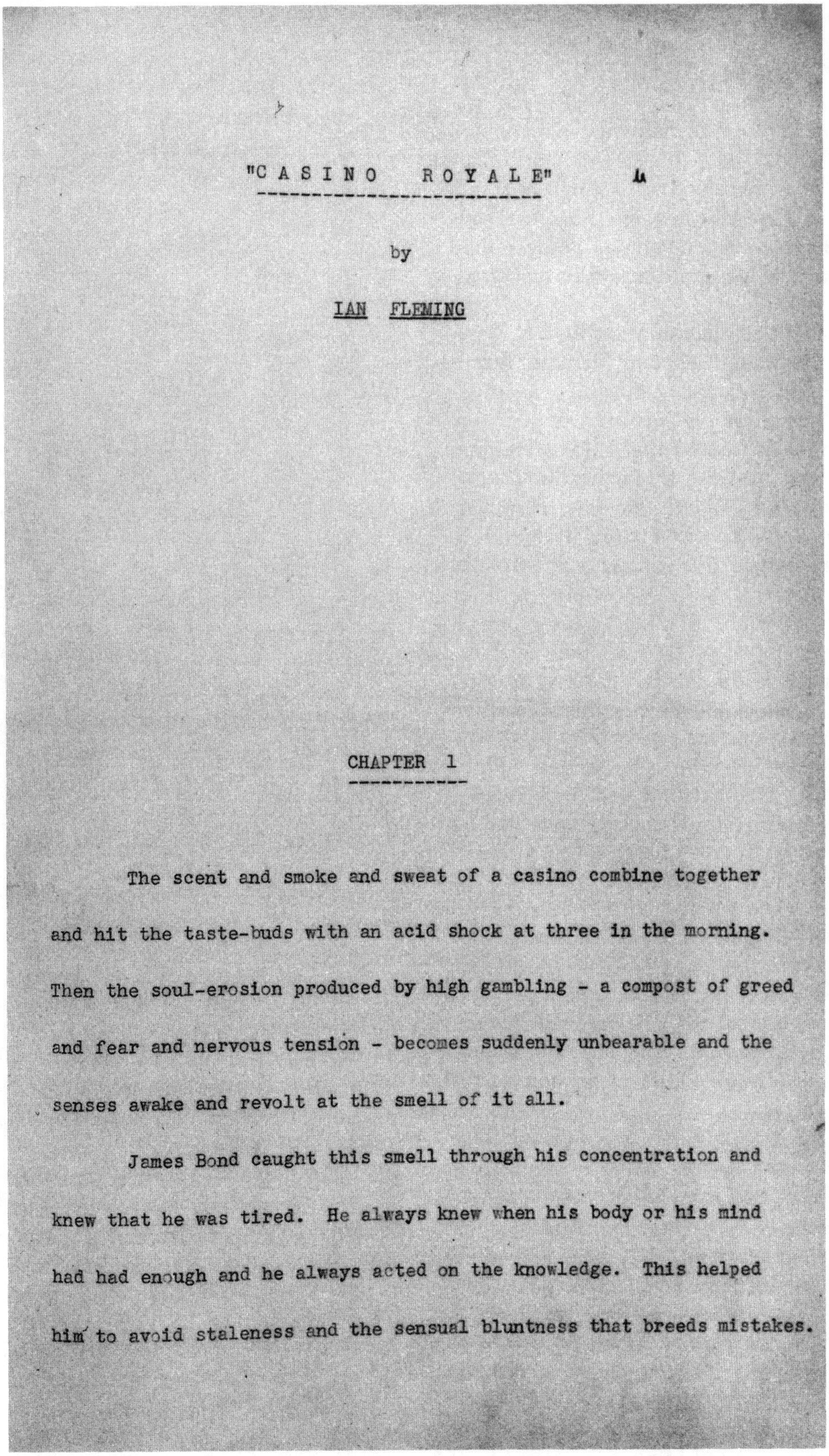

"C A S I N O   R O Y A L E"
----

by

IAN FLEMING

CHAPTER 1

The scent and smoke and sweat of a casino combine together

and hit the taste-buds with an acid shock at three in the morning.

Then the soul-erosion produced by high gambling - a compost of greed

and fear and nervous tension - becomes suddenly unbearable and the

senses awake and revolt at the smell of it all.

James Bond caught this smell through his concentration and

knew that he was tired. He always knew when his body or his mind

had had enough and he always acted on the knowledge. This helped

him to avoid staleness and the sensual bluntness that breeds mistakes.

Typescript page from Fleming's first novel, Casino Royale *(Manuscript Division, Lilly Library, Indiana University)*

ployees of the Metropolitan-Vickers Electrical
Company, who had been accused of espionage
and sabotage. Fleming's knowledge of the language allowed him to converse with Russian na-
tionals, and, in addition to doing a creditable job
of covering the trial, he acquired firsthand information about Moscow which was to be useful in a
later assignment. He also requested an interview
with Joseph Stalin, who sent him an autographed
letter of refusal which became one of his most trea-
sured possessions.

In 1933 Fleming's grandfather Robert Fleming died. Ian Fleming, believing that his father
had, perhaps unintentionally, done his sons an injustice in leaving all of the income from his fortune to his widow, assumed that Robert Fleming
would rectify this injustice by bequeathing some
of his own wealth to Valentine's sons. However,
Robert Fleming left his entire fortune of three million pounds in trust for his widow. It was then to
pass to his surviving son, Valentine's brother
Philip. Shortly after the reading of his grandfather's will, Fleming was offered the post of assistant general manager of the Far Eastern division
of Reuters at a salary of eight hundred pounds
per year. Knowing that his salary as an employee
of Reuters would never be a great deal higher
and that no inherited income was forthcoming,
he refused on the grounds that "I wouldn't be
able to keep up with the Joneses of Singapore."
He left Reuters in order to take up a career in business, which he hoped would prove to be more re-
munerative. His first position was with a firm of
merchant bankers, Cull and Company. Two years
later he joined a firm of stockbrokers, Rowe and
Pitman, as a junior partner. His annual income
suddenly rose to more than two thousand
pounds, and he was able to afford a home of his
own.

Fleming's first home was a converted Baptist chapel on Ebury Street, which he decorated
in gray, dark blue, and black. He began to entertain quite frequently, particularly a group of
friends to which he gave the title *Le Cercle
gastronomique et des jeux de hasard*. He also began
to collect books, encasing them in expensive
black boxes with which he lined the windowless
walls of the converted nave that served as his living room. Percy Muir, a noted expert on rare
books, located for Fleming first editions of works
which introduced significant new discoveries in science, medicine, and the history of ideas. The Ian
Fleming Collection of 19th-20th Century Source
Material Concerning Western Civilization, which

Dust jacket designed by Fleming for the first British edition of
Casino Royale

is now in the Lilly Library at Indiana University,
includes such works as a copy of Marie Curie's
1903 doctoral dissertation on the isolation of ra-
dium and a copy of Sigmund Freud's *Die Traum-
deutung* (1900; translated as *The Interpretation of
Dreams*, 1913).

Fleming was a noted womanizer. He attributed his ruthlessness with women to his mother's
domineering nature and, in particular, to her
refusal to allow him to marry Monrique de
Mestral. Others thought that he never actually
knew a woman in any but the carnal sense. John
Pearson's 1966 biography of Fleming quotes one
of his mistresses, who says that "he looked on
women just as a schoolboy does, as remote, mysterious beings. He could never hope to understand
them, but if he was lucky he felt he might occasionally shoot one down." Fleming's attitude toward
women is surely one of the reasons for the un-

even quality of James Bond's relationships with the female characters in his novels.

In 1939 Fleming was given an opportunity to interrupt his routine as a junior partner at Rowe and Pitman for the purpose of accompanying a British trade mission to Russia and Poland. Ostensibly, Fleming was covering the event as a representative of the London *Times;* in fact, he was preparing a report for the Foreign Office on anything he observed that might help the British assess Russia's potential usefulness as an ally in the war which was now imminent. Fleming was chosen for this assignment because of his knowledge of Russian, his experience as a journalist, and the insights and acquaintances he had acquired during his previous visit to Moscow. This assignment, in turn, helped to bring about one of the most important events of his life: his appointment as personal assistant to the director of Naval Intelligence during World War II.

Adm. Sir Reginald Hall, director of Naval Intelligence during World War I, had employed as his personal assistant a former stockbroker, Claude Serocold, whose experience had made him invaluable as a complement to the career military men around him. Hall suggested to Adm. John Godfrey, the new director of Naval Intelligence, that he should look for someone with a similar background to serve as his own personal assistant. Godfrey consulted the governor of the Bank of England, Montagu Norman, who undertook an intensive but confidential survey of the records of promising young men in London's business world. Norman finally suggested only one candidate, Fleming. Godfrey, having interviewed Fleming, had him commissioned as a lieutenant in the Naval Reserve and assigned to the Department of Naval Intelligence. Fleming was later promoted to commander, the rank that he eventually assigned to James Bond.

In 1941 Fleming accompanied Godfrey to the United States for the purpose of establishing relations with the American intelligence services. In New York he met Sir William Stephenson, "the quiet Canadian," who became a lifelong friend. Stephenson allowed Fleming to take part in a clandestine operation against a Japanese cipher expert who had an office in Rockefeller Center, and Fleming later embellished this story and used it in his first James Bond novel, *Casino Royale* (1953; republished as *You Asked for It,* 1955). Stephenson also introduced Fleming to Gen. William Donovan, who had just been appointed coordinator of information and who

Fleming, circa 1954

later became director of the U.S. Office of Strategic Services. At Donovan's request Fleming wrote a lengthy memorandum describing the structure and functions of a secret-service organization, and parts of this memorandum were later included in the charter of the OSS. In appreciation, Donovan presented Fleming with a .38 Police Positive Colt revolver inscribed "For Special Services." Fleming later wove fantasies around this weapon, suggesting that the services for which he had received it had been of a violent character.

Fleming visited North America again during the war to prepare a report on Stephenson's training school for secret agents located in Oshawa, Ontario. He took part in the training course himself and did extremely well. One of his assignments was to swim underwater at night to a derelict vessel moored in a lake, attach an inactive limpet mine to its hull, and escape without being seen. The story of that swim, suitably embroidered, became one of the most important scenes in Fleming's second Bond novel, *Live and Let Die* (1954). He also succeeded in planting a dummy bomb in the Toronto power station under the eyes of guards who had been warned that this "attack" was to take place. Other trainees from Stephenson's school tried to sneak into the power station and failed. Fleming telephoned the managing director for an appointment, representing himself as a member of a British engineering firm, and walked in—and out—without question.

At the end of the training course, Stephenson told Fleming that the intelligence services had located a spy in a Toronto hotel, and ordered him to burst into the hotel room and shoot the spy without giving him a chance to draw his own gun. The occupant of the hotel room was actually a former member of the Shanghai Water Police who made a profession of surviving such attempts on his life. The presence of a live target and the use of live ammunition gave the exercise the verisimilitude necessary to allow Stephenson to determine which of his trainees were capable of killing a man in cold blood. Fleming was not. He got as far as the landing outside the hotel room, but, after a long pause, he turned and left. Stephenson and Fleming's fellow trainees were very amused and not very sympathetic, and Fleming found the experience intensely embarrassing. After the war he occasionally confided to one or another of his friends (as a matter of great secrecy) that he had once had to kill a man in the line of duty. The circumstances surrounding this alleged killing varied considerably, although the discrepancies were never noted during Fleming's lifetime because the friends to whom he told the story kept it in confidence. Most of these fantasies eventually appeared in the Bond books, along with the central fantasy of a man who, licensed to kill in cold blood, dislikes doing so but always succeeds.

One of Fleming's most exciting assignments during World War II was the command of Number 30 Assault Unit, which he called "My Red Indians." It was modeled on a German unit under Obersturmbandführer Otto Skorzeny, which went into captured areas with the first wave of troops and gathered up all available intelligence material. As the Allies advanced across North Africa and then across Europe, he determined the nature and location of intelligence material and directed his commandos to it. On the whole the unit carried out its tasks so well that it was eventually removed from Fleming's control and placed under the direct command of Adm. Sir Bertram Ramsay.

In 1944 Fleming was sent to Kingston, Jamaica, to attend a conference. He was accompanied by his friend Ivar Bryce, who had a home in Jamaica. The weather was miserable, but in spite of the rain Fleming was so enchanted with the island that he asked Bryce to find him a piece of land there on which to build a house. Bryce located a suitable place on the bay at Oracabessa, and after the war Fleming built a house which he called Goldeneye. It was there that he wrote the James Bond novels.

After his discharge from the navy in 1945 Fleming returned to journalism as manager of the foreign news service for the Kemsley (later Thomson) newspapers, including the London *Sunday Times*. Before accepting Kemsley's offer, however, he insisted on a guarantee of a two-month paid vacation so that he could spend January and February of each year at Goldeneye. Fleming remained in this position for most of the rest of his life, although his power and prestige gradually declined through the 1950s because of internal economy measures and because of the inability of his foreign news service to compete with organizations such as UPI, AP, and Reuters. In 1953 Fleming also became "Atticus," a post once held by an earlier writer of espionage fiction, John Buchan. As Atticus he wrote a weekly column of more or less sophisticated gossip.

In 1946 Fleming, experiencing pain and a sensation of tightness in his chest, visited a cardiologist. Two years later, he suffered a recurrence of the chest pain along with kidney trouble. He was smoking between sixty and seventy cigarettes a day and drinking inordinate quantities of gin. Despite his gradually failing health Fleming remained physically active, particularly during the part of the year that he spent in Jamaica. He greatly enjoyed underwater swimming, and he took a personal interest in the fauna in the bay at Oracabessa. He called one unusually friendly octopus Pussy Galore, a name which he later gave to a character in *Goldfinger* (1959).

Fleming's Jamaican property was very beautiful, with a large garden, a private beach, and an unobstructed view across the bay, but the house itself was uncomfortable. At Goldeneye, Fleming combined his penchant for physical ruggedness with a desire for expensive singularity which bordered upon eccentricity. For most of the time that he owned the house it had no telephone and no hot water, and the living room had a blue concrete floor which the native servants polished with slices of orange, with the result that the residents' bare feet were always sticky. A narrow banquette ran around three sides of the dining room table, cutting into the diners' thighs, and the

Fleming with a copy of the American edition of his first novel (photograph by Maurey Garber)

food was abominable, although Fleming always insisted that it was delightfully plain Jamaican cooking.

In 1946 one of Fleming's guests at Goldeneye was Anne Rothermere, née Charteris, wife of Fleming's friend Viscount Esmond Rothermere. She and Fleming had carried on a casual romance before and during the war, but during her visit to Goldeneye they began to feel seriously attracted to one another. They continued to meet, and in 1951 Viscount Rothermere sued for divorce, naming Fleming as corespondent. His wife did not contest the action. When Fleming went to Goldeneye for his annual holiday in January 1952, she went with him to await the final divorce decree.

The period of waiting which Rothermere and Fleming endured at Goldeneye that winter was, naturally, a time of great tension. She found relief in painting. Fleming, who had been talking for years about writing what he called "the spy story to end all spy stories," finally decided to try it. For three hours every morning and for two hours every afternoon he interrupted his Golden-

eye routine of swimming and sunbathing to record the first adventure of James Bond, namesake of a well-known ornithologist whose *Birds of the West Indies* (1936) was one of Fleming's favorite books.

Fleming chose this rather plain name because, admiring W. Somerset Maugham's Ashenden stories and the novels of Graham Greene and Eric Ambler, he originally intended to write realistic espionage fiction centering around the type of featureless gray protagonist that those authors often used. However, his vivid imagination and love of the dramatic, combined with the self-imposed pressure of producing a new Bond novel every year, led him into giving Bond personal idiosyncrasies and into placing him in thoroughly improbable situations. As a result, his books never approached those of Maugham, Ambler, and Greene in realism, depth, or complexity. He wrote not for the sake of making thematic statements or contributing to the development of a genre, but for the sake of entertaining himself and his readers and making a great deal of money. However, it is hardly fair to conclude, as

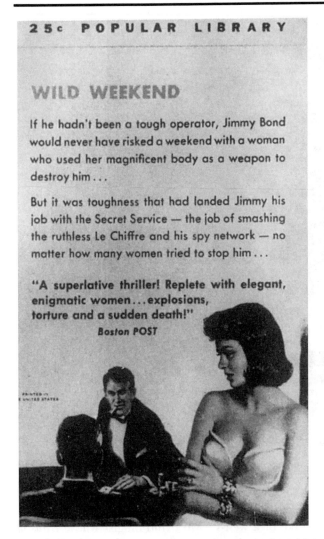
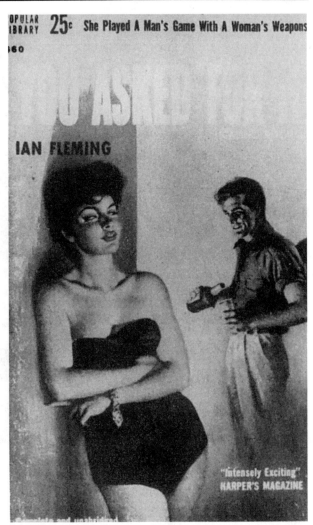

Front and back covers of the first American paperback edition of Casino Royale, *which was republished with this new title*

some critics have done, that Fleming's work has no merit at all. The James Bond novels are, unquestionably, popular formula fiction rather than great—or even good—literature, and at their worst they are improbable, repetitive, and abominably structured. However, at their best they are entertaining, spectacularly imaginative, and highly readable. A reviewer for the *Daily Telegraph* (26 April 1955) observed that Fleming's third novel, *Moonraker* (1955; republished as *Too Hot to Handle*, 1957), was "A fantastic piece of nonsense. I didn't believe a word of it. But I couldn't put the book down until it was finished."

Because Bond's physical appearance is modeled on Fleming's own—a tall and lean man with black hair, gray eyes, and high cheekbones—and because his adventures include romanticized versions of events in which Fleming is known to have participated, the question of Fleming's identi-

fication of Bond with himself, or with an idealized concept of himself, naturally arises. In some respects Bond does externalize Fleming's drives and fantasies: he enjoys the finest food and drink, makes love to the most beautiful and affectionate women, and defeats the most fiendish villains. On the other hand, Bond is unquestionably a fictional creation, consciously and deliberately developed, whom Fleming manipulated according to the requirements of his plots and, later, in response to critical observations and popular demand. Bond's accomplishments do reflect a vivid wish-fulfillment fantasy that arose, to some extent, from his experiences; but, as Fleming's fan mail suggests, similar fantasies are equally vivid in the minds of many readers. Fleming knew that, and he exploited it consciously and skillfully. As a result, although the Bond novels romanticize incidents from Fleming's life and dwell on wish-fulfillment fantasies, the autobiographical and psychological elements in these books are quite deliberate and, for the most part, superficial.

Among the romanticized autobiographical incidents in Fleming's first novel is an epic baccarat game between Bond and the villain, Le Chiffre, which was suggested by an occasion during World War II when Fleming, visiting Lisbon with Godfrey on navy business, tried to defeat a group of Portuguese gamblers at baccarat. In the real-life game the Portuguese soundly beat Fleming, but that was, of course, one of the details that he altered when he turned the event into fiction. The scene in which two Bulgar assassins blow themselves up in an attempt to murder Bond is based on an identical failure on the part of two assassins who tried to murder Franz von Papen in Ankara during World War II, and Bond's killing of a Japanese cipher expert is based on the much less violent operation in which Fleming had participated in New York in 1941.

Shortly after he finished *Casino Royale*, Fleming and Anne Rothermere were married in the town hall at Port Maria, Jamaica, with Noel Coward as principal witness. The next day Fleming flew to New York with his wife and the completed typescript of his novel. A few months later he gave the typescript to a friend, William Plomer, an author and one of the readers for Jonathan Cape, who passed it along to other readers. They liked the book, and it was scheduled for publication in the spring of 1953. About this time Anne gave birth to a son, Caspar.

Fleming made substantial changes to the typescript before the book was published, particularly in the style. He divided compound sentences into simple ones and replaced general terms such as "the middle of the week" with specific terms such as "Tuesday." He also eliminated some of the more obvious clichés; for example, he replaced "or I'll eat my hat" with "if I'm not mistaken." Far fewer changes of this kind were necessary in the typescripts of the later books, but he did have to make changes in the typescripts of all his books to correct at least some of his numerous factual errors. In *Casino Royale*, for example, he had to substitute "Marchall headlights" for his original reference to "Chagall headlights." The most significant changes involved the celebrated torture scene in which Le Chiffre attacks Bond's private parts with a carpet beater. No one who read the typescript was absolutely sure what ef-

fect such treatment would have in reality, but they felt, understandably, that it was rather lively stuff for a book which was to be published by a reputable and respected firm. Even after Fleming had toned it down by changing some of the language and by substituting a knife for the pair of rusty scissors with which Le Chiffre originally threatened Bond, that scene provoked a great deal of discussion. The real arguments about sadism in the Bond books, however, did not begin until after the publication of *Dr. No* (1958).

The reviews of *Casino Royale* were generally good both in Britain and in the United States; one reviewer described Fleming as "a kind of supersonic John Buchan" (*Listener*, 23 April 1953), and another said that "If Bulldog Drummond had had brains, this is the kind of work he would have done" (*Harper's*, May 1954). Fleming persuaded Jonathan Cape to give him a higher royalty on his next book, and he observed with delight that his royalty—although not, of course, his advance—was equal to Ernest Hemingway's. He also began to investigate the possibility of a film sale. Although he enjoyed writing the Bond books, at least for the first few years, his intention was to make the fortune which had, so far, eluded him.

As Fleming planned his second novel, *Live and Let Die,* he began consciously to perceive and to interpret events in terms of their suitability for use in his books. During a plane trip to Jamaica in 1953, for example, he made notes which became the source for the account of Bond's plane trip in the novel. On occasion he deliberately set about having an adventure so that he could describe it in one of his books, as he did when he and a close friend, Ernest Cuneo, made a round of the major Harlem nightclubs so that Fleming could use them as background for some of the scenes in *Live and Let Die.* However, although these Harlem scenes are highly entertaining in themselves, they have little to do with the plot, and Fleming's indulgence in this kind of interpolated set piece was to become one of the weakest points in the structuring of his novels.

Live and Let Die contains no scene of torture as vivid as the one in *Casino Royale*, but it does help to establish the trend of mayhem in Fleming's books by having Bond commit far more acts of violence than he does in the earlier story. For example, at one point in the novel, Bond's American associate, Felix Leiter, is dropped into a shark tank. His body is returned to Bond, bloody and maimed, with a note saying, "He disagreed

Fleming's library in his home at Sevenhampton, near Surndon, which contained his collection of nineteenth- and twentieth-century works that influenced the development of Western civilization (Lilly Library, Indiana University)

with something that ate him." Bond retaliates against the author of this biting satire by kicking him into the same tank and listening to the grunts of the sharks as they hit. This type of poetic justice, which is a common characteristic of earlier thriller literature written by such authors as Buchan, Edgar Wallace, and Leslie Charteris, occurs frequently in Fleming's novels.

Although Fleming had not yet succeeded in making a film sale by the time *Live and Let Die* was published, when he wrote his next novel, *Moonraker,* he visualized it in terms of a screenplay. He later used this cinematic perspective as an excuse for the episodic quality of the novel, explaining in an unpublished 1956 letter, "I originally thought of this book as a film and the reason why it breaks so badly in half as a book is because I had to more or less graft the first half of the book onto my film idea in order to bring it up to the necessary length." In fact Fleming was never at his best in handling the transitions between the dramatic episodes which are the strength of the Bond books—he simply stuck them together with the literary equivalent of

Scotch tape and chewing gum. *Moonraker* is actually one of his better-constructed novels, but, as his letter indicates, even here he had structural difficulties. The first half of the book concerns an epic bridge game between Bond and the villain, Drax, which resembles both the baccarat game in *Casino Royale* and the round of golf that Fleming would incorporate into his seventh novel, *Goldfinger.* The game itself is suspenseful and colorful, but it has nothing to do with the rest of the novel except to suggest that, since Drax cheats at cards, he is probably capable of other forms of skulduggery. Further, the tension which builds up between Bond and Drax during the game makes it difficult to believe that Bond's boss, who is present at the game, would choose Bond, rather than one of the other three operatives considered for the assignment, to investigate the death of a security officer assigned to Drax. The second half of the book, which Fleming refers to in his letter as "my film idea," concerns Drax's threat to drop a rocket on the center of London. Ironically, by the time *Moonraker* was made into a film in 1978, this plot was out of

Front cover and flap from the dust jacket for the 1954 first British edition of Fleming's second James Bond novel

date, so that the film owes almost nothing to Fleming's original idea.

By the time *Moonraker* was published, the Bond books had begun to achieve modest popular success in both the United States and Britain, and this growing popularity was fostered by the first of the elaborate advertising campaigns which came to be associated with the Bond books. In the United States, for example, Macmillan ran full-page color advertisements showing a cordial bottle with "Moonraker" on the label and lines such as "The sensational new 100 proof spinechilling concoction," and "WARNING. Take dosage only in sitting, prone, or supine position. If apathy continues, consult your psychiatrist." In part as a result of this campaign, *Moonraker* was reasonably successful commercially, although the Bond stories were still far from the height of their popularity.

Encouraged by the success of *Moonraker*, Fleming continued with his plan of writing an annual Bond novel, and he continued to draw much of the material for these novels from his own experiences and those of his friends. He acquired some of the source material for his fourth novel, *Diamonds Are Forever* (1956), from a former schoolmate, Philip Brownrigg, who was then a se-

nior executive with De Beers, the world's largest diamond corporation. Brownrigg supplied Fleming with factual information about diamond mining and smuggling, and Fleming added to it the gadgetry and glitter which were becoming increasingly important in his books. He also included in *Diamonds Are Forever* episodes which take place in Saratoga, New York, where Fleming had attended horse races with his friends Bryce and Cuneo. Other episodes take place in Las Vegas, Nevada, which Fleming and Cuneo, who appears in the book as a heroic taxi driver named Ernie Cureo, had visited for the specific purpose of allowing Fleming to use it as one of the settings for this book.

Fleming's use of all of this source material makes *Diamonds Are Forever* one of his most self-indulgent and loosely structured books. For example, because he had been fascinated by the mud baths which he had visited at Saratoga, he included in *Diamonds Are Forever* a graphic description of Bond's experience in a coffin full of smelly, 110-degree mud; this scene, like many of Fleming's set pieces, has little to do with the rest of the story. The same is true of much of the information that Fleming provides about the pipeline of stolen diamonds that Bond has been sent to in-

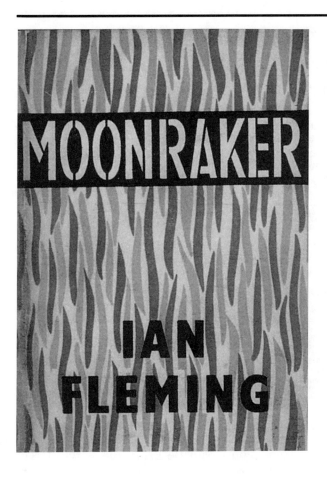

Dust jacket designed by Fleming for the first British edition of his third James Bond novel

vestigate. Furthermore, Fleming made the error, which he was to repeat in a few of his later novels, of providing no clear-cut villain to serve as a focal point for the action. The Spang brothers are hackneyed gangster types who seldom appear in the story and whose actions, like Bond's, are exciting in themselves but often unrelated to what is supposed to be the main story line.

Despite its serious structural flaws, *Diamonds Are Forever* was reasonably successful commercially because, although much of it is neither logical nor probable, most of it is exciting. It also includes an interesting variety of settings, such as a restored Western town in which Bond engages in an uncharacteristic fistfight, and a luxurious Victorian train on which Bond is kicked insensible by a pair of gangsters who ceremoniously don football boots for the purpose.

Although his first four books were by no means commercial failures, after he wrote *Diamonds Are Forever*, Fleming became discouraged with the Bond series and acutely discontented

with the comparatively small financial returns he was receiving. Therefore, when Gregory Ratoff offered him six thousand dollars for the film rights to *Casino Royale*, Fleming accepted because he could see no possibility of a better offer in the immediate future. As a result, this is the only Bond book which cannot be used by the production company which now owns the film rights to the other titles and to the Bond character. The film of *Casino Royale*, released in 1967 by Columbia Pictures, is a spoof of the more conventional Bond films, which were by that time well established. It features David Niven as an aging Bond and Woody Allen as his nephew, Jimmy Bond.

Fleming's discouragement with reference to Bond was lightened to some extent by the appearance at Kemsley House of a Russian who claimed to have firsthand information about an organization called Smiert Spionam (SMERSH), which Fleming had heard about in the late 1940s and had used in *Casino Royale* and *Live and Let Die*. This information was apparently inaccurate, but Fleming made good use of it in depicting Bond's Russian adversaries in his next novel, *From Russia, with Love* (1957). He also heightened the verisimilitude of the story by inserting an author's note beginning with the characteristically offhand assertion, "Not that it matters, but a great deal of the background to this story is accurate," and including the exact address of SMERSH headquarters in Moscow.

Fleming was given the opportunity to collect further material for *From Russia, with Love* when Sir Ronald Howe, assistant commissioner of Scotland Yard, arranged for him to attend the conference of the International Police Organization (Interpol) in Istanbul. The Interpol conference itself was of little interest to Fleming, but he was fascinated by Istanbul. He became friendly with a Turkish businessman, Nazim Kalkavan, who showed him around the city. Kalkavan, who provided the inspiration for Bond's friend Darko Kerim in *From Russia, with Love*, made a remark which Fleming paraphrased in the novel as, "But I am greedy for life. I do too much of everything all the time. Suddenly one day my heart will fail. The Iron Crab will get me as it got my father. But I am not afraid of The Crab. At least I shall have died from an honourable disease. Perhaps they will put on my tombstone 'This Man Died from Living Too Much.'" Fleming, who had his own recurrent problems with the "Iron Crab," found in this attitude an affirmation of the kind

SECRET AGENT

No. 007

The double zero means that he has killed an enemy in personal combat. The number seven identifies James Bond, one of the toughest secret agents in the world.

This case started with Hugo Drax, an eccentric millionaire who cheated at cards. Bond's mission was to find out why. For Drax was also the mysterious genius behind a top-secret guided-missile project.

The hunt took Bond to one of the world's most exclusive gambling clubs, to the dangerous rocket-testing area and to the passionate arms of a woman who was very beautiful and very brave.

Bond knew that when you play against a man like Drax the bets are fabulously high. What he didn't know was that the final stake would be his own life and that once again he must kill or be killed!

An explosive mixture of gambling, danger, sex, chills and murder!

TOO HOT TO HANDLE

(MOONRAKER)

by
IAN FLEMING
Author of LIVE AND LET DIE, a writer whom the Associated Press calls "super-special...with blows below the belt the way Mickey Spillane delivers them!

Front and back covers for the first American paperback edition of Moonraker, *which was republished with this new title*

of life he had chosen and a justification for the kind of death he expected to meet as a result.

From Russia, with Love is one of Fleming's best novels, in part because it is more carefully structured than most of his other books. There are a few interpolated scenes, such as one in which girls are fighting in a Gypsy camp, but on the whole the individual events in the story fit together comparatively well. Its basic premise—that the Russian Secret Service wants to ruin Bond's reputation by filming him in bed with a female Russian agent and then killing them both—is somewhat farfetched, but within the world of the Bond books it is by no means impossible.

The characterizations in *From Russia, with Love* are also better than those in Fleming's earlier novels. Fleming never came anywhere near

creating such realistic characters as Ambler's Arthur Abdel Simpson or John le Carré's George Smiley, primarily because most of the action in the Bond novels takes place because of the requirements of the plot. However, Darko Kerim, who has a rudimentary philosophy of life and a rather eccentric sense of humor, is one of Fleming's best characters, and, although none of his female characters is really well-rounded (in the literary sense), Tatiana Romanova is one of the most charming.

During his period of discouragement following the publication of *Diamonds Are Forever,* Fleming had considered killing Bond off, and, although he decided against it, he concluded *From Russia, with Love* with a scene in which Bond, stabbed with a poisoned blade which had been con-

["yebionna mat!" The gross obscenity was a favourite with General G. His hand slapped down on the desk.

39

CHAPTER SIX. [DEATH WARRANT

~~Bond~~ General G's hand slapped down on the desk. 'Comrade, there certainly is 'a man called Bond' as you put it' His voice was sarcastic. *'James Bond. (he pronounced it 'jems)* 'And nobody, myself included, could think of this spy's name! We are indeed forgetful . No wonder the Intelligence Apparat is under criticism.'

General Vozdveshensky felt he should defend himself and his department. 'There are countless enemies of the Soviet Union, Comrade ˇeneral' he protested. If I want their names, I send to *the* ~~Records Department~~ *Central Index* for them. Certainly I know ~~this~~ the name of this /Bond'. He has been a great trouble to us at different times. But today my ~~mind~~ mind is full of other names/~~of~~ *—names of* people who are causing us trouble today, this week. ~~Comxannatxxnamenhan~~ I am interested in football, but I cannot remember the names of every foreigner who has scored a goal against the ˇ Dynamos.'

~~fffhhtnanhannnnntfnnanfnnnn~~ 'ˇou are pleased to joke, Comrade!. said ˇeneral G to underline this out of place comment, "~~but~~ This *for one* is a serious matter and I/admit my fault in not remembering the *notorious* name of this ~~famous~~ agent. Comrade Colonel Nikitin will no doubt refresh our memories further, but I recall that this Bond had at least twice f ustrated the operations of SMERSH. That is' he added ~~quickly~~,' before I ~~hannnnn~~ assumed control of the Department. There was this affair in France, at that Casino town. The man Le Chiffre. An excellent leader of the ˇParty in France. He foolishly got into some money troubles. But he would have got out of them if this man Bond had not interfered. ~~Imhadmtmnmaan~~ I recall that the Department had to act quickly and liquidate ~~him~~ the Frenchman. The executioner should have dealt with the Englishman at the same time , but he didn not. Then there was this negro of ours in ᴴarlem. A great man -- one of the greatest foreign agents we have ever employed, and with a vast network behind him. There was some business about a treasure in the ˇaribbean, I forget the details. ~~But~~ This Englishamn was sent out by the Secret Service and smashed the whole organisation and killed our man. It was a great reverse, and again my predecessor should have proceeded

Revised typescript page for Fleming's fifth James Bond novel, From Russia, with Love, *one of his favorites among his books (Manuscript Division, Lilly Library, Indiana University)*

Dust jacket designed by Fleming and Richard Chopping for the first British edition of From Russia, with Love

cealed in the toe of a villainess's boot, crashes to the floor. This ending naturally aroused a great deal of comment, as it was meant to do. Iain Hamilton, a friend of Fleming's, wrote him a jocular letter of protest (unpublished): "I have said harsh words about this fellow in the past but, by George, you can't go and let an ugly old trollop kick him to death with an absurdly poisoned boot. This won't do at all." In a letter of 1 May 1957 Fleming replied, "Surely a man can have a dose of Fugu poisoning (a particularly virulent member of the curare group obtained from the sex glands of the Japanese globe fish) without at once being written off. Pray spare your tears." A more public explanation appeared in the newspapers in the form of a medical bulletin from Sir James Molony, physician to the British Secret Service in Fleming's books, declaring James Bond to be alive and well and recovering from a dose of Fugu poisoning. As the high-powered advertising campaign for *From Russia, with Love* got under way, the bulletins from Sir James were accompa-

nied by entries in the "Personals" sections of various newspapers, addressed to characters in the story: one such advertisement, addressed to Bond himself, warns him that "Rosa Klebb may have poisoned knife blade concealed in toe of shoe. Look alive."

From Russia, with Love received glowing reviews, many of which not only assess this particular novel, but also comment on the growing importance of Bond as a popular hero. These reviews discuss in some detail the wish-fulfillment aspect of the character, particularly his professional and amatory prowess and his enjoyment of an exciting and at times luxurious life-style untouched by inflation, taxes, or mass-produced shoddy goods. As these reviews suggest, Fleming was by now committed to writing formula-based escapist fiction which included certain elements that the public had come to expect: emphasis on expensive brand-name products; feminine capitulation (immediate or eventual) to Bond's charms; Bond's survival of fiendish tortures, deadly perils, acts of God, and assorted other unpleasantries; exotic, or seemingly exotic, settings; and the presence of outrageously ugly villains with grandiose schemes for world domination.

Following the success of *From Russia, with Love,* the London *Daily Express* offered Fleming fifteen hundred pounds per book for permission to publish Bond's adventures in comic-strip form. Despite the advice of friends who feared that this might cheapen Bond, Fleming agreed. He also agreed to write his first non-Bond book, an account of the work of the International Diamond Security Organization (IDSO), which had been formed by the Diamond Corporation to discourage smuggling. Although some of the material that Fleming collected was suppressed for reasons of industrial security and personal privacy, *The Diamond Smugglers* became a very successful series in the London *Sunday Times* before being published in book form in 1957. The success of *The Diamond Smugglers* led to a second nonfiction series for the London *Sunday Times,* based on travels financed by the newspaper, describing and commenting on famous and exotic places. Some of the material that Fleming collected for these essays served as the basis for his descriptions of the settings in his later novels, and the essays themselves were collected in book form as *Thrilling Cities* (1963).

By the time Fleming left Jamaica with the typescript of *From Russia, with Love,* he had already decided on the setting for his next book,

/ Insert 2.1. /

"I had intended to play golf this afternoon – a lesson with
at
I'm
have priority among
my hobbies. My tendency to un-cock the wrists too early
with the mid-irons will have to wait." The eyes rested incuriously on
Bond.
"You play golf, Mr Bond?"
Bond raised his voice,
"Occasionally when I'm in England."
"And where do you play?"
"Swinley."
"Ah – a pleasant little course. I have recently joined
the Royal St. Marks. Sandwich is close to one of
my business interests. Do you know it?"
"I have played there."
"What is your handicap?"
"Nine."
"That is a coincidence. So is mine. We must have
a game one day." Mr Goldfinger slipped his feet to
the ground & picked up his tin wings. He said to Mr
Pont. "I will be with you in five minutes" & walked
slowly off towards the stairs.
Bond was amused. This social sniffing at him
had been done with just the right casual touch of
the tycoon who didn't really care if Bond was
alive or dead, but since he was there & alive, might as
well place him in an approximate category.

A manuscript page inserted into the typescript for Goldfinger *(Lilly Library, Indiana University)*

106

Dr. No. Fleming's friend Bryce had invited him to accompany an expedition whose purpose was to assess the well-being of a colony of flamingos on Inagua Island in the Bahamas. In addition to exploring the marshy island, Fleming had talked with a member of the expedition, Dr. Robert Murphy, about the guano harvests of South America, where bird droppings are collected for fertilizer. Fleming later combined his impressions of Inagua with what Dr. Murphy had told him, filtered it through his imagination, and created in the fictional island of Crab Key a suitable setting for the sinister Dr. No. The plot, in which a thoroughly up-to-date villain uses a privately owned island as a base for deflecting American missiles fired from Turks Island, came from a television script which Fleming had written for an abortive NBC series.

The most controversial scene in *Dr. No* is one in which Bond, imprisoned by Dr. No, seeks escape through a tunnel prepared to test the endurance of Dr. No's victims up to the moment of their supposedly inevitable demise. Having been knocked down by an electric shock and burnt, screaming, in a heated segment of pipe, Bond mashes twenty giant tarantulas into a "writhing, sickening mess of blood and fur," crawls over the pulped tarantulas, and stops to catch his breath before tumbling headfirst down a shaft and being knocked unconscious when he hits the sea at 40 MPH. He clings to a convenient cable strung across the inlet, in which, recovering consciousness just in time, he watches the fish eat his blood until a fifty-foot squid tries to eat the rest of him. Some reviewers felt that this episode was unacceptably violent. Then, recalling scenes of bloodshed in the earlier Bond books, these reviewers protested against Fleming's romanticized view of mayhem in general. These were not by any means the first objections to the violence in Fleming's books, but they were the first signs of a comprehensive attack.

The two most influential blasts at Fleming's work in general which were provoked by *Dr. No* were Paul Johnson's "Sex, Snobbery and Sadism" in the *New Statesman and Nation* (5 April 1958) and Bernard Bergonzi's "The Case of Mr. Fleming" in *Twentieth Century* (March 1958). These writers expressed disapproval not only of the violence, but also of the gambling, drinking, sexual permissiveness, and materialism found in the Bond books. Other critics, maintaining that the Bond stories were highly entertaining tales of adventure which ought not to be taken too seriously, deplored the narrow-mindedness of the objectors. All this controversy, of course, did no harm to the sales of Fleming's books, and he continued to include the disputed elements in his fiction.

One aspect of the argument over the violence in the Bond books concerns the question of whether it is relieved by humor. Fleming himself often expressed disingenuous surprise at the seriousness with which some critics took scenes which he regarded as funny, although he could hardly have failed to recognize the extent to which he made use of "inside" jokes which are incomprehensible to anyone unfamiliar with the real-life people and events that Fleming parodied. Some of the humor in the Bond novels, however, is more general; for example, Fleming used some rather adolescent sexual puns, including M's telling Bond, in reference to a jeweler's loop, "Don't push it in. Screw it in" (*Diamonds Are Forever*), and a genealogist's telling him that the Bond family's coat of arms features three golden bezants (balls), to which Bond replies, "That is certainly a valuable bonus" (*On Her Majesty's Secret Service*, 1963). Other examples of humor in the Bond novels occur in conjunction with the violence itself: these include the note attached to Felix Leiter's shark-mauled body; Dr. No's startling demise under a twenty-foot heap of guano; and Bond's reference to his assignment in *From Russia, with Love* as "pimping for England." Even Fleming's grimmest book, *You Only Live Twice* (1964), includes a scene in which the lobster that Bond has been served by his well-meaning Japanese host flips over and wanders off across the dinner table, prompting Bond to exclaim, "Good God, Tiger! . . . The damn thing's alive!" Despite these examples, humor is certainly not as important in Fleming's stories as it is in thrillers written by such authors as Buchan and Charteris, and it is unquestionably much less important here than it is in the Bond films. As the torture scenes in *Casino Royale* and *Dr. No* suggest, the infliction and the endurance of pain play an important part in the Bond novels, but it is hardly fair to define them, as some critics have done, as utterly humorless orgies of sadomasochism.

As a means of escaping from the controversies surrounding his books and from the increasingly unpleasant problems that he was encountering at this time in his position on the Kemsley newspapers, Fleming often spent weekends in or near Sandwich so that he could play the Royal St. George golf course. As he played, Fleming

Fleming and Belgian mystery writer Georges Simenon (Lilly Library, Indiana University)

worked out an imaginative, if dishonest, way to defeat a villainous opponent at golf. This scheme became the basis of a preliminary encounter between Bond and the villain of Fleming's next novel, *Goldfinger*. Letters which began to arrive as soon as the book was published pointed out that the stratagem Fleming had devised would not work in real life, and that in any case it was not nearly so creatively reprehensible as the novel suggested. One of Fleming's friends, for example, wrote to tell him that they would not raise an eyebrow at that sort of thing at *his* club. Nevertheless, the golf game in *Goldfinger* is one of the best known and most popular scenes in the Bond novels, and it became an equally successful sequence in the filmed version of the story. Unfortunately, however, the novel itself is one of Fleming's poorest, and the effectiveness of the golf scene in the first half of the story makes the ineffectiveness of the main plot line even more glaringly apparent.

One of the central weaknesses of *Goldfinger* is that it lacks plausibility, even by the undemand-

ing standards of Fleming's usual style. For example, Goldfinger, knowing who Bond is and hating him because of his triumph in the golf game and because Bond has discovered that Goldfinger cheats at cards, wants Bond, for no convincing reason, to be his assistant. Further, Goldfinger's plot to infiltrate Fort Knox is described in excruciating detail, a type of error into which Fleming, to do him justice, seldom fell. Most important, although Fleming often repeated such situations as fights in moving vehicles, the sexual surrender of previously unresponsive women, and castration-fantasy tortures, in *Goldfinger* he carried such repetitions to the point of self-parody. The book does include a few original and entertaining elements, such as the character of Oddjob (a squat Korean bodyguard who kills people with his hat and eats pet cats), but these are not sufficient to compensate for its shortcomings. The reviews of *Goldfinger*, although they were not entirely negative, were the worst that Fleming had ever received.

Even before these reviews appeared, Fleming, discouraged, exhausted again, and suffering from chest pains, sciatica, and kidney trouble, decided that he could not face the prospect of writing another novel. His next book, *For Your Eyes Only* (1960), is a collection of five short stories. He had already written one of them during his most recent trip for the London *Sunday Times,* and he adapted three of the others from plot outlines that he had developed for an abortive James Bond television series for CBS.

One of the stories in *For Your Eyes Only,* "Quantum of Solace," is presented in the form of a narrative told to Bond by a dinner host; it concerns the breakup of a marriage because of the failure of each of the partners in turn to provide the other with a necessary minimum of comfort: a "quantum of solace." Each of the other four stories in the book is based on the kind of adventure which would ordinarily have formed one of the more striking scenes in a Bond novel. Such scenes readily presented themselves to Fleming's imagination, and by using the short-story form he spared himself the effort of working out any more than the separate, disconnected episodes. Reviews of *For Your Eyes Only* were generally polite, but it was clear that Fleming was running out of ideas and energy.

Finding the production of his annual Bond book increasingly difficult, Fleming was more anxious than ever to make a film sale which, he felt, would bring him the kind of financial reward for which he had long hoped. He was therefore delighted when Bryce, who had become acquainted with a talented young producer, Kevin McClory, proposed a three-way collaboration on a film: Fleming would provide the character of Bond and help to write the script, Bryce would put up the money for the film, and McClory would produce and direct it. Accordingly, Fleming and McClory worked together on a story outline, and Jack Whittingham, a well-known British scriptwriter, was brought in to work on the screenplay. The final draft therefore incorporated the work of Fleming, McClory, and Whittingham. Fleming eventually decided to terminate his association with McClory and Whittingham and to sell the film rights to the character of Bond to an established film company. However, he assumed that he had the right to use as the basis for his next novel the story that he, McClory, and Whittingham had produced. McClory disagreed, and when *Thunderball* (1961) was about to be published, he brought his case to court, claiming that

Fleming and his wife, Anne, January 1962

the novel was based on a film story to whose development he had made substantial contributions.

On 25 March 1961 Fleming attended a hearing at which the court, because of the investment which Jonathan Cape had already made in printing *Thunderball* and in advance publicity, permitted the publication of the book. However, the court made it clear that its action did not prejudice McClory's pending suit in any way, and two years later McClory was awarded the film rights to *Thunderball* as well as substantial damages paid by Fleming's codefendant, Bryce. Three weeks after the 1961 hearing, Fleming attended a conference at the headquarters of the Kemsley—now Thomson—newspapers, in the course of which he had his first major heart attack. He was taken to the London Clinic, where he made a surprising recovery. He amused himself during his convalescence by writing a children's book, *Chitty-Chitty-Bang-Bang* (1964-1965), which was based on stories of a magic car that Fleming had told his son. *Chitty-Chitty-Bang-Bang* was later made into a film, released in 1968.

Because of his physical condition, Fleming was ordered to limit himself to three ounces of hard liquor a day. Appalled, he wrote to a friend in the Ministry of Agriculture, Fisheries, and

Food to ask what liquor has the highest alcohol content per ounce. His friend recommended Green Chartreuse (102 proof), followed by Benedictine and Yellow Chartreuse (74 proof) and then by whiskey, brandy, and rum (70 proof). However, as he began to feel better, Fleming gradually returned to his former drinking habits as well as to his heavy smoking.

Despite the *Thunderball* suit and his heart attack, not everything that happened to Fleming in 1961 was unpleasant. Sales of his books increased noticeably after *From Russia, with Love* was included in a list of President John F. Kennedy's ten favorite books. Arthur Schlesinger, Kennedy's press secretary, has since claimed that Kennedy was not in fact a great admirer of the Bond books, but, true or not, the publicity had its effect. More importantly, Fleming finally made the film deal that he had been thinking about for so many years. Harry Salzman, a Canadian producer, had taken out an option on the film rights to the Bond books, but he had been unable to secure the backing of a major film company. Another producer, Albert "Cubby" Broccoli, became Salzman's partner and succeeded in negotiating a contract with United Artists. Fleming was guaranteed a minimum of one hundred thousand dollars per movie, but because of the great commercial success of the Bond film series, his profits were actually much higher. Broccoli and Salzman formed a company, Eon Productions, and planned to begin their series with *Thunderball*. However, because of McClory's pending suit, they filmed *Dr. No* instead. The 1962 film was a success, and they went on to make *From Russia, with Love* (1963) and then *Goldfinger* (1964). Fleming read the scripts, made suggestions, and was present during some of the filming, but the movies themselves were in the hands of Broccoli and Salzman. Although Fleming felt that he had incorporated humor into his books, chiefly in the form of tongue-in-cheek exaggerations, the producers wanted a broader kind of humor, and they began using the one-liners and send-ups which have become hallmarks of the Bond films.

Fleming enjoyed much of the humor in the Bond films, but he was pained by jokes which detract from Bond's status as a British gentleman. In reading the script of the third Bond film, *Goldfinger,* for example, he objected to a scene in which Bond, looking into a woman's eyes, sees in them the reflection of an assailant approaching with a blackjack. At the last moment Bond swings the girl around so that it is she who is coshed.

"Bond," wrote Fleming in the margin, "wouldn't do this to a girl!" Nevertheless, this film, which features the first of the famous Bond cars and a great deal of sophisticated gadgetry and stunt work, was even more popular than the first two had been. Many students of the Bond films date the beginning of the Bond-film cult from the release of *Goldfinger,* and it certainly became the major commercial success for which Fleming had long hoped. Ironically, he never enjoyed the profits from this film, which was released in the year of his death.

Despite the *Thunderball* hearing, his heart attack, and the film deal, Fleming had his next novel ready for publication in 1962. *The Spy Who Loved Me* is significantly different from the other Bond novels because it is narrated by the heroine, Vivienne Michel; Bond does not even appear until more than halfway through the book. The major events of this story—Vivienne's early sexual traumas, her encounter with Bond, and their lovemaking—follow a pattern which can be found in almost every Bond novel, but the emphasis on the heroine becomes the controlling factor in this one. *The Spy Who Loved Me* is, in fact, a woman's love story, and a surprisingly perceptive one, although it suffers from overwriting and outrageous sentimentalism. Predictably, however, Fleming's audience was disappointed by the absence of a major villain, a world-threatening conspiracy, and the trappings of the good life. Even reviewers who thought that *The Spy Who Loved Me* was a reasonably good novel in itself protested that it was not what readers expected a Bond story to be. *The Spy Who Loved Me* was, and remains, Fleming's least popular novel.

His publishers' apprehensive reception of the typescript of *The Spy Who Loved Me* had led Fleming to anticipate the negative reaction that the book received, so even before it was published he had begun working on a more traditional Bond novel which would, he hoped, achieve the kind of success that some of the earlier Bond stories had achieved, and, to some extent, it did. Despite the undereffectiveness of its villain and a few tediously lengthy digressions into genealogy and biological warfare, *On Her Majesty's Secret Service* is the best book that Fleming produced after *Dr. No.* It includes several exciting chases, such as a ski scene which became an important sequence in the filmed version of the story; a love affair which is serious enough to terminate, briefly, in marriage; and the brand-name products and opulent settings which had become

Dust jackets for the British editions of two of Fleming's James Bond novels

hallmarks of the Bond novels. The villain's machinations and Bond's love affair relate to one another only tangentially, but by this time Fleming's readers had become so accustomed to the episodic quality of his plots that very few reviewers even mentioned it. The reviews of *On Her Majesty's Secret Service* were better than Fleming's reviews had been for five years, and its sales, boosted by the publicity regarding President Kennedy's enjoyment of the Bond books and by the success of the first two Bond films, were excellent. When Pan Books put out the paperback edition, they printed one million copies and had to print more a few months later.

Shortly before the publication of *On Her Majesty's Secret Service*, Fleming left England for Japan to collect background material for his penultimate novel, *You Only Live Twice*. In part because of his own failing health, he was particularly fascinated by what he perceived as the Japanese preoccupation with death, and *You Only Live Twice* is filled with death-oriented scenes and imagery. Although there is no shortage of deaths by violence

in Fleming's earlier novels, those were the deaths of people who did not want to die; in this book Fleming displays an obsession with death itself which is carried to the point of morbidity.

Fleming's excessive concern with death is most evident in his depiction of the villain of *You Only Live Twice*, a nightmarish figure whose scheme is the least adequately motivated and the most macabre in the entire Bond series. With no thought of world domination or of wealth, he creates a garden for suicides solely to give himself the pleasure of furnishing others with the opportunity to destroy themselves by means of poisonous plants, a piranha pool, or steaming fumaroles. Fleming's state of mind also affected the character of Bond, who, even in *On Her Majesty's Secret Service*, seems older, more subdued, and more tired than he does in the earlier novels. In *You Only Live Twice*, Bond is reflective and even poetic, quoting the haiku verse from which the novel takes its title: "You only live twice: / Once when you are born, / and once when you look death in the face." He is also less tough and

Dust jacket for the British edition of Fleming's 1964 James Bond novel, which takes its title from a haiku by Matsuo Bashō: "You only live twice: / Once when you are born, / and once when you look death in the face"

more sentimental than ever before. *You Only Live Twice* is imaginative and eminently readable, but it is, in comparison with the earlier Bond novels, a depressed and tired story written by a depressed and tired man.

Fleming went to Goldeneye as usual in January 1964 to work on what was to be his last novel, *The Man with the Golden Gun* (1965). He found the book almost impossible to write, partly because he could no longer work for long periods of time and partly because, although he would not yield to his illness by failing to produce his annual book, the joy had long gone out of his writing. Not surprisingly, *The Man with the Golden Gun* is the least original of Fleming's novels. It includes, among other repetitions, a fight on a train which derives from similar scenes in *Diamonds Are Forever* and *From Russia, with Love* and the device of having Bond gain access to the vil-

lain by being employed by him, as he does in *Goldfinger* and *On Her Majesty's Secret Service*. It also includes the use of a dossier like those in *Casino Royale* and *Live and Let Die*, providing not only factual information about the villain, but also a pseudosophisticated psychological analysis which is not entirely serious: in this case, the suggestion that Scaramanga became a hired killer because of a traumatic childhood experience involving the shooting of a bull elephant in heat.

In addition to being repetitious *The Man with the Golden Gun* is even less plausible than Fleming's other novels. It relies heavily on coincidence, and the characters often indulge in unaccountable behavior. For example, Bond, who has killed innumerable adversaries—including some who, like the crane operator in *Dr. No* and the night guard in *On Her Majesty's Secret Service*, never even saw him coming—repeatedly refuses to kill Scaramanga under circumstances which he regards as unsporting. The novel culminates in a wildly improbable scene in which Bond agonizes over the fact that he is duty-bound to kill Scaramanga, who, wounded and apparently unarmed, eats a raw snake and then recites a Roman Catholic prayer for the dying—in Latin. Fleming undoubtedly wrote this scene, as he wrote many others, with tongue-in-cheek; however, because of the weakness and unevenness of the novel as a whole, this scene comes across as painfully poor melodrama masquerading as suspense.

Fleming was very dissatisfied with *The Man with the Golden Gun*, and he intended to edit it heavily. However, on a rainy summer day, despite a bad cold, he insisted on attending a committee meeting at the Royal St. George golf club. The next day he suffered a hemorrhage, and that evening he was taken to nearby Canterbury Hospital, where he died shortly after one o'clock in the morning of 12 August 1964, at the age of fifty-six. His last recorded words were an apology to the ambulance attendants for having inconvenienced them.

The Man with the Golden Gun was published posthumously, followed by *Octopussy, and The Living Daylights* (1966), two short stories which resemble those in *For Your Eyes Only*. The paperback editions of this book also include "The Property of a Lady," a short story which had appeared in Sotheby's annual report for 1963. Shortly after Fleming's death, Glidrose Productions, the company which controls the James Bond copyright, commissioned Kingsley Amis (under the name of

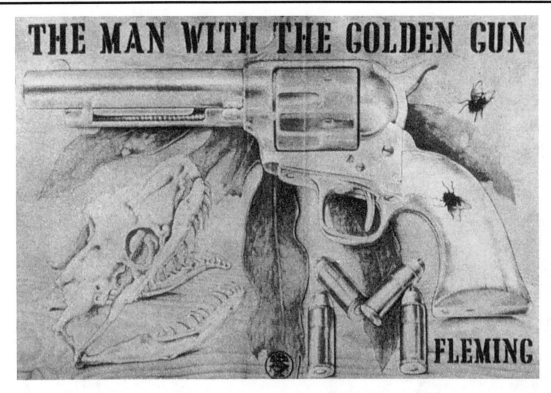

Dust jacket for the 1965 first British edition of the last James Bond novel by Fleming. He died after completing the first draft.

Robert Markham) to write an original Bond novel, *Colonel Sun* (1968). More recently, Glidrose commissioned John Gardner to write *Licence Renewed* (1981) and *For Special Services* (1982). Eon Productions, now controlled not by Broccoli and Salzman but by Broccoli alone, has filmed almost all of Fleming's original titles as well as Gardner's first Bond book. Chiefly because of the popularity of the Bond films, James Bond Fan Clubs are active in the United States, Great Britain, and Canada, holding annual conventions and selling such items as film posters and models of the Bond cars and guns.

Critical opinion regarding the quality of Fleming's books and his own importance in the field of espionage fiction is radically divided. The following observation by Amis, originally published shortly after Fleming's death, still reflects the viewpoint of his supporters: "Ian Fleming has set his stamp on the story of action and intrigue, bringing to it a sense of our time, a power and a flair that will win him readers when all the protests about his supposed deficiencies have been forgotten. He leaves no heirs." Fleming's detractors, on the other hand, view his work as ephemeral and hopelessly inferior. As Leroy L. Panek writes, "No publisher today would even consider printing *Casino Royale,* and if it were not for

the films, James Bond would mean as little to the contemporary consciousness as, say, Okewood of the Secret Service. It is, then, historical accident which has made a public figure of a muddled hero created by a third-rate hack." There is very little moderate opinion on the subject; whatever its other shortcomings, at least Fleming's work does not inspire indifference. Nevertheless, the truth is probably somewhere in the middle. Fleming's books are superficial, implausible, and erratically structured, and they have unquestionably been overshadowed in popularity by the Bond films, which are even more superficial, implausible, and erratically structured. On the other hand, Fleming's work is, for the most part, imaginative, readable, and, most importantly, outrageously entertaining. Fleming himself remarked in an interview, quoted by Amis, that he was in "the business of getting intelligent, uninhibited adolescents of all ages, in trains, aeroplanes and beds, to turn over the page."

Interview:

"Interview: Ian Fleming," *Playboy,* 11 (December 1964): 97-106.

Bibliography:

Iain Campbell, *Ian Fleming: A Catalogue of a Collection* (Liverpool: Iain Campbell, 1978).

Christopher Lee (left) and Roger Moore (right) as James Bond in a scene from the 1974 movie
The Man with the Golden Gun *(United Artists)*

Biographies:

John Pearson, *The Life of Ian Fleming* (London: Cape, 1966; New York: McGraw-Hill, 1966);

Bruce A. Rosenberg and Ann Steward, *Ian Fleming* (Boston: Twayne, 1989).

References:

Kingsley Amis, *The James Bond Dossier* (London: Cape, 1965; New York: New American Library, 1965);

Mary Wickham Bond, *How 007 Got His Name* (London: Collins, 1966);

Ann S. Boyd, *The Devil with James Bond* (Richmond, Va.: Knox, 1967; London: Collins, 1967);

Ivar Bryce, *You Only Live Once: Memories of Ian Fleming* (London: Weidenfeld & Nicolson, 1975);

Oreste del Buono and Umberto Eco, eds., *The Bond Affair*, translated by R. A. Downie (London: Macdonald, 1966);

Richard Gant, *Ian Fleming: The Man with the Golden Pen* (New York: Mayflower-Dell, 1966);

John E. Gardner, *Ian Fleming's James Bond* (New York: Avenet, 1987);

Sheldon Lane, ed., *For Bond Lovers Only* (London: Panther, 1965);

Percy Muir, "Ian Fleming: A Personal Memoir," *Book Collector*, 14 (Spring 1965): 24-33;

Leroy L. Panek, *The Special Branch: The British Spy Novel, 1890-1980* (Bowling Green, Ohio: Bowling Green University Popular Press, 1981);

Eleanor Pelrine and Dennis Pelrine, *Ian Fleming: Man with the Golden Pen* (Wilmington, Del.: Swan, 1966);

Lars Ole Sauerberg, *Secret Agents in Fiction: Ian Fleming, John le Carré and Len Deighton* (New York: St. Martin's Press, 1984);

O. F. Snelling, *007 James Bond: A Report* (London: Holland, 1964; New York: Signet, 1965);

Lycurgus M. Starkey, *James Bond: His World of Values* (Nashville: Abingdon, 1966);

William Tanner, *The Book of Bond or Every Man His Own 007* (London: Cape, 1965; New York: Viking, 1965);

Colin Watson, *Licence to Kill* (London: Eyre & Spottiswoode, 1971), pp. 233-251;

Henry A. Zeigler, *Ian Fleming: The Spy Who Came In with the Gold* (New York: Duell, Sloan & Pearce, 1965).

Papers:

Correspondence, typescripts, interview notes, annotated copies of Fleming's books, and Fleming memorabilia are at the Lilly Library, Indiana University. Additional material is owned by Glidrose Productions.

William Golding

(19 September 1911 -)

This entry was updated by Bernard Oldsey (West Chester University of Pennsylvania) from his entry in DLB 15: British Novelists, 1930-1959: Part One.

See also the Golding entries in DLB 100: Modern British Essayists: Second Series *and* DLB Yearbook: 1983.

BOOKS: *Poems* (London: Macmillan, 1934; New York: Macmillan, 1935);

Lord of the Flies (London: Faber & Faber, 1954; New York: Coward-McCann, 1955);

The Inheritors (London: Faber & Faber, 1955; New York: Harcourt, Brace & World, 1962);

Pincher Martin (London: Faber & Faber, 1956; New York: Capricorn, 1956); republished as *The Two Deaths of Christopher Martin* (New York: Harcourt, Brace & World, 1957);

Sometime, Never: Three Tales of Imagination, by Golding, John Wyndham, and Mervyn Peake (London: Eyre & Spottiswoode, 1956; New York: Ballantine, 1957);

The Brass Butterfly: A Play in Three Acts (London: Faber & Faber, 1958); republished with an introduction by Golding (London: Faber & Faber, 1963);

Free Fall (London: Faber & Faber, 1959; New York: Harcourt, Brace & World, 1960);

The Spire (London: Faber & Faber, 1964; New York: Harcourt, Brace & World, 1964);

The Hot Gates and Other Occasional Pieces (London: Faber & Faber, 1965; New York: Harcourt, Brace & World, 1966);

The Pyramid (London: Faber & Faber, 1967; New York: Harcourt, Brace & World, 1967);

The Scorpion God: Three Short Novels (London: Faber & Faber, 1971; New York: Harcourt Brace Jovanovich, 1971);

Darkness Visible (London: Faber & Faber, 1979; New York: Farrar, Straus, Giroux, 1979);

Rites of Passage (London: Faber & Faber, 1980; New York: Farrar, Straus, Giroux, 1980);

A Moving Target (London: Faber & Faber, 1982; New York: Farrar, Straus, Giroux, 1982);

Nobel Lecture, 7 December 1983 (Leamington Spa, U.K.: Sixth Chamber, 1984);

The Paper Men (London: Faber & Faber, 1984; New York: Farrar, Straus, Giroux, 1984);

An Egyptian Journal (London & Boston: Faber & Faber, 1985);

Close Quarters (London: Faber & Faber, 1987; New York: Farrar, Straus, Giroux, 1987);

Fire Down Below (London: Faber & Faber, 1989; New York: Farrar, Straus, Giroux, 1989);

To the Ends of the Earth (London: Faber, 1991).

PLAY PRODUCTION: *The Brass Butterfly*, Oxford, New Theatre, April 1958.

MOTION PICTURE: *Lord of the Flies*, screenplay by Golding, British Lion Films, 1963.

William Golding

RADIO: "Our Way of Life," *Third Programme*, BBC, 15 December 1956;

Miss Pulkinhorn, Third Programme, BBC, 20 April 1960;

Break My Heart, Third Programme, BBC, 3 February 1962.

OTHER: Jack Biles, *Talk: Conversations with William Golding*, foreword by Golding (New York: Harcourt Brace Jovanovich, 1970).

SELECTED PERIODICAL PUBLICATIONS—
UNCOLLECTED: "The Writer in His Age," *London Magazine*, 4 (May 1957): 45-46;

"Children's Books: Senior Bookshelf," *Listener*, 58 (December 1957): 953;

"In Retreat," review of *A Hermit Disclosed*, by Raleigh Trevelyan, *Spectator*, 204 (25 March 1960): 448-449;

"Raider," review of *John Paul Jones*, by Samuel Eliot Morrison," *Spectator*, 204 (20 May 1960): 741;

"Miss Pulkinhorn," *Encounter* (August 1960): 27-32;

"Man of God," review of *The Sabres of Paradise*, by Leslie Blanch, *Spectator*, 205 (7 October 1960): 530;

"Prospect of Eton," review of *Eton*, by Christopher Hollis, *Spectator*, 205 (25 November 1960): 856-857;

"Thin Partitions," review of *Some Reflections on Genius, and Other Essays*, by Russell Brain, *Spectator*, 206 (13 January 1961): 49;

"The Rise of Love," review of *The Characters of Love*, by John Bayley, *Spectator*, 206 (10 February 1961): 194;

"Androids All," review of *New Maps of Hell*, by Kingsley Amis, *Spectator*, 206 (24 February 1961): 263-264;

"All or Nothing," review of *The Faithful Thinker*, edited by A. C. Harwood, *Spectator*, 206 (24 March 1961): 410;

"Before the Beginning," review of *World Prehistory*, by Grahame Clark, *Spectator*, 206 (26 May 1961): 768;

"Thinking as a Hobby," *Holiday*, 31 (August 1961): 8, 10-13;

"Exile, Poverty, Homecoming," *Holiday*, 33 (April 1963): 10, 16-19;

"Advice to a Nervous Visitor," *Holiday*, 34 (July 1963): 42-43, 93-97, 125-126;

"The Best of Luck," *Holiday*, 35 (May 1964): 12, 14-17;

"The Condition of the Novel," *New Left Review* (January-February 1965): 34-35;

"Egypt and I," *Holiday*, 39 (April 1966): 32, 36, 38, 40, 42-44.

William Golding achieved international fame and wide critical acceptance with his first published novel, *Lord of the Flies*, in 1954. Since that time his fictional canon has won Golding a special niche in the pantheon of modern British fiction. It is a niche that deserves to be inscribed with the phrase *sui generis*, for Golding's fiction does not fit within any modern school of writing. Although his work can be categorized as broadly Christian in outlook, it advocates no specific church or political system, and it does not represent any ethnic subdivision within the British Isles. Each of his works, moreover, has been an attempt to treat a different subject in a different time and place in a different manner. As

Golding himself declared, during a *Third Programme* radio discussion, "There's really very little point in writing a novel unless you do something that either you suspected you couldn't do, or which you are pretty certain nobody else has tried before. I don't think there's any point in writing two books that are like each other. . . .

"I see, or I bring myself to see, a certain set of circumstances in a particular way. If it is the way everybody else sees them, then there is no point in writing a book."

None of this means that Golding has been a wild literary experimenter or originator of philosophical ideas. He has worked well within the pale of recognizable forms (of the novel and allegory) and an outline of Judeo-Christian morality. In some respects, he is as conventional a writer as H. G. Wells; and like Wells he sees things from a perspective that is personal, corrective, and highly original. Unlike Wells (at least the early Wells), he does not believe in the efficacy of science; and he writes with the contained fervor, the subdued musicality and sensitivity of a poet, an entranced seer. In his novels we pause at the depths of childhood's depravity; we peer down into the deep free-fall well of birth and rebirth; we teeter at the top of a spire, with the last nail in hand; and we are brought into the presence of something truly awful, perceiving the gap between man and God.

It is with the discerning eye of the poet that Golding views matters. In his conservatism and his allusiveness, he works in prose much as T. S. Eliot did in verse. With an amateur's background in paleontology and a student's knowledge of Greek, Latin, and Anglo-Saxon literature, he has brought past and present together, trying to shore up the ruins of a post-Belsen, post-Hiroshima world in a desperate attempt to preserve sanity and morality. His works bear traces of Egyptian hieratics, Homer, St. John of Patmos, St. Augustine, John Bunyan, Daniel Defoe, R. M. Ballantyne, Joseph Conrad, Albert Camus and Wells. But despite all the influences, allusions, borrowings, echoes, and almost parodistic contradictions that pervade Golding's fiction, he has paradoxically emerged as one of the most original post-World War II British novelists, and one of those who have gained the widest of audiences outside their native land.

This achievement is all the more impressive, and somehow indicative, when one considers that Golding published his first novel (*Lord of the Flies*, by which he is most widely known) at the age of forty-three, while still an unknown schoolmaster. Nine years previously he had been discharged from the Royal Navy as a lieutenant; and the war appears to have been a most important influence on him, awakening both man and writer from what he himself has described as a long, delayed "adolescence." Before the war his life was all of a piece, fitting the pattern one might very well expect for a young man born into an English, middle-class, academic family during the early part of the century. Afterward, his fiction would reflect and yet break that pattern with works reaching well beyond the parochial.

William Gerald Golding was born on 19 September 1911 in St. Columb Minor, near Newquay, in Cornwall. His father, Alec Golding, was a distinguished schoolmaster from a family that had produced a long line of schoolmasters. His mother, Mildred, was an early suffragette. Golding admired his father as a great polymath; he saw him as a representative of a world that was sane and logical. But if one were looking for signs of things to come, it would have to be noted, as it was by Golding in an autobiographical aside, that the *Titanic*, that great symbol of rationalistic amelioration, sank just seven months after he was born. Later he remembered his mother confiding in him, when he was very young, that her awareness of the world as "an exhilarating but risky place" dated from the day she learned that the *Titanic* went down.

Golding's childhood was rather idyllic and isolated. As he says in "Billy the Kid," until he reached school age, he knew no one outside his own family, remembered nothing but walks with his parents or his nurse, Lily, and "long holidays by a Cornish sea." He had read much for his age but was not good with figures. Much like his character Sammy Mountjoy in *Free Fall* (1959), he was an in-school dreamer, his head full of tantalizing images that struggled for expression. He had a passion for words and "collected them like stamps or birds' eggs." When he was supposed to be doing his multiplication tables or learning his Collect, he would instead make up lists of words or chant them inside his head—words like "deebriss and Skirmashar, creskent and sweeside." He looked at pictures, drew ships and airplanes, and "waited for the bell."

The boy's love of "words in themselves" flowered into a love of literature. Golding was much taken with Greek and the *Odyssey*; he read the classics of childhood and those of adulthood during his early years, making pretty much a muddle of both. "I am personally stunned," he later remarked, "when I think of what a passionless pattern I made of it all. If we revisit our childhood's reading we are likely to discover that we missed the satire of *Gulliver*, the evangelism of *Pilgrim's Progress*, and the loneliness of *Robinson Crusoe*." He read George Alfred Henty, Robert Michael Ballantyne, Edgar Rice Burroughs, and Jules Verne as well, long before he realized that they "require an innocence of approach which, while it is natural enough in a child, would be a mark of puerility in an adult." Seeing them from a larger view was to be of personal literary significance, but at the time the classics of childhood satisfied him as they were—and as he was: "They held me rapt. I dived with the Nautilus, was shot round the moon, crossed Darkest Africa in a balloon, descended to the centre of the earth, drifted in the South Atlantic. . . ."

When he was about twelve, Golding tried his hand at writing a novel. It was to be in twelve volumes and, unlike the kinds of works he had been reading, was to incorporate a history of the rise of the trade-union movement. He never forgot the opening sentence of this magnificent opus: "I was born in the Duchy of Cornwall on the eleventh of October, 1792, of rich but honest parents." That sentence set a standard he could not maintain, he playfully admitted, and nothing much came of the cycle.

After completing his secondary schooling (at the Marlborough School, where his father was a master), Golding entered Brasenose College, Oxford, intending to take a degree in science. More than two years went by before he decided that he had erred in his choice of curriculum, and he turned to the study of English literature. Once there, his interests veered as far away from science and the modern world as possible, in the direction of Anglo-Saxon studies. This fascination with primitive subjects and ancient means of expression remains apparent in much of his writing. So does his academically split personality— his humanities-versus-science point of view, and his habit of conducting literary experiments that smack of the laboratory he rejected.

Golding entered Oxford in 1930 at the age of nineteen; he emerged in 1935 with a B.A. in English and a diploma in education. The year before graduation he managed to publish a volume of verse in a series Macmillan Publishers had set up for budding poets. Simply entitled *Poems*, these pieces are undistinguished enough for their author to wish they might be lost sight of; but

they do indicate that Golding, two decades before his first fictional success, aspired to write with the compression and intensity of a poet. Like other twentieth-century novelists, including William Faulkner and Ernest Hemingway, he can be viewed as a "failed" poet who applied the lessons of demanding verse to the writing of prose narrative.

After leaving Oxford, Golding was employed as a social worker in a London settlement house, and, somewhat like Sammy Mountjoy, he wore "several hats"—writing, acting, and producing for an experimental theater. In 1939 he married Ann Brookfield, an analytical chemist, and in that same year he followed family tradition by taking a position as a teacher, of English and philosophy, at Bishop Wordsworth's School in Salisbury, Wiltshire. It was here, in the section of England celebrated in Anthony Trollope's Barset novels, that Golding was destined to find fame and live with his wife and children, David and Judith, for most of his adult life. But first there was to be that catastrophic interruption of life and work known as World War II.

Golding had what many of his countrymen refer to as "a good war." Aside from seven months when he was stationed in New York and another such period spent at the Naval Research Establishment, he was engaged in active sea duty. "I spent five years in the Royal Navy," he declared in a 1980 interview. "What did I do? I survived. I worked my way down, starting on cruisers in the North Atlantic as an ordinary seaman and ending up in command of a rocket ship. . . ." Here and elsewhere Golding has tended to make light of his own war experiences, remembering in one instance that his men used to call him "Schoolie," in reference to his teaching background. Another time he assured an interviewer that his reputation for ferocity in action came from the fact that a nervous tic twisted his face into a grin during moments of stress. But Lieutenant Golding, who remembered his mother's words about the sinking of the *Titanic*, was himself present when the *Bismarck* was sunk. He saw action against battleships, submarines, and aircraft, and took his rocket ship to France on D day.

After returning to his post at Bishop Wordsworth's School in 1945, Golding settled down to teaching and attempting to further his literary career. Except for a few minor reviews and magazine articles, he was unsuccessful, although he did produce three manuscript novels. All that

Golding has divulged about these manuscripts is that they were attempts to please publishers and that eventually they convinced him that he should write something to please himself. What one might have expected from him is a work based on his war experiences, something like Richard Aldington's *Death of a Hero* (1933) or, more likely, Nicholas Monsarrat's *The Cruel Sea* (1951). It is indicative of Golding's artistic temperament that what he brought forth instead was *Lord of the Flies*, a story of some English schoolboys marooned on a desert island during some future war.

Most of Golding's fame still rests on *Lord of the Flies*. In fact, there are two kinds of Golding readers: those who know or appreciate only the first of his novels and those who go beyond it to an appreciation of the entire canon, sometimes preferring one of the later works as his "best" (such as *The Inheritors*, 1955, for which the author himself has expressed a preference). The popular myth about *Lord of the Flies* is that it met with immediate success upon publication, in both Britain and the United States. The truth is that it ran into difficulties from the very beginning. After being rejected by twenty-one publishers, the manuscript finally reached Faber & Faber, where Charles Monteith, seeing the merits of the work, agreed to publish it. Early reviews of the book were mixed. In a brief notice for the *New Statesman*, Walter Allen said it was a "skilfully told" story but one that was "rather unpleasant and too easily affecting." It was thrown into sometimes not very flattering comparison with Richard Hughes's 1929 work *The Innocent Voyage* (published as *A High Wind in Jamaica* in Great Britain). Louis Halle, in *Saturday Review*, announced that the "integrity" of Hughes's book was "perfect," while Golding's account, intimidated by "textbook anthropologists," left the reader with nothing more than "the dead stick of an academic conception." In his *Herald Tribune* review, Dan Wickenden was less severe: "Attempting rather more than *A High Wind in Jamaica*," he declared, "Mr. Golding's book may achieve a little less, but it seems to this reviewer to belong on the same shelf."

Despite the mixed reviews, *Lord of the Flies* sold well in England from the time of its first publication, and in 1955 Golding was elected to the Royal Society of Literature. But the novel's reception in the United States was considerably different. The original Coward-McCann edition (1955) sold fewer than three thousand copies and was soon allowed to go out of print. The book had, however, found influential advocates, especially academic critics, who began recommending it to their students; and, when the Capricorn paperback edition was published in 1959, Golding's work soon began to replace J. D. Salinger's *The Catcher in the Rye* as the favorite novel on American college campuses. In 1961, at age fifty, Golding could afford to resign his post at Bishop Wordsworth's School, and after a year as writer in residence at Hollins College in Virginia, he devoted himself fully to writing. By 1980 *Lord of the Flies* was, remarkably enough, in its ninety-seventh printing, having sold more than seven million copies during the quarter century it had been in publication.

At the simplest narrative level, *Lord of the Flies* can be read as a boys' adventure story in the tradition of Ballantyne's *The Coral Island* (1857), or as something of a survival story in the manner of *Robinson Crusoe* (1719) and *The Swiss Family Robinson* (1813). In this instance, the story revolves around a group of English schoolboys who are marooned on a desert island when the plane evacuating them from Britain crashes, killing the adults aboard. The island, it would appear, lies in the Indian or the Pacific Ocean. The time is the near future when a catastrophic, and perhaps atomic, war is in progress, threatening civilization as we know it.

Reflecting their national background, the boys on the island initially establish a form of democratic government and a division of labor. One of the older boys, Ralph, is chosen leader and keeper of the flame, a signal fire that is to be kept burning atop a hill to attract rescuers. Ralph is attended by his brain-trust friend Piggy and the strangely perceptive Simon. Jack, another of the "big-uns," becomes leader of the hunters, a faction that eventually resorts to ritualistic murder. In their atavistic pursuits, Jack and his tribe recapitulate primitive rites of propitiation, making obeisance to what they call "The Beast," and erecting a pig's head as their totemic device. This is the emblem for Golding's title of the book: "Lord of the Flies" refers not only to the Judeo-Christian figure of Beelzebub and the Devil, but also, in Greco-Roman tradition, to Zeus (sometimes referred to as "god of flies and death"), and quite possibly, as James R. Baker maintains, the Bacchus-Dionysus figure of *The Bacchae*, a work Golding knew "by heart."

Simon sees this totemic lord of the flies as nothing more than a "Pig's head on a stick," and yet he falls under its spell when the head seemingly admonishes him: "Fancy thinking the Beast was something you could hunt and kill. You knew, didn't you? I'm part of you? Close, close, close! I'm the reason it's no go? Why things are what they are?" Helping form one of the most dramatic sections of the book, this speech is delivered (as Golding himself has done it in personal appearances) in the penetrating voice of a schoolmaster bullying one of his charges.

With the death of Simon, the seer of the book, and with Ralph about to be hunted down and killed, Jack and his by now thoroughly savage cohorts are on the brink of triumph when the adult world intervenes in the form of a naval officer dressed in a white-drill uniform. The officer greets these grimy and bewildered boys with a speech full of misunderstanding: "Jolly good show," he says; "Like the Coral Island." It is this sudden reversal, something of a deus ex machina ending, that annoyed and angered some critics. Kenneth Rexroth saw it as an example of the way in which Golding falsely "rigged" his fiction; and James Gindin, in his " 'Gimmick' and Metaphor in the Novels of William Golding," viewed it as a typical weakness in the author's work.

Golding himself has explained his thematic purpose and the reason for the conclusion he devised: "The theme is an attempt to trace the defects of society back to the defects of human nature. . . . The whole book is symbolic in nature except the rescue in the end where adult life appears, dignified and capable, but in reality enmeshed in the same evil as the symbolic life of the children on the island. The officer, having interrupted a man-hunt, prepares to take the children off the island in a cruiser which will presently be hunting its enemy in the same implacable way. And who will rescue the adult and his cruiser?"

The conclusion was not intended, then, as a concession to happy endings. What it provides instead of specious gimmick or conventional deus ex machina is a vital change of focus: the boys, who have grown almost titanic in their struggle, are suddenly seen as boys, some as merely tots, dirty-nosed and bedraggled. And then a retrospective irony occurs: if they have been fighting our battle, we realize—with both hope and dismay—that mankind is still in something of a prepuberty stage, with a propensity for backsliding into savagery.

In some important ways Golding's first novel foreshadows his later themes and methods.

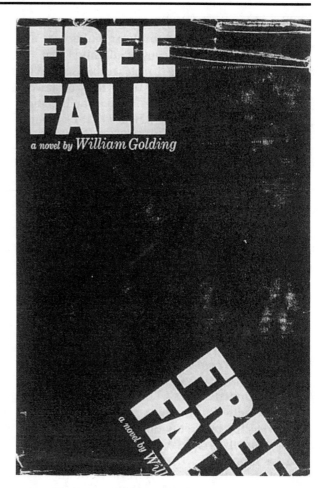

Dust jacket for the 1960 American edition of Golding's novel in which an artist-writer tells his story in a series of confessional flashbacks

The book is, for example, a tour de force, something of an experiment worked out in isolation. Also, it takes its lead from previous works of literature, as Carl Niemeyer makes clear in his article "The Coral Island Revisited"; and it acts as a counterstatement to at least one of these works, as Frank Kermode indicates in his analysis of Ballantyne's novel and Golding's as contradictory documents in the history of ideas and ideals. Most importantly, it combines the visual richness and precise observation of realistic fiction with the mythopoeic propensities usually associated with fable and allegory. As Bernard S. Oldsey and Stanley Weintraub have observed, "The essence of Golding's art resides exactly within the area of overlap."

A remarkable first novel on any terms, *Lord of the Flies* was at first much less praised on novelistic grounds than as sociological, psychological, or religious tract, as pure parable, fable, or myth. John Peter's early article, "The Fables of William

Golding," set much of the critical tone. E. L. Epstein, in the Capricorn edition afterword, and Claire Rosenfield, in "Men of Smaller Growth," analyzed the work as a fictionalized version of primitive psychology and anthropology. Frederick Karl, oversimplifying the political allegory, declared that "When the boys on the island struggle for supremacy, they re-enact a ritual of the adult world, as much as the Fellows in [C. P.] Snow's *The Masters* work out the ritual of a power struggle in the larger world." The temptation to force the novel into an allegorical box was strong, since the story is evocative, and the characters seem to beg for placement within handy categories of meaning. But Golding is a simply complicated writer; and (so much the better for the novel as novel) none of the boxes fit precisely. Ian Gregor and Mark Kinkead-Weekes wisely concluded that "Golding's fiction has been too complex and many sided to be reducible to a thesis and a conclusion. *Lord of the Flies* is imagined with a flexibility and depth which seem evidence of finer art than the polish and clarity of its surface."

The Inheritors (1955), published a year after *Lord of the Flies*, has been praised as an even more powerfully and consistently imagined work than its predecessor. Another tour de force using a primitive setting, it shares certain thematic and technical characteristics with *Lord of the Flies*. Both works proceed from the idea—impressed by Belsen and Hiroshima on Golding—that civilization does not necessarily guarantee civilized acts.

In his first novel Golding asked what would happen to those elements of civilization brought to a primitive setting by a group of schoolboys. In *The Inheritors* he asks what might have happened when the last of the Neanderthals met and were conquered by early Homo sapiens. Taking his lead this time from Wells rather than Ballantyne, Golding once again made his novel into a literary counterstatement. As epigraph for the book, he selected a passage from Wells's *Outline of History* (1920) that describes Neanderthal man as an ugly, repulsive brute, inferior in all ways to our own immediate ancestors, and quite possibly "the germ of the ogre in folklore." Casually read, the epigraph might simply be seen as a dim starting point for *The Inheritors*. Critics soon realized, however, that the epigraph was ironic, and that, as John Bowen put it, "Once again something has been stood on its head—after *Coral Island*, H. G. Wells' *Outline of History*." Golding would later explain the reason for using the epi-

graph and give evidence of his own reactive method of writing. He declared that Wells's *Outline of History* played a considerable part in his own upbringing because it was accepted as a kind of rationalist's gospel by his father. But Golding came to see it as "too neat, too slick." When he reread it as an adult, he came across Wells's depiction of Neanderthal man and thought to himself: "This is just absurd," and decided to do something about correcting that picture.

In *The Inheritors* the tribes of Lok and Tuami replace (on a somewhat grown-up level) those of Ralph and Jack. This time Golding seems to contradict the "real," or unstated, conclusion of his first novel, since this time he allows the more "civilized" of the tribes to triumph and thus become the inheritors of the earth. But the contradiction is only seeming, for although Tuami's people are Homo sapiens and appear to represent a step upward in man's climb, they are eventually revealed as being more savage in their vicious, lusting nature than Lok's subsapien folk. Like the youthful members of Jack's band of savage hunters, Tuami's people represent the Descent of Man, not simply in the Darwinian sense, but in the Biblical sense of the Fall. Peculiarly enough, the boys slide backward, through their own bedevilment, toward perdition; and Lok's Neanderthal tribe hunches forward, given a push by their Homo sapiens antagonists, toward the same perdition. In Golding's view, there is precious little room for evolutionary slippage: progression in *The Inheritors* and retrogression in *Lord of the Flies* have the same results. The Descent of Man and Man's Fall (that is to say, rationalism versus religion, the scientific view versus spiritual vision) constitute the crux of Golding's constant thematic structuring. This is true for all of his literary endeavors, but nowhere is it more apparent than in *The Inheritors*.

Another trait of Golding's that becomes apparent in *The Inheritors* is his utilization of one character in the role of seer or perceiver—such as Simon in *Lord of the Flies*, Sammy Mountjoy in *Free Fall*, and Dean Jocelin in *The Spire* (1964). In fact, the visual richness and revelatory power of the author's own work demonstrate the role he assigns to such characters. In *The Inheritors* two levels of perception are represented: Lok, the Neanderthal paterfamilias, discovers the possibilities of "like," of simile and metaphor, and dimly perceives his own fate. Tuami, a leader among the Homo sapiens, is a primitive artist who is shown carving the bone handle of a knife while he consid-

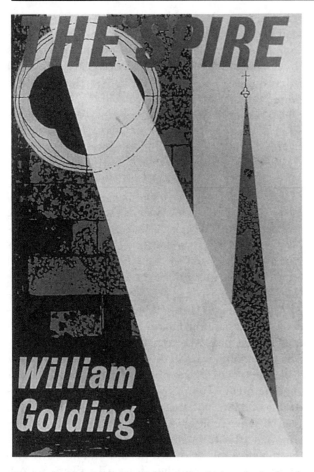

*Dust jacket for Golding's 1964 novel, which ends the decade
of his most notable achievement, beginning with* Lord of the
Flies *in 1954 and including five novels*

ers killing the chieftain, Marlan. His humanistic
conclusion is apparent in the second of two questions he contends with: "What was the use of
sharpening it [the knife] against a man? Who
would sharpen a point against the darkness of
the world?"

To conclude *The Inheritors*, Golding once
again resorted to a radical shift in viewpoint. The
first ten chapters of the novel are done sympathetically from the viewpoint of Lok and his family.
In this respect, as psychologist Dale B. Harris declares, "Golding beats all the psychologists in his
conceptualization and portrayal of a limited mentality combined with an affect life rather fully
developed—which is what cultural anthropologists and psychologists would assume about a sub-
sapiens level of evolution." Chapter 11 of the
book modulates the narrative point of view. With
the death of his mate, Lok is reduced from "he"
to "it," and the reader for the first time comes to
see him as the Homo sapiens have, as an animal:
"It moved faster, broke into a queer loping run

that made the head bob up and down and the
forearms alternate like the legs of a horse. It
stopped.... It put up a hand and scratched
under its chinless mouth." This chapter of transition, in which Lok—lover, father, and family
comic—is reduced to an "it," may well be one of
the most effective things Golding has written.

The twelfth and last chapter of the book is
also remarkable. It is only about ten pages long
but accomplishes, in respect to the presentation
of Tuami's tribe, what the first two hundred
pages do for Lok's tribe. With tremendous compression, chapter 12 functions, in effect, as
"Book II." By the time we reach it, only five or
six days have elapsed since the beginning of the
story, but ages pass as Lok's people give way to
Tuami's in the focus of the narrative. We are provided a new and wider scope of vision; and
through the more sophisticated Tuami, we learn
to decode the meaning of the double story.

By publishing his third novel in three years,
Pincher Martin (1956), Golding appeared to be
making up for lost time. But he was not simply re-
peating himself. The new work made use of contemporary times and some of the author's war experience in the navy. In its own way, it proved as
distinctive as Golding's previous novels. By now,
however, critics were able to discern a kind of fiction that could be called "Goldingesque." Here
again was the tour de force approach; here again
the isolated setting, the poetic precision of detail,
the allegorical mode in conjunction with the novelistic, the ambiguous and cleverly planned conclusion. Here also was the utilization of previous
works of literature, for both thematic and technical purposes.

In fact, *Pincher Martin* may be Golding's
most allusive work. It contains echo after echo of
Shakespeare, John Milton, T. S. Eliot, Conrad,
and a host of lesser writers. The title comes directly from a minor World War I adventure yarn
by H. P. Dorling called *Pincher Martin*. The setting may have been borrowed from a poem by Michael Roberts entitled "Rockall," the name
Golding's protagonist applies to his island. The
ending is an adaptation of a peculiar technique
used by both Ambrose Bierce and Hemingway
on earlier occasions. Moreover, Golding's novel
contains many parallels to various mythical patterns, particularly those involving Satan and Prometheus. "I shit on your heaven," Pincher cries
out in one place, and, in another, "I am Atlas. I
am Prometheus."

When the novel was republished in the United States (1957), it came out under the title of *The Two Deaths of Christopher Martin*, presumably because an American audience might not understand the implications of "pincher" as a designation for "thief," but also because the novel does contain two versions of death. Paradoxically, it is a tale both of a man's epic struggle for existence and of a man who is already dead—or who lives only through the last flickering of his will not to be destroyed. Christopher ("Pincher") Martin, survivor of a torpedoed destroyer in World War II, makes desperate efforts to stay alive, alone, on a barren rock in the North Atlantic. It is "A single point of rock, peak of a mountain range, one tooth set in the ancient jaw of a sunken world. . . ." Strong as is his will to survive, he cannot survive by will alone. And when we reach the last pages of the story, we are not sure that he survived at all. In the first chapter Martin seems to have kicked off his seaboots to lighten his weight and stay afloat; yet on the last page we discover that his body has been washed ashore with the boots still on.

Like much of modern writing, *Pincher Martin* concerns man existing in a state somewhere between life and death, at the outermost limits of endurance and imagination, on a stage as circumscribed as that of Samuel Beckett or Harold Pinter, in a situation as circumscribed as Jean-Paul Sartre's *No Exit* (1945). In the depiction of Martin's toothlike island, details take on a nightmarish clarity and horror, much as they do in Bierce's "An Occurrence at Owl Creek Bridge." Bierce's well-known story about the hanging of a Southern spy during the Civil War opens with the hanging miraculously averted by the snapping of the rope as the victim drops. Or so it seems. The story ends with the spy's body actually dangling from the rope and works on the basis of what has been dubbed "postmortem consciousness," an imaginative concept of the brain's continuing to work after death, for a time. Another well-known story that makes use of this concept and the ending technique is Hemingway's "The Snows of Kilimanjaro" (1938) in which, again, it is difficult to tell exactly when the protagonist dies.

Not only is it difficult to tell when Christopher Martin dies, but whether he has had two lives as well as two deaths, and whether he is to be viewed as Promethean hero or Satanic villain. Golding himself thought he had left little room

for doubt, as his analysis for the *Radio Times* indicates:

> Christopher Hadly Martin had no belief in anything but the importance of his own life. . . . The greed for life which was the mainspring of his nature forced him to refuse the selfless act of dying. He continued to exist separately in a world composed of his own murderous nature. His drowned body lies rolling in the Atlantic but the ravenous ego invents a rock for him to endure on. It is the memory of an aching tooth. Ostensibly and rationally he is a survivor from a torpedoed destroyer: but deep down he knows the truth. He is not fighting for bodily survival but for his continuing identity in face of what will smash it and sweep it away—the black lightning, the compassion of God. For Christopher, the Christ-bearer, has become Pincher Martin who is little but greed. Just to be Pincher is purgatory; to be Pincher for eternity is hell.

These are unmistakable words, but they also represent what is known as "the intentional fallacy," and in a later interview Golding was willing to admit that the author might be the last person in the world to ask about his own writing.

Martin comes off better than merely the personification of sheer ego and negation, because of the artistic intensity of his imagination and the Promethean quality of his struggle. As with Milton's heroically fashioned Satan, Golding's Pincher Martin is given an extra magnitude—perhaps beyond that conceived by the writer. John Peter sees this novel as a fable organized as carefully as a poem, its compelling symbols "integrated into a pattern . . . where the meaning is difficult to exhaust." With final ambiguity of theme as well as of form, *Pincher Martin* will always pose a reading problem. Has the author wrought better than he thought? Does one take his word and accept this as a story of man's evil nature and illimitable pride (the ancient sin of hubris), or does one go beyond the author's word to the work itself and find there as well the heroic struggle of a single human being to establish his own rock of existence, holding on against all odds? This basic ambiguity lies at the core of all man's knowledge and creation. Evil as he has been, Pincher Martin mirrors the author's own ability to create—to envision and to name. "I am netting down this rock with names and taming it," Martin tells himself. "What is given a name is given a seal."

The role of creative artist is even more directly associated with the protagonist of Golding's next novel, *Free Fall*. Sammy Mountjoy, whose

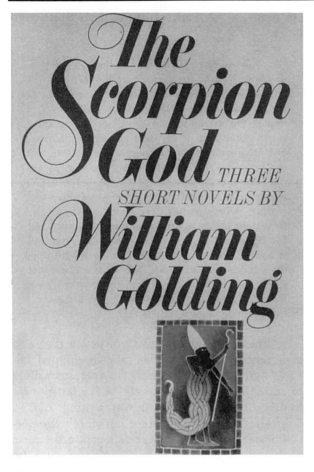

Dust jacket for the American edition of Golding's 1971 collection of three unconnected novellas. It was his only book between 1967 and 1979.

paintings "hang in the Tate," has "walked by stalls in the market-place where books, dog-eared and faded from their purple, have burst with a white hosanna." Now he is engaged in telling his own story in a book of his own making: "My darkness," he says, "reaches out and fumbles at a typewriter with tongs. Your darknes reaches out with your tongs and grasps a book. There are twenty modes of change, filter and translation between us."

Sammy tells his story through a series of confessional flashbacks. He has traveled quite some distance from his beginnings as a bastard born in a place called, with Bunyanesque bluntness, "Rotten Row." Somewhere in his climb to "Paradise Hill" he has fallen from grace, so that he is "a burning amateur, torn by the irrational and incoherent, violently searching and self-condemned." What makes Sammy fall is the central mystery of the story; his confessional search is punctuated by the thematic refrain of "When did I lose my freedom?"

His line of existence runs from Rotten Row and his mother, whom he sees in cloacal terms as the end of a tunnel, blocking the view back. But his fall is not natal. Infancy and childhood have, in his view, their own protective innocence. Even when he watches a little girl, Evie, urinate like one of the boys, standing up, and when he himself attempts to desecrate a church by urinating on its altar, Sammy finds himself guiltless by virtue of the animal state of childhood. He answers the question of "Here?" with absolution: "Not here." It is not *here* that he falls from grace.

When his mother dies, Sammy is adopted by Father Watts-Watt and comes under the contradictory tutelage of Nick Shales (benevolent rationalist) and Rowena Pringle (sanctimonious Christian). It is she who accuses young Sammy of reading smut into the Bible, and sends him to the headmaster to be punished for a landscape sketch he draws. Held a certain way, the sketch depicts private aspects of the human body. Perceiving the boy's wit and artistic ability, the headmaster withholds punishment and allows Sammy to follow his natural talent rather freely, except in Pringle's class. Eventually, on Sammy's graduation day, the headmaster provides the young man with a vital piece of advice: "If you want something enough, you can always get it provided you are willing to make the appropriate sacrifice. . . . But what you get is never quite what you thought; and sooner or later the sacrifice is always regretted."

This advice is held in narrative abeyance; it comes only some twenty pages from the end of the novel. By this time we have followed Mountjoy through numerous selfish acts and peccadilloes. We have watched him try on a Communist hat and take a wife, Taffy. We have observed him unsuccessfully struggle to erect a bridge between Nick Shales's presentation of physical laws, in respect to the conservation of energy, and Miss Pringle's presentation of Moses' burning bush and its metaphysical energy. We have seen him brought to the point of almost betraying himself and his comrades as he is tortured in a German prisoner-of-war camp. We have also seen him entrap, seduce, desecrate, and perhaps destroy a beautiful, if rather weak-minded, girl named Beatrice Ifor. In respect to all these instances except the last, Sammy has raised his anguished question of "Here?" and answered "Not here." In respect to Beatrice (whose name indicates Dantean temptation and a disjunctive *if-or* choice), the question is raised but left unanswered.

We discover that Sammy has debauched Beatrice in every sexual manner possible, only to leave her and marry someone else. But Sammy's fall begins with an act of free will, before the actual seduction takes place. Right after graduation, with the headmaster's words still ringing in his ears, Sammy retreats to the escarpment of the nearby river. It is a day of days as wood pigeons coo, rabbits thump, and butterflies murmur sexily—"for musk was the greatest good of the greatest number." Here in a bower of bliss, Sammy realizes joys of the flesh, autoerotically, knowing how "to sow my seed from the base of the strong spine." In so doing, he asks himself what is worth sacrificing for, and the answer is "Beatrice Ifor." What will he sacrifice for her white, unseen body? The next-to-last word in this section of the book is "Everything." The last word is "Here?" And there is no answer, except what the auditor of this confession cares to supply. Sammy's "free fall" occurs within this budding grove. The actual sullying of Beatrice is afterclimax.

The tortuous scenes of Sammy in a prisoner-of-war camp are anticlimactic, too, although necessary. Through a long series of questionings, his Nazi captors perceive his weakness. He is made to stand in a small, damp closet (somewhat like a toilet stall, or "bog"). When he explores the floor of this unlighted cell with his hand, Sammy believes that he touches a dismembered penis (the symbol of his own and Beatrice's downfall), and he screams. It is at this point in Golding's tangled tale that the reader begins to understand the difference between Sammy Mountjoy and Pincher Martin. Sammy escapes the machinations of the camp psychiatrist, Dr. Halde, by making use of man's last resource, prayer. It is all concentrated in his cry of "Help me! Help me!"—a cry which Pincher Martin stubbornly refuses to utter. In this moment of desperate prayer, Sammy spiritually bursts open the door of his own selfishness. It remains for the camp commandant to open the physical door of the dark cell, apologizing for the inhumane treatment of his prisoner with these words: "Dr. Halde does not know about peoples."

The dismembered "penis" in the cell, Sammy's remembrance of "Ma" in their family bog, the episodes of early micturition and masturbation, as well as the boy's sketch with hidden private parts—all of these thematic elements are

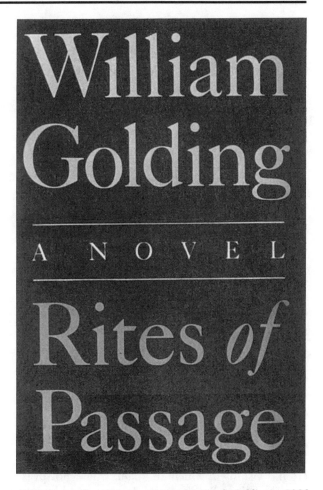

Dust jacket for the American edition of Golding's 1980 novel, for which he won the Booker McConnell Prize

brought together in the penultimate chapter of the book. This chapter makes it clear why Sammy is making his confession and doing penance. He goes to visit Beatrice Ifor, who is in a mental institution. Her hair has been cut short like a boy's; her skin has coarsened; her body is of a piece, from shoulder to hip the same thickness. As she turns around under a nurse's direction, she moves "like the figure in a cathedral clock." And then, as Sammy reports the episode, "Beatrice pissed over her skirt and her legs and her shoes and my shoes. The pool splashed and spread." After such knowledge, what forgiveness? Sammy flees from the institution, with the mad twittering of birds in his ears. His only recourse now is to tell his story, hoping for a Pentecostal sign.

Free Fall is preeminently a novel of atonement. Its pattern is that imposed by the mind of the protagonist-writer, who searches through the jumbled past seeking some means of exculpation.

Golding's next work, *The Spire*, is an example of the novel as metaphor. Set in the fourteenth century, it stands as an allegory of aspiration and inspiration with respect to art, both holy and profane, literary and architectural. It follows the pattern of the architectural pile it describes: the progress of the spire is the progress of the novel. What this book shares with *Free Fall* is the question suggested by the headmaster of Sammy Mountjoy's school: What is one willing to sacrifice to obtain one's desire? And the answer once again is "Everything."

Dean Jocelin, protagonist of *The Spire*, is obsessed with the belief that it is his divine mission to raise a four-hundred-foot tower and spire above his church (a fictional version of Salisbury Cathedral). His colleagues protest vainly that the project is too expensive and the edifice unsuited for such a shaft. His master builder (obviously named Roger Mason) calculates that the foundations and pillars of the church are inadequate to support the added weight, and fruitlessly suggests compromises to limit the shaft to a lesser height. The townspeople—amoral, skeptical, and often literally pagan—are derisive about "Jocelin's Folly" (a play on the name *Jocelin*, implying "God's fool"). But Jocelin forces the work onward more by his "blazing will" than by his piety. He has visions in which an angel, whose hot presence he often feels behind him, urges him on. He obtains tainted money from his worldly aunt, Lady Alison, on the basis of postcoital royal whim. He blackmails Mason and his army of builders to proceed with the construction by making it impossible for them to get work elsewhere. And Mason, who opposes each stage of the enterprise, knowing that his reputation as well as his freedom are becoming as undermined as the cathedral's foundations, reluctantly goes on with the work, and the spire rises.

The foundations shudder; the pillars sing under their increasing burden; the chaos in the church brings an end to all worship within; the chaos outside alienates Jocelin from the chapter as well as the community; the builder's unruly mercenaries drink, fornicate, murder, and brawl away their leisure hours; but the work goes on. Jocelin neglects all his spiritual duties to be up in the tower overseeing the workmen himself, all the while choosing not to see within and without himself what might interrupt the spire's dizzying climb. The physical and emotional wreckage increases along with Jocelin's monomania, as pride, stubbornness, and self-delusion only accelerate

his relentlessness. "The folly isn't mine," he tells himself; "It's God's folly."

The intensity of Golding's narrative encloses the reader in the hysterical mind of the Dean in the same way that the range of metaphorical treatment of the spire, integral to the theme, evokes the Dean's feverish, oscillating states of mind. The spire, maimed, like his spine at the close, is successively the mast of a ship, the Ark of God, a "diagram of prayer," the phallus of a supine man, a "dunce's cap," a "stone hammer . . . waiting to strike." A second symbol, less pervasive but almost as intriguing as the spire itself, is that of the apple tree. Two lines given to Jocelin are set in italics: *"There is no innocent work. God knows where God may be."* And: *"It's like the apple tree!"* This last seems primarily a reference to the fact that the great spire, like the trunk of a tree, thrusts grandly upward, but also thrusts in other directions, many of which—like the mixed nature of man's motives and works—are too complex to be seen at first view. But it also seems inescapable that Golding has chosen an apple tree rather than any other because it is his intention to remind us of that most notorious of trees, whose fruit precipitated man's expulsion from Eden. Again Golding returns to the most obsessive subject in his fiction—The Fall.

The spire rises and stands against all odds—against "facts" and storm. Only Jocelin, after placing the last nail in the top, falls, a victim of a mysterious ailment in his spine (probably cancer), which seems the physical equivalent of the angel that he feels pressing him on. Whether he has been urged by Satan, God, or his own pride (much like that of Pincher Martin) is a moot question. But good Father Adam, as he leans over the dying Dean, sees a tremor of his lips that might be interpreted as a mute cry of *"God! God! God!"* and thus out of the charity of his office, he lays "the Host on the dead man's tongue."

With the publication of *The Spire* in 1964, Golding concluded a remarkable decade of literary creativity and in 1965 received the honor of Commander of the British Empire. The decade from 1954 to 1964 stands as the major period of his career in the minds of most critics. Nothing he published afterward has received anything like the critical attention accorded his first five novels. His next novel, *The Pyramid* (1967), was a disappointment to his admirers and met with a harsh reception. Denis Donoghue, writing for the *New York Review of Books*, called it "an embarrassment, a disaster," and even Golding's most faithful adherents wondered if the book was indeed a novel or if it contributed anything to the author's reputation. To some it seemed merely three weak stories jammed together to produce a salable book.

Bernard F. Dick has defended the unity of *The Pyramid* while admitting that it is a secondary work lacking "the mosaic exactness of the author's best work." He views it as something of a bildungsroman, "cast in the form of three selected episodes in the life of a narrator, spanning a period from the early 1930's through 1963." A dispenser's son and future chemist, Oliver is a product of a tiny country village called, with full implication, Stilbourne. Here he undergoes three learning experiences representing defeat through lack of sufficient love. The first involves his semiseduction of a pretty and promiscuous young woman of the lower classes. The second concerns his disillusionment with another young woman whom he considers his true love (under the guidance of a homosexual director of musicales, he realizes that this young woman, Imogen, is as worthless as her singing). The third and last episode centers on Oliver's early ambition to become a great musician (he becomes a chemist instead), and on the antic activities of his former music teacher, the now elderly and eccentric Miss Dawlish, who believes that "Heaven is music." Through her and his own life's choices, Oliver comes to understand that everything in life must be measured by "the price paid in love." Here Golding plays a variation on the theme of sacrifice which dominates both *Free Fall* and *The Spire*. Sammy Mountjoy and Dean Jocelin err in sacrificing too much; Oliver fails by sacrificing too little. In comparison to the earlier novels, however, *The Pyramid* seems little more than the kind of semicomic novel that has so often dominated English fiction—a provincial tale told with a certain amount of charm and social insight, but lacking in intensity.

The same thing cannot be said about *The Scorpion God* (1971), a straightforward collection of three unconnected novellas. As Arnold Johnston declares, these pieces "reflect several of Golding's characteristic interests: the classical period, in the previously published 'Envoy Extraordinary' (1956); prehistory, in 'Clonk Clonk,' which deals, like *The Inheritors* . . . with the adventures of early men; and Egyptology, in the title piece, which centers on the death of a pharaoh from the late Middle Kingdom and the efforts of his jester . . . to avoid perishing according to the custom with the ruler." "Envoy Extraordinary" was published originally in the collection *Sometime, Never: Three Tales of the Imagination* (1956). It is a wry piece of comic writing that was turned into an extended play under the title of *The Brass Butterfly*, which was produced at the New Theatre in Oxford (1958). The plot is rather simple: Phanocles, an Alexandrian Greek inventor, turns up at the court of the Emperor (one of the Caesars) bearing models of three inventions and the idea for a fourth. The Emperor rejects them all, including a cannon, a steam engine, and a printing press. He prefers his own aristocractic and humanistic ways, rejecting science out of hand. At the end of the play, he sends Phanocles away with a line taken in part from a once-popular song: "Phanocles, my dear friend—I want you to take a *slow* boat to China." Although the tone of the story and play is light, Golding still shows his own attitude toward scientific and rationalistic amelioration.

A good amount of comic fun also runs through the other two stories in *The Scorpion God*. In a prehistoric setting, "Clonk Clonk" tells of an ancient tribe of Homo sapiens who call themselves The Leopard Men and have such names as Rutting Rhino, Stooping Eagle, and Charging Elephant for the men, and Palm, Minnow, and She Who Names the Women for the women. The title comes from an incident in which one of the men, lowly Chimp, discovers that the bones in his ankle make a noise when he moves it—"clonk, clonk." A longer title might have encapsulated the entire tale: "How Chimp Had His Name Changed to Wounded Leopard and Got to Marry She Who Names the Women."

"The Scorpion God" is somewhat more serious, its dark humor a matter of historical irony. Here Golding returned to one of his early interests, Egyptology. "I am," he once said, "an Ancient Egyptian, with all their unreason, spiritual pragmatism and capacity for ambiguous belief." As an epigraph for *The Pyramid* he used a portion of *The Instructions of Ptah-hotep*; and in *Free Fall* he has Sammy Mountjoy dream of being a descendant of Egyptian kings. In "The Scorpion God," he depicts the deadly and yet hilarious efforts of characters who bear such names as The God, Head Man, Pretty Flower, and Liar. The emperor-god must run a race each year to prove he is still capable of moving the sun, moon, and Nile River in proper fashion. He is also supposed to copulate with his young daughter, Pretty Flower, who does a Salome-like dance, but to no avail. When it becomes obvious that the emperor is incapable of these tasks, he decides to seek his death and to undergo full and proper burial, taking with him all his treasures, including his vizier-jester, whose name is, appropriately enough, Liar. How Liar extricates himself from this situation and escapes from the Head Man is an action-filled piece of farce. The narrative method here is oblique, and the reader must dig for all the comically mythical meanings imbedded in the action.

Delightful as the pieces in *The Scorpion God* might be, they do not stand as major works of fiction. And like those elements that went into the making of *The Pyramid*, they give the appearance of having been thrown together. Since Golding published nothing for quite some time afterward, these last works—uncharacteristic as they were—seemed to betoken waning powers and possibly an early literary demise. When *Darkness Visible* finally appeared in 1979, one reviewer summed up the situation in this quizzical manner:

> Whatever became of William Golding?
> During the late 1950s and early 1960s, he enjoyed a period of high critical esteem.... But after the publication of *The Spire* in 1964, Golding's work and reputation declined severely, and he himself vanished from the literary scene. Had he died? Or was he simply the stunned victim of "future shock"?

Golding's first real novel in fifteen years, *Darkness Visible* provided a somewhat reassuring answer. The author had resurfaced with enough of his skill intact to depict some of the ways in which the modern world was going to hell with itself. Appropriately enough, the new book took its title from the opening scene in *Paradise Lost* (1667), in which Satan discerns the contours of his new domain after his fall. Its thematic scenario is derived in equal parts from William Butler Yeats's "The Second Coming" (1921) and the apocalyptic revelations of Ezekiel and St. John of Patmos. In novelistic form, Golding informed his audience once again that "The center cannot hold," chaos is upon us, and it *is* the fire this time.

Fire flares up from almost every page of *Darkness Visible*. The very first scene of the book describes a fire during the London blitzkrieg—and out of its flames toddles a child, a burning babe, who eventually grows up to be a Pentecostal prophet. This perhaps demented, perhaps prescient figure known as Matty Septimus Windrove (or Windrow, Wildwort, Windrap, as well as a half-dozen other variations on the last name) is all the

protagonist the book is allowed. Part 1 of the novel is devoted to his search for both identity and a sense of mission. "Who am I?" he asks; "What am I? What am I for?" The diary Matty keeps contains a partial answer, derived from conversations he has with guiding spirits. In the final climactic section of the novel, we see his grotesquely burned figure become a true example of holocaust—a burnt sacrifice, offered up on the altar of modern terrorism.

The means by which terror arrives in the small English town of Greenfield, where Matty first attends the local foundlings' school and where he later works as a groundskeeper, is revealed in part 2 of the story. This section depicts the growth of Sophy Stanhope into a brilliant, beautiful young woman and evil incarnate. Sophy and her twin sister, Toni, a professional terrorist trained by Arabs, pool their efforts in launching a firebombing and kidnapping. They are assisted by two paramilitarists, former members of Her Majesty's Forces, who have discovered the combined pleasures of drugs, sex, and violence.

The third and final part of this book revolves around the pathetic ineffectuality of some senior citizens of Greenfield: Sim Goodchild, owner of a bookstore; Edwin Bell, former headmaster; and Sebastian Pedigree, a compulsive pederast who had been a teacher of the young Matty. These three old men function somewhat like a Greek chorus, bewailing the speeded-up ruination of civilization brought on by jet planes, television, drugs, rampant sex, electronic bugging, secret service activities, and terrorism. Each of them searches for some means of personal exoneration, and each takes a different message from the prophet Matty.

Although readers may disagree about the moral and religious messages emanating from *Darkness Visible*, most of them would probably agree that this is one of Golding's canonical works without being one of his best. Only partly does it fuse today's headlines with elements of the Old and New Testaments. The result reads like a series of interlinking mysteries that have not quite been solved. Golding performs some interesting mirror tricks amidst flame and shadow, adjusting the narrative angle and scope of vision. He allows the reader to see as through a glass, darkly; and while the effect and technique are appreciable, he does not have the power to make enough of the darkness visible. Perhaps that is why, behind the cries of the faltering old men, the author's own voice can be heard: it is a voice

William Golding, 1970

crying out in a modern wilderness, confusedly, as though the writer has lost his way and, to some extent, his sense of an audience.

The next year, however, Golding did much more to assure admirers that he had indeed made a comeback. A literate and crafty sea yarn, *Rites of Passage* (1980) is an extraordinary tour de force that has something in common with Herman Melville's *Billy Budd* (1924), Conrad's *Nigger of the 'Narcissus'* (1897), and even Samuel Taylor Coleridge's *Rime of the Ancient Mariner* (1798). Typical of the reception with which this later work met is the concluding comment of George Stade's *New York Times* review: "*Rites of Passage* is as skillful and resonant as the best of William Golding's other novels, which are among the best written by any Englishman these past 25 years."

The narrator-protagonist of the story is a snobbish young Englishman named Edmund Talbot, who is outward bound to take his place in colonial government and who reports his passage to a powerful and urbane patron—an unnamed nobleman, himself a translator of Jean Racine's dramas. The time is the first quarter of the nineteenth century, in the wake of the Napoleonic

Wars. The physical passage is "from the south of Old England to the Antipodes," in this case, Australia. It takes place aboard a ripe old hulk of the line that has been transformed into an emigrants' ark, replete with sheep, cattle, plants, and a strange assortment of sailors and passengers.

Among these are a clergy-hating captain, a naive and sacrificial clergyman (with the give-away initials of J. C.), a bisexual Billy Budd of a sailor (Billy Rogers), a loud and insistent rationalist (quite willing to kill an albatross), a nymphomaniacal "lady," and her alcoholic and flatulent protector. These, among others, undergo various personal rites of passage—from bachelorhood to marriage, innocence to perversion, ignorance to understanding, life to death. But the central rite is a sacrilegious baptism to which the Reverend Mr. Colley is subjected. As this ship of fools and saints crosses the equator, his sailor assailants dip the minister into a tarpaulin font filled with foul liquids that include urine.

Golding places this and other key actions behind narrative veils that must be pulled aside by the reader. Some of these incidents are relayed to Edmund Talbot, who finally moves from blind snobbery to perceptive justness in his own rite of passage. Everything we know comes from a diary that Talbot keeps; and part of Golding's achievement here stems from his ability to parody the sometimes pompous and lush memoir style of the late eighteenth and early nineteenth centuries. In describing a fellow passenger, for example, Talbot indites these lines: "Miss Zenobia is surely approaching her middle years and is defending indifferent charms before they disappear forever by a continual animation which must surely exhaust her as much as they tire the beholder. A face that is never still cannot be subjected to detailed examination. May it not be that her parents are taking her to the Antipodes as a last resort?"

The book contains parodistic touches of Henry Fielding and Tobias Smollett, and it is something of a "good read," like one of the Captain Horatio Hornblower stories. In typical Golding fashion, however, characters and plot take on allegorical density and weight. Aboard this ship of state, the military tyranny of Captain Anderson rules. It dominates the burgeoning humanism of Talbot, the rationalism of Mr. Prettiman, the hedonism of Miss Zenobia Brocklebank, and the naive religiosity of the Reverend Mr. Colley. In the struggle between church and state, Colley is no match for the captain, who humiliates the clergyman and helps establish an attitude among the ship's crew which eventually leads to Colley's final degradation and suicide. The unworldly and unprepared minister proves to be his own worst enemy, but the particular instrument of his fall is the devilishly handsome sailor, Billy Rogers—as the reader discovers in an oblique and ambiguous passage near the end of the book: "Billy Rogers was laughing like a bilge pump when he come away from the captain's cabin. He went into the heads and I sat by him. Billy said he'd knowed most things in his time but he had never thought to get a chew off a parson." Golding camouflages the real meaning of this passage, relating the incident through the unsuspecting Mr. Prettiman, who has heard of it through one of the crewmen, and who thinks that Colley has cultivated the filthy habit of chewing tobacco. Only after due pause does the reader—along with Talbot—realize the full purport of the incriminating words.

Rites of Passage provides readers with still another instance of Golding's virtuosity and moral stamina. In respect to technique, his handling of a nineteenth-century style and narrative frame sets Golding well above the usual level of today's novelists. As for morality, he is still working out of a central dictum that he issued years ago in an appropriately titled essay, "On the Crest of the Wave" (1960), in which he states: "Our humanity rests in the capacity to make value judgments, unscientific assessments, the power to decide that this is right, that wrong, this ugly, that beautiful, this just, that unjust." This is the lesson finally perceived by Edmund Talbot in *Rites of Passage*, and it is the thematic core of Golding's fiction.

Rites of Passage was awarded the Booker Prize, the highest literary award in Britain, in 1981. Golding has received honorary degrees from the University of Warwick (1981), Oxford University (1983), and the Sorbonne (1983). He was honored with the Nobel Prize for Literature in 1983. He published another novel, *The Paper Men*, in 1984, the year in which he was made Companion of Literature, a Royal Society of Literature award.

The Paper Men is the weakest of Golding's later works, as Golding here fails to achieve artistic distance from his somewhat autobiographical subject. It is perhaps most like *Free Fall*—with a narrator who is once again an artist compulsively driven to reexamine his sinful life. Wilfred Townsend Barclay, the ironically conceived dipsomaniac, novelist, and narrator of *The Paper Men*, be-

lieves he is a penitent undergoing a religious crisis, but reveals himself as simply a sadistic egoist experiencing a kind of literary delirium tremens.

Golding's *To the Ends of the Earth* (1991) comprises his novels *Rites of Passage, Close Quarters* (1987), and *Fire Down Below* (1989). This sea trilogy charts the voyage to Australia begun in *Rites of Passage* and includes a foreword by the author, in which he discusses the relationship of fiction to history. He also details the alterations he has made for this edition. The trilogy has been critically acclaimed, some reviewers hailing it as Golding's masterpiece.

Now in his eighties, William Golding is old enough to have addressed three generations of readers. Essentially, his own impulse toward writing was stimulated by World War II and its attendant evils. He wrote, as a kind of inspired schoolmaster or lay minister, in didactic tones about moral and religious issues. His constant themes have been original sin and man's fall, as well as the necessary commitment to free will—the choice between doing good or doing evil.

His first five novels, especially *Lord of the Flies*, met with wide acceptance at home and abroad. For a period of approximately fifteen years, Golding enjoyed a position of both popular and critical acclaim. But then matters changed abruptly. Younger readers found new literary idols—in Hermann Hesse, Kurt Vonnegut, Jr., and J. R. R. Tolkien. Readers of a feminist bent cried out for and received books of the kind written by women such as Doris Lessing and, later, Margaret Drabble. As a result of the war in Vietnam, the activities of counterculture and terrorist groups, the general phenomenon of the so-called drug scene and the generation gap, there seemed little need for the allegorical and mythic sermons of an aging schoolmaster.

Like many novelists before him, Golding must have realized that his old world, bad as it might have been, no longer existed. For a decade and a half, he turned silent, allowing only a few odd pieces to be gathered together and published. Like some literary Lazarus, however, he reemerged with the publication, first, of *Darkness Visible* and then of the *To the Ends of the Earth* trilogy. With these works he achieved a good measure of reconsideration, as well as a considerable amount of self-satisfaction.

Golding's strength lies in the imaginative presentation of other times and other places with figures that are potentially allegorical. It is probably in his ability to visualize in clearly poetic prose, in mythic form, with a sense of holy and profane wit, that he surpasses other modern novelists. *Lord of the Flies* and *The Inheritors*, along with the *To the Ends of the Earth* trilogy, perhaps best demonstrate the qualities mentioned by the Swedish Academy in awarding the Nobel Prize to Golding for a series of novels that "with the diversity and universality of myth illuminate the human condition in the world today."

Interviews:

Anonymous, "Portrait," *Time*, 70 (9 September 1957): 118;

Owen Webster, "Living with Chaos," *Books and Art* (March 1958): 15-16;

Frank Kermode, "The Meaning of It All," *Books and Bookmen* (October 1959): 9-10;

Webster, "The Cosmic Outlook of an Original Novelist," *John O'London's* (28 January 1960): 7;

John W. Aldridge, "Mr. Golding's Own Story," *New York Times Book Review*, 10 December 1961, pp. 56-57;

"The Well Built House," in *Authors Talking* (London: BBC Broadwater Press, 1961);

Maurice Dolbier, "Running J. D. Salinger a Close Second," *New York Herald Tribune Books*, 20 May 1962, pp. 6, 15;

Douglas M. Davis, "Golding, the Optimist, Belies His Somber Pictures and Fiction," *National Observer*, 1 (7 September 1962): 4;

Anonymous, "*Lord of the Flies* Goes to College," *New Republic*, 148 (4 May 1963): 27-28, 29-30;

Davis, "A Conversation with William Golding," *New Republic*, 148 (4 May 1963): 28-30;

James Keating, "The Purdue Interview of William Golding," in the *Casebook Edition of William Golding's "Lord of the Flies,"* edited by James R. Baker and Arthur P. Ziegler, Jr. (New York: Putnam's, 1964);

Bernard F. Dick, "The Novelist Is a Displaced Person: An Interview with William Golding," *College English*, 26 (March 1965): 481-482;

Jack I. Biles, *Talk: Conversations with William Golding* (New York: Harcourt Brace Jovanovich, 1970).

Bibliographies:

James R. Baker, Bibliography, in *William Golding: A Critical Study* (New York: St. Martin's Press, 1965);

Jack I. Biles, "A William Golding Checklist," *Twentieth Century Literature*, 17 (April 1971): 107-122;

J. Don Vann, "William Golding: A Checklist of Criticism," *Serif*, 8 (June 1971): 21-26.

References:

Howard S. Babb, *The Novels of William Golding* (Columbus: Ohio State University Press, 1970);

James R. Baker, *William Golding, A Critical Study* (New York: St. Martin's Press, 1965);

Jack I. Biles and Carl R. Kropf, "The Cleft Rock of Conversion: *Robinson Crusoe* and *Pincher Martin*," *A William Golding Miscellany, Studies in the Literary Imagination*, 2 (October 1969): 17-43;

Biles and Robert O. Evans, eds., *William Golding: Some Critical Considerations* (Lexington: University Press of Kentucky, 1979);

John Bowen, "Bending Over Backwards," *Times Literary Supplement*, 23 October 1959, p. 608;

Bernard F. Dick, *William Golding* (New York: Twayne, 1967);

E. L. Epstein, "Notes on *Lord of the Flies*," *Lord of the Flies* (New York: Capricorn, 1959), pp. 249-255;

James Gindin, *Harvest of a Quiet Eye: The Novel of Compassion* (Bloomington: Indiana University Press, 1971);

Martin Green, "Distaste for the Contemporary," *Nation*, 190 (21 May 1960): 451-454;

Peter Green, "The World of William Golding," *Review of English Literature*, 1, no. 2 (1960): 62-72;

Ian Gregor and Mark Kinkead-Weekes, *William Golding, A Critical Study* (London: Faber & Faber, 1967);

Samuel Hynes, *William Golding* (New York & London: Columbia University Press, 1964);

Arnold Johnston, *Of Earth and Darkness: The Novels of William Golding* (Columbia & London: University of Missouri Press, 1980);

R. Jones, "William Golding: Genius and Sublime Silly-Billy," *Virginia Quarterly Review*, 60 (Autumn 1984): 675-687;

Frank Kermode, "Coral Islands," *Spectator*, 201 (22 August 1958): 257;

Kermode, "The Novels of William Golding," *International Literary Annual*, 3 (1961): 11-29;

Millar Maclure, "Allegories of Innocence," *Dalhousie Review*, 40 (Summer 1960): 144-156;

Stephen Medcalf, *William Golding* (Essex, U.K.: Longmans, 1975);

William Nelson, *William Golding's "Lord of the Flies": A Source Book* (New York: Odyssey, 1963);

Carl Niemeyer, "The Coral Island Revisited," *College English*, 22 (1960): 241-245;

Bernard S. Oldsey and Stanley Weintraub, *The Art of William Golding* (New York: Harcourt, Brace & World, 1965);

Oldsey and Weintraub, "*Lord of the Flies*: Beelzebub Revisited," *College English*, 25 (November 1963): 90-99;

John Peter, "The Fables of William Golding," *Kenyon Review*, 19 (1957): 577-592;

V. S. Pritchett, "Secret Parables," *New Statesman*, 61 (2 August 1958): 146-147;

Philip Redpath, *William Golding* (Totowa, N.J.: Barnes & Noble, 1986);

Virginia Tiger, *William Golding: The Dark Fields of Discovery* (London: Calder & Boyars, 1974);

John Wain, "Lord of the Agonies," *Aspect*, 3 (April 1963): 56-67.

Graham Greene
(2 October 1904 - 3 April 1991)

This entry was updated by Richard Hauer Costa (Texas A & M University) from his entries in DLB 15: British Novelists, 1930-1959: Part One and DLB Yearbook: 1985.

See also the Greene entries in DLB 13: British Dramatists Since World War II: Part One; DLB 77: British Mystery Writers, 1920-1939; *and* DLB 100: Modern British Essayists: Second Series.

BOOKS: *Babbling April* (Oxford: Blackwood, 1925);

The Man Within (London: Heinemann, 1929; Garden City, N.Y.: Doubleday, Doran, 1929);

The Name of Action (London: Heinemann, 1930; Garden City, N.Y.: Doubleday, Doran, 1931);

Rumour at Nightfall (London: Heinemann, 1931; Garden City, N.Y.: Doubleday, Doran, 1932);

Stamboul Train (London: Heinemann, 1932); republished as *Orient Express* (Garden City, N.Y.: Doubleday, Doran, 1933);

It's a Battlefield (London: Heinemann, 1934; Garden City, N.Y.: Doubleday, Doran, 1934; revised edition, New York: Viking, 1962);

England Made Me (London & Toronto: Heinemann, 1935; Garden City, N.Y.: Doubleday, Doran, 1935); republished as *The Shipwrecked* (New York: Viking, 1953);

The Bear Fell Free (London: Grayson & Grayson, 1935; Folcroft, Pa.: Folcroft, 1977);

The Basement Room, and Other Stories (London: Cresset, 1935);

Journey Without Maps (London & Toronto: Heinemann, 1936; Garden City, N.Y.: Doubleday, Doran, 1936);

A Gun for Sale: An Entertainment (London & Toronto: Heinemann, 1936); republished as *This Gun for Hire* (Garden City, N.Y.: Doubleday, Doran, 1936);

Brighton Rock (New York: Viking, 1938; London & Toronto: Heinemann, 1938);

The Lawless Roads (London & Toronto: Longmans, Green, 1939); republished as *Another Mexico* (New York: Viking, 1939);

The Confidential Agent (London & Toronto: Heinemann, 1939; New York: Viking, 1939);

Twenty-Four Short Stories, by Greene, James Laver, and Sylvia Townsend Warner (London: Cresset, 1939);

The Power and the Glory (London & Toronto: Heinemann, 1940); published simultaneously as *The Labyrinthine Ways* (New York: Viking, 1940); republished as *The Power and the Glory* (New York: Viking, 1946);

British Dramatists (London: Collins, 1942);

The Ministry of Fear: An Entertainment (London & Toronto: Heinemann, 1943; New York: Viking, 1943);

The Little Train (Norwich: Jarrold, 1946; New York: Lothrop, Lee & Shepard, 1958);

Nineteen Stories (London & Toronto: Heinemann, 1947; New York: Viking, 1949);

The Heart of the Matter (Melbourne, London & Toronto: Heinemann, 1948; New York: Viking, 1948);

Why Do I Write?, by Greene, Elizabeth Bowen, and V. S. Pritchett (London: Marshall, 1948; Folcroft, Pa.: Folcroft, 1969);

The Third Man and The Fallen Idol (Melbourne, London & Toronto: Heinemann, 1950);

abridged as The Third Man (New York: Viking, 1950);

The Little Fire Engine (Norwich: Jarrold, 1950); republished as The Little Red Fire Engine (New York: Lothrop, Lee & Shepard, 1953);

The Lost Childhood, and Other Essays (London: Eyre & Spottiswoode, 1951; New York: Viking, 1952);

The End of the Affair (Melbourne, London & Toronto: Heinemann, 1951; New York: Viking, 1951);

The Little Horse Bus (Norwich: Jarrold / London: Parrish, 1952; New York: Lothrop, Lee & Shepard, 1954);

The Living Room: A Play in Two Acts (Melbourne, London & Toronto: Heinemann, 1953; New York: Viking, 1954);

The Little Steamroller: A Story of Adventure, Mystery and Detection (London: Parrish, 1953; New York: Lothrop, Lee & Shepard, 1955);

Essais Catholiques, translated (into French) by Marcelle Sibon (Paris: Editions du Seuil, 1953);

Twenty-One Stories (London, Melbourne & Toronto: Heinemann, 1954; New York: Viking, 1962);

Loser Takes All (Melbourne, London & Toronto: Heinemann, 1955; New York: Viking, 1957);

The Quiet American (Melbourne, London & Toronto: Heinemann, 1955; New York: Viking, 1956);

The Potting Shed: A Play in Three Acts (New York: Viking, 1957; London, Melbourne & Toronto: Heinemann, 1958);

Our Man in Havana: An Entertainment (London, Melbourne & Toronto: Heinemann, 1958; New York: Viking, 1958);

The Complaisant Lover: A Comedy (London, Melbourne & Toronto: Heinemann, 1959; New York: Viking, 1961);

A Burnt-Out Case (London, Melbourne & Toronto: Heinemann, 1961; New York: Viking, 1961);

In Search of a Character: Two African Journals (London: Bodley Head, 1961; New York: Viking, 1961);

A Sense of Reality (London: Bodley Head, 1963; New York: Viking, 1963);

Carving a Statue: A Play (London: Bodley Head, 1964);

The Comedians (London: Bodley Head, 1966; New York: Viking, 1966);

Victorian Detective Fiction: A Catalogue of the Collection Made by Dorothy Glover & Graham Greene, by Greene and Dorothy Glover, edited by Eric Osborne (London, Sydney & Toronto: Bodley Head, 1966);

May We Borrow Your Husband? And Other Comedies of the Sexual Life (London, Sydney & Toronto: Bodley Head, 1967; New York: Viking, 1967);

Modern Film Scripts: The Third Man, by Greene and Carol Reed (London: Lorrimer, 1968; New York: Simon & Schuster, 1969);

Collected Essays (London, Sydney & Toronto: Bodley Head, 1969; New York: Viking, 1969);

Travels With My Aunt: A Novel (London, Sydney & Toronto: Bodley Head, 1969; New York: Viking, 1970);

A Sort of Life (London, Sydney & Toronto: Bodley Head, 1971; New York: Simon & Schuster, 1971);

Collected Stories (London: Bodley Head/Heinemann, 1972; New York: Viking, 1973);

The Pleasure-Dome: The Collected Film Criticism, 1935-40, edited by John Russell Taylor (London: Secker & Warburg, 1972); republished as *Graham Greene on Film: Collected Film Criticism, 1935-1940* (New York: Simon & Schuster, 1972);

The Honorary Consul (London, Sydney & Toronto: Bodley Head, 1973; New York: Simon & Schuster, 1973);

Lord Rochester's Monkey: Being the Life of John Wilmot, Second Earl of Rochester (London, Sydney & Toronto: Bodley Head, 1974; New York: Viking, 1974);

The Return of A. J. Raffles: An Edwardian Comedy in Three Acts Based Somewhat Loosely on E. W. Hornung's Characters in "The Amateur Cracksman" (London, Sydney & Toronto: Bodley Head, 1975; New York: Simon & Schuster, 1976);

The Human Factor (London, Sydney & Toronto: Bodley Head, 1978; New York: Simon & Schuster, 1978);

Doctor Fischer of Geneva, or the Bomb Party (London: Bodley Head, 1980; New York: Simon & Schuster, 1980);

Ways of Escape (London: Bodley Head, 1981; New York: Simon & Schuster, 1981);

Monsignor Quixote (Toronto: Lester & Orpen Dennys, 1982; London: Bodley Head, 1982; New York: Simon & Schuster, 1982);

J'Accuse: The Dark Side of Nice (London: Bodley Head, 1982);

Getting to Know the General: The Story of an Involvement (London: Bodley Head, 1984; New York: Simon & Schuster, 1984);

The Tenth Man (London: Bodley Head, 1985; New York: Simon & Schuster, 1985);

The Captain and the Enemy (London: Bodley Head, 1988; New York: Viking, 1988);

Yours, Etc.: Letters to the Press, 1945-1989 edited by Christopher Hawtree (New York: Viking Penguin, 1990);

The Last Word and Other Stories (London: Reinhardt, 1990; New York: Viking, 1991).

Editions and Collections: *Three Plays* (London: Mercur, 1961);

Graham Greene: The Collected Edition, with introductions by Greene (London: Bodley Head/ Heinemann, 1970-);

The Portable Graham Greene, edited by Philip Stratford (New York: Viking, 1973; Harmondsworth, U.K.: Penguin, 1977);

Shades of Greene: The Televised Stories of Graham Greene (London: Bodley Head/Heinemann, 1975; New York: Penguin, 1977);

Why the Epigraph? (London: Nonesuch, 1989);

Reflections (London: Reinhardt, 1990; New York: Viking, 1991).

PLAY PRODUCTIONS: *The Living Room*, London, Wyndham's Theatre, 16 April 1953;

The Potting Shed, New York, Bijou Theatre, 29 January 1957; London, Globe Theatre, 5 February 1958;

The Complaisant Lover: A Comedy, London, Globe Theatre, 18 June 1959; New York, Ethel Barrymore Theatre, 1 November 1961;

Carving a Statue, London, Haymarket Theatre, 17 September 1964; New York, Gramercy Arts Theatre, 30 April 1968;

The Return of A. J. Raffles, London, Aldwych Theatre, 4 December 1975;

Yes and No and *For Whom the Bell Chimes*, Leicester, Haymarket Studio, 20 March 1980.

MOTION PICTURES: *Twenty-one Days*, screenplay by Greene and Basil Dean, Columbia, 1937; rereleased as *21 Days Together*, Columbia, 1940;

The Future's in the Air, commentary by Greene, Strand Film Unit, 1937;

The New Britain, commentary by Greene, Strand Film Unit, 1940;

Brighton Rock, screenplay by Greene and Terence Rattigan, Pathé, 1946; rereleased as *Young Scarface*, Mayer-Kingsley, 1952;

The Fallen Idol, screenplay by Greene, British Lion, 1948; rereleased, Selznick International, 1949;

The Third Man, screenplay by Greene, British Lion, 1949; rereleased, Selznick International, 1950;

The Stranger's Hand, screenplay by Green and John Stafford, British Lion, 1954; rereleased, Distributors Corporation of America, 1955;

Loser Takes All, screenplay by Greene, British Lion, 1956; rereleased, Distributors Corporation of America, 1957;

Saint Joan, screenplay by Greene, United Artists, 1957;

Our Man in Havana, screenplay by Greene, Columbia, 1960;

The Comedians, screenplay by Greene, M-G-M, 1967.

OTHER: *The Old School: Essays by Divers Hands*, edited by Greene (London: Cape, 1934);

H. H. Munro, *The Best of Saki*, introduction by Greene (London: Lane, 1950; New York: Viking, 1961);

The Spy's Bedside Book: An Anthology, edited by Greene and Hugh Greene (London: Hart-Davis, 1957; New York: Carroll & Graf, 1985);

Ford Madox Ford, *The Bodley Head Ford Madox Ford*, volumes 1-4 edited by Greene (London: Bodley Head, 1962-1963);

An Impossible Woman: The Memoirs of Dottoressa Moor of Capri, edited by Greene (London, Sydney & Toronto: Bodley Head, 1975; New York: Viking, 1976);

Victorian Villainies, edited by Greene and Hugh Greene (Harmondsworth, U.K. & New York: Viking, 1984).

SELECTED PERIODICAL PUBLICATIONS—
UNCOLLECTED:
FICTION
"The Lieutenant Died Last," *Collier's*, 105 (29 June 1940): 9-10;

"Men at Work," *New Yorker*, 17 (25 October 1941): 63-66;

"Proof Positive," *Harper's*, 195 (October 1947): 312-314;

"A Drive in the Country," *Harper's*, 195 (November 1947): 450-457;

"The Hint of an Exploration," *Commonweal*, 49 (11 February 1949): 438-442;

"The Third Man," *American Magazine*, 147 (March 1949): 142-160;

"Church Militant," *Commonweal*, 63 (6 January 1956): 350-352;

"Dear Dr. Falkenheim," *Vogue*, 141 (1 January 1963): 100-101;

"Dream of a Strange Land," *Saturday Evening Post* (19 January 1963): 44-47;

"Beauty," *Esquire*, 59 (April 1963): 60, 142;

"Root of All Evil," *Saturday Evening Post*, 237 (7 March 1964): 56-58;

"Invisible Japanese Gentlemen," *Saturday Evening Post*, 238 (20 November 1965): 60-61;

"Blessing," *Harper's*, 232 (March 1966): 91-94;

"Story," *Vogue*, 149 (1 January 1967): 94-95.
NONFICTION
"Middle-brow Film" *Fortnightly*, 145 (March 1936): 302-307;

"Ideas in the Cinema," *Spectator*, 159 (19 November 1937): 894-895;

"Self-Portrait," *Spectator*, 167 (18 July 1941): 66, 68;

"H. Sylvester," *Commonweal*, 33 (25 October 1949): 11-13;

"The Catholic Church's New Dogma: Assumption of Mary," *Life*, 29 (30 October 1950): 50-52;

"Malaya, The Forgotten War," *Life*, 31 (30 July 1951): 51-54;

"The Pope Who Remains a Priest," *Life*, 31 (24 September 1951): 146-148;

"The Return of Charlie Chaplin: An Open Letter," *New Statesman and Nation*, 45 (27 September 1952): 344;

"Indo-China," *New Republic*, 130 (5 April 1954): 13-15;

"Last Act in Indo-China," *New Republic*, 132 (9 May 1955): 9-11; (16 May 1955): 10-12;

"The Catholic Temper in Poland," *Atlantic Monthly*, 197 (March 1956): 39-41;

"In Search of a Character," *Harper's*, 224 (January 1962): 66-74;

"Return to Cuba," *New Republic*, 149 (2 November 1963): 16-18;

"Nightmare Republic," *New Republic*, 149 (16 November 1963): 18-20;

"Reflections on the Character of Kim Philby," *Esquire*, 70 (September 1968): 110-111.

Graham Greene was a writer who lived his life under the torment of faith. In his fictional world, where evil dominates, good-bad men are put in situations where their individual capacities for evil and good inevitably collide, where what is at stake transcends integrity. If the character is really good while seeming bad, nothing will serve him better than his vulnerability. Greene paved hell with heavenly intimations until, finally, innocence—that is, freedom from a controlling guile or cunning—takes over everything, even corruption, and a state that Greene called grace is reached. In Greene's major novels, the protagonist's fall is always fortunate because it strips him of everything, including his disguises: bad Catholic (Scobie in *The Heart of the Matter*, 1948), bad writer (Bendrix in *The End of the Affair*, 1951), drunken diplomat (Brown in *The Comedians*, 1966), flawed clergyman (the whiskey priest in *The Power and the Glory*, 1940), inept idealist (Pyle in *The Quiet American*, 1955). Always in the wings, urging the character on, is a figure he will have to discern on his own, a figure called, for want of a better name, God.

God, in fact, hardly enters Greene's fiction until *A Gun for Sale* (1936), when the killer Raven, trapped by a betrayal, reaches out for a God he does not believe in. Later, action is allegorized in God's image, as in *The Power and the Glory*. The journal entries of Sarah Miles in *The End of the Affair* show her infidelity with Bendrix pitted against God's will in such a way as to make God an actual character. Consistently, in the key works, Greene used God as a kind of reference. What happens over and over in Greene is like something that occurs perhaps once in Ernest Hemingway's work—near the end of *The Sun Also Rises* (1926). When Brett Ashley informs Jake Barnes that deciding not to be a bitch is "sort of what we have instead of God," Jake replies, "Some people have God . . . quite a lot." It is usually that way in Greene's religious novels: God either honored in the breach or dishonored in the observance.

During his earliest period, Greene dealt often, in both his long and his short fiction, with the initiation of a youngster into the adult world, that is, the transformation by experiences which can sometimes prove cruel and disillusioning. Later, in his three most deeply and problematically "religious" novels, Greene depicts rites of passage in such a way that good and evil are indistinguishable. Pinkie in *Brighton Rock* (1938) believes the only way to survive is to rewrite the golden rule: cause pain to everyone lest they inflict it on you. The whiskey priest in *The Power and the Glory* finds companionship among criminals that was unknown to him when the pious came kissing his hand. Major Scobie in *The Heart of the Matter* is cor-

rupted by pity. Greene is the supreme exemplar in twentieth-century fiction of the guilt-obsessed writer who has worked through corruption-of-innocence so thoroughly that he has brought it out on its other side as innocence-of-corruption.

Graham Greene was born 2 October 1904 at Berkhamstead, Hertfordshire, England, to Charles Henry Greene, headmaster of Berkhamstead School, and Marion R. Greene. He was one of six children. The parents were cousins, both born with the family name Greene, and Robert Louis Stevenson was Marion's first cousin.

Although *The Lost Childhood and Other Essays* (1951) is the title of a memoir Greene wrote in his forties, there is no writer in whom less of childhood has been lost. The penance childhood pays to disillusion is a common theme in his earliest stories. Many of these stories are analogues of the painful life he appears to have led "on a border" between two "countries," that of his family and that of the school where his father was headmaster. It is difficult to know how much of Greene's proclaimed hatred of school was intellectual and how much, in the words of Douglas Jerrold, was "merely emotion recollected in hostility to life in general." Peter Quennell, his contemporary at Berkhamstead, recalls Greene as a potential Pierrot, a wearer of a "rather woebegone mask" concealing "a great capacity for cynical humor. . . . [Reading his books] I sometimes feel that I am confronting the spirited schoolboy in a more accomplished and more portentous guise." Greene wrote an often quoted memoir ("The Revolver in the Corner Cupboard," in *The Lost Childhood, and Other Essays*) of how, at seventeen, he put one live round in a six-shooter, spun the chamber, placed the muzzle against his head, and pulled the trigger. He recorded "an extraordinary sense of jubilation" over his adventure with Russian roulette, whose savor he compared to a drug he craved. It was only after his sixth dose—he reports taking the revolver with him when he went up to Oxford—that he could pay it a permanent farewell. "I wasn't [by now] even excited. I was beginning to pull the trigger as casually as I might take an aspirin tablet." But his schoolboy desire to banish boredom never left him. He was to go on waging his war against it for the next sixty years.

Greene entered Berkhamstead School in 1915 and left in 1921, when he was seventeen. He shares with a distinguished list of upper middle-class English writers of his generation, such as George Orwell, Robert Graves, and Malcolm Lowry, the intense nostalgia for schooldays which they hated and, therefore, love to recall. Berkhamstead School was the place where evil became an article of faith, "a land of stone stairs and cracked bells ringing early [where] one was aware of fear and hate. . . . One met for the first time characters, adult and adolescent, who bore about them the genuine quality of evil. . . . And so faith came to one—shapelessly, without dogma, a presence about a croquet lawn, something associated with violence, cruelty, evil across the way. One began to believe in heaven because one believed in hell, but for a long time it was only hell one could picture with a certain intimacy." This sense of hell as more credible than heaven is another way of saying that corruption acquired innocence. It would be a theme on which the writer would never tire of playing.

In his fiction the world is always under siege. "It was the fusion of the morbid and the sentimental," declares David Pryce-Jones, likening Greene's novelistic landscape to perpetual war, "a matter of watching the familiar, the old, the safe being transformed or adapted or blown to bits." It is not surprising, then, that in a writer for whom adolescence lay like a dread palimpsest over everything, stories whose protagonists are boys should trace in capsule the interweaving of innocence and corruption. Written nearly twenty years apart, "The Basement Room" (1935) and "The Destructors" (1954) are parables of goodness subverted.

In "The Basement Room," the author's childhood is symbolized dually by the worlds of the nursery, where young Philip Lane spends most of his time, and the basement living room of Philip's idol, the butler Baines, and his bitchy wife. When his parents go on holiday, Philip penetrates the green baize door of childhood into Baines's quarters, where he lives every word of the butler's made-up stories. However, in the dramatically limited perception of the boy, fantasy gives way to a series of too-intimate-too-soon brushes with the world of adults. Philip is startled, during one of his flights beyond the baize door, to find Baines kissing a girl, Emmy, whom he has introduced as his niece. Philip is, finally, the witness to a struggle between the Baineses which ends with the woman falling down the staircase to her death. "The whole house had been turned over to the grown-up world," Philip feels. He will shut it all out. Let them keep to their world; he will keep to his. He runs away only to be found by a policeman. In his innocence about

involvements with the secrets of adults, he blurts out, "It was all Emmy's fault!" He had adored Baines: "Baines had involved him in secrets, fears he didn't understand. That was what happened when you loved—you got involved; and Philip extricated himself from life, from love, from Baines."

In 1948 "The Basement Room" became the film *The Fallen Idol*, the first of two symbiotic efforts that joined Graham Greene as scenarist and Carol Reed as director (the other was *The Third Man* a year later). Film-writer Greene changed storyteller Greene's ending by having Baines cleared when Philip's innocence is detected by an alert inspector. The original ending, though it flawed the story, is vintage Greene. Philip dies sixty years after the incident, a lonely isolate who has grown up shunning human involvements.

By reversing every assumed value, the later story, "The Destructors," flips innocence into an unaccustomed controlling position over corruption. Time and place—the World War II blitzkrieg of London—are ripe for it, and Greene makes the most of his opportunity. Philip Lane has grown to early teens as Trevor, son of a patrician family reduced by the war to neighborhood caste. Trevor joins the Wormsley Common Gang, who know him only as "T." He takes over the gang by audacity, making it clear there is to be no more kids' stuff—petty thievery or cadging rides from unwary conductors. Instead, they will systematically demolish the common's last standing buildings, a house and loo belonging to an elderly man who has offered them chocolates, a gesture they view as a bribe. They dub Thomas, the householder, "Old Misery." They work, Greene writes, "with the seriousness of creators—and destruction after all is a form of creation." They will dismantle Old Misery's house, with its two-hundred-year-old corkscrew staircase, from the inside, bring down to their level a building that, to Trevor, is invisibly held up "by opposite forces."

Opposite forces generate, as they do all of Greene's longer works, this short story, which leads off a list of Greene's own favorites ("I believe I have never written anything better"). T. and his gang dispossess the old man, but they are not thieves; they burn his seventy bank notes one by one. T. admits to wanting "to see Old Misery's face when we're through," but he denies hating him. "There'd be no fun if I hated him." For Trevor, hate and love—opposing forces—are "soft . . . hooey. There's only things."

There was a wealth of dissatisfaction in his indulgence; he knew the whole time he took his revenge for the poor opinion he had of it.

THE HOME FROM HOME   75

at the moment towards his fair or his dark angel. Then it was as well to add a few details: "Something rather lean," and in another mood: "Curved but not too curved." He didn't, he told me, find the place very satisfactory; shop-girls and nursery-maids adding a little to their wages on the slant were pitiably lacking in finesse. I think it was the theatre rather than the play which exercised its fascination over Major Grant; he liked the idea of ordering a woman, as one might order a joint of meat, according to size and cut and price. ~~Price was important; Major Grant was a poor man; he couldn't afford the highest quality.~~ Presently he ~~changed his butcher,~~ shifting his custom to an address in Hanover Street, and faded out of my knowledge, ~~other voices coming in between as I tuned in to new stations, but~~ occasionally the old voice ~~from Savile Row broke through Paris, Berlin, London Regional~~: "Like a pig in a poke. That's what I enjoy. Never know what you are going to get." "And if they were not quite up to mark?" "I take what comes," the voice would say, "I always accept 'em."

"Having to construct something upon which to rejoice."

Miss Kilvane lived in the Cotswolds in a strange high house like a Noah's ark with a monkey puzzle tree and a step-ladder of terraces. The rooms were all tiny and of the same shape, like the rows of rooms in an advertising exhibition or in the brothel quarter of an eastern city. The rooms were packed with china ornaments, old Staffordshire and Woolworth pieces and Goss presents from Bournemouth. She was a follower of the Regency prophetess, Joanna Southcott, had a manuscript collection of her prophecies, two counterpanes the prophetess had made, seals and locks of hair and a Communion glass engraved with little ludicrous symbolical figures. She was old and innocent and terribly sure of herself; she took down Joanna's life

Revised page proof for Journey Without Maps *(Sotheby's auction catalogue, 15 July 1974)*

They maneuver Thomas into his own loo, then lock the door behind him. While they put finishing touches on the demolition, he, half suspecting, ponders the Bank Holiday and an unfavorable horoscope ("They speak in parables and double meanings"). The gang makes him "comfortable" by passing in a blanket and throwing buttered penny buns and sausage rolls over his wall. Early next morning, a driver starts the lorry that he has parked by Thomas's house. The lorry, having been tied to a strut of the house, completes Trevor's fiendish achievement. The driver, even in the face of Old Misery's misery, breaks into convulsive laughter—opposing forces at work to the end: "Nothing personal, but you got to admit that it's funny." "The Destructors," like "The Basement Room," is about youth at bay. In the first, goodness loses out to forces it cannot understand; in the second, to forces it understands all too well. Innocence and depravity—opposing forces—have joined hands.

There is something compelling about authors who travel to exotic places for their materials, make wars or revolutions vital parts of the action, and install heroes who somehow perform honorably despite a paralysis of spirit. Where the Ernest Hemingway hero comes out of early crucibles purged of all posturing except the ultimate posture of never showing the scars or talking about how he got them, the Greene hero records his daily grappling with the demons of a "despairing romanticism" that is associated with boredom.

Greene wonders "how all those who do not write, compose or paint can manage to escape the madness, the melancholia, the panic fear which is inherent in the human situation." One wonders how close *his* situation, up to the age of thirty, brought him to despair, so conventional was it. After graduation from Berkhamstead School, he read modern history at Balliol College, Oxford. While there, as a perverse prank, he joined the Communist party as a dues-paying member—the amount he paid has been estimated at twenty-eight cents—for a period variously reported as from four to six weeks. That caprice would haunt Greene thirty years later.

Greene, a lifelong socialist, was fairly consistently pro-Marxist: supporting Charlie Chaplin, favoring Fidel Castro, and saying if it came to a choice he would rather live in the Soviet Union than in America—a statement Greene insisted was quoted out of context. His later friendship with the ultraconservative Evelyn Waugh, although largely founded on their shared religion,

often stood poised in uneasy truce. Waugh regarded socialism as the root of most modern heresy, and Greene resented the conservatism of Catholic custom and fashion. Despite these differences, neither novelist found any temptation to doubt the doctrine of the Fall.

He took a second-class degree at Oxford in 1925. Engagement and an initially happy marriage to a Catholic, Vivien Dayrell-Browning, in 1927 followed his conversion to the Church of Rome in 1926, but even though he would be known as a "Catholic writer," so notable an event as his conversion resists, in Greene's retelling, even a semblance of drama.

In the decade following his conversion Greene worked initially as a literary journalist and then as an editor on the London *Times*, a job he relinquished only after the publication of his first novel, *The Man Within* (1929), and the guarantee from Heinemann and Doubleday of a six-hundred-pound advance. The title of the book comes from Sir Thomas Browne's epigraph, "There's another man within me that's angry with me." Pryce-Jones notes that significantly the work contains many of the characteristic themes Greene was to work out later. Andrews is a foreshadowing of Greene's early heroes, a young man dogged by recollections of a desperate childhood and a brutal father, a smuggler disguised as a London businessman. To wreak vengeance on his father for his own lost innocence, Andrews anonymously informs to the excisemen about the smugglers. When the smugglers are acquitted in court despite Andrews's defiant testimony, they revenge themselves on the woman he loves. Her death by suicide is the final in a booklong series of betrayals. Andrews gives himself up to the police as her murderer. His fate looks ahead to that of Greene's perhaps prototypical betrayer-penitent, Scobie of *The Heart of the Matter*, a book that came two decades later. *The Man Within* was a modest success, selling 8,000 copies.

Greene became a popular success with *Stamboul Train* (1932; published in the United States as *Orient Express*, 1933). He employs the train speeding from Ostend to Istanbul as the setting for his first thriller of international espionage. The novel is segmented into five parts, each a major station on the route and each propelling the action forward. Involved is a gallery of typecast personages à la Agatha Christie and John Buchan: a Communist revolutionary, a Jewish merchant, a chorus girl, and a lesbian journalist. Pryce-Jones regards this novel as a distinct ad-

First page of the manuscript for The Power and the Glory *(Harry Ransom Humanities Research Center, University of Texas, Austin)*

vance on the three apprentice works, in which Greene's attempts to reveal his characters' inner lives were like "clumsy asides in a play." In *Stamboul Train* "the lull of the journey is an illusion: one and all are being borne to a destiny as much as to a destination, and they will be harried all along the line—Czinner the revolutionary, Coral the dancer with a bit-part waiting for her in Constantinople, Myatt the Jew with a deal in currants which will clinch a monopoly. Although all have ultimate purposes in making the journey, the very fact of travelling deviates or at least deflects them from their purposes. That is in the nature of life." And betrayal prior to a fall is in the nature of Greene. Czinner, his revolutionist's zeal disguising the innocence of the idealist, falls farthest; he has misapprehended the distance between actuality and aspiration most falsely. Coral only wants an ideal marriage, Myatt a better business. But Czinner seeks a juster world. The climax of the novel is Czinner's debate with Colonel Hartep, a strong-arm Fascist. As Pryce-Jones observes, Czinner knows that idealism is heroic in a world of Harteps: "He goes to his death pleased that the anomalies which made his life a torture are to be solved at last. He proves that he is as strong as Colonel Hartep, foreshadowing the relation of the priest and the lieutenant in *The Power and the Glory.*"

Stamboul Train was followed by two novels, *It's a Battlefield* (1934), a work deriving from Joseph Conrad's 1907 work *The Secret Agent* (the hero is even named Conrad Drover), about the repercussions in the lives of various Londoners of the conviction of a Communist for the murder of a policeman, and *England Made Me* (1935; published in the United States as *The Shipwrecked,* 1953), about the empty lives of a Swedish tycoon named Krogh and those around him.

In *It's a Battlefield*, Conrad Drover replaces Czinner as the man whose innocence is betrayed by the tragically fortuitous in life. His brother Jim is in prison for killing a policeman who had given offense to his wife, Milly. Like Czinner, Drover seeks justice in the void, but his imprisoned brother is the Communist. As Pryce-Jones points out, the central issue of the book, which is the moral problem of Jim's responsibility, is obscured by political implications. The novel underscores the never-relaxed tension in every Greene novel during his earliest phase, before he began equating elements of his plots with religious doctrine. For him, innocence is not antithetical to corruption but often accessory to it. A man such as

Jim Drover can be innocent at heart even when taking an action—the killing of a hurtful police official—that is deemed harmful to society. When innocence persists in the face of society's relentless formulations against it, as with revolutionary idealists such as Czinner and the Drover brothers, it becomes cruel and ironic, and in the long run more deadly than corruption.

England Made Me, a carefully constructed book with each scene, like the stops in *Stamboul Train*, leading to final betrayal and murder, presents the clearest vision of this interaction of innocence and corruption. In *England Made Me*, Greene assumes a wasteland where justice is not even sentimentalized, where any protest against Krogh's world of high-handed finance is stifled. Krogh may represent Krupp, the industrial complex that was feeding Hitler's armies with munitions, steel, and machinery. Pryce-Jones declares that this novel reveals Greene's awareness of a new kind of classlessness that was evolving in the 1930s. In "The Destructors," Trevor, the onetime rich kid reduced by war to being leader of a street gang, will parody gentility as a man in a high silk hat. Trevor is classless. In the earlier *England Made Me*, all the principals—Krogh, Kate and Anthony Farrant, Minty—share this in common: they are déclassé.

But they are not without mercy. The past, for twins Anthony and Kate, is childhood (innocence), but it cannot survive its encounter with a corrupted present that is controlled by the industrialist. Even Krogh, in long passages of interior monologue, recognizes that his life, unexamined except for profit and loss, narrows him crucially. When Anthony Farrant finally defies his tormentor and arranges to leave Sweden for England, he is already doomed. Nobody can afford to ignore or dismiss him as an innocent; he must die violently because he has found out too much about Krogh.

In this hellhole of a world, the real hero may be Minty, the seedy journalist whose livelihood depends on reporting Krogh's movements. He remembers school, not innocently, but as Greene did: a place of public humiliations and private disasters. Minty has reached the bottom of the hole and knows there is no salvage rope. If he does not grasp for a hold, he will not slip. The emblem of his survival is the spider he keeps trapped under his tooth glass. In the later novels, as Pryce-Jones notes, "Minty's tooth-glass has been lifted, and the characters tempt God to prove His existence. But [here] the tooth-glass is still over the spider. Krogh seems invincible under the glass because he has blotted out self-awareness most completely. Anthony and Kate could also remain under the glass if Anthony had not tried to tip it over from within."

Both *It's a Battlefield* and *England Made Me* were ignored by the public on both sides of the Atlantic. By 1935, bored and experiencing marital problems, Greene, with a £350 advance from Heinemann and Doubleday, hiked through the jungles of Liberia. The result was *Journey Without Maps* (1936), the first evidence that Greene would win recognition as a travel writer, too.

Up to a point, the itinerant Greene bears an affinity to his contemporary George Orwell. The Greene who trekked through Liberia, Mexico, and the Congo saw the same endemic poverty, shabbiness, and human misery that forever turned Orwell, whose early years were spent as a civil policeman in Burma, against officialdom and empire. Although both seem to penetrate to the heart of what in a later day would be called the Third World, Orwell's vision extends to *other* worlds, to a possible beyond. In *Journey Without Maps*, Greene scoffs at utopian blueprints, whether Wellsian visionist or Orwellian revisionist, for his journeys, whose maps were inner as well as outer, "represented a distrust of any future based on what we are."

Greene's distrust of "what we are" leads, then, neither to the inverted utopias of Orwell nor, as John Updike wrote of Catholics Waugh and Muriel Spark, to a "faith [that] serves as a crystalline index, an unseen whetstone sharpening the satiric knife, a settled judgment upon a foolish world." It is not that Greene is any more serious than other pessimistic writers, but that he is unable to stand above the fray armed with symbolic patterns embodying the human condition, like T. S. Eliot, or, like Waugh, with the fortifying conviction that only in unremitting anachronism lies salvation.

A clue to where Greene was heading—his commitment to dealing with his own crisis of faith even though it could not yet make itself known to him with the clarity of a controlling philosophy—is that he was drawing a distinction between drama and melodrama. The distinction prompted him, for a time, to partition his fiction into novels and "entertainments." His reputation rising with every book, these labels caused little stir either in him or in his growing audience. A work such as *A Gun for Sale* (published in the United States as *This Gun for Hire*, 1936) is a thriller, fast-paced and suspenseful, that includes chase, confession, and betrayal. The opening is one of the best known in all of Greene's works: "Murder didn't mean much to Raven. It was just a new job. You had to be careful. You had to use your brains. It was not a question of hatred. He had seen the minister only once: he had been pointed out to Raven as he walked down the new housing estate between the little lit Christmas trees—an old, rather grubby man without any friends, who was said to love humanity." It is flawless in the Greene manner—melodrama heightened by the cinematic effects he learned as film critic, beginning in 1935, on the London *Spectator*. In one take, the passage captures the killer, the victim, whose innocence (he "was said to love humanity") invites the response corruption makes when it is threatened, and Greene's Christian icons, those artificially lit tiny Christmas trees. Their shining signifies, at once, the commercialization of Christmas and the lost solemnity and radiance of the birth they are supposed to honor. The action moves against the Christian myth. Looking at a plaster model of the Christmas crèche, Raven lights on "the swaddled child," calling him "the little bastard." An outcast himself, he then speaks of "this business of no room at the inn," and another character later thinks of Raven simultaneously with "the little lighted crib."

Raven's path, then, follows Christian signposts. Along with Raven's fascination with primitive Christianity is his Judas complex. Although his moral code, sanctioning murder, may be warped, he does observe it honorably: "I don't go back on a fellow who treats me right," he says, adding later, "It's not the killings I mind, it's the double-crossing." But, as A. A. DeVitis observes, *A Gun for Sale* is predominantly secular in its outlook. it is an entertainment. Betrayed by Anne Crowder, the only person he ever trusted, and by the world, Raven remains to his death a nonbeliever. The religious note is held in abeyance.

Brighton Rock (1938) was a milestone in Greene's career. Following his usual classification system, Greene first had it listed as a novel, then as an entertainment. In subsequent editions, Greene reclassified it as a novel. DeVitis puts Greene's reasons well: "What had been before *Brighton Rock* a deeply felt religious outlook became with this novel the frame of reference within which the action developed. . . . [Now] it was Greene's Roman Catholicism that gave coherence and meaning to the narratives."

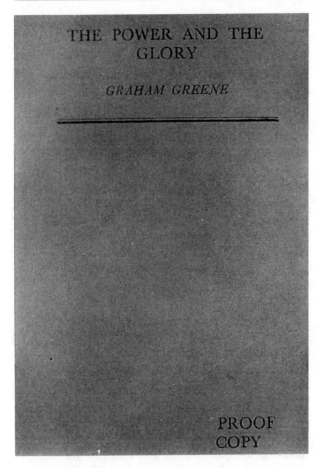

THE POWER AND THE
GLORY

GRAHAM GREENE

PROOF
COPY

*Bound proofs for Greene's award-winning novel, which had
its origins in his 1937-1938 trip to Mexico*

Brighton Rock deals overtly with the questions of sin, damnation, and salvation. It begins, like *A Gun for Sale*, in the manner of a thriller: "Hale knew, before he had been in Brighton three hours, that they meant to murder him. With his inky fingers and bitten nails, his manner cynical and nervous, anybody could tell he didn't belong—belong to the early summer sun, the cool Whitsun wind off the sea, the holiday crowd." The reader plunges straight into danger, "the undertow of suspense and fear," as Elizabeth Bowen called it, praising the opening of the novel for its wonderful scene-setting.

Hale has thrown in his lot with Colleoni's gang, and it is for this that Pinkie Brown and his rival mob are seeking to kill him. Hale has betrayed Kite, the leader of Pinkie's gang, to Colleoni, and Pinkie is seeking revenge for Kite's murder in order to prove himself, at seventeen, a worthy successor. It is, in fact, Raven, the central figure of *A Gun for Sale*, who has killed Kite. Therefore, the initial conflict in *Brighton Rock*

grows out of the earlier book, another indication that *Brighton Rock* began as an entertainment. Raven seems to be an unretouched photo of the more clearly pictured Pinkie.

Knowing that a witness is his only means of safety, Hale picks up Ida Arnold, a big friendly woman. But he becomes Pinkie's victim anyway, slain during the few minutes when Ida is in another room tidying up. Ida, unwilling to accept the cause of his death as "natural," determines to track down his murderer. Her unremitting pursuit of Pinkie provides a motif dear to Greene's heart: the chase. Pinkie—or, as he is often referred to, the Boy—finds himself obliged to marry, in spite of his feeling of revulsion, a pathetic sixteen-year-old waitress named Rose who might have turned evidence against him. Rose, like Pinkie, is a slum-born Roman Catholic. There is a grisly—and fake—suicide pact, which is thwarted by Ida. Pinkie is blinded by his own vitriol and jumps over a precipice to his death. When the novel concludes, Rose is pregnant with the child of the dead killer.

Given this sort of plot recital, *Brighton Rock* might be discounted as little different from a run-of-the-mill crime novel. But Greene, partially in *A Gun for Sale* and fully in *Brighton Rock*, is bringing tough-guy violence to the level of a moral dialectic that reflects, as R. W. B. Lewis writes, "a relation between two kinds or levels of reality: a relation between incommensurable and hostile forces; between incompatible worlds; between the moral world of right and wrong, to which Ida constantly and confidently appeals, and the theological world of good and evil inhabited by Rose."

Pinkie is the kind of character that fascinated Greene in Marjorie Bowen's *The Viper of Milan*: "perfect evil walking the world where perfect good can never walk again." Critical reaction against the book and its central couple was strong, with that of playwright Sean O'Casey most devastating of all: "Here," wrote O'Casey of *Brighton Rock*, "the Roman Catholic girl of sixteen and the boy of seventeen, respectively, are the most stupid and evil mortals a man's mind could imagine." One may concur with O'Casey about Pinkie, but it would be more accurate to call Rose innocent rather than stupid. Paired with Pinkie, she reinforces Greene's pervasive theme of the coexistence of corruption and innocence. Rose is the center of innocence, the point of purity in the dark picture, the object of treachery. She illustrates Greene's preoccupation with the kind of innocence that he identifies in the heroines of Henry James—always an object of admiration to Greene, who, as a free-lance literary journalist, was even then writing his finest criticism on the creator of Isabel Archer.

The religious theme comes to the fore in the confessional scene after Pinkie's death. It clarifies, for the first time in his fiction, Greene's ideas about sin and redemption. Rose expresses to a priest her conviction that Pinkie is damned and says she wants to be damned too. The priest speaks of the "appalling . . . strangeness of the mercy of God." When Rose mentions that Pinkie was a Catholic, the priest answers, summing up not only the theme of this novel but a major theme in all of Greene's religion-oriented works: "*Corruptio optimi est pessima.* . . . I mean—a Catholic is more capable of evil than anyone. I think perhaps because we believe in him—we are more in touch with the devil than other people." The priest—Greene's spokesman?—holds out hope for Pinkie, but the reader, like Rose, knows he was incapable of love. The Catholic church does not demand, as the priest tells Rose, "that we believe any soul is cut off from mercy," but Pinkie has deliberately and willfully evaded it. Rose is left at the end carrying Pinkie's unborn child, walking toward "the worst horror of all." These are the final words of the book, and they are ambiguous. One can only surmise that Rose's fate will be self-pity, disbelief, and loss of faith.

Brighton Rock is the quintessential example of that series of fast-paced works in which politics and religion, rightly understood, merge and which Greene, until the 1970s, labeled entertainments: *The Confidential Agent* (1939), *The Ministry of Fear* (1943), and *The Third Man* (1950). The epigraph to *The Honorary Consul* (1973) is from Thomas Hardy: "all things merge in one another—good into evil, generosity into justice, religion into politics. . . ." This sense of the blending of politics and religion helps explain why, according to Frank D. McConnell, "Greene often seems most 'religious' when he is writing about spies and policemen . . . and most 'political' when he is writing about priests and saints."

In *The Power and the Glory* (1940), a book about Mexico, Pinkie's counterpart, who, like him, seems hell-bent on damnation, will accept humbly the mercy offered. The gaping pit is still there, but in *The Power and the Glory*, as J. P. Kulshrestha succinctly puts it, "we also see the outsoaring spirit which rises up to heaven and the comedy is all divine." *The Power and the Glory*, like Malcolm Lowry's *Under the Volcano* (1947), with

Graham Greene, 1948

which it is often compared, is a religious novel but not an ecclesiastical one. R. W. B. Lewis writes of the remarkable interplay "of sacred and obscene love, of beauty and extreme ugliness, of comedy and deadly peril . . . a rich multiplicity of action beyond anything Greene had previously achieved."

Greene went to Mexico in the late winter of 1937-1938. He had been commissioned by a London publishing house, Longmans, Green, to study the plight of the Mexican Catholic church, which had for more than a decade been engaged in a running feud with the revolutionary government. Nothing was further from his thoughts in Mexico than the writing of a novel, Greene recalls in his preface to the Viking Critical Edition of *The Power and the Glory*. He was in Villahermosa when by accident he came on traces of his principal character. A villager told him of the last priest in the state. The priest had baptized the villager's son, giving him a girl's name, for he was so drunk he could hardly stand for the ceremony, let alone remember a name. Afterward he had disappeared into the same mountains on the borders of Chiapas through which Greene, astride a mule, rode that winter on his way to Las Casas, where the churches were still standing but with priests *prohibido*. It was not a happy journey. The West was edging its way to World War II, the Italian pope was dying, and Greene was suffering from dysentery and the knowledge that he might be as much persona non grata in England as British diplomats were in Mexico. A libel action had been brought against him by Shirley Temple for remarks he had made in a film review for *Night and Day*. The case was settled for £3,500, including £2,000 for Temple, but at the time Greene feared he might be arrested on his return. So it was that he extended his stay to eight weeks and accumulated material for his best novel.

The incidents on which the plot of *The Power and the Glory* are based can be found in his second travel book, *The Lawless Roads* (1939; published in the United States as *Another Mexico*, 1939), a straightforward plea for the religious practices of Catholicism. Since the provinces of Tabasco and Chiapas were remote and communication was virtually nonexistent, the physical conditions of the journey proved somewhat similar to those of his journey through Liberia. Once again Greene was lonely and bored, and once again he was able to compare the civilized world with the primitive, only this time the primitive was Catholic, not pagan. Then, too, *Brighton Rock*, with its explicitly religious message, had intervened between the two "journey" books. His opposing forces were now a variation on previous ones: the instinctive faith of men versus materialism. "The war is declared," writes Pryce-Jones, placing his finger squarely on the question of whether faith ameliorates or intensifies poverty: "The war between the God of faith and the Devil of the twentieth century, and if the Mexicans must stay hopelessly poor in order to keep their faith, then there is very little help for it."

The Power and the Glory enables Greene to deploy his opposite forces in an Aristotelian fashion. Complication in the Mexican interior leads inevitably to tragic resolution. Religion and materialism are embodied by a priest and a police lieutenant. As soon as the two protagonists, never named except by their vocations, are matched, Greene's most powerful novel takes on the air of a parable. The action is right out of the entertainments—a chase—but much extended. Triangulated by three legs (three meetings), the action moves from the first, in a village where the priest has sought refuge and celebrated mass, to a second, in a prison where the priest is confined on a charge of drunkenness, to the final, the arrest leading to his execution.

The priest is tracked by a mestizo—a half-caste—who forces him to return to the village to at-

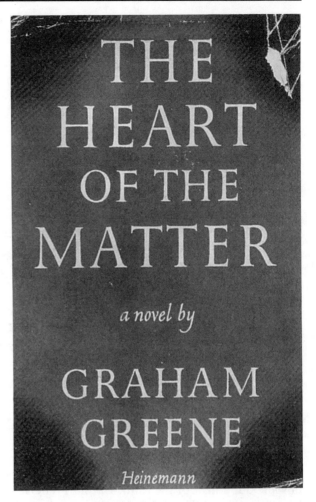

Dust jacket for Greene's 1948 novel, about a Catholic who wills his damnation by committing suicide

tend to a dying gangster, a grown-up Pinkie, a Catholic who might be saved by confession and whom the police have used as an involuntary decoy in their ambush. The priest's case is not as extreme as Pinkie's, for the former has the plea of suffering from his earnest moral intentions whenever he is sober enough to concentrate. By paying with his life, he attains salvation, which apparently was denied Pinkie. Greene's question, as a Catholic writer, is whether the priest is a saint. Pryce-Jones is cogent on this point, which he answers in the affirmative. The priest becomes a saint "because of the stress towards repentance set up by his sins, much as Rose is something of a saint because of her shouldering of the burdens of Pinkie's sins. . . . Certainly the priest never fails to mortify himself whenever his conscience is brought into play: perhaps his self-knowledge should be seen as humility instead of realism. He admits to the lieutenant that he had

145

stayed in the province partly to have the satisfaction of being the last priest when the others had run way, and partly out of pride, and he is angrily answered by the lieutenant that he will be a martyr. 'Oh no. Martyrs are not like me. They don't think all the time—if I had drunk more brandy, I shouldn't be so afraid,' the priest replies."

In *Ways of Escape* (1981) as well as in his introduction to *The Power and the Glory* in the collected edition of his books published by Bodley Head and William Heinemann, Greene acknowledges that *The Power and the Glory* was written to a thesis, the only one of his novels so written. The thesis is Christian dogma, without which the novel would become *Brighton Rock* written larger, a superior thriller about a policeman hunting down a priest, romanticized by a setting more exotic than a holiday resort and peopled by figures that rise to something approaching archetypal significance. But with a belief in a Christian God, the priest and Maria, the woman who shelters him, the mestizo, and the gangster all share in this one inescapable existence conditioned by their maker. They cannot properly be distinguished by the individual moral consideration of their actions, for every action, even drunkenness, lechery, or killing, is in God's image.

Edmund Wilson once noted of another novel about a man of the cloth, Harold Frederic's *The Damnation of Theron Ware* (1896), that a work of fiction whose hero is relentlessly humiliated can be significant but cannot be deemed great. *The Power and the Glory* is Greene's plea for the priest's heroic, or, in religious terms, saintly, status despite constant self-humiliation, a status that allows him to die for his faith despite his impulse for self-preservation. Given the fortification of belief, *felix culpa* (doctrinally translated as the "fortunate fall") takes on imperatives no less deterministic than the *hamartia* ("tragic flaw" or "error") of classical tragedy. In Greene, the humiliated, like the humble, can inherit the earth. He has said that of all his novels the one that most satisfies him is *The Power and the Glory*.

From a book which redeems hatefulness and disguises spirituality as depravity, it is only a short step to the creation of a world like that of the West African colony in *The Heart of the Matter* (1948). Greene's policeman-protagonist, Major Scobie, reflects that in such a cruel climate one could love people almost as God loves them, knowing the worst. Scobie will abandon this abstract, bitter charity. He falls in love with a woman not his

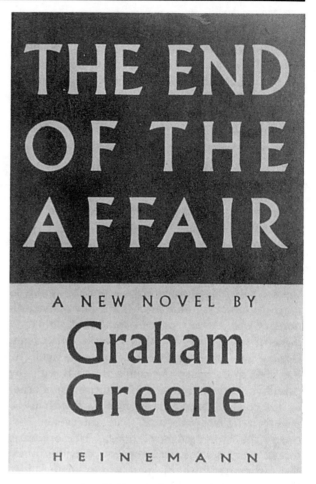

Dust jacket for Greene's 1951 novel, a story of adulterous and divine love

wife. His mortal sin reveals to him the radiance of the truth he has betrayed.

Scobie is another one of Greene's self-humiliating saints. In fact, in this book the Catholic Scobie is actually defined by his pity, both of self and of his fellows. His suicide at the end of the novel occasioned a storm of controversy in Roman Catholic literary circles. Evelyn Waugh wrote in *Commonweal* upon the publication of *The Heart of the Matter*: "To me the idea of willing my own damnation for the love of God is either a very loose poetical expression or a mad blasphemy, for the God who accepted that sacrifice could be neither just nor lovable."

If one has to be a Christian to be convinced of the apotheosis of the whiskey priest in *The Power and the Glory*, one has to disbelieve, in order to praise the later work, that the tenets of any organized religion should be invoked as aesthetic considerations. DeVitis puts the question especially well: "The point . . . is not why Greene uses a religious theme but how; it is important to decide whether or not his use of a religious theme invalidates the novel as a work of art. And to do so, Greene must be considered as a novelist who is a Catholic, not as a dilettante of religion and theology. . . . The problem then of whether Major Scobie is 'saved' or not according to the teachings of the Catholic Church becomes a minor consideration; for the novel presents a personal moral—Scobie's moral—which may not coincide with that of orthodox Catholicism."

DeVitis goes on to mount a strong case for considering Scobie as a modern tragic hero and accepting his Catholicism as something akin to the fatality of Greek drama. For Major Scobie, pity is the keynote of human existence. He soliloquizes about the futility of any expectation of happiness: "What an absurd thing it was to expect happiness in a world so full of misery. . . . If one knew . . . the facts, would one have to feel pity even for the planets? If one reached what they called the heart of the matter?"

The plot is by far the most complex of any Greene novel so far. Suffice it to say that Scobie is pitiful—or rather "pity-full"—in a literal sense. A middle-aged police officer in British West Africa, he is a loser, like Eliot's Prufrock, able merely to fill out a scene, unable to obtain promotion. He feels only pity for his wife, Louise. To avoid making her unhappy over his various failures, he unwisely borrows money from the merchant Yusef, who, by a complicated net of circumstances, will blackmail Scobie into smuggling diamonds for him. The book's love triangle is completed when a torpedoed ship brings Helen Rolt into the pattern of Scobie's unhappiness. He falls in love with her because she is pathetic. Scobie realizes his love for Helen is only an effect of his pity. Nevertheless, his affair drones on and is exposed. Louise goads him into attending communion and the confessional as tests of his repentance. With the smuggling of diamonds comes his realization that he is "one of those whom people pity" and further awareness that his corruption corrupts others. He tacitly agrees to the murder of his houseboy, Ali, by one of Yusef's henchmen. He knows that he has destroyed Ali to keep from bringing hurt to either Helen or Louise, and he determines to set them free of him. He reasons that if he kills himself he will stop crucifying God; and it is God whom he loves above all things.

Much of the latter part of the book becomes slightly dramatized inner dialogue be-

tween Scobie and God, almost Bunyanesque in intensity. At the end of the novel, a priest returns to give comfort to the living, to reestablish the norm of the church and to give hope for Scobie's soul, even though he committed suicide. In *The Heart of the Matter*, as DeVitis emphasizes, Scobie can love infinite goodness, but he cannot trust it, since it allows unreasonable anguish. In other words, Greene poses in this novel something of the same moral dialectic as in his first: the terrible wages of innocence, of goodness, in a world that will not—or, in its present corruption, cannot—honor it. Greene daringly pits his hero against God: "Scobie becomes at once a traitor, a scapegoat, and a hero; his sense of pity, an image of his love for God, assumes the proportions of a tragic flaw. It is incontestable that he suffers more than he deserves; but whether or not he is damned becomes unimportant in a consideration of his heroism."

In the maturity of Greene's forties, the chiaroscuro world of childhood and adolescence—that world that he, in his essay "The Young Dickens," insists is the determinant of everything for the writer—became a prism through which the beam of grace penetrated into unlikely places. For his first two major religious novels he had conferred controversial sainthood on a whiskey priest in the Mexican interior and unlikely salvation on a compromised, life-negating functionary in an African outpost. For the final of the three books on which his reputation will likely rest, Greene chose his own country for his setting and a writer of novels for his hero.

In *The End of the Affair* (1951), the religious theme is inseparable from the plot. Greene clothes adultery in holy writ. He also demonstrates that he can write a powerful love story on two levels—the earthbound and the divine—while making each level reinforce the other. The plot is easily summarized. Maurice Bendrix hopes to write a novel about a civil servant and takes Sarah, the wife of a ministry official, out to lunch. It is wartime, and London is under the blitzkrieg. They have an affair which ends abruptly, leaving Bendrix unhappy and jealous. After a lapse of two years—by now the war is over—Bendrix meets Henry, the deceived husband, and the chance encounter leads to the explanation of Sarah's conduct. The story is told in both past and present tenses. Bendrix is the narrator, but a forty-page interlude consisting of Sarah's diary, to which Bendrix is illicitly made privy after he has jealously set a private investigator on

Sarah's trail, becomes a dramatic device which enables Greene to give Sarah's account of the affair.

Such a plot recital evokes little of the mystic spirit of the novel. Although Bendrix serves as a first-person version of Henry James's "central intelligence," he moves through the book with a combination of unflattering self-awareness and cosmic diffidence, and he is not changed in any apparent way by the extraordinary developments around him. The spiritual development of Sarah is the pivot around which the action (or the *reaction*) revolves. Until this book, the conversions of the good-bad characters in Greene were either tentative or ambiguous or both. Sarah Miles finds a true reconciliation. Although *The End of the Affair* leaves Sarah's end uncertain—the reader cannot be sure whether she has become a Catholic—there is no doubt that she has become an Antigone, deserting life—in this case, her lover—for a higher commitment—in this case, God.

During an air raid which interrupts his lovemaking with Sarah, Bendrix is knocked down by a door. Sarah sees his hand extending from beneath the door and grasps it, assuming that he is dead. She explains her extremity in the diary Bendrix reads a few days before her death:

> "I knelt down on the floor; I was mad to do such a thing; I never even had to do it as a child . . . I hadn't any idea what to say. Maurice was dead. Extinct. There wasn't such a thing as a soul. Even the half-happiness I gave him was drained out of him like blood. He would never have the chance to be happy again—with anybody, I thought; somebody else could have loved him and made him happier than I could, but now he won't have that chance. I knelt and put my head on the bed and wished I could believe. Dear God, I said—why dear, why dear?—make me believe. I can't believe. Make me. I said, I'm a bitch and a fake and I hate myself. I can't do anything of myself. *Make* me believe. I shut my eyes tight, and I pressed my nails into the palms of my hands until I could feel nothing but the pain, and I said, I will believe. Let him be alive, and I *will* believe. Give him a chance. Let him have his happiness. Do this, and I'll believe. But that wasn't enough. It doesn't hurt to believe. So I said, I love him and I'll do anything if You'll make him alive. I said very slowly, I'll give him up forever, only let him be alive with a chance, and I pressed and pressed and I could feel the skin break, and I said, people can love without seeing each other, can't they, they love You all their lives without seeing You, and then he came in at the door, and he was alive, and I thought now the agony of being without him starts, and I

> wished he was safely dead again under the door."

Sarah now addresses her diary directly to God, who becomes a kind of epistolary monitor. Bendrix thinks there is another rival for Sarah's affections. His efforts to expose her as a double infidel provide most of the surface action. But it is "those things invisible" that truly generate this complex novel. Little does Bendrix realize that the unknown "he" should have a capital letter. By the time he learns the truth, he also knows that Sarah has made her vow, abandoned the flesh, and it is too late—she is dying of lung congestion.

The End of the Affair is a modern religious novel that cannot be for everyone. It relies on the reader's believing that something even proclaimed atheists might do in an emergency can change the bargainer's life forever. Specifically, Greene requires acceptance of at least four fictionally unearned developments—miracles—the most implausible of which is the gratuitous insertion of evidence that when very young Sarah had been secretly baptized as a Catholic by her mother.

The End of the Affair is the most sectarian of Greene's novels. Ten years later, in *A Burnt-Out Case* (1961), Greene returned to a shabby setting that calls to mind *The Heart of the Matter*. He also moved beyond mounting a case for any particular dogma. He beaches his Faustian seeker, appropriately named Querry, in a Congo leprosarium where, like other Greene heroes, he experiences a rebirth of concern for human suffering and becomes martyred by it. Querry is a Catholic architect of world renown who has sought refuge in the leprosarium, where his spiritual impasse equates to the lepers' physical condition. He has come to the end of his tether, a stage further even than Scobie or Bendrix. "I haven't enough feeling left for human beings to do anything for them out of pity." In the Congo, however, his rehabilitation becomes possible because he sees the worst of suffering. His rebirth apparent in his efforts to design a new hospital, Querry dies meaninglessly, a victim of the mistaken assumptions and stupidities of others.

Although political considerations do not override his novels as they do those of Orwell, Greene did not escape unscathed the right-wing repressions of America in the 1950s. Early in 1952, through the American consul in Saigon, Greene applied for a visa to enter the United States. That he was admitted briefly amid difficul-

148

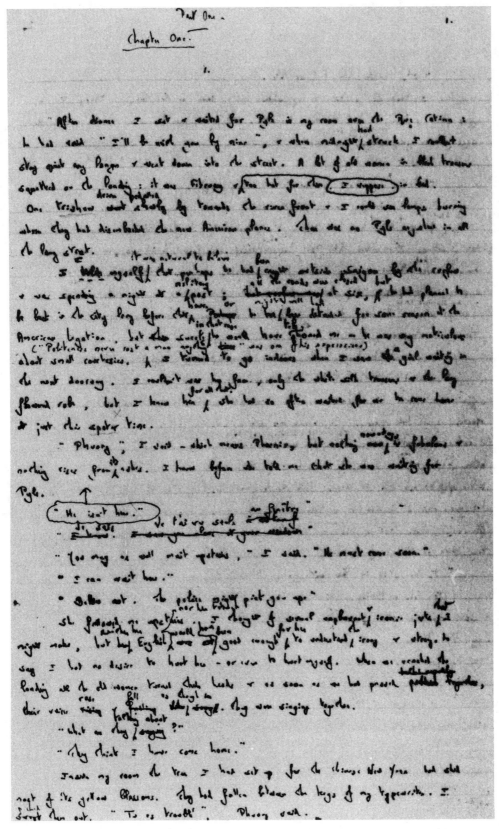

First page from the manuscript for The Quiet American *(Sotheby's auction catalogue, 21-22 July 1980)*

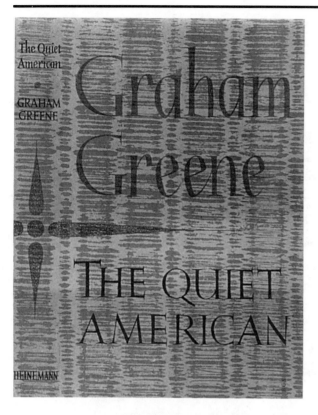

Dust jacket for Greene's "Vietnam novel"

ties and then denied the visa Greene blamed on the United States attorney general. "That it could seriously be thought that Graham Greene would carry the contagion and infect us is a fair measure of the intelligence and the precision of the authors of the McCarran Act," editorialized *Commonweal.* "McCarran and McCarthy might sacrilegiously have met Mr. Greene on his arrival, with bell and book and candle to drive from his spirit the last few traces of germs." As is usually the case, the rebuff became grist for the writer's mill. Eviction generated journalistic invective: a spirited defense of the concept of "disloyalty" and an open letter, "Dear Mr. Chaplin," castigating Sen. Joseph McCarthy and his Hollywood supporters and urging British writers and actors to refuse to sell stories or appear in films sponsored by any organization that included "these friends of the witch-hunter."

Greene's view of loyalty and disloyalty is a version of a remark Gertrude Stein is said to have made in conversation with American soldiers in Paris after World War II. "The Germans," she charged, "had never learned to disobey." For Greene, "loyalty forbids us to comprehend sympathetically our dissident fellows; but disloyalty encourages us to roam experimen-

tally through our human mind; it gives to the novelist the extra dimension of sympathy."

In *The Quiet American* (1955), his "Vietnam novel," Greene dramatizes the necessity of disloyalty in the face of a destructive idealism. Although his most polemical novel came more than three years after the denial of his visa, some American reviewers saw a connection, and nearly all criticized the book for its anti-American fervor. The novel counterpoises Fowler, an English journalist, and Pyle, the American of the title. Fowler, middle-aged, sophisticated, and safe, is a self-proclaimed atheist who nevertheless frequently addresses himself to God. Pyle is thirty-two, Harvard-reared, innocent, and full of intellectual idealism, enthusiasm, and danger. Greene brings into vivid relief the old problem—the fearful price of innocence—and shows, as Bernard Shaw does in his major plays, that behind innocence lurk unconscious arrogance and a self-righteous streak of moral blindness.

In *The Quiet American* and in *The Comedians* (1966), Greene succeeds in compressing political differences into the differences that exist among human beings. The latter's title does not refer to conscious laughter but rather to the rituals of the commedia dell'arte, in which the principals either play parts thrust on them by circumstance or enact roles meant to cover up their true selves. The hero, Brown, is a theist turned nihilist (Greene denied that Brown's being a former Catholic makes *The Comedians* still another Catholic novel) who maintains that, since he has not limited himself to believing in anything, he is open to everything. Brown's idea that everything can be contained in nothing is a further application of the innocence-of-corruption motif. He ends his Haitian odyssey in continued disbelief and despair. His innocent nihilism does not blunt the book's larger philosophy, illustrated by the fate of the other "comedians": man needs to believe in some set of values if he is to avoid despair.

The Comedians was apparently Greene's signal that he would no longer write about no-longer-young, not-quite-happy men with tedious and/or dangerous jobs in seedy locales. He puts in the mouth of Brown words that loom as the shape of Greene to come: "When I was a boy I had faith in the Christian God. Life under his shadow was a very serious affair; I saw Him incarnated in every tragedy.... Now that I approached the end of life, it was only my sense of humor that enabled me sometimes to believe in Him. Life was a comedy, not the tragedy for which I had been pre-

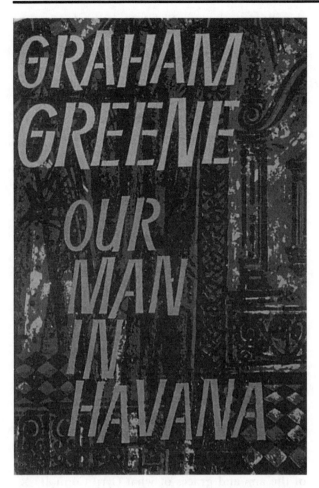

Dust jacket for Greene's 1958 novel, which he called "really a grey comedy, not a black comedy. . . . Perhaps in some ways it is a black comedy after all."

pared, and it seemed to me that we were all . . . driven by an authoritative practical joker towards the extreme point of comedy."

If Querry of *A Burnt-Out Case* fingered his lack of faith like a sore he wanted to get rid of, Greene may well have fingered his guilt-obsessed Scobies like sores *he* wanted to get rid of. After *A Burnt-Out Case*, it is the moments of rich if bitter comedy that scintillate in Greene's books. Critics, he writes in *Ways of Escape*, "were too concerned with faith and no faith to notice that in the course of the blackest book I have written I had discovered comedy." In *Our Man in Havana* (1958) and *Travels With My Aunt* (1969), he gives expression fully to his gift for comedy. *Our Man in Havana*, despite Greene's measured contradictory disclaimer ("It is really a grey comedy, not a black comedy. . . . Perhaps in some ways it is a black comedy after all"), is another one of those works he labeled entertainments, and this one follows the usual meaning of the word more than,

perhaps, the melodramas. The novel combines exciting satire on the exploits of the British secret service abroad with wry commentary on Fulgencio Batista's decadent Cuba with its stupid bureaucracy, which may have reminded Greene of postwar Austria. *Travels With My Aunt* is a jeu d'esprit about a dotty old lady with a delightfully wicked past. Aunt Augusta takes it upon herself to initiate her inhibited middle-aged nephew into grotesqueries beyond his conception. Their trip becomes a montage of places where Greene had set his previous books. They board some of the same trains—the Orient Express, for instance.

The central point of much of Greene's writing has been suicide, in Catholic doctrine the most deadly sin. In Greene's play *The Living Room* (1953), his interpretation of it is not a doctrinal one. The audience is left feeling that the heroine's (Rose Pemberton's) soul is saved, if anyone's is, and the message of the play is not Catholic propaganda but of far wider appeal. It is a plea to believe in a God who Father Browne, the girl's confessor, admits may not exist, but belief can only do good not ill, and without it we cannot help ourselves. Although Rose's suicide will probably be the only answer visible to most people, Father Browne's unshaken faith, his calm acceptance of her death, implies that there is another, but that the struggle for it must be unceasing.

Another play, *The Potting Shed* (1957), makes combined use of the Lazarus theme and the framework of the detective story. James Callifer has come to his father's deathbed hoping to learn what in his life makes him incapable of experiencing any deeply felt emotion. In the second act it is learned that James had been a suicide at fourteen but had been returned to life after the boy's Uncle William had promised God his only valuable possession—his faith—to spare the boy he loved. This miracle is crucial and strongly reminiscent of the miracles in *The End of the Affair*. After God answers Sarah Miles's prayer, sparing Bendrix, she proceeds to greater and greater awareness of His existence. Unlike Sarah, William Callifer goes on in his existence without faith until he is given proof of the miracle.

The Complaisant Lover: A Comedy (1959) stands in relation to the earlier pair of plays as *Our Man in Havana* relates to the novels and the preceding entertainments. This play is a brisk, witty, oftentimes farcical treatment of the triangle situation Greene had used in several of his novels as well as in *The Living Room*. But where the emphasis in the novels and the first play falls on the

Dust jacket for Greene's comedy about a dotty old lady with a delightfully wicked past

emotional and spiritual complications of characters involved in basically tragic situations, in *The Complaisant Lover* it falls on the comic involvements of a domestic tragedy.

The Honorary Consul (1973) is a religious-political novel by a writer who had mellowed since *The Quiet American* eighteen years earlier. It relates the story of the politically motivated kidnapping of Charlie Fortnum, a minor British functionary in South America. The novel's major characters exemplify the kinds of personal sacrifices one must make in order to live in good conscience in a world where there is too much tyranny and injustice. A minor machismo novelist endures privation; a priest joins the radical underground movement; a physician gives up a lucrative Buenos Aires practice. All three hope their sacrifices will in some way help the poor. One reviewer found it a melodramatic "mixture of violent action and religious speculation that is simply what Greene does best [while establishing]

the idea of the great church beyond our time and place."

The Human Factor (1978) allows Greene to venture into territory previously explored by John le Carré. It is about a double agent named Castle who seeks to help black South Africans—friends of his black wife—and becomes a mole, leaking information to the Russians. The leak is discovered, the wrong man murdered, and the Russians whisk Castle off to Moscow. Denis Donoghue believes that the book is based on Greene's loyalty to his old friend Kim Philby, the British intelligence officer who defected to the Soviet Union in 1963.

By 1973, at age sixty-eight, Greene was "drawing into perspective." So writes Philip Stratford in his introduction to *The Portable Graham Greene* (1973). "Few [other complete men of letters] have resisted definition better. . . . His pursuit fiction was criminal-centered; his Catholic novels skirted heresy; his journalism espoused unpopular causes; his comedies were sad and his politics paradoxical." John Lehmann, a literary historian of the period whose writers achieved early prominence in the 1930s, finds no such difficulty in "fixing" Greene: "He has pursued speed in dialogue, simplicity in prose structure and in his diction. He is thus extremely readable and has none of the airs and graces of what Cyril Connolly . . . has called the 'Mandarin style'. And he is . . . interested . . . in the ordinary and suburban scene of working lives. He has, in fact, exactly the same claim to be called a realist as they, and can make squalor smell as efficiently as Orwell. But *within* that world his preoccupations are entirely different."

As Greene closed in on his eightieth year, he published his twenty-first and twenty-second novels, *Doctor Fischer of Geneva, or the Bomb Party* (1980) and *Monsignor Quixote* (1982), plus a revealing memoir, *Getting to Know the General* (1984), which appeared a few weeks before his eightieth birthday. Both short novels—156 and 221 pages, respectively—return to "Greeneland," that is, to the terrain of man's fall. In *Doctor Fischer*, these are failure, betrayal, and boredom, fictionally implemented by such Greene staples as Russian roulette (de facto) and suicide (botched). In *Monsignor Quixote*, there is Greene's deployment of "opposite forces," announced thirty years beforehand in the classic short story "The Destructors" and here made dialectically vibrant in a running dialogue, frequently softened by wine, between a

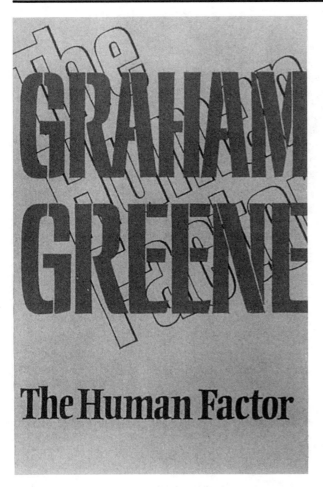

Dust jacket for Greene's 1978 spy thriller, which may have been inspired by the defection of Greene's friend British intelligence officer Kim Philby

Quixote figure and a Sancho figure contrasting and comparing Communism and Catholicism.

The narrator of *Doctor Fischer* is Alfred Jones, a middle-aged Englishman with a minor secretarial job in a Swiss chocolate firm, who meets, falls in love with, and marries Anna-Luise Fischer, the very young daughter of the famous man of the title. Fischer, inventor-tycoon of "Dentophil Bouquet," the best-selling toothpaste in Europe, has, in the manner of the Duke in Robert Browning's "My Last Duchess," murdered his wife, Anna-Luise's mother, for "betraying" him by indulging her taste for music with a minor clerk. His revenge only exacerbating his despair, Fischer makes a hobby of dinner parties that are spiritually of a Grand Guignol character: laboratory experiments in the depths of human greed and self-degradation. Rightly perceiving that the rich are not less but more pathetically greedy than the poor, Fischer invites to his repasts a gallery of affluent grotesques whom Anna-Luise

dubs the "Toads." He humiliates them in various ways, which they gladly tolerate for the sake of the expensive "presents" they know he will give them at the end of the ordeal. As Frank McConnell notes in *Commonweal*, they are "like the tests of a vengeful Jehovah eager to see, not who might be saved, but whom he can damn." Greene's sense of man's depravity has intensified since *A Burnt-Out Case*. He leaves nothing ambiguious in his misanthropism. Anna-Luise dies—absurdly—and Jones, after a bungled suicide attempt, agrees reluctantly to attend Doctor Fischer's last supper. The party, McConnell wisely observes, "is a kind of communal Russian roulette." Looking at the dead body of Fischer, Jones thinks: "This . . . was the bit of rubbish I had once compared in my mind with Jehovah and Satan."

For McConnell, with *The Honorary Consul* and *The Human Factor*, this book forms a trilogy that suggests Franz Kafka's major unfinished books, *The Trial* and *The Castle*. He writes, "Just as Kafka banishes all virtues but Hope from his characters' moral repertoire, so Greene banishes all but Love. And in both cases, the odd and fascinating allegories that result are in fact acts of a distinctively modern, existential Faith in the very center of the abyss."

Monsignor Quixote appears to constitute the subsuming statement—part comedy, part allegory, all compelling—that culminates for Greene his innocence-of-corruption theme. Recently elevated to the rank of monsignor, Father Quixote teams up with a Communist ex-mayor whom he dubs Sancho Panza, and together they set off across Spain for Madrid to buy the purple socks and bib that are the insignia of the new monsignor's rank. They encounter as many windmills as their literary ancestors. Their mutual ineptitude scandalizes the bishop and nearly lands them in jail. A night in a brothel, a confession of an undertaker, an X-rated movie, and other adventures never disturb the pair's innocence. Through all of these adventures, which have their obvious parallels with Cervantes' novel, there is a running dialogue comparing Communism and Catholicism, but in the most human and personal terms, it is free from the intense emotional charges that longtime Greene watchers will remember from his earlier years.

Thomas F. Staley concludes that Greene's concern, dramatized first in his early masterpiece *The Power and the Glory*, remains steadfast in *Monsignor Quixote*—the transforming power of illusion

Graham Greene

and the transforming power of love: "For Greene, love lies deeper than faith. Both Quixote and Sancho realize this at the end. After the priest dies, Sancho, the avowed Communist and dear friend, says, 'I wish I could come upon St. Paul now by accident and for the first time.' "

Greene managed throughout the 1980s to maintain a steady publication pace, but what curious books he produced. *J'Accuse* (1982), which is hardly a book at all, does no honor to its distinguished namesake. It is an exposé of links among the police, the courts, and the underworld in Nice, the French Riviera city ten miles from Antibes, where Greene lived as a semirecluse in a modest two-room apartment overlooking the harbor. The background for *J'Accuse* dates from 1960 when Greene was in Africa doing research for *A Burnt-Out Case*. He became friendly with a French-Swiss family living there. Six years later, when he moved to Antibes, he discovered the family was living not far away in Juan-Les-Pins. They renewed their friendship; the wife became Greene's secretary, and the daughter, Martine, a surrogate niece.

Martine worked as a TV announcer in

Monte Carlo and in 1972 married a suave real estate salesman named Daniel Guy. They divorced in 1979. The settlement, says Greene, was "monstrous." Martine got custody of the two children, but she had to live within five hundred yards of her ex-husband and could never leave work later than 8:30 P.M.. According to Martine, Daniel snatched their older child after the settlement, roughing up his father-in-law, while Martine sprayed Daniel with tear gas. Afterward, the French courts gave Daniel custody of the child. To the rescue of his friend's daughter came Greene. First he caused a small sensation by returning his Legion of Honor to the French government (it was returned to him with the word that it could be forfeited only in death or disgrace). Then Greene appealed to Alain Peyrefitte, a fellow writer and minister of justice under former President Valéry Giscard d'Estaing. His own investigation, Greene charged, had revealed that Daniel had served three prison terms for crimes of theft and violence in the 1960s. Although a special investigator agreed with Greene that the situation was "horrifying," nothing substantive was done; Green decided to write and publish his polemic, a pale soundalike of Emile Zola's courageous stand on the Alfred Dreyfus case nearly a century ago. Legal battles followed but with no redress for Greene's side.

The year 1984 saw the publication of still another slim book—*Getting to Know the General*—which may provide the only clues Greene gave to the guarded side of the traveling man in his seventies. It is a memoir of Omar Torrijos Herrera, the Panamanian strongman through whose skillful diplomatic maneuvering the Panama Canal was returned to Panama in 1978. Torrijos was also a romantic figure who could have stepped out of a novel by Graham Greene. In fact, he did step out of it. The novel Greene wanted to write was to have been called *On the Way Back*; it was to be about a woman who is invited to interview Panama's leader and who nearly becomes the lover of the leader's closest friend. The novel was aborted, a victim of the tyranny that truth can impose on fiction when it is not only stranger but stronger. In its place, built from the same blocks of remembrance, is this memoir of a six-year involvement between the most international of living authors and a revolutionary with a touch of the poet. It was in August 1981, while packing for his fifth trip to Panama, that Greene received word that Torrijos had died in a plane crash. He was moved to declare that "I have never lost as good a friend as Omar Torrijos." Although Greene had said substantially the same thing when Evelyn Waugh died, there is no book to prove it. *Getting to Know the General* is Greene's eulogy for General Torrijos, but it is a lot more besides. The book is based on Greene's four trips to Panama, expenses paid, as the guest of an admirer—Torrijos—before, during, and after the book's centerpiece: the Washington signing by Torrijos and President James Earl Carter of a pair of treaties under which the United States agreed to relinquish control of the canal by the year 2000. With Greene joining another "temporary Panamanian," Colombian novelist Gabriel García Márquez, in the Torrijos entourage, the twelve pages devoted to the signing produce the memoir's first real interest (after 130 pages). Up to then, Greene's book might better have been titled *Getting to Wait for the General*. But in Washington, Greene's portrait of the Panamanian leader deepens.

"I am nervous," Torrijos tells Greene, "but Carter is more nervous and that comforts me a little." Torrijos expresses dismay that Carter had in-

vited the South American military dictators—Jorge Rafael Videla of Argentina, Augusto Pinochet of Chile, Hugo Banzer-Suarez of Bolivia, Alfredo Stroessner of Paraguay. He would have preferred only those moderates who had supported him in his long negotiations—from Colombia, Venezuela, Peru.

Someone has said, perhaps only partly in jest, that if another general—Dwight D. Eisenhower—had appointed Hemingway ambassador to Cuba in the 1950s, the Bay of Pigs disaster might never have occurred under President John F. Kennedy in the early 1960s. Whether, with dictators, the pen can ever be mightier than the sword is doubtful. Nevertheless, it is a virtue of this book to bring Latin American strongmen and their politics down to something more human than media-vantage stereotype. Thus, on his final journey as Torrijos's posthumous emissary (January 1983), Greene returns to Nicaragua as a signal to the Sandinista leaders that the Torrijos spirit is still alive in Panama. He visits Cuba, where, at their first meeting since 1966, Greene finds a Castro who says he is reading *Monsignor Quixote*. Greene goes finally to a jungle village built by refugees from El Salvador, who had been rescued from their perilous exile in Honduras by Torrijos.

The book promised to be as controversial among American readers as his anti-U.S. novel *The Quiet American* thirty years before. But Greene was not an ideologue; he lived his life under a torment of faith of which his political views are the merest suggestion. Anyone interested in knowing about the enormous commitment in sweat and sacrifice that went into building the Panama Canal and the extraordinary dramas behind its disposition should not look into this brief memoir. What the reader gets are sidebars of the master storyteller's craft; and his pictures are not only of General Torrijos but of his associates, the byproducts, in this case, of the abandoned novelist.

If *The Tenth Man* (1985) should have proved the final work by Greene published in his lifetime, it would have been, in the worst sense, ironic. This 30,000-word melodrama, described by its publisher as Greene's "newly discovered novella," dates from the midst of World War II—1944—when the 40-year-old author was doing some screenwriting for M-G-M. Greene, who declares in his straight-faced introduction that he remembered the manuscript only as a film-script outline of a few pages, purports now to welcome the "discovery" and even hints that he finds it superior in craft to his rightly celebrated scenario for *The Third Man*. The opening, in fact, is vintage Greene. Thirty imprisoned Frenchmen draw lots to determine which three of them will be executed in retaliation for three slayings by the resistance. The wealthiest of the prisoners, Jean-Louis Chavel, an attorney, draws one of the unlucky lots, but cheats death by signing away his fortune and ancestral home to the family of a young clerk—the tenth man—who takes his place before the firing squad. This opening section provides a model of economy, the sort of taut writing and plotting that were trademarks of the "entertainments" of Greene's earliest period. However, once Greene allows the war to end and the lawyer to return to the estate that is no longer his, the novella turns wholly implausible. *The Tenth Man* sold briskly in England and the United States. The film adaptation of *The Tenth Man* (1988), starring Anthony Hopkins as Chavel, thus fulfilled, after forty-odd years, the work's original intent.

Asked point-blank by Anthony Burgess when he was going to get the Nobel Prize, Greene replied that when he was asked the same question by a Swedish journalist, he had said he was looking forward to getting a bigger prize than the Nobel. "Which one?" asked Burgess. "Death," Greene answered, followed immediately by a request that they end the interview and have lunch. Green received his bigger prize on 3 April 1991, at the age of eighty-six.

As a novelist, Greene's ruling passion was an awareness of man's aboriginal corruption. His characters cannot dismiss that sense at the heart of things that life has no meaning, that life cheats when original sin is blurred. And this endless burrowing for the corruption within testifies to Greene's battle as a novelist for the survival of consciousness. Greene directed his characters to relentless probes within themselves for that deepest level of corruption known to the underground man, that aspect that he can only with the most agonizing difficulty acknowledge to himself.

Interviews:
Martin Shuttleworth and Simon Raven, "The Art of Fiction III: Graham Greene," *Paris Review*, 1 (Autumn 1953): 24-41;
"New Honor and a New Novel: Interview," *Life*, 60 (4 February 1966): 43-44;

G. D. Phillips, "Graham Greene: On the Screen: Interview," *Catholic World*, 209 (August 1969): 218-221;
Michael Mewshaw, "Greene in Antibes," *London Magazine*, 17 (June-July 1977): 35-45;
Marie-Françoise Allain, *The Other Man: Conversations with Graham Greene* (London: Bodley Head, 1983);
John Vinocur, "Graham Greene: Waiting for the Words," *International Herald Tribune*, 8 March 1985, p. 7;
John Mortimer, "I'm an Angry Old Man, You See," *The Spectator*, 14 June 1986, pp. 9-12.

Bibliographies:
William Birmingham, "Graham Greene Criticism: A Bibliographical Study," *Thought*, 27 (Spring 1952): 72-100;
Francis Wyndham, *Graham Greene, Bibliographical Series of Supplements to British Book News on Writers and Their Work, No. 67* (London: Longmans, Green, 1955);
Maurice Beebe, "Criticism of Graham Greene: A Selected Checklist with an Index to Studies of Separate Works," *Modern Fiction Studies*, 3 (Autumn 1957): 281-288;
Phyllis Hargreaves, "Graham Greene: A Selected Bibliography," *Modern Fiction Studies*, 3 (Autumn 1957): 269-280;
Jerry Don Vann, *Graham Greene: A Checklist of Criticism* (Lexington: University of Kentucky Press, 1970);
Robert H. Miller, *Graham Greene: A Descriptive Catalog* (Lexington: University of Kentucky Press, 1979);
R. A. Wobbe, *Graham Greene: A Bibliography and Guide to Research* (New York & London: Garland, 1979);
A. F. Cassis, *Graham Greene: An Annotated Bibliography of Criticism* (Metuchen, N.J. & London: Scarecrow Press, 1981).

Biography:
Norman Sherry, *The Life of Graham Greene, Volume 1: 1904-1939* (New York: Viking Penguin, 1989).

References:
Judith Adamson, *Graham Greene and Cinema* (Norman, Okla.: Pilgrim Books, 1984);
Jacob H. Adler, "Graham Greene's Plays: Technique versus Value," in *Graham Greene: Some Critical Considerations*, edited by Robert O.

Evans (Lexington: University of Kentucky Press, 1963);

Walter Allen, *Tradition and Dream: The English and American Novel from the Twenties to Our Time* (London: Phoenix House, 1964);

Kenneth Allott and Miriam Farris Allott, *The Art of Graham Greene* (New York: Russell & Russell, 1951);

John Atkins, *Graham Greene: A Biographical and Critical Study* (New York: Roy Publishers, 1958; revised, London: Calder & Boyards, 1966);

Atkins, "Two Views of Life: William Golding and Graham Greene," *Studies in the Literary Imagination*, 13, no. 1 (1980): 81-96;

W. H. Auden, "The Heresy of Our Time," *Renascence*, 1 (Spring 1949): 23-24;

Saul Bellow, "The Writer as Moralist," *Atlantic Monthly*, 211 (March 1963): 58-62;

Gwenn R. Boardman, *Graham Greene: The Aesthetics of Exploration* (Gainesville: University of Florida Press, 1971);

Arthur Calder-Marshall, "Graham Greene," in *Living Writers: Being Critical Studies Broadcast in the B.B.C. Third Programme*, edited by Gilbert Phelps (London: Sylvan, 1947), pp. 39-47;

Calder-Marshall, "The Works of Graham Greene," *Horizon*, 1 (May 1940): 367-375;

A. F. Cassis, "The Dream as Literary Device in Graham Greene's Novels," *Literature and Psychology*, 24 (1974): 99-108;

Francis X. Connolly, "Inside Modern Man: The Spiritual Adventures of Graham Greene," *Renascence*, 1 (Spring 1949): 16-24;

Donald P. Costello, "Graham Greene and the Catholic Press," *Renascence*, 12 (Autumn 1959): 3-28;

Beekman W. Cottrell, "Second Time Charm: The Theatre of Graham Greene," *Modern Fiction Studies*, special Greene issue, 3 (Autumn 1957): 249-255;

Maria Couto, *Graham Greene: On the Frontier: Politics and Religion in the Novels* (New York: St. Martin's Press, 1988);

Richard Creese, "Abstracting and Recording Narration in *The Good Soldier* and *The End of the Affair*," *Journal of Narrative Technique*, 16 (Winter 1986): 1-14;

David Daiches, "The Possibilities of Heroism," *American Scholar*, 25 (Winter 1956): 94-106;

A. A. DeVitis, *Graham Greene* (New York: Twayne, 1964; revised, 1986);

Denis Donoghue, "Secret Sharer," *New York Review of Books*, 19 February 1981, pp. 14-18;

William D. Ellis, Jr., "The Grand Theme of Graham Greene," *Southwest Review*, 41 (Summer 1956): 239-250;

Quentin Falk, *Travels in Greeneland: The Cinema of Graham Greene* (London & New York: Quartet Books, 1984);

Georg M. A. Gaston, *The Pursuit of Salvation: A Critical Guide to the Novels of Graham Greene* (Troy, N.Y.: Whitson, 1984);

Richard Gilman, "Up from Hell with Graham Greene," *New Republic*, 29 January 1966, pp. 25-28;

Alan Grob, "*The Power and the Glory*: Graham Greene's Argument from Design," *Criticism*, 2 (Winter 1969): 1-30;

Henry A. Grubbs, "Albert Camus and Graham Greene," *Modern Language Quarterly*, 10 (March 1949): 33-42;

David Leon Higdon, "Saint Catherine, Von Hugel 28714 and Graham Greene's *The End of the Affair*," *English Studies*, 62, no. 1 (January 1981): 46-52;

Richard Hoggart, "The Force of Caricature: Aspects of the Art of Graham Greene, with Particular Reference to *The Power and the Glory*," *Essays in Criticism*, 3 (October 1953): 447-462;

Samuel Hynes, ed. *Graham Greene: A Collection of Critical Essays* (Englewood Cliffs, N.J.: Prentice-Hall, 1973);

Douglas Jerrold, "Graham Greene, Pleasure-Hater," *Harper's*, 205 (August 1952): 50-52;

Richard Kelly, *Graham Greene* (New York: Frederick Ungar, 1984);

Frank Kermode, "Mr. Greene's Eggs and Crosses," in his *Puzzles and Epiphanies* (New York: Chidmark, 1963), pp. 176-187;

Francis L. Kunkel, *The Labyrinthine Ways of Graham Greene* (New York: Sheed & Ward, 1959);

F. N. Lees, "Graham Greene: A Comment," *Scrutiny*, 19 (October 1952): 31-42;

Laurence Lerner, "Graham Greene," *Critical Quarterly*, 5 (1963): 217-231;

R. W. B. Lewis, "The Trilogy," in his *The Picaresque Saint: Representative Figures in Contemporary Fiction* (New York: Lippincott, 1959), pp. 239-264;

Lewis and Peter J. Conn, eds., *The Power and the Glory: Text and Criticism* (New York: Viking, 1970);

David Lodge, *Graham Greene* (New York: Columbia University Press, 1966);

François Mauriac, "Graham Greene," in his *Men I Hold Great* (New York: Philosophical Library, 1951), pp. 124-128;

Mary McCarthy, "Graham Greene and the Intelligentsia," *Partisan Review*, 11 (Spring 1944): 228-230;

Frank D. McConnell, "Perspectives: Graham Greene," *Wilson Quarterly*, 5 (Winter 1981): 168-186;

James L. McDonald, "Graham Greene: A Reconsideration," *Arizona Quarterly*, 27 (Winter 1971): 197-210;

Marie-Beatrice Mesnet, *Graham Greene and the Heart of the Matter* (Westport, Conn.: Greenwood, 1972);

Jeffrey Meyers, ed., *Graham Greene: A Revaluation* (New York: St. Martin's Press, 1990);

Conor Cruise O'Brien, "A Funny Sort of God," *New York Review of Books*, 18 October 1973, pp. 56-58;

Sean O'Faolain, "Graham Greene: I Suffer; Therefore, I Am," in his *The Vanishing Hero: Studies in Novelists of the Twenties* (London: Eyre & Spottiswoode, 1956), pp. 73-97;

Paul O'Prey, *A Reader's Guide to Graham Greene* (New York: Thames and Hudson, 1988);

George Orwell, "The Sanctified Sinner," in *The Collected Essays, Journalism and Letters of George Orwell*, edited by Sonia Orwell and Ian Angus (New York: Harcourt, Brace & World, 1968);

Gene D. Phillips, S. J., *Graham Greene: The Films of His Fiction* (New York: Teachers College Press, Columbia University, 1974);

Orville Prescott, "Comrade of the Coterie," in his *In My Opinion* (Indianapolis: Bobbs-Merrill, 1952), pp. 92-109;

V. S. Pritchett, "The World of Graham Greene," *New Statesman* (4 January 1958);

David Pryce-Jones, *Graham Greene* (New York: Barnes & Noble, 1967);

Peter Quennell, *The Sign of the Fish* (London: Collins, 1960);

Michael Routh, "Greene's Parody of Farce and Comedy in *The Comedians*," *Renascence*, 26 (Spring 1974): 139-151;

Anne T. Salvatore, *Greene and Kierkegaard: The Discourse of Belief* (Tuscaloosa: University of Alabama Press, 1988);

Marc Silverstein, "After the Fall: The World of Graham Greene's Thrillers," *Novel*, 22 (Fall 1988): 24-44;

Roger Sharrock, *Saints, Sinners and Comedians: The Novels of Graham Greene* (Notre Dame, Ind.: University of Notre Dame Press, 1984);

Martin Shuttleworth and Simon Raven, "The Art of Fiction III: Graham Greene," *Paris Review*, 1 (Autumn 1953): 25-41;

Philip Stratford, *Faith and Fiction: Creative Process in Greene and Mauriac* (Notre Dame, Ind.: University of Notre Dame Press, 1964);

Stratford, Introduction to *The Portable Graham Greene* (New York: Viking, 1973);

Brian Thomas, *An Uncertain Fate: The Idiom of Romance in the Later Novels of Graham Greene* (Athens: University of Georgia Press, 1988);

John Updike, "The Passion of Graham Greene," *New York Review of Books*, 16 August 1990, pp. 16-17;

Richard J. Voorhees, "The World of Graham Greene," *South Atlantic Quarterly*, 50 (July 1951): 389-398;

Ronald Walker, *The Infernal Paradise: Mexico and the Modern English Novel* (Berkeley & Los Angeles: University of California Press, 1978);

Peter Wolfe, *Graham Greene: The Entertainer* (Carbondale: Southern Illinois University Press, 1972);

George Woodcock, "Mexico and the English Novelist," *Western Review*, 21 (Autumn 1956): 21-32;

Morton Dauwen Zabel, "Graham Greene: The Best and the Worst," in his *Craft and Character in Modern Fiction* (New York: Viking, 1957), pp. 76-96.

Papers:

The Harry Ransom Humanities Research Center, University of Texas, Austin, has manuscripts and typescripts of most of Greene's books, plus working drafts and final manuscripts of various short stories and articles, as well as much of his correspondence. There are Greene holdings at the Lilly Library, Indiana University; the Pennsylvania State University Library; the Library of Congress; and the British Library.

David Jones

(1 November 1895 - 28 October 1974)

This entry was updated by Vincent B. Sherry, Jr. (Villanova University) from his entry in
DLB 20: British Poets, 1914-1945.

See also the Jones entry in DLB 100: Modern British Essayists: Second Series.

BOOKS: *In Parenthesis* (London: Faber & Faber, 1937; New York: Chilmark, 1962);

The Anathemata: Fragments of an Attempted Writing (London: Faber & Faber, 1952; New York: Chilmark, 1963);

Epoch and Artist: Selected Writings, edited by Harman Grisewood (London: Faber & Faber, 1959; New York: Chilmark, 1963);

The Fatigue (Cambridge: Rampant Lions, 1965);

The Tribune's Visitation (London: Fulcrum, 1969);

An Introduction to the Rime of the Ancient Mariner (London: Clover Hill, 1972);

The Sleeping Lord and Other Fragments (London: Faber & Faber, 1974; New York: Chilmark, 1974);

The Kensington Mass (London: Agenda, 1975);

Use & Sign (Ipswich, U.K.: Golgonooza Press, 1975);

The Dying Gaul, and Other Writings, edited by Grisewood (London & Boston: Faber & Faber, 1978);

Introducing David Jones: A Selection of His Writings, edited by John Matthias (London & Boston: Faber & Faber, 1980);

The Roman Quarry and Other Sequences, edited by Grisewood and René Hague (London: Agenda, 1981; New York: Sheep Meadow, 1981);

The Narrows (Budleigh Salterton, Devon, U.K.: Interim, 1981).

RECORDING: *Readings from the Anathemata, In Parenthesis*, [and] *The Hunt*, Argo PLP 1093, 1967.

SELECTED PERIODICAL PUBLICATIONS— UNCOLLECTED:

POETRY
"The Narrows," *Anglo-Welsh Review*, 22 (Autumn 1973): 8-12; republished in *Agenda*, 11-12 (Autumn/Winter 1973/1974): 12-16.

NONFICTION
"Langland's 'Piers Plowman,' " letter to the editor, *Listener*, 4 April 1957, pp. 563-564;

"Lost Languages," letter to the editor, *Times* (London), 20 August 1958, p. 9;

"Amends to a Prophet," letter to the editor, *Times* (London), 12 August 1961, p. 7;

"Christianity and Poetry," letter to the editor, *Times Literary Supplement*, 22 July 1965, p. 616;

"Fragments of an Attempted Autobiographical Writing," *Agenda*, 12-13 (Winter/Spring 1975): 98-108.

David Jones seemed to enter the company of major modern poets when, at a 1937 reception for the publication of his first work, the book-length poem based on his experience in World War I, William Butler Yeats rose from the crowd and intoned: "I salute the author of *In Parenthesis*." Later T. S. Eliot, in a "Note of Introduction" to the second edition (1961) of *In Parenthesis*, included David Jones with Ezra Pound, James Joyce, and himself in the inner circle of modernist writers. But as late as 1980 it was necessary to entitle a selection of his poetry *Introducing David Jones*. As the youngest member of his literary generation, and the slowest to have his work published, Jones has been late in gaining popular recognition. He lived largely apart from the public literary world, pursuing in seclusion his other crafts of painting and engraving and lettering, illustrating his books, and writing theoretical essays on history and religion, art and literature. But he is increasingly regarded as an important, innovative poet who has extended and refined the techniques of literary modernism.

David Michael Jones was born on 1 November 1895 outside London at Brockley in Kent, the youngest of three children to an English mother, Alice Ann Bradshaw Jones, and a Welsh father, James Jones, who instilled in his son an enthusiasm for Welsh culture and history. He left grammar school in 1909 and entered Camber-

David Jones, November 1965 (photograph by Mark Gerson)

well School of Art, which, if nothing else, reinforced his aversion to becoming a "commercial artist." But the outbreak of war took away the immediate need of earning a living. He first tried to enlist in the Artists' Rifles, "was rejected as deficient in expansion of chest," and subsequently joined the Royal Welsh Fusiliers. Siegfried Sassoon and Robert Graves served as officers in the same regiment, but Jones, who remained at the rank of private throughout the war, never made their acquaintance. He served in Flanders from December 1915 through June 1916 and received a leg wound at the Somme River in France in July 1916. He returned in October to the northern front, where he remained until March 1918, when he was evacuated with a severe case of trench fever. As a soldier he labeled himself "a knocker-over of piles, a parade's despair," but the war was undoubtedly the most important experience of his life. Later he felt that "the particular Waste Land that was the forward area of the West Front had a permanent effect upon me and has affected my work in all sorts of ways"—for example, a painting strategy taken from positional warfare: "I like looking out on to the world from a reasonably sheltered position."

Jones reentered art school at Westminster on a government grant in 1919. Lacking direction, for a while he considered reenlisting for the

Archangel expedition against the new Bolshevik regime. In January 1921 he visited Ditchling Common in Sussex, a guild of Catholic artists and workmen under the direction of Eric Gill, a polemical essayist and sculptor. His regimen of work and prayer, and the religious, sacramental importance given to art at Ditchling, appealed deeply to Jones. He entered the Catholic church in September 1921 and joined Ditchling Common in January 1922. Gill hoped to "knock some corners off him," but Jones was unable to acquire the workmanlike behavior of the guild. Gill thought of the artist's table as an altar for an offering to God, but on his table Jones mounted a heap of books, discarded brushes, and paint cans with crushed cigarette ends in them. He failed to learn carpentry, and he kept chaotic accounts. But he finally learned and mastered the trade of engraving, which admitted him to Ditchling Common and earned the greater part of his living until 1933. He lived with the Gill family (he was engaged for a while to Gill's second daughter) until 1924 at Ditchling, then until 1927 at Capel-y-ffin in the Black Mountains on the Welsh border. Here he met René Hague, master printer and typesetter for his books, commentator on his work, correspondent, and later editor of his letters. Periodically he would visit a Benedictine monastery at Caldey Island, Pembrokeshire, and his parents' cottage by the sea at Portslade, Sussex.

Jones's poetry is thoroughly modernist in practice: highly allusive, discontinuous, a juxtaposition of "fragments" drawn from history and literary culture and his own experience. And, following his experience, the poetry pictures man in the two images of soldier and artist. Although soldiers inflict and endure unreasonable hardships, they possess a fundamental dignity based on a Christian acceptance of suffering. But man is first of all a maker of art (*maker* is a term from Gill's workshop). Art, as Jones's impractical temperament would have it, is essentially gratuitous, intransitive; it serves no social purpose; it is, ideally, a free hymn of praise to God, and as such resembles the gift offerings of sacrament.

Jones began writing *In Parenthesis* while visiting his parents' cottage in 1928. In early 1929 he rejoined the Gill family at Pigotts, a large farmhouse in Buckinghamshire, where he worked with Gill on printing and engraving until 1933. Few letters survive from these years; it was a fertile but feverish period; he completed sixty paintings in 1930 alone. Straining to finish *In Parenthesis* brought on the first of his nervous breakdowns in the early autumn of 1933. A London neurologist diagnosed the problem as "shell-shock," a delayed reaction to the war; to Jones it evinced the "neurasthenia" of the war generation. The doctor sent him on a Mediterranean cruise to Cairo and Jerusalem in the spring of 1934. Improvement was surprisingly quick; by the second day out of port he was playing shuffleboard and deck tennis and enjoying the sea air.

He returned to England in the summer of 1934 to complete *In Parenthesis*. His income was less secure, since he had abandoned engraving in 1933. The only regular paycheck Jones had in fact ever drawn was from the army; he could never force himself to work for money alone. His parents now regularly supplemented the small amount he earned from the occasional sale of a painting. He lived alternately as a guest at the Yorkshire home of Helen Sutherland, an art collector and later his personal patron, and in Sidmouth at the Fort Hotel.

In Sidmouth, Jones received regular visits from Prudence Pelham. His relationship with her was undoubtedly the most important relationship with a woman in his life. Her vivacity remedied his depressions. She darned his socks, made him gifts ranging from money to filched pewter teapots, supplied him with books, and gave suggestions for the final revisions of *In Parenthesis*. Jones had drawn a map of the Flanders front to aid his memory in writing; it bears page references to the manuscript before and after revisions, and shows that nearly fifty pages were deleted in 1935. He also saw the need now to provide notes for the text, in the manner of Eliot's *The Waste Land* (1922). These thirty-four pages of notes discuss esoteric details of trench warfare or explain the allusions and symbolism. He rewrote his preface several times, and he made drawings for a frontispiece and endpiece. The frontispiece depicts a soldier in a racked, sacrificial posture, his uniform askew and one boot missing—the last detail a comic private reference to the night an artillery attack caught Jones sleeping with one boot off. As late as 1936 he and Hague wished to have the book printed in folio columns, a newspaper format that was probably meant to emphasize its documentary quality. The manuscript was presented to Faber and Faber through Eliot early in 1937, and it was published in June 1937.

The narrative of *In Parenthesis* follows the experience of Jones's platoon from disembarkation in November 1915 to the Somme battle in July 1916, where John Ball, Jones's counterpart, is

wounded in the leg, and his whole platoon is annihilated. The book is divided into seven parts, each bearing a title and a quotation from the sixth-century Welsh heroic poem *Y Gododdin*. The parallel with this earlier work provides a kind of epic perspective on the action and has caused the book to be called "a modern epic" by many critics.

But *In Parenthesis* eludes even the simple categories of novel or poem. Long sections of prose are interspersed with verse—and Jones provided no help by referring to the book only as a "writing." Like a novel, *In Parenthesis* has characters—the members of John Ball's platoon—who live, develop, interrelate, and ultimately die. As in most novels, the narrator occasionally adopts their perspectives to intensify the action, and John Ball adds a special personal dimension through frequent flashbacks and interior monologues. At the same time, *In Parenthesis* is unmistakably poetic in its language, a cadenced prose that breaks naturally into verse. The ritual quality of military life, which to Jones suggests a Christian analogy and thus a whole religious vision to mitigate the suffering of war, lends cadence to the language. The poetry is descriptive and dramatic by turns. The rhythmical evocation of events is punctuated by the dramatic speech of soldiers, whose army cockney, to Jones's ear at least, "reached real poetry." A poetic intensity is achieved by numerous allusions to classical myths, the Bible, and the imaginary heroic literature of the past.

This imaginary past and the present meet at the center of the book, in the middle part of the middle section, where a young infantryman, "Dai Greatcoat," rises to speak a "Boast" in the manner of ancient heroic poetry. His set of adventures includes the major conflicts of Western history, legends, and myths. He is a kind of Universal Soldier, who testifies to the eternal reality of war. But his boast differs from the vaunts of heroes such as Achilles and Hector. He sees himself as much a passive instrument as an agent of force—"I was the spear in Balin's hand / that made waste King Pellam's land"—a paradox that reflects the modern soldier's passive role in the new technological warfare.

Several reviews in the popular press joked about the recondite contents of "Davy Jones's Locker," but the first fifteen hundred copies of *In Parenthesis* sold quickly, and a second impression of one thousand was made in 1938. The *Sunday Times* and most literary journals proclaimed it highly. Herbert Read, writing for the *London Mer-*

cury (July 1937), found it "as near a great epic of the war as ever the war generation will reach," displaying "the noble ardour of the *Chanson de Roland* and the rich cadences of the *Morte d'Arthur*." Eliot called it "a work of genius." With the publication of the second British (1961) and first American (1962) editions, Stephen Spender wrote for the *New York Times Book Review* (15 April 1962) that this "monumental elegy of World War I" had been too long neglected. *In Parenthesis* has since remained continuously in print.

Until 1939 Jones continued to live at the Yorkshire home of Helen Sutherland and in Sidmouth at the Fort Hotel. When visiting London, he stayed in Chelsea with his friend Thomas Burns, editor of the *Tablet*. He received small royalties from the sale of *In Parenthesis*, and occasionally there came a windfall, such as the Hawthornden Prize for *In Parenthesis* (one hundred pounds) in 1938. But his anxiety about money increased constantly in the years before and during World War II. After the death of his mother in 1937, he depended more and more on the generosity of his friends. By 1939 he was relying on a monthly check from Helen Sutherland, gifts from the collector James Ede, and the proceeds of a fund organized by Kenneth Clark to benefit Jones and several other artists. His stubborn refusal now to sell his paintings—he needed to be surrounded by his work, he claimed, in order to see the "direction" it was taking—lay at the root of his troubles. The news of Prudence Pelham's marriage in early 1939 injected a new tension. "Human relationships are so heart-rending in a way," he confided to James Ede in a letter: "I love her very much and our friendship has meant everything to me. So naturally, however much this may be 'a good thing,' I've naturally had a twisting, trying to get all the tangled delicate emotional bits and pieces tied up and sorted out. I only tell you this because of the intimate friendship we have and I wanted to tell you. *It is all private to you and Helen. I'm sure you'll understand that* [Jones's emphasis]." It was probably the radical disorder of his personal life and finances that caused him, in 1939, to flirt briefly with the program for order in *Mein Kampf* (1924). He would later maintain that fellow feelings for the German-front fighters in World War I had led him to dismiss the "reports of Nazi cruelty and nihilism as propaganda, like the stories of soldiers crucified on hay ricks in the Great War." In any case, he perceived the error before the outbreak

of war. To correct himself he tried to become absorbed in his art.

Shortly after finishing *In Parenthesis*, Jones had started a work provisionally titled "The Book of Balaam's Ass," a medley of voices and anecdotes in the freewheeling style of soldiers' postwar conversations. It lacked the narrative element of *In Parenthesis*, however, and could not achieve even the coherence of continuity. He abandoned it after struggling with it for several years. At the same time he began his second booklength poem, *The Anathemata*, as a series of experimental "fragments," which would not be completed and published until 1952.

In 1940 Jones returned to London to be near his aging father. Thomas Burns had gone to work at the British embassy in Madrid, and he allowed Jones to live in his Chelsea home until it was sold. The impermanence and solitude at Chelsea, in addition to his unrelieved financial worries, brought about a relapse of his nervous disorder in 1941. A doctor's certificate disqualifying him from Industrial Service reads:

> In 1932 [1933] he had a nervous breakdown and developed symptoms of mental depression—a depressive psychosis. The condition was severe. The course has been marked by improvement with relapses.
>
> He has been unfit for consecutive work in his own profession for nearly ten years. He is unstable, and under stress of duty would relapse.

He declined treatment for his condition, however, and moved to Sheffield Terrace, in Kensington, where he remained through the duration of the war. His finances continued to be unpredictable. Finally, in June 1944 Ede devised a scheme which, although it did not change the source of his income, at least remedied the uncertainty of its arrival. A group of friends and admirers would pay sums regularly into Jones's bank account, and he would reward the donors with paintings or inscriptions at his own discretion. These stipends allowed him to continue work on the fragments of *The Anathemata* through the war.

While staying with Sutherland in the summer of 1946, Jones suffered the last and most serious of his nervous breakdowns. He would later recall that "the main symptom was being frightened. The Bible often mentions men's knees knocking together; it was really like that; it was worse when I was at home...." His friends put him under psychiatric care at Bowden House, a nursing home at Harrow-on-the-Hill,

Frontispiece by Jones for In Parenthesis

where he remained until late 1947. He seemed to respond quickly and enthusiastically to the "frontal attack" of psychoanalysis. The doctors required him to confront his problems in written form, and he composed long passages on matters related to his condition. He tried to explain his personal neurosis as the problem of every artist in the modern technological world: they must experience a neurotic conflict between utile and gratuitous things. Another cause of neurosis lay in his lack of social status; he was afraid of being an outsider, even an impostor, in the upper-class world of his patrons. But he denied any sexual element in his neurosis, asserting that his failure to marry did not derive from any fear of sex, rather, that the artistic vocation can be a calling to a single life.

By the end of 1947 Jones had recovered sufficiently to move into a room in Northwick Lodge, a residential hotel in Harrow. Here, in a bay window overlooking the hill, his painting flourished. He also drafted many of the essays collected later in *Epoch and Artist* (1959) and *The Dying Gaul, and*

Other Writings (1978). He completed the project of writing and rewriting, arranging and rearranging the fragments of *The Anathemata*, which in 1951 Eliot persuaded him to publish with Faber and Faber. Jones composed footnotes that he included with the text, and wrote a long preface on the situation of the modern artist. He also supervised the reproduction in halftones of seven inscriptions, one painting, and one woodcut, and he did the inscriptional lettering for the cover.

The Anathemata tells the history of man-as-artist and his artifacts (his anathemata), and in a parallel fashion relates the historical development of British culture. Although history is not treated in linear sequence—there is a modernist, mosaiclike organization of fragments—the poem's eight parts interrelate in various ways. Part one follows the development of early man as artist, and part two, in roughly chronological form, views the emergence of the first Mediterranean cultures and traces the voyages of early tin traders to Britain. The motif of the sea voyage then links the middle sections of the poem (parts three through six), in which ships reach the site of London variously in Anglo-Saxon, Victorian, late medieval, and early Britonic times. Different world cultures thus penetrate the island. The last two sections celebrate the activity of the Catholic Mass and return the poem to its thematic center. Man's artifacts resemble sacramental offerings to God; the priest lifting the wafer of bread in the Mass is the supreme artist. The Mass also serves as the unifying occasion of the poem, which begins with the scene of a priest consecrating the bread and ends, 194 pages later, with the elevation of the sacrament. The Mass thus provides a kind of infinite moment; its sacrament is the timeless archetype of all the artifacts catalogued in the poem. Jones always regarded *The Anathemata* as a more sophisticated work than *In Parenthesis*; the conception of art as sacrament dictates the shape of the later poem, whereas the war book follows the simpler pattern of narrative.

The poem's overriding sacramental metaphor also establishes a liturgical tone and incantatory quality for the poetic voice, but the style, like that of *In Parenthesis*, defies simple classification. Prose mingles with verse, and the mode shifts from epic to lyric, from historical chronicle to dramatic monologue. Jones makes a concerted attempt at dramatic immediacy: in the preface he asks the reader to speak the poem aloud; his own lyric voice frequently pierces the text; and there are several dramatic monologues by different historical personages. The longest of the poem's eight parts, the fifth, is the dramatic monologue of "The Lady of the Pool," a lavender seller in late-medieval London, who seems to live in an eternal present, having "entertained" the captains of most of the voyages to the island. Jones felt that the dramatic monologue "showed the way to make the past part of the Now," and the lady, like Dai Greatcoat in *In Parenthesis*, gives her strong speaking presence and character-in-voice to the materials of history and myth. But the poem's subject and vocabulary may seem remote and difficult. The diction bristles with foreign languages, and recondite words can create the impression of verbal density.

None of the poem's initial reviewers failed to notice its difficulty; some could see nothing else. Hayden Carruth, writing for the *Partisan Review* (September-October 1953), labeled it a "devastating conclusion" to the kind of difficult poetry cultivated by the modernists. The *Times Literary Supplement* saw "too many arcane allusions for a reader to grasp the meaning within its magic." Even W. H. Auden and T. S. Eliot, both of whom praised the poem categorically, worried so much about its difficulty that they produced long and detailed (and contradictory) instructions on how to deal with the notes. Most critics, however, echoed Auden's judgment in *Encounter* (February 1954) that "it is one of the most important poems of our time." Winfield Townley Scott, Kathleen Raine, and Emyr Humphreys all accepted its difficulty as necessary, and judged it, with Harman Grisewood, who reviewed the poem for the *Dublin Review* (Autumn 1952), "a major work of poetic innovation." Jones particularly liked Raine's assessment, in the *New Statesman* (22 November 1952), of the poem's "obscurity": "Such is the paradox of our time that the more a poet draws on objective tradition, the less on subjective experiences, the more obscure he will seem." Misprints resulting from unusual and foreign words were corrected in the second British edition of 1955. *The Anathemata* won the Russell Loines Memorial Award of the American National Institute of Arts and Letters in 1954—the first non-American work to do so—and an American edition followed in 1963.

Jones remained at Northwick Lodge until 1964, when its demolition forced him to move into Monksdene Hotel, also at Harrow-on-the-Hill, where he lived until 1970. No serious nervous relapse occurred in this period, and his financial circumstances were improving. In connection with Ede's financial scheme, he now regularly produced inscriptional poems for the important occasions in his friends' lives: a river-marriage poem in Welsh for the wedding of Welsh friends, a blessing in Latin for a baptism or confirmation. Prudence Pelham left him a legacy at her death in 1952 to supplement the income he received through Ede's plan. In 1964, when Helen Sutherland left him six thousand pounds, his assets were sufficient for Ede to arrange a guaranteed annuity. At the age of sixty-eight Jones had attained a degree of secure comfort. He received more visitors in his room at Harrow. Although he welcomed the conversation, his own speech was often painfully deliberate and tentative; he seemed to struggle with "the complication of what he has to say and the desire to get it exactly right." A new visitor had to learn not to fill a pause in the discussion with a new topic (one "asked 'Did you ever meet Chesterton?' between 'ap— ' and '—palling' "). His famous visitors included Auden, who, Jones would later confide, could never stop talking, and Igor Stravinsky, who would always remember the sight of Jones swaying to and fro in his chair, listening to a Gregorian chant on a portable gramophone he kept beneath his bed. His letters became longer; they took on the decorative quality of his inscriptions, done in different inks to create beautiful polychromatic effects.

The letters were also becoming discursive in a way that reflected his increasing attention to essay writing. Grisewood collected about twenty-five essays under the title *Epoch and Artist* in 1959. These were divided into four subjects: Welsh culture, the religious quality of art, early British history, and contemporary art and literature. The volume drew fire from Frank Kermode, who considered the attempt to view art as sacrament a backward step, "a kind of atavism, an inability to think, however sophisticatedly, in any but primitivistic terms." But Harold Rosenberg of the *New Yorker* (22 August 1964) claimed that the essays were fully alive to contemporary aesthetic problems, judging them "the most acutely relevant writing on contemporary form and value to have appeared in years." Jones's concern about the validity of traditional symbols and the fading awareness of history was, according to Rosenberg, legitimate and necessary. Rosenberg also perceived "the difference between him and the usual elegist of cultural decline: while conscious of being surrounded by modern decadence, instead of devoting himself

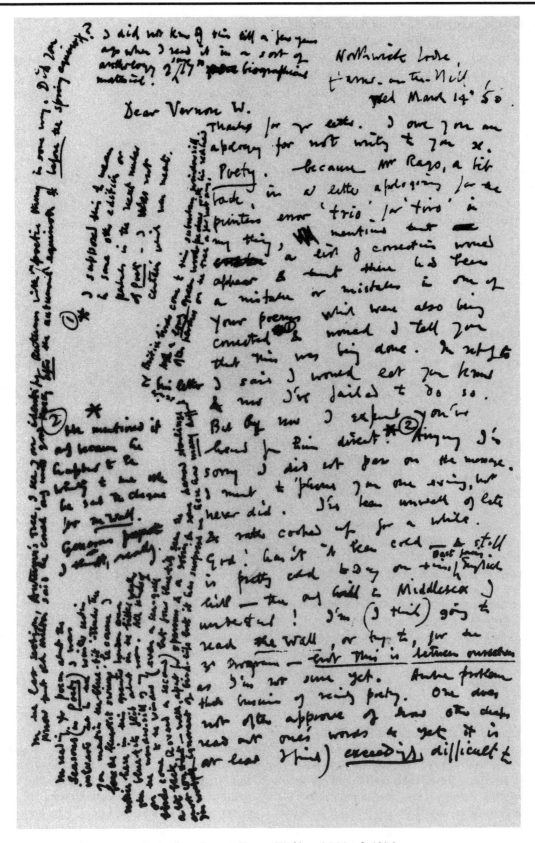

Letter from Jones to Vernon Watkins, 14 March 1956

to denouncing examples of it, he takes pleasure in the questions the decadence raises for him." This acclaim expressed the interest and admiration of an audience that had grown since the republication of *In Parenthesis* in a Viking Compass edition in 1963; the Viking edition of *The Anathemata* in 1965 further expanded the readership. Jones felt increasingly grateful to his American readers, "chaps who are *far* more receptive, willing to worry-out the meaning of a thing, more generous, naive—yes, perhaps, but more open, yes, more perceptive, not so inhibited and unresponsive as the English— . . ."

In March 1970 Jones fell, broke his leg, and suffered a slight, nondebilitating stroke. From the hospital he went to Calvary Nursing Home, also at Harrow, where he continued to write and revise the group of shorter poems collected and published as *The Sleeping Lord* in March 1974. His careful editing and shaping of these pieces becomes clear when one looks at the poetic manuscripts, published in 1981 as *The Roman Quarry and Other Sequences*, edited by Harman Grisewood and René Hague. Several of the "fragments" in *The Sleeping Lord* (all but the last are complete dramatic or lyric units) date from the early 1940s; others, like the title poem, were written as late as 1967. A special issue of *Agenda* in 1967 had collected six of these poems; two others, published in 1965 and 1969 in limited editions (*The Fatigue* and *The Tribune's Visitation*), and an excerpt from "The Book of Balaam's Ass" completed the collection. As with *In Parenthesis* and *The Anathemata*, Jones supervised the layout and typography of the book, attempting to balance prose and verse on the page. He also designed the cover and reproduced the inscriptions he had made for the two limited editions.

Excluding the introductory lyric and the final piece from "The Book of Balaam's Ass," the poems fall into two contrasting groups: four dramatic monologues by Roman soldiers in Jerusalem, hearkening back to Jones's own visit while recovering in 1934, and three lyric invocations of Celtic antiquity, derived from early Celtic mythology and literature. In "The Wall" and "The Dream of Private Clitus," perplexed Roman legionnaires complain from their outpost of the empire about the decay of the founding myths of the Roman republic. In "The Fatigue," a Roman principalis (equivalent to sergeant) directs the military detail for the Crucifixion of Christ; although he realizes the implications of the event, the jaded mood of imperial decadence prevails

David Jones, 1964 (photograph by Mark Gerson)

against his conversion. A tribune surprises his soldiers in their garrison in "The Tribune's Visitation"; the officer confesses his private dismay at the corruption of the original innocence of Rome. The speakers in "The Wall" and the audience for the other Roman poems are all legionnaires of mixed provincial recruitment—German and Celtic as well as Roman—and demonstrate as such the heterogeneous nature of the empire, the problems of a political order removed from its local origins. By contrast, the Celtic poems praise the virtues of local, rooted culture. "The Tutelar of the Place" celebrates the spirit of place in the person of a female "tutelar," an earth goddess who protects those of her own "place, time, demarcation, hearth, kin, enclosure" against the encroachment of a Roman Empire or a modern megalopolis. "The Hunt," which is based on the episode of Arthur's chasing the fabulous beast Trywth, invokes the sanctity of Welsh places, viewing Arthur as a Christ who rides and dies for the healing of the land. The longest of the Celtic poems is "The Sleeping Lord," which envisions Arthur asleep beneath the landscape of modern Wales. Like James Joyce's Finn asleep beneath Dublin, Arthur waits to be awakened to restore Wales to its ancient inheritance.

The artistry of voice and characterization may be the most striking features of the last poems. The Roman speakers reach a condensed, bitter eloquence to fit their disenchantment. A new contemporary accent falls here, too; into the Roman monologues Jones dubs the idiom of the modern cockney army. This joking anachronism may be traced back to the cockney speech he heard in the streets of Jerusalem under the British Mandate, but it also conveys the similarity he perceives between the late empire and the twentieth century. The Celtic poems, thick with references to Welsh geography and history and legend, also employ the formulaic language of early Welsh poetry. "The Sleeping Lord," for instance, is spoken in great part through the persona of the Welsh bard stationed in Arthur's household to deliver his funeral eulogy.

The characterization of the old poet in "The Sleeping Lord" might afford an antagonistic critic a portrait of Jones himself as an aging poet:

> But now that he was many winters old, the diverse nature of what he had read had become sadly intermeddled and very greatly confused.

Philip Toynbee, for example, labeled Jones "an eccentric figure on the periphery of English poetry." Critics in the United States and Britain, however, generally welcomed the new work. Peter Scupham, in the *New Statesman* (24 May 1974), praised the new "open dramatic quality running through the book." In the *Spectator* (4 May 1974), Seamus Heaney acclaimed Jones "an extraordinary writer," who has "returned to the origin and brought something back, something to enrich not only the language but people's consciousness of who they have been and who they consequently are." Reviewing the book in *Poetry* (January 1975), John Matthias outlined an intelligent American response to Jones, a response "conditioned by an encounter in his work with sheer *otherness*, things otherwise opaque made numinous by the craft of the maker. . . . In remembering, and in encountering things other, we are changed."

In 1973 *Agenda* commissioned Jones to write a poem for a second special issue. He resumed work on "The Kensington Mass," which he had begun in the early 1940s but subsequently lost, and it was published as a "work in progress" in 1974. In 1975 Agenda Editions brought out a softcover edition of the poem, including a series of manuscript drafts. These reveal Jones building his repetitive incantatory syntax by layers, draft by draft; the poem takes shape like a clay model built up by a sculptor's hand. He continued to work on the poem until his death on 28 October 1974.

The London *Times* obituary of 29 October repeated the comparison frequently drawn between David Jones and William Blake. Both were painters and poets; both were unusual and difficult artists to their contemporaries; both would belatedly receive the fame they deserved. The number of full-length critical studies of Jones steadily grows, and there are chapbooks ranging from personal appreciations to detailed explications. Jones's diversity of interests also invites treatment by historians and theologians, and the very difficulty of closing categories around him allows him to keep company with most major modern writers. The title of Jones's last book of poetry is mildly prophetic. Like the Sleeping Lord beneath the treasures of Wales, Jones's achievement waits, under the complex deposits of history and culture and religion, under the many layers of magic and strangeness, to be wakened and fully appreciated.

Letters:

Letters to Vernon Watkins, edited by Ruth Pryor (Cardiff: University of Wales Press, 1976);

List of Letters by David Jones, compiled by Charles J. Stoneburner (Granville, Ohio: Limekiln, 1977);

Letters to William Hayward, edited by Colin Wilcockson (London: Agenda, 1979);

Dai Greatcoat: A Self-Portrait of David Jones in His Letters, edited by René Hague (London & Boston: Faber & Faber, 1980);

Letters to a Friend, edited by Aneirin Talfan Davies (Swansea, U.K.: Triskele, 1980);

Inner Necessities: The Letters of David Jones to Desmond Chute, edited by Thomas Dilworth (Toronto: Anson-Cartwright, 1984).

Bibliography:

Samuel Rees, *David Jones: An Annotated Bibliography and Guide to Research* (New York & London: Garland, 1977).

Biographies:

René Hague, *David Jones* (Cardiff: University of Wales Press & Welsh Arts Council, 1975);

William Blisset, *The Long Conversation: A Memoir of David Jones* (Oxford & New York: Oxford University Press, 1981).

References:

Agenda, special Jones issue, 5 (Spring/Summer 1967);

Agenda, special Jones issue, 11-12 (Autumn/Winter 1973/1974);

Bernard Bergonzi, *Heroes' Twilight: A Study of the Literature of the Great War* (London: Constable, 1965; New York: Coward-McCann, 1965), pp. 198-212;

David Blamires, *David Jones: Artist and Writer* (Manchester: Manchester University Press, 1971; Toronto: University of Toronto Press, 1972);

William Blissett, "David Jones: 'Himself at the Cave Mouth,'" *University of Toronto Quarterly*, 36 (April 1967): 259-273;

Blissett, "*In Parenthesis* Among the War Books," *University of Toronto Quarterly*, 42 (Spring 1973): 258-288;

Thomas Dilworth, "The Anagogical Form of *The Anathemata*," *Mosaic*, 12 (Winter 1979): 183-195;

Dilworth, *The Liturgical Parenthesis of David Jones* (Ipswich, U.K.: Golgonooza Press, 1979);

Dilworth, "The Parenthetical Liturgy of David Jones," *University of Toronto Quarterly*, 42 (Spring 1973): 241-257;

Paul Fussell, *The Great War and Modern Memory* (New York & London: Oxford University Press, 1975), pp. 144-154;

René Hague, *A Commentary on The Anathemata of David Jones* (Wellingborough, U.K.: Christopher Skelton, 1977; Toronto: University of Toronto Press, 1977);

Jeremy Hooker, *David Jones: An Exploratory Study of the Writings* (London: Enitharmon, 1975);

John H. Johnston, *English Poetry of the First World War* (London: Oxford University Press, 1964; Princeton: Princeton University Press, 1964), pp. 284-340;

Roland Mathias, ed., *David Jones: Eight Essays on His Work as Writer and Artist* (Llandysul, U.K.: Gomer, 1976);

Samuel Rees, *David Jones* (Boston: Twayne, 1978);

Harold Rosenberg, "Aesthetics of Crisis," *New Yorker* (22 August 1964): 114-122;

Vincent B. Sherry, Jr., "David Jones's *In Parenthesis*: New Measure," *Twentieth Century Literature*, 28 (Winter 1982);

Sherry, "A New Boast for *In Parenthesis*: The Dramatic Monologue of David Jones," *Notre Dame English Journal*, 14 (Spring 1982): 113-128;

Sherry, "The Roman Quarry of David Jones: Signs and Wonders," *Chesterton Review*, 9 (February 1983): 46-55;

Elizabeth Ward, *David Jones, Mythmaker* (Manchester, U.K.: Manchester University Press, 1983).

Papers:

The National Library of Wales, Aberystwyth, has the manuscripts of *In Parenthesis* and *The Anathemata* as well as Jones's personal library; the Fisher Rare Book Library at the University of Toronto holds the letters to René Hague; and the Beinecke Rare Book Library at Yale University has the letters to Harman Grisewood.

Arthur Koestler

(5 September 1905 - 3 March 1983)

This entry was updated by Sidney A. Pearson, Jr. (Radford University) from his entry in DLB Yearbook: 1983.

BOOKS: *Von Weissen Nächten und Roten Tagen* (truncated version, Kharkov: Ukranian State Publishers for National Minorities, 1934);

Menschenopfer Unerhört (Paris: Editions du Carrefour, 1937); republished as *L'Espagne ensanglantée* (Paris: Editions du Carrefour, 1937); enlarged as *Spanish Testament* (London: Gollancz, 1937);

The Gladiators, translated by Edith Simon (London: Cape, 1939; New York: Macmillan, 1939);

Darkness at Noon, translated by Daphne Hardy (London: Cape, 1941; New York: Macmillan, 1941);

Scum of the Earth (London: Gollancz, 1941; New York: Macmillan, 1941);

Arrival and Departure (London: Cape, 1943; New York: Macmillan, 1943);

The Yogi and the Commissar (London: Cape, 1945; New York: Macmillan, 1945);

Twilight Bar: An Escapade in Four Acts (London: Cape, 1945; New York: Macmillan, 1945);

Thieves in the Night (London & New York: Macmillan, 1946);

Insight and Outlook (London & New York: Macmillan, 1949);

Promise and Fulfillment: Palestine 1917-1949 (London & New York: Macmillan, 1949);

The Age of Longing (London: Collins, 1951; New York: Macmillan, 1951);

Arrow in the Blue: An Autobiography (London: Collins/Hamilton, 1952; New York: Macmillan, 1952);

The Invisible Writing (London: Collins/Hamilton, 1954; New York: Macmillan, 1954);

The Trail of the Dinosaur, and Other Essays (London: Collins, 1955; New York: Macmillan, 1955);

Reflections on Hanging (London: Gollancz, 1956; New York: Macmillan, 1957);

The Sleepwalkers: A History of Man's Changing Vision of the Universe (London: Hutchinson, 1959; New York: Macmillan, 1959);

The Lotus and the Robot (London: Hutchinson, 1960; New York: Macmillan, 1961);

Arthur Koestler (© Fay Godwin)

Hanged by the Neck: An Exposure of Capital Punishment, by Koestler and C. H. Rolph (Cecil Rolph Hewitt) (Harmondsworth, U.K. & Baltimore: Penguin, 1961);

The Act of Creation (London: Hutchinson, 1964; New York: Macmillan, 1964);

The Ghost in the Machine (London: Hutchinson, 1967; New York: Macmillan, 1968);

Drinkers of Infinity. Essays 1955-1967 (London: Hutchinson, 1968; New York: Macmillan, 1969);

The Case of the Midwife Toad (London: Hutchinson, 1971; New York: Random House, 1972);

The Roots of Coincidence (London: Hutchinson, 1972; New York: Random House, 1972);

169

The Call-Girls (London: Hutchinson, 1972; New York: Random House, 1972);

The Challenge of Chance, by Koestler, Sir Alister Hardy, and Robert Harvie (London: Hutchinson, 1973; New York: Random House, 1974);

The Heel of Achilles. Essays 1968-1973 (London: Hutchinson, 1974; New York: Random House, 1975);

The Thirteenth Tribe. The Khazar Empire and Its Heritage (London: Hutchinson, 1976; New York: Random House, 1976);

Janus: A Summing-Up (London: Hutchinson, 1978; New York: Random House, 1978);

Bricks to Babel: Selected Writings With Comments by the Author (London: Hutchinson, 1980; New York: Random House, 1981);

Kaleidoscope (London: Hutchinson, 1981);

The Stranger on the Square, by Koestler and Cynthia Koestler (London: Hutchinson, 1983).

Collection: The Danube Edition of Koestler's works is being published in Great Britain by Hutchinson (1965-) and in the United States by Macmillan (1967-1970) and Random House (1982-).

OTHER: R. H. S. Crossman, ed., *The God That Failed*, includes an essay by Koestler (New York: Harper, 1950);

Alexander Weissberg, *The Accused*, foreword by Koestler (New York: Simon & Schuster, 1951);

Suicide of a Nation? An Inquiry Into the State of Britain Today, edited by Koestler (London: Hutchinson, 1963; New York: Macmillan, 1964);

Beyond Reductionism: New Perspectives in the Life Sciences, edited by Koestler and J. R. Smythies (New York: Macmillan, 1970);

"Humor and Wit," *Encyclopædia Britannica*, 15th Edition (1974).

Whoever would undertake the formidable task of writing the intellectual history of the twentieth century would be well advised to include in it the works of Arthur Koestler and the controversies they helped to spawn. These controversies were both bitter and continuous throughout Koestler's career because with each of his books he peeled away another layer of twentieth-century consciousness. Many of these arguments, especially those centered on the political realities of communism, were among the most heated intellectual battles of the twentieth century. In his

most powerful novel, *Darkness at Noon* (1941), Koestler explored the psychology of an individual Marxist so thoroughly that the novel itself has become inseparable from our general understanding of Karl Marx and the Marxists. Koestler's portrait of the revolutionary personality is so sharply drawn that it must be counted among the indispensable pieces in the intellectual mosaic of modern Western man.

Arthur Koestler was born on 5 September 1905 in Budapest, Hungary, which was then part of the Hapsburg Empire. His parents, Henrik and Adela Jeiteles Koestler, were prosperous middle-class Jews, proud of their heritage yet fully assimilated into Germanic culture. When World War I broke out, Koestler's parents moved to Vienna, where he received his early education. His elementary education completed, he decided to study science and engineering. His parents enrolled him in a *Realschule*, a school that specialized in science and modern languages. In 1922 he enrolled at the University of Vienna, where the climate of postwar politics quickly pushed his scientific interests into the background. Attracted to Zionism, he became involved in Zionist activities, and in 1926 he left school, with his studies incomplete, for Palestine, where he lived and worked on an Israeli kibbutz. In 1927 he went to work for the Ullstein chain of German newspapers as a Middle East correspondent. By June 1929 he had left the Middle East and was sent to work for the Ullstein News Service in Paris. He returned to Berlin in September 1930 and became science editor for *Vossische Zeitung*, one of the Ullstein newspapers. In 1932, disillusioned with Zionism, he secretly joined the German Communist party, but within a few months he was found out and was forced to resign his editorship. He went to work full-time for the party, taking a series of assignments that eventually led him to the Soviet Union (1932-1933), back to Western Europe (1933-1936), and finally to the Spanish civil war (1936-1937), undercover as an English journalist. He gradually became disillusioned with the party and the fruits of the Russian revolution and made a formal break with the party during the Spanish civil war. When World War II broke out, he was in France, where he was captured after the country fell to the invading Germans. He eventually escaped to England, where he worked with the BBC during the remainder of the war. After the war he resumed his occupation as a journalist, covering the birth of Israel. He became a British citizen and from the security of his adopted country engaged in the political battles that helped to make him one of the most controversial figures of his day.

Koestler's fluency in foreign languages helped to make his transition to writing in English easier than for most writers similarly situated. His mother tongue was Hungarian (Magyar), but he never wrote in it professionally. As a student in Vienna he pursued a course of study that emphasized modern languages along with science, and by the time he began to write professionally for Ullstein his first language was German. While living in France after the Spanish civil war and his apostasy from the party, Koestler wrote some articles in French, but German remained his literary language. His first two novels, *The Gladiators* (1939) and *Darkness at Noon*, were originally written in German and were translated into English by others. After *Darkness at Noon*, all of his professional writing was in English.

Koestler's domestic life is perhaps best described as "cosmopolitan." His first marriage was in 1935, during his active party days, to Dorothy Asher. At the time Koestler considered marriage a bourgeois institution that had been replaced by what was then called the "new proletarian morality." Nevertheless he did marry, not out of any sense of propriety but rather because they were living in Switzerland at the time, and Dorothy's passport was about to expire—it was either marriage or deportation for her. After a few months of marriage both parted company without bitterness or rancor. They remained good friends afterward, and during the Spanish civil war Dorothy was instrumental in gaining Koestler's release from one of Gen. Francisco Franco's jails. After a series of affairs during the next decade, Koestler met and eventually married his secretary Mamaine Paget in 1950. Mamaine and her twin sister had been prominent debutantes in England during the 1930s, and the marriage seems to have been happy initially. But within a year Koestler and Mamaine separated, evidently with mixed emotions on both sides. Mamaine died after a prolonged period of ill health in 1954. In the meantime Koestler had begun an affair with his secretary Cynthia Jefferies Patterson, whom he married in 1965. Cynthia was twenty-two years Koestler's junior, but their marriage proved to be his most durable, and apparently happiest, partnership. Cynthia was absolutely devoted to her husband, even to the point of joining him in suicide in 1983.

In terms of subject matter Koestler's career may be divided into two distinct periods. The first period, from the mid 1930s until the mid 1950s, is marked not only by the dominance of political issues but also by the single-minded intensity of his work. He later wrote that the desire to understand the nature of modern politics was the inspirational basis for all of his most creative writing. The second period, from the mid 1950s until his death in 1983, stands in sharp relief with the first period because it seems apolitical and eclectic by comparison. In his later writing Koestler consciously eschewed political polemics in order to pursue his lifelong interest in modern science, especially with reference to the philosophical meaning of the post-Newtonian revolution. But this dichotomy is more apparent than real. The conceptual linkage between the two periods becomes more evident when we ask, as Koestler did, what accounts for the curious fascination so many intellectuals have had for Marxist totalitarianism? It was Koestler's conclusion, derived in large measure from the results of his early work, that this fundamental question could not be satisfactorily answered apart from an inquiry into the origins of modern science. Totalitarian political ideologies, he thought, were rooted in the inability of modern science to give a sufficiently rational and truthful account of the human condition to satisfy man's natural longing for spiritual meaning. It is a more correct reading of Koestler's writing to see the second period as a logical and deeper outgrowth of the first.

Koestler joined the Communist party, he later wrote in *The God That Failed* (1950), out of many of the same impulses that prompt a person to embrace a church and a religion: "I became converted because I was ripe for it and lived in a disintegrating society thirsting for faith." This initial experience colored his subsequent interpretations of Communist psychology, as it was more akin to an act of faith than an act of reason. He saw himself as engaged in a morally pure enterprise—a grand experiment in creating the City of God in the here and now—as devoted to a pure utopia and in revolt against a polluted society. "To the psychiatrist," he wrote, "both the craving for Utopia and the rebellion against the status quo are symptoms of social maladjustment. To the social reformer, both are symptoms of a healthy rational attitude." When he left the Communist party in 1937, it was with a sense the party had betrayed, had left him, rather than the other way around. His commitment to utopia was still in-

Cynthia and Arthur Koestler (© Times Newspapers Limited)

tact, but he no longer saw the party as the vehicle to get from here to there. The problem with the revolution was that noble ends had become corrupted by ignoble means.

In Koestler's work the disparity between revolutionary ends and means is the modern version of the classic problem of the proper relationship between theory and practice. In one of his most influential essays he symbolized this dilemma as the problem of "The Yogi and the Commissar." These, he said, are the representative types of men who dominate all political debate, but from opposite ends of the political spectrum. At one end is the yogi, who represents the ethic of pure means. He believes that means alone count and will not compromise his moral integrity in pursuit of any end, no matter how noble, if that pursuit entails corrupt means. For all practical purposes then, the yogi is unable to act politically, but this scarcely seems important because his goal is not politics but rather communion with

the Absolute. At the other end of this idealized spectrum stands the pure form of the commissar mentality. The mirror image of the yogi in every respect, he is the supreme political activist who conceives of all morality in terms of the ends sought. There are no "immoral" means, merely "ignoble" ends. In the final analysis, Koestler argues, all political choices are reduced to a choice between the yogi and the commissar. The tragedy of twentieth-century politics is not only that it is dominated by the commissar types—that is more or less inevitable in every era—but that we have forgotten altogether the morality of the yogi, and the yogi is the only brake on the commissar's actions. Attempts to find what Koestler calls ideological "halfway houses" between these extremes are doomed to failure at the outset because they are divorced from the real world of political action. Practical participation in politics necessarily means an initial commitment to the commissar mentality—the personality of the modern revolutionary who is the symbol of the contemporary political dilemma.

Given these dilemmas inherent in the yogi-commissar continuum, Koestler arrived at the conclusion that all revolutions are doomed to failure from the beginning. The yogi and the commissar define the limits of political possibilities. This fundamental fact of political life limits the ability of political action to solve permanently the problems of the human condition. But it does not thereby follow from this analysis that all attempts at revolution will fail for the same reasons. Some will fail because excessive concern with means will prevent them from reaching their goal. Others will fail because their fixation on the end will lead them to ignore means, and corrupted means will prevent them from ever reaching their end. In terms of politics, the common bond between the yogi and the commissar is the experience of failure. What remains for the student of modern politics therefore is an empirical analysis of the specific causes of revolutionary failure. Koestler explored this problem in a trilogy of novels on the nature of revolutionary ethics: *The Gladiators*, *Darkness at Noon*, and *Arrival and Departure* (1943). Each novel was intended to depict a separate aspect of revolutionary morality in terms of the yogi and the commissar.

Koestler's first novel, *The Gladiators*, is a fictionalized account of the revolt of Spartacus's army of slaves and gladiators against Rome during the first century B.C. The date of publication is significant. At that time European Communist parties were splitting into factions and debating the course of the Russian revolution. It was, for many, turning out far differently under Joseph Stalin than they had expected. But what if Leon Trotsky had succeeded Lenin and not Stalin? Would it have made any difference in the later course of the revolution? Koestler's answer is that it *might* have made a difference, but not in terms of the ultimate success or failure of the revolution. If Trotsky had been more scrupulous than Stalin in his choices of means, the revolution would have been crushed; and if he had remained loyal to the ends of the revolution as defined by Marx, he would have had to act precisely as Stalin had done. In *The Gladiators*, Koestler portrayed the course of a revolution in which the means are allowed to dominate the end. The aim of Spartacus's revolt is to build a "Sun State," a gladiator-slave conception of utopia. So powerful is the dream that it inspires slaves and intellectuals throughout Italy to follow

Spartacus. Along the way the dream runs afoul of the "Law of Detours," the hidden law of all revolutionary movements that decrees that the leader must be ruthless in pursuit of the goal. But Spartacus has seen too much suffering and is too solicitous of the feelings of his followers, who do not understand the political necessity of the Law of Detours, and at a critical moment he fails to do what he must to build the Sun State; he fails to kill one of his subordinate commanders who has wantonly destroyed a town. After this the people no longer flock to his banner, and the Romans finally crush his revolt. Koestler's first lesson of revolutionary ethics is that to follow the morality of the yogi, the morality of means, is the surest road to defeat.

Koestler's second lesson of revolutionary ethics is the consequence of following the morality of the commissar. What would happen if the revolutionary leader were ruthless in pursuit of the final, eschatological end of human history, the perfect utopia that would abolish all human suffering and misery? Could the noblest end imaginable for a revolution justify the most savage means to bring it about? This course of political action was the subject of his most powerful work, *Darkness at Noon*.

The backdrop for *Darkness at Noon* is the Russian revolution and the infamous Moscow Purge Trials of the 1930s, although these historical events are never specifically mentioned by name. Stalin is a shadowy figure in the minds of the characters, referred to simply as "Number One." The physical action of the novel is slight. It consists of the arrest, interrogation, trial, and execution during the purges of one of the "Old Guard," Commissar N. S. Rubashov. The real heart of the novel is the intellectual unfolding of the revolutionary ethic in the mind of Rubashov. His personal problem is to understand where the revolution went wrong and reconcile his duty to the end of the revolution with his duty to the party that is the agent of that future. Rubashov has been singled out for public trial and execution, as opposed to a silent death in anonymity, precisely because of his lifelong dedication to the party and its goals. For reasons ordained by history, reasons that cannot be understood except through the eyes of the faithful, the revolution has reached a point at which it needs blood sacrifices to serve as examples to the still backward peasant and proletariat masses. Only the most dedicated party members, such as Rubashov, have been chosen for this special role because only they can be trusted not to betray the party in public trials—to confess to crimes they did not commit as a "last service to the Party."

At first Rubashov is reluctant to confess to these patently phony charges. He has come to doubt the truth that the party is supposed to embody and cannot render any last service. But his first interrogator, Comrade Ivanov, is confident that when Rubashov has time to think his thoughts out to their logical conclusion, he will confess of his own free will and not as the result of any physical torture. It is here, in the dialectic between Rubashov and his interrogators, first Ivanov and then Gletkin, that the full horror of the revolutionary mind-set is revealed. In the end Ivanov is right—Rubashov works out in his mind the logic of the revolutionary ideal and comes to will what the party wills, even his own death. When Gletkin finally puts a bullet in the back of Rubashov's neck, it comes as no surprise to the reader. But the intellectual agreement between Rubashov and Gletkin is a stunningly powerful and thought-provoking conclusion. It spawned a controversy over the nature of the Marxian revolutionary idea and its demonstrable appeal to many intellectuals that has never abated. Indeed, *Darkness at Noon* may be the prototypical and paradigmatic novel explaining such appeals.

At this point in the development of Koestler's approach to revolution, many of his friends and critics alike were left with certain problems of their own regarding his exact intentions. If the political morality of both the yogi and the commissar end in disaster, and there are no other options, what then is the basis for political action? Here, it must be said, Koestler was far better at diagnosing the problems than at prescribing remedies. The closest he came to exploring the contemporary basis of political activism in the light of his yogi-commissar spectrum was in his third novel, *Arrival and Departure*.

Arrival and Departure is the story of Peter Slavek, a vaguely East European refugee literally washed ashore in the country of "Neutralia" (Portugal) during the opening months of World War II. Like Koestler, Peter is a former party member who is disillusioned by the course of the revolution. Though a former commissar-type, he is not a yogi-type either. He is trying to find some halfway position between these two extremes. His problem in terms of fighting the Fascists is that outside of the movement he can find no rationale for political action. How can he act

without some goal that only the party can provide? His answer is that he cannot act, and so he remains in Neutralia, where he is confronted with conflicting arguments as to what he ought to do. As with the case of Rubashov, the central drama of the novel is in the mind of Peter as he tries to think through what he must do: rejoin the party, join the Fascists, remain neutral, or flee to England and fight for a cause that is less than perfect. Each of these choices carries certain implications in terms of a choice between what Koestler calls "expediency" versus "morality." In the end Peter chooses England, as did Koestler, but it is out of a sense of "decency" rather than moral reasoning. This is because Peter sees reason run amok in the modern world, and reason can no longer be the measure of men's deeds. Peter's choice does not make him a hero, because there is neither God nor classical reason by which his actions can be judged. Living midway between the yogi and the commissar is Koestler's equivalent to modern man's intellectual purgatory.

The reception of and reaction to Koestler's dramatic indictment of revolutionary morality was partly delayed by World War II. After the war, however, the full fury of the intellectual storm over Koestler's work began to break. The reaction in France was especially strong. The Leftist newspaper *Les Temps Moderne*, edited by Jean-Paul Sartre with Maurice Merleau-Ponty, two of the most influential French philosophers, was particularly outspoken in its criticisms. Merleau-Ponty collected his articles and published them as *Humanism and Terror* (1947), the most systematic Leftist critique of *Darkness at Noon* in the postwar years. There was, however, a certain irony in Merleau-Ponty's defense of Stalin's purges, for in defending revolutionary terror he affirmed the truth of Koestler's portrait of Rubashov more effectively than any work defending Koestler. These acrimonious intellectual debates in France were recorded in a fictional form by Simone de Beauvoir in *The Mandarins* (1954). The reaction to Koestler in England was slightly different. The more skeptical British habits of mind had difficulty accepting his thesis that Rubashov would confess for reasons of ideological motivation. In George Orwell's *Nineteen Eighty-Four* (1949), the victim, Winston Smith, confesses to certain crimes, but only following psychological torture—Orwell would have none of the "last service to the party" thesis. Everywhere the debates came more and more to ask the questions "What were the political motivations of the Communists and fellow travelers of the 1930s? Was Rubashov *really* an accurate portrait of the typical party member?"

The psychology and personal motivations of party members and fellow travelers led to a surge in what might be termed "confessional" writings during this period—autobiographical accounts by former party members on what attracted them to the Russian revolution in the first place. Were they duped by clever Soviet propaganda, or did they know full well what was going on and what they were doing from the beginning? The most widely read of these books was a collection of confessional accounts appropriately entitled *The God That Failed*. In it Koestler had the lead essay, and his personal account immediately took on an authority of near-biblical proportions. If there is an indispensable personal account of the "Pink Decade" by a former party member, it is surely this essay by Koestler. The other contributors were Ignazio Silone, André Gide, Stephen Spender, Louis Fischer, and Richard Wright. Koestler followed up this brief memoir of his party days with an impressive two-volume autobiography that took his personal story up to the eve of his joining the party in 1932, *Arrow in the Blue* (1952), and *The Invisible Writing* (1954). Autobiographical writing about the years after he left the party may be found in his fiction, essays, and historical writings, and in *The Stranger on the Square* (1983). This incomplete final volume of Koestler's autobiography, written jointly with his wife Cynthia and described as "an experimental autobiography by two hands," often presents contrasting views of Koestler's private and public life.

Koestler's last political fiction for almost two decades was *The Age of Longing* (1951). It was intended to be his final statement on the nature of politics in the mold of the yogi and the commissar. The general mood of the novel is a pessimism that is unusual even for Koestler's generally pessimistic worldview. Composed during the zenith of Stalin's postwar power, it conveys to the reader the general impression that Koestler is expecting the imminent outbreak of World War III. The setting is Paris, Bastille Day in the late 1950s—in the near-enough future to have a necessary element of immediacy about it. As with most of Koestler's novels, the physical action is slight. The action is almost all intellectual, in this case debates among Parisian intellectuals over the *real* threat to peace in Europe: some blame the Americans, and others the Russians; some say the

threat is more spiritual than political. All of the characters, in one way or another, long for a lost faith that none has known since his youth—faith in politics or faith in God. All are caught in some sort of political halfway position that prevents them from acting effectively in politics. Evidently for Koestler, postwar Paris lacked even that sense of decency that managed to move Peter in *Arrival and Departure*.

Most of the participants in these arguments are Leftist intellectuals who are unable to break out of their Marxist habits of thought in order to see the world aright. Only Julien, a disillusioned former party member, understands what is going on but is unable to convince anyone else that he is right. Julien is a Cassandra who tries to speak but is mute insofar as those around him are concerned. Julien no longer believes in "the West," and he appears to be motivated by no other cause than an unrelenting hostility to the "Free Commonwealth" (Koestler's euphemism for the Soviet Union). In the end no one listens, and the novel closes with rumors of Russian paratroopers landing just outside Paris. A new French underground is being formed, but without even a glimmer of the hope and spirit that animated the World War II resistance.

By the mid 1950s the polemics over the true nature of Marxism and revolution had reached a dead end for Koestler. When he bid a formal farewell to these political battles in 1955, it was not because he thought the issues had been settled, but rather, as he said, because he had nothing more original to say. He had exhausted his creative energies on the subject. Yet it is also important to note that more was involved here than a simple decision to abandon politics. It is apparent in some of Koestler's later work, fiction and nonfiction alike, that he was searching for a more rational mode of political knowledge than was being provided by the images of the yogi and the commissar. Koestler had always been impressed by the rupture between political theory and practice; all of his novels are predicated on that assumption. But he was still troubled by the inability of modern political theory to explain adequately the most salient features of modern politics. The reason for this gap, he thought, lay in a general failure of modern scientific thinking. The paradox was that most scientists were apolitical by nature and were only dimly aware, at most, of the impact science was having on the political world. The general result of this state of affairs was a profound misunderstanding both by scientists and the general public of the limits and possibilities of modern science. This was most conspicuous for those social and political theories, such as Marxism, that claimed to be "scientific." Koestler turned to the history and study of science because he was convinced that political theory could not advance beyond the sterility of debates between the Left and the Right until both sides had a better understanding of science itself.

The failure of modern political theory, so evident in the failed revolutions of the twentieth century, was linked, Koestler argued, to certain outmoded notions of science carried over from an earlier time. Marx and the Marxists are the very embodiment of that failure, since they are the children of a now obsolete view of science. Marx had argued for a class structure of knowledge because he saw the human mind formed in a materialistic and deterministic world—such were the lessons of Sir Isaac Newton applied to political thought. But, as Koestler understood it, twentieth-century science was nonmaterialistic, at least in the nineteenth-century meaning of the term, and probabilistic in its form. And, in any case, Koestler had always held that scientific truth, whatever it might be, was independent of any particular class structure in society. All of this added up to the notion that the first order of business in the restoration of reason to human affairs was the construction of a nonmaterial, probabilistic theory of the human mind. This task required an inquiry into the very origins of modern science and into its development until the twentieth century. It was this enterprise, a new science of the human mind suitable for the twentieth century, that occupied most of Koestler's work for the next quarter-century.

Koestler's major study of the science of the mind was in the form of a nonfiction trilogy, *The Sleepwalkers* (1959), *The Act of Creation* (1964), and *The Ghost in the Machine* (1967). In addition to these larger studies, Koestler authored several interesting diversionary excursions into sidelight areas of modern science: *The Case of the Midwife Toad* (1971), *The Roots of Coincidence* (1972), and a book he wrote with Sir Alister Hardy and Robert Harvie, *The Challenge of Chance* (1973). These last two works were serious studies of extrasensory perception (ESP) and the various implications of probability theory in human psychology. (Koestler left $600,000 to promote university study of psychic phenomena.)

The most impressive, as well as the most controversial, of Koestler's trilogy was *The Sleepwalk-*

ers. In broad outline, it is a survey of scientific thought from the early Greeks through the Newtonian revolution in physics. The primary emphasis, however, is on the period from Nicolaus Copernicus through Galileo Galilei, and Koestler deals with the issue of how the science of astronomy changed man's conception of himself. What helped to make Koestler's history both unique and controversial was his thesis on how science operates and develops. He challenged the widespread notion that there is a definite line between what scientists are wont to call "superstition" and science per se. Much of the inspiration for scientific discovery comes, he said, from an awe of the supernatural. Properly understood, religion and science are not polar-opposite ways of knowing, but rather are complementary. In arguing for this view of science Koestler questioned the accepted notion that scientific knowledge can be traced along a linear notion of historical development, one in which science is the progressive accumulation of knowledge and the shrinking of superstition. His basic proposition is that science proper is not necessarily progressive in character; that there is no clearly definable boundary between science and superstition (the "science" of one epoch quickly dissolves into the "superstition" of the next); and that science, instead of following a straight line of progress into the twentieth century, follows "a wild zig-zag which alternates between progress and disaster."

Koestler's emphasis in *The Sleepwalkers* was on the creativity of the scientific enterprise, and he steadily denied that the act of creativity is itself a scientific phenomenon. It is a mysterious working of the mind that can not be reduced to material causes. The flaw in scientific reasoning, however, is that in the contemporary world, knowledge has outstripped man's ability to control science; science now threatens to control man. The evolution of the human mind was too slow to cope with these changes, and the very future of the human species is in jeopardy. "Progress by definition can never go wrong; evolution constantly does; and so does the evolution of ideas, including those of the 'exact sciences.'" And since natural evolution had not equipped men to deal with the objects of their own creation, Koestler was prepared to suggest that man would somehow have to wrest from nature control over his own evolution. It was the only way man could regain control over science. Here, it must be said, Koestler may have been far more insightful in diagnosing a problem of modern science than prescribing a remedy, a fact he seems to have acknowledged later in his novel *The Call-Girls* (1972).

In *The Act of Creation* and *The Ghost in the Machine*, Koestler sought to diagnose the nature of human creativity analytically, not historically as he had done in *The Sleepwalkers*. The longest and most difficult of all of Koestler's books, *The Act of Creation* is almost an encyclopedia of knowledge and of his speculative thinking on the mystery we call "human creativity." He begins his study with an impressive inquiry into various forms of creativity—humor, wisdom, poetry, art, and creative writing. All of these acts of creation must be understood within a hierarchy of knowledge that tends to abolish any relevant distinctions between "wholes" and "parts," which is the way most scientists classify knowledge. It is a curious hierarchy without an apex because each apparent whole is in reality but a part of a larger whole; no whole or part can be understood as an end in and of itself. Wholes and parts present themselves to the mind with what Koestler calls a "Janus effect." "The members of a hierarchy, like the Roman god Janus, all have two faces looking in opposite directions." Wholes and parts are linked only through the mind in a mysterious joining of these wholes and parts that is the very essence of the act of scientific creation. The basic principles of this conception of hierarchy can be stated as follows:

> The laws of the higher cannot be reduced to, nor predicted from the lower level; the phenomenon of the lower level and their laws are implied in the higher level, but the phenomenon of the higher order if manifest in the lower level appear as unexplainable and miraculous.

These relationships between parts and wholes are the ultimate objects of science, but the linkage between them through the workings of the human mind is not itself a scientific act. It is one of the defects of the contemporary science of the mind—by which Koestler means primarily the behavioral psychology of B. F. Skinner and company—that it continues to operate not only from mechanistic assumptions but also as if wholes and parts of reality are in fact radically separate entities. Behavioral psychology, in brief, repeats all of the old, materialistic assumptions about the mind that have led Marxists into the abyss of Stalin's totalitarian politics. Unless the behaviorists alter their understanding of science, they will be led inevitably into the same fatal errors of the commissar's ethos. In *The Ghost in the*

Machine, Koestler delivers his most devastating critique of behaviorism: "An age is drawing to a close in the history of psychology: the age of the dehumanization of man. Words like 'purpose,' 'volition,' 'introspection,' 'consciousness,' 'insight,' words which have been banned as obscene from the vocabulary of the so-called 'Behavioral Sciences,' are triumphantly reasserting themselves—not as abstract philosophical concepts, but as indispensable descriptive tools without which even a rat's actions in an experimental maze do not make sense."

Although Koestler thought that behaviorism would collapse of its own internal contradictions and the accumulated weight of scientific knowledge, he was not optimistic about the ultimate future of a rational science of the mind. His science had a certain quality of desperation about it that grew more pronounced with the passage of time—as if science were "the god that must not fail." He saw science in general as the last line of resistance against a chaotic, threatening, and perhaps even demonic universe. Since political revolution could not cure the dilemmas of the human condition, science was the only alternative. But he did not really expect this to happen. Rationality and civility were a thin veneer over man as a species of animal that had not really evolved very much since genesis. In his essay on capital punishment, he wrote, "Deep inside every civilized being there lurks a tiny Stone Age man, dangling a club to rob and rape, and screaming an eye for an eye." The application of science to the ills of the human condition required at a minimum two preconditions. First, the *right* science had to be chosen for application. How could this be done when most working scientists still thought in terms of parts and wholes that are distinct from one another? Second, any application of science implied a conscious political act. How could the cure be applied without encountering the old nemesis of political action, the images of the yogi and the commissar? This problem of trying to bring modern science to bear on politics was the subject of his last work of fiction, *The Call-Girls*.

The Call-Girls may be the least read of all Koestler's fiction. This is most unfortunate, because it may also be his best work after *Darkness at Noon*. Surely his wittiest and most playful book, it displays a strong sense of humor that readers of Koestler's other work might not have suspected. The setting is an academic conference, high in a remote Alpine village, where the greatest scientific minds of the age have been assembled for the expressed purpose of formulating a "plan" for the salvation of mankind through science. The pretentious title of the conference is "Approaches to Survival," and it has been hastily called by Nobel Prize-winning physicist Nikolai Solovief, one of the original members of the "Manhattan Project" team that built the first atomic bomb. The other almost equally distinguished participants represent a broad spectrum of scholarly, scientific opinion on the science of the human mind as it is currently understood. The tragedy of the conference is that each of these scientists has only a partial view of science qua science but fervently believes that their part is a whole. Naturally these various parts are logically incompatible, and there is no agreement on what would constitute a viable synthesis between them. Furthermore, even if the participants could agree on a single course of action and proposal, there is considerable doubt that any government would pay any attention to them.

The various scientific ideas are presented in the form of academic papers, read and debated at the conference. Here Koestler is at his best in breathing life into the scientific controversies that are normally only matters of esoteric interest for specialists. As for the specific proposals, they range from the bizarre to the frightening to the oddly plausible. But while the reader may be intrigued by arguments that he has never heard, the participants themselves are engaged in a sham debate. They know each other intimately, having delivered these same papers repeatedly at previous conferences, and they are even then preparing to leave for still more conferences where the same issues will be rehashed again. Each of these intellectual "call girls" resembles a modern Sisyphus, endlessly and impotently struggling against something inevitable. But Koestler also leaves the reader with the impression that much of what is produced by modern science may have much in common with the Augean stables—without a Hercules to clean them out. In the end the conference breaks up with predictably nothing to show for the efforts. The participants depart for their next conference with the threat of World War III in the background. "In view of the international situation, however, nobody could be sure whether they would reach their destination."

With *The Call-Girls*, even science had apparently exhausted itself as a subject of interest for Koestler. In *The Thirteenth Tribe* (1976) he attempted to trace the origins of European Jewry

to a non-Semitic people. His basic thesis was that the roots of European anti-Semitism were irrational because European Jews were not really Semitic people to begin with. Koestler's history was, to say the least, controversial. Most serious scholars of the subject dismissed the book rather curtly, and rightly so. It was an unfortunate epitaph for his scattered writings on Israel and Jewish affairs. His earlier novel on life in an Israeli kibbutz, *Thieves in the Night* (1946), and his reporting of the creation of Israel in *Promise and Fulfillment* (1949) remain interesting, though relatively minor, pieces of Koestler's work.

Even in death Arthur Koestler was characteristically controversial. He died in a double suicide with his wife—a suicide evidently prompted by the effects of leukemia and Parkinson's disease on his health. The Koestlers were members of the voluntary euthanasia society EXIT. Koestler became one of its vice-presidents in 1981, writing a preface to the group's *Guide to Self-Deliverance* on how to commit suicide. Humans, he wrote, unlike animals, do not die "peacefully and without fuss in old age." Koestler's death was apparently peaceful, unlike the demise of his fictional commissars.

Bibliography:
Frank Day, *Arthur Koestler: A Guide to Research* (New York: Garland, 1987).

Biographies:
Pierre Debray-Ritzen, *Arthur Koestler* (Paris: Herne, 1975);
Sidney A. Pearson, Jr., *Arthur Koestler* (Boston: G. K. Hall, 1978);
Iain Hamilton, *Koestler: A Biography* (London: Secker & Warburg, 1982; New York: Macmillan, 1982);
Mark Levene, *Arthur Koestler* (New York: Ungar, 1984).

References:
Jeni Calder, *Chronicles of Conscience. A Study of George Orwell and Arthur Koestler* (London: Secker & Warburg, 1968);
Bernard Crick, "Koestler's Koestler," *Partisan Review*, 2 (1982): 274-283;
Harold Harris, ed., *Astride the Two Cultures—Arthur Koestler at 70* (London: Hutchinson, 1975);
Harris, ed., *Stranger on the Square: Arthur and Cynthia Koestler* (New York: Random House, 1984);

Maurice Merleau-Ponty, *Humanism and Terror*, translated by John O'Neill (Boston: Beacon Press, 1969);

Murray A. Sperber, ed., *Arthur Koestler: A Collection of Critical Essays* (Englewood Cliffs, N.J.: Prentice-Hall, 1977).

C. S. Lewis
(29 November 1898 - 22 November 1963)

This entry was updated by Eugene McGovern from his entry in
DLB 15: British Novelists, 1930-1959: Part One.

See also the Lewis entry in DLB 100: Modern British Essayists: Second Series.

BOOKS: *Spirits in Bondage*, as Clive Hamilton (London: Heinemann, 1919);

Dymer, as Hamilton (London: Dent, 1926; New York: Dutton, 1926);

The Pilgrim's Regress: An Allegorical Apology for Christianity, Reason and Romanticism (London: Dent, 1933; New York: Sheed & Ward, 1935; revised edition, London: Bles, 1943; New York: Sheed & Ward, 1944);

The Allegory of Love: A Study in Medieval Tradition (Oxford: Clarendon Press, 1936; New York: Oxford University Press, 1958);

Out of the Silent Planet (London: Bodley Head, 1938; New York: Macmillan, 1943);

Rehabilitations and Other Essays (London & New York: Oxford University Press, 1939);

The Personal Heresy, by Lewis and E. M. W. Tillyard (London & New York: Oxford University Press, 1939);

The Problem of Pain (London: Bles & Centenary Press, 1940; New York: Macmillan, 1944);

The Screwtape Letters (London: Bles, 1942; New York: Macmillan, 1943);

Broadcast Talks (London: Bles, 1942); republished as *The Case for Christianity* (New York: Macmillan, 1943);

A Preface to "Paradise Lost" (London & New York: Oxford University Press, 1942; revised and enlarged, 1959);

Christian Behaviour (London: Bles, 1943; New York: Macmillan, 1943);

C. S. Lewis, 1950

Perelandra (London: Bodley Head, 1943; New York: Macmillan, 1944);

The Abolition of Man (London: Oxford University Press, 1943; New York: Macmillan, 1947);

Beyond Personality: The Christian Idea of God (London: Bles, 1944; New York: Macmillan, 1945);

179

That Hideous Strength (London: Bodley Head, 1945; New York: Macmillan, 1946);

The Great Divorce (London: Bles, 1945; New York: Macmillan, 1946);

Miracles (New York: Macmillan, 1947; London: Bles, 1947);

Arthurian Torso, by Lewis and Charles Williams (London & New York: Oxford University Press, 1948);

Transposition (London: Bles, 1949); republished as *The Weight of Glory* (New York: Macmillan, 1949);

The Lion, The Witch and the Wardrobe (London: Bles, 1950; New York: Macmillan, 1950);

Prince Caspian (London: Bles, 1951; New York: Macmillan, 1951);

The Voyage of the "Dawn Treader" (London: Bles, 1952; New York: Macmillan, 1952);

Mere Christianity (London: Bles, 1952; New York: Macmillan, 1952);

The Silver Chair (London: Bles, 1953; New York: Macmillan, 1953);

The Horse and His Boy (London: Bles, 1954; New York: Macmillan, 1954);

English Literature in the Sixteenth Century, Excluding Drama, volume 3 of the *Oxford History of English Literature* (Oxford: Clarendon Press, 1954);

The Magician's Nephew (London: Bodley Head, 1955; New York: Macmillan, 1955);

Surprised by Joy: The Shape of My Early Life (London: Bles, 1955; New York: Harcourt, Brace, 1956);

The Last Battle (London: Bodley Head, 1956; New York: Macmillan, 1956);

Till We Have Faces (London: Bles, 1956; New York: Harcourt, Brace, 1957);

Reflections on the Psalms (London: Bles, 1958; New York: Harcourt, Brace, 1958);

Studies in Words (Cambridge: Cambridge University Press, 1960);

The Four Loves (London: Bles, 1960; New York: Harcourt, Brace, 1960);

The World's Last Night, and Other Essays (New York: Harcourt, Brace, 1960);

A Grief Observed (London: Faber & Faber, 1961; Greenwich, Conn.: Seabury Press, 1963);

An Experiment in Criticism (Cambridge: Cambridge University Press, 1961);

They Asked for a Paper (London: Bles, 1962);

The Discarded Image (Cambridge: Cambridge University Press, 1964);

Letters to Malcolm (London: Bles, 1964; New York: Harcourt, Brace & World, 1964);

Poems, edited by Walter Hooper (London: Bles, 1964; New York: Harcourt, Brace & World, 1965);

Screwtape Proposes a Toast (London: Collins, 1965);

Studies in Medieval and Renaissance Literature, edited by Hooper (Cambridge: Cambridge University Press, 1966);

Of Other Worlds: Essays and Stories, edited by Hooper (London: Bles, 1966; New York: Harcourt, Brace & World, 1967);

Spenser's Images of Life, edited by Alistair Fowler (Cambridge: Cambridge University Press, 1967);

Christian Reflections, edited by Hooper (London: Bles, 1967; Grand Rapids, Mich.: Eerdmans, 1967);

Narrative Poems, edited by Hooper (London: Bles, 1969; New York: Harcourt Brace Jovanovich, 1972);

Selected Literary Essays, edited by Hooper (Cambridge: Cambridge University Press, 1969);

God in the Dock, edited by Hooper (Grand Rapids, Mich.: Eerdmans, 1970); republished as *Undeceptions* (London: Bles, 1971);

Fern-seed and Elephants, edited by Hooper (London: Fontana, 1975);

The Dark Tower, edited by Hooper (London: Collins, 1977; New York: Harcourt Brace Jovanovich, 1977);

On Stories and Other Essays, edited by Hooper (New York: Harcourt Brace Jovanovich, 1982);

Boxen: The Imaginary World of the Young, edited by Hooper (London: Collins, 1985);

Present Concerns (San Diego: Harcourt Brace Jovanovich, 1986).

Collections: *The Complete Chronicles of Narnia*, 7 volumes (Harmondsworth, U.K.: Penguin, 1965; New York: Macmillan, 1970);

A Mind Awake: An Anthology of C. S. Lewis, edited by Clyde S. Kilby (London: Bles, 1968; New York: Harcourt, Brace & World, 1969);

The Joyful Christian (New York: Macmillan, 1977);

Space Trilogy (New York: Macmillan, 1978);

The Essential C. S. Lewis (New York: Macmillan, 1988).

C. S. Lewis has several reputations. He was an important and respected critic and literary scholar, specializing in medieval and Renaissance English literature. To the public he has been well known for fifty years as an expositor and defender of Christian beliefs. And in his remarkably varied canon—drama and biography are the only genres to which he made no contribution—there is fiction in sufficient amount, and of sufficient interest, to give him considerable standing as a novelist.

Clive Staples Lewis was born on 29 November 1898 in Belfast, Ireland, into the comfortable household of Albert James Lewis, a solicitor, and Flora Augusta Hamilton Lewis. His mother died when he was nine years old; his only sibling, three years his senior, was Warren Hamilton Lewis (1895-1973), the author of *The Splendid Century* (1953) and other works on seventeenth- and eighteenth-century France. C. S. Lewis attended several schools in Belfast and in England, but the most important part of his preuniversity education came during the two-and-a-half years he spent as a private pupil of W. T. Kirkpatrick (1848-1921), a man revered by Lewis for the intellectual training he provided. Lewis entered Oxford in 1917, then joined the army and served in France with the Somerset Light Infantry. He was wounded in 1918 and returned to Oxford in 1919. His undergraduate career was distinguished by his receiving firsts in three courses: honour moderations (Greek and Latin literature), greats (philosophy and history), and English. His first academic appointment was a temporary position at Oxford in 1924-1925 as a tutor in philosophy, taking the place of a tutor who was spending a sabbatical year in America. In 1925 Lewis was elected a fellow of Magdalen College, Oxford, as a tutor in English language and literature. He held this position until 1954, when he left Oxford to accept the chair of medieval and Renaissance literature at Magdalene College, Cambridge. He married Joy Davidman Gresham (1915-1960), an American poet and novelist, in 1956. His death on 22 November 1963, from heart failure following an extended illness, came on the same day as did those of John F. Kennedy and Aldous Huxley.

Though Lewis was the English tutor at Magdalen College, his early studies in philosophy were frequently put to use during the 1930s. It often happened that too few students were reading English to keep Lewis occupied, and in such terms he took students in philosophy, politics, and history. He was known as a demanding tutor and as a superb lecturer. His was a strong personality, and he became well known in Oxford, his views provoking both agreement and disagreement. Helen Gardner has said of him: "He aroused warm affection, loyalty, and devotion in his friends, and feelings of almost equal strength

among innumerable persons who knew him only through his books. But he also aroused strong antipathy, disapproval, and distaste among some of his colleagues and pupils, and among some readers. It was impossible to be indifferent to him." The antipathy Lewis aroused seems to have played a part in his never having been offered a professorship at Oxford and in his defeat by C. Day Lewis in the election for professor of poetry in 1951.

One of Lewis's important activities was the Oxford Socratic Club, founded in 1942 to sponsor weekly debates on "the *pros* and *cons* of the Christian religion." Lewis was the president of the Socratic Club for its first twelve years, and he was its most frequent and best-known speaker. Even more important than the Socratic Club was "the Inklings," an informal group that gathered weekly for reading and criticism of works in progress. It was centered on Lewis, with Charles Williams and J. R. R. Tolkien playing major roles. John Wain—poet, novelist, biographer of Samuel Johnson, one of Lewis's pupils, and later a "junior member" of the Inklings—has given (in his autobiography, *Sprightly Running*, 1962) a striking, and not altogether flattering, picture of Lewis in both the Socratic Club and the Inklings.

Lewis's first scholarly work was *The Allegory of Love: A Study in Medieval Tradition* (1936), which received the Gollancz Memorial Prize for Literature in 1937 and which is credited with providing a seminal reading of Sir Edmund Spenser. Other important scholarly works are *English Literature in the Sixteenth Century, Excluding Drama* (1954, volume three in the *Oxford History of English Literature*) and *A Preface to "Paradise Lost"* (1942; revised and enlarged, 1959). Many of his wide-ranging essays are collected in *Studies in Medieval and Renaissance Literature* (1966) and *Selected Literary Essays* (1969).

Lewis's early ambition was to be a poet, and his first two published volumes, *Spirits in Bondage* (1919) and *Dymer* (1926), were poetry. They were followed in 1933 by *The Pilgrim's Regress*, a polemical book modeled on John Bunyan's *Pilgrim's Progress* (1678) and fairly described by its subtitle, *An Allegorical Apology for Christianity, Reason and Romanticism*. Lewis later judged that *The Pilgrim's Regress* suffered from "needless obscurity, and an uncharitable temper," and critics have tended to agree with that evaluation.

Out of the Silent Planet (1938), a fairly short piece of science fiction, was Lewis's first novel. A Cambridge philologist named Elwin Ransom is abducted to Mars (Malacandra) by Weston, a world-famous physicist who is determined to help mankind spread to other planets and to the rest of the universe (an enterprise Lewis deplored), and Devine, a man interested in interplanetary matters only for the money to be made by exploiting the natural resources and the inhabitants of other planets. Earth is Thulcandra, the planet of the novel's title, silent because it is under the control of the Bent One. On Malacandra, Ransom escapes from Weston and Devine and lives for a time with some of the inhabitants. He becomes familiar with "eldila" (angels) and discovers that the planet is the home of three distinct rational species, corresponding to artisans, poets, and philosophers. Weston and Devine kill an inhabitant and are brought to trial, with Ransom serving as interpreter for the court. Lewis provides some satire when Ransom translates Weston's florid expression of ideas from Bernard Shaw (*Back to Methuselah*, 1922) and Olaf Stapleton (*First and Last Men*, 1931) into simple language. Weston and Devine are found guilty and are forced to return to Earth. Ransom accompanies them, protected from the villains by eldila. Lewis soon began a sequel to *Out of the Silent Planet*, but abandoned the attempt when it was perhaps one-fourth finished. This fragment was published in 1977 as *The Dark Tower* in a volume that also contains the rest of Lewis's short fiction: four stories and another fragment of an unfinished novel, "After Ten Years."

The second of Lewis's science-fiction novels to be published was *Perelandra* (1943). Ransom is sent to Venus (Perelandra) to prevent a Fall from taking place there. That is, Perelandra has not seen a counterpart of the eating of the forbidden fruit that occurred on Earth; there is an imminent danger of such an event, however, and Ransom's task is to avert it. The tempter is Weston, whose devotion to science is now forgotten and who is so corrupted as to be called "the Unman." The conflict takes the form of a learned and profound debate that occupies one-fourth of the novel, Weston offering the temptation to the Perelandran Eve and Ransom arguing against him. The debate ends in a physical fight, followed by a long chase that ends in Weston's death. Perelandra has been saved, and the guiding intelligences of the other planets gather to celebrate in a great dance of elaborate imagery.

The final book of Lewis's space trilogy is *That Hideous Strength* (1945), the longest of the three novels and the one with the most complicated structure. All of the action takes place on

Earth, in and around a university town. The National Institute of Coordinated Experiments (NICE) enlists the help of Mark Studdock, a young sociologist, in order to approach his wife. Jane Studdock is subject to dreams in which she can locate the grave of Merlin. The NICE wants to find the grave, revive Merlin, and make use of his magical powers. Ransom appears again, this time as the director of a company that succeeds in finding Merlin and defeating the NICE.

Lewis packs *That Hideous Strength* with scenes from college politics, bureaucracy, journalism, and married life, and he has much to say about academic ambition, education, equality and obedience, language and abuses of it, scientism and social science, vivisection, magic, the legend of King Arthur, and medieval cosmology, a subject he treated more fully in 1964 in his somewhat neglected scholarly work, *The Discarded Image*. All of this is kept under an impressive control, with the many discursive elements never interfering with the narrative.

It was rather unusual for a scholar in 1938 to choose other planets for the settings of novels, but Lewis had too many predecessors in science fiction for him to be called a pioneer in the genre. He gave his reasons for his choice in two essays, "On Stories" (1947) and "On Science Fiction" (1955). He chose science fiction, he said, for the opportunity it gave, by the otherness of its unfamiliar settings, to the operation of the imagination on the fantastic. Some critics have faulted Lewis for the small attention he gave to scientific hardware. It was an objection he did nothing to meet: "The most superficial appearance of plausibility—the merest sop to our critical intellect—will do." On the way to Malacandra, for instance, Weston "explains" to Ransom that the spacecraft is powered by "exploiting the less observed properties of solar radiation," and, when Ransom has to be gotten to Perelandra, he is simply transported by eldila.

Some critics have claimed to detect an "anti-scientific" streak in Lewis, giving as evidence the treatment that science and scientists receive in the space trilogy. If the charge is that Lewis believed there are other ways than science to study reality and to acquire knowledge, then he would be glad to plead guilty. But when J. B. S. Haldane, in 1946, made the charge that Lewis depicted science and scientists unfairly, Lewis responded vigorously with "A Reply to Professor Haldane." The only real scientists who appear in the novels (Weston and William Hingest, a hero

Lewis's drawing of Screwtape

in *That Hideous Strength*) are treated with a good deal of respect. Ridicule and contempt are dealt only to Devine, greedy for wealth in *Out of the Silent Planet* and, having become Lord Feverstone, for power in *That Hideous Strength*, and to a few fuddled bureaucrats. As Lewis replied to Haldane, "If anyone ought to feel himself libelled by *That Hideous Strength* it is not the scientist but the civil servant: and, next to the civil servant, certain philosophers." Logical positivists were prominent among the "certain philosophers," and Lewis had attacked their views on ethics and aesthetics in *The Abolition of Man* (1943), a short and important book.

Critical response to the space trilogy has been generally favorable, with science-fiction authors Arthur C. Clarke and Marjorie Hope Nicholson (*Voyages to the Moon*, 1948) giving Lewis high marks for the quality of his conception and for the skill of its execution. C. N. Manlove (*Modern*

Fantasy, 1975) entered a dissenting opinion in his chapter on *Perelandra*.

Two items of Lewis's religious fiction were published in the 1940s. *The Screwtape Letters* (1942) is a collection of thirty-one letters of advice and guidance from Screwtape, an experienced devil, to Wormwood, a young tempter who is dealing with his first human patient. Screwtape's counsel concerns the patient's dealings with his family, his falling in love and his becoming a Christian, popular culture and its fads, and the effect of the Zeitgeist. Alas for Wormwood, the patient is killed in an air raid while doing his duty and with his soul at peace; Wormwood has failed, and Screwtape reminds him that forgiveness has no place in the lowerarchy. The book was a huge success, and many essayists have since chosen to cast their efforts in the form of "Screwtape Letters." A striking fact about *The Screwtape Letters* is the offhand way in which

Screwtape views World War II. The letters appeared in successive issues of a weekly religious newspaper, the *Guardian*, through the second half of 1941 and then were collected into a book. Those were dark days in Britain, but Screwtape attaches little importance to the war: "I am not in the least interested in knowing how many people in England have been killed by bombs. In what state of mind they died, I can learn from the office at this end. That they were going to die sometime I knew already. Please keep your mind on your work."

The Great Divorce (1945) also appeared first in weekly installments in the *Guardian*. It is a dream vision in which the narrator accompanies a busload of souls from hell on a trip to the outskirts of heaven. Each chapter is an episode in which a soul has to wrestle with its sin—selfishness, lust, greed, arrogance—and decide either to repent and win heaven or to refuse and return to hell. An important part is played by the soul of novelist and poet George MacDonald, whose fantasies *Phantastes* (1858) and *Lilith* (1895) Lewis loved, and who serves as a guide for the narrator, much as Virgil served as a guide for Dante.

Another major activity of Lewis's during the war was his speaking on Christianity to groups of servicemen. His voice was found to be very good for radio broadcasting, so he proceeded to give four series of talks over the BBC. These talks were later collected and published as *Mere Christianity* (1952). George Orwell was contemptuous of the book when it appeared ("chummy little wireless talks"), but it has become the best-known of Lewis's works and has sold many millions of copies. There is nothing ironic in the title *Mere Christianity*. It is a phrase Lewis found in the works of Richard Baxter, a Puritan theologian. The "mere" refers to that which is common to the beliefs of all Christians, Protestant, Catholic, and Orthodox; "mere Christianity" is Christianity without sectarian additions.

It was unusual for an Oxford don to write science fiction in 1938, but it was less surprising than Lewis's next venture in fiction. Yearly between 1950 and 1956 there appeared the seven volumes of the "Chronicles of Narnia": *The Lion, The Witch and the Wardrobe* (1950), *Prince Caspian* (1951), *The Voyage of the "Dawn Treader"* (1952), *The Silver Chair* (1953), *The Horse and His Boy* (1954), *The Magician's Nephew* (1955), and *The Last Battle* (1956). These are stories written expressly for children. There is (as Lewis pointed out) "no love interest and no close psychology"; the vocabulary is simple; the action is exciting; children have large roles; and the chapters are of uniform length for convenience in reading aloud. Narnia is a world other than ours. It can be entered only by certain children and only at certain times. Narnian time runs independently of English time: a Narnian year may be much longer or much shorter than an English year. Through each of the stories strides Aslan, a huge lion. It is Aslan who creates Narnia (in *The Magician's Nephew*), sacrifices his life for one of the human children (in *The Lion, The Witch and the Wardrobe*), protects Narnia in times of trouble, and draws the curtain at the close of Narnian history (in *The Last Battle*).

Lewis provided a good deal of information about his methods and his intentions in the Narnian stories in several essays collected in *Of Other Worlds* (1966). "All of my seven Narnian books," said Lewis, "and my three science fiction books, began with seeing pictures in my head. At first they were not a story, just pictures. The *Lion* all began with a picture of a Faun carrying an umbrella and parcels in a snowy wood. This picture had been in my mind since I was about sixteen. Then one day, when I was about forty, I said to myself: 'Let's try to make a story about it.'" Once embarked on the Narnian stories, he said, "I thought I saw how stories of this kind could steal past a certain inhibition which had paralyzed much of my own religion in childhood. Why did one find it so hard to feel as one was told one ought to feel about God or about the sufferings of Christ? I thought the chief reason was that one was told one ought to. An obligation to feel can freeze feelings. . . . But supposing that by casting all these things into an imaginary world, stripping them of their stained-glass and Sunday school associations, one could make them for the first time appear in their real potency? Could one not thus steal past those watchful dragons?"

This is not to say that Lewis took the stories as an opportunity to introduce his readers to the content of the New Testament. Lewis hoped that Narnia might prepare the imagination to receive the New Testament, rather than to reject it with distaste, but the stories are not at all a retelling of the Gospels. What Aslan does is not what Christ did in his time on earth, said Lewis, but what Christ might do were there to be a world like Narnia. This has not prevented the use of the Narnia stories in ways that would have exasperated their author. Readers have described how

Two Kinds of Memory.

Oh still vacation, silver
Pause and relaxing of severer laws,
Oh Memory the compassionate,
Forever in the quiet pools of reverie
How you refresh the past, how you refashion it!

But iron Memory, tyrant
Importunate by night! whose lucid torture
Still back into the merciless,
Unalterable fact and choking halter of
The finished past, without appeal, coërces us.

Well did our fabling elders
Appoint two differing powers to rule with joint
Authority the underworld:
Persephone, the lost and found, the ineffable
Lady of spring and death, august and wonderf'—

And Hades unevaded,
Stern and exact, whom neither prayers can turn
Nor lapse of ye... s can mitigate;
On Orpheus when, the second time, he forfeited
Eurydice, he gazed, precise, unpitying.

His mercies even are cursed
Mockeries of life, cold, cold as lunar rock,
And all his famed Elyzium
Worthless, if former joys in all their earth lines
Must there recur, mechanically, dizzily.

And round forever, borne for
No goal, caught in a circular rut, the soul
Re-lives her past—Orion on
His quarry and upon his foe the warrior
Ever pursuing and forever triumphing.

Thus Thus hoarding and recording
He keeps the mummied past. In her it sleeps,
Dreams, stirs... then soft! the magical
Blendings and overgrowings, and the tenderness
Of budded spring makes green the graves of tragedies;

And joys remembered, poising
One moment on the past which was their home,
Spread wings, and then with arrowy,
Swift flight in airy song are off to light upon
The branches of the sun-shot woods of Paradise.

Manuscript for "Two Kinds of Memory" (Sotheby's auction catalogue, 14 March 1979)

185

they have used the stories in Sunday-school classes, the students turning from Luke to *The Voyage of the "Dawn Treader"* and from *The Last Battle* to Revelation.

Narnia has been a great popular success. The sales of the "Chronicles" have gone into the millions. There have been an animated film version on television, recordings from Caedmon, posters and maps, bumper stickers, a jigsaw puzzle, and a calendar. Some critics, Madeleine L'Engle among them, have been enthusiastic about the "Chronicles of Narnia." Others have rejected these fairy tales, but usually, it seems, for ideological reasons, not literary ones. The theological element in the stories seems excessive to some readers, while others have objected to the violence of some of the battles and to the large place the stories give to such conventional virtues as courage, honesty, and self-control. J. R. R. Tolkien was among those who were sharply critical of his friend's children's stories, apparently because he thought they were too allegorical. (Lewis insisted the stories were not allegories.)

Lewis's last novel was *Till We Have Faces* (1956), a retelling of the myth of Cupid and Psyche. The setting is about 250 B.C. in Glome, a semibarbarous land on the fringes of the Hellenic world. The narrator is Orual, queen of Glome, an ugly woman and the older half-sister of the beautiful Psyche. Most of the novel is autobiography offered by the elderly Orual in support of her complaint against the gods for the life she was given to lead. She was treated unfairly by the gods, she says, and she is blind to what is obvious to the reader: throughout her life she has exhibited a possessive love that she needs to repent before she dies. (In pointing to the possibility of tyranny that lies in a love that is both self-sacrificing and possessive, Lewis was returning to a theme he had considered in *The Screwtape Letters* and in *The Great Divorce*.)

In the space trilogy, especially in *Perelandra*, Lewis had displayed unusual powers for description of landscapes and physical events, but his characters did not need to be more than consistent and believable. Not before *Till We Have Faces* did Lewis show he could produce a complete and thoroughly convincing portrait, and in this novel he has not one but three impressive creations. In addition to the complex and nuanced Orual, there is the Fox, a Greek slave who first is a tutor for Orual and Psyche and later is Queen Orual's adviser and foreign minister, and Bardia, a soldier and lifelong friend, who serves as the military leader of Glome.

Till We Have Faces surprised and puzzled many readers. It seemed to be very unlike the rest of Lewis's work. The novel included several themes that had appeared earlier, especially the doctrine that pagan myths are not simply falsehoods but are, rather, profoundly important bearers of truth; there was also the emphasis on the spiritual danger of a determinedly self-sacrificing love. But the ambiguity of the story, the psychological emphasis on feelings, the importance given to subjective interpretations of events, the viewing of a world almost entirely through the mind of one character (and that character a woman)—all of this was a surprise, coming from Lewis. Lewis thought it was perhaps his best work, and a good many readers have agreed. But there have been dissenters, readers who have enjoyed most, or all, of Lewis's other work but who were disappointed by this novel; there have also been admirers of *Till We Have Faces* among those who have little regard for the rest of Lewis's writings.

On their publication, Lewis's novels received respect and admiration on both sides of the Atlantic, with substantial and generally quite favorable reviews in both the *Times Literary Supplement* and the *New York Times*. While it has been well received, however, Lewis's fiction has not often attracted the attention of the most celebrated critics. Lionel Trilling and Edmund Wilson, for example, seem to have never commented on his work. There are several ways in which Lewis's novels are quite different from most of those that were deemed, in the middle of this century, to be serious and important novels. Except for *Till We Have Faces*, they were science fiction or children's novels, and these were, and are, considered unlikely genres in which to find important works. They were not experimental in structure, language, or perspective, and they did not attempt to break with the novel's conventional form. Lewis saw little of importance in the insights of psychoanalysis and Marxism. World War I did not represent for Lewis the watershed that it was for many writers of his generation, and World War II and atomic bombs did not reveal to him depths of human depravity, or of impotence and futility in the face of evil, that he had not suspected in the past. Finally, his novels are accessible to the general reader; they do not need the explication and analysis that have been found necessary, or useful, in dealing with the fiction of Charles Williams and Flannery O'Connor, to mention two other writers whose Christianity had an important place in their work.

It is a surprising fact that Lewis's popularity seems to have increased steadily since his death. The breadth of his appeal can be gauged by noting that Eugene McCarthy, Ronald Reagan, and Margaret Thatcher all reported their admiration for his writings. Irving Kristol, Jacques Barzun, W. H. Auden, Alan Paton, and Loren Eiseley are among the distinguished writers who have quoted Lewis with respect and approval. There are some who have judged otherwise. George Steiner delivered a sneer in *Language and Silence* (1967): Lewis is one of "The Enemy," those "who divide study of literature with the pursuit of elegance or science fiction. . . . The Enemy represents cosiness, frivolity, mundane cliques, the uses of culture for mutual adulation or warmth. . . . The Enemy is the Establishment of the mind. His brow is middle and his tone is suave." B. F. Skinner tried to dispose of *The Abolition of Man* in his *Beyond Freedom and Dignity* (1971), and Kathleen Nott was severely condemnatory in her *The Emperor's Clothes* (1953).

Perhaps the most surprising aspect of Lewis's popularity is that it is largely based in that famous person "the general reader." This is a reader to whom books are important though he may have no professional or academic stake in the books he chooses to read. This reader may, or may not, have formal training in philosophy, literature, history, or theology. Many of these general readers have reported that they owe more to Lewis than to any other author, or to any teacher, they have ever encountered. To read Lewis, they say, as Lewis said of reading Spenser, is to grow in mental health.

Letters:

Letters of C. S. Lewis, edited by W. H. Lewis (New York: Harcourt, Brace & World, 1966; London: Bles, 1966);

Letters to an American Lady, edited by Clyde S. Kilby (Grand Rapids, Mich.: Eerdmans, 1967; London: Hodder & Stoughton, 1969);

They Stand Together: The Letters of C. S. Lewis to Arthur Greeves, edited by Walter Hooper (New York: Macmillan, 1979; London: Collins, 1979);

Letters to Children (New York: Macmillan, 1985; London: Collins, 1985).

Bibliography:

Walter Hooper, "A Bibliography of the Writings of C. S. Lewis," in *Light on C. S. Lewis*, edited by Jocelyn Gibb (London: Bles, 1965; New York: Harcourt Brace Jovanovich, 1976), pp. 117-160.

Biographies:

Roger Lancelyn Green and Walter Hooper, *C. S. Lewis: A Biography* (New York: Harcourt Brace Jovanovich, 1974; London: Collins, 1974);

A. N. Wilson, *C. S. Lewis: A Biography* (New York: Norton, 1990).

References:

Owen Barfield, Introduction to *Light on C. S. Lewis*, edited by Jocelyn Gibb (London: Bles, 1965), pp. ix-xxi;

Humphrey Carpenter, *The Inklings: C. S. Lewis, J. R. R. Tolkien, Charles Williams, and Their Friends* (London: Allen & Unwin, 1978; Boston: Houghton, Mifflin, 1979);

Nevill Coghill, "The Approach to English," in *Light on C. S. Lewis*, pp. 51-66;

James T. Como, ed., *"C. S. Lewis at the Breakfast Table" and Other Reminiscences* (New York: Macmillan, 1979);

Austin Farrer, "The Christian Apologist," in *Light on C. S. Lewis*, pp. 23-43;

Walter Hooper, *Past Watchful Dragons: The Narnian Chronicles of C. S. Lewis* (New York: Macmillan, 1974);

Peter J. Schakel, ed., *The Longing for a Form: Essays on the Fiction of C. S. Lewis* (Kent, Ohio: Kent State University Press, 1977);

Chad Walsh, *The Literary Legacy of C. S. Lewis* (New York: Harcourt Brace Jovanovich, 1979).

Papers:

Many of Lewis's papers are housed at the Bodleian Library, Oxford, and in the Marion E. Wade Collection at Wheaton College, Wheaton, Illinois.

Malcolm Lowry

(28 July 1909 - 27 June 1957)

This entry was written by Ronald Binns for
DLB 15: British Novelists, 1930-1959: Part One.

SELECTED BOOKS: *Ultramarine* (London: Cape, 1933; revised edition, Philadelphia: Lippincott, 1962; London: Cape, 1963);

Under the Volcano (New York: Reynal & Hitchcock, 1947; London: Cape, 1947);

Hear Us O Lord from Heaven Thy Dwelling Place (Philadelphia: Lippincott, 1961; London: Cape, 1962);

Lunar Caustic, edited by Earle Birney and Margerie Bonner Lowry (New York: Grossman, 1968; London: Cape, 1968);

Dark as the Grave Wherein My Friend Is Laid, edited by Douglas Day and Margerie Bonner Lowry (New York: New American Library, 1968; London: Cape, 1969);

October Ferry to Gabriola, edited by Margerie Bonner Lowry (New York: World, 1970; London: Cape, 1971);

Notes on a Screenplay for F. Scott Fitzgerald's Tender Is the Night, by Lowry and Margerie Bonner Lowry (Bloomfield Hills, Mich.: Bruccoli Clark, 1976).

Malcolm Lowry's reputation rests largely on a single novel, *Under the Volcano* (1947), the semiautobiographical account of an expatriate Englishman's disintegration through despair and dipsomania in Mexico at the end of the 1930s. Although hailed by some reviewers as a masterpiece, the book was slow to win acceptance as a major modern work. Lowry found it impossible to repeat the virtuoso writing and dazzling intensity of vision which are to be found in this novel, and some of the book's leading themes—exile, alienation, failure, self-destruction—became synonymous with the subsequent course of his life. It is sometimes difficult to separate the colorful and romantic legend of Lowry the alcoholic and suicide from the plots of his fiction, which repeatedly explore the sufferings of a disturbed and self-doubting individual who is often a writer. Lowry ended his life in obscurity, having succeeded in finding a publisher for only a fraction of his writing. When he died in 1957, his most recent pub-

Malcolm Lowry

lishing contract, with Random House, had long since been terminated by his publishers, and his two published novels were out of print. The gradual revival of interest in Lowry's writing after his death eventually led to the posthumous publication of a variety of novels and stories, many of which he had never completed to his own satisfaction. Almost all of these later works are autobiographical and describe Lowry's troubled life and career in the context of journeys he made with his wife through Mexico, Canada, and Italy. Reviewers and critics have generally found these later works disappointing. Interest in Lowry's life was reawakened by Douglas Day's popular 1973 biography, which won the 1974 National Book Award for biography, and by the National Film Board of Canada's prizewinning documentary *Volcano* (1976).

Clarence Malcolm Lowry was born in New Brighton, near Liverpool, on 28 July 1909 to Arthur Osborne and Evelyn Boden Lowry. His father was a wealthy businessman, and Lowry had a conventional English upper-class upbringing. He was sent away to private boarding schools to be educated, and a place was made available for him at Cambridge University. It was expected that he would thereafter dutifully enter the family business as his three elder brothers had done. Lowry rebelled; perhaps he never forgave his parents for christening him Clarence, a name irresistibly comic to British ears, and which he never used. As a teenager he began to drink heavily, and when he was seventeen, he demanded to be allowed to go to sea, a naively romantic ambition derived in part from reading the early plays of Eugene O'Neill. His long-suffering father consented, and in May 1927 Lowry shipped out to Yokohama, Japan, from Liverpool, working as a deckhand on the SS *Pyrrhus*. He returned five months later, disillusioned but haunted by the experience. The trip marked the final break with his family.

In later life Lowry was to claim that his childhood had been one of misery and neglect, but such claims seem unfounded. Lowry was fond of fabricating romantic legends about his past, making his life seem somehow the inevitable result of early circumstances. The scar on his leg, which he melodramatically boasted was the result of a gunfight in China, actually came from a childhood mishap with a bicycle, and the benign picture of early adolescence portrayed in his story "Enter One in Sumptuous Armour" is almost certainly an accurate one for him.

Lowry's literary aspirations first surfaced in the poems and stories, some parodying popular fiction, which he wrote for the *Leys Fortnightly*, a school magazine. His voyage to the Far East subsequently furnished him with material for half a dozen stories, which he later expanded into his first novel, *Ultramarine* (1933). The style and content of Lowry's first full-length work of fiction were strongly influenced by two literary contacts he made soon after leaving home in 1927. A fan letter to the American poet and critic Conrad Aiken resulted in an important friendship. Aiken coached the young writer, who rewarded him by writing *Ultramarine* in a style reminiscent of

Aiken's own novel *Blue Voyage* (1927), itself an imitation of James Joyce's *Ulysses* (1922). Aiken, laconically acknowledging the influence of his clotted prose and interior monologue techniques on his young disciple, suggested that Lowry should have called his novel "Purple Passage." Lowry was equally excited by *The Ship Sails On* (1927), a translation of a grim, pessimistic novel about a young man's experiences at sea, by the Norwegian writer Nordahl Grieg. Lowry promptly made a pilgrimage to meet Grieg and regarded the book with awe for several years afterward.

In fall 1929, performing one last act of filial duty before estranging himself from his family for life, Lowry enrolled at Cambridge University. There he drank heavily and remained aloof from academic life, shutting himself away to work on drafts of *Ultramarine*. His years at Cambridge were overshadowed by tragedy. In Lowry's first term his roommate, Paul Fitte, committed suicide. This death had a traumatic impact on the young writer, and in later life he was to hold himself responsible for it. There is some evidence that the nineteen-year-old Fitte was a homosexual threatened with exposure by a blackmailer, but the exact nature of his relationship with Lowry is unknown. This suicide haunted Lowry for the rest of his life, and he made oblique references to Fitte's death in much of his later fiction—although not in his first novel, which was published a year after he was graduated.

Ultramarine tells the story of a sensitive, educated young man's voyage to the Far East. Because of his socially superior background, Dana Hilliot finds himself envied and disliked by the other crew members, and he determines to win their acceptance. After weeks of loneliness and vengeful brooding, Hilliot is finally invited to help out as a ship's fireman; his painful progress from alienation to integration within the ship's community is complete.

Lowry's treatment of the ports and countries Hilliot encounters en route is perfunctory; his real interest lay in the landscapes of the mind. Hilliot is bullied by the ship's cook, and he is mocked by the crew because of his sexual inexperience. These torments are luridly magnified in his imagination. He decides to visit a brothel but endlessly vacillates, disturbed by premonitions of catching syphilis and dying horribly. In the friction occurring inside the hero's psyche, in the differing pulls of terror and desire, lie the energies of the novel. There are passages of real power in

Lowry and his first wife, Jan, in Cuernavaca, Mexico, 1937

the book, and it was an extraordinary tour de force for a twenty-three-year-old writer, but in many respects it remains an unsatisfactory novel. Dana Hilliot's experiences as a sailor seem too inconsequential to carry the significance Lowry attaches to them, and the book's displays of learning and wit often seem obscure and redundant. As a narrative *Ultramarine* is not very compelling, and the problems of finding an interesting subject to write about and of maintaining the reader's interest in it continued to dog Lowry throughout his career. In later years he regarded *Ultramarine* as an embarrassment; it was "not worth reading," he brusquely informed an inquiring student in 1951.

Reviewers were unenthusiastic. Derek Verschoyle, writing in the *Spectator*, found the novel "disastrously mannered," with the collage techniques producing "no unity of impression." Of the fifteen hundred copies of *Ultramarine* printed, barely half were sold. The novel remains a curiosity piece, the eventual appearance of *Under the Volcano* having given it a retrospective significance which in itself it lacks. It was a testing ground for the interior-monologue techniques

which Lowry was to use so much more effectively in his masterpiece, published fourteen years later. Lowry planned to rewrite *Ultramarine* but devoted little time to the project. The first edition has never been reprinted, and the revised edition which appeared after his death incorporates only a handful of minor changes.

The publication of this precocious first novel enabled Lowry to regard himself seriously as a writer. The book's poor sales were not of financial significance to him, since his wealthy father was generously prepared to finance the literary career of his erring son, partly in an effort to exercise some control over his drinking (a strategy that failed absolutely). From Cambridge, Lowry drifted down to London for a few months, where he mixed with the bohemian set and became friendly with Dylan Thomas. In April 1933 Lowry's career of restless exile began in earnest. He traveled to Spain with Aiken, and there he met Jan Gabrial, a pretty, footloose American girl with literary ambitions of her own. After a whirlwind courtship they were married in Paris on 6 January 1934. The marriage was not a success, and two stories Lowry had published at this time, "Hotel Room in Chartres" and "In Le Havre," record its fractious early days. Jan soon fled home to New York, leaving Lowry alone in France.

At this time Lowry was working on "In Ballast to the White Sea," a lengthy psychological novel about a Cambridge student and his relationships with his girlfriend, a brother who commits suicide, and a Norwegian novelist. The book seems to have been an imaginative fusion of Lowry's obsessions and experiences between 1927 and the mid 1930s. It preoccupied him, on and off, until the end of the decade, by which time it was a thousand pages long. Aiken described it as "brilliant," but Lowry was unable to find a publisher. The manuscript was later destroyed in a fire.

In 1935 Lowry followed his wife to New York. His heavy drinking there soon resulted in his incarceration in the psychiatric ward of the city's Bellevue Hospital. Lowry was shattered by his experiences among the insane, and when he was released after a stay of three or four weeks, he immediately wrote a short novel about it. "The Last Address" is a naked account of the hell of Bellevue, seen through the eyes of a cultured English drunkard who is obsessed with Herman Melville and the house where *Moby-Dick* (1851) was completed. Many years later Lowry confessed his strong sense of identification with Melville, "mostly because of his failure as a writer and his whole outlook generally. His failure for some reason absolutely fascinated me and it seems to me that from an early age I determined to emulate it, in every way possible."

The feeling that, as a writer, he was a failure haunted Lowry through much of his life, and indeed in commercial terms he was. Dissatisfied with his Bellevue novel, he rewrote it in a less pessimistic version entitled "Swinging the Maelstrom," at the climax of which the hero decides to join the crew of a loyalist ship traveling to the civil war in Spain. Lowry was unable to find a publisher for either story, and in 1952 he considered the possibility of mixing the two drafts together in a single narrative entitled *Lunar Caustic* (a name for silver nitrate, once used to try to cure syphilis). Publishers remained uninterested, and the idea was only put into practice after Lowry's death, in a version edited by his widow, Margerie Bonner Lowry, in collaboration with the Canadian poet Earle Birney.

Lunar Caustic (1968) favors the bleak vision of Lowry's original draft. The Englishman Bill

Margerie Bonner Lowry

Plantagenet wakes up in Bellevue Hospital confused about his identity and his past. He loses all sense of time, and as the days pass he begins to establish a relationship with three of the ward's inmates: Garry, a violent teenager with a propensity for telling stories with ominous endings; Kalowski, a confused old man; and Battle, a burly Negro who semaphores messages through the windows to the outside world. Plantagenet recognizes in these individuals facets of his own personality taken to absurd and distressing extremes. Like Garry, he is a maker of fictions; like Kalowski, he is a rootless, dispossessed wanderer; like Battle, he cannot communicate meaningfully with other people. What Plantagenet witnesses, in effect, are the horrifying realities of his own character embodied in the caricatures of madness. Released from the hospital, he thankfully takes refuge from life once more in the consolations of alcoholic withdrawal.

Lunar Caustic is a powerful, spare, shocking work, and the wit and humor which often appear in Lowry's writing are strikingly absent. The novel has appeared in many editions since its belated appearance in 1968, when reviewers generally gave it a rapturous reception, praising the book for its compassion and visionary power. An anonymous writer in the *Canadian Forum* hailed *Lunar Caustic* as a "haunting little masterpiece," and it remains one of the few pieces of writing by Lowry, other than *Under the Volcano*, to have won critical recognition.

In 1936 Malcolm and Jan Lowry patched up their marriage and traveled to Los Angeles and then to Mexico, where they settled in Cuernavaca. Once again their relationship deteriorated; Lowry indulged in bouts of heavy drinking, and Jan went off with other men. The following year she left him for the last time, and they never saw each other again. Lowry was stunned when Jan later had published a short story, "Not with a Bang," which charted the final stages of their tortured marriage with painful accuracy. Alone in Mexico, Lowry sank into despair, having arrived at what he claimed was a "condition of amnesia, breakdown, heartbreak, consumption, cholera [and] alcoholic poisoning." He traveled to Oaxaca in search of the best mescal in Mexico, and there he befriended Juan Fernando Márquez, a Mexican Socialist. The two men went on wild drinking sprees together, and on at least one occasion Lowry ended up in jail. In 1938 Lowry returned to Los Angeles.

Throughout this period Lowry had been working on the first draft of *Under the Volcano*, an autobiographical novel about his anguished experiences in Mexico. By 1939 he had completed a third draft, which he submitted, unsuccessfully, to many publishers. Once again his fortunes had hit rock bottom. That same year he met Margerie Bonner, a former actress. It was, they later claimed, love at first sight. When his American visa expired, she immediately abandoned her job as a secretary and went north to live with Lowry in Vancouver, British Columbia. He obtained a divorce, and the couple was married on 2 December 1940. For the next fourteen years they lived in a succession of squatter's cabins on the foreshore at Dollarton, on the Burrard Inlet, just outside Vancouver. Lowry later memorialized their legendary existence as makeshift pioneers in his much-anthologized story "The Forest Path to the Spring." It was at Dollarton that Lowry worked on his final revisions of *Under the Volcano*. In June 1944 their shack burned down in a fire which may have been deliberately started by Lowry himself; it was, pointedly, the fifth anniversary of his first encounter with Margerie Bonner. "In Ballast to the White Sea" was destroyed, but Lowry's other work was saved. Homeless, they traveled east to stay with friends at Niagara-on-the-Lake, Ontario. It was there, on Christmas Eve 1944, that the final draft of Lowry's masterpiece was completed.

Under the Volcano tells the tragic story of Geoffrey Firmin, a cultured, middle-class Englishman who is drinking himself to an early grave in a Mexican town after being abandoned by his young American wife, Yvonne. All of the novel—with the exception of the first chapter, which is set in 1939—takes place on 2 November 1938 and charts Firmin's last twelve hours and demise. Firmin, until recently the town's British consul, is unemployed as a result of the severing of diplomatic relations between Britain and Mexico in the aftermath of the 1938 oil crisis. His personal disintegration is mirrored in the world at large: Mexico is in a state of political turbulence, and Europe is sliding toward a Fascist victory in Spain and the eventual apocalypse of World War II. Unexpectedly, Yvonne returns to Firmin, but their tentative efforts to rediscover their love for one another are frustrated by the intrusive presence of Laruelle, a retired French film director, and Firmin's half-brother, Hugh, a journalist. Both men have previously had affairs with Yvonne, and the emotional friction generated by her return to Mexico moves to a bloody climax in which Firmin is assassinated by Fascists, and his wife dies under the hooves of a runaway horse.

In a 2 January 1946 letter to the publisher Jonathan Cape, Lowry described the novel as being "concerned with the guilt of man, with his remorse, with his ceaseless struggling towards the light under the weight of the past, and with his doom. The allegory is that of the Garden of Eden. The drunkenness of the Consul is used on one plane to symbolize the universal drunkenness of mankind during the period immediately preceding the [Second World] war."

Under the Volcano is a dense, complex novel of many dimensions. Most immediately it offers a dazzling portrait of the agonies of an alcoholic, but equally it is a novel of Mexico, of love, of conflicting political ideologies, and of myth and magic. Lowry juxtaposes the extremes of the Mexican landscape—its snowcapped volcanoes and dark ravines, its vegetative luxurance and human squalor—to provide a lurid, epic backdrop to his story of a damned soul. Unexpected coincidences, sinister animals such as the constantly ap-

Malcolm Lowry circa 1950, Bowen Island, British Columbia

pearing pariah dogs, and multitudinous literary allusions repeatedly suggest the mysterious presence of strange occult forces. The consul, it is hinted, is Adam, about to be expelled from Eden; he is Christ, the sacrificial scapegoat for man's sins; he is Dante, journeying through an inferno of the damned; he is also Faust, due to be cast into hell for abusing his powers. Lowry's employment of myth and allegory in the novel remains suggestive rather than systematic, evoking vestiges of a lost order which the consul seeks but cannot find. The novel strives for the timelessness of myth but remains firmly rooted in the historical realities of the 1930s, which intrude finally in the consul's murder by a Fascist's bullet.

Lowry once remarked that *Under the Volcano* "started off" as a political parable, and judged by the values of Hugh Firmin, who is a left-wing idealist, the other three principal characters are found wanting. Laruelle is a promiscuous playboy, a self-centered artistic failure who has gone to seed. The consul plays the stock market and is involved in an illicit property deal. Yvonne is the wealthy daughter of a capitalist, with little awareness of what is happening in the world around her. But Hugh himself is a flawed figure, his utopi-

anism represented as slightly comic. Despite all his talk of revolutionary commitment, the only time Hugh holds a rifle is when he shoots at wooden ducks in a fairground booth; Laruelle describes him sarcastically as "a professional indoor Marxman." The one figure in *Under the Volcano* not subjected to a critical irony is the revolutionary Socialist Juan Cerillo (based on Lowry's friend Márquez). It is significant that Cerillo does not make a direct appearance in the novel; he remains an ideal, a brief, fleeting figure in Hugh's memory. Lowry's background was a conservative one, but in the mid 1930s, influenced by Jan, who was possibly a member of the Communist party, and by his friendship with Márquez, the novelist's politics shifted sharply to the left. Hugh Firmin represents Lowry's ironic portrait of himself a few years earlier; by the time *Under the Volcano* was published, the novelist's politics had altered and increasingly began to resemble the cynical quietism of the consul. In 1949, consenting to the idea that the novel be abridged for a paperback edition, Lowry suggested that the figure of Juan Cerillo be expunged from its pages.

Under the Volcano remains a profoundly ambiguous novel, open to many interpretations,

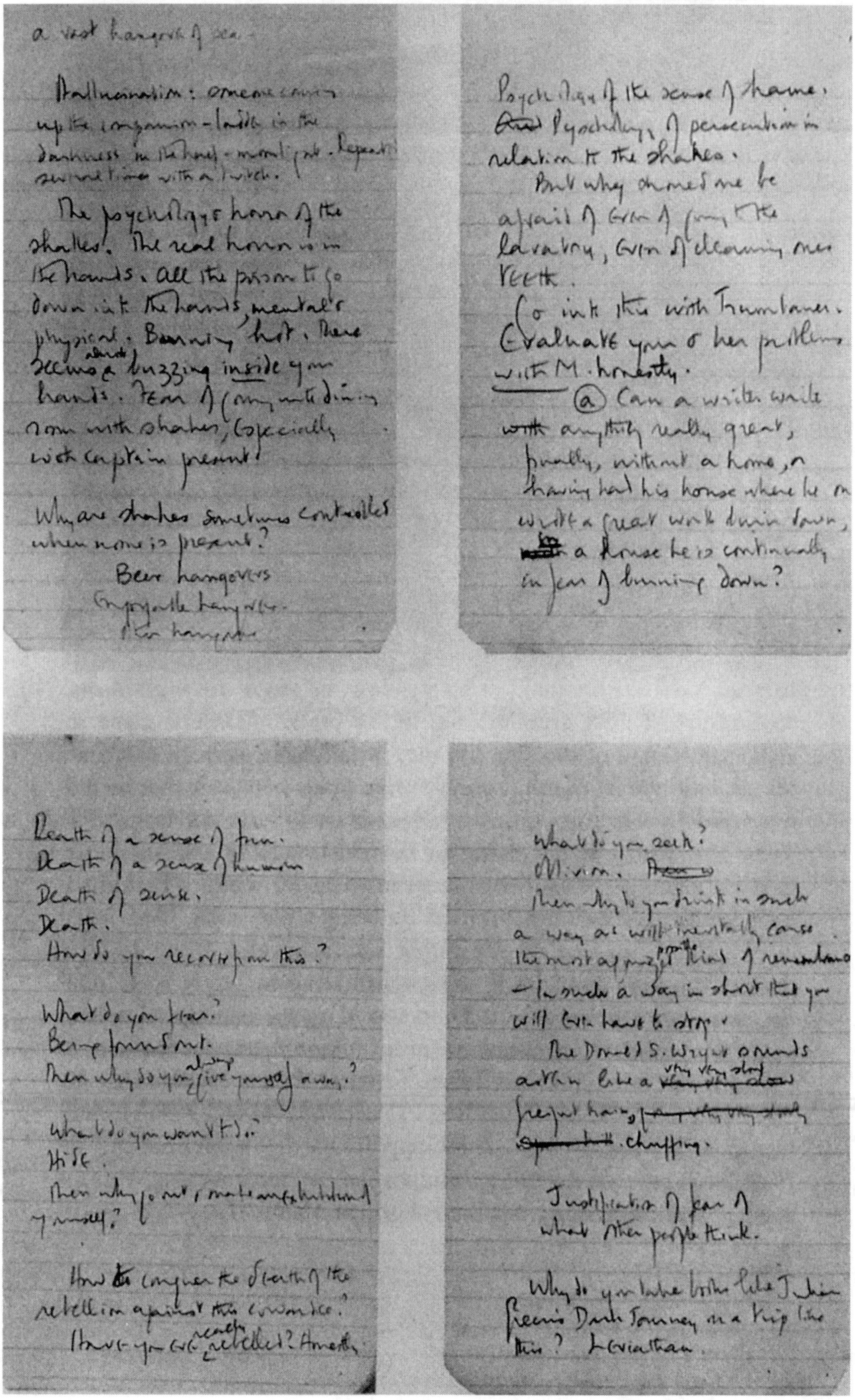

a vast hangover of sea -

Hallucination: someone comes up the companion-ladder in the darkness in the [illegible] - moonlight. Repeats several times with a twitch.

The psychological horror of the shakes. The real horror is in the hands. All the poison to go down into the hands, mental & physical. Burning hot. There seems already a buzzing inside your hands. Fear of going into dining room with shakes, especially with captain present.

Why are shakes sometimes controlled when none is present?

Beer hangovers
[illegible] hangover
[illegible] hangover

Psychology of the sense of shame. Psychology of persecution in relation to the shakes.

But why should one be afraid of even of going to the lavatory, even of cleaning ones teeth.

Go into this with [illegible]. Evaluate your own problems with M. honestly.

(a) Can a writer write with anything really great, finally, without a home, or having had his house where he wrote a great work burn down, or a house he is continually in fear of burning down?

Death of a sense of fun.
Death of a sense of humour
Death of sense.
Death.
How do you recover from this?

What do you fear?
Being found out.
Then why do you always give yourself away?

What do you want to do?
Hide.
Then why not, make an exhibition of yourself?

How to conquer the death of the rebellion against this cowardice? Have you ever really rebelled? Honestly.

What do you seek?
Oblivion.
Then why do you drink in such a way as will inevitably cause the most appropriate kind of remembrance — in such a way in short that you will even have to stop.

The [illegible] sounds are like a very very slow frequent hammering, chuffing.

Justification of fear of what other people think.

Why do you take books like Julian Green's Dark Journey on a trip like this? Leviathan.

Lowry's notes on his alcoholism

though its ambiguities have not always been welcomed; H. R. Hays in the *New York Times Book Review* complained that the author's "final moral intention is somewhat obscure." Some notices were hostile, condemning the book as turgid, negative, and decadent. Lowry was particularly upset by Jacques Barzun's review in *Harper's*, which caustically remarked, "Mr. Lowry is on the side of good behaviour, eager to disgust us with tropical vice. He shows this by a long regurgitation of the materials found in *Ulysses* and *The Sun Also Rises*." Other reviewers were enthusiastic. John Woodburn, in the *Saturday Review of Literature*, called the novel "A work of genius . . . magnificent, tragic, compassionate and beautiful"; writing in *Partisan Review*, Elizabeth Hardwick praised Lowry's "astonishing and often brilliant images." *Under the Volcano* sold six thousand copies in the first month of publication and was on the bestseller charts for months. In Britain it was a different story. Reviewers were lukewarm or hedged their praise with damning qualifications, and the first edition was eventually remaindered. In the *Spectator*, D. S. Savage found the novel promising but complained that its "scenic descriptions" were "somewhat imprecise," adding that "Mr. Lowry writes rather prolixly; a slight thread of incident carries too heavy a burden of reflections and perceptions."

Several of the American reviews were highly perceptive and raised issues which Lowry scholars are still debating today. In the *New York Herald Tribune Weekly Book Review*, Mark Schorer saw *Under the Volcano* as above all a metaphysical novel, concerned with "the deeper reality of man's fall from grace, the drama of how we are damned and who shall be saved." William York Tindall disagreed; writing in *College English*, he asserted that Lowry's interests were essentially political. Others pointed to the curious dualism of the novel: George Maybury in the *New Republic* found it neither realistic nor neatly symbolic; Hardwick noted the evocation of the *déraciné* of the 1920s beneath the 1930s setting. Charles J. Rolo in *Tomorrow* placed Lowry firmly in the experimental modernist tradition and saluted the novel's "brilliant" portrait of a private universe, adding that "its merit hinges neither on characterisation nor plot, which are virtually nonexistent."

No critical consensus about *Under the Volcano* has emerged. Many critics have regarded it as essentially a symbolic novel which evokes timeless, archetypal images and myths. Much attention has

been given to Lowry's use of folklore and literary allusion; by far the fullest study of this aspect of the novel is David Markson's *Malcolm Lowry's "Volcano": Myth, Symbol, Meaning* (1978). Others have argued that the mythic level of the novel is of secondary importance to Lowry's treatment of social and historical themes. The most accessible account of Lowry's masterpiece is that contained in Day's biography. Day describes *Under the Volcano* as "the greatest religious novel of this century" and analyzes five major elements in the narrative: landscape, characterization, politics, the occult, and religion. It is clear that *Under the Volcano* will continue to provoke critical discussion and disagreement for many years to come; the many hiatuses and ambiguities of Lowry's multileveled, mannered, encyclopedic narrative seem to invite multiple interpretations.

In 1945 Lowry and his wife set out for Mexico, partly so that he could show her the places he had written about in *Under the Volcano*, and partly because he wanted to renew his friendship with Márquez. The trip was not a success. A publisher sent Lowry an unfavorable reader's report on his novel, and in despair Lowry made a half-hearted suicide attempt. Later he discovered that Márquez had been shot dead in a barroom brawl six years earlier. Finally the couple was deported after Lowry stubbornly refused to pay a small bribe to two minor immigration officials. Undaunted by these disastrous experiences, Lowry immediately decided to write a novel about his fruitless quest for his dead friend. *Dark as the Grave Wherein My Friend Is Laid* went through three drafts but was then abandoned. An edited version appeared posthumously in 1968. Reviews were mixed. In the *Atlantic*, John Wain praised Lowry's evocation of Mexico but condemned his subjectivism and the narrow range of his material. The book has since received little critical attention, generally being regarded as more a travel journal than a novel. Richard Hauer Costa summarized the opinions of many Lowry scholars when he wrote that as far as Lowry's career after *Under the Volcano* is concerned, "the maker gives way to the autobiographer."

Lowry himself was anxious and unsure about his writing in the period after *Under the Volcano*. He contemplated a further autobiographical novel about Mexico entitled "La Mordida" but abandoned it in confusion. He also made notes for "The Ordeal of Sigbjorn Wilderness," a short novel based on memories of people he had known at Cambridge University, but then gave

Dust jacket for Lowry's posthumously published short-story collection

that up, too. Lowry derived little comfort from the fuss which attended the eventual publication of *Under the Volcano* in 1947. "Success is like some horrible disaster," he wrote, loathing his brief moment as a celebrity.

Lowry took refuge from his writing difficulties in drink and travel. In 1946 he and Margerie sailed to Haiti from New Orleans, traveling to New York on their return. The following year the couple journeyed via the Panama Canal to France and Italy and did not return until the spring of 1949. Back once more in British Columbia, they visited Gabriola Island in the Strait of Georgia as part of an unsuccessful attempt to find a new home. These experiences were to form the material for almost all Lowry's subsequent work, though none of the later fiction was to match the intensity of his masterpiece. *Dark as the Grave Wherein My Friend Is Laid* reveals the compulsive quality of Lowry's memories of Mexico from 1936 to 1938; no other experience was ever as important to him.

Upon his return to Canada in 1949 Lowry found himself with nothing to write about. Mexico seemed exhausted as a subject; he was in despair. He then abandoned fiction altogether and

occupied his time working on a screenplay of F. Scott Fitzgerald's *Tender Is the Night* (1934). The result was a script of quirky originality, 455 pages long. Lowry, though he was a keen moviegoer, knew nothing about the making of films or the writing of screenplays, and he failed to find a buyer for his script. It remains an impressive, if colorful, imaginative reconstruction. To Lowry it was psychologically an important achievement. After six years of false starts and uncertainty, he had at last managed to finish something.

Writing the Fitzgerald screenplay seems to have given Lowry's morale a much-needed boost. In the four years that followed he worked hard, producing a sequence of linked stories as well as drafts of his final novel. Some of these stories were collected after Lowry's death in the prizewinning volume *Hear Us O Lord from Heaven Thy Dwelling Place* (1961). Stories such as "Through the Panama," "Strange Comfort Afforded by the Profession," "Elephant and Colosseum," and "Present Estate of Pompeii" hark back to the time, just a few years earlier, when Lowry's creativity had been paralyzed by the feeling that he had written himself out. They dramatize states of despair and uncertainty which are

Lowry at Dollarton, 1953

subjected to ironic scrutiny and, finally, are rendered into comedy. By far the most popular of these stories from the 1950s is "The Forest Path to the Spring," a lyrical account of the years Lowry and Margerie spent in the squatters' community at Dollarton. The long, flowing sentences convey the change of the seasons and the rhythms of the natural landscape with a brilliance perhaps unmatched since D. H. Lawrence's *The Rainbow* (1915). Lowry's economy of style makes the story a far more compelling memorial to his long sojourn in British Columbia than his more ambitious last novel, *October Ferry to Gabriola* (1970).

Lowry left *October Ferry to Gabriola* unfin-

ished at his death. He had completed a first draft but planned many revisions. The novel describes a long day's journey by coach and ferry from Dollarton to Gabriola Island, off the British Columbia coast. As he travels toward the island, Ethan Llewelyn, an unemployed lawyer, looks back over his life, recalling the early days of his marriage and the traumatic memory of a college friend's suicide. Most of the novel takes place inside Llewelyn's mind, as it roams to and fro among his memories. Although Lowry made some attempt to provide a realistic framework for the novel, he was patently more interested in autobiographical reverie than in matters of characterization or plot, or even a consistent time scheme. Difficulties over *October Ferry to Gabriola* resulted in the termination of Lowry's contract with Random House. The complaints of Lowry's editor that the book lacked clarity and narrative interest were proved justified by reviewers' reactions to the edited version of the novel published in 1970. Notices were sympathetic but critical; Robert Nye in the *Guardian* described the novel as "a rather sketchy and scratchy book, thirty-seven chapters, some of them little more than recipes for situations."

In 1954 Lowry and his wife left Canada and flew to Europe. He was shocked and depressed by the termination of his contract, and the last three years of his life were a sorry record of alcoholism, despondency, and restless travel. Lowry seems to have written little during these years. In February 1956 the couple rented a cottage in the village of Ripe on the south coast of England. The novelist died there on 27 June 1957 from an overdose of sleeping tablets after a drunken quarrel with his wife. He was forty-seven.

Malcolm Lowry's place in modern literature remains a matter of some dispute, and the problem of evaluating his achievement has been compounded by controversies over the record of his life and about the methods adopted in the posthumous editing of his later fiction, much of which was left incomplete at the time of his death. Matthew Corrigan has described the published text of *Dark as the Grave Wherein My Friend Is Laid* as a pastiche, "neither Lowry's novel nor his manuscript." The orthodox verdict is that Lowry was an author who burned himself out after writing a single masterpiece. He has been described as a compulsive autobiographer, not a novelist at all, except by accident. His other writings have been generally judged as too restrictively autobiographical to be successful works of fiction. Lowry's oeuvre rests on uneasy aesthetic foundations, since the self-mythologizing of a romantically damned and doomed artist is not something that lends itself to repetition. The doom either arrives, as it does for Geoffrey Firmin in *Under the Volcano*, or it is eluded, as at the deflationary and disappointing climax of *Dark as the Grave Wherein My Friend Is Laid*. Ironically, the theme worked best on the one occasion that Lowry gave serious attention to matters of plot, characterization, and social and historical background—the conventional materials of the social novel, a genre which he otherwise disdained. Stripped of these supports, Lowry's highly personal vision ran the risk of appearing complacent and self-regarding. It is a matter of continuing debate whether or not Lowry's career developed after *Under the Volcano*. Some critics have suggested that the editors of the posthumously published manuscripts have failed to understand Lowry's intentions and have misrepresented them in their choice of narrative material. It has been argued that the later stories and novels are not simply autobiographical jottings or failed attempts to imitate *Under the Volcano* but deliberately experimental works which significantly enlarge the possibilities of metafiction. Irrespective of these disagreements, it seems clear that Lowry's dense and difficult prose style, together with the narrow range of his fictional interests, makes it unlikely that his appeal will ever be widespread.

Letters:

Selected Letters of Malcolm Lowry, edited by Harvey Breit and Margerie Bonner Lowry (Philadelphia: Lippincott, 1965; London: Cape, 1967);

The Letters of Malcolm Lowry and Gerald Noxon, 1940-1952, edited by Paul Tiessen (Vancouver: University of British Columbia Press, 1988).

Biographies:

Douglas Day, *Malcolm Lowry: A Biography* (New York: Oxford University Press, 1973);

Tony Bareham, *Malcolm Lowry* (New York: St. Martin's press, 1989).

References:

Chris Ackerley, *A Companion to Under the Volcano* (Vancouver: University of British Columbia Press, 1984);

Jonathan Arac, "The Form of Carnival in *Under the Volcano*," *PMLA*, 92 (May 1977), 481-489;

Ronald Binns, "Beckett, Lowry and the Anti-Novel," in *The Contemporary English Novel*, edited by M. Bradbury and D. Palmer (London: Arnold, 1979), pp. 88-111;

Binns, "Materialism and Magic in *Under the Volcano*," *Critical Quarterly*, 23 (Spring 1981): 21-32;

Malcolm Bradbury, "Malcolm Lowry as Modernist," in his *Possibilities: Essays on the State of the Novel* (New York: Oxford University Press, 1973), pp. 181-191;

Roger Bromley, "The Boundaries of Commitment: God, Lover, Comrade—*Under the Vol-*

cano as a Reading of the 1930's," in *1936: The Sociology of Literature. Volume One: The Politics of Modernism*, edited by Francis Barker (Colchester, U.K.: University of Essex Press, 1979), pp. 273-296;

Anthony Burgess, "Europe's Day of the Dead," *Spectator*, 20 January 1967, p. 74;

Matthew Corrigan, "Malcolm Lowry, New York Publishing, and the 'New Illiteracy,'" *Encounter*, 35 (July 1970): 82-93;

Richard Hauer Costa, *Malcolm Lowry* (New York: Twayne, 1972);

Rosemary Creswell, "Malcolm Lowry's Other Fiction," in *Cunning Exiles: Studies of Modern Prose Writers*, edited by Don Anderson and Stephen Knight (Sydney: Angus & Robertson, 1974), pp. 62-80;

Richard K. Cross, *Malcolm Lowry: A Preface to his Fiction* (Chicago: University of Chicago Press, 1980);

Dale Edmonds, "*Under the Volcano*: A Reading of the 'Immediate Level,'" *Tulane Studies in English*, 16 (1968): 63-105;

Sherrill Grace, *The Voyage That Never Ends: Malcolm Lowry's Fiction* (Vancouver: University of British Columbia Press, 1984);

David Markson, *Malcolm Lowry's "Volcano": Myth, Symbol, Meaning* (New York: Times Books, 1978);

William H. New, *Malcolm Lowry* (Toronto: McLelland & Stewart, 1971);

New, *Malcolm Lowry: A Reference Guide* (Boston: Hall, 1978);

J. Douglas Porteous, *Landscapes of the Mind: Worlds of Sense and Metaphor* (Toronto: University of Toronto Press, 1990);

Andrew Pottinger, "The Consul's 'Murder,'" *Canadian Literature*, 67 (Winter 1976): 53-63;

Charles J. Rolo, "The New Novel," *Tomorrow*, 7 (May 1948): 53-55;

Anne Smith, ed., *The Art of Malcolm Lowry* (New York: Barnes & Noble, 1978);

Paul Tiessen, ed., *Apparently Incongruous Parts: The Worlds of Malcolm Lowry* (Metuchen, N.J.: Scarecrow Press, 1990);

John Wain, "Another Room in Hell," *Atlantic Monthly*, 222 (August 1968): 84-86;

Ronald G. Walker, *Infernal Paradise: Mexico and the Modern English Novel* (Berkeley: University of California Press, 1978);

Barry Wood, "Malcolm Lowry's Metafiction," *Contemporary Literature*, 19 (Winter 1978): 1-25;

George Woodcock, ed., *Malcolm Lowry: The Man and His Work* (Vancouver: University of British Columbia Press, 1971).

Papers:

The major Lowry manuscript collection, including drafts of published and unpublished fiction, poetry, letters, and the Fitzgerald screenplay, is at the University of British Columbia.

Hugh MacDiarmid

(11 August 1892 - 9 September 1978)

*This entry was updated by Kenneth Buthlay (University of Glasgow) from his entry in
DLB 20: British Poets, 1914-1945.*

SELECTED BOOKS: *Annals of the Five Senses*,
as C. M. Grieve (Montrose, U.K.: C. M.
Grieve, 1923);

Sangschaw (Edinburgh & London: Blackwood,
1925);

Penny Wheep (Edinburgh & London: Blackwood,
1926);

A Drunk Man Looks at the Thistle (Edinburgh & London: Blackwood, 1926; edited by John C.
Weston, Amherst: University of Massachusetts Press, 1971; edited by Kenneth Buthlay, Edinburgh: Scottish Academic Press,
1987);

Contemporary Scottish Studies, First Series, as Grieve
(London: Parsons, 1926; enlarged edition,
Edinburgh: Scottish Educational Journal,
1976);

Albyn, or Scotland and the Future, as Grieve (London: Paul, Trench & Trübner, 1927);

The Present Position of Scottish Music, as Grieve
(Montrose, U.K.: C. M. Grieve, 1927);

To Circumjack Cencrastus (Edinburgh & London:
Blackwood, 1930);

First Hymn to Lenin and Other Poems (London: Unicorn Press, 1931);

Second Hymn to Lenin (Thakeham, U.K.: Valda
Trevlyn, 1932);

Scots Unbound and Other Poems (Stirling, U.K.:
Mackay, 1932);

Scottish Scene, by MacDiarmid and Lewis Grassic
Gibbon (James Leslie Mitchell) (London:
Jarrolds, 1934);

Stony Limits and Other Poems (London: Gollancz,
1934);

At the Sign of the Thistle (London: Nott, 1934);

Selected Poems (London: Macmillan, 1934); enlarged as *Speaking for Scotland: Selected Poems*
(Baltimore: Contemporary Poetry, 1946);

Second Hymn to Lenin and Other Poems (London:
Nott, 1935);

Scottish Eccentrics (London: Routledge, 1936; New
York: Johnson Reprint, 1972);

Scotland, and the Question of a Popular Front against

Hugh MacDiarmid, May 1936

Fascism and War (Whalsay, U.K.: Hugh MacDiarmid Book Club, 1938);

The Islands of Scotland (London: Batsford, 1939;
New York: Scribners, 1939);

Cornish Heroic Song for Valda Trevlyn (Glasgow: Caledonian Press, 1943);

Lucky Poet (London: Methuen, 1943; enlarged edition, London: Cape, 1972);

Poems of East-West Synthesis (Glasgow: Caledonian Press, 1946);

A Kist of Whistles (Glasgow: Maclellan, 1947);

Cunninghame Graham: A Centenary Study (Glasgow: Caledonian Press, 1952);

Francis George Scott: An Essay on the Occasion of His Seventy-fifth Birthday (Edinburgh: Macdonald, 1955);

In Memoriam James Joyce (Glasgow: Maclellan, 1955);

Stony Limits and Scots Unbound and Other Poems (Edinburgh: Castle Wynd Printers, 1956);

Three Hymns to Lenin (Edinburgh: Castle Wynd Printers, 1957);

The Battle Continues (Edinburgh: Castle Wynd Printers, 1957);

Burns Today and Tomorrow (Edinburgh: Castle Wynd Printers, 1959);

The Kind of Poetry I Want (Edinburgh: Duval, 1961);

Collected Poems (New York: Macmillan, 1962; Edinburgh & London: Oliver & Boyd, 1962; revised edition, New York: Macmillan / London: Collier-Macmillan, 1967);

The Company I've Kept (London: Hutchinson, 1966; Berkeley: University of California Press, 1967);

A Lap of Honour (London: MacGibbon & Kee, 1967; Chicago: Swallow Press, 1969);

The Uncanny Scot, edited by Buthlay (London: MacGibbon & Kee, 1968);

A Clyack-Sheaf (London: MacGibbon & Kee, 1969);

Selected Essays, edited by Duncan Glen (London: Cape, 1969; Berkeley: University of California Press, 1970);

More Collected Poems (London: MacGibbon & Kee, 1970; Chicago: Swallow Press, 1970);

Selected Poems, edited by David Craig and John Manson (Harmondsworth, U.K.: Penguin, 1970);

The Hugh MacDiarmid Anthology, edited by Michael Grieve and Alexander Scott (London: Routledge & Kegan Paul, 1972);

Metaphysics and Poetry (Hamilton: Lothlorien, 1975);

Complete Poems, 2 volumes, edited by Grieve and W. R. Aitken (London: Brian & O'Keeffe, 1978).

RECORDINGS: *Hugh MacDiarmid Reads His Own Poetry* (Claddagh);

A Drunk Man Looks at the Thistle (Claddagh);

Whaur Extremes Meet (Tuatha).

OTHER: *The Golden Treasury of Scottish Poetry*, edited, with an introduction, by MacDiarmid (London: Macmillan, 1940);

Harry Martinson, *Aniara*, adapted from the Swedish by MacDiarmid and Elspeth Harley Schubert (London: Hutchinson, 1963);

Bertolt Brecht, *The Threepenny Opera*, translated by MacDiarmid (London: Eyre Methuen, 1973).

Hugh MacDiarmid has long been considered the greatest Scottish poet since Robert Burns. That might not be the most impressive of distinctions, but his admirers would add that his work has dimensions beyond Burns's, and that in a contemporary context a just appreciation would place it alongside Ezra Pound's and T. S. Eliot's. If so, the question that immediately confronts us is why MacDiarmid should have received so little attention in comparison with these celebrated names.

Perhaps there are two main reasons for his lack of renown: the extreme unevenness of his output and the fact that much of the best of it is in Scots. To appreciate the latter requires of most readers (even Scottish readers, whose anglicized educational system requires of them little or no knowledge of their native languages) a special effort to extend and sustain their linguistic receptivity. Those who have most influence in matters of literary reputation in Britain have proved unwilling to make such an effort in MacDiarmid's case. Their literature is not, and never has been, British. It is *English* literature—an ambiguous term which can readily lay claim to Irishmen such as William Butler Yeats and James Joyce and Welshmen such as Dylan Thomas, but balks at a professedly Anglophobe Scottish nationalist who did his best work in Scots. And that is the case even when they regard that language as a mere dialect of what they call, equally ambiguously, "English." It seems that only an English critic who is himself something of an outsider, Anthony Burgess, is willing to learn much about the historical status of Scots alongside his own language or to approach modern work in Scots in a receptive frame of mind. Burgess, at any rate, has no doubt that MacDiarmid is a major poet.

Hugh MacDiarmid was born Christopher Murray Grieve to James and Elizabeth Graham Grieve on 11 August 1892 in Langholm, Dumfriesshire, near the border with England. His father was a rural postman, and most of his relatives worked in the local tweed mills or on farms.

C. M. Grieve (photograph by Eddie Armstrong)

A crucial factor in his boyhood was the happy accident whereby the family found accommodation in the same building as the town library, from which he borrowed books in such quantities that he used a clothes basket to transport them.

He was educated at Langholm Academy, where one of his early teachers was Francis George Scott, an outstanding song composer of his day, who was later to collaborate closely with the poet. From Langholm he went to Edinburgh in 1908 as a pupil-teacher at Broughton Junior Student Centre but turned to journalism in 1910. He was by that time actively involved in socialist politics, having joined the Independent Labour party at the age of sixteen.

After a variety of jobs on local newspapers in Scotland and Wales, he joined the Royal Army Medical Corps in 1915 and served as a sergeant in Greece and France. While on sick leave following bouts of malaria, he married Margaret Skinner in 1918, and when he was demobilized in the following year, the couple made their home in Montrose, Angus.

In the course of the next decade Grieve made this little town the center of what came to be called the Scottish Renaissance movement, through his efforts to revive a sense of national identity in cultural and political life. He had returned from a war fought ostensibly for the rights of small nations, and his ultimate aim was to regain for Scotland the place in Europe and the comity of nations which it had lost in the

course of assimilation by England. To this end he channeled his formidable energies into a national propaganda movement while earning his living as a reporter on the local newspaper, holding office as town councillor and justice of the peace, and writing a vast amount of prose and the solid body of poetry on which he staked his claim as a creative artist. During this period he became a founding member of the National Party of Scotland and the Scottish center of P.E.N.

Like any other ambitious author in the Scotland of his day, he began by writing entirely in English, and the first signs of the literary revival that was claimed for Scotland were detected in *Northern Numbers* (1920-1922), a series of three anthologies of contemporary poetry which he edited and to which he contributed verse in English. His own first book, *Annals of the Five Senses* (1923), was likewise in English: a collection of experimental prose pieces, erratic but bearing tokens of extraordinary talent, and a few specimens of his poetry.

His early poems in English were sufficiently impressive to earn him a reputation as the outstanding poet of his generation in Scotland, but, with few exceptions, they have not stood up well to the test of time. Their main interest today is perhaps in the way in which they exhibit his struggle to bring a Georgian-flavored English to terms with tendencies that attracted him in recent European poetry.

Grieve first used the name Hugh MacDiarmid in October 1922, in the *Scottish Chapbook*. The immediate reason for this was probably to avoid the charge of writing too much for the magazine of which he was editor, but it was also convenient for him to attribute his work in Scots to MacDiarmid rather than to Grieve, under which name he had achieved a considerable reputation by following the prevailing wisdom and writing entirely in English.

As it happened, one of the factors in his turning to writing poems in Scots was his awareness of the part played by the deployment of neglected linguistic resources of various sorts in recent European literary developments. Hitherto he had been inclined to relegate writing in Scots to the domestic backyard, rather as the Scots speech of his childhood was excluded from the precincts of education. Scots—before the union with England a national language with a healthy literature that claimed its place in Europe—had been progressively degraded for political and religious reasons. The adoption of an English translation of the Bible at the Reformation, the departure of king and court for London at the Union of Crowns in 1603, and the abolition of the Scots parliament in 1707 marked the stages of its decline. It fragmented into regional dialects and was subjected to social prejudices; its prose development was aborted; and its poetic revival in the eighteenth century, culminating in the work of Burns, was inevitably restricted in range. After Burns came too many imitators with minimal literary standards, and by MacDiarmid's time to write in Scots seemed to confine one inescapably to a corner of minor verse.

In 1922, however, he began to explore the language not only in its literature but in dictionaries and other linguistic works and suddenly discovered that his empathy with certain Scots words was releasing a fresh, untapped creative potential. One of his first Scots poems to result from this research, "The Watergaw," which grew around a cluster of unfamiliar expressions encountered in a linguistic study by Sir James Wilson, was immediately recognized as being of exceptional quality by good judges of poetry, including the critic Denis Saurat, who declared it to be a veritable masterpiece and translated it and other early MacDiarmid poems into French.

The standard response of English readers to a poem such as "The Watergaw" is to say that some of the vocabulary is so strange to them that they are unable to make anything of the poem. But the vocabulary was quite as unfamiliar to Saurat and to the vast majority of Scottish readers who have, in the subsequent, seventy years, shared his high opinion of it.

Perhaps the most useful approach would be to look at some seemingly simple poems in which the language MacDiarmid uses is not so very far removed from "standard" English. In "Empty Vessel," for example, the linguistic problem does not go much beyond recognizing a few Scots cognates of common English words and knowing that a *cairney* is a small heap of stones marking some feature of the landscape or a grave. What is less easily accounted for is the effortless skill in rhythm and image which holds the balance in this tiny poem between a girl singing to her dead child and the music of the spheres, rocked by cosmic winds, while the all-compassing light bends over creation:

> I met ayont the cairney
> A lass wi' tousie hair

> Singin' till a bairnie
> That was nae langer there.

> Wunds wi' warlds to swing
> Dinna sing sae sweet,
> The licht that bends owre a'thing
> Is less ta'en up wi't.

(*ayont*: beyond; *tousie*: tousled; *wunds*: winds; *warlds*: worlds; *owre*: over; *a'thing*: everything; *ta'en up wi't*: deeply concerned with it)

Or take the poem "Scunner," which is concerned with sexual love. The literal meaning of that familiar, colloquial Scots expression, *scunner*, is "disgust; a shudder betokening physical or moral repugnance." But there is in the poem a suggestion of affection for the "disreputable" Scots word, which subtly conveys the psychological perception on which the poem is based: that the element in the woman's sexuality which from one angle seems repugnant to him, from another angle provides the savor which makes him relish the experience. The word *scunner* is so crucial to his meaning, and so patently without an English equivalent, that one feels the poem's existence depended upon that word being available to him. And so the poem acts out one of the theoretical arguments for the value of Scots:

> Your body derns
> In its graces again
> As the dreich grun' does
> In the gowden grain,
> And oot o' the daith
> O' pride you rise
> Wi' beauty yet
> For a hauf-disguise.

> The skinklan' stars
> Are but distant dirt.
> Tho' fer owre near
> You are still—whiles—girt
> Wi' the bonnie licht
> You bood ha'e tint
> —And I lo'e Love
> Wi' a scunner in't.

(*derns*: hides; *dreich grun'*: drab ground; *gowden*: golden; *hauf-*: half-; *skinklan'*: glittering; *fer owre*: far too; *whiles*: sometimes; *bood ha'e tint*: should have lost; *lo'e*: love)

This poem also suggests a characteristic of MacDiarmid's use of Scots which he felt linked him with certain avant-garde writers of the time, particularly Joyce: it liberated him from the ele-

Councillor CHRISTOPHER M. GRIEVE

Grieve was elected to the Montrose town council as an Independent Socialist in 1922 (photograph by A. S. Milne).

ment of moral censorship which seemed to him to have been built into literary English.

As "Hugh MacDiarmid" took over from C. M. Grieve in the 1920s, a steady flow of poems in Scots followed. In deciding to write in Scots he based himself in the dialect speech of his boyhood—his native tongue—but allowed himself freedom to use any Scots expression that appealed to him, regardless of its historical or geographical distribution. It did not matter to him whether a word was categorized as obsolete or obsolescent or extant only in some dialect area remote from his home ground: what mattered was the use he could make of it in a poem. On the theoretical level, he made a strong case for what has been called his "synthetic" Scots, appealing to comparable developments in recent revivals of other long-neglected languages and pointing out that his "synthetic" procedure was just an extension of the principle actually followed by Burns, allegedly a model of "naturalness" in language. He also argued for Scots as an expression of national psychology not otherwise available to Scotsmen, one deeply rooted in the sound system of the language: "There are certain old Scots words which (apart altogether from their precise original signification) have a significance of sound and shape which may prove infinitely suggestive. . . . I think that if Scottish artists will hunt out all these old words, the mere shapes and sounds of them will suggest to them effects which they cannot at present contrive, and if they set to and secure these effects the results will constitute a Scottish idiom—a Scottish scale of sound-values and physico-psychical effects completely at variance with those of England." But the most persuasive evidence of the value of what he was doing lay in the quality of the poetry he produced. Compared with his earlier work in English, it is much more tightly knit, richer and more powerful in its sound effects, and at the same time more concrete and more suggestive in its imagery—the very thing at which Pound and the imagists were aiming. Above all, he rapidly found his individual voice in Scots and with it a style which rooted the speculative, metaphysical bent of his mind in an earthy, virile vernacular.

Certain deliberate tours de force apart, even the most unfamiliar items in his Scots vocabulary do not, as used by him, give that impression of artificiality associated with a rarefied diction. Some are vivid illustrations of the imaginative life inherent in the process of word formation itself: for example, *yow-trummle* (a late cold spell which comes in a northern summer after the sheep have been shorn—hence the trembling of the ewes), and *how-dumb-deid* (middle of the night), in which the first element in the compound is the *howe* (hollow) occurring in place names. On the other hand a proverbial expression about the weather, "there was nae reek i' the laverock's hoose that nicht" (there was no smoke—hence warmth—in the lark's house that night), in a leap of metaphor conveys that it was a cold, wild night.

MacDiarmid's first two poetry collections, *Sangschaw* (1925) and *Penny Wheep* (1926), consist mainly of short, highly charged Scots poems of which the finest are perhaps "Empty Vessel," "The Bonnie Broukit Bairn," and "The Eemis Stane." These poems show his characteristic sense of the earth, with its earthiness affectionately conveyed through the associations of the vernacular but strongly visualized in a cosmic setting. By far the most difficult, from the lexical point of view, is "The Eemis Stane." The earth is seen as at once a dead star adrift in space and a stone in the cosmic graveyard, inscribed with mysterious words which human history has obscured:

> I' the how-dumb-deid o' the cauld hairst nicht
> The warl' like an eemis stane
> Wags i' the lift;
> An' my eerie memories fa'
> Like a yowdendrift.

> Like a yowdendrift so's I couldna read
> The words cut oot i' the stane
> Had the fug o' fame
> An' history's hazelraw
> No' yirdit thaim.

(In the still center of the dead of night, cold at harvest-time, / The world like a loose stone / Shakes in the sky; / And my eerie memories fall / Like snow driven down by the wind. / / Like snow driven down by the wind, so that I couldn't read / The words cut out in the stone / Had the moss of fame / And the lichen of history / Not buried them.)

Along with these short lyrics MacDiarmid began writing longer poems and "suites" of poems in Scots, and his next venture was intended as a major, book-length work which would stake the claim of Scots to regain its place in contemporary European literature. The composer Scott supplied the title of this poem or poem sequence, *A Drunk Man Looks at the Thistle* (1926), and he also assisted the author in deciding which items in a proliferating mass of material should be eliminated from the work prior to publication, and what the order for those retained should be. This assistance suggests a weakness on MacDiarmid's part where the shaping of large-scale forms was concerned, and it was undoubtedly a real weakness which was to bedevil his subsequent determination to turn himself into an epic poet. In the case of *A Drunk Man Looks at the Thistle*, however, he succeeded in organizing an extraordinary variety of material around key images which generate a dynamic symbolism pervading the work as a whole. The whiskey imbibed by the protagonist—the national "spirit," now much adulterated—liberates a stream of consciousness from which separable, fully formed poems, along with much else worthy of interest, emerge as he gazes intently at the thistle in the moonlight. Thistle and moon are the poet's archetypal symbols, around which figures of speech and patterns of thought constellate in astonishing profusion. Or perhaps a better suggestion of

how they function is to be found in Pound's words: "The image . . . is a radiant node or cluster; it is a *vortex*, from which, and through which, and into which, ideas are constantly rushing."

The thistle is of course the Scottish national emblem, and at one level the problem the Drunk Man sets himself—how to "pluck figs from thistles"—is the problem of writing the poem itself, which is aimed at bringing to fruition the stunted growth of MacDiarmid's native Scots tradition. This task involves on the one hand an attempt at scourging contemporary Scotland into awareness of its degenerate condition by a series of scathing satirical attacks. It also involves an effort toward restoring the international context of the old national tradition by absorbing into the texture of his work Scots adaptations of poems by modern German, French, Belgian, and Russian writers—plus a passage from Dante and a network of literary allusions including a reference to Eliot's *The Waste Land* (1922), which MacDiarmid confidently set out to rival.

On another level, giving the poem its metaphysical dimension, the thistle embodies prickly philosophical questions confronting all mankind, as the Drunk Man sees in the tension between its jagged leaves and incongruous blossoms an epitome of the human dilemma between matter and spirit, and in its unpredicted shape a challenge to the belief that life itself has an intelligible purpose. The fluctuation of the poem from one level to another is related to an idea which runs through a great deal of MacDiarmid's work in addition to *A Drunk Man Looks at the Thistle*. The critic Gregory Smith diagnosed as the distinguishing feature of Scottish literature a tendency to combine opposites or contraries, which he designated "the Caledonian Antisyzygy." What especially excited MacDiarmid about this observation was that he discerned a similar tendency in modern European literatures, and so, if he succeeded in reviving the essential spirit of his national tradition, he would be working in harmony with up-to-date European developments. But the concept of antisyzygy, or the combination of opposites, was in fact an ancient one, going far beyond recent literary tendencies to the function of the human imagination itself (as described for example in Samuel Taylor Coleridge's and William Blake's accounts of that faculty) and informing many European and Eastern philosophies as the principle of *coincidentia oppositorum*, whereby existence itself is a dynamic, creative tension between polar opposites. MacDiarmid's declared philosophical posi-

Yet Hae I Silence Left.

Yet hae I Silence left, the croon o' a'.

Tho' her, wha on the hills langsyne I saw
liftin' a forehead o' perpetual snaw.

Tho' her, wha in the how-dumb-deid o' nicht
Kythes, like Eternity in Time's despite.

Tho' her, withooten shape, wha's name is Daith.

Tho' Him, unkennable abies by faith.

— God whom, gin e'er He saw a man 'ud be
E'en mair dumfoonert at the sicht than he!

But Him, whom nocht in Man or Deity
Or Daith or Dreid or loneliness can touch,
Wha's deed owre often and has seen owre much.

O I hae Silence left, the croon o' a'.

                                   Hugh M'Diarmid.

Page from a draft for the conclusion of A Drunk Man Looks at the Thistle

tion at the beginning of *A Drunk Man Looks at the Thistle*—"whaur extremes meet"—is another rendering of the same principle, and thus the speculative, metaphysical ramifications of his poem have an underlying connection with his efforts to put into practice a specifically Caledonian aesthetic of antisyzygy.

Around what Smith called "the 'polar twins' of the Scottish Muse," MacDiarmid puts into orbit his antimonies of the real and the ideal, passion and intellect, body and soul, lust and love, beauty and ugliness, God and man, life and death, chaos and cosmos, being and essence, oblivion and eternity. The process of the poem is a romantically self-lacerating one, resulting in the total exhaustion of the poet, but it is the speculative stamina he brings to the longer, more sustained passages that ensures that the work is no mere showcase for the more immediately attractive specimens of his art, but that rare thing, a genuine modern long poem. It was written at a time when H. J. C. Grierson's work on John Donne and others was alerting the twentieth century to what its poets could learn from the metaphysicals of the seventeenth century. And, using the term in its several senses, MacDiarmid's "metaphysical" anatomy of the thistle may be seen as a splendid celebration of opportunities thus rediscovered for poetry:

> Plant, what are you then? Your leafs
> Mind me o' the pipes' lood drone
> —And a' your purple tops
> Are the pirly-wirly notes
> That gang staggerin' owre them as they groan.
>
> Or your leafs are alligators
> That ha'e gobbled owre a haill
> Company o' Heilant sodgers
> And left naething but the toories
> O' their Balmoral bonnets to tell the tale.
> . . . .
> The thistle in the wind dissolves
> In lichtnin' as shook foil gi'es way
> In sudden splendours, or the flesh
> As Daith lets slip the infinite soul;
> And syne it's like a sunrise tint
> In grey o' day, or love and life,
> That in a cloody blash o' sperm
> Undae the warld to big't again,
> Or like a pickled foetus that
> Nae man feels ocht in common wi'
> —But micht as easily ha' been!
> Or like a corpse a soul set free
> Scunners to think it tenanted
> —And little recks that but for it
> It never micht ha' been at a',

> Like love frae lust and God frae man!
> . . . .
> 'Let there be Licht,' said God, and there was
> A little: but He lacked the poo'er
> To licht up mair than pairt o' space at aince,
> And there is lots o' darkness that's the same
> As gin He'd never spoken
> —Mair darkness than there's licht,
> And dwarfin't to a candle-flame,
> A spalin' candle that'll sune gang oot.
> —Darkness comes closer to us than the licht,
> And is oor natural element. We peer oot frae't
> Like cat's een bleezin' in a goustrous nicht
> (Whaur there is nocht to find but stars
> That look like ither cats' een),
> Like cat's een, and there is nocht to find
> Savin' we turn them in upon oorsels;
> Cats canna.

(*mind*: remind; *lood*: loud; *pirly-wirly notes*: grace notes; *gang*: go; *haill*: whole; *Heilant sodgers*: Highland soldiers; *toories*: pompoms; *syne*: then; *tint*: lost; *blash*: shower; *big't*: build it; *ocht*: anything; *scunners*: shudders; *a'*: all; *poo'er*: power; *aince*: once; *gin*: if; *spalin'*: guttering; *een*: eyes; *goustrous*: stormy; *nocht*: nothing; *oorsels*: ourselves; *canna*: can't)

Only quotation on a massive scale could suggest the inventive powers which sustain this astonishing work. *A Drunk Man Looks at the Thistle* is one of the great poems of the century.

MacDiarmid's problem was, inevitably, how to follow it. He struggled for four years before taking the plunge with his next work, a much longer poem in Scots called *To Circumjack Cencrastus* (1930). As the poem reveals, domestic and professional troubles played a large part in his difficulties, acerbated by an ill-fated move to London and then to Liverpool. The key factor in his decision to leave Scotland for London in 1929 was the offer of a job on *Vox*, a magazine founded by Compton Mackenzie to cater to the growing interest in the new medium of radio. The magazine was inadequately financed, and MacDiarmid soon had to contend with the scourge of the 1930s, unemployment, along with a succession of personal problems culminating in divorce and separation from his two children.

Mackenzie said of the writing of *To Circumjack Cencrastus* that, under these conditions, it was only by a miracle that any sort of book appeared at all, and it is certainly true that the work shows signs of having been patched together in a desperate attempt to salvage pieces from at least two different projects. One of these projects was the pursuit of Cencrastus on a highly metaphysical level, Cencrastus (the name

JOIN THE

HUGH MACDIARMID BOOK CLUB

Organised to secure publication for a constant stream of revolutionary Scottish Literature, devoted to anti-English separatism.

The majority of the entire Scottish electorate votes for the Left, but this is not only nullified in practice by the English connection but is so far almost entirely unreflected in journalism and publishing. Mr. MacDiarmid's aim is the establishment of a Scottish Workers' Autonymous Communist Republic and a revival of literature in the distinctive Scottish tradition.

SEND NO MONEY, but sign this form and post it to the Secretary, Hugh MacDiarmid Book Club, Whalsay, via Lerwick, Shetland Islands :—

I agree for one year from this date to accept on publication the four or five books to be issued during the ensuing twelve months, at preferential rates to Club members, by the Hugh MacDiarmid Book Club, also the weekly paper, *Red Scotland*, and the monthly *Hammer and Thistle*, at a total inclusive rate, including postage, of 40/- [books to be paid for on delivery, and the *Red Scotland* and *Hammer and Thistle* annual subscriptions (10/- each) on receipt of the first issues of these.]

Name ....

Address ....

....   *Date*....................

(Please fill in in clear block letters.)

HUGH MACDIARMID'S BOOKS INCLUDE :—

Poetry: A Drunk Man looks at the Thistle; Selected Poems; Stony Limits; First Hymn to Lenin; Second Hymn to Lenin, etc., etc.

Criticism: At the Sign of the Thistle; Contemporary Scottish Studies; Scottish Scene, etc., etc.

Biography: Scottish Eccentrics, etc., etc.

Fiction: Annals of the Five Senses; Five Bits of Millar, etc., etc.

Politics: Albyn, or Scotland and the Future, etc., etc.

Music: The Present Condition of Scottish Music.

Agriculture: Rural Reform (with Lord Passfield and others.)

(Thirty titles in all.)

Early Club issues will include *Cornish Heroic Song for Valda Trevlyn* and *The Red Lion* (a poetical gallimaufry of the Glasgow slums). Further Club news in *Red Scotland* weekly.

Circular for the Hugh MacDiarmid Book Club

of a snake the poet encountered in his exploration of John Jamieson's Scots dictionary) being conceived as the mythological world-serpent or "the underlying unifying principle of the cosmos," and the meaning of "to Circumjack" being "to lie round or about." The other main project was an attempt at reviving the ethos, not just of Lowland Scotland, but of the ancient Celtic civilization, which included Ireland, Scotland, Wales, and Cornwall. This attempt centered on what MacDiarmid hoped would be a dynamic myth, "The Gaelic Idea," conceived as a counterbalance to "The Russian Idea" projected by Fyodor Dostoyevski and radically transformed by Lenin. Since Cencrastus was intended to have a historical dimension, his movements traceable in world history, one can see how these two strands might have been woven together imaginatively in the work, but the poet failed to carry out this integration. Lacking the cohesion of imagery achieved in *A Drunk Man Looks at the Thistle*, *To Circumjack Cencrastus* obstinately remains full of awkward gaps which MacDiarmid in the end tried to plug with an assortment of bits and pieces, thus ensuring that the work was (as he had said it would be) "a much bigger thing than *A Drunk Man*," but merely in terms of length. Readers may find the bulk of the poem such an indigestible mixture that they are likely to miss some of the good things in it.

MacDiarmid's difficulties in the unhappy period which followed were compounded by his political leanings. He was increasingly drawn to communism (a communism cut very much to his own Scottish pattern, though he did become a card-carrying member of the Communist party in 1934), but he believed that the best immediate prospect for his own country, in the existing circumstances, lay in the adoption of the Social Credit economic policies of Clifford Hugh Douglas. His efforts to get a Douglas plan accepted as the economic program of the National Party of Scotland led to his expulsion from that party in 1933, and he was convinced that the forces operating against him in his increasingly desperate struggle to make a living and support his second wife, Valda Trevlyn (whom he married in 1932), and their child, as well as to get his literary work published, were largely political in motivation.

It is, however, a mistake to suppose, as some commentators have done, that MacDiarmid in the 1930s confined his talents as a poet to political propaganda, resulting in hymns to Lenin and that sort of thing. He wrote what he called "Hymns to Lenin," certainly, but they are not what anyone else would be likely to call hymns, and the second of the three, in particular, is an assertion of the supremacy of the work of art over all politics, Lenin's included:

> Your knowledge in your ain sphere
> Was exact and complete
> But your sphere's elementary and sune by
> As a poet maun see't.
>
> Unremittin', relentless,
> Organized to the last degree,
> Ah Lenin, politics is bairns' play
> To what this maun be!

(*ain*: own; *sune by*: soon past; *maun*: must)

The two hymns written in the early 1930s were intended to take their place in the first volume of "Clann Albann," a huge autobiographical poem planned for five volumes. Indeed, *First Hymn to Lenin and Other Poems* (1931) and *Scots Unbound and Other Poems* (1932) were presented as interim selections of samples from the first volume—the title of which, "The Muckle Toon," indicated

MacDiarmid and his second wife, Valda, outside their cottage in Biggar, 1951

their connection with MacDiarmid's birthplace, Langholm—and other material intended for inclusion in it remained for decades forgotten in periodicals. The poems not published in *First Hymn to Lenin and Other Poems* and *Scots Unbound and Other Poems* include some excellent longer poems, such as "Whuchulls" and "By Wauchopeside"—a fact which indicates that MacDiarmid was unable to find a place even for some of the best of his poems in the little volumes he did manage to get published.

His first four volumes of poetry had been published by the old Scottish establishment of Blackwood's, but now he had to fall back on the modest resources of the Unicorn Press, for which he worked in London, and a small press in Stirling. A short spell of employment as a public-relations officer in Liverpool was followed by a period of bare subsistence in a borrowed cottage in Surrey, and in 1932 he returned to Scotland in an attempt to eke out a living from journalism in Edinburgh.

The breakup of his first marriage and separation from his children had brought about a return in the poet's imagination to the Langholm

of his childhood, with a wry review of his relationships with his kinsfolk and a search for the restorative powers of the images with which the surrounding countryside had first nurtured his inner life.
Above all, "a perfect maze of waters is aboot the
Muckle Toon," and so the work intended for the
first volume of "Clann Albann" is full of the imagery of water, which takes him through the
search for the sources of his own creative powers
ultimately to the source and evolutionary potential of life itself. "Water Music" is one of the most
striking poems which emerged from this search:
a verbal tour de force addressed to James Joyce,
celebrating the dynamic multifariousness of the
rivers Wauchope, Esk, and Ewes in a rhythmic
apotheosis of the Scots lexicon:

> Wheesht, wheesht, Joyce, and let me hear
>   Nae Anna Livvy's lilt,
> But Wauchope, Esk, and Ewes again,
>   Each wi' its ain rhythms till't.

> Archin' here and arrachin there,
>   Allevolie or alleman,
> Whiles appliable, whiles areird,
>   The polysemous poem's planned.

> Lively, louch, atweesh, atween,
>   Auchimuty or aspate,
> Threidin' through the averins
>   Or bightsome in the aftergait.

(*wheesht*: hush; *till't*: to it; *archin'*: flowing smoothly; *arrachin*: tu-
multuous; *allevolie*: volatile; *alleman*: orderly; *appliable*: compli-
ant; *areird*: troublesome; *louch*: downcast; *atweesh*: betwixt;
atween: between; *auchimuty*: trickling; *aspate*: in flood; *averins*:
cloudberries; *bightsome*: ample; *aftergait*: outcome)

The verve of such lines carries the reader along,
willing for the sake of the verbal music to forgo
the usual semantic sustenance, until

> you've me in your creel again,
>   Brim or shallow, bauch or bricht,
> Singin' in the mornin',
>   Corrieneuchin' a' the nicht.

(*creel*: spell; *brim*: swollen; *bauch*: dull; *corrieneuch-
in'*: gossiping)

In the experiments with dictionary Scots
which he made about this time, rhythmic and
other relationships in the *sound* of his language
are of vital importance in stimulating the reader
to respond to the life of the poems. But with
MacDiarmid's tendency to push experimental

techniques to the extreme, as if to find out just
how much they could stand, he was beginning, in
such works as "Scots Unbound," to lose his rhythmic touch and so to overwhelm the reader with a
sense of sheer verbalism. Clearly he could not go
much further in that particular direction. And although he could still in 1932 produce one of his
most perfect poems, "Milk-wort and Bog-cotton,"
that was to be the last of his truly great Scots lyrics:

> Cwa' een like milk-wort and bog-cotton hair!
> I love you, earth, in this mood best o' a'
> When the shy spirit like a laich wind moves
> And frae the lift nae shadow can fa'
> Since there's nocht left to thraw a shadow there
> Owre een like milk-wort and milk-white cotton hair.

> Wad that nae leaf upon anither wheeled
> A shadow either and nae root need dern
> In sacrifice to let sic beauty be!
> But deep surroondin' darkness I discern
> Is aye the price o' licht. Wad licht revealed
> Naething but you, and nicht nocht else concealed.

(*cwa'*: come away; *laich*: low; *lift*: sky; *nocht*: nothing; *wad*:
would; *dern*: hide; *sic*: such)

MacDiarmid began to write more and more
poems in English, as the "Clann Albann" scheme
became ever less likely to be carried out, and his reversion to English was made to seem more emphatic when the publisher of his next collection,
Stony Limits and Other Poems (1934), deleted from
the manuscript two of the most substantial works
in Scots. (The two poems were restored in *Stony
Limits and Scots Unbound and Other Poems*, 1956.)
One of these, "Ode to All Rebels," is his longest
sustained achievement in Scots since *To
Circumjack Cencrastus*, while the other, "Harry
Semen," explores the theme of fascinated revulsion at the human sexual process as powerfully
and memorably as anything in that vein in *A
Drunk Man Looks at the Thistle*.

The change from Scots back to English, in
which language the vast majority of Mac-
Diarmid's later poems were written, accompanied
a move which might have been expected to result
in some new orientation. In 1933 he left Scotland
for Whalsay, in the Shetland Islands, where at
any rate physical survival was less of a problem
for him, his courageous new wife, and their infant son. In other respects, however, he felt his isolation acutely, and he was to remain there in virtual exile for the next eight years.

Hugh MacDiarmid (photograph by Gordon Wright)

The later poems in English suggest a turning away from the lyrical aspects of poetry. There are propaganda pieces—most of the propaganda being Douglasite rather than communist—in which the all-important message is sometimes put across at a crude level of versifying, as in "The Belly-Grip." There are experiments with scientific, technical, or otherwise recondite vocabularies, rapidly taken to breaking point as was his wont, but achieving some brilliant effects along the way. For example, the first part of "In the Caledonian Forest" is verbalistically supersaturated to a degree which is likely to repel readers, but in the second part they are lured back against all the odds with the following:

The gold edging of a bough at sunset, its pantile
    way
Forming a double curve, tegula and imbrex in one,
Seems at times a movement on which I might be
    borne
Happily to infinity; but again I am glad
When it suddenly ceases and I find myself
Pursuing no longer a rhythm of duramen
But bouncing in a diploe in a clearing between
    earth and air

Or headlong in dewy dallops or a moon-spairged
    fernshaw
Or caught in a dark dumosity or even
In open country again watching an aching spargosis
    of stars.

There are also much longer, meditative poems which may make use of recondite lexical resources for special effects but which owe their power to the sustained concentration of an endlessly speculative mind coiling itself around the curious, multifarious lore of a lifetime's reading. The most impressive of these is "On A Raised Beach," a sustained meditation on the world of stones, the beginning and end of creation, seen in the hard, clear light of the Shetland Islands. The stones on the raised beach are geological clues to the mystery of the universe, and they are represented at the beginning of the poem by a great pile of recondite words seemingly as hard to penetrate as the stones. But as the poet proceeds to explore the imagery he finds indefatigably for the "barren but beautiful reality" of this bleak world, he does in the end achieve on his own terms the miracle of "bread from stones":

This is no heap of broken images.
. . . .
What happens to us
Is irrelevant to the world's geology
But what happens to the world's geology
Is not irrelevant to us.
We must reconcile ourselves to the stones,
Not the stones to us.
Here a man must shed the encumbrances that muf-
    fle
Contact with elemental things, the subtleties
That seem inseparable from a humane life, and go
    apart
Into a simple and sterner, more beautiful and more
    oppressive world,
Austerely intoxicating; the first draught is overpow-
    ering;
Few survive it. It fills me with a sense of perfect
    form,
The end seen from the beginning, as in a song.
It is no song that conveys the feeling
That there is no reason why it should ever stop,
But the kindred form I am conscious of here
Is the beginning and end of the world,
The unsearchable masterpiece, the music of the
    spheres,
Alpha and Omega, the Omnific Word.

In this poem and in "Stony Limits," his noble elegy to a fellow visionary of the desert, Charles M. Doughty, MacDiarmid used his isolation in the wilderness to give resonance to verse of massive dignity. But the strain of his increasingly fanatical demands on himself—"immense exercise of will, / Inconceivable discipline, courage, and endurance, / Self-purification and antihumanity"—resulted before long in a mental and physical breakdown. He spent some time in a hospital in 1935 and on his return launched himself into a series of projects for vast, epic works, none of which was ever executed, or at any rate published, on the scale on which they were conceived, though the remainder of his poetic career was largely devoted to them.

Second Hymn to Lenin and Other Poems (1935) strikes one as a clearing of his desk of short poems (including pieces of the rejected "Ode to All Rebels" recast in English) before committing himself absolutely to these huge projects. The first of them, "Cornish Heroic Song for Valda Trevlyn," seems to have been an attempt to carry out on a much larger canvas what *To Circumjack Cencrastus* had failed to achieve but his long "Lament for the Great Music" had again heralded: a celebration of the unique Celtic contribution to civilization in all its aspects. The other main project was called "Mature Art" or "A Vision of World Language" and was conceived as a "poetry of fact" aimed at presenting as many facets as possible of the world of information and ideas impacting on the mind of a "harbinger of the epical age of Communism." Two of an intended four parts of this work were eventually published as *In Memoriam James Joyce* (1955) and *The Kind of Poetry I Want* (1961).

Meanwhile, MacDiarmid had returned to mainland Scotland, conscripted for war work in 1941. At the age of fifty he worked as a fitter in the copper shell-band department of an engineering works in Glasgow and then moved to service as a ship's engineer until the end of the war, when his job was eliminated, and he rejoined the unemployed.

In 1950 he was awarded a civil-list pension of £150 a year for his services to literature and moved soon afterward to the farm worker's cottage near Biggar in Lanarkshire where he stayed until his death from cancer in 1978. An honorary doctorate from Edinburgh University signaled his recognition by the academic establishment in Scotland, and visits to various Communist countries and to North America indicated a growing international reputation. In his own view, the crucial breakthrough occurred in 1962 with the publication in New York of *Collected Poems*, a partial but very substantial collection of his poems. This volume made the range of his work known at last—even in London, though the gradual buildup of critical appreciation occurred elsewhere—and there was now widespread acknowledgment of his public stature as the Grand Old Man of Scottish literature: a part which he played with great aplomb and a certain subversive relish. Inwardly he continued in his seventies the pursuit of those unrealized epic schemes which haunted him till almost the end.

The samples of his epic "poetry of fact" which appeared in 1955 and 1961 contain some pioneering attempts at extending the range of poetry to take in areas long considered to have become foreign to its nature, notably through his use of scientific, technical, and other apparently prosaic materials for purposes of analogy. Although these works have proved stimulating to later poets, particularly Edwin Morgan, they tend to be overwhelmed by an obsessive cataloguing of itemized pieces of information or labeling of specimens. MacDiarmid now conceded only a minimal distinction between poetry and prose, so that the contents of his notebooks and stacks of press clippings could supply the substance of his epics with little verbal manipulation by the poet himself. He could on occasion do fascinating and imaginative things with passages of prose taken from writers who often had very different purposes in mind, but his determination to project everything onto an epic scale resulted in the erection of a top-heavy Tower of Babel which he propped up with some epic wishful thinking.

All of MacDiarmid's poetry became available in the two massive volumes of *Complete Poems* (1978), and it is now a straightforward matter for readers to judge for themselves what part of his total output is worthy of the immense energy and ambition he brought to it. No one could take the risks MacDiarmid repeatedly took and not be vulnerable on a grand scale, but even his disasters have an awesome grandeur about them, and the best of his work is a delight of the highest order which no one who cares for poetry should allow himself to miss:

> For you rin coonter to the rhythms o' thocht,
> Wrenched oot o' recognition a' words fail
> To haud you, alien to the human mind,
> Yet in your ain guid time you suddenly slip,
> Nae man kens hoo, into the simplest phrase,
> While a' the dictionary rejoices. . . .

(*rin coonter*: run counter; *haud*: hold; *kens hoo*: knows how)

Letters:
The Letters of Hugh MacDiarmid, edited by Alan Bold (London: Hamish Hamilton, 1984).

Interviews:
Duncan Glen, "A Conversation," *Akros,* 5 (April 1970): 9-72;

George Bruce, "An Interview," *Akros,* 5 (April 1970): 73-77;

Walter Perrie, Interview with MacDiarmid, in his *Metaphysics and Poetry* (Hamilton, U.K.: Lothlorien Publications, 1975);

Alexander Scott, "An Interview with Hugh MacDiarmid," *Studies in Scottish Literature,* 14 (1979): 1-22.

Biography:
Alan Bold, *MacDiarmid* (London: John Murray, 1988).

References:
Akros, special MacDiarmid issue, 12 (August 1977);

Kenneth Buthlay, "The Appreciation of the Golden Lyric: Early Scots Poems of Hugh MacDiarmid," *Scottish Literary Journal,* 2 (July 1975): 41-66;

Buthlay, *Hugh MacDiarmid (C. M. Grieve)* (Edinburgh: Oliver & Boyd, 1964; revised edition, Edinburgh: Scottish Academic Press, 1982);

David Daiches, "Hugh MacDiarmid and Scottish Poetry," *Poetry,* 72 (July 1948): 202-218;

Kulgin D. Duval and Sydney Goodsir Smith, eds., *Hugh MacDiarmid: A Festschrift* (Edinburgh: Duval, 1962);

Nancy K. Gish, *Hugh MacDiarmid: The Man and His Work* (London: Macmillan, 1984);

Duncan Glen, *Hugh MacDiarmid (Christopher Murray Grieve) and the Scottish Renaissance* (Edinburgh: Chambers, 1964);

Glen, ed., *Hugh MacDiarmid: A Critical Survey* (Edinburgh: Scottish Academic Press, 1972);

Charles I. Glicksberg, "Hugh MacDiarmid the Marxist Messiah," *Prairie Schooner,* 26 (Fall 1952): 325-335;

Peter McCarey, *Hugh MacDiarmid and the Russians* (Edinburgh: Scottish Academic Press, 1987);

Edwin Morgan, *Essays* (Cheadle Hulme, U.K.: Carcanet New Press, 1974), pp. 194-221;

Morgan, *Hugh MacDiarmid* (Harlow, U.K.: Longman, 1976);

Harvey Oxenhorn, *Elemental Things: The Poetry of Hugh MacDiarmid* (Edinburgh: Edinburgh University Press, 1984);

P. H. Scott and A. C. Davis, eds., *The Age of MacDiarmid: Essays on Hugh MacDiarmid and his Influence on Contemporary Scotland* (Edinburgh: Mainstream, 1980);

Scottish Literary Journal, MacDiarmid memorial number, 5 (December 1978); MacDiarmid issue, 15 (November 1988);

Roderick Watson, *MacDiarmid* (Milton Keynes, U.K.: Open University Press, 1985).

Papers:
Most of MacDiarmid's papers are in Edinburgh University Library and the National Library of Scotland, Edinburgh. Others are in the libraries of Yale University; the State University of New York, Buffalo; and the University of Delaware, Newark.

George Orwell
(Eric Arthur Blair)
(25 June 1903 - 21 January 1950)

This entry was written by David Morgan Zehr (University of Alabama) for
DLB 15: British Novelists, 1930-1959: Part Two.

See also the Orwell entry in DLB 98: Modern British Essayists: First Series.

BOOKS: *Down and Out in Paris and London* (London: Gollancz, 1933; New York & London: Harper, 1933);

Burmese Days (New York: Harper, 1934; London: Gollancz, 1935);

A Clergyman's Daughter (London: Gollancz, 1935; New York: Harper, 1936);

Keep the Aspidistra Flying (London: Gollancz, 1936; New York: Harcourt, Brace, 1956);

The Road to Wigan Pier (London: Gollancz, 1937; New York: Harcourt, Brace, 1958);

Homage to Catalonia (London: Secker & Warburg, 1938; New York: Harcourt, Brace, 1952);

Coming Up for Air (London: Gollancz, 1939; New York: Harcourt, Brace, 1950);

Inside the Whale, and Other Essays (London: Gollancz, 1940);

The Lion and the Unicorn: Socialism and the English Genius (London: Secker & Warburg, 1941);

Animal Farm (London: Secker & Warburg, 1945; New York: Harcourt, Brace, 1946);

Critical Essays (London: Secker & Warburg, 1946); republished as *Dickens, Dali and Others* (New York: Reynal & Hitchcock, 1946);

Nineteen Eighty-Four (London: Secker & Warburg, 1949; New York: Harcourt, Brace, 1949);

Shooting an Elephant, and Other Essays (London: Secker & Warburg, 1950; New York: Harcourt, Brace, 1950);

England Your England and Other Essays (London: Secker & Warburg, 1953); republished as *Such, Such Were the Joys* (New York: Harcourt, Brace, 1953);

A Collection of Essays (Garden City, N.Y.: Doubleday, 1954);

The Orwell Reader: Fiction, Essays, and Reportage (New York: Harcourt, Brace, 1956);

The Collected Essays, Journalism, and Letters of George Orwell, 4 volumes, edited by Sonia Or-

George Orwell

well and Ian Angus (London: Secker & Warburg, 1968; New York: Harcourt, Brace & World, 1968);

Orwell, the War Broadcasts, edited by W. J. West (London: Duckworth / BBC, 1985).

OTHER: "Fascism and Democracy" and "Patriots and Revolutionaries," in *The Betrayal of the Left*, edited by Victor Gollancz (London: Gollancz, 1941).

George Orwell's remarkable international reputation is primarily due to his last two novels, *Animal Farm* (1945) and *Nineteen Eighty-Four* (1949), which have spoken to the Cold War consciousness with such force and intimacy that conceptions such as Big Brother, "doublethink," and the apocalyptic date 1984 have become virtually mythic elements in our culture. Although Orwell became England's most prominent political writer during the 1940s, he was equally honored for his pragmatic, commonsensical habit of mind and for his uncompromising commitment to intellectual integrity. In fact, his career is a testimony to the enduring power of a moralist who tenaciously clings to the values of common decency, social justice, and respect for the individual. When Orwell died in January 1950, V. S. Pritchett eulogized him as a "saint" and as the "conscience of his generation."

Orwell was a complex, paradoxical figure who once described himself as a "Tory anarchist," a phrase which expressed his complex unification of radical and conservative impulses. Although he became a militant socialist after 1936, he was a fervent anti-Communist and persistently attacked the "smelly little orthodoxies" which he felt had corrupted intellectual liberty. While he was committed to the power of the writer to influence and affect the direction of his society and its political order, he was convinced that ideological commitment would destroy the power of a writer: "To write in plain, vigorous language one has to think fearlessly, and if one thinks fearlessly one cannot be politically orthodox." He hated expediency (whether political or literary), sympathized with the poor and the underdog, opposed imperialism and aristocratic privilege, and became England's most vigorous spokesman for popular culture during the 1940s. He repeatedly defended the normative values of ordinary, bourgeois life, felt a persistent nostalgia for the order and stability of the pre-1914 world, and believed in the embryonic power within common, ordinary Englishmen. He became, in the words of one writer, a "revolutionary patriot." Orwell's career—as novelist, essayist, and political pamphleteer—finally serves as a kind of barometer to an understanding of the conflicts and mood of the 1930s and 1940s and of the situation of the liberal writer working in a time of cultural and political crisis.

Eric Arthur Blair (he never legally changed his name to George Orwell) was born on 25 June 1903 at Motihari in Bengal, India, where his fa-ther was an undistinguished administrator in the Opium Department of the Government of India. He was the second child of Richard Walmsley and Ida Mabel Limouzin Blair. His mother returned to England with her children by 1905, although his father did not return permanently until 1911, when he retired. These early years in England, living at Henley-on-Thames, a very Edwardian town, would come to represent a period of happiness and security that affected Orwell's consciousness for the rest of his life. And yet he was also aware of conflicts. Years later he described himself as a member of the "lower-upper-middle class," a phrase which was meant to contrast the family's social rank (as servants of king and country) with their middle-class economic status. Although the family was by no means impoverished, Orwell was later to insist that in this kind of "shabby-genteel family . . . there is far more *consciousness* of poverty than in any working-class family above the level of the dole." His awareness of having an ambivalent social position and of money's extraordinary importance would become prominent themes in Orwell's first four books and helped to shape his attitudes to what he came to see as the privileged intelligentsia.

In September 1911 he was sent to St. Cyprians, a snobbish and expensive school, where he was to be prepared for entrance into one of the good public schools of England. The rigorous commitment to education and to the building of character at St. Cyprians was to make Orwell a promising candidate for public school, but the four years that he spent there also had a profound emotional impact on him, which he recorded in his posthumously published *England Your England and Other Essays* (1953). This world was one in which money, position, and privilege seemed to be the determinate values, and Orwell came to feel like an alien in a foreign land. He remembers that the rich boys were openly favored and that he was reminded of his own tenuous economic status by being denied things because, he was told, his parents could not afford them. While a critic such as Anthony West finds the paradigm of the world of 1984 expressed in Orwell's recollections of favoritism, arbitrary rules, and the omnipotence of the system, it is perhaps more important to understand that during these years Orwell began to develop his antipathy toward authoritarian or institutionalized rule and began to develop an embryonic theory about victims and victimizers. This awareness of a fundamental conflict between the individual and a larger social structure would become an important social subject in his writing of the 1930s and a political subject in his work of the 1940s.

In the spring of 1916, Orwell sat for scholarship examinations for entrance into a public school. He narrowly missed a place at Eton but was accepted into Wellington, where he spent the first nine weeks of 1917; however, because of the war, a place opened up in the scholarship class at Eton, and in May 1917 he enrolled there. The atmosphere at Eton was much more open than at St. Cyprians: it was a freer intellectual environment, one in which individuality and intellectual freedom were encouraged. Orwell was later to say that the great virtue of the school was its "tolerant and civilized · atmosphere which gives each boy a fair chance of developing his individuality." Immediately after the war Eton gained the reputation of being "Bolshie"; there was a popular recoil against convention and authority, and Orwell's outspoken, cynical stance thrived in this atmosphere. Cyril Connolly, a contemporary at Eton, remembers that at the time Orwell rejected "the war, the Empire, Kipling, Sussex, and Character." It was perhaps not unnatural that he should react against the values of his upbringing, education, and class, and yet, during these years, the values of patriotism, tradition, and tolerance were also deeply ingrained within him.

In December 1921 Orwell left Eton, but he suddenly felt displaced—both socially and psychologically. While the majority of his scholarship class went off to Oxford or Cambridge, there is no indication that Orwell wanted to go to either university nor is there any evidence that he felt any other particular sense of direction—including the desire to become a writer. While the Far East may have exerted a strong romantic pull for him (his father had been in India and he had a grandmother in Burma), his parents must have seen his relatively sudden decision to apply to the Indian Imperial Police as the logical consequence of his upbringing and family tradition. Early in 1922 he took the India Office examinations for the Indian Imperial Police and listed Burma as the first of his choices. On 27 October 1922 he sailed for Rangoon, Burma, where he was to be stationed as assistant superintendent of police and to begin what would become a five-year interval between his Etonian skepticism and the beginning of his literary apprenticeship.

The effect of the Burmese experience on Orwell is difficult to gauge, but there is no indication that he found himself comfortable in an atmosphere in which the natives were hostile and the English jingoistic. The work was generally dull and routine, and Orwell is remembered as being solitary, unsocial, and eccentric. He apparently found the social and psychological pressures associated with being a British sahib completely antithetical to the open intellectual environment at Eton, and this experience must have convinced him of the impossibility of accommodating himself to a conformist, establishment society. Perhaps another significant aspect of this five-year exile is that when he returned to England he had not yet read James Joyce, Marcel Proust, Virginia Woolf, Aldous Huxley, André Gide, T. S. Eliot, Ernest Hemingway, Ezra Pound, or any of the other major modernists who emerged during the second and third decades of the twentieth century. Prior to Burma he had been an enthusiastic reader, indulging himself mostly with William Thackeray, Charles Dickens, William Shakespeare, Rudyard Kipling, Jonathan Swift, Bernard Shaw, A. E. Housman, Samuel Butler, and Somerset Maugham. When he returned to England his sensibility and literary imagination were not much different from what they were when he left England in 1922, and his early work was primarily influenced by his reading of Victorian and Edwardian writers.

In August 1927 Orwell returned to England on leave. The following month he resigned his post and declared to his parents his intention of becoming a writer—a profession for which he had shown little inclination or promise up to that time. He moved to London in the autumn of 1927, and for the first time in his life he felt free from complex social pressures associated with his family, his schools, and his life in Burma—all of which had pressured him to adopt prescriptive codes of thought and behavior. The choice of becoming a writer, therefore, complexly involved the whole question of his social and psychological identity.

Early in 1928 Orwell put on some old rags and ventured into the East End of London in order to investigate the netherworld of the impoverished and unemployed. Why he voluntarily submerged himself into this underground world, which he had been taught to fear and despise, and continued to make such forays into it over the next three years, is not easy to answer. In 1936 he suggested that his quest for such experiences reflected the "bad conscience" he had when he returned from Burma: "I was conscious of an immense weight of guilt that I had got to expiate.... I felt that I had got to escape not merely from imperialism but from every form of man's dominion over man. I wanted to submerge myself, to get right down among the oppressed, to be one of them and on their side against their tyrants." While this explanation of the evolution of a socialist probably has its element of truth, it takes no account of his own adventurous spirit, and says nothing about his motivation to become a writer or his attempt to break free from the bonds of his class and upbringing. Whatever the complex psychological reasons that drove Orwell to descend into the social abyss, these experiences proved to be formative in the shaping of his consciousness.

In the spring of 1928 Orwell traveled to Paris, where he remained for eighteen months. Ostensibly he had gone there in order to live more cheaply than in London, but undoubtedly he was also drawn by the mystique of the bohemian, artistic life. However, while in Paris he showed a disciplined commitment to his late-chosen career. He had several articles published in Parisian newspapers, the subjects of which—unemployment, Burma, popular culture, political power, poverty, and social oppression—reflected what would continue to be his dominant interests. He also wrote two novels and some short stories, all of which were rejected. He returned to England at the end of 1929 and continued to write about his experiences. The first demonstrations that he was developing his own narrative voice are seen in "The Spike" and "A Hanging," which were published in *Adelphi* in 1931. What he had achieved for the first time with these two pieces was a successful blending of imaginative writing and reportage, and it was this fusion of two techniques that would give form to his first book.

The first version of *Down and Out in Paris and London* (1933) was completed in October 1930, initially titled "A Scullion's Diary." This early draft was written in the form of a diary and included only his Parisian experiences. The first publisher he submitted it to found it interesting but too short and fragmentary. Orwell then expanded it, adding the complementary section on London, altered the structure, and resubmitted it, only to have it rejected again. When T. S. Eliot, representing Faber and Faber, rejected it in February 1932, Orwell became severely dejected and began to look for a regular job. In April 1932 he took a teaching position at The Hawthorns, in Hayes, Middlesex, a middle-class private school for boys (although he changed

schools once, he continued to teach until December 1933). Finally, through the personal intervention of a friend, Orwell's manuscript was given to Victor Gollancz, who agreed to publish it. Orwell requested that it be brought out pseudonymously, and suggested four names to Gollancz: P. S. Burton, Kenneth Miles, George Orwell, and H. Lewis Allways, and expressed a preference for George Orwell. Gollancz made the final decision on the name. The book was published on 9 January 1933, and the first printing sold out almost immediately and was followed by second and third printings.

Down and Out in Paris and London is a buoyant, lively first book about an unidentified narrator who lives a marginal existence among the working class and the unemployed, first in Paris and then in London. It is important to remember that Orwell added the London section in order to make his manuscript more marketable, because the two sections are quite different and reflect conflicting literary impulses. The Paris section is imaginatively conceived, using evocative scenes and a tenuous story line to interweave the narrator's experiences with representative experiences of Parisian lowlife. Although the Orwellian narrator tells the reader in the first chapter that "Poverty is what I am writing about," there is a fundamental conflict between the avowed social purpose and the actual dramatic development of the material in the Paris section. This first half reflects the preoccupations of the novelist rather than those of the documentarist. Orwell appears to have been romantically fascinated by unfamiliar experiences, "queer tales," and individuals who "lived lives that were curious beyond words." The narrator becomes primarily a raconteur, retelling anecdotes and experiences with a boyish, vigorous, individualized voice, and although he virtually starves with his friend Boris and later engages in eighteen-hour workdays at the expensive "Hotel X," the cheerful spirits and vigorous narrative of this first half are never dampened.

In the London section there is a complete change of mood as the narrator dons rags and goes down and out among the East Enders while he waits for a promised job. The narrator is no longer a raconteur: he now functions as a research worker and a detached social critic. There are some interesting scenes that demonstrate how deeply ingrained is the narrator's class consciousness, but the motivating impulse is primarily sociological. He gives an honest, objective portrait of tramps and suggests how current laws only serve to perpetuate their condition. As the work moves toward a conclusion, Orwell abandons any illusion of a dramatized narrative: he includes a three-page description of the slang of the London poor and describes the various types of housing available for the destitute with no attempt to transform the material imaginatively, as he does in the Paris section. While this work was generally well received, it also reflected Orwell's conflicting desires to produce an imaginative work of art and to expound directly on social issues and conditions about which he felt deeply.

By December 1933 Orwell had finished his second book, *Burmese Days* (1934). Then, shortly before Christmas 1933, he entered Uxbridge Cottage Hospital seriously ill with pneumonia (he later claimed that the climate of Burma had ruined his health), and after recovering he resigned his teaching position. He returned to his parents' home in Southwold in January 1934 and began writing *A Clergyman's Daughter* (1935), which was completed by October of that year. He seems to have almost obsessively committed himself at this time to his writing and the formation of his career. He had some difficulty finding a publisher for *Burmese Days*. Victor Gollancz rejected it for fear of giving libelous offense to colonials in Burma and India. Harper and Brothers, in New York, after requesting some minor stylistic alterations, published it on 25 October 1934 (Gollancz finally brought this novel out in London in June 1935).

Burmese Days provides a finely drawn, convincing portrait of the provincial, chauvinistic British community in the backwater village of Kyauktada. With no sense of moral direction or purpose, these English colonials sit around the European Club, bored, recalling an idealized British Raj that never existed, and fostering tenuous relationships through alcohol and their mutual vilification of the Burmese. The pukka sahib code, which dictates that all white men must "hang together" and which implicitly forbids any kind of social relationship with the natives, is the unimaginative social orthodoxy that has replaced private values and an authentic moral code. Despite the clear political overtones of the novel, its dominant mood of claustrophobic oppression is not so much political as social and psychological. The novel's portrait of the social and moral bankruptcy of the English colonials leads to an incisive examination of the psychological effects of living under a repressive social orthodoxy.

John Flory, the novel's protagonist, is a thirty-five-year-old timber merchant who marches through the novel castigating British hypocrisy and the colonial habit of mind. Although repelled by the innate inequalities of imperialism and by the mindless jingoism of his fellow colonials, he neither leaves Burma (as Orwell had done) nor pronounces open rebellion against the system and ethic that so repel him. He is a weak, lonely, neurotic figure who is as much a victim of tyranny as are the Burmese. At one point he muses on the oppression that has morally paralyzed him: "Free speech is unthinkable. All other kinds of freedom are permitted. You are free to be a drunkard, an idler, a coward, a backbiter, a fornicator; but you are not free to think for yourself. Your opinion on every subject of any conceivable importance is dictated for you by the pukka sahib's code." For Orwell, this implicit regimentation of thought (so thoroughly developed in *Nineteen Eighty-Four*) is as serious an issue as the political evils of imperialism, for it stunts the development of internally defined values and morality and usurps the freedom and individuality of the individual. Although Flory endures this bleak life through a screen of anesthetics—books, gardening, drinking, work, women, and shooting—it is when the young Elizabeth Lackersteen enters into the plot that he sees a possible escape from his guilt-ridden, secret world. But he finds in the superficial, priggish Elizabeth neither a profound personal love (and thus a viable private life) nor the revelation of a partner in rebellion (as Julia is for Winston Smith in *Nineteen Eighty-Four*). When this attempt to establish a separate community of two fails, and he suffers public disgrace through the machinations of a powerful native, he turns to his final anesthetic—suicide. If John Atkins is correct when he suggests that Flory is a portrait of what Orwell thought he would have become if he had remained in Burma, then we can more fully appreciate Orwell's sense of emancipation once he had freed himself from this debilitating world. *Burmese Days* was Orwell's first novel, and while it reflects his traditionalist conception of the form, it is the best of his early novels and demonstrates his facility for handling a large body of experience and transforming it into a coherent narrative. During the first half of the 1930s there is no reference in his essays, reviews, or letters to any belief about the novelist's responsibilities. Rather, the primary influences on his early fiction were writers such as Thomas Hardy, George Gissing, H. G. Wells, Arnold Bennett,

Orwell (second from right) at the Independent Labour Party Summer School, 1937

and Maugham. He once identified Maugham as the novelist who had influenced him most.

In *A Clergyman's Daughter*, published on 11 March 1935, Orwell continued to examine the problematic relationship between an individual and a repressive, middle-class society that limits him with its rigid, exhausted values. This episodic novel tells the story of Dorothy Hare, the overworked only child of an acrimonious Church of England rector. Beset by both social and internal pressures that she is unable to cope with, Dorothy suffers a case of amnesia, which provides the vehicle for her escape from her hometown and her subsequent journeys into the hop fields of Kent, the social netherworld of London, and the lower-middle-class life of a fourth-rate private school. Orwell's own ambivalence in the novel is seen in the fact that he alternately casts Dorothy as his central subject, focusing on her crisis of self, and as a mere device for dramatizing his own experiences—he had also picked hops in Kent, been on the bum in London, been arrested (intentionally), and had taught in a private school. Although many of his works are strikingly autobiographical, this is one instance when

he appears to have been more at the mercy of his material than in control of it.

In the portrayal of the bleak, provincial world of Knype Hill with which the novel opens, Orwell's debt to Wells and Bennett is apparent. Dorothy is entrapped by a debilitating world of habit and convention which has sapped her physical and spiritual vitality and deprived her of any sense of personal meaning or purpose. While the social texture of this shabby world is finely rendered, Orwell's attempt to portray Dorothy as a pathologically disturbed woman—whose masochism, morbid fear of sex, and severe self-repression have their origins in certain experiences of her childhood—betrays all too clearly the casualness of his flirtation with literary Freudianism. Although Dorothy's crisis of self ceases to be the focus when we next see her in the hop fields of Kent, this section is described with a vitality and affection that reflect Orwell's persistent belief in the essential goodness and moral endurance of the working class. The third part of the novel is a short, expressionistic section that dramatizes the experience of about a dozen vagrants (including Dorothy) who spend a long, cold night in Trafalgar Square. This is Orwell's only truly experimental endeavor (it is clearly influenced by the Circe chapter of James Joyce's *Ulysses*); while it is interesting, it is an unsuccessful experiment which neither propels the action nor further delineates the character of Dorothy. At the end of the novel, Dorothy, having had various experiences and having lost her religious belief, returns to Knype Hill and to the hollow ritual of her previous life. Because her return is given authorial affirmation, it is impossible to escape the assumption that this unsatisfying end (which provides no resolution to Dorothy's crisis of self) reflects at once Orwell's longing for an ordered, communal world and his failure to discover such an affirmative, creative location within his society at this time. While parts of this novel are interesting, it is the least controlled, least unified work in Orwell's canon, and during the 1940s he refused to allow it to be republished.

In October 1934 Orwell left his parents' home in Southwold and moved to Hamstead, on the outskirts of London, where he became a part-time assistant in a bookshop, Booklovers Corner. The bookshop was owned by the Westropes, who were members of the Independent Labour party (ILP), a left-wing, egalitarian, anti-Communist, antimilitarist party that Orwell was to join in 1938. This period probably marks the beginning of his formal political education. He began *Keep the Aspidistra Flying* in February 1935, completed it by the end of the year, and it was published by Gollancz on 20 April 1936.

Gordon Comstock, the protagonist of *Keep the Aspidistra Flying*, is a struggling poet and an "angry young man" who believes that the modern world is dead and morally bankrupt and so gives up his job at an advertising agency; declares war on money, success, and all the bourgeois values associated with respectability, and takes a part-time job at a bookstore. He is a solipsistic hero whose festering bitterness and obsession with money overshadow the entire novel. Although he initially idealizes the bohemian life of the impoverished poet, his consciousness is still anchored in the money world, and he still accepts middle-class values. As a result he becomes caught up in a self-pitying, adolescent obsession with money that saps his personal energies and his ability to write and that disrupts his relationship with his girlfriend, Rosemary. The novel attempts to identify Comstock's malaise with the decay and fatigue of his culture and provides

some acute criticism of contemporary England, but it is difficult to believe that Comstock is anything but a petulant neurotic trapped in his own perverse consciousness. An uneven novel, it lacks the vigor, pace, and imaginative depth of his later writing. But the novel does contain two particularly fine chapters: the one describing Gordon and Rosemary's disastrous Sunday outing, and the one chronicling Gordon's drunken squandering of the fifty dollars he receives from the sale of a poem to a California magazine. What is significant about this novel is the nature of the affirmative ending that Orwell gives it.

While Gordon's petulant rebellion is finally discredited, there is no transformation of personal protest into political commitment. While many of Orwell's contemporaries (such as W. H. Auden, Stephen Spender, and C. Day Lewis) were becoming politically engaged, Orwell had not yet developed a political commitment, and this novel appears clearly to reject socialism. The novel's criticism of socialism is based on the belief either that it has become rooted among the upper-middle class or that it has come to signify little more than a Wellsian vision of utopia. Comstock finds an alternative to his self-destructive rebellion not in politics, but in a sudden idealization of ordinary, normative values, which he sees embodied in the lower-middle class. When Rosemary reveals that she is pregnant, his sense of decency (a highly valued word in Orwell's moral lexicon) is awakened, and he agrees to marry her and take his old job back. Rather than feeling betrayed or defeated, he recognizes that it is not in isolation, but as a member of a vital community that he can discover and express personal meaning, and reenter the "stream of life." Comstock, and perhaps Orwell, suddenly sees within the lower-middle class the nonintellectual spirit that has preserved and transmitted the unspoken, moral-ethical code and the instinctive vitality that have maintained the continuity of English civilization (a set of attitudes that would have a prominent role in the composition of *Animal Farm* and *Nineteen Eighty-Four*). This novel is the first of Orwell's books in which we see the clear beginnings of his idealization of the ordinary in English life and of his commitment to traditional values. Becoming an apologist for the traditional and decent values in English culture did not, however, signify an end to Orwell's adversary role as a social critic; rather, it would temper and humanize his politics and would provide a basis of belief that would keep his politics pragmatic and concrete. It was out of this radical-conservative tension that the idiosyncratic nature of Orwell's politics emerged.

Nineteen thirty-six was one of the pivotal years in Orwell's life. He married Eileen O'Shaughnessy on 9 June 1936. His relationship with this strong, independent woman (she was completing her M.A. in psychology) gave a new optimism and security to his life and very likely influenced the affirmative ending of *Keep the Aspidistra Flying*. In April 1936 he rented The Stores, a general store in Wallington, which he retained until 1939; when he was not writing, Orwell ran the store and took care of his garden and his goats. Until this time Orwell had remained curiously unaffected by the highly charged political atmosphere in England, but two significant experiences of 1936 fostered his transformation into a political writer. First, in January 1936 Victor Gollancz asked him to write a book on the conditions of the unemployed and the working class in the coal-mining districts of Yorkshire and Lancashire. The resulting book, *The Road to Wigan Pier* (1937), contains his first clear identification with socialist aims and ideals. The second experience was his involvement in the Spanish civil war, which began on 17 July 1936. Orwell went to Spain in December 1936 as a journalist but almost immediately joined a combat unit in order to fight fascism. His experiences there deepened his commitment to socialism and produced a passionate distrust of the Communist party. This was probably the single most significant experience of his life, and it led him to write in 1947: "Every line of serious work that I have written since 1936 has been written, directly or indirectly, *against* totalitarianism and *for* democratic Socialism, as I understand it." However, Gollancz felt compelled to add a critical foreword to *The Road to Wigan Pier*, taking issue with Orwell's unorthodox socialism, and refused to publish *Homage to Catalonia* (1938) because of what he saw as its heretical political point of view, suggesting the degree to which Orwell was outside the dominant mainstream of leftist politics during the mid 1930s. He was on his way to becoming not only an important socialist writer, but a morally committed dissident in an age that had become infatuated with orthodoxy.

The Road to Wigan Pier (published as a main selection of the Left Book Club in March 1937, with an initial printing of 43,690 copies) demonstrates Orwell's fundamental alienation from the political orthodoxy of his age. The first half of the book records and describes in documentary fashion the squalid living conditions that he encountered in the economically depressed areas of Yorkshire and Lancashire. However, it was the idiosyncratic second half that disturbed so many at the time. In this section Orwell traces his own intellectual journey, from childhood and Burma to the present, focusing on how his class attitudes were formed and the process by which he developed into a socialist; but this discussion also leads up to his incisive criticism of socialism. Although he adamantly expresses his commitment to the ideals of socialism, he insists that English socialism has become corrupted by external influences: "Socialism, at least in this island, does not smell any longer of revolution and the overthrow of tyrants; it smells of crankishness, machine worship and the stupid cult of Russia." His own bêtes noires are perhaps revealed when he says that "One sometimes gets the impression that the mere words 'Socialism' and 'Communism' draw towards them with magnetic force every fruit-juice drinker, nudist, sandal-wearer, sex-maniac, Quaker, 'Nature Cure' quack, pacifist and feminist in England." He also indicts the intelligentsia, who, he suggests, have completely lost touch with the best virtues and values of English common culture. Orwell became convinced that a leftist orthodoxy, if it were not informed and tempered by such traditional values as common decency, individualism, justice, and liberty, was *capable* of transforming his world into an impersonal, totalitarian system. Therefore, it is important to understand that Orwell's idiosyncratic concept of being a political writer represented not just a commitment to extra-Parliamentary action, but also a defense "of what was still sound in civilization." An example of Orwell's frame of mind in 1936 is seen in his encounter with a Communist at a leftist meeting; when the young man began vilifying the bourgeoisie, Orwell interrupted him and said, "Look here, I'm a bourgeois and my family are bourgeois. If you talk about them like that I'll punch your head."

When Orwell came to write *Homage to Catalonia* (published 25 April 1938), he set out to write not a history of the war or a political documentary but a personal memoir that would chronicle his subjective experience of the drudgery of war, of a social revolution, and of an interparty political conflict. In so doing he was able successfully to transform the documentary into both a descriptive and an expressive form that has made this one of Orwell's most popular books. Although

Orwell (second from right) at the Aragon front, 1937

his involvement in Spain was relatively short (December 1936 - June 1937), it profoundly influenced the direction and shape of his personal and literary imagination. The disillusionment and anger that he felt over the dubious, self-serving role of the Communist party in Spain, and over what he saw of the extensive rewriting of history for the purposes of propaganda and deception, provided the seminal experiences that would inform and structure *Animal Farm* and *Nineteen Eighty-Four*. And yet, his experiences of comradeship and community in Spain furthered his belief in the essential goodness and potential power of the common people—and the vigor, buoyancy, and élan with which *Homage to Catalonia* is written testifies to the personal significance of these experiences.

Orwell apparently went to Spain with the intention of writing articles, but he was almost immediately enthralled by the romantic, revolutionary atmosphere of Barcelona in December 1936: tipping had been forbidden, ceremonial forms of speech had been replaced by the term *comrade*, shops and cafes had been closed, and churches were being systematically demolished. Con-

fronted for the first time by a primitive, spontaneously formed community that was unified by a common cause and by a shared commitment to human ideals, Orwell claims that he "recognized it immediately as a state of affairs worth fighting for," and so he joined a militia unit. He had come to Spain with letters of introduction from the Independent Labour party office in London, and so the ILP office in Barcelona enrolled him in the militia of its sister party in Spain, the POUM (he was listed on the roll as "Eric Blair, grocer").

In the early chapters of *Homage to Catalonia* we witness a systematic, realistic debunking of the glamour and romanticism of a war that had achieved the status of an international crusade. Although Orwell insists that the political side of the war bored him, he recognizes a fundamental schism between the strategy of the Communists on the one hand and the Socialists and anarchists on the other. The POUM and the anarchists believed that a social revolution was interdependent with the war, while the Communists felt that a social revolution should be postponed until the war was won. While Orwell was sympathetic to the

Socialist-anarchist position, he accepted the pragmatism of the Communist position, and he applied to transfer into the Soviet-controlled International Brigades. But before he was able to do so, he was involved in the May fighting in Barcelona between the POUM and the Civil Guards, and the subsequent representation of the POUM by the Communists as a "fifth column" Fascist movement. Apparently overwhelmed by a sense of historical and political urgency, Orwell disrupts the unity of his otherwise predominantly experiential book in order to devote two chapters to a detached, documentary overview of the political conflicts that had frustrated a social revolution in Catalonia and led to the suppression of the POUM, and to an examination of the propaganda that had been written in order to obscure the truth of these events. In 1946 Orwell agreed that these two chapters "must ruin the book," but insisted that he had no other choice but to include them. He quotes articles from the *Daily Worker* and other papers in order to point out contradictions, incongruities, and ideological distortions of historical fact in the Communist treatment of the POUM (so pervasive was the Communist influence at the time that much of the left-wing press accepted the Communist propaganda). In a 1938 review of Arthur Koestler's *Spanish Testament*, Orwell quoted this sentence from Koestler's book: "If those who have at their command printing machines and printer's ink for the expression of their opinions, remain neutral in the face of such bestiality, then Europe is lost." The dangerous role that propaganda and censorship could play was brought home to Orwell in 1938 when the editors of *New Statesman* agreed to publish an article of his on the war and then, when they learned it dealt with the suppression of the POUM, changed their minds because it "controverted editorial policy."

Back on the Aragon front, Orwell was wounded through the neck on 20 May 1937; one of his vocal cords was damaged, leaving his voice altered for the rest of his life. When he returned to Barcelona in June, the POUM had been outlawed, and he lived like a fugitive, sleeping in deserted churches and parks at night, until he and his wife (she had come to Barcelona in February to work at the ILP office) managed to cross the border into France, after some of his comrades had already been arrested. If Orwell had gone to Spain to fight against fascism, he returned with a more complex understanding of power politics, and with the recognition that it was totalitarian-

ism that was a threat to the liberty of Europe and to England's liberal heritage. And it was precisely this recognition that made Orwell a member of a very select community of European left-wing writers who had become disillusioned with communism, a group which included Koestler, Ignazio Silone, and Franz Borkenau. However, the fact that only nine hundred copies of *Homage to Catalonia* had been sold by the time of his death, and that it was not even published in America until 1952, testifies to the limited readership that the work attained and perhaps helps to clarify why he would seek new aesthetic forms in the 1940s for the expression of his political ideas.

During 1938-1939 Orwell entered into a period of profound cultural anxiety and intense political militancy. Disillusioned with the failure of liberal politics to stop fascism, he felt convinced that a coming war would only accelerate the totalitarian direction of the modern world, and he became militantly antiwar. He suggested to Cyril Connolly that they begin to prepare for illegal antiwar activities and told him in December 1938: "Everything one writes now is overshadowed by this ghastly feeling that we are racing towards a precipice, and, though we shan't actually prevent ourselves or anyone else from going over, must put up some sort of fight." It was during this period that Orwell first gained a prominent reputation as an unmasker of political hypocrisy and self-deceit and as a pragmatic political thinker. In March 1938 a turbercular lesion on one lung began to hemorrhage, and he spent five months in a sanatorium. During Orwell's period of recovery the novelist L. H. Meyers anonymously gave him three hundred pounds so that he could go to Morocco for his health. He and Eileen left in September 1938 for Marrakech, where he wrote *Coming Up for Air*. They returned to London in the spring of 1939.

Coming Up for Air (published on 12 June 1939) is narrated by George Bowling, a middle-aged, nonintellectual, lower-middle-class insurance salesman who is acutely responsive to the political insecurities of 1938. As we might expect, the novel is permeated with a sense of the inevitability of the coming war and the horrors that will accompany it, and yet much of the power of the novel is derived from its counterpointing of the pre-1914 world in which Bowling grew up with the acute contemporaneity of the world of 1938. Bowling, preoccupied with the shabbiness and anxiety of his world, has a Proustian experience in which a newspaper headline triggers his memory, imaginatively catapulting him back into his Edwardian childhood and a nostalgic re-creation of that apparently stable, secure, permanent world. When Bowling later decides to make an actual journey to his childhood hometown, his nostalgia is predictably shattered, and he awakes to a more realistic understanding that there is no escape from the dangers and threats of the contemporary world. And yet his memory of the past, and of a cultural heritage, gives him a moral resiliency.

The novel is a cautionary tale to the extent that its intention is to awaken the lower-middle and middle classes from their "semi-anaesthesia" into an awareness of the political realities of 1938, and to mobilize them into an active, conscious, political force. What frightens Bowling (and very likely Orwell) is not just the coming war, but his vision of the after war: "The world we're going down into. The kind of hate-world, slogan-world. The coloured shirts, the barbed wire, the rubber truncheons. The secret cells where the electric light burns night and day, and the detectives watching you while you sleep. And the processions and the posters with enormous faces and the crowds of a million people all cheering for the Leader till they deafen themselves into thinking that they worship him. . . ." Although this is unquestionably an intensely political novel, its emphasis on the value of the past transforms it into a profound cultural work. Orwell seeks to reanimate the memory of a pre-World War I consciousness in order to remind ordinary Englishmen of their resources of strength, which he believes reside in a common cultural heritage. The past in this novel comes to represent the vigor of an authentic, shared moral tradition which Englishmen must once again become conscious of in order to judge and understand the present; if that tradition is lost, Orwell says, the English people will be culturally and morally disarmed before the real threat of totalitarianism. What Orwell is saying through Bowling is that the preservation of the past in a communal memory represents the imaginative capacity of the large body of common, ordinary Englishmen not only to endure, but to become active agents in resisting those forces which would sever English life from its cultural roots. Orwell often idealized Bowling's class, and the reader is shown that his resiliency of character makes him the kind of person who will survive and who will preserve the human heritage; but Orwell's challenge in this novel was to awaken Bowling's class to an active

role in the determination of their own future. This is the first novel in which Orwell successfully integrates his political consciousness and his personal vision within a developing fictional narrative. In so doing he departed from the realistic novel and instead chose a lyrical, expressive form which permitted him greater interplay of his vision and imagination. This is also the first of his novels to be a relative commercial success.

The outbreak of war in 1939 intensified Orwell's feelings of anxiety and pessimism. In his finest essay of the 1930s, "Inside the Whale," completed shortly after the start of the war, he exhibited a sharply accelerating tone of pessimism and near hysteria: "The literature of liberalism is coming to an end and the literature of totalitarianism has not yet appeared and is barely imaginable. As for the writer, he is sitting on a melting iceberg; he is merely an anachronism, a hangover from the bourgeois age, as surely doomed as the hippopotamus." During 1939-1940 Orwell was planning a three-volume saga, tentatively titled "The English People," which might have demonstrated the resiliency of his liberal concept of the novel by unifying his political militancy with his commitment to English common culture within a traditional fictive framework. Whether the work was too ambitious for him, or whether he was simply unable at this traumatic time to synthesize his imagination and conscience, is difficult to say, but he never got beyond the planning stages of this work. It is clear from his writing at the time that his fears of cultural apocalypse were virtually overwhelming him. In 1941 he told readers of *Partisan Review*, "Only the mentally dead are capable of sitting down and writing novels while this nightmare is on. . . . There is such a doubt about the continuity of civilization as can hardly have existed for hundreds of years. . . ." He feared that England as he knew it—a liberal-bourgeois tradition with which he identified his own values, worldview, sensibility, and vocation— was in the process of being radically displaced.

The war influenced him in another significant way: while he developed a growing antipathy toward politics, his militant antiwar stance of 1938-1939 yielded now to an equally militant patriotism. He tried several times to enlist in military service but was turned down because of his precarious health (lesions on his lung). He found an outlet for his patriotism and for his continuing revolutionary feelings through two means: first, he joined the Home Guard in June 1940 (serving as a sergeant until November 1943), and second, he

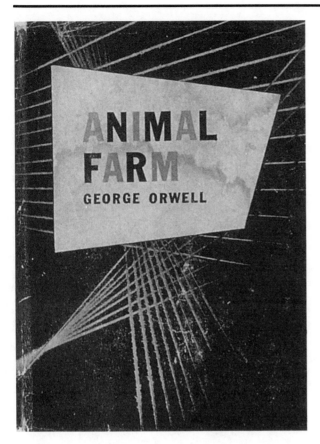

Dust jacket for Orwell's 1945 indictment of communism

In August 1941 he finally found "essential service" by joining the BBC as talks assistant (later as talks producer) in the Indian section of its Eastern Service, where he remained until November 1943. While at the BBC he witnessed a great deal of propaganda (from both sides), which served to heighten his fears that the concept of objective truth was fading out of the world. In 1942, responding to the political twisting of historical fact by the Nazis, Russians, and others, he wrote: "The implied objective of this line of thought is a nightmare world in which the leader, or some ruling clique, controls not only the future but *the past*. If the Leader says of such and such an event, 'It never happened'—well, it never happened. If he says that two and two are five, well, two and two are five. This prospect frightens me much more than bombs. . . ." When he resigned from the BBC in November 1943, he joined the *Tribune* as literary editor, and began writing *Animal Farm*. Also, in June 1943 he and Eileen adopted a baby, whom they named Richard Horatio Blair.

Animal Farm was written between November 1943 and February 1944, but was not published until August 1945, principally as a result of political objections that arose over the book's attack on Joseph Stalin and the Soviet Union. It was turned down by publishers in England (including T. S. Eliot at Faber and Faber) and America. One American publisher rejected it because, he said, Americans were not in the mood for animal stories. Orwell, fearing implicit censorship and convinced of the urgency of his message, considered publishing it himself as a two-shilling pamphlet. Finally, Secker and Warburg agreed to publish it, but it was still held for publication until the end of the war, ostensibly because of lack of paper, but more likely because it was still deemed imprudent to publish something attacking the Soviet Union when it was a valuable ally of the West. When the novel was finally published, the magnitude of its success surprised Orwell as much as anyone. The first edition sold out the first month, and by the spring of 1946 it was being translated into nine languages. After the Book-of-the-Month Club in America chose it as a selection, it sold more than a half-million copies, relieving him from financial worries for the first time in his life.

began to formulate what can only be called a "myth" of an English cultural heritage, which embodied both his patriotism and his faith in the potential power of the common, ordinary Englishman. While this "myth" probably has its beginnings in *Coming Up for Air*, he sets it forth in "My Country Right or Left" (1940), in which he defines patriotism as a "devotion to something that is changing but [which] is felt to be mystically the same," and then develops it more complexly in his pamphlet *The Lion and the Unicorn: Socialism and the English Genius* (1941). The pamphlet is an ambitious attempt to reconcile his conservative and radical impulses as he tries to reactivate the consciousness of a common cultural heritage among Englishmen in a time of crisis. He suggests that English culture is "continuous, it stretches forth into the future and the past, there is something in it that persists, as in a living creature." In addition, he continues his attack on intellectuals for their severance from the renewing moral sources of the common culture of their country, and he stresses his belief in the compatibility of socialism (without dominance by intellectuals) with English common culture.

The specific political purpose that had aroused Orwell's sense of urgency was his desire to explode the myth of the Soviet Union as the paradigm of the socialist state. He also wanted to expose the dangers of totalitarianism, which he saw reflected in the politics of expedience, the devaluation of objective truth, and the systematic manipulation of the common people through propaganda. This fable about the animals who overthrow their human oppressors only to be oppressed once again by those animals who were once their comrades has been used to support various ideological points of view. However, while Orwell clearly indicts the betrayal of the revolution that occurs on Marsh Farm, there is no indication that the revolution itself is being satirized. When Old Major, the political visionary who represents Karl Marx, describes the plight of the animals—their lack of freedom, their misery, their powerlessness—in his declaration of the principles of Animalism, it is clear that he is describing allegorically the relationship between the working class and the rich, landowning upper class of any society. The revolution that occurs spontaneously (it is significant that it is not activated by the conspiracy of a privileged few) establishes an idyllic, primitive community that is reminiscent of Orwell's depiction of Barcelona in December 1936. While the revolution itself is entirely affirmed, the major question is why it fails, why it proves to be only temporary.

Orwell's identification of what exactly goes wrong on the Animal Farm is more complex than many readers give him credit for; he suggests several causes: the perverse drive for power among those who already possess it, the lack of intelligence and memory among the lower animals (which makes them powerless against the autocracy of the pigs), and, perhaps most important, the idea that to alter merely the *shape* of a society is insufficient as a revolutionary goal. The pigs clearly represent a savage critique of an intellectual, elite class. Because they organize and supervise the operations of the farm, they establish themselves as an isolated, privileged class; as a result, Orwell suggests, they are displaced from the renewing work of the farm, from the communal life of the other animals, and from the tempering moral sources of their origin. Thus isolated from the sources of their cultural and moral strength, they become as deracinated and self-serving as Orwell believed many British left-wing intellectuals had become.

But Orwell also dramatically emphasizes that the animals' lack of a cultural heritage (seen in their lack of memory and in their illiteracy, which deprive them of a conscious past) renders them powerless against the totalitarian oppres-

Orwell with his adopted son, Richard, circa 1945

sion of the pigs. Their lack of a verifiable history and of a historical consciousness (what Orwell was trying to awaken in common-culture Englishmen in *Coming Up for Air* and in *The Lion and the Unicorn*) makes them easily subject to the manipulative uses of language and power. As they repeatedly witness the falsification of history and the rewriting of the seven commandments of Animalism, their disquiet is appeased only when they are convinced that "their memories had been at fault." Thus, the decay of the revolution stems not simply from the consolidation of power by the pigs but also from the animals' lack of a conscious moral-cultural tradition, for they have no heritage of justice and equality on which to fall back. Without the agency of memory, which could preserve the ideals of the revolution and enable them to shape the future of their own society, the prerevolutionary shape of the farm is gradually restored, although under a different leadership.

In 1947 Orwell said that *Animal Farm* was "the first book in which I tried, with full consciousness of what I was doing, to fuse political purpose and artistic purpose into one whole." His

226

fable is a remarkably effective integration of a political message within a unified fictional narrative, and it is significantly a radical departure in form from his documentaries and fiction of the 1930s. The use of the fable, the simplicity of style, and the notable absence of a narrative or authorial voice provide *Animal Farm* with the potential for a mythic quality that engages a deeper level of consciousness than either realistic fiction or the essay. While this is very likely Orwell's most perfect literary production, the form of the fable does limit the emotional and psychological complexity of the story, which is the limitation that Orwell sought to transcend in the more complex *Nineteen Eighty-Four*.

Although by 1945 Orwell had achieved an international reputation and relative economic security, his last years continued to be wrought with tension. In the spring of 1945 he resigned from his job as literary editor at the *Tribune* and traveled to Europe as a war correspondent. While he was in Europe, his wife died on 29 March 1945 during an operation apparently for cancer. Later in that year he became vice-chairman of the Freedom Defense Committee, which was headed by Herbert Read and which was established in order to fight for civil liberties. In February 1946 Secker and Warburg published a collection of his finest essays, *Critical Essays* (published in the United States as *Dickens, Dali and Others*). He had been dreaming since the early 1940s about the possibility of escaping to an island in the Hebrides (off Scotland), where he could garden and have sufficient peace to work; and in May 1946 he finally rented a house on Jura, in the Outer Hebrides, where he lived until shortly before his death. It was there that he wrote most of *Nineteen Eighty-Four* (he had been making notes for his final work since 1944, and had originally entitled it "The Last Man in Europe"), completing the first draft in October 1947. Two months later his tuberculosis again forced him into a sanatorium, where he spent seven months, unable to work for the majority of that time. He returned to Jura at the end of July 1948 and completed *Nineteen Eighty-Four*. The book was published on 5 June 1949, and in its first year sold some 45,000 copies in England and more than 170,000 copies in America.

In *Nineteen Eighty-Four* Orwell envisions a time in the near future when the world has been divided into three super states, each of which is ruled by a system of oligarchical collectivism that has brutally eliminated privacy, intellectual free-

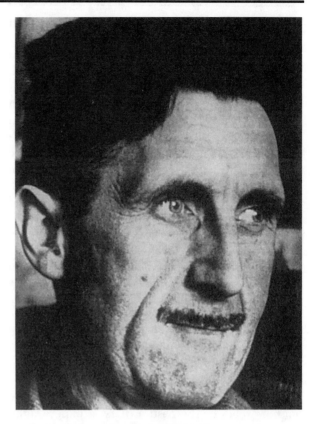

George Orwell, 1946

dom, friendship, and the autonomy of the individual, and each of which has systematically deprived its inhabitants of a verifiable history and of the resources of a cultural consciousness. It is a mistake to read this work as a fatalistic prophecy of the death of civilization, for Orwell's primary purpose is to magnify and distort disturbing conditions, tendencies, and habits of thought that he saw existing in the world, so that they could be recognized and arrested. What makes *Nineteen Eighty-Four* a more powerful, disturbing dystopia than such works as Aldous Huxley's *Brave New World* (1932) and Eugene Zamyatin's *We* (1924), both of which he had read, is, first, the temporal proximity of its setting (only thirty-five years from its publication, whereas Huxley's and Zamyatin's imagined futures are set hundreds of years away), and second, the disturbing familiarity and plausibility of the world that Orwell constructs. Because the social world of 1984 is not that far removed from the reader's own experience, he becomes involved in a more profound, intimate way than he does in Huxley's remote chrome-and-glass society. Orwell wanted his readers to understand not only the intellectual-theoretical foundations of this future society, but to experience the dull, shabby horror of living in such a world.

The first two-thirds of *Nineteen Eighty-Four* portrays the future as a schizoid, psychotic world, but Orwell counterpoints this disturbing portrait by showing that an awareness of the past (which the Party is determined to extirpate from human consciousness) provides a means of understanding the present and becomes the single resource by which the novel's protagonist, Winston Smith, can preserve his sanity and establish his individuality. While the world of 1984 has virtually erased the private, subjective life, Winston surreptitiously begins his diary (itself a political crime) in order to give form to his "ancestral memory," a vague term which is used to express the recesses of his cultural consciousness, his shadowy sense of the past, and his last vestiges of a communal human spirit. The motivation for Winston's revolt is not so much political as it is cultural and historical—he seeks to validate his "ancestral memory" by seeking out ordinary, bourgeois experience (a quest not entirely dissimilar to Flory's, Comstock's, or Bowling's). Toward this end he gathers relics of the past: a diary, a paperweight, and Charrington's upstairs room, where he and Julia make love. There is a timeliness and peace about this bourgeois room, and it becomes a place where he and Julia can establish (albeit temporarily) a normative and private life. This "pocket of the past" is both an escape from the nightmarish world of Oceania and a place where they can recover the sources of ordinary human experience, which the Party recognizes as an embryonic threat to its control and therefore seeks to extinguish. It is important to remember that this work, like previous works of Orwell's, does not simply assert a nostalgia for the past, but asserts the value and significance of the past to human consciousness, and therefore to the preservation of human liberty and the human heritage.

The only hope outside of himself that Winston feels lies in his quasi-faith in the proles, who comprise 85 percent of the population (a large figure which suggests that it comprises the majority of common, ordinary Englishmen, what Orwell elsewhere referred to as the "big public"). Winston believes that they have unconsciously preserved the ordinary values and habits of life through an "ancestral transmission of the human spirit," and yet he finds in them no potential for acting upon their instincts, or even of becoming conscious of their instinctual heritage. The proles are strikingly evocative of a pre-1914 working-

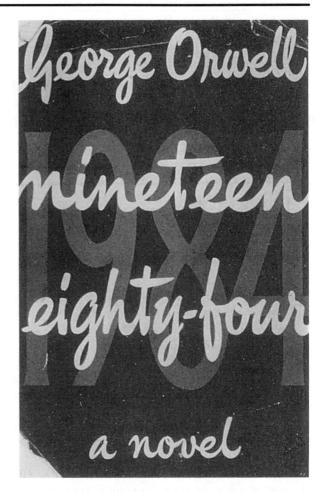

Dust jacket for Orwell's 1949 novel. "I don't believe that the kind of society I describe will arrive, but I believe something resembling it could arrive," Orwell wrote.

class world, a class that Orwell periodically idealized, but whose "semi-anaesthesia" he feared would abet their own oppression. The image of the working-class woman who sings as she hangs up her clothes defines for Winston the abiding human spirit that the Party has not extinguished, but, finally, the proles are no more conscious of their past or of their heritage than are the animals in *Animal Farm* and are vulnerable to the same kind of oppression.

The last third of *Nineteen Eighty-Four*—dominated by the interpolated chapters from Emmanuel Goldstein's "The Theory and Practice of Oligarchical Collectivism," and Winston's systematic "re-education" in the Ministry of Love as O'Brien expounds on the theoretical foundations of Ingsoc—does not effectively develop or resolve the thematic or plot elements established in the first two-thirds. It is in this section that Orwell's focus appears to shift away from the dramatic framework and toward the direct, unfiltered expression of his political purpose. By the close of the novel, Winston's final obliteration and the mute survival of the proles suggest Orwell's pessimistic outlook in 1948 for the survival of England's liberal heritage, a pessimism which he was repeatedly expressing elsewhere (as in statements such as, "When you are on a sinking ship, your thoughts will be about sinking ships"). There is no doubt that this grim, powerful, affecting work has continued to express the latent insecurities and anxieties of our age.

For Orwell, the problem of making people conscious of what was happening around them, as well as awakening a critical habit of mind that would resist the political rationalizations of power politics, had been his most significant literary challenge since 1936. In *Nineteen Eighty-Four* he found a form capable of meeting that challenge by fusing realism and fantasy: realism enabled him to establish a recognizable world and to express some of his most deeply felt social and cultural attitudes; fantasy enabled him to construct a mythic framework that would dramatize the nightmarish quality of the political society of 1984 and to affect the deepest resources of the reader's imagination. Although the work was immediately successful, it coincided with the emergence of the Cold War consciousness, and because it was often used to support political points of view that Orwell never intended, he was provoked to respond directly to such "misreadings":

> It has been suggested by some of the reviewers of *Nineteen Eighty-Four* that it is the author's view that this, or something like this, is what will happen inside the next forty years in the Western world. This is not correct. I think that, allowing for the book being after all a parody, something like *Nineteen Eighty-Four could* happen. This is the direction in which the world is going at the present time, and the trend lies deep in the political, social and economic foundations of the contemporary world situation.
>
> Specifically the danger lies in the structure imposed on Socialist and on Liberal capitalist communities by the necessity to prepare for total war with the U.S.S.R. and the new weapons, of which of course the atomic bomb is the most powerful and most publicized. But danger lies also in the acceptance of a totalitarian outlook by intellectuals of all colours.
>
> The moral to be drawn from this dangerous nightmare situation is a simple one: *Don't let it happen. It depends on you.*

Despite Orwell's continued preoccupation

with politics and with the fate of his civilization, in the last years of his life he was planning long essays on Joseph Conrad, George Gissing, and Evelyn Waugh—suggesting his renewed interest in the traditional forms of the novel. Laurence Brander reports that during the closing months of his life Orwell was "ready to turn from politics and polemics to the normal preoccupation of the literary artist in our time, the study of human relationship." On 13 October 1949 he married Sonia Brownell, whom he had known for about five years, and on 21 January 1950 he died of tuberculosis at the University of London Hospital, at the age of forty-six.

Although his experiences and the temper of his age transformed George Orwell into a political writer, he never ceased to affirm the value of a nonideological tradition of the novel and to celebrate the normative values of English cultural life. Indeed, he remained committed to a manifestly liberal tradition of the artist: he continued to see art as a means of enlarging one's sympathies and testifying to one's humanity, and to see the writer as a central social intelligence, capable of affecting human awareness, transmitting moral values, influencing the order and direction of society, and celebrating the values and vitality of the common, ordinary person. And it is for these reasons, and not simply because of his last two novels, that Orwell continues to speak with so much vigor and clarity.

Bibliography:
Jeffrey and Valerie Meyers, *George Orwell: An Annotated Bibliography of Criticism* (New York: Garland, 1977).

Biographies:
Peter Stansky and William Abrahams, *The Unknown Orwell* (New York: Knopf, 1972);
Stansky and Abrahams, *Orwell: The Transformation* (New York: Knopf, 1980);
Bernard Crick, *George Orwell: A Life* (Boston: Little, Brown, 1980);
Averil Gardner, *George Orwell* (Boston: Twayne, 1987).

References:
Keith Alldritt, *The Making of George Orwell: A Literary History* (New York: St. Martin's Press, 1969);

John Atkins, *George Orwell: A Literary Study* (London: Calder, 1954);

Gordon Beadle, "George Orwell and the Spanish Civil War," *Duquesne Review*, 16 (Spring 1971): 3-16;

Laurence Brander, *George Orwell* (London: Longmans, Green, 1954);

Peter Buitenhuis and Ira B. Nadel, eds., *George Orwell: A Reassessment* (New York: St. Martin's Press, 1988);

Jenni Calder, *Chronicles of Conscience: A Study of George Orwell and Arthur Koestler* (London: Secker & Warburg, 1968);

Cyril Connolly, *Enemies of Promise* (London: G. Rutledge & Son, 1938; republished, New York: Macmillan, 1948);

Issac Deutcher, "*1984*—The Mysticism of Cruelty," in his *Russia in Transition and Other Essays* (London: Hamilton, 1957), pp. 230-245;

T. R. Fyvel, "George Orwell and Eric Blair: Glimpses of a Dual Life," *Encounter*, 13 (July 1959): 60-65;

Miriam Gross, ed., *The World of George Orwell* (New York: Simon & Schuster, 1971);

Harold J. Harris, "Orwell's Essays and 1984," *Twentieth Century Literature*, 4 (January 1959): 154-161;

Christopher Hollis, *A Study of George Orwell: The Man and His Works* (London: Hollis & Carter, 1956);

Irving Howe, "Orwell: History as Nightmare," in his *Politics and the Novel* (New York: Horizon, 1956), pp. 235-251;

Samuel Hynes, ed., *Twentieth Century Interpretations of 1984: A Collection of Critical Essays* (Englewood Cliffs, N.J.: Prentice-Hall, 1971);

David L. Kubal, *Outside the Whale: George Orwell's Art and Politics* (Notre Dame: University of Notre Dame Press, 1972);

Q. D. Leavis, "The Literary Life Respectable," *Scrutiny*, 9 (September 1940): 173-176;

Robert A. Lee, *Orwell's Fiction* (Notre Dame: University of Notre Dame Press, 1969);

Jeffrey Meyers, *A Reader's Guide to George Orwell* (New Jersey: Littlefield, 1977);

Meyers, ed., *George Orwell: The Critical Heritage* (London: Routledge & Kegan Paul, 1975);

Philip Rahv, "The Unfuture of Utopia," *Partisan Review*, 16 (July 1949): 743-749;

Alok Rai, *Orwell and the Politics of Despair: A Critical Study of the Works of George Orwell* (Cambridge: Cambridge University Press, 1988);

Richard Rees, *George Orwell: Fugitive from the Camp of Victory* (London: Secker & Warburg, 1961);

Philip Rieff, "George Orwell and the Post-Liberal Imagination," *Kenyon Review*, 16 (Winter 1954): 49-70;

Alan Sandison, *The Last Man in Europe* (New York: Harper & Row, 1974);

Christopher Small, *The Road to Miniluv* (Pittsburgh: University of Pittsburgh Press, 1975);

Richard I. Smyer, *Primal Dream and Primal Crime: Orwell's Development as a Psychological Novelist* (Columbia: University of Missouri Press, 1979);

Jerome Thale, "Orwell's Modest Proposal," *Critical Quarterly*, 9 (1962): 365-368;

Lionel Trilling, "George Orwell and the Politics of Truth," in his *The Opposing Self* (New York: Viking, 1955), pp. 151-172;

Trilling, Introduction to *Homage to Catalonia* (Boston: Beacon, 1952), pp. v-xxiii;

Anthony West, *Principles and Persuasions* (London: Eyre & Spottiswoode, 1958);

Raymond Williams, *George Orwell* (New York: Viking, 1971);

Williams, ed., *George Orwell; A Collection of Critical Essays* (Englewood Cliffs, N.J.: Prentice-Hall, 1974);

George Woodcock, *The Crystal Spirit: A Study of George Orwell* (Boston: Little, Brown, 1966);

Alex Zwerdling, *Orwell and the Left* (New Haven: Yale University Press, 1974).

John Osborne

(12 December 1929 -   )

*This entry was updated by Arthur Nicholas Athanason (Michigan State University)
from his entry in* DLB 13: British Dramatists Since World War II: Part Two.

BOOKS: *Look Back in Anger* (London: Faber &
Faber, 1957; New York: Criterion, 1957);
The Entertainer (London: Faber & Faber, 1957;
New York: Criterion, 1958);
Epitaph for George Dillon, by Osborne and An-
thony Creighton (London: Faber & Faber,
1958; New York: Criterion, 1958);
The World of Paul Slickey (London: Faber & Faber,
1959; New York: Criterion, 1961);
*A Subject of Scandal and Concern: A Play for Televi-
sion* (London: Faber & Faber, 1961);
Luther (London: Faber & Faber, 1961; New York:
Criterion, 1962);
Plays for England: The Blood of the Bambergs [and]
Under Plain Cover (London: Faber & Faber,
1963; New York: Criterion, 1964);
Tom Jones: A Screenplay (London: Faber & Faber,
1964; New York: Grove, 1964; revised edi-
tion, New York: Grove, 1965);
Inadmissible Evidence (London: Faber & Faber,
1965; New York: Grove, 1965);
A Patriot for Me (London: Faber & Faber, 1966;
New York: Random House, 1970);
A Bond Honoured, adapted from Lope de Vega's
La Fianza Satisfecha (London: Faber & Faber,
1966);
Time Present [and] *The Hotel in Amsterdam* (Lon-
don: Faber & Faber, 1968);
The Right Prospectus: A Play for Television (London:
Faber & Faber, 1970);
Very Like a Whale: A Play for Television (London:
Faber & Faber, 1971);
West of Suez (London: Faber & Faber, 1971);
A Gift of Friendship: A Play for Television (London:
Faber & Faber, 1972);
Hedda Gabler, adapted from Henrik Ibsen's play
(London: Faber & Faber, 1972; Chicago: Dra-
matic Publishing Company, 1974);
A Sense of Detachment (London: Faber & Faber,
1973);
A Place Calling Itself Rome, adapted from
Shakespeare's *Coriolanus* (London: Faber &
Faber, 1973);
The Hotel in Amsterdam (London: Evans, 1973);

John Osborne, 1966 (photograph by Mark Gerson)

The Picture of Dorian Gray: A Moral Entertainment,
adapted from Oscar Wilde's novel (London:
Faber & Faber, 1973);
*The End of Me Old Cigar and Jill and Jack: A Play
for Television* (London: Faber & Faber, 1975);
Watch It Come Down (London: Faber & Faber,
1975);
*You're Not Watching Me, Mummy and Try a Little
Tenderness: Two Plays for Television* (London:
Faber & Faber, 1978);
*A Better Class of Person: An Autobiography 1929-
1956* (London: Faber & Faber, 1981; New
York: Dutton, 1981);
*A Better Class of Person: An Extract of Autobiography
for Television and God Rot Tunbridge Wells* (Lon-
don & Boston: Faber & Faber, 1985);

Strindberg's The Father and Ibsen's Hedda Gabler, adapted by Osborne (London & Boston: Faber & Faber, 1989);

Déjà Vu (London: Faber & Faber, 1990);

Almost a Gentleman (London: Faber & Faber, 1991).

PLAY PRODUCTIONS: *The Devil Inside Him,* by Osborne and Stella Linden, Huddersfield, Theatre Royal, 29 May 1950;

Personal Enemy, by Osborne and Anthony Creighton, Harrogate, Grand Opera House, 1 March 1955;

Look Back in Anger, London, Royal Court Theatre, 8 May 1956, 151 [performances]; transferred to Hammersmith, London, Lyric Theatre, 5 November 1956; New York, Lyceum Theatre, 1 October 1957, 407;

Epitaph for George Dillon, by Osborne and Creighton, Oxford, Oxford Experimental Theatre Club, 26 February 1957; London, Royal Court Theatre, 11 February 1958, 38; transferred as *George Dillon* to London, Comedy Theatre, 29 May 1958; New York, John Golden Theatre, 4 November 1958, 23;

The Entertainer, London, Royal Court Theatre, 10 April 1957, 36; transferred to London, Palace Theatre, 10 September 1957; New York, Royale Theatre, 12 February 1958, 97;

The World of Paul Slickey, London, Palace Theatre, 5 May 1959;

A Subject of Scandal and Concern: A Play for Television, London, BBC Television, 6 November 1960; Nottingham, 1962; New York, New Theatre Workshop, 7 March 1966, 3;

Luther, London, Royal Court Theatre, 27 July 1961, 28; transferred to London, Phoenix Theatre, 5 September 1961; New York, St. James Theatre, 25 September 1963, 212;

Two Plays for England: The Blood of the Bambergs and *Under Plain Cover,* London, Royal Court Theatre, 19 July 1962, 60;

Inadmissible Evidence, London, Royal Court Theatre, 9 September 1964, 40; transferred to London, Wyndham's Theatre, 17 March 1965; New York, Belasco Theatre, 30 November 1965, 167;

A Patriot for Me, London, Royal Court Theatre, 30 June 1965, 53; New York, Imperial Theatre, 5 October 1969, 49;

A Bond Honoured, adapted from Lope de Vega's *La Fianza Satisfecha,* London, Old Vic, 6 June 1966;

Time Present, London, Royal Court Theatre, 23 May 1968, 39; transferred to London, Duke of York's Theatre, 11 July 1968;

The Hotel in Amsterdam, London, Royal Court Theatre, 3 July 1968, 47; transferred to London, New Theatre, 5 September 1968;

West of Suez, London, Royal Court Theatre, 17 August 1971, 32;

Hedda Gabler, adapted from Henrik Ibsen's play, London, Royal Court Theatre, 28 June 1972, 40;

A Sense of Detachment, London, Royal Court Theatre, 4 December 1972, 39;

The End of Me Old Cigar, London, Greenwich Theatre, 16 January 1975, 26;

The Picture of Dorian Gray: A Moral Entertainment, adapted from Oscar Wilde's novel, London, Greenwich Theatre, 13 February 1975, 26;

Watch It Come Down, London, Old Vic, 24 February 1976;

The Father, adapted from August Strindberg's play, South Bank, London, Cottesloe Theatre, 26 October 1988, 49.

MOTION PICTURES: *Look Back in Anger,* screenplay by Nigel Kneale with additional dialogue by Osborne, Woodfall, 1959;

The Entertainer, screenplay by Osborne and Kneale, Woodfall, 1960;

Tom Jones, screenplay by Osborne, adapted from Henry Fielding's novel, Woodfall, 1962;

The Charge of the Light Brigade, screenplay by Osborne and Charles Wood, adapted from Alfred, Lord Tennyson's poem, Woodfall, 1968;

Inadmissible Evidence, screenplay by Osborne, Woodfall, 1968.

In 1975 American psychoanalyst Rollo May wrote: "It is easier in our society to be naked physically than to be naked psychologically or spiritually—easier to share our body than to share our fantasies, hopes, fears, and aspirations, which are felt to be more personal and the sharing of which is experienced as making us more vulnerable." Although written about contemporary American society, May's compassionate comment on the courage it takes to be vulnerable transcends its cultural context and describes the artistic vision of the prominent postwar British dramatist John Osborne, who has attempted to use the theater as a weapon to destroy old and outmoded ways of thinking and responding to life.

In 1957 Osborne wrote: "I do not like the kind of society in which I find myself. I like it less and less. I love the theatre more and more because I know that it is what I always dreamed it might be: a weapon. I am sure that it can be one of the decisive weapons of our time." Osborne believes that the theater must be based on caring how people feel and live. Although he concedes that there is room for many kinds of theater, he is most concerned with "the one that offers a vital, emotional dynamic for ordinary people, that breaks down class barriers, and all the many obstacles set in the way of feeling." Correspondingly, Osborne holds the firm opinion that "we need a new feeling as much as we need a new language.... Out of the feeling will come the language."

In a 1958 interview with Robert Muller of the *Daily Mail*, Osborne clarified further his mission to make people feel: "I want people to see life through my mirror, to feel my image. If it gets as far as that, if they feel, then I've made my contribution. What they do with those feelings afterwards is somebody else's business. Politicians. Journalists. Those sort of people." Given these intentions, it is understandable that Osborne found that the theater itself presented (as critic Gabriel Gersh has suggested) "a brave enough cause, and he embarked on it with a clear image of the enemy and simple plan of action. The theater belongs to the middle class. The middle class do not care. They must be made to care...." In a BBC television interview in 1962, Osborne stated that "the reason I have not written overt 'social message' plays is because I prefer to treat 'personal relationships' ... these are the things that interest me most." As for presenting any plans for political or social action to remedy the imperfections of this plainly flawed contemporary life, Osborne disclaims such responsibility, believing that it is not the playwright's task. On this very issue, critic A. V. Carter has remarked that Osborne "does not pretend to solve, simply to electrify by language the current feeling of futility. He had, and still has, the ear of the postwar generations. We know he has the talent to be the voice. Is it his task to go beyond? Perhaps there is a very positive value in merely standing against the tide, if you think the current of events is moving in the wrong direction."

Osborne gained international fame in 1956 when *Look Back in Anger* was presented at the Royal Court Theatre. Since that time he has been surrounded by controversy, which he has not only permitted, but which he has also, in the words of Cameron Northouse and Thomas P. Walsh, "frequently inflamed . . . by lashing out at his critics and countrymen, both in his plays and elsewhere, with an overpowering poignancy and sense of conviction combined with an artful use of the barbed phrase." To date he has written more than twenty plays, as well as eight television dramas and five screenplays, and has contributed numerous articles and commentaries on the theater and contemporary society.

Because his maturation as an artist has been inextricably connected with his training in the theater, he does not believe that anyone can write easily for the theater who does not work in it. Appropriately enough, he has taken time from his busy writing schedule to direct three West End productions (*The World of Paul Slickey* in 1959, the 1965 revival of *Inadmissible Evidence*, and Charles Wood's *Meals on Wheels* in 1965) and to act in three films (*First Love*, 1970, *Get Carter*, 1971, and *Tomorrow Never Comes*, 1978) and three television dramas (*The Parachute*, 1968, *The First Night of Pygmalion*, 1969, and *Lady Charlotte*, 1977). He has also taken time to participate in numerous political and social protests and to lead battles against newspaper drama critics and the Lord Chamberlain's censorship control of the theater.

Born on 12 December 1929 in Fulham, a suburb of London, John James Osborne is the only son of Thomas Godfrey Osborne, then a commercial artist and copywriter of lower-middle-class Welsh descent, and Nellie Beatrice Grove Osborne, then a barmaid with higher aspirations. In his lengthy essay "They Call It Cricket," published in 1957 in *Declaration*, Osborne recalls, with considerable affection and sensitivity, several vivid childhood recollections of his parents and their contrasting temperaments and family backgrounds. However, Osborne cannot look back upon his childhood in Fulham with any genuine pleasure, for much of it was spent on the edge of poverty and personal poor health. Although only a child during World War II, he remembers quite vividly his father's death by tuberculosis in 1941, the air raids, and the general excitement of the war—events which have had profound and lasting effects upon both Osborne and his writing. Osborne learned at an early age what it was to be poor, for during most of the war he lived with his widowed mother in Fulham, where they at one time subsisted on as little as twenty-two shillings and sixpence (then $3.12) a week.

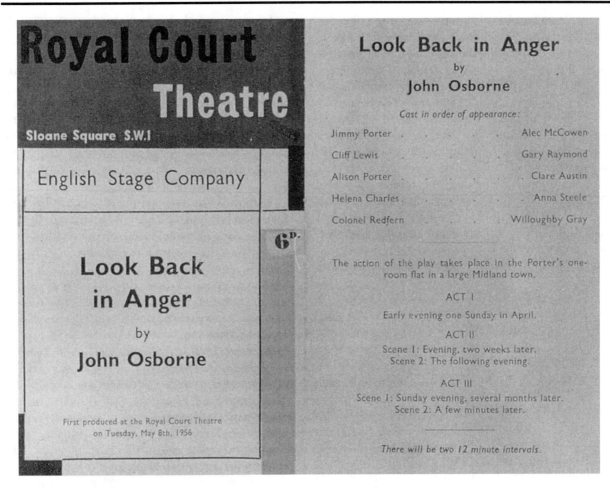

Program cover, cast list, and synopsis of scenes for the third 1957 Royal Court revival of the play that gave rise to the label "angry young man"

Osborne's school days were filled with a great deal of bitterness and acrimony as well as extended periods of illness. He attended several day schools and then, when he was sixteen, went (through the financial assistance of a charitable institution) to St. Michael's College, which Osborne has denigrated as an obscure and "rather cheap boarding school" in North Devon. Although he has dismissed the education he received there as "worth no mention," Osborne did remain at St. Michael's for slightly less than two years to receive his General School Certificate. After leaving St. Michael's, he received no other formal education and as a result is, for the most part, self-educated, unlike most of the postwar young intellectuals who went on to study at universities. After spending some time at home, he took jobs on several trade journals for about six months at each, but he soon became disillusioned with journalism and drifted, obliquely, into theater by accepting a job as tutor for child actors in a provincial touring company. Shortly thereafter, Osborne was found to be unqualified as a teacher, and he was relieved of his tutorial responsibilities and invited instead to stay on as assistant stage manager and eventually as an actor in the company. Osborne made his acting debut at the Empire Theatre, Sheffield, in March 1948 as Mr. Burrells in Joan Temple's *No Room at the Inn* and for the next seven years made the rounds of the provincial repertory theaters as a competent actor specializing in characterizations of old men.

Osborne's play-writing career began nearly a decade before the production of *Look Back in Anger*. While a repertory actor, Osborne began writing plays—many of them collaborative efforts with other actors—on the side. During this period he wrote five unsuccessful "bottom drawer" plays, three of which were *The Devil Inside Him* (co-authored with Stella Linden and produced in Huddersfield in 1950), *Personal Enemy* (written with Anthony Creighton and produced in Har-

Kenneth Haigh and John Osborne, 1956

rogate in 1955), and the Ur-version of *Epitaph for George Dillon* (coauthored with Creighton and produced in a highly revised form at the Royal Court Theatre in 1958). Of these three plays, only *Epitaph for George Dillon* has been published. Although Osborne has dismissed *The Devil Inside Him* and *Personal Enemy* as juvenilia unworthy of publication, both of these early plays have merit. In its depiction of a poetically gifted Welsh youth cruelly mistreated by both his family and village community, *The Devil Inside Him* presents a sensitive portrait of a young artist; and in its depiction of the psychological destruction of an American family from within by a paranoid mother, *Personal Enemy* presents an often compelling portrait of the McCarthy era in America during the early 1950s. When *Personal Enemy* was produced at Harrogate in 1955, Osborne encountered his first difficulties with the Lord Chamberlain's Office, which refused to license the play unless sizable portions dealing with homosexuality were deleted from the script. Osborne and Creighton complied with the Lord Chamberlain's demands, but the truncated version that resulted rendered the play incoherent and pointless.

Osborne's third apprentice play to be produced, *Epitaph for George Dillon*, was written in 1954 in London during odd breaks between spells of repertory work all over the provinces. Osborne and Creighton completed the script in five weeks and sent copies of it to every theater management in London, but the script was rejected by all. In 1957, when Osborne was an established international celebrity for *Look Back in Anger*, *Epitaph for George Dillon* received its world premiere (an undergraduate production) at Oxford University. Drama critics from London who covered the event found the play disappointing, but significant in that in its principal roles could be found the rough sketches for such later success-hungry heroes as Jimmy Porter in *Look Back in Anger* and Archie Rice in *The Entertainer* (1957).

Despite two intrusive and clumsily handled flashback sequences which the script then contained, *Epitaph for George Dillon* was nonetheless found well worth bringing to London. Its first professional performance (in which the two flashback sequences had been virtually eliminated) was given at the Royal Court Theatre on 11 February 1958 by the English Stage Company. The title role was played by Robert Stephens.

Like *The Devil Inside Him, Epitaph for George Dillon* is a portrait of an artist as a young failure, and like its predecessor *Personal Enemy*, it is also an intense study of a young writer struggling to bear up under the smothering attention and oppressiveness of a matriarchal household. More specifically, however, in *Epitaph for George Dillon*, the title character is a young, out-of-work actor-playwright who unscrupulously sponges off the goodwill of the Elliots, a suburban London family of limited means and sophistication. George, who believes that the world owes him a living, accepts the generosity of the Elliots to their faces (especially the goodwill of Mrs. Elliot, who sees him as a surrogate for her son who was killed in the war) but ridicules them behind their backs. George, however, finds himself drawn toward Mrs. Elliot's unmarried sister, Ruth Gray, who rebuffs him. Frustrated by Ruth's attitude, George turns his attention to the ignorant and uncomprehending Josie Elliot, a sluttish, teenage girl who is infatuated with him. Desperate for success, George finally achieves bittersweet fame when a ruthless fly-by-night theatrical producer turns his latest play into a tawdry popular success. Meanwhile, George, who has recovered from a mild case of tuberculosis, returns to the Elliot family, doomed to marry the pregnant Josie to save her good name and to accept the congratulations on his success with his play, which he knows is artistically worthless.

The London critics' reception of the Royal Court production of *Epitaph for George Dillon* was mixed. Despite its unevenly distributed dramatic interest, the play was nonetheless seen as one of promise by most reviewers, who repeated the earlier observation that the play contained the prototype for later Osborne characters. In *Epitaph for George Dillon*, critic R. B. Marriott of the *Stage* noted that "Osborne's interest, and uncanny understanding of failure and decay, and the integrity and strange hope that can be found in their midst, are evident in the lives of the ordinary suburban family with whom George Dillon ... comes to live." In Osborne's portrait of George Dillon, Marriott also saw "one of the most pitiable of creatures, a would-be creator without much talent, doomed to mediocrity." *Epitaph for George Dillon* may be an apprentice play containing serious flaws, but these flaws are understandably those of a young playwright finding his way.

After the disappointing failure of *Personal Enemy* in 1955, Osborne returned to acting, having left the repertory circuit before the play's production. He went to London, where he encountered long periods of unemployment and "lived" in a public library because it was warmer than his "digs." During one of these periods, Osborne wrote his first solo play, *Look Back in Anger*. He submitted copies of the script to every theatrical agent in London and to many of the West End producers, but it was rejected by all.

In responding to the English Stage Company's advertisement soliciting plays by new British playwrights, Osborne sent a copy of *Look Back in Anger* to George Devine, the artistic director of the company, at the Royal Court Theatre in July 1955. The English Stage Company had just been founded to provide a theater and proper conditions in London where contemporary playwrights—preferably, English playwrights—could express themselves without having to submit to the increasing restrictions of the commercial theater. Through the support of the British Arts Council and the English Stage Company, Devine set out to create conditions "where the dramatist is acknowledged for what he is—the fundamental creative force in the theatre; and where the play, the discovery of the truth of its style, and the interpretation of the dramatist will be carried out with a sense of responsibility towards him, with the same seriousness of purpose that it is carried out in all good classical theatres and opera houses. I mean a theatre where the play is more important than the actors, the director, the designer. I mean a theatre where the various elements of interpretation will be placed in their balance. To this end I devised a method of staging which would only require the minimum of scenic elements, so that it was the play and not the look of it which would make its impact on the public, and would throw the necessity for creating the situation and the mood much more on the actors and on to the director."

When the script of *Look Back in Anger* arrived through the post, Devine and Tony Richardson, then a young director on the staff of the English Stage Company, knew instantly that it was just what they had been looking for—as Devine later described it, "the bomb that would blow a hole in the old theatre and leave a nice-sized gap, too big to be patched up." Devine promptly accepted the play for production in the company's first season. When Devine learned that Osborne was an out-of-work actor, he invited him to join the English Stage Company as an actor for the spring 1956 season. Osborne accepted and appeared in the productions of Ronald Duncan's

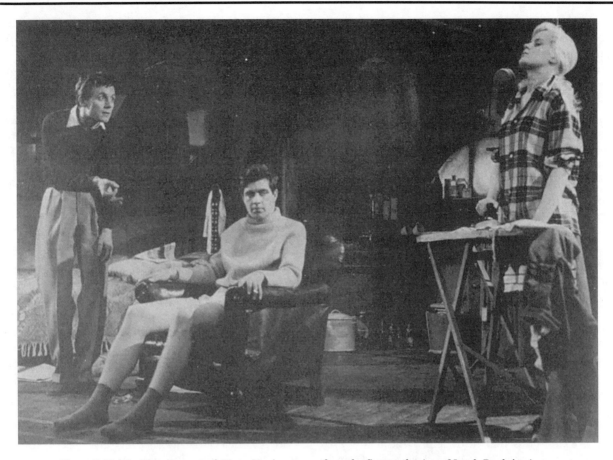

Kenneth Haigh, Alan Bates, and Mary Ure in a scene from the first production of Look Back in Anger

Don Juan and *The Death of Satan*, Jean Girau-doux's *The Apollo of Bellac*, Nigel Dennis's *Cards of Identity* and *The Making of Moo*, and Bertolt Brecht's *The Good Woman of Setzuan*.

Look Back in Anger premiered on 8 May 1956, the company's third production of the season. It was directed by Richardson, and the principal roles of Jimmy Porter and his wife, Alison, were played by Kenneth Haigh and Mary Ure. The critical reception of the first performance is now legendary. Most of the reviewers had mixed reactions: they acknowledged Osborne's obvious dramatic talent, but they did not care for the play. Harold Hobson saw much merit in the play, but only Kenneth Tynan gave the play an unreservedly favorable review—a review that has become almost as famous as Osborne's play, particularly this comment: "I agree that *Look Back in Anger* is likely to remain a minority taste. What matters, however, is the size of the minority. I estimate it at roughly 6,733,000, which is the number of people in this country between the ages of twenty and thirty. And this figure will doubtless be swelled by refugees from other age-groups

who are curious to know precisely what the contemporary young pup is thinking and feeling. I doubt if I could love anyone who did not wish to see *Look Back in Anger*. It is the best young play of its decade." The one idea that all reviewers seemed to share was their view of the play as chiefly a social commentary on postwar England—particularly the England of the 1950s welfare state. Few critics looked beneath Jimmy Porter's invective to see the intimate human drama that exists there.

Despite its great amount of social commentary, *Look Back in Anger* is as much "a play about what it means to give and receive love" as it is a play about the rebellion of the educated, lower-class young man against current society. As James Gindin puts it, "Jimmy Porter does rant against bishops and 'posh' Sunday papers, against any form of aristocratic gentility or pretense, but his invective is part of a plea for human honesty and vitality, for people to live emotionally as fully and as deeply as they can."

There is in fact little discussion of political problems in *Look Back in Anger*, although it is in-

237

ferred that Jimmy Porter is also a political rebel. Jimmy's frustration is based on other, more immediate concerns: a wife who will not surrender completely to him (not even in the intimate act of sexual intercourse) and who persists in withholding herself from him in the deeper recesses of her thoughts and feelings. Jimmy justly resents her exclusion of him and lashes out savagely at her calculated indifference to his emotional and spiritual needs.

When *Look Back in Anger* first opened at the Royal Court Theatre, it was celebrated as a new form of play writing, as the first shocking sound of the authentic voice of postwar British society. It was the first dramatic work to give rise to the glib and fashionable labels "kitchen-sink" school and "angry young man." *Look Back in Anger* is in fact a well-made play in the same manner as Henrik Ibsen's plays. It is traditional in form, not experimental. It does not speak with the voice of one generation or class but, rather, with the voice of humanity. In plot and dramatic situation, it has marked affinities with the works of August Strindberg, D. H. Lawrence, and Tennessee Williams.

In the play, Jimmy Porter, a twenty-five-year-old, working-class man with a provincial university education, runs a sweet stall with his friend Cliff Lewis in a large Midlands town (presumably Derby) during the mid 1950s. With Jimmy's wife, Alison—whose upper-class social background Jimmy can neither forget nor forgive—Jimmy and Cliff share a cramped, one-room flat in a Victorian garret. Jimmy, who is outraged by the apathetic humanity he sees around him and by his own inability to effect an entrance into the power structure of the upper classes, has a quick wit and a determination to shock, particularly the more gently nurtured, such as his own wife. Alison, in turn, is both infatuated and frightened by Jimmy's passionate intensity but chooses to protect herself from it by responding to his bitter outpourings with calculated indifference and an air of resigned exhaustion. A bright and articulate young man, Jimmy is (in Osborne's words) "anxious to give a great deal, and is deeply angry and hurt because no one seems interested enough to take it—including his wife." Simple, uneducated, and loving, Cliff is, like Alison, infatuated with Jimmy's charisma but, unlike Alison, chooses to respond to it in a more giving and generous manner.

When Alison's friend Helena Charles comes to stay with the Porters, she is shocked by what she finds and sends for Alison's father, Colonel Redfern. Alison's mother had been bitterly opposed to her daughter's marriage, and now, at last, Alison, who is expecting a baby, agrees to go home. But, apparently, Helena's bitter hatred of Jimmy has also turned to infatuation, for in Alison's absence she stays on and becomes Jimmy's mistress. Some months later, having lost her baby, Alison returns. She is unable to live without Jimmy, and Helena, realizing that these two cannot continue to exist without one another, however unhappy their life together, withdraws. When Cliff also departs at the end of the play to better his social and financial prospects, the future for both Jimmy and Alison is indeed bleak. The human buffer that Cliff once provided between them in moments of crisis will no longer be there. And Alison's baby, which could have taken Cliff's place in their triangular relationship, will never be. Jimmy and Alison must depend more than ever now on fantasy games to fill this void and to achieve what moments of intimacy and peaceful coexistence they can in their precarious marriage.

With the success of *Look Back in Anger*, Osborne found himself, overnight, regarded as a critic of society or, more precisely, a reflector of his generation's attitudes toward society. Of course the concern and feeling for intimate personal relationships that are displayed in *Look Back in Anger* may indeed have social and moral implications. But what really moves Osborne in this play seems to be the inability of people to understand and express care for each other better—particularly in their language and their emotional responsiveness. What is new and experimental about *Look Back in Anger*, in British drama, is the explosive character of Jimmy Porter and his brilliant and dazzling vituperative tirades, in which a renewed delight in a Shavian vigor and vitality of language and ideas is displayed with virtuoso command. Also, like Tennessee Williams's *A Streetcar Named Desire* (1947), the play provides an intimate portrait of an extremely troubled working-class marriage (riddled with psychological problems and sexual frustrations), which was, in its way, a theatrical first for British drama. John Elsom has also suggested that "the success of *Look Back in Anger* destroyed several inhibiting myths about plays: that the theatre had to be genteel, that heroes were stoical and lofty creatures, that audiences needed nice people with whom to identify." He goes on to comment, "Osborne also demonstrated that it was possible to write vivid and powerful speeches without making them sound verbally narcissistic. . . . He had also given the first telling expression in modern British theatre to the theme of social alienation."

Despite a somewhat mixed press—with the exception of Harold Hobson's and Kenneth Tynan's glowing reviews—*Look Back in Anger* ran for eighteen months in London, and Osborne was awarded the *Evening Standard* Drama Award in 1956 for most promising British playwright. New Yorkers, too, were impressed with the play when it opened on 1 October 1957 (with the original London cast) at the Lyceum Theatre. It ran for 407 performances, had a second Broadway production at the 41st St. Theatre beginning in November 1958, and toured the United States and Canada. *Look Back in Anger* received the New York Drama Critics Circle Award for the best foreign play of the 1957 Broadway season. The play was taken to Russia by Wolf Mankowitz and Oscar Lewenstein in 1957 as part of the World Youth Festival.

Look Back in Anger has enjoyed more revivals (both professional and amateur) than any other Osborne play to date. It has startled audiences in France, Germany, Italy, Holland, Poland, Sweden, Yugoslavia, Russia, and the United States. Much of its popularity is, of course, based on its crucial historical significance in postwar British drama, but its chief appeal seems to be (and no doubt will continue to be) the challenge that the role of Jimmy Porter provides for young actors. Long after people have forgotten about the era of the "angry young man" and the doldrums of welfare-state England, there will still be productions of *Look Back in Anger* (such as the 1980 Broadway revival starring Malcolm McDowell) in which talented young actors will display their own original interpretations of the Hamlet-like Jimmy Porter.

The English Stage Company's production of *Look Back in Anger* brought about several marked changes in Osborne's public and private life. It began an artistic collaboration between Osborne and Tony Richardson that was to last almost ten years and to culminate in their cofounding of Woodfall Films, Limited. Richardson has directed the stage and film versions of *Look Back in Anger* and *The Entertainer*, *A Subject of Scandal and Concern* (a play for television), *Luther*, and *Tom Jones* (a screenplay for which Osborne received an Academy Award in 1964). Having been granted a divorce in 1957 from his first wife, Pamela Elizabeth Lane (a repertory actress whom he met

and married in 1951), Osborne married actress Mary Eileen Ure at the Chelsea Register Office on 11 August 1957. Shortly thereafter, Osborne purchased a mews flat on Woodfall Street in Chelsea, and because of the financial success of *Look Back in Anger*, he began paying income tax for the first time in his life. In 1962 Osborne's marriage to Ure ended in divorce.

If there had been any doubt that Osborne could write a play with more than one fully developed character, it was dispelled by *The Entertainer*, which firmly established his importance in postwar British drama. Essentially an in-depth portrait of three generations of the Rice family (who make up almost the entire cast of the play), *The Entertainer* demonstrates once again Osborne's gift for invective and his deep compassion for failures. In addition to being a portrait of three generations of an English middle-class theatrical family, *The Entertainer* can also be seen as a depiction of the past, present, and future of contemporary England. Principally, however, this play is Osborne's requiem for the dying music hall and the vital part of English life that it represents.

The Entertainer enjoys the distinction in Osborne's canon of being his first play commissioned by an actor. When Laurence Olivier had first seen a performance of *Look Back in Anger* at the Royal Court Theatre, he (unlike John Gielgud) had disliked the play intensely. At the persuasion of George Devine (a close friend of Olivier's) and American dramatist Arthur Miller, who was greatly impressed with the play, Olivier saw *Look Back in Anger* a second time with Miller and changed his mind. Olivier, then forty-nine years old, went backstage to see Osborne, who was twenty-six, and apologized to him for his original, negative reaction, asking Osborne if he had a part for him in his next play. Osborne's reply at the time was noncommittal. However, he sent Olivier the first act of *The Entertainer* as soon as he had finished it, and this portion of the play was enough to persuade Olivier to accept the part of Archie Rice, a seedy, fifth-rate music-hall comedian. He felt an immediate interest in the character—an interest that deepened with time. Almost ten years later, in an interview with Kenneth Tynan, Olivier described the role of Archie Rice as "the most wonderful part that I've ever played" in a modern play. In the English Stage Company's production of *The Entertainer*, which premiered at the Royal Court Theatre on 10 April 1957, Olivier gave one of the most bril-

Jocelyn Herbert's set for the Diet of Worms scene in the first production of Luther *(photograph by Sandra Lousada)*

liant performances of his acting career in what has been considered one of the finest acting parts in English written since World War II.

Dedicated to A. C. (presumably, Anthony Creighton), *The Entertainer* is written in three acts or, more precisely, an overture and thirteen short scenes or music-hall "turns." Its action is set in a large English seaside resort during the Suez Canal crisis in the autumn of 1956, when England, with France and Israel, invaded Egypt but were forced by pressure from the United States to withdraw.

Osborne takes great precautions at the outset of *The Entertainer* to explain the symbolic significance of the play's music-hall milieu: "The music hall is dying, and, with it, a significant part of England. Some of the heart of England has gone; something that once belonged to everyone, for this was truly a folk art. In writing this play, I have not used some of the technique of the music hall in order to exploit an effective trick, but because I believe that these can solve some of the eternal problems of time and space that face

the dramatist, and, also, it has been relevant to the story and setting. Not only has this technique its own traditions, its own convention and symbol, its own mystique, it cuts right across the restrictions of the so-called naturalistic stage. Its contact is immediate, vital, and direct." Like Shaw, Osborne owes a particular indebtedness to the turns and stock-character types of the English music-hall tradition, and, in *The Entertainer* particularly, he set out to capitalize on the dramatic as well as the comic potential of these values. For example, by conceiving each scene of this play as a music-hall turn, Osborne enables the audience to see both the "public" Archie performing his trite patter before his "dead behind the eyes" audience and the "private" Archie performing a different comic role of seeming nonchalance before his own family.

The music-hall tradition, like the spirit of modern England, is dying, and Osborne relates the fortunes of the Rice family, by implication, to the state of postwar England valiantly trying to keep up appearances. Or, as the *Newsweek* theater critic expressed it: "*The Entertainer* is a compassionate study in decay. In the disintegration of both the Rice family and the institution of vaudeville itself, one can find the symbol of a tired and declining England."

In *Heartbreak House* (1920), Shaw dramatized the plight of modern England as a ship of state foundering on the rocks of pre-World War I disillusionment, futility, pessimism, and decay. Osborne, approximately forty years later, envisions post-World War II England as a tatty, crumbling music hall where Archie Rice, standing before a *tableau vivant* of a nude wearing Britannia's helmet and holding a bulldog and trident, jokingly admonishes his apathetic audiences not to "clap too hard, we're all in a very old building."

Although critics have labeled *The Entertainer* as Brechtian epic in style because of Osborne's use of loose, episodic construction and musical numbers and patter addressed directly to the audience, the play, in actuality, has been derived, as Osborne has firmly asserted, directly from the English music-hall tradition which he himself had experienced ever since childhood.

Like the Brechtian epic, however, the English music-hall tradition does acknowledge the audience as an essential participant in the play's action. In *The Entertainer*, for example, the audience plays a dual role: they are, at one and the same time, the audience in Archie's theater for whom he performs his tired comic patter and jingoistic patriotic songs, and they are also the intellectually aware audience of Brechtian epic whose complacency is shaken when Archie transfers his care and concern to them at the end of the play.

In the character of Archie Rice, Osborne has created another universal type of the modern world, infinitely disturbing in his utter hopelessness and despair. There is much perceptivity in the *Observer* critic's analogy that "Archie Rice is Jimmy Porter grown old and disintegrated. His cynicism has slumped into apathy, his ideals are dissolved in alcohol, his future is in the hands of the bureaucrats." Touring the English provinces in fifth-rate nude shows, Archie is constantly in debt and has a habit of alleviating his sorrows through women and drink. His life has collapsed into a sordid round of drunken domestic bickerings, unfaithfulness, self-pity, and humiliation. Like one of T. S. Eliot's hollow men, Archie finds his present precarious and his future hopeless; however, that in no way deters him—even at the play's end—from finding some source of valorous endurance within himself that can enable

him to resist defeat and to go on with the struggle of life.

Critic John Raymond (who considers Osborne a "virulent and biting nostalgic") believes that *The Entertainer* "is a genuine piece of twentieth century folk-art, a grotesque cry of rage and pain at the bad hand history is dealing out to what was once the largest, most prosperous empire in the world. . . ." He views Osborne as "a dramatist, concerned to harrow us with pity, love and the vanished past, not a journalist or even a descriptive writer." Nonetheless, despite its many dramatic merits and its allegorical implications concerning postwar England, *The Entertainer*, unlike *Look Back in Anger*, has enjoyed very few professional revivals. Perhaps the chief reason for this is the demanding role of Archie Rice. Olivier's seemingly definitive interpretation has no doubt intimidated other contenders from taking up this acting challenge.

Osborne's highly successful use of music-hall technique in *The Entertainer* encouraged him to employ it for a second time in his next full-length effort, *The World of Paul Slickey*, a musical satire of the London press, to whom he vituperatively dedicated the play: "I dedicate this play to the liars and self-deceivers; to those who daily deal out treachery; to those who handle their professions as instruments of debasement; to those who, for a salary cheque and less, successfully betray my country; and those who will do it for no inducement at all. In this bleak time when such men have never had it so good, this entertainment is dedicated to their boredom, their incomprehension, their distaste."

Ostensibly an attack on Fleet Street and the yellow press, the play's real targets are debased public taste which craves scandal, and the "common man" who makes himself the object of the mass media's contempt by allowing his tastes and interests to be manipulated by them. Its hero, Jack Oakham (alias Paul Slickey), a twenty-eight-year-old "scoop" reporter for the *Daily Racket*, is an appealing blend of a ruthless Pal Joey and a compassionate Miss Lonelyhearts who is striving for ideals in a corrupt commercial world of admass values.

Under Osborne's own stage direction, *The World of Paul Slickey* opened at the Palace Theatre in London on 5 May 1959 and received perhaps the worst critical reception of any West End production since the war. As Osborne wittily put it, *The World of Paul Slickey* and he had received "the worst notices since Judas Iscariot." This is per-

Program cover for the first production of Osborne's one-act satiric lessons for his countrymen

haps not surprising, since the playwright did not spare anyone, including the theater critics, in the play's fierce assault on the unhealthy state of 1950s England, which Osborne felt needed to take a good, serious look at itself.

Most critics agree that in *The World of Paul Slickey* Osborne attempts to satirize too much at once, and as a result, his efforts prove ultimately excessive and futile. Critic George Wellwarth, however, admires the intensity and frankness of the play's anger and consequently considers it one of Osborne's artistically best plays. Critic Richard Findlater, on the other hand, deplores the results of Osborne's efforts but admires the playwright's intentions in writing *The World of Paul Slickey*, which he perceives as being a wish to create a "kind of *Threepenny Opera* of post-war England; to give teeth to the poor old English musical; to extend both its form and content; to break down, still further, the barrier between musical and non-

musical theatre; to challenge the old audience and bring in the new; to say something loud and clear—in theatrical terms—about the shams of a dying social order under the shadow of the H-Bomb."

Osborne's first play for television, *A Subject of Scandal and Concern*, was first transmitted by the BBC on 6 November 1960 as part of its New Writing series. The principal role of George Jacob Holyoake, the last person to be imprisoned in England for blasphemy, was played by Richard Burton. Resembling a truncated three-act play, *A Subject of Scandal and Concern* is an accurately researched historical documentary structured on Brechtian epic format and set within the frame of a modern-day narrator-lawyer who patronizingly introduces the viewing audience in epic fashion to this "straight-forward account of an obscure event in the history of your—well—my country" and fills in with incidental but pertinent information where necessary. Act 1 traces the events that culminate in Holyoake's trial for blasphemy. Act 2 depicts the actual courtroom proceedings, and act 3 deals with the aftermath of Holyoake's conviction and imprisonment.

Osborne's two primary historical sources for *A Subject of Scandal and Concern* were the published transcript of the trial, *The Trial of George Jacob Holyoake, on an Indictment for Blasphemy, before Justice Erskine, and a Common Jury, at Gloucester, August the 15th, 1842* (1842), and Holyoake's own *de profundis* of his six-month imprisonment, *The History of the Last Trial by Jury for Atheism in England: A Fragment of Autobiography* (1851). From these two works, Osborne extracted actual dialogue and incorporated it so deftly into the context of his play that it is almost impossible to distinguish between Osborne's words and Holyoake's. This successful experiment with the fusion of dialogue served as excellent preparation for Osborne's combining Martin Luther's words with his own in his next full-length stage play, *Luther* (1961).

Much about Holyoake makes him an ideal dramatic subject for Osborne. A follower of the Socialist reformer Robert Owen, Holyoake was only twenty-five (the same age as Jimmy Porter) when he stood trial. Despite his imprisonment for blasphemy, Holyoake became a popular figure in the nineteenth-century English social struggle, winning a remarkable circle of distinguished friends that included William Gladstone. The virtual founder of the cooperative movement in England, Holyoake was a courageous man who contributed enormously through his writings, lectures, and debates to the progress in England of freedom of speech, free thought, a free press, the education of the working people, and woman's rights.

In his study *Osborne* (1969), critic Martin Banham suggests that Osborne's three principal concerns in *A Subject of Scandal and Concern* are, in fact, "man's right to dissent, his freedom of thought, and a society that allows him the dignity of speaking the truth." Critical reaction to the teleplay was decidedly negative. Guy Taylor of the *Stage*, for example, thought the play was a "mass of heavy dialogue, pretentious, uninspired and as a result as dull as can be." Nonetheless, this television play had enabled Osborne to try his hand at writing for another dramatic medium and to gain the necessary skills in Brechtian epic to dramatize for the stage the life of another historical religious rebel, Martin Luther.

In *Luther*, Osborne effectively demonstrated once again that he could skillfully handle historical material and made good use of documentary sources for the reconstruction of dialogue. By selecting a sixteenth-century historical figure as his protagonist, Osborne gained a vehicle of expression more acceptable to spectators who had found the proximity of Jimmy Porter's slings and arrows too close for comfort. Furthermore, history can add other dimensions, particularly those of remoteness, stature, objectivity, and even of tragedy. Osborne's *Luther* is a psychological study of Martin Luther the private man and not Martin Luther the public religious figure and instigator of the Protestant Reformation. Like *Epitaph for George Dillon*, *Look Back in Anger*, and *The Entertainer*, it shares the theme of loss of faith.

Luther was undoubtedly Osborne's riposte to those who doubted that he had it in him to write a play of historical significance. Osborne's fascination for someone such as Martin Luther is not surprising. One of the greatest religious rebels of all time, Luther for a time bowed to neither princes nor popes to obey the dictates of his own conscience. Like Osborne, Luther was humbly born, and through the assertion of his vituperative rhetoric he, like Osborne, scored a victory for the individual against authority.

Luther is a solid, diligently researched chronicle play that took Osborne almost two years to write. It documents a span of twenty-two years in Luther's life and uses many of Luther's own pronouncements (particularly the unusual imagery of anuses and bowels) and blends them effectively with Osborne's own strong prose. The external facts of Luther's life are, in general, accurately observed, and in the particular aspects stressed by the play the documentation is well detailed. *Luther* leans perhaps a little too trustingly on Brecht's *The Life of Galileo* (1955), both in substance and episodic style of construction, and it lacks a stern dramatic line of its own. Yet, at the same time, with an admirable economy of means it presents the audience with an authentic psychological portrait of a man and his time. In fact, like *The Life of Galileo*, much of the beauty of *Luther* relies on what the spectator actually sees, for the play depends very heavily on stage effects, music, decor, costumes, lighting, directorial compositions, and stage properties.

The first performance of *Luther* was a tryout at the Theatre Royal in Nottingham on 26 June 1961 by the English Stage Company, which brought the play to the Royal Court Theatre in

THE BLOOD OF THE BAMBERGS
by JOHN OSBORNE
Directed by JOHN DEXTER

Cast in order of appearance

Wimple	JAMES COSSINS
Cameraman	JOHN MAYNARD
Lemon	BILLY RUSSELL
Floor Assistant	BARBARA KEOGH
Brown	GLYN OWEN
Taft	GRAHAM CROWDEN
Withers	ANTON RODGERS
Guards	TONY CAUNTER JIMMY GARDNER
Russell	JOHN MEILLON
1st Footman	CHARLES LEWSEN
2nd Footman	NORMAN ALLEN
3rd Footman	JOHN MAYNARD
Woman	AVRIL ELGAR
Melanie	VIVIAN PICKLES
Archbishop	ALAN BENNETT
1st Reporter	ROBIN CHAPMAN
2nd Reporter	BARBARA KEOGH
3rd Reporter	TONY CAUNTER
4th Reporter	CONSTANCE LORNE
5th Reporter	JIMMY GARDNER

Scene 1   The Cathedral

Scene 2   The Palace

Scene 3   The Cathedral

Film sequence by John Dexter, Desmond Davies and Tony Gibbs

INTERVAL

UNDER PLAIN COVER
by JOHN OSBORNE

Directed by JONATHAN MILLER

Cast in order of appearance

Postman	BILLY RUSSELL
Tim	ANTON RODGERS
Jenny	ANN BEACH
Stanley	GLYN OWEN
1st Reporter	ROBERT EASTGATE
2nd Reporter	DONALD TROEDSEN
3rd Reporter	ROBIN CHAPMAN
4th Reporter	TONY CAUNTER
Bridegroom's Mother	CONSTANCE LORNE
Bride's Mother	AVRIL ELGAR
Bridegroom's Father	JAMES COSSINS
Bridegroom	JOHN MAYNARD
Bridegroom's Brother	NORMAN ALLEN
Bride's Father	JIMMY GARDNER
Waiter	CHARLES LEWSEN
Guests	BARBARA KEOGH PAULINE TAYLOR

The action takes place in a suburban home in Leicester
and at a wedding reception in London.

Cast lists for the first production of Two Plays for England

London on 27 July. The part of Luther was played by Albert Finney. The play is divided into twelve scenes that are bridged by terse and barked announcements of time and place in Brechtian epic fashion by a gaunt sixteenth-century knight (a symbol of the bloody age). The story of Luther's growth from conscience-ridden monk to revolutionary opponent to papal authority is unfolded by means of a series of stage effects, long set speeches (designed more to provoke thought rather than arouse emotions) that recall Shaw's *Saint Joan* (1923) and Brecht's *The Life of Galileo*, and a succinctly dramatic dialogue that often exploits to superb effect the coarsely carnal vocabulary of the German miner's son who became the founder of the Lutheran church.

If *Luther* seems to fall into chapters rather than scenes, it is perhaps because Osborne limited his historical research for this play to primarily one source. The themes of *Luther*, all its main points, and almost all of its protagonist's key lines are excerpted quotes by Luther from *Young Man Luther* (1958), a psychoanalytical and historical study by American psychoanalyst Erik H. Erikson, who views Luther's actions as almost exclusively the result of his anal obsession. Osborne's debt to this study is extensive. Osborne even adheres to Erikson's explanation that Luther's hatred of the paternalism of the pope and the established church stemmed from his hatred of his own father. Osborne departs from Erikson, however, when he fails to dramatize Luther's decision not to support—indeed actively to help suppress—the revolt of the Swabian peasants over a matter with which Luther would obviously have sympathized. In his informative article "Luther and Mr. Osborne," Gordon Rupp meticulously documents Osborne's use and misuse of historical fact in *Luther* and concludes that despite its frequent liberties with history, the play is nonetheless an achievement for which he can find many reasons to be grateful.

Critical response to *Luther* was, in general, quite enthusiastic. The play was voted the best new work of the 1963-1964 season by the New York Drama Critics Circle and won the Antoinette Perry (Tony) Award for best play in 1964. *Luther* is unquestionably an important play that solidified Osborne's international reputation. On 18 August 1961 Osborne wrote "A Letter to My Fellow Countrymen" and telegraphed it to the *Tribune* from Valbonne, France, where he had gone to write. In this, which is perhaps one of the best-known letters of the decade, Osborne vents much of the anger and frustration—but in a highly distilled and concentrated manner—that he unleashed in *Look Back in Anger*, *The Entertainer*, and *The World of Paul Slickey* against what he thought to be the inept and apathetic political leadership of his country. Public reaction to Osborne's letter was immediate and intense, compounded by misunderstanding, rage, and agreement. What many failed to see was that Osborne cared about England as deeply as, if not more than, they did and that he cared enough to try to do something. But to many, the audacity of Osborne's act was un-English and unforgivable.

After the international success of *Luther*, Osborne turned his attention once again to comic satire and wrote two revuelike one-acts, *The Blood of the Bambergs* and *Under Plain Cover*, which he jointly titled *Two Plays for England* (1962). These one-acts interestingly bridge the artistic gap for Osborne between *Luther* and *Inadmissible Evidence* (1964) by demonstrating his experimentation with comedy of manners and his treatment, like that of Jean Genet, of an intimate marital relationship. As their title implies, *Plays for England* are satiric lessons for Osborne's countrymen, and Osborne seems to have made no effort to universalize the ideas in these plays, for their themes are presented in such a way that only an English audience could fully appreciate the satiric points being made.

Essentially a satirical exploration of the monarchy industry and its mindless worship by the general public, *The Blood of the Bambergs* concerns a royal wedding in a contemporary mythical kingdom. On the eve of the royal wedding of Princess Melanie and Prince Wilhelm, the latter is killed instantly in a sports-car crash. Wilhelm's younger brother, Heinrich, the rightful successor, is a homosexual. To ensure that there will be heirs, a plot is designed to prevent Heinrich's succession to the throne. Alan Russell, a bearded Australian press photographer with a marked facial re-

semblance to Prince Wilhelm, is discovered to be the illegitimate son of the late king. The minister of culture takes immediate advantage of this good fortune and whisks Russell off to the palace to be shaved and prepared for his forced marriage to Princess Melanie the next day. Danger to the state must be averted, implies Osborne, no matter how much lying and corruption are involved. In return for his service to the state, Russell will be bribed handsomely for the "claustrophobia and overwhelming boredom" he will have to endure as monarch.

A hasty glance at the fairy-tale plot of *The Blood of the Bambergs* quickly reveals that Osborne's one-act is a modern satirical reworking of Anthony Hope Hawkins's *The Prisoner of Zenda* (1894). Alan Brien, in fact, saw the play as "a satirical charade designed to clobber the monarchy industry. It is *The Prisoner of Zenda* played to wound, *The Apple Cart* revamped to hit where it hurts. And intermittently, it is funny, savage and accurate."

Of the two *Plays for England*, *Under Plain Cover* is by far the more effective dramatic achievement. According to the play's director, Jonathan Miller, *Under Plain Cover* "seems to be a play in two minds. One half deals tenderly with the sexual privacy of marriage, while the other half is a hot, somewhat pamphleteering attack on the excesses of the yellow press. It is hard to marry these two dramatic textures in one evening's performance. . . ." In this play, Tim and his wife, Jenny, live with their two children in a little house in suburban Leicester. They are very much in love, and their marriage is firmly based on a highly successful sadomasochistic relationship. Tim and Jenny are in fact role-playing clothes fetishists who order their costumes through the mail under plain cover. Tim and Jenny realize that their fantasy world is not the real world; they recognize only too well their isolation from reality and the boundaries along which they tread. When Stanley Williams, a newspaper reporter, reveals that Tim and Jenny are unknowingly brother and sister, their happy and innocent world is promptly destroyed. Although the rule book of the National Union of Journalists specifically states, "No intrusion on private grief," Stanley persists in tormenting Tim and Jenny in order to drum up more sensational news copy. For the sake of a scoop, Jenny is married off to a "decent fellow" as soon as possible, and Tim is left "on his own" to shift as best he can. Love, however, wins out, and Jenny returns to live in seclu-

Nicol Williamson and Sheila Allen in a scene from the first production of Inadmissible Evidence *(photograph by Zoë Dominic)*

sion with Tim. The play ends with Stanley once again knocking at their door. But Tim and Jenny, within the darkened interior, will not hear.

Under Plain Cover is, according to R. B. Marriott, "a wonderfully imaginative and honest revelation of ordinary private life that ends on a heart-piercing cry for understanding and tolerance." Ostensibly a plea for sexual tolerance, the play is not condoning sexual abnormality but instead is making a plea for individuality. This play, says the drama critic of the *Times*, "is fired with Osborne's characteristic negative patriotism [the individual before society], a rooted mistrust of all public institutions, contempt for the conformist majority and instinctive support for people who practice individuality in defiance of social pressure." Granted, Osborne does indeed

continue in this play his personal feud with the press (which he commenced with *The World of Paul Slickey*), but this aspect of the play is only of secondary interest. In the play's duologue scenes between Tim and Jenny, the *London Magazine* found Osborne's play writing for once was "not thrashing about, yelling at the top of his voice, but whispering gently and clearly of the delectable, undeniable value of a relationship which conformity would frown on, and, if it could, destroy.... Osborne's couple are given us with such straight-faced candour and allowed, without bathos, a genuine mutual tenderness, that they come out as nice, sensible, moral people." Osborne himself has stated that since *Luther* he has become more and more concerned with private grief than public sorrow. One cannot weigh this concern too heavily in arriving at an understanding of *Under Plain Cover*.

Assessing *The Blood of the Bambergs* and *Under Plain Cover* together, Osborne's intention in writing *Two Plays for England* seems to be to examine the public games to which people willingly sacrifice their personal values and freedom in *The Blood of the Bambergs*, and the private games to which persons must resort in order to achieve or establish some semblance of personal independence from the conforming pressures of society in *Under Plain Cover*. R. B. Marriott finds the two *Plays for England* inextricably linked by Osborne's passion for people and his country, which was first fully apparent in *The Entertainer*: "for those who can respond to Osborne's work in the spirit that gives these plays their embracing title, much more is in them. One realises that Osborne is a satirist with a heart, a critic with love, angry because life is not made better than it is. As all his plays so far belong one to the other, so one can see that when the blasting has passed, there will be a play of hope and affirmation, these vital qualities for living being already implicit, if not easily recognisable, in all his works."

On 25 May 1963 Osborne married the film critic Penelope Gilliatt; they have a daughter, Nolan Kate. This marriage lasted approximately four years, ending in divorce in 1967.

Two Plays for England was followed two years later by *Inadmissible Evidence*, a play that unquestionably demonstrated a major step forward in Osborne's play-writing career. Although by the same hand as *Look Back in Anger*, *Inadmissible Evidence* was the product of a more mature artistic mind. *Inadmissible Evidence* is quite different from anything that Osborne had previously attempted, and it proved that he could successfully break all the dramaturgic rules.

In size, structure, and intention, *Inadmissible Evidence* was, up to that point in his career, his most ambitious undertaking. It runs nearly three hours in playing time, and in both its length and its massive reliance on psychological and rhetorical dialogue, rather than on a conventional narrative line, it can be compared with Eugene O'Neill's *The Iceman Cometh* (1946) or Edward Albee's *Who's Afraid of Virginia Woolf?* (1962).

The first performance of *Inadmissible Evidence* was given at the Royal Court Theatre on 9 September 1964 by the English Stage Company. The principal role of Bill Maitland was played by Nicol Williamson. This play picks up Osborne's chronicle of the state of contemporary England where *Look Back in Anger* and *The Entertainer* left off. Through the persona of Bill Maitland, a

"failed" London solicitor, *Inadmissible Evidence* also brings Osborne back to the contemporary English scene in the embattled first person. Maitland, whose professional and private life is on the point of deterioration, is an apt successor to Jimmy Porter and Archie Rice.

Inadmissible Evidence opens with a Kafkaesque courtroom dream sequence that foreshadows the fate of the play's protagonist. Bill Maitland, a thirty-nine-year-old London solicitor of some standing and experience, is on trial before his own conscience for "having unlawfully and wickedly published and made known ... a wicked, bawdy and scandalous object"—himself. Although he pleads not guilty to the court's indictment of him, his life is presumably the inadmissible evidence that he dares not produce in mitigation. Like Holyoake, Maitland has purposefully discarded the service of learned counsel and has elected to conduct his own self-defense, in which he admits to being "only tolerably bright," irredeemably "mediocre," and incapable of making decisions. Trapped in a limbo of helplessness and oppression, Maitland is a prisoner of a nightmarish existence of his own making. He can no longer distinguish between hallucinations and reality, and his original quickness of mind has declined into vagueness.

As his nightmare dissolves into reality, Maitland arrives for a day's work in his law office, where he sits in judgment of himself and others. Thereafter the play contains itself within Maitland's office and proceeds through two days, during which he suffers the final throes of a complete nervous breakdown. In short, the remainder of the play attempts to explain Maitland's opening condition, and—through two days of concentrated dramatic action—to summarize his precarious existence. Professionally he can no longer deal either with his staff or with his clients in their sad cases of divorce and sexual misdemeanors. The law society is after him for some obvious use of false evidence, and he cannot reach the legal colleagues and friends he wants on the telephone. He takes tranquilizers endlessly and forgets things. After each disappointment he rallies, taunts his staff, and clutches for the nearest secretary.

Unable to relate to those around him, including his clients, Maitland alienates them by either absorbing himself in his own matrimonial troubles or, in the case of Mr. Maples, finding himself unable to concentrate on his client's painful story of his trouble with the police for a homosexual offense. Helplessly, Maitland watches everyone around him withdraw from contact with him. In desperation he tries to force a personal response from his staff, his secretaries, his clients, his wife, his daughter, and lastly, his mistress, but the more anxious he becomes to reach them, the more self-protective and distant they become. One by one, they walk out on him. When his mistress, Liz, abandons him, she removes any hope of salvation for him, and his ending is inevitably one of black despair and total spiritual collapse.

Essentially a journey through the static spiritual hell of Maitland's mind, *Inadmissible Evidence* dramatizes a living, mental nightmare that culminates, as Maitland's alienation is pushed to its inevitable end, in a complete nervous breakdown. The play is principally a tour-de-force monologue for one actor, for its secondary characters are mere dream figures and metaphors that externalize the intense conflict going on within Maitland's disintegrating mind.

Inadmissible Evidence is an astonishing and exhausting dramatic experience that contains some of Osborne's finest writing to date. Constructed with great technical skill and deeply moving in its treatment, it is Osborne's study of personal disintegration and despair which demonstrates a marked psychological advance in Osborne's play writing. Having realized from his earlier plays that the factual situation in his drama is usually secondary to the verbal situation, Osborne has, according to Wilfrid Sheed, "turned the whole play into a verbal situation, a talk-nightmare as opposed to an image-nightmare. He has converted all his actual happenings into mental events, and has reduced his characters to one. . . . This leaves him free to wrestle with the central psychological data without cluttering the place with weak secondary characters and significant plot twists. . . . He has, in brief, locked himself up in one skull and found there all the rottenness and stagnation and aimlessness of a whole society." Sheed further suggests that in this play, Osborne presents a hero "who is so totally merged with society's evils that you can no longer tell who has done what to which. Society is to blame for him, but he is equally to blame for it. The Osborne man is victim and executioner, debaser and debased—and either way he loses. In bullying his subordinates, he is imitating one of society's unpleasant aspects; in crawling to them, he is imitating another. Society is ourselves, and the man who would flay the one must flay the other."

In *Inadmissible Evidence*, Osborne has taken Jimmy Porter's harangues of invective and self-pity, Archie Rice's music-hall patter, and Martin Luther's vituperative diatribes and carried them to their logical artistic end: he has created a play that is a brilliant tirade of self-pleading delivered by the typically alienated Osborne protagonist in his own existential self-defense. Despite his impressive artistic achievement in *Look Back in Anger*, *The Entertainer*, and *Luther*, it was not until *Inadmissible Evidence*, in many ways his finest play, that Osborne found his own distinctive and undiluted voice, which owed no debt to any writer but Osborne himself. The play's general critical reception reflected this assessment of Osborne's achievement. In this vintage Osborne work can be found all the qualities that have characterized his particular dramatic style and appeal: his gift for the stunning verbal tirade and the rhetoric of insult, anguish, and pain. Here, too, can be found synthesized many of Osborne's obsessive themes of revolutionary individualism, which may be found in their embryonic forms even in his first apprentice efforts, *The Devil Inside Him* and *Personal Enemy*—namely, those themes that the *Times* critic so succinctly summed up in 1962 as "rooted mistrust of all public institutions, contempt for the conformist majority, and instinctive support for people who practice individuality in defiance of social pressure."

Osborne followed *Inadmissible Evidence* the next year with another equally impressive dramatic achievement: *A Patriot for Me*, a vast chronicle play set against the background of the Austro-Hungarian Empire at the turn of the century and involving the intelligence game that was prevalent in Europe at that time. The play concerns the decline and fall of the Hapsburg empire and its mighty Imperial and Royal Army as reflected through the tragic military career of one of its most outstanding officers, Capt. Alfred Victor Redl (1864-1913).

A Patriot for Me is inspired, at least in part, by Robert B. Asprey's biography of Redl, *The Panther's Feast* (1959), which recounts how the young, intelligent, and ambitious Redl was able to fight his way to a commission in the elitist Austro-Hungarian Imperial and Royal Army despite his humble, working-class origins, then into the War College of the General Staff, and finally into the Intelligence Bureau. While a member of the Intelligence Bureau, he was blackmailed, because of his homosexuality and heavy debts, into becoming a spy for Tsarist Russia. According to Asprey, Redl succeeded for nearly twelve years in leading a double life: "by day, a bright conscientious officer heavily decorated for his outstanding service; by night, an evil man intent on satisfying his lust and selling his country to pay the cost. Caught by chance early in 1913, he was allowed to commit suicide." Asprey in his biography, like Osborne in his play, effectively uses Redl's tragic career to point out "the danger of military supremacy in governmental affairs, especially that accruing from a General Staff concept; the lack of progress made by society in the homosexual problem—any officer today falling into this perversion is still subject to blackmail for reasons familiar to Redl; and the ease with which bureaucracy, sheltered by the sacrosanct curtain of official secrecy, can hide its errors from the people it represents."

In Osborne's portrait of Redl, the alienated protagonist achieves its ultimate expression. In this sweeping historical drama, Osborne succeeds, through consummate artistry and skill, in arousing the audience's care and concern for a protagonist purposefully endowed with seemingly insurmountable unsympathetic characteristics. Osborne, in fact, seemed to have consciously tried to make it difficult for viewers to respond empathetically to Redl; and, in his portrait of this desperate and hunted human being, he challenges the audience with the ultimate test of their capacity to see beyond the surface abrasiveness of the character and perceive with compassion and understanding the compelling inner humanity of the man.

Regrettably, *A Patriot for Me*, which won the *Evening Standard* Drama Award for best play, was presented only at the Royal Court Theatre for a limited engagement during the summer of 1965. The Lord Chamberlain's office had demanded such extensive deletions in the script—even to the removal of entire, crucial scenes—that the English Stage Company formed a private club so that *A Patriot for Me* could be presented intact.

Since 1965 Osborne has written six full-length plays (*Time Present*, 1968; *The Hotel in Amsterdam*, 1968; *West of Suez*, 1971; *A Sense of Detachment*, 1972; *The End of Me Old Cigar*, 1975; and *Watch It Come Down*, 1976), five dramatic adaptations (*A Bond Honoured*, 1966; *Hedda Gabler*, 1972; *A Place Calling Itself Rome*, 1973; *The Picture of Dorian Gray*, 1973; and *The Father*, 1988), eight television plays (*The Right Prospectus*, 1970; *Very Like a Whale*, 1971; *A Gift of Friendship*, 1972; *Jill and Jack*, 1974; *Almost a Vision*, 1976 [unpub-

lished]; *You're Not Watching Me, Mummy*, 1978; *Try a Little Tenderness*, 1978 [unperformed]; and *A Better Class of Person: An Extract of Autobiography for Television*, 1985), one dramatic monologue for television, *God Rot Tunbridge Wells* (1985), and the first volume of his autobiography, *A Better Class of Person* (1981), which spans his life from 1929 to 1956. Though this productive output is impressive, much of it lacks the passionate vitality and impact that typified Osborne's earlier work. The five adaptations and eight television plays, though often deft, seem ultimately to be dramatic exercises marking time during a fallow period for a gifted dramatist, and they are finally disappointing. The six full-length plays contain pointed commentary on the cultural and sociopolitical decline of England in the late 1960s and in the 1970s, but many of their chief concerns have been better dealt with by Osborne in earlier plays. The overriding topicality and parochialism of these six plays have greatly limited their scope and impact and, undoubtedly, the extent of their production abroad.

Time Present, staged at the Royal Court Theatre in 1968, fails to break new ground. The play's actress-protagonist, Pamela, is beleaguered by the need to adapt to a present from which she feels herself spiritually isolated and alienated. To critic Simon Trussler, Pamela is like a "sister to Jimmy Porter in that she draws on the ever diminishing resources of the past—as personified in the life of her old-style actor father—and lets the relationships and requirements of the present crumble around her."

Winner of the *Evening Standard* Drama Award for the best play of 1968, *The Hotel in Amsterdam* is indeed a well-crafted and effective ensemble play which demonstrates Osborne's firm control of his material. Set in a suite in a first-class hotel in Amsterdam, the play concerns three English couples who escape for a weekend away from their movie-producer boss, K. L. The *Spectator* critic observed that if the play had been written "by a good television script writer, the story of a bitchy drunken middle-aged author working in film, spending a weekend in Amsterdam with his upper-class wife, a genial ex-public school film editor and his wife, and the producer's secretary who has brought her working-class painter husband, all trying to get away from the producer, would be banal, irritatingly limited in its range of theatrical conversation, and probably repulsively boring. . . ." He contended, however, that "written by Osborne it is almost perfectly con-

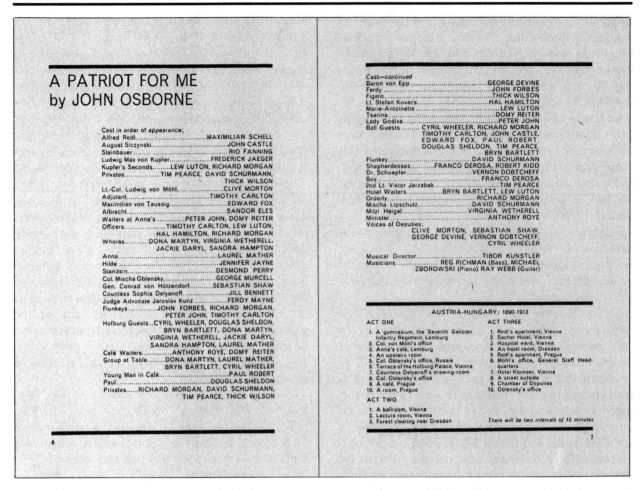

Cast list and synopsis of scenes for Osborne's 1965 play about the decline and fall of the Austro-Hungarian Empire

structed, uses the same elements with infuriatingly disturbing success, and above all, by thrusting its roots deep down into general truth, it becomes though intensely personal, particular and limited in its literal scope, both part of universal experience and universally comprehensible."

In *West of Suez* (1971), Wyatt Gillman, an elderly British writer and television personality, and his four formidable daughters and their husbands have gathered for a holiday on an indeterminate (but formerly British) Caribbean island which is currently experiencing extreme political unrest. Much of the play concerns discussions and confrontations between members of the family and, in turn, their encounters with various outsiders. The political unrest on the island eventually breaks into revolution, and Gillman, who could have been a capable leader, becomes instead a pointless victim of assassination. Though *West of Suez* evokes strong Chekhovian overtones in its presentation of a British colonial heritage in decline, its characters and their situation—

despite Osborne's efforts to create an ensemble play—are never satisfyingly developed and explored. Nonetheless, J. W. Lambert, in the *Sunday Times*, believed that in this play, "Osborne has taken a great bound forward" in his growth as a serious dramatist. John Russell Taylor also perceptively observed that *West of Suez*, despite its flaws, is a major work in which Osborne seems to be siding with the conservatives more than in any other play.

A Sense of Detachment (1972) is essentially an ensemble play for four actors and two actresses. The work defies easy description, as Michael Billington in the *Guardian* observed: "How to describe John Osborne's *A Sense of Detachment* at the Royal Court? A thinking man's *Hellzapoppin*? A spiky, satirical, inconsequential collage? An attack on our own heartless, loveless, profiteering society in which language is corrupted daily? A moving threnody for a dying civilization? The paradox of this (to me) provocative, innovatory and exciting work is that it manages to be all of these things, moving outwards from purely theatrical satire to an eloquent examination of the world at large ... sustainedly entertaining. It is full of Osborne's characteristic rancid eloquence. And it goads, provokes and agitates its audience as only a truly vital theatrical work can."

Like *Two Plays for England, The End of Me Old Cigar* (1975) demonstrates once again Osborne's gift for outrageous social satire. In this play, the widowed Lady Regine Frimley (née Myra Steinitz from Hackney) supports herself and her young "husband," Stan, by inviting prominent men and women from contemporary British cultural life and the mass media to her country house for intimate (but discreet) liaisons with each other. John Elsom noted the play's "slaughterous first act ... followed by a sentimental second...." He went on to comment upon its poor critical reception, "not an unusual fate for Osborne's plays, for many had received 'mixed' reviews, except that this time critical impatience seemed to give way before plain boredom."

Watch It Come Down (1976) was the first play by Osborne to be staged by England's National Theatre Company since their production of his *A Bond Honoured* in 1966. In *Watch It Come Down*, which is set in a country home converted from a former railway station, film director Ben Prosser and his wife, Sally, reach a crisis in their relationship. As they attempt to work out their problem, they draw the rest of their household into the conflict. Critical and audience reception of this most recent, full-length Osborne play was mixed, but the play nonetheless demonstrated Osborne's penetrating understanding of conflicting human emotions and his marked ability to create memorable confrontations between vital and compelling characters who can express their anguish with lacerating fluency.

Osborne's efforts with dramatic adaptation, on the other hand, have been in general less successful. A one-act adaptation of Lope de Vega's Renaissance tragedy *La Fianza Satisfecha, A Bond Honoured* (1966) was specially commissioned by the National Theatre Company. Its plot centers around the almost tender love of a young nobleman, Leonido, for his sister, Marcela. In Osborne's adaptation, there is, according to Simon Trussler, a "half-hearted attempt to transmute the motiveless malignity of Lope's vicious hero, Leonido, into a kind of adolescent existentialism...." But Osborne, Trussler concludes, is unable to sustain the idea. Osborne's 1972 adaptation of Ibsen's *Hedda Gabler* is both a faithful and

successful rendering of the original into English. *A Place Calling Itself Rome* (1973), an imaginative reworking of Shakespeare's *Coriolanus* in a modern idiom, is not only an effective treatment of the original but also a compelling drama of contemporary life and politics. *The Picture of Dorian Gray: A Moral Entertainment* (1973) is a courageous attempt on Osborne's part to adapt the melodramatic vitality of Oscar Wilde's well-known novel for the stage while preserving (to use Osborne's own words) "its feeling of wilful courage and despair, the two qualities only too clearly embodied in the spirit of Wilde himself." Unquestionably, however, Osborne's most successful dramatic adaptation to date is his 1988 new English version of August Strindberg's *The Father* (an adaptation also specially commissioned by the National Theatre Company), which he undertook with the determination that if "anyone were to become the keeper of the unpredictable [Strindbergian] flame [in Britain], the task should be recklessly entrusted to [him]." Osborne was convinced that he was "uniquely placed by temperament, tradition, similarities of experience and personal style to ... carry the Strindberg torch into the [British] arena." In Osborne's opinion, "the ferocity of the battle between the Captain and [his wife] Laura [which *The Father* depicts] apprehends far more than an isolated account of the battle between the sexes. [Strindberg's] constant reversion to lyricism of agonizing power, his astonishing modernism, his sense of the nineteenth century receding and, with it, the disintegration of structures of faith, moral philosophy and accepted notions of romantic love, put him, as [David Leveaux, director of the National Theatre production] said to me, 'in the Great and Unreasonable camp of the humanists.'" Sheridan Morley, in his *Punch* review of the National Theatre production, perceptively noted that one of its many virtues is its "scathing adaptation by John Osborne, whose line in chauvinist rage and marital loathing seemed to mark him out as a natural Strindbergian for our times."

In April 1968 Osborne married actress Jill Bennett. They were divorced in August 1977, and since 2 June 1978, Osborne has been married to journalist Helen Dawson.

Despite an understandable unevenness in his works (an unevenness more strongly noticeable in the plays that follow *A Patriot for Me*), Osborne's canon is impressive, rich, and vital. In his artistic maturation, he has courageously man-

John Osborne, August 1981 (photograph by Mark Gerson)

aged to grow beyond the somewhat narrowly personal tone of *Look Back in Anger* without losing much of his original fire and vitality. He is a committed dramatist whose allegiance is principally to his art and not to political fashion, and like many artists, his concern is with people first and ideas afterward. *New York Times* drama critic John E. Booth has aptly described Osborne as a "passionate rebel against much that he finds oppressive and stagnant in the life of his countrymen." What Osborne most wants is to spur people he thinks have been too passive for far too long to feel deeply. He has, in fact, described his plays as "lessons in feeling."

With the possible exceptions of Simon Gray and Trevor Griffiths, Osborne has inspired few, if any, imitators. According to critic Gabriel Gersh, it is fairly clear why not: Osborne "has, in the first place, been continuously in search of a style. To date he has experimented with the well-

made play, the music-hall, overlapping Chekhovian dialogue, Brechtian chronicle, courtroom drama, the musical, and the one-act satire. But the only convention he has made his own is the tirade. And here we come to the main reason for his uselessness as a model. Osborne's tirades are not formal rhetorical constructions like, say, those of Giraudoux. They are amplifications of his own voice."

Osborne has little regard for understatement, flippancy, or other such clever devices that people use to mask their emotions. Critic Susan Sontag has perceptively observed that "Osborne's plays are full of unembarrassed passion; he relishes it. The best parts are the bravura solo passages of dense, intricate complaint and diatribe. The plays come marvellously alive when somebody launches into a virtuoso cadenza of invective, telling off somebody else (who lapses into silence), or passionately castigating the state of things in general."

The strong response that plays such as *Look Back in Anger* and *Inadmissible Evidence* still continue to arouse in members of Osborne's generation and in theater audiences in general testifies to Osborne's unerring capacity to touch on many of the critical, social, and psychological problems of his age and, even more important, to his intuitive ability to put people's fears and feelings into words for them more accurately than most can for themselves. Osborne understands profoundly Russian writer Aleksandr Herzen's prescription for revolutionary artists: "You can work on men only by dreaming their dreams more clearly than they can dream them themselves, not by demonstrating their ideas to them as geometrical theorems are demonstrated." One cannot help but agree with critic Irving Wardle of the *Times* that "It is the memory of Jimmy Porter and Bill Maitland that brings audiences back to [Osborne's] work hoping that the same thing will happen again; that another unrepentant egoist will step forward and compel them to acknowledge their own kinship with that scornful, guilt-ridden, challenging face. Ugly as they may be, Osborne's heroes are living creatures raising their voices to wake the dead." Even when their contemporary social impact no longer provides the vitality for Osborne's drama, his plays will still remain "lessons in feeling" and his protagonists symbolic figures who themselves embody the essence of their anxious times.

Bibliographies:

Shirley Jean Bailey, "John Osborne: A Bibliography," *Twentieth Century Literature*, 7 (1961): 118-120;

Cameron Northouse and Thomas P. Walsh, *John Osborne: A Reference Guide* (Boston: G. K. Hall, 1974);

Kimball King, *Twenty Modern British Playwrights: A Bibliography, 1956-1976* (New York & London: Garland, 1977).

References:

Ruediger Ahrens, "History and the Dramatic Context: John Osborne's Historical Plays," *Fu Jen Studies: Literature and Linguistics* (Taipei), 16 (1983): 49-75;

Kenneth Allsop, *The Angry Decade* (London: Owen, 1958), pp. 96-132, 135-140;

Michael Anderson, *Anger and Detachment: A Study of Arden, Osborne and Pinter* (London: Pitman, 1976), pp. 21-49;

Martin Banham, *Osborne* (Edinburgh: Oliver & Boyd, 1969);

Mark Brady, "Looking Back at the Language of Anger," in *Four Fits of Anger: Essays on the Angry Young Men* (Udine, Italy: Campanotto, 1986), pp. 150-170;

John Russell Brown, ed., *Modern British Dramatists: A Collection of Critical Essays* (Englewood Cliffs, N.J.: Prentice-Hall, 1968), pp. 9-10, 47-57, 117-121;

Brown, *Theatre Language: A Study of Arden, Osborne, Pinter, and Wesker* (New York: Taplinger, 1972), pp. 118-157;

David Cairns and Shaun Richards, "No Good Brave Causes?: The Alienated Intellectual and the End of the Empire," *Literature and History*, 14 (Autumn 1988): 194-206;

Alan Carter, *John Osborne* (Edinburgh: Oliver & Boyd, 1969);

Joseph Chiari, *Landmarks of Contemporary Drama* (London: Jenkins, 1965), pp. 109-115;

Robert G. Egan, "Anger and the Actor: Another Look Back," *Modern Drama*, 32 (September 1989): 413-424;

John Elsom, *Post-War British Theatre* (London: Routledge & Kegan Paul, 1976), pp. 72-81;

Harold Farrar, *John Osborne* (New York & London: Columbia University Press, 1973);

G. S. Fraser, *The Modern Writer and His World* (Harmondsworth, U.K.: Penguin, 1964), pp. 223-233;

Steven H. Gale, "John Osborne: Look Forward in Fear: Thematic Developments, 1965-1980," in *Essays on Contemporary British Drama*, edited by Hedwig Bock and Albert Wertheim (Munich: Max Heuber, 1981), pp. 5-29;

Bamber Gascoigne, *Twentieth Century Drama* (New York: Hutchinson, 1962), pp. 196-198;

James Gindin, *Postwar British Fiction* (Berkeley: University of California Press, 1963), pp. 51-64;

Ronald Hayman, *British Theatre Since 1955: A Reassessment* (Oxford: Oxford University Press, 1979), pp. 34-38;

Hayman, *John Osborne* (New York: Ungar, 1972);

Arnold P. Hinchliffe, *John Osborne* (Boston: Twayne, 1984);

D. L. Hirst, *Comedy of Manners* (London: Methuen, 1979), pp. 81-96;

John Osborne: A Symposium (London: Royal Court Theatre, 1966);

Andrew Kennedy, *Six Dramatists in Search of a Language* (Cambridge: Cambridge University Press, 1975), pp. 192-212;

Laurence Kitchin, *Drama in the Sixties* (London: Faber & Faber, 1966), pp. 185-191;

John Lahr, "Poor Johnny One-Note," in his *Up Against the Fourth Wall* (New York: Grove, 1970), pp. 230-245;

Frederick Lumley, *New Trends in Twentieth Century Drama* (London: Barrie & Rockliff, 1967), pp. 221-232, 255;

John Mander, *The Writer and Commitment* (London: Secker & Warburg, 1961), pp. 179-211;

Charles Marowitz, with Tom Milne and Owen Halle, *The Encore Reader* (London: Methuen, 1965);

Benedict Nightingale, "The Fatality of Hatred: On John Osborne," *Encounter*, 58 (May 1982): 63-70;

Malcolm Page, comp., *File on Osborne* (London & New York: Methuen, 1988);

Gordon Rupp, "Luther and Mr. Osborne," *Cambridge Quarterly*, 1 (Winter 1965-1966): 28-42;

John Russell Taylor, *Anger and After*, revised edition (London: Methuen, 1969), pp. 39-66;

Taylor, ed., *John Osborne: Look Back in Anger, A Casebook* (London: Macmillan, 1968);

Simon Trussler, *John Osborne* (London: Longmans, 1969);

Trussler, *The Plays of John Osborne: An Assessment* (London: Gollancz, 1969);

Kenneth Tynan, *Tynan on Theatre* (Harmondsworth, U.K.: Penguin, 1964), pp. 130-132, 173-176, 205-207;

Tynan, *Tynan Right & Left* (New York: Atheneum, 1967), pp. 5-6;

Tynan, *A View of the English Stage* (Frogmore, U.K.: Granada, 1976);

Irving Wardle, *The Theatre of George Devine* (London: Cape, 1978);

George E. Wellwarth, *The Theater of Protest and Paradox*, revised edition (New York: New York University Press, 1971), pp. 254-269;

Katharine J. Worth, *Revolutions in Modern English Drama* (London: G. Bell, 1973), pp. 67-85.

Anthony Powell

(21 December 1905 -   )

This entry was written by James Tucker for
DLB 15: British Novelists, 1930-1959: Part Two.

SELECTED BOOKS: *Afternoon Men* (London: Duckworth, 1931; New York: Holt, 1932);

Venusberg (London: Duckworth, 1932); republished with *Agents and Patients* (1952);

From a View to a Death (London: Duckworth, 1933); republished as *Mr. Zouch: Superman* (New York: Vanguard, 1934); republished as *From A View to A Death* (Boston: Little, Brown, 1968);

Caledonia (N.p.: Privately printed, 1934);

Agents and Patients (London: Duckworth, 1936); republished with *Venusberg* (1952);

What's Become of Waring (London: Cassell, 1939; Boston: Little, Brown, 1963);

John Aubrey and His Friends (London: Eyre & Spottiswoode, 1948; New York: Scribners, 1948; revised edition, London: Hogarth, 1988);

A Question of Upbringing (London: Heinemann, 1951; New York: Scribners, 1951);

Two Novels: Venusberg, and Agents and Patients (New York: Periscope-Holliday, 1952);

A Buyer's Market (London: Heinemann, 1952; New York: Scribners, 1953);

The Acceptance World (London: Heinemann, 1955; New York: Farrar, Straus & Cudahy, 1955);

At Lady Molly's (London: Heinemann, 1957; Boston: Little, Brown, 1957);

Casanova's Chinese Restaurant (London: Heinemann, 1960; Boston: Little, Brown, 1960);

The Kindly Ones (London: Heinemann, 1962; Boston: Little, Brown, 1962);

The Valley of Bones (London: Heinemann, 1964; Boston: Little, Brown, 1964);

The Soldier's Art (London: Heinemann, 1966; Boston: Little, Brown, 1966);

The Military Philosophers (London: Heinemann, 1968; Boston: Little, Brown, 1968);

Books Do Furnish a Room (London: Heinemann, 1971; Boston: Little, Brown, 1971);

Two Plays by Anthony Powell: The Garden God and *The Rest I'll Whistle* (London: Heinemann, 1971; Boston: Little, Brown, 1971);

Photograph by Mark Gerson

Temporary Kings (London: Heinemann, 1973; Boston: Little, Brown, 1973);

Hearing Secret Harmonies (London: Heinemann, 1975; Boston: Little, Brown, 1975);

Infants of the Spring (London: Heinemann, 1976; New York: Holt, Rinehart & Winston, 1978);

Messengers of Day (London: Heinemann, 1978; New York: Holt, Rinehart & Winston, 1978);

Faces in My Time (London: Heinemann, 1980; New York: Holt, Rinehart & Winston, 1981);

The Strangers All Are Gone (London: Heinemann, 1982; New York: Holt, Rinehart & Winston, 1983);

O, How the Wheel Becomes It! (London: Heinemann, 1983; New York: Holt, Rinehart & Winston, 1983);

The Fisher King: A Novel (London: Heinemann, 1986; New York: Norton, 1986);

Miscellaneous Verdicts: Writings on Writers, 1946-1989 (London: Heinemann, 1990).

OTHER: *Barnard Letters 1778-1884*, edited by Powell (London: Duckworth, 1928);

Novels of High Society from the Victorian Age, introduction by Powell (London: Pilot, 1947);

Brief Lives; and Other Selected Writings of John Aubrey, edited by Powell (London: Cresset, 1949; New York: Scribners, 1949);

E. W. Hornung, *Raffles*, introduction by Powell (London: Eyre & Spottiswoode, 1950);

The Complete Ronald Firbank, preface by Powell (London: Duckworth, 1961);

"Reflections on the Landed Gentry," in *Burke's Landed Gentry* (London: Burke's Peerage Publications, 1965);

Jocelyn Brooke, *The Orchid Trilogy*, introduction by Powell (London: Secker & Warburg, 1981).

SELECTED PERIODICAL PUBLICATIONS—
UNCOLLECTED: "The Other Amiel I," *Cornhill*, no. 966 (December 1945): 481-488;

"The Other Amiel II," *Cornhill*, no. 967 (April 1946): 78-86;

"George Orwell: A Memoir," *Atlantic Monthly*, 220 (October 1967): 62-68;

"The Flight From Romanticism: Picasso's Great Harlequinade," *Encounter*, 40 (February 1973): 53-55.

Although Anthony Powell produced five charming, self-contained, intermittently profound novels before World War II and has published two plays, his place as a major writer of fiction rests upon *A Dance to the Music of Time*, the roman-fleuve in twelve volumes—*A Question of Upbringing, A Buyer's Market, The Acceptance World, At Lady Molly's, Casanova's Chinese Restaurant, The Kindly Ones, The Valley of Bones, The Soldier's Art, The Military Philosophers, Books Do Furnish a Room, Temporary Kings,* and *Hearing Secret Harmonies*—which came out between 1951 and 1975. The life of its narrator, Nicholas Jenkins, and the life of Powell have many similarities, though the work is

not pure autobiography. Like Jenkins, Powell comes from an ancient, aristocratic Welsh lineage but has been comprehensively anglicized. Powell had a standard upper-class English education at Eton and Balliol College, Oxford. The son of a regular army officer, he was born early in the century and worked at various times in publishing, films, and literary journalism and was himself an army officer during World War II.

In all these respects, Powell and his creation, Jenkins, have marked resemblances, and it is Powell's achievement to have composed from this deft mix of autobiography and fiction a work which gives a vivid, amusing, shrewd, and passably balanced account of upper-class Britain between 1914 and 1975, and which presents a consistent plea for tolerance, moderation, humaneness, and sensitivity.

Regarding himself as a poor maker of plots, Powell deliberately chose a form requiring other skills, and *A Dance to the Music of Time* has a drifting, apparently inconsequential quality which suits his view of life as comprising constant fluke and surprise. He establishes his settings and his people with such precision—nobody can better portray the well-off, well-bred, twentieth-century English male—that the books can stand some excursions into flagrant coincidence or even fantasy.

For the most part Powell is writing about a fairly small and privileged social class. He treats them with a perception, irony, and verve which allow him to find much of general significance and interest within the limited subject matter. All the same, he has felt it necessary to answer detractors who condemn novels about "small aristocratic societies" on the grounds that they shut out the ordinary concerns of the rest of the world. In *Messengers of Day* (1978), the second volume of his memoirs, he writes: "When it comes to general implications of behaviour, Oedipus was king of Thebes; Hamlet Prince of Denmark." There remains an impression, though, that while Powell does find large topics of wide relevance within the restricted group he depicts, he perhaps lacks the wish and the ability to portray the most profound human conflicts; and it is, of course, such portrayals which enable *Oedipus Rex* and *Hamlet* to excite a universal response, regardless of the plays' confined, aristocratic backgrounds.

In autumn 1926, after leaving Oxford with a third-class degree in history, Powell joined the London publishing house of Duckworth, a post ar-

Drawing by Powell in the Eton Candle, *1922*

ranged through Thomas Balston, a director at Duckworth and friend of Powell's father. It was while working here that Powell first seriously began to consider writing fiction and set about making some preparatory notes. In due course, Duckworth would bring out four of his five prewar novels, all five entertaining, light but not lightweight. Even while planning the first, *Afternoon Men* (1931), his mind was on something larger, or so he claims in retrospect: "The original de-

sign for my first novel was . . . not without resemblance to the initial framework of . . . *A Dance To The Music of Time*; and, allowing for inexperience, the treatment is perhaps less different from the long novel than has sometimes been suggested by critics."

Powell would prefer the term *comic* to *satirical* as a description of *Afternoon Men* and was surprised that reviewers greeted it as an attack on contemporary behavior. ("These drones are not worth paper and print," wrote the reviewer for *Civil Service Opinion*.) Powell says he believed himself to be portraying the kind of life he was leading then without too much satirical distortion. *Afternoon Men* is certainly a very funny and generally good-humored book, but the reader is almost bound to feel that the fairly aimless collection of young, middle- or upper-middle-class people is being lampooned and that, in their trivialization of life, they mirror to some degree a section of current British society. It is a book very largely about parties and outings.

Afternoon Men opens with an invitation to a party for its hero, William Atwater, and ends with an invitation to another. This kind of cyclic construction, which Powell employs to reflect what he regards as the patterned nature of life, is frequently used as a structural feature in the *Music of Time* books. Atwater is a mild, rather languid young man who works in a museum, though the novel does not deal much with his work. The novel concerns his search for love with a series of women who seem calculatedly to have devoted their lives to emotional shallowness. Atwater's timid yearning for something profound is sure to fail and does so, in comic, often grotesque situations throughout the book. They are situations where a glimmer of sadness may also be spotted occasionally. Although the tragic elements are always overwhelmed by the comic, the novel's message is clear: life ought to be deeper and more purposeful than the norm here. Such a reflection would kill the book by triteness, so the touches of melancholy must be delicate. In *Messengers of Day*, Powell comments that he thought of the book as "an urban pastoral . . . depicting the theme of unavailing love."

There is little plot in *Afternoon Men* but instead a series of set pieces linked by Atwater and other entertaining characters. Humor springs largely from one or two clownish figures and from the laconic, self-centered, frequently abrasive conversation. This is very much a novel of dialogue, a factor which must have attracted and assisted Riccardo Aragno, who adapted it for a stage run of four weeks at the New Arts Theatre Club, London, opening on 22 August 1963. In no other of his novels does Powell employ so much direct speech, generally preferring to fix a character through elaborate description and analysis. In *Afternoon Men* he expertly depicts the banality of the lives under scrutiny by having characters talk with a remorseless, plodding simplicity, as if half-baked, half-drunk, or half-asleep after too many nights on the town: some are afternoon men in the sense that this is when they get out of bed.

Looking back on the book, Powell has called the dialogue "abrupt," as if this were a failing. In fact, the terseness must surely have been carefully chosen to match the novel's unexpansive, blasé personnel. It is revealing that in *Messengers of Day* Powell recalls the impact made on him by Ernest Hemingway's *The Sun Also Rises* (1926), at about the time he was planning *Afternoon Men*, particularly in the treatment of dialogue: "the naturalistic, vocable, banal, even inane, purposeless exchanges that are their own purpose, on account . . . of an undercurrent of innuendo and irony." Powell, who saw something similar in the work of Ronald Firbank and in Thomas Hardy's peasant talk, adopted the technique for *Afternoon Men*.

The novel received some good notices, including one by Edith Sitwell in a general article: "Mr. Powell is by far the most amusing and incisive observer of what has been known vulgarly as the 'bright young people.' " *Afternoon Men* sold about three thousand copies. Encouraged, Powell brought out *Venusberg* (1932) in the following year. This novel has another young man as hero, and he, too, suffers pain through rejected love, though he does collect the girl at the end. Lushington is a no more thrustful figure than Atwater, and these two books must have given Powell practice in creating the kind of unassertive, sensible, amiable male central figure who would narrate the *Music of Time* and hold it together.

Venusberg is set chiefly in a Baltic capital based substantially on Helsinki (then generally called Helsingfors), which Powell had visited during two Oxford vacations after his father was posted there with a British military mission in 1924. From Helsinki he made a weekend trip to the Estonian capital Reval (or Tallinn). The town in *Venusberg* is an amalgam of these two capitals and, so Powell has been told, comes out as "an ap-proximation to Riga, capital of Latvia, which I did not visit."

Venusberg, a lavishly ironic love story of great charm and delightful wry humor, is a more systematically plotted book than *Afternoon Men* and actually moves toward a quite powerful dramatic climax: an assassination, though one which goes poignantly awry when the wrong people are killed. Partly because of wider geography, the book has a considerably more diverse set of characters than *Afternoon Men*, and the moods of the second book are also much more various than those of the first. In *Venusberg*, Powell catches hauntingly the pervasive sense of social disruption in this part of the world following the Russian Revolution. It is sharply personified in several émigré characters down on their luck, some of them flourishing aristocratic titles which may or may not amount to anything. Powell had met the models for two of these figures as he toured Europe during his long vacation of 1924. One of them, "Count" Bobel, is a magnificent comic creation who, at the same time, relays a sinister and powerfully threatening influence throughout. *Venusberg* moves with remarkable accomplishment among comedy, menace, melancholy, and tragedy, and contains one of the most tenderly composed love affairs found anywhere in Powell's work. It involves Lushington and the wife of a hilariously ponderous but endearing local professor. Powell is not generally a good creator of women, but in this novel Frau Mavrin has admirable warmth, sweetness, and steel. For the most part, Powell's females are combative and/or phlegmatic, and his descriptions of love affairs, as well as the act of lovemaking, tend to seem unimpassioned and bleakly ritualized.

One technical mannerism in *Venusberg* recurs throughout Powell's work. Although the plot is resolved by what, for Powell, is a decidedly vigorous incident—the assassination—it is not seen firsthand by Lushington but reported to him later, reported, in fact, by one of the book's most amusing supernumeraries, Pope, a valet. Powell will often filter accounts of dramatic events in this way, thus willfully dissipating their impact. Particularly in the *Music of Time* books, his interest and his talent will be seen to lie not in the invention and striking presentation of powerful happenings but in the elaborate embellishment of generally quite small-scale events through discursive, even circuitous, witty prose. To Powell, incident is incidental.

Venusberg was well received by reviewers, and its humor was especially praised. Like *Afternoon Men*, the book sold about three thousand copies. It did not match the first novel in immediately attracting an American publisher, despite what might appear to be the tactical inclusion of a U.S. diplomat, Cortney. Shortly after publication of the book, Powell accepted a suggestion from Duckworth—which was feeling the effects of the Depression—that he should take a cut in salary from three hundred pounds a year to two hundred pounds and attend the office only in the mornings. Powell thought he would have more time for novel writing and literary journalism, though he soon discovered that he could rarely make himself produce fiction in the afternoons and that there was little journalistic work on offer.

After *Venusberg*, Powell appeared to take a conscious turn toward a different kind of novel in *From a View to a Death* (1933). Again, a young man is the major character, but this young man, Arthur Zouch, who is egocentric, amoral, and arduously on the make, is very different from Atwater and Lushington. Although he is a professional artist, aesthetic refinement has not reached his soul. He sees himself as a superman and has little of the genial compliance which characterizes both Atwater and Lushington: Zouch means to make things happen rather than have them happen to him. Powell has put to one side the passive hero, descendant of T. S. Eliot's Prufrock and Hemingway's Jake Barnes. Zouch proposes to burst his way, by marriage and any other method he can find, into the landed, if faded, Passenger family. It soon becomes apparent, however, that, energetic, ruthless, and clever though Zouch may be, he ultimately will meet disaster. In his irritable way, Mr. Passenger, too, is a superman; and he and his forebears have been at it longer and do it better. In these first three books (as, possibly, in the *Music of Time*) Powell appears to be interested in societies under threat, either from their own languor and foolishness or from huge political reverses or from calculated infiltration by arrivistes. *Afternoon Men* and *Venusberg* looked at the process in cities. *From a View to a Death* moves out into the heartland of privilege, an English country estate, though a small one. Here, the menace seems easily disposed of, almost offhandedly disposed of. Passenger and his property are more secure and intact at the end than when the book opens, though there is, possibly, one reservation to be made: late in the novel

Powell introduces a London acquaintance of Zouch, a hiking journalist named Fischbein, who leads rambles across Passenger's land. Fischbein and his followers seem to represent some sort of encroaching urban menace to the country set.

From a View to a Death is in some senses a harsher book than either of its predecessors, and in others more wholeheartedly, even laboriously, devoted to comedy—comedy which at times approaches farce. Especially at the beginning, Powell moves about among a collection of eccentric and half-witted rural figures, as if keen to get the reader laughing early. Zouch himself, although his name is part of the title of the first American edition of the book, disappears for quite long periods, and the novel seems to lose focus occasionally. It deliberately eschews the drifting charm of *Afternoon Men* and the tender melancholy of *Venusberg* and is harsher, though still from time to time very funny: the satirist Evelyn Waugh admired it, writing in *Harper's Bazaar*, "Except Mr. Anthony Powell, whose *From a View to a Death* delighted me, I cannot name any novelist who seems really worth watching." (By this time, Waugh was a friend of Powell's but probably would not have provided blurb notices on the basis of comradeship.) *From a View to a Death* received all-around acclaim, with the reviewer for the *New York Evening Post* getting as close as any to the right evaluation: "brilliantly written, witty and bitter." However, the *Egyptian Gazette* reviewer wrote: "The story is written cleverly and seems to me worthless. . . . Such books have a sociological interest, but that is no excuse for writing them." Sales in Britain of Powell's third novel were slightly higher than for the first two novels. In the United States they were dismal.

On 1 December 1934 Powell married Lady Violet Packenham and so became part of a large, aristocratic family that bears some resemblances to the Tolland family, into which Jenkins marries in the *Music of Time*. Constant Lambert, a composer and a friend of Powell, arranged the wedding music but was not well enough to attend the ceremony, owing to the aftereffects of a party the night before. Lambert would provide some basis for the character of Hugh Moreland in the *Music of Time*. Powell and his wife settled into a flat in Great Ormond Street, London, living on about eight hundred pounds to nine hundred pounds a year: not wealth, but a comfortable income at that time. By now Powell was part of what might reasonably be called a London literary coterie. They tended to review each other's work, and it is wise to regard the acclaim in some of these contemporary notices with decent reserve. Besides Waugh, Powell knew Cyril Connolly, the critic; Elizabeth Bowen, the novelist; Edith Sitwell, the poet; and Desmond MacCarthy, the critic. Through Connolly he met Dylan Thomas, then about twenty, whose work was beginning to find recognition.

Agents and Patients (1936) was the last of Powell's novels to be published by Duckworth. The book achieves another change of direction, a further extension of range. Money has become an important concern, and we hear hints of the "slump." In *Faces in My Time* (1980), the third volume of his memoirs, Powell says he detects a "persistent sense of nervous tension" in the book. This quality does exist, despite wit and humor as successful as those in any of the earlier works. Powell recalls that in this fourth novel he wanted to treat the differences between characters who "do" and those who "have things done to them": that is, between such characters as Atwater and Lushington, men to whom things happen, and Zouch, one who tries disastrously to cause them to happen. In *Agents and Patients* there is another central, young male figure, Blore-Smith. But in his case terms such as languor, passiveness, self-effacement—all of which might be applied to Atwater and Lushington—become quite inadequate. Blore-Smith is a sucker, a victim.

Two glossy, scheming men of the world, Maltravers and Chipchase (the very names suggest sophisticated dirty work), seek to lift this innocent's funds from him to back their own enterprises in, respectively, filmmaking and psychiatry. They mean to find comfort and self-advancement, if possible without the banalities of hard work. Through an amusing turn of the plot, Blore-Smith steals from them the woman they both want, but it is clear that she will now take over control of Blore-Smith's life, for as long as it suits her, in place of these two stylish con men. Powell seems to be saying that those who are born to be led, milked, and put-upon will stay that way and that those who lead, milk, and impose are similarly unchangeable: at the end, Blore-Smith is still having to shell out for the debts of Maltravers and Chipchase, and these two are engaged in new projects to be financed by others. In a small rush of self-assertion, Blore-Smith tells them he means to lead his own life once more, "Not the life foisted on me by you two. . . . The real thing." All the same, we last see him apparently stunned by all that has happened

and trying to sidestep a homosexual approach from the unnerving Colonel Teape, this an added version of the "patient-agent" theme, homosexual relationships having their passive-active partners.

A bleak thesis is implied by the novel. If we are all trapped in our given personalities, none of us is free: Blore-Smith remains a dupe; Maltravers and Chipchase persist as knaves. This grim view of predestined lives is lightened by some excellent comic incidents (including Blore-Smith in a brothel) and by several magnificently bizarre minor characters. The book has pace and exuberance, and its dialogue for the most part is suitably brisk, devious, and shallow.

Large changes took place at this time in Powell's life. At the end of 1936 he ended his part-time appointment with Duckworth and signed a six-month contract to write film scripts for Warner Bros. at Teddington on the outskirts of London. For fifteen pounds a week, rising to twenty pounds—big money for him then—he turned out screenplays for what was known as the "quota," a system devised to protect jobs in the British film industry by stipulating that United Kingdom cinemas must show a percentage of home-produced work. This period as a scenario hack—during which he was harnessed for three weeks on one project with Terence Rattigan, already a known playwright through the success of *French Without Tears* (1936)—would provide material for the *At Lady Molly's* volume (1957) in the *Music of Time*. Although nothing written by Powell at Teddington ever reached the screen, he believes the experience taught him something about narrative construction, including a technique useful for someone undertaking a long novel: the need to prepare early for what would come later.

In May 1937 he and his wife set out by sea for the United States and Hollywood where, so he had been told, there was a chance of writing for a new film, *A Yank at Oxford*. They rented an apartment in Beverly Hills, and Powell did what he could to find work. No new novel was under way. He heard Hemingway give an address about a film he had helped make on the Spanish civil war, and at Culver City Studios in July 1937, Powell had lunch with F. Scott Fitzgerald, who was working on *A Yank at Oxford*. Although Powell did not work on the film, he gave Fitzgerald advice on English idiom and social nuances. Under the byline "A Reporter in Los Angeles," Powell contributed two articles to the London-based magazine *Night and Day*. Powell's articles dealt with a production of *Macbeth* by an all-black cast and with the Hemingway film.

The Powells returned to Britain in August 1937, Hollywood having provided no work for him. Powell was without a job but after a while began reviewing for the *Daily Telegraph* and the *Spectator*. He was also able to start a new novel and, toward the end of 1938 or at the beginning of 1939, completed *What's Become of Waring*. The uncertainty about dates is his own, but 1938 would seem the more likely, since by March 1939 the book had been published by Cassell. It is an amusing novel, notable particularly for its use of a narrator with scarcely any character development, a narrator who would appear the most obvious precursor yet of Nicholas Jenkins, particularly as both work in publishing and both are writers. The narrator is a degree less obtrusive than Jenkins in that he does not even rate a name. His role, beautifully managed, is to observe with mild irony and to keep the plot moving.

About this book, the term *plot* can be used in its simple, storytelling sense. *What's Become of Waring* is a pleasantly constructed tale with a central, mildly intriguing mystery: the narrator and the publishing firm that employs him try to discover the identity of one of the firm's most successful authors despite his attempts at concealment. At times the book appears to be a deliberate amassing of negations: an unnamed, featureless narrator in search of an author with no discernible identity, who turns out to have done no original work. It seems as though Powell is saying something about the thinness at this stage of his own fictional resources. Clever and polished though it may be, the novel is also strikingly inward looking and narrow in its preoccupation with books, writing, and publishing. The novel's mystery is resolved about three-quarters of the way through after sizable hints, and from then on the reader becomes aware of how frail the characterization and structure have been.

Because of its background, *What's Become of Waring* has sometimes been taken as a portrayal of the Duckworth office during Powell's time there. He says, though, that Balston, by then retired, found nothing exceptionable when he read the typescript and wished the book well; nor did the other directors at Duckworth object. However, they would not increase the advance payment on royalties, and Powell went elsewhere to find a publisher. The novel came out six months

before war started in an atmosphere, Powell believes, unfavorable to the sale of fiction. It sold 999 copies, and the remaining stock was later burned in storage during an air raid.

Powell's interest in the occult, which would reappear in the *Music of Time*, provides some amusing episodes in *What's Become of Waring*. Spiritualist séances, agnostically but not dismissively treated, contribute to the mild tension. Powell sometimes suggests he believes that not everything can be explained rationally. He concludes *Faces in My Time*, for instance, with an account of a telephone call at his home on the day after Constant Lambert died and at a time that Lambert had regularly rung. When Powell lifted the receiver there was silence, then a click as the connection was cut.

Despite the failure of *What's Become of Waring* to do much for Powell's prospects as an author, by the late 1930s he had come to be recognized as one of several significant novelists who had emerged in Britain since World War I and who were experimenting with the attenuation of form. In *Twilight on Parnassus* (1939), G. U. Ellis discussed Powell alongside Hemingway, Evelyn Waugh, Wyndham Lewis, and Aldous Huxley and, for one writing almost contemporaneously, made remarkably shrewd estimates of Powell's first four novels. Ellis also gave hints, with considerable acumen, about Powell's likely development. He found Powell the most accomplished of those new novelists who were determined not to impose on their fiction the kind of undue shapeliness and organization which must be "regarded as largely false when compared with the inconsequence and indetermination of experience." *Afternoon Men* he believed particularly telling as an accurate representation of life: that is, going nowhere very much, most of it empty and void of real meaning. (He, like Powell, regards the book as unsatirical.) Ellis thought Waugh the better moralist and Powell the better artist. What was not yet possible for Ellis to discover in these early books is Powell's continual assertion in later works that, although to arrange events in a novel toward some dramatic payoff or tidy resolution may be a falsification of things as they are in reality, some sort of pattern to life does exist, based on what Powell calls in *Messengers of Day* "the inexorable law of coincidence": repetition, interweaving, and balance produced by fluke.

Even if *What's Become of Waring* did not suggest that by 1939 Powell was temporarily written out as a novelist, the fact that he produced no

The Allied Military Attachés at Field Marshal Bernard Montgomery's Tactical Headquarters on the Netherlands/German frontier, November 1944. Powell is second from right.

new work of fiction for twelve years afterward might indicate something of the sort. It is true that for part of this period he was serving as a soldier, and he has said that in wartime he could not achieve the state of calm he needed to write novels. The war ended in 1945, six years before the first volume of the *Music of Time* appeared, a period largely devoted by Powell to his work on John Aubrey. As soon as *What's Become of Waring* was finished, he began making notes for the Aubrey biography. This seventeenth-century antiquarian and writer had interested Powell for some years as illustrating a new and stimulating type of sensibility for the period: "the appreciation of the oddness of the individual human being." Further attractions were that Aubrey's family, like Powell's, came originally from the Welsh marches and that Aubrey had lived for a while in Wiltshire, as had Powell.

When war broke out in September 1939, Powell wanted to enter the army at once, but he was nearly thirty-four years old and regarded as rather elderly. With the help of a little influence he was eventually able to join the Welch Reg-

iment—in which his father had served as a regular officer—on 11 December 1939 at Haverfordwest in southwest Wales. The three war novels of the *Music of Time—The Valley of Bones* (1964), *The Soldier's Art* (1966), and *The Military Philosophers* (1968)—reflect Powell's army service pretty closely: he believes that the first two of those books give a more authentic portrait of Welsh troops than he can achieve in memoirs.

Powell spent the early part of his service as a second lieutenant in Northern Ireland: Gosford Castle, in County Armagh, the location of the Divisional Tactical School during the war, provides a model for Castlemallock in *The Valley of Bones*. Then, in January 1941 he was posted to the Third Politico-Military Course at the Intelligence Training Centre in Cambridge, and after that to a war intelligence course at Matlock, Derbyshire. By now he had been transferred from the Welch to the Intelligence Corps and in the spring of 1941 was promoted to first lieutenant. Having been rejected as a liaison officer with the Free French because he did not speak the language well—Jenkins has a similar failure—he was

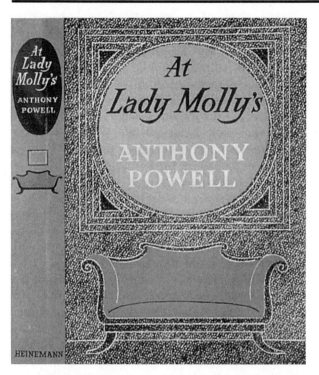

Dust jacket for Powell's 1957 novel, the fourth volume of
A Dance to the Music of Time

sent to Military Intelligence Liaison in London. This period provided many of the incidents and several of the characters for *The Military Philosophers*. M.I.L. maintained relations with foreign contacts of the army in London and some Allied and neutral countries. Several of the foreign military attachés in the novel are lifted directly from life, and the commanding officer of the section in *The Military Philosophers*, Lt. Col. Lysander Finn, Victoria Cross, is based on the second-in-command at M.I.L., Maj. A. E. Ker, V.C. Powell's particular duty was to liaise with the Poles, whose attaché, Maj. Gen. Bronislow Regulski, becomes Bobrowski in the novel. Not long after joining M.I.L., Powell was promoted to captain.

As relief from the tensions produced by the bombing of London, Powell spent many evenings reading seventeenth-century background for the projected work on Aubrey. He had little to do with what literary life went on in wartime London, though he occasionally met George Orwell—who remained a friend until his death—and was repeatedly urged by Cyril Connolly to produce something for the magazine *Horizon*, which Connolly was then editing. Powell never did. In February 1943, for about nine weeks, he became a military assistant secretary in the Cabinet Office, a post carrying the rank of major. He does

not consider himself to have been a success in this post and, after this short interlude, returned to M.I.L., this time dealing with Czech and Belgian forces. His experiences in this capacity provided further material for *The Military Philosophers*. By the end of 1944 the Allies had reached the German frontier, and Powell was able to accompany a party of foreign attachés on a Continental tour, as described in the novel. Powell—like Jenkins in the novel—was astonished and delighted to find that one town in Normandy where the party stayed briefly was Cabourg, on which Marcel Proust had partly based his Balbec, and *The Military Philosophers* contains a passage of pastiche Proust in celebration. During this foreign excursion, Powell visited Field Marshal Bernard Law Montgomery's headquarters and brilliantly records in the novel his impressions of the great soldier.

For his war service Powell was awarded several orders: the White Lion (Czechoslovakia), the Oaken Crown and Croix de Guerre (Luxembourg), and the Leopold (Belgium). By late summer 1945 his army career was nearing its end. *The Military Philosophers* describes the Thanksgiving For Victory service at St. Paul's Cathedral on August 19, an occasion when, through one of those enormous coincidences so liked by Powell, Jenkins is assigned to look after a Latin American attaché, who turns out to be married to the former Jean Templer, Nicholas's first real love. In fact, the attaché, Col. Carlos Flores, reintroduces them, though nothing develops from that encounter. (A further coincidence is hinted at: Flores may have been in a party of South Americans seen by Jenkins at the Ritz in *The Acceptance World* [1955], thirteen years before. Powell half makes this suggestion in the novel, but later said he decided not to pursue the possibility, just as life leaves some matters unclear.)

While on leave at this time Powell wrote two articles for the *Cornhill Magazine* on the Swiss nineteenth-century diarist Henri-Frédérique Amiel, whose *Journal Intime* covers a period between 1847 and 1881. Powell says he was impressed by Amiel's ability to analyze human character. We may speculate about other elements in Amiel's work which attracted Powell. In "The Other Amiel I," Powell compares him in some respects with Proust. There is, too, in this article a quoted description by Amiel of a sexual experience, and the mood is much like Powell's treatment of several such encounters in his fiction: "For the first time I received a woman's favours and, frankly,

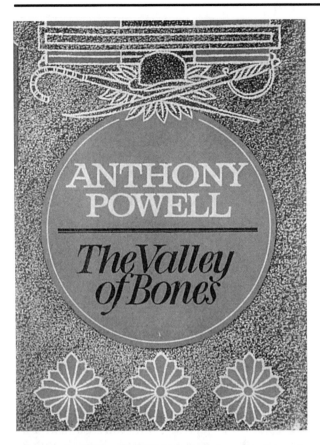

Dust jacket for Powell's 1964 novel, the seventh volume of
A Dance to the Music of Time

compared to what the imagination assumes or expects, they are a small matter. It was like a bucket of cold water." In "The Other Amiel II," Powell records that "an Amiel untormented by half a dozen different points-of-view would ... be no Amiel." Powell's later prose style—full of parentheses, backtracking, qualifications—often seems shaped to impart simultaneously several competing versions of a thought or incident.

Late in 1945 Powell began putting into order his notes on Aubrey, with a view to starting work on the biography. His three months of demobilization leave began in September, and by Christmas he had established a program of steady research and writing, most of it conducted in the Bodleian Library, Oxford, much as Jenkins prepares his book on Robert Burton's *Anatomy of Melancholy* in *Books Do Furnish a Room* (1971). In his memoirs, Powell describes how painstaking scholarship acted in some way as a stimulus to novel writing, and while completing the Aubrey book, he had already started thinking about the composition of a very large work of fiction. He was still reviewing for the *Daily Tele-*

graph and the *Spectator* at this time and in 1947 took up a part-time post supervising novel-reviewing for the *Times Literary Supplement*. By now Powell had become one of a group of literary men who would meet at the Authors' Club in Whitehall Court. Members included Malcolm Muggeridge, then writing leaders for the *Daily Telegraph*; Hugh Kingsmill, literary editor of the *New English Review*; Douglas Jerrold, its editor and the chairman of Eyre and Spottiswoode publishers; and Graham Greene, managing director of that firm. Powell took the Aubrey biography to Eyre and Spottiswoode after the Oxford University Press offered an unsatisfactory advance. There were delays in publishing, and some acrimony. Powell recalls that Greene told him: "It's a bloody boring book, anyway." In fact, for such a scholarly work, *John Aubrey and His Friends* (1948) is full of life and warmth, catching well Aubrey's eccentric, intelligent, and vulnerable personality, and has gone into several reprints. Although by now feeling himself ready to begin a novel, Powell next accepted an invitation to collect and edit some original Aubrey material for publication: *Brief Lives; and Other Selected Writings of John Aubrey* (1949).

At this time Powell did not know how many volumes his long novel would run to, but he did know it would be more than one. Believing that many authors went on producing what were virtually the same characters in book after book, though with different names and in fresh circumstances, he wanted to break out from the confines of the eighty-thousand-word novel. The roman-fleuve would allow him to recognize the problem openly and continue with established characters through successive volumes. During the late 1940s, while visiting the Wallace Collection in London, he saw Nicolas Poussin's painting *A Dance to the Music of Time* and felt he had at last found the theme and title of his work.

Jenkins refers to the picture at the start of *A Question of Upbringing* (1951): "The Seasons, hand in hand and facing outward, tread in rhythm to the notes of the lyre that the winged and naked greybeard plays." He—and Powell—regard the painting as an image of how time and life may bring people into contact with each other, separate them for a while, and then perhaps push them together again "in evolutions that take recognisable shape." These evolutions make up this twelve-volume chronicle of upper-class British manners from early in the century to the 1970s. Scores of major characters dance their

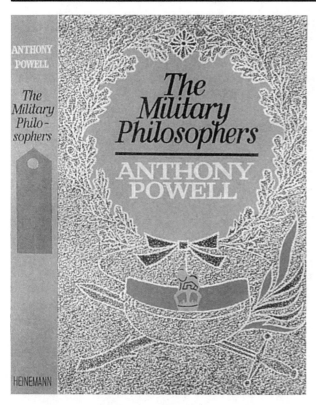

Dust jacket for Powell's 1968 novel, the ninth volume of
A Dance to the Music of Time

way in and out of one another's lives—and especially one another's beds—often in seemingly random style; yet when the whole sequence is seen together there is some sort of order. To put it more strongly than that would be wrong; but music and dance do imply a system, harmony, pattern.

A Question of Upbringing introduces Nicholas Jenkins as the kind of character he will be throughout the sequence: reflective, good-natured, sensitive, intelligent, diffident—occasionally to the point of passiveness. The book also presents an uncertainty never resolved through the sequence: how old is the narrator at the period when recounting this or that book of the twelve? Is he at a point where he can see the outcome of all the matters he recalls for us? Or are the later events of the *Music of Time* still unfolding as Jenkins recounts the earlier ones? Occasionally this imprecision causes basic confusions. There are moments when the narrator seems to know everything that will take place, and his tone at the opening of *A Question of Upbringing* suggests that he does. Yet at times—seemingly for the sake of suspense or surprise in the storytelling—he will be deluded by false appearances, though his position as one

recollecting, rather than living through, events should allow him to know the full truth.

A Question of Upbringing, which takes in a period between 1921 and 1924, is set mainly at Jenkins's public school, at his university, and in France, where he goes to improve his use of the language. Also, he visits the homes of two school friends who will be important figures in succeeding volumes, Charles Stringham and Peter Templer. These three have about them a poise, casualness, and high-spiritedness which the book and much of the rest of the sequence present as admirable when seen against the plodding, careerist energy and gaucherie of another pupil, Kenneth Widmerpool. At least in terms of space taken on the page, Widmerpool is the chief character of the *Music of Time* after Jenkins, a great comic creation in the early and middle books whom, later in the series, Powell skillfully turns into a figure of considerable evil, though still touched by farce.

In fact, one of Powell's main themes is presented in the contrast developed throughout the twelve books between Jenkins and Widmerpool. Widmerpool, in this first book and in the rest, is one of life's aggressors, a tireless seeker for the main chance. Although he has great triumphs—after, not at, school—and although Jenkins sometimes sadly compares his own progress with what Widmerpool has achieved, there is no point in the *Music of Time* where Widmerpool is viewed as other than ludicrously inferior to Jenkins and his friends. Of course, novels have rarely favored accomplished materialists, but Powell is doing more than following that literary tradition. Against Widmerpool's frenzied and ruthless self-seeking, the sequence sets Jenkins's imperturbable loyalty to his own values, his respect for people, his charm and style. Some critics have seen this contrast as one between the "man of will"—Widmerpool—and the "man of imagination"—Jenkins. On a deeper level, it is the difference between a man who is nothing but ambition, a sort of burlesque Faust, and another who represents enduring standards of humaneness, creativity, and artistic appreciation in a shoddy world. There is, it must be said, a trace of snobbery in the way Powell presents this contrast. Jenkins, Stringham, and Templer come from families with either lineage or money or both, whereas Widmerpool's father operated at a rather low level of commerce, selling liquid manure to the gentry. It is hard to accept a view of character which implies that a boy not up to the mark at

Nicolas Poussin's A Dance to the Music of Time *(Wallace Collection, London)*

Eton on account of class deficiencies and social ineptitude will probably turn out to be a corrupt, sexually incompetent monster, as Widmerpool does.

A Question of Upbringing drew good notices, with particular commendation for its wit and intelligence, and quickly went into three impressions. The *Times Literary Supplement* critic detected hints that there might be a sequel. In 1952 Powell and his family moved from London to their present home, The Chantry, Near Frome, in Somerset. He appears in *Burke's Landed Gentry* as "Powell of The Chantry," his pedigree—registered with the College of Arms in 1964—claiming connection with the so-called Second Royal Tribe of Wales and going back to the fourth century. Powell continued reviewing and also served, from 1952 to 1958, as literary editor of *Punch*, a post which left him some free time.

Parties, dinners, and dances take up much

of the next novel, *A Buyer's Market* (1952). Occasionally the reader hears something of people's work—Jenkins, now twenty-one or twenty-two, is in publishing and thinking about writing a novel—but nightlife is what really counts. The book's crises tend to be social gaffes (a torrent of sugar falls from a sprinkler on Widmerpool; Sir Magnus Donners, a rich and very bourgeois industrialist, grows morbidly gleeful when talking about punishments for young girls). As if concerned to make the most of rather slight material, Powell's prose, never especially plain in the *Music of Time*, becomes laboriously facetious in portions of this book.

All the same, several set pieces are brilliantly executed and seem to contain powerful, satirical comment by Powell on the fragility and preposterousness of his pleasure-seeking, well-heeled world. Nicholas ends up one night at a party in the house of a Mrs. Andriadis, currently very close to Stringham. The company has some dubious elements but on the whole is reasonably chic. Among the guests, though, is a rather disreputable friend of Nicholas's parents, E. Bosworth Deacon, an artist and political activist. First, he becomes involved in a rowdy argument with one of the entertainers. Then, about to leave, he gathers up some pamphlets—entitled *War Never Pays!*—which he had been distributing outside before the party and had placed under a chair. The door is opened and the wind scatters these papers throughout the house: radical literature disturbing the activities of social butterflies.

Jenkins develops quickly in *A Buyer's Market* and has his first sexual relationship—with Gypsy Jones, a combative, gamine associate of Mr. Deacon. It is a perfunctory coupling and described in sentences so woolly and wordy that at least one critic thought Jenkins failed to make it. He does lose his virginity, but he achieves negligible pleasure and sparks no passion in Gypsy. The reader may recall Amiel's "bucket of cold water."

During *The Acceptance World* and *At Lady Molly's* Widmerpool's business career moves very briskly forward, but his love life seems desperately jinxed. Catastrophically, he attempts in *At Lady Molly's* to consummate his engagement with Mildred Haycock, a notorious bed hopper who is totally unsuitable for Widmerpool (not that any woman in the novel does seem suitable). Widmerpool's ambition has apparently done basic damage to his emotional apparatus, possibly even to his sexual apparatus. Jenkins, too, has advanced, but in his own fashion. By the beginning of *The Acceptance World* he has written one novel and is contemplating another, and he and Templer's sister, Jean—who is married to a man called Duport—start a love affair, beautifully described by Powell. Toward the end of *At Lady Molly's*, Jenkins is engaged to Lady Isobel Tolland, one of Lord Warminster's ten children, whom he knows at first sight he will marry. In this contrast between their somewhat magical, instant rapport and poor Widmerpool's continual sexual rebuffs, the reader is meant to see further evidence that Jenkins's approach to life is the better and more blessed.

His career changes. By the start of *At Lady Molly's* he has moved on from publishing to film scripting, and his second novel is completed before the end of *At Lady Molly's*: it is 1934, and, now in his late twenties, Jenkins spots his first gray hair. Friends from school and university

keep him in touch with the intense political life of the period. Modish, intellectual socialism and its response to the Depression are deftly and amusingly ridiculed in these two books, especially in *The Acceptance World*. There is an occasional darkening where Powell seems to suggest that the political naiveté and foolhardiness of eminent figures such as the popular novelist St. John Clarke, who turns suddenly Marxist, caused the collapse of traditional British social values at the time. (In a *New Review* interview with Alan Brownjohn, published in September 1974, Powell says he came to regret the conservatism in these reflections.) Society is in flux during these two books: Quiggin, a Marxist friend of Jenkins at the university, steals Templer's wife, Mona, in *The Acceptance World*; but she deserts him in *At Lady Molly's* for Lord Erridge, Earl of Warminster, Jenkins's brother-in-law, a left-winger who cannot always suppress traces of distinguished birth. Some see hints of Powell's friend Orwell here, especially in the common determination to jettison privilege. But Orwell had no aristocratic lineage, and the differences from Erridge are more substantial than the resemblances with him. Powell himself had acquired a social distinction between the publication dates of these two books: in 1956 he became a Commander of the Order of the British Empire.

Nicholas has married when *Casanova's Chinese Restaurant* (1960) opens, and much of this volume is concerned with showing the strains of long-term relationships on an assortment of couples, including Edward VIII and Mrs. Wallis Warfield Simpson; although we never meet them, their troubles and the abdication are often mentioned and give eminent endorsement to the thesis that sexual liaisons generally bring discomfort, or worse. The abdication is presented as a further symptom of social breakup. Through friendship with the composer Moreland, Jenkins enters the rather grubby margins of bohemia, and these scenes contrast well with a stately family conclave at the home of Lady Warminster, Isobel's stepmother: Erridge has announced his intention to fight for the Republic in Spain (Orwell also fought there), but Erridge cannot take it for long and is soon home.

Despite some customarily subtle observation and a fine evocation of the period from 1933 to 1937, Powell in *Casanova's Chinese Restaurant* sometimes seems unsure where he is going, and the book has sluggish, repetitive passages. Widmerpool, on whom the success of the series so

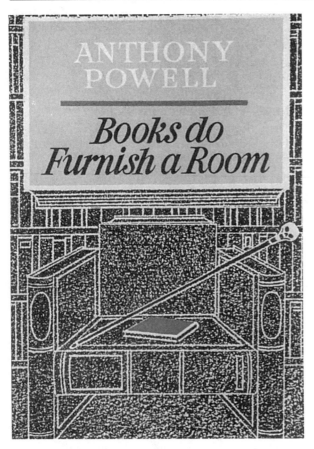

Dust jacket for Powell's 1971 novel, the tenth volume of
A Dance to the Music of Time

much depends, appears only briefly and to no real purpose. Drawbacks of the narrative method for a work of such length—the single observer who cannot be everywhere—become apparent for a while, and the difficulty goes even deeper. Powell never entirely solves the problems that spring from having a narrator who is in some ways a participant and in others the very detached voice of the author.

During 1962, the year that his next novel, *The Kindly Ones*, was published, Powell became a trustee of the National Portrait Gallery, a position he continued to hold until 1976. *The Kindly Ones* is in some ways the first of the war books, though outside the actual trilogy set between 1939 and 1945. In *The Kindly Ones* Powell boldly shifts chronology back in the opening chapter to Jenkins's childhood at Stonehurst, near Aldershot, where his father was stationed while waiting to fight in World War I. Then, in a later section bristling with coincidences, we move forward to the weeks just before the outbreak of World War II. The scene is a seaside hotel run by Albert

Creech, who was the family's cook at Stonehurst. Jenkins's Uncle Giles—prominent throughout the early books—has died at the hotel, and there are some belongings to be sorted out. Giles, a superbly drawn, cantankerous, shady figure, has occasionally in the previous books provided the narrator with a usefully aggressive, worldly, though unreliable second opinion on things. At the hotel, several other characters from earlier books also turn up by chance, including one, besides Albert, from the Stonehurst days. Powell is here stretching likelihood so as to suggest the patterned and cyclic nature of time: war and rumors of war are shown as part of the cycle. The Greek Furies, whose savagery men tried to placate with the inappropriate title "The Kindly Ones," were lurking after the Sarajevo assassination in 1914—with which the early part of the book ends—which led to World War I; and they lurk again after the Russo-German pact of August 1939—with which chapter 3 closes—which made World War II a certainty. It is a somberly effective juxtaposition by Powell.

Before the end of the book, Jenkins is trying to get into the army (as is his father), and Widmerpool already holds a commission. The volume is much concerned with the onus of those who have position and privilege to defend the system when it is threatened: posthumously, Giles, like St. John Clarke earlier, is censured for his casual or negative attitude to the established order. It is a deeply conservative, even feudal, doctrine, but one which is honestly—and amusingly—treated; it is also one which, in real life, seems to have motivated many in 1939, including Powell and Waugh.

Jenkins has what might be called a peaceful war. The three books generally known as the war novels—*The Valley of Bones*, *The Soldier's Art*, and *The Military Philosophers*—earn the description by covering the period rather than showing Jenkins fighting. We do hear of battles, but they are far off. In *The Military Philosophers*, Jenkins, as a major, gets close to the advancing Allied armies during a trip to Europe with some foreign attachés. By then, though, the war is coming to an end, and Jenkins is primarily interested in tracing historical and literary associations of the places he visits. These three books demonstrate more than any of the others that Powell is little interested in writing about action but has evolved a prose the most natural tone of which is thoughtful, unhurried, undramatic, even antidramatic. His method of composition—repeated rewrites

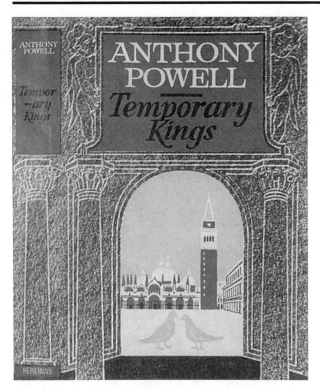

Dust jacket for Powell's 1973 novel, the eleventh volume of
A Dance to the Music of Time

with a gradual progress from thirty to fifty to eighty words and so on—may have something to do with this low regard for rapid pace.

Some striking changes do take place in these three books, though. Widmerpool's army career soars, and for a considerable time he has Jenkins, lower in rank, within his power. More startling is the decline of Stringham. Once a figure of aristocratic grace and savoir faire, compared with whom Widmerpool appeared a plodding fool, Stringham turns up in *The Soldier's Art* as a waiter in the officers' mess, debilitated by alcoholism and likely now to be humiliated by crude members of the mess. Somehow, though, even in these circumstances he retains dignity and charm, and no amount of military rank can make Widmerpool his superior. It is in these books that Widmerpool's role as a blundering clown veers toward something considerably worse: he will be indirectly responsible for Stringham's death, and possibly for Templer's, in both cases through abuses of power.

The war books are notable, too, for the reintroduction of the remarkable female character who will later marry Widmerpool. Pamela Flitton, first seen as a child in *A Buyer's Market*, moves through *The Military Philosophers* as a fierce

sexual predator, bedding with many of the male characters. Through these relationships she establishes for the later books of the *Music of Time* an invaluably elaborate crisscross of relationships. Such interweavings are the very fabric of the *Music of Time*. Powell is not always interested in making very much of these surprising "evolutions," to pick up the word from *A Question of Upbringing*. There is not necessarily any result or any sharp and obvious effect on the narrative. The novel merely asserts that these are the kinds of inconsequential flukes that help make up life. And because there is often no apparent motive for these coincidences—no pressure on Powell to round off a plot, for instance—they become acceptable and more or less credible.

During *Books Do Furnish a Room* and *Temporary Kings* (1973), covering late 1945 to late 1959, Pamela develops spectacularly, even garishly. Her marriage to Widmerpool eventually provides her with a title when he is made a life peer, but this does not inhibit her strenuous promiscuity. She becomes involved with political, literary, and film men, and possibly a schoolboy. The frenetic quality she displays tints these two books in general, as if Powell wished to ensure vividness in the narrative as his long work neared its conclusion; Pamela may also be an attempt to compensate for the earlier scarcity of positive women. Whatever the reason for her blazing emergence, she seems a somewhat desperate stratagem.

Jenkins has resumed a scholarly and literary life after demobilization, beginning preparations for his book on Robert Burton as soon as he is released. His novels are by now well known but out of print. Toward the end of *Temporary Kings* he is in his fifties with a son near the age of conscription. Pamela dies from a drug overdose after an unsatisfactory affair with Russell Gwinnett, an American academic, and Moreland also dies after much illness. These tenth and eleventh books introduce many new characters, some of them brilliantly individual, vital, and—in several cases—comic. Lindsay Bagshaw, known for some uncertain reason as Books-Do-Furnish-A-Room-Bagshaw, is a magnificently complex and amusing figure, as is Daniel Tokenhouse, retired army major, in his seventies and now a vehemently ideological left-wing painter. Despite the inventiveness put into such creations, the late books of the *Music of Time* illustrate a difficulty in the roman-fleuve: characters built up over many volumes take on a solidity that is hard to match in new ones within the scope of one or two closing books, and the contrast can be unsettling. It is true, though, that by the end of *Temporary Kings* many of the original personnel of the series have died or otherwise disappeared.

In 1974 Powell was made an honorary fellow of Balliol College. Each book of the *Music of Time* had earned him critical esteem, and long before the final volume appeared, his standing as a major novelist of the twentieth century was assured. Some idea of how he regards his own work may be found in his reply to a request from a book club in 1974 to allow one of his volumes to be included in a special scheme. The proposal was that he should nominate a favorite book from among those he had written and sign five hundred copies of it. Other distinguished authors were participating. Powell said he would not contemplate it because he could not select a favorite, any more than he would name one of his children as his favorite.

Hearing Secret Harmonies (1975), the final volume of the *Music of Time*, closes with Jenkins tending a bonfire in the garden of his country house. The scene completes a circle, that favorite Powell mannerism. *A Question of Upbringing* opened with Jenkins watching street workmen grouped around a fire, and his mind was led then to thoughts of the past, and from there to wider speculations about the patterns and convolutions of time. Now, at the end of the final book, as smoke swirls again and Jenkins recalls the workmen's brazier, Powell implies that some of these patterns and convolutions have worked themselves out. It is as if time pauses momentarily, having achieved some measure of order. The novel ends with a reference back to Poussin: "Even the formal measure of the Seasons seemed suspended in the wintry silence."

Widmerpool undergoes enormous psychological change in this volume, renouncing the world and enlisting in a cult devoted to mysterious rites: *Hearing Secret Harmonies* shows Powell's interest in the occult at its darkest. Having lost some of his reason but none of his energy, Widmerpool eventually drops dead while overdoing things on a run with his new friends; because the book ends in 1971, he would be approaching seventy. Even in self-abasement Widmerpool will push himself to excel and push himself, finally, too hard. It is a slightly strained, yet basically convincing thesis. In any case, Widmerpool's removal allows Jenkins to dominate the last pages, and it is apparent that he retains the qualities Powell regards as necessary for the worthwhile

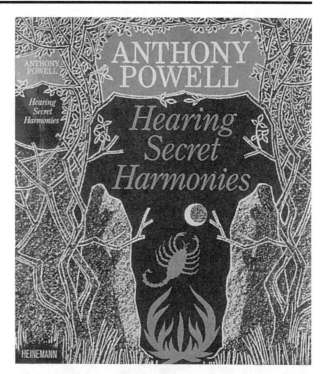

Dust jacket for Powell's 1975 novel, the twelfth and final volume of A Dance to the Music of Time

life: moderation, sensitivity, quiet independence of mind, and some creative skill, vigor, and integrity.

In 1971, while the *Music of Time* volumes were still coming out, Powell's two plays, *The Garden God* and *The Rest I'll Whistle*, were published, both entertaining studies of sexual tensions that read well enough but have not been staged. His memoirs, with the overall title *To Keep the Ball Rolling*, provide a fascinating parallel with the *Music of Time*: actual autobiography against fictionalized autobiography. After a ponderous genealogical start in *Infants of the Spring* (1976)—Jenkins has a similar, more attractive session about lineage in *The Valley of Bones*—the memoirs become lively and wide-ranging. Powell can give valuable glimpses of many twentieth-century figures in literature, journalism, academe, and the army. Here and there a recollection falls a little flat, and readers might long for the novelist's imagination to take hold of an incident or piece of conversation and make something significant of it beyond the circumstances of the moment. Yet because fact circumscribes the writer of memoirs, these anecdotes have to stand alone, and a few seem frail.

Encounters with Orwell, Waugh, Connolly, Guy Burgess, Donald Maclean, James Thurber,

Dylan Thomas, Field Marshal Montgomery, and Fitzgerald are rivetingly described, though. And the memoirs contain several valuable insights into a novelist's mind and his methods when at work: they are particularly revealing about the way actual experiences and people may be transmuted into material for fiction. Of course, if the reader puts *To Keep the Ball Rolling* alongside the *Music of Time*, he can see that happening for himself.

Powell, who became an honorary member of the American Academy of Arts and Letters in 1977, has recently completed his memoirs and continues to review books for the *Spectator*. As well as critical acclaim, the *Music of Time* has achieved popular success through many paperback editions of the books. Powell is recognized as the exponent of a consistent, unextreme philosophy of life; as a great creator of upper-class and/or artistic male characters; as a wit; and as a fine evoker of period.

Interviews:

W. J. Weatherby, "Taken from Life," *Twentieth Century*, 170 (July 1961): 50-53;

Alan Brownjohn, "Profile of Anthony Powell," *New Review*, 1 (September 1974): 21-28;

Julian Jebb, "Anthony Powell's Dreams," *Listener*, 94 (11 September 1975): 347-348.

Biography:

Neil McEwan, *Anthony Powell* (New York: St. Martin's Press, 1991).

References:

Bernard Bergonzi, *Anthony Powell*, Writers and Their Work, 144 (London: Longmans, Green, 1962);

Laurie Frost, *Reminiscent Scrutinies: Memory in Anthony Powell's A Dance to the Music of Time* (Troy, N.Y.: Whitston, 1990);

Michael Gorra, *The English Novel at Mid-Century: From the Leaning Tower* (New York: St. Martin's Press, 1990);

Robert K. Morris, *The Novels of Anthony Powell* (Pittsburgh: University of Pittsburgh Press, 1968);

John Russell, *Anthony Powell, A Quintet, Sextet and War* (Bloomington: Indiana University Press, 1970);

Robert L. Selig, *Time and Anthony Powell: A Critical Study* (Rutherford, N.J.: Fairleigh Dickinson University Press, 1991);

Hilary Spurling, *A Handbook to Anthony Powell's Music of Time* (London: Heinemann, 1977); republished as *Invitation to the Dance: A Guide to Anthony Powell's "Dance to the Music of Time"* (Boston: Little, Brown, 1978);

James Tucker, *The Novels of Anthony Powell* (London: Macmillan, 1976; New York: Columbia University Press, 1976).

Terence Rattigan

(10 June 1911 - 30 November 1977)

This entry was updated by Susan Rusinko (Bloomsburg State College) from her entry in
DLB 13: British Dramatists Since World War II: Part Two.

BOOKS: *French Without Tears* (London: Hamish Hamilton, 1937; New York: Farrar & Rinehart, 1938);

After the Dance (London: Hamish Hamilton, 1939);

Flare Path (London: Hamish Hamilton, 1942);

While the Sun Shines (London: Hamish Hamilton, 1944; New York: French, 1945);

Love in Idleness (London: French, 1945);

The Winslow Boy (London: Hamish Hamilton, 1946; New York: Dramatists Play Service, 1946);

Playbill: The Browning Version and Harlequinade (London: Hamish Hamilton, 1949; New York: French, 1950);

Adventure Story (London: French, 1950);

Who Is Sylvia? (London: Evans, 1951);

The Deep Blue Sea (London: Hamish Hamilton, 1952; New York: Random House, 1952);

Collected Plays of Terence Rattigan, volume 1 (London: Hamish Hamilton, 1953)—includes *French Without Tears, Flare Path, While the Sun Shines, Love in Idleness*, and *The Winslow Boy*;

Collected Plays of Terence Rattigan, volume 2 (London: Hamish Hamilton, 1953)—includes *The Browning Version, Harlequinade, Adventure Story, Who Is Sylvia?*, and *The Deep Blue Sea*;

The Sleeping Prince (London: Hamish Hamilton, 1954; New York: Random House, 1954);

Separate Tables: Table by the Window and Table Number Seven (London: Hamish Hamilton, 1955; New York: Random House, 1955);

Variation on a Theme (London: Hamish Hamilton, 1958);

Ross (London: Hamish Hamilton, 1960; New York: Random House, 1962);

Man and Boy (New York: French, 1963; London: Hamish Hamilton, 1964);

Collected Plays of Terence Rattigan, volume 3 (London: Hamish Hamilton, 1964)—includes *The Sleeping Prince, Separate Tables, Variation on a Theme, Ross*, and *Heart to Heart*;

A Bequest to the Nation (London: Hamish Hamil-ton, 1970; Chicago: Dramatic Publishing Company, 1971);

In Praise of Love: Before Dawn, After Lydia (London: Hamish Hamilton, 1973); *After Lydia* revised as *In Praise of Love: A Comedy* (New York: French, 1975);

Cause Célèbre (London: Hamish Hamilton, 1978);

Collected Plays of Terence Rattigan, volume 4 (London: Hamish Hamilton, 1978)—includes *Man and Boy, A Bequest to the Nation, In Praise of Love: Before Dawn* and *After Lydia*, and *Cause Célèbre*.

PLAY PRODUCTIONS: *First Episode*, by Rattigan and Philip Heimann, London, Q Theatre, 11 September 1933 (transferred 26 January 1934 to Comedy Theatre); New York, Ritz Theater, 17 September 1934, 40 [performances];

French Without Tears, London, Criterion Theatre, 6 November 1936, 1,030; New York, Henry Miller's Theater, 28 September 1937, 111; revised as *Joie de Vivre*, music by Robert Stolz, lyrics by Paul Dehn, London, Queen's Theatre, 14 July 1960, 4;

After the Dance, London, St. James's Theatre, 21 June 1939, 60;

Follow My Leader, by Rattigan and Anthony Maurice, London, Apollo Theatre, 16 January 1940;

Grey Farm, by Rattigan and Hector Bolitho, New York, Hudson Theater, 3 May 1940, 35;

Flare Path, London, Apollo Theatre, 13 August 1942, 679; New York, Henry Miller's Theater, 23 December 1942, 14;

While the Sun Shines, London, Globe Theatre, 24 December 1943, 1,154; New York, Lyceum Theater, 19 September 1944, 39;

Love in Idleness, London, Lyric Theatre, 20 December 1944, 213; produced again as *O Mistress Mine*, New York, Empire Theater, 23 January 1946, 452;

Terence Rattigan (photograph by Mark Gerson)

The Winslow Boy, London, Lyric Theatre, 23 May 1946, 476; New York, Empire Theater, 29 October 1947, 218;

Playbill: The Browning Version and Harlequinade, London, Phoenix Theatre, 8 September 1948, 245; New York, Coronet Theater, 12 October 1949, 69;

Adventure Story, London, St. James's Theatre, 17 March 1949, 108;

Who Is Sylvia?, London, Criterion Theatre, 24 October 1950, 381;

A Tale of Two Cities, adapted by Rattigan and John Gielgud from Charles Dickens's novel, 1950;

The Deep Blue Sea, London, Duchess Theatre, 6 March 1952, 513; New York, Morosco Theater, 5 November 1952, 132;

The Sleeping Prince, London, Phoenix Theatre, 5 November 1953, 274; New York, Coronet Theater, 1 November 1956, 60;

Separate Tables: Table by the Window and *Table Number Seven*, London, St. James's Theatre, 22 September 1954, 726; New York, Music Box Theater, 25 October 1956, 332;

Variation on a Theme, London, Globe Theatre, 8 May 1958, 132;

Ross, London, Haymarket Theatre, 12 May 1960, 762; New York, Eugene O'Neill Theater, 26 December 1961, 159;

Man and Boy, London, Queen's Theatre, 4 September 1963, 69; New York, Brooks Atkinson Theater, 12 November 1963, 54;

All on Her Own, televised, 25 September 1968; Kingston-on-Thames, 1974; London, 1974; produced again as *Duologue*, London, Kings Head Theatre, February 1976, 15;

A Bequest to the Nation, Haymarket, London, Theatre Royal, 23 September 1970, 124; televised as *Nelson—A Portrait in Miniature*, London, ATV, 21 March 1966;

In Praise of Love: Before Dawn and *After Lydia*, London, Duchess Theatre, 27 September 1973, 131; *After Lydia* produced as *In Praise of Love*, New York, Morosco Theater, 10 December 1974;

Kay Hammond, Rex Harrison, Roland Culver, and Robert Fleming in a scene from the first production of French Without Tears

Cause Célèbre, London, Her Majesty's Theatre, 4 July 1977, 282.

MOTION PICTURES: *French Without Tears*, screenplay by Rattigan, Anatole de Grunwald, and Anthony Asquith, Paramount, 1939;

The Day Will Dawn, screenplay by Rattigan, de Grunwald, and Patrick Kirwin, Paul Soskin Production, 1940; released in the United States as *The Avengers*, 1942;

Quiet Wedding, screenplay adapted by Rattigan and de Grunwald from Esther McCracken's play, Universal, 1941;

Uncensored, screenplay adapted by Rattigan, Wolfgang Wilhelm, and Rodney Ackland from Oscar E. Millard's writings, 20th Century-Fox, 1943;

English Without Tears, screenplay by Rattigan and de Grunwald, 1944; released in the United States as *Her Man Gilbey*, Universal, 1949;

The Way to the Stars, screenplay by Rattigan, 1946; released in the United States as *Johnny in the Clouds*, United Artists, 1946;

Brighton Rock, screenplay adapted by Rattigan and Graham Greene from Greene's novel, Associated British Picture Corporation, 1947;

Bond Street, screenplay by Rattigan, de Grunwald, and Ackland, 1948;

While the Sun Shines, screenplay by Rattigan and de Grunwald, Stratford, 1950;

The Winslow Boy, screenplay by Rattigan and de Grunwald, Eagle Lion, 1950;

The Browning Version, screenplay by Rattigan, Universal, 1952;

The Sound Barrier, screenplay by Rattigan, David Lean, 1952; released in the United States as *Breaking the Sound Barrier*, United Artists, 1952;

The Final Test, screenplay by Rattigan, Rank, 1954;

The Man Who Loved Redheads, screenplay by Rattigan, United Artists, 1955;

The Deep Blue Sea, screenplay by Rattigan, 20th Century-Fox, 1955;

The Prince and the Showgirl, screenplay by Rattigan, Warner Bros., 1957;

Separate Tables, screenplay by Rattigan and John Gay, United Artists, 1958;

The V.I.P.s, screenplay by Rattigan, M-G-M, 1963;

The Yellow Rolls Royce, screenplay by Rattigan, M-G-M, 1965;

Goodbye, Mr. Chips, screenplay adapted by Rattigan from James Hilton's novel, M-G-M, 1969;

A Bequest to the Nation, screenplay by Rattigan, Hal Wallis, 1973.

TELEVISION: *The Final Test*, BBC, 1951;
Heart to Heart, BBC, 1962;
Ninety Years On, BBC, 1964;
Nelson—A Portrait in Miniature, ATV, 1966;
All on Her Own, BBC 2, 1968;
High Summer, Thames Television, 1972.

RADIO: *Cause Célèbre*, BBC, Radio 4, 27 October 1975.

OTHER: "An Appreciation of His Work in the Theatre," in *Theatrical Companion to Noel Coward*, by Raymond Mander and Joe Mitchenson (London: Rockliff, 1957);

Harold French, *I Swore I Never Would*, foreword by Rattigan (London: Secker & Warburg, 1970);

Charles Castle, *Noel*, with a contribution by Rattigan (Garden City, N.Y.: Doubleday, 1973), pp. 123-125, 243-244;

Logan Gourlay, ed., *Olivier*, with a tribute by Rattigan (London: Weidenfeld & Nicolson, 1973), pp. 129-135.

SELECTED PERIODICAL PUBLICATIONS—
UNCOLLECTED: "Concerning the Play of Ideas," *New Statesman and Nation* (4 March 1950): 241-242;

"The Play of Ideas," *New Statesman and Nation* (13 May 1950): 545-546;

"What Audiences Want to See," *Times*, 27 August 1964, p. 11;

"Mr. Anatole de Grunwald," *Times*, 21 January 1967, p. 10.

During a career that spanned nearly forty years, from the early 1930s to the 1970s, Terence Rattigan wrote twenty-four dramas for the stage and more than thirty film, television, and radio plays. He demonstrated striking development in comedy, farce, and romance and versatility with history plays, plays about celebrated English court trials, and, most important, his studies of flawed or failed average, middle-class characters, reminiscent of Robert Browning's. Frequently associated with Noel Coward as the last of the major dramatists in the well-made-play tradition, he felt shunned by the stage revolution in London in the mid 1950s. Yet, diversifying and intensifying his themes and style, he continued to write until his death in 1977.

Rapidly changing times and the interaction of personal lives with the events of those times form the subject matter of his dramas. Conflicts between fathers and sons, marital mismatches, the English habit of repressed emotion, sexual hypocrisies, and the right of the most insignificant individual to be heard and understood are themes that recur in his works, regardless of genre. Early comedies, the middle serious dramas, and the later mellowed, yet still problematic, character studies of his last plays contain these themes from *First Episode* in 1933 through *Cause Célèbre* in 1977.

The traditions of the Scribean well-made play and the English problem play have haunted the reviews and criticism of Rattigan's dramas. What was frequently overlooked was his adaptation of these traditions to serve his own purposes of style and theme. Influenced by Anton Chekhov, Bernard Shaw, and John Galsworthy, he was not in any way an imitator of them. Even more he resisted the experimental trends of the Brechtian socially committed theater and the absurdist techniques, both hallmarks of the stage revolution of his time. Rattigan not only survived the turbulence in British drama initiated by John Osborne's *Look Back in Anger* (1956) but increasingly dramatized the personal and social problems dealt with by the newer dramatists. Indeed, as the stage freedoms of the 1950s were followed by the abolition of censorship in the 1960s, his plays became more open and direct about sensitive subject matter such as homosexuality. Deep-rooted and painful ambivalences in characters became increasingly important as conflicts caused by emotional repression and hypocritical attitudes on sexual matters took their toll on the young as well as the middle-aged.

The action-packed plots of the early comedies about schoolboys and university students

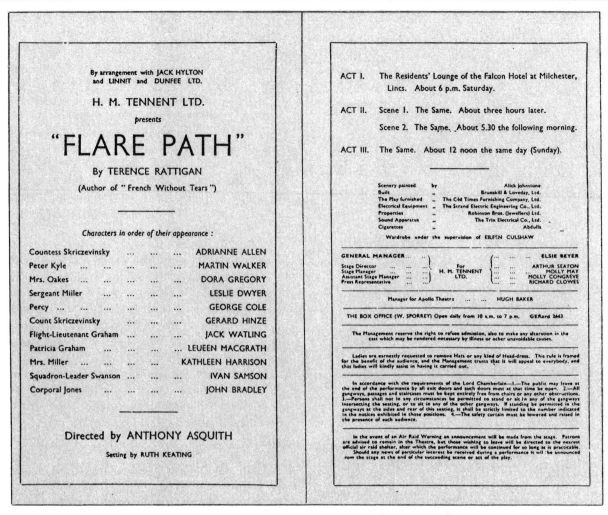

By arrangement with JACK HYLTON
and LINNIT and DUNFEE LTD.

H. M. TENNENT LTD.

presents

"FLARE PATH"

By TERENCE RATTIGAN

(Author of " French Without Tears ")

Characters in order of their appearance :

Countess Skriczevinsky	ADRIANNE ALLEN
Peter Kyle	MARTIN WALKER
Mrs. Oakes	DORA GREGORY
Sergeant Miiler	LESLIE DWYER
Percy	GEORGE COLE
Count Skriczevinsky	GERARD HINZE
Flight-Lieutenant Graham	JACK WATLING
Patricia Graham	LEUEEN MACGRATH
Mrs. Miller	KATHLEEN HARRISON
Squadron-Leader Swanson	IVAN SAMSON
Corporal Jones	JOHN BRADLEY

Directed by ANTHONY ASQUITH

Setting by RUTH KEATING

ACT I.   The Residents' Lounge of the Falcon Hotel at Milchester, Lincs. About 6 p.m. Saturday.

ACT II.   Scene I. The Same. About three hours later.

          Scene 2. The Same. About 5.30 the following morning.

ACT III. The Same. About 12 noon the same day (Sunday).

Scenery painted	by	Alick Johnstone
Built	"	Brunskill & Loveday, Ltd.
The Play furnished	"	The Old Times Furnishing Company, Ltd.
Electrical Equipment	"	The Strand Electric Engineering Co., Ltd.
Properties	"	Robinson Bros. (Jewellers) Ltd.
Sound Apparatus	"	The Trix Electrical Co., Ltd.
Cigarettes	"	Abdulla

Wardrobe under the supervision of EILEEN CULSHAW

GENERAL MANAGER ... ... ELSIE BEYER

Stage Director	For	ARTHUR SEATON
Stage Manager	H. M. TENNENT	MOLLY MAY
Assistant Stage Manager	LTD.	MOLLY CONGREVE
Press Representative		RICHARD CLOWES

Manager for Apollo Theatre ... ... HUGH BAKER

THE BOX OFFICE (W. SPORREY) Open daily from 10 a.m. to 7 p.m.   GERrard 2663

The Management reserve the right to refuse admission, also to make any alteration in the cast which may be rendered necessary by illness or other unavoidable causes.

Ladies are earnestly requested to remove Hats or any kind of Head-dress. This rule is framed for the benefit of the audience, and the Management trusts that it will appeal to everybody, and that ladies will kindly assist in having it carried out.

In accordance with the requirements of the Lord Chamberlain—1.—The public may leave at the end of the performance by all exit doors and such time be open. 2.—All gangways, passages and staircases must be kept entirely free from chairs or any other obstructions. 3.—Persons shall not in any circumstances be permitted to stand or sit in any of the gangways intersecting the seating, or to sit in any of the other gangways. If standing be permitted in the gangways at the sides and rear of this seating, it shall be strictly limited to the number indicated in the notices exhibited in those positions. 4.—The safety curtain must be lowered and raised in the presence of each audience.

In the event of an Air Raid Warning an announcement will be made from the stage. Patrons are advised to remain in the Theatre, but those wishing to leave will be directed to the nearest official air raid shelter, after which the performance will be continued for so long as is practicable. Should any news of particular interest be received during a performance it will be announced from the stage at the end of the succeeding scene or act of the play.

Cast list, synopsis of scenes, and credits for the first production of Rattigan's 1942 play, the first of three plays about World War II

gradually gave way to complex and sharply poignant character studies. Although the later works are characterized by some of the techniques of the well-made play, Rattigan increasingly explored the repressed psychological problems of flawed, middle-class characters such as the Winslow family in *The Winslow Boy* (1946), the schoolmaster Crocker-Harris in *The Browning Version* (1948), the desperately unhappy upper-middle-class housewife, Hester Collyer, in *The Deep Blue Sea* (1952); of famous historical characters such as T. E. Lawrence in *Ross* (1960) and Horatio Nelson in *A Bequest to the Nation* (1970); and of characters embroiled in famous English legal cases, such as Alma Rattenbury in his last play, *Cause Célèbre*. In a decided departure from the slickness of the *pièce bien faite*, Rattigan's dramas did not conclude with artificially happy endings but with unresolved or only partially resolved conflicts and ambivalences of the unhappy or tortured characters.

The disillusionment his characters experience is countered by the dignity with which they confront their problems and carry on with what remains of their lives. The characters, unsentimentally portrayed, are the more sympathetic for their flaws. Some proof of their enduring quality is seen in the constant revivals of the plays. In 1981 and 1982 productions at New York's Roundabout Theatre of *The Winslow Boy* and *The Browning Version* drew impressive notices from critics such as John Simon. To achieve character-centered drama, Rattigan adapted well-made-play conventions to his dramatization of the damaging effects of repressive, intolerant societal attitudes toward aberrant behavior.

Terence Mervyn Rattigan was born on 10 June 1911, the coronation year of George V, to William Frank Arthur and Vera Houston Rattigan in London. Before being pensioned from the foreign service late in 1922, Frank Rattigan held diplomatic posts in Europe, serving as acting high commissioner in Turkey and British minister in Romania. While his parents lived abroad, Terence and his older brother, Brian, lived with their paternal grandmother in South Kensington, London.

Mr. Hornbye's School at Sandroyd, Harrow, and Trinity College, Oxford, provided Terence with the education that was intended to prepare him for a diplomatic career like his father's. Included in this experience were summers spent at foreign-language schools in France and Germany. However, at Harrow, which he attended from 1925 to 1930 on a scholarship, Rattigan read Chekhov, Galsworthy, and Shaw; he wrote a short play on which he received the criticism, "French execrable; theatre sense first class"; and, in general, he began dreaming of becoming a famous playwright in whose dramas would appear the famous actors and actresses of his time. In 1930 he entered Oxford on a history scholarship, where his dramatic interests only intensified. At Oxford he wrote for the *Cherwell*, acted briefly, but, most importantly, began writing plays in collaboration with friends. His academic pursuit of history (later dramatized in his plays about Alexander the Great and Lord Horatio Nelson) was soon replaced by his interest in theater, and after some debate, he persuaded his parents to finance him in a two-year trial writing period in London, on the condition that if things did not work out, he would pursue diplomacy or banking as a career. Just before the trial period expired, the resounding popular success of *French Without Tears* (1936) launched Rattigan on a career from which he never veered.

Foregoing his examinations for diplomacy, Rattigan enjoyed his first professional production with *First Episode* in 1933. Written with Philip Heimann, the play is a romantic farce dealing with sexual escapades of university students involved with visiting professional actresses. During the 1930s, he coauthored three additional plays: *Follow My Leader* (with Anthony Maurice, produced in 1940); an adaptation of Charles Dickens's *A Tale of Two Cities* (with John Gielgud, not produced until 1950); and *Grey Farm* (with Hector Bolitho, produced in 1940). *First Episode*, in a mixed notice in the London *Times*, was praised for its farcical moments. *Follow My Leader*, a satirical farce on Adolf Hitler, fared less well, possibly because of the untimeliness of its production during the Battle of Britain. The *Times* reviewer was "surprised that the author of *French*

Without Tears could do no better than Ruritania without over much laughter." *Grey Farm*, produced only in New York, with Oscar Homolka in the leading role, received a negative review from Brooks Atkinson. All four plays remain unpublished, although the manuscript of *First Episode* was discovered in 1977 during Michael Darlow's research for a BBC program on Rattigan. Naim Attalah, who also commissioned the 1979 Darlow-Hodson biography of Rattigan, purchased an option on the play, but to date it has not been revived. Of particular interest in the manuscript are the self-revealing crossed-out references to homosexuality.

French Without Tears, Rattigan's first produced solo play, is a farce about schoolboys in summer language school on the Riviera. Running for 1,030 performances, the play broke existing box office records in London and enjoyed success on the Continent and in the United States. With one stroke Rattigan's reputation as a writer of well-made plays and light comedies was established. Much less successful, *After the Dance* (1939) is a serious drama in the Chekhovian manner about the generation gap during the period between the two wars. Published in 1939, *After the Dance* was underrated by critics and theatergoers, possibly because of the events of the time.

Rattigan enlisted in the Royal Air Force in April 1940, shortly after the news of Hitler's attack on Denmark and Norway. Darlow and Hodson write that Rattigan was nearly rejected as a result of a bad interview, but the board decided to take a chance on him and assured him that he could always write for camp concerts in his spare time. After basic training, Rattigan served as a wireless operator in Coastal Command, later as flight lieutenant and gunnery officer with 422 Squadron. Afterward he was seconded to the RAF film unit.

Flare Path (1942), written during hazardous patrol duty, is the first of three dramas about the war. The play provides a mixture of comedy and intensely emotional moments in the lives of a pilot, who flies bombing missions from an English airfield, and his wife. After reading the reviews, Rattigan commented on finding himself at long last "if not exactly as a professional playwright, at least a promising apprentice who had definitely begun to learn the rudiments of his job." W. A. Darlington called Rattigan a "real dramatist and not a competent hack," particularly in regard to his handling of characterization. Darlow and Hodson regard the play as

Eugene Deckers, Michael Wilding, and Hugh McDermott in a scene from the first production of While the Sun Shines

Rattigan's departure from the style of his previous plot-centered plays, for in *Flare Path* the "accumulation of incidents and scenes between an ensemble of characters . . . depends on a central outside event—a night bomber raid on Germany." A farce about servicemen, *While the Sun Shines* (1943), and a romantic comedy about civilian life during the war, *Love in Idleness* (1944), retitled *O Mistress Mine* when produced in 1946 in New York, complete the trio. All three plays were produced in the West End, with *While the Sun Shines* running for more than 1,100 performances, but only 39 on Broadway.

Rattigan had been employed during the 1930s as a scriptwriter for Warner Bros., and although unnoticed, he had gained valuable technical experience for the many films he later wrote about the war, about flying, and about the life of the average man during the war. Even though his film writing had provided him with necessary finances, it was secondary to his love for the stage.

If *Flare Path* called critical attention to his talent as a serious playwright, it was *The Winslow Boy* that won for him his first major critical and popular acclaim. Although Rattigan's public-school principles seem to dominate the play thematically, stylistically his concentration on character development is strong, and the characterizations of Ronnie Winslow's father, sister, and attorney fascinated audiences wherever the play was performed. The play is about the celebrated Archer-Shee case, in which a young naval cadet was charged with stealing a five-shilling postal order. His father, at the cost of his health and financial well-being, carried the case to the highest courts to clear the boy's name. The drama emphasizes the cherished English right of even an insignificant schoolboy to be heard. The grandson of distinguished British lawyers, Rattigan added noted trials to his already established interests in history, diplomats, and the upper-class civilian and military life he knew so well.

Rattigan's interest in youth as subject matter for plays led to *The Browning Version*, considered by many to be his best work, and continued throughout his career to his last play, *Cause Célèbre*. In *The Browning Version* the emphasis, however, remains on the schoolmaster rather than on the student, Taplow. For many reasons the play has sustained its appeal to new generations of theatergoers. A tautly written one-act play, *The Browning Version* has the severity of a classical tragedy, its action unfolding over a twenty-four-hour period during a schoolmaster's last day of teaching. Crocker-Harris, known to the schoolboys as "the Crock," has been fired after nearly twenty years of teaching the classics to schoolboys who have long regarded him only as a butt for their jokes. He is dealt one blow after another, including being denied a pension. In an attempt to make the situation easier, the headmaster has asked him to speak at the commencement exercises before, rather than after, a more popular master. In the swiftly moving scenes of the play Taplow presents Crocker-Harris with a copy of Browning's translation of Aeschylus's *Agamemnon*, giving his wife, Millie, cause later to taunt him with the remark that the gift was appeasement for a passing grade. At one time able to communicate his love for the classics to his students, Crocker-Harris has known for some time that this is no longer the situation. He also has known for some time that Millie has been unfaithful, the latest affair involving a popular young master. In a masterfully understated scene, he tells Millie that he is leaving her when he moves to his new position in an inferior school and then calmly asks her to sit down to supper before the food gets cold. Confronting the long years of failure as master and husband, Crocker-Harris does muster dignity even in his bleak life. His is a middle-class tragedy that Rattigan later repeats with Hester Collyer in *The Deep Blue Sea*. He remains Rattigan's most satisfyingly dramatized character and, like so many others in Rattigan's plays, is drawn from a person he once knew.

Rattigan's handling of the one-act play is faultless in *The Browning Version*. A superb creator of scenes by virtue of what he claimed as Chekhovian influence, he is in no other work so much the master of this technique. This compressed study of a failed schoolmaster contains in a quintessential way themes on which Rattigan elaborates in many variations in his later plays. John Simon, in his review of a 1980 production of *The Browning Version* at the Roundabout Theater in New York, described it as "the most rousing and uncheatingly uplifting drama in New York today." Hav-

ing underestimated "Terence Rattigan and his often impeccable craftsmanship" in the past, he wrote that he "can only hope that the fine gentleman I remember from an interview I once did with him will, even posthumously, accept my apology." Having already won the Ellen Terry Award in 1947 and the New York Drama Critics Circle Award in 1948 for *The Winslow Boy*, Rattigan was honored a second time with the Ellen Terry Award in 1948 for *The Browning Version*.

Harlequinade, a farce about a provincial touring acting company, accompanied *The Browning Version* under the collective title of *Playbill* (1948). Like its companion play, it is built around a personal experience, Rattigan's one-line appearance as an actor in an Oxford University production of *Romeo and Juliet*, with professional stage actresses Edith Evans and Peggy Ashcroft. The double bill, or the play consisting of two or more loosely joined acts, increasingly became a hallmark of Rattigan's dramatic structure.

Relationships between men and boys, peripheral in his first success, *French Without Tears*, gradually became central in the succeeding dramas. The progression of this theme can be traced from *The Winslow Boy* to *The Browning Version*, and even to dramas such as *Adventure Story* (1949). Rattigan's first history play, *Adventure Story* depicts Alexander the Great as he conquers the world in act 1 and then as he reflects in act 2 on the legacy he has inherited from his father and on the emptiness of that power. Again, the play's construction is two-part: the rise to power in all its action and the reflection on that power in all its passivity. Some reviewers questioned the anticlimactic nature of act 2, and Rattigan himself talked on several occasions of wanting to revise his favorite play.

The disillusionment pervading the second half of *Adventure Story* continues in *Who Is Sylvia?* (1950), an ironic farce in which a father searches for a feminine ideal in his successive mistresses. With its autobiographical echoes, the play deals with a son who attempts an understanding of his father's diplomatic career and his rakish lifestyle.

Mixed reviews of both *Adventure Story* and *Who Is Sylvia?* may have partially prompted Rattigan's initiation of a debate on the theater in the *New Statesman and Nation* in 1950, in a letter he wrote on the play of ideas. Drawn into the debate were James Bridie, Benn Wolfe Levy, Peter Ustinov, Sean O'Casey, Ted Willis, Christopher Fry, and Bernard Shaw. Defensive about being la-

A scene from the first New York production of Separate Tables: *(front) Margaret Leighton, Phyllis Neilson-Terry, Eric Portman, William Podmore, and May Hallatt; (back) Donald Harron and Ann Hillary*

beled a popular playwright of entertainment, Rattigan described his view of the theater as a place in which people were moved to laughter or to tears rather than bored with propaganda. He used his invention, Aunt Edna, the average, middle-class, middlebrow audience member, as a symbol of his point of view. At times the debate became acrimonious and irrelevant, but Rattigan's keen injury at the label was obvious.

In 1953 Rattigan's first two volumes of *Collected Plays* were published, with prefaces elucidating his dramatic theories. Among the more frequently mentioned theories are the goal of theater to move an audience to laughter or to tears, the insistence on workmanship and craft in play construction, the effectiveness of the simplest words such as "yes" or "never" well placed and timed, the Chekhovian sense of implicit rather than overt expression, and, perhaps above all, the primacy of character over plot.

In spite of some disappointment about his

previous two plays and in spite of the play-of-ideas debate, the 1950s were golden years for Rattigan. He was adapting his plays as films, and original screenplays such as *The Sound Barrier* (1952) were providing ample means for his lavish life-style. Moreover, the stage plays *The Deep Blue Sea* (1952), *The Sleeping Prince* (1953), and *Separate Tables* (1954) received wide acclaim and firmly established Rattigan as the leading dramatist of the time.

The Sleeping Prince, a romantic fantasy-comedy with Laurence Olivier and Vivien Leigh cast in the stage production (with Olivier and Marilyn Monroe in the film version, *The Prince and the Showgirl*, 1957), was written for the occasion of Queen Elizabeth's coronation. But for all its charm and glamour, this romance ironically appeared between two plays—*The Deep Blue Sea* and *Separate Tables*—whose characters stand out in stark contrast to both the characters and mood of *The Sleeping Prince*.

In *The Deep Blue Sea* the loneliness, frustration, and emotional and sexual deprivation lurking between the lines in the earlier plays become concentrated in one character, confirming in Rattigan's style what some critics described as the art of humiliation. Hester Collyer, an upper-middle-class Englishwoman, experiences the painful lack of passion in her husband, a successful judge, and an equally painful absence of considerateness in her lower-class, ex-flyer lover.

More delicately portrayed are the characters of *Separate Tables*, a double bill consisting of *Table by the Window* and *Table Number Seven*. In what many consider Rattigan's most aesthetically pleasing drama, his confident characterization is at its finest, not only of the main characters but of the delightful minor characters who create a rich Chekhovian texture for the dramatic action and who serve as vehicles for his attitudes about what in a later play a character refers to as the "vice-Anglais." *Separate Tables*, with *The Browning Version* and *The Deep Blue Sea*, demonstrates Rattigan's best play writing.

Table by the Window, the first of two short plays set in a shabby provincial boarding hotel in the seaside town of Bournemouth, concerns the events caused by the arrival of Anne Shankland, a fashion model who has discovered the whereabouts of her ex-husband John, a journalist and former Labour politician. Now forty, she has divorced her second husband and needs John, who, in the meantime, has developed a close and comfortable relationship with Miss Cooper, the manageress. In a series of delicately yet powerfully constructed scenes, Rattigan explores the various emotional and sexual needs of people such as John and Anne, which though mutually destructive, must be fulfilled. Vulnerabilities are strong, causing John and Anne to decide to reconcile. They are mutually dependent. The more solid, but less driven, liaison between John and Miss Cooper falls victim to the sexual-emotional needs of John and Anne. With John's lower-class background and Anne's more delicate upper-class attitudes toward sex, the two types of characters precede Jimmy and Alison Porter in John Osborne's *Look Back in Anger* by two years. The love-hate relationship between John and Anne represents a prominent theme of modern drama which has been successfully explored in Tennessee Williams's *A Streetcar Named Desire* (1947) and Edward Albee's *Who's Afraid of Virginia Woolf?* (1962). In Rattigan's second act, *Table Number Seven*, the same Bournemouth Hotel residents

are present, with the focus this time on two new characters, Major Pollock and Sybil Railton-Bell. Major Pollock, painfully shy with women, commits sexual offenses in dark theaters and is reported in the local newspapers, much to the shock of the inhabitants. Sybil Railton-Bell is an equally painfully shy spinster who is virtually a prisoner of her dominant mother, Lady Railton-Bell. Despite the mother's tyranny, Sybil can communicate with the major as with no one else. The climax occurs when at the usual breakfast ritual, Sybil defies her mother for the first time in her life in full hearing of the other boarders. Again, as in *Table by the Window*, Rattigan is at his best in the delineation of ineffectual, vulnerable, flawed characters and in his satire on repressive societal attitudes toward sex. Originally, the major's acts were to be homosexual, but because of the censorship laws of the time, Rattigan changed the sexual focus. The change worked so well that when he thought later that he might revert to his original premise, he decided not to, since the play should be a "plea for the understanding of everyone" rather than for "tolerance specifically of the homosexual."

The two leads of each play were portrayed superbly by Margeret Leighton and Eric Portman, their performances balanced by the comic relief provided by the other inhabitants of the hotel. The blend of pathos and comedy begun as early as *Flare Path* is nearly perfect in *Separate Tables*. The double bill received almost unanimous acclaim both in London and New York. W. A. Darlington, referring to Rattigan as the "most consistently successful of our dramatists," observed that the playwright "seems to be hitting off with uncanny exactness and deft economy of words characters for whose weakness he feels a pitiful understanding." Brooks Atkinson praised the "dramatic shorthand" which can be fully understood only by British audiences. He applauded Rattigan's "knack for British understatement" that had "resulted in a taut and lucid drama about human desperation," concluding that *Separate Tables* is Rattigan's best play.

Ironically, even as *Separate Tables* was enjoying a two-year run, the Royal Court stage exploded with the 1956 production of *Look Back in Anger*, and the avant-garde's first wave of innovation hit London stages. Rattigan's next three plays felt the impact of that wave. Receiving few positive reviews, *Variation on a Theme* (1958), an updated version of the Camille story with strongly existential overtones, opened with Margaret Leigh-

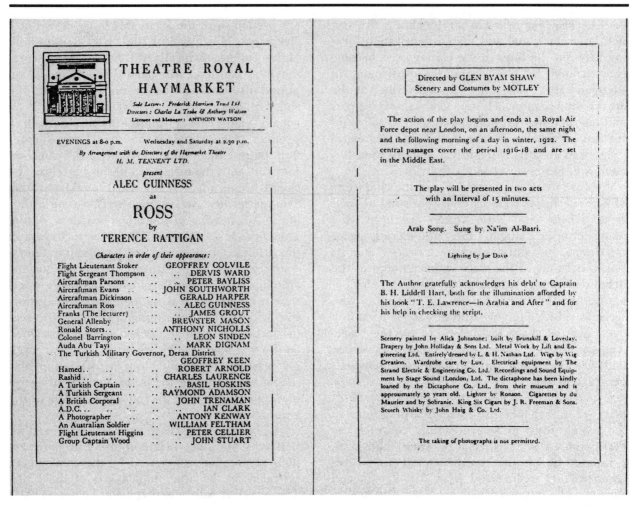

THEATRE ROYAL
HAYMARKET

Sole Lessees: Frederick Harrison Trust Ltd.
Directors: Charles La Trobe & Anthony Watson
Licensee and Manager: ANTHONY WATSON

EVENINGS at 8·0 p.m.   Wednesday and Saturday at 2.30 p.m.
By Arrangement with the Directors of the Haymarket Theatre
H. M. TENNENT LTD.
present
ALEC GUINNESS
as

ROSS
by
TERENCE RATTIGAN

Characters in order of their appearance:

Flight Lieutenant Stoker	GEOFFREY COLVILE
Flight Sergeant Thompson	DERVIS WARD
Aircraftman Parsons	PETER BAYLISS
Aircraftman Evans	JOHN SOUTHWORTH
Aircraftman Dickinson	GERALD HARPER
Aircraftman Ross	ALEC GUINNESS
Franks (The lecturer)	JAMES GROUT
General Allenby	BREWSTER MASON
Ronald Storrs	ANTHONY NICHOLLS
Colonel Barrington	LEON SINDEN
Auda Abu Tayi	MARK DIGNAM
The Turkish Military Governor, Deraa District	
	GEOFFREY KEEN
Hamed	ROBERT ARNOLD
Rashid	CHARLES LAURENCE
A Turkish Captain	BASIL HOSKINS
A Turkish Sergeant	RAYMOND ADAMSON
A British Corporal	JOHN TRENAMAN
A.D.C.	IAN CLARK
A Photographer	ANTONY KENWAY
An Australian Soldier	WILLIAM FELTHAM
Flight Lieutenant Higgins	PETER CELLIER
Group Captain Wood	JOHN STUART

Directed by GLEN BYAM SHAW
Scenery and Costumes by MOTLEY

The action of the play begins and ends at a Royal Air Force depot near London, on an afternoon, the same night and the following morning of a day in winter, 1922. The central passages cover the period 1916-18 and are set in the Middle East.

The play will be presented in two acts with an Interval of 15 minutes.

Arab Song. Sung by Na'im Al-Basri.

Lighting by Joe Davis

The Author gratefully acknowledges his debt to Captain B. H. Liddell Hart, both for the illumination afforded by his book "T. E. Lawrence—in Arabia and After" and for his help in checking the script.

Scenery painted by Alick Johnstone; built by Brunskill & Loveday. Drapery by John Holliday & Sons Ltd. Metal Work by Lift and Engineering Ltd. Entirely dressed by L. & H. Nathan Ltd. Wigs by Wig Creation. Wardrobe care by Lux. Electrical equipment by The Strand Electric & Engineering Co. Ltd. Recordings and Sound Equipment by Stage Sound (London) Ltd. The dictaphone has been kindly loaned by the Dictaphone Co. Ltd., from their museum and is approximately 50 years old. Lighter by Ronson. Cigarettes by du Maurier and by Sobranie. King Six Cigars by J. R. Freeman & Sons. Scotch Whisky by John Haig & Co. Ltd.

The taking of photographs is not permitted.

Cast list, synopsis of scenes, and credits for the first production of Rattigan's 1960 play based on the life of T. E. Lawrence

ton playing the leading role of Rose Fish. Homosexual relationships, obliquely handled in earlier plays, are dealt with directly in Rattigan's most discursive play up to this time. The title of the play refers to the theme of Alexandre Dumas *fils*'s 1852 play *La Dame aux Camélias* (*Camille*), the story of a courtesan with a heart of gold. Rattigan, as the title suggests, varies the theme considerably. With Margaret Leighton in mind for the lead part, Rattigan dedicated the play to her. Just as Anne Shankland, the model in *Table by the Window*, derived in part from Jean Dawnay, a friend who served as hostess for Rattigan's parties, *Variation on a Theme* bears some faint resemblance to Margaret Leighton's marriage to Laurence Harvey. The story involves Rose Fish, who has been married three times and is considering a fourth marriage, when Ron, a young ballet dancer, comes into her life. Involved in a homosexual relationship at the time, he falls in love with Rose. She eventually gives up her marriage plans for a more uncertain

life with Ron. The play ends with the mismatch of a younger man and older woman with unequal needs, boding problems in the future. Rattigan's own homosexual relationships resembled the amatory relationships discussed by the characters in the course of the play. Indeed, the compressed and delicately understated characterizations of his earlier plays here give way to a directness and discursiveness that evoked mainly negative reactions from critics such as Harold Hobson. Shelagh Delaney is said to have written her more delicately spun play about homosexuals, *A Taste of Honey* (1958), in reaction to seeing her favorite actress, Margaret Leighton, "wasting her time" in such a play.

Unlike *Variation on a Theme*, *Ross* (1960), about a man who fled from himself and based upon the life of T. E. Lawrence, more than held its own in the waves of theatrical innovations. Written from Rattigan's unproduced film script for "Lawrence of Arabia," *Ross*, which dramatized

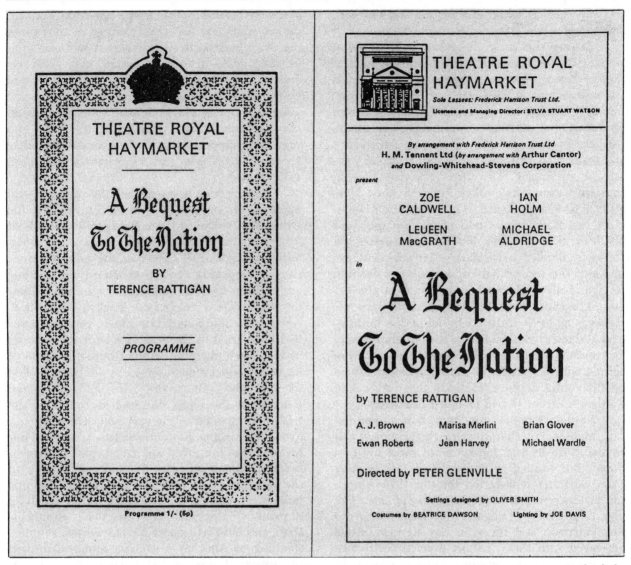

Program cover and title page for the first stage production of Rattigan's tribute to Lord Horatio Nelson, written to raise funds for the restoration of the Cutty Sark

homosexuality—indeed, rape—repeated the major success of earlier plays, running for more than 700 performances.

In *Man and Boy* (1963), his third play dealing directly with the homosexual theme, Rattigan again confronted father with son. This story is based on the last days before the suicide of the confidence man, match-industry king Ivar Kreuger. Like *Variation on a Theme*, its reception was mixed, in spite of its fascinating treatment of the con man Antonescu as a man without a soul—as Rattigan put it, a man who tried to be a devil. All three plays of the late 1950s and early 1960s deal with contemporary moral problems.

By 1963 Rattigan, feeling keenly his label as an old-fashioned writer of well-made plays, had absented himself from the English stage for artistic reasons and, later, from England for a year as a tax exile. He lived lavishly, traveled often in the United States, Italy, France, and the Bahamas, and devoted much time to writing for film, television, and radio. Movie spectaculars such as *The V.I.P.s* (1963) and *The Yellow Rolls Royce* (1965) provided him with ample means. A 1969 filmed musical adaptation of James Hilton's *Goodbye, Mr. Chips* starred Peter O'Toole in the title role, with Petula Clark as his wife, Kathy. An unproduced television script on Russian dancer Vaslav Nijinsky and a powerful 1962 television play about political corruption, *Heart to Heart* (with Ralph Richardson and Kenneth More), were only a few of the many projects in which he was involved as writer during his self-imposed, seven-year absence from the English stage.

During this exile, he wrote another occasional play for television, this one at the suggestion of Prince Philip as a means of raising funds for restoration of the *Cutty Sark*. *Nelson—A Portrait in Miniature*, televised in 1966, was rewritten as *A Bequest to the Nation* for Rattigan's return to the London stage in 1970. The stage play in turn was made into a film in 1973, with Rattigan writing the screenplay. The stage version deals with the tempestuous love affair between Lord Horatio Nelson and Emma, Lady Hamilton, especially her flagrant violation of socially approved behavior. The first half of the play focuses upon Nelson's family, particularly his wife and his nephew, the second half upon Nelson's decision to fight fully uniformed in full view of the enemy. The conflicts of the drama in both parts are Nelson's as he is tortured by his wife's faithfulness and tolerance, shamed by the outlandish public conduct of his mistress, and sensitively concerned with the truths of the adult world forced on his young nephew. He is in the tradition of Rattigan's earlier flawed or failed characters.

Rattigan's penetrating studies of contemporary middle-class characters reach their most discursive form in *After Lydia*, one of two plays of a double bill entitled *In Praise of Love* (1973). *After Lydia* was later lengthened for the 1974 American production and retitled *In Praise of Love*. The play is based on Rattigan's experience with the Rex Harrison and his wife, Kay Kendall, while he stayed with them a short time in California. She was then in the terminal stages of cancer. In the play Rattigan examines the ways in which the husband, son, and friend of a terminal cancer patient deal with the situation. Lydia Crutwell, the wife of a failed-novelist-turned-journalist, attempts to keep the news of her illness from her husband and from her son Joey, an aspiring playwright. In the meantime her husband knows that she is dying, but he tries to hide his knowledge from her. They continue to play this game until her friend, a successful American novelist, arrives. The painful, long-awaited confrontation is catalyzed by the husband's apparent indifference to viewing their son's first play on television. As with Crocker-Harris earlier, long repressed emotions on the part of son, father, and mother explode in a strong scene. Both father and son, heretofore uncommunicative, seem to be approaching some basis for an understanding as the play ends with Lydia's exit. Again, a father-son conflict and

a flawed marital relationship, this time between the novelist and his wife, emerge as themes as the three males—all writers—react to Lydia's impending death in their respective ways. The second of the works, *Before Dawn*, although played by the same impressive cast of *After Lydia*, was a failure as a reworking of the Victorien Sardou play *La Tosca* (1887). Unlike Rattigan's earlier and very loose modernizing of the Camille legend in *Variation on a Theme*, this adaptation is very close and strained.

Having been honored with the rank of Commander, Order of the British Empire, on the Queen's Birthday in 1958, Rattigan was knighted in 1971. Late in 1975 Rattigan began a two-year losing struggle with cancer of the bone marrow. But he lived long enough to attend the opening on 4 July 1977 of his last stage play, *Cause Célèbre*, about a celebrated English court trial. Alma Rattenbury and her much younger lover had been tried in the mid 1930s for the murder of her much older husband. Unusual because of its precedent-setting defense in which each lied to save the other, the case had fascinated Rattigan at the time. The intense drama of the trial was sustained to the very end, when the jury exonerated Alma Rattenbury and convicted her lover. Later, the lover was freed, but too late to prevent Alma's suicide. Maintaining fidelity to the outcome of the case, Rattigan used a fictional head jurywoman as a framework within which he dramatized the real-life case. The drama is Rattigan's most passionate plea for society's understanding of Alma as a woman, immoral though she appeared to be by 1930s standards. The symbol for society is the jurywoman, Mrs. Davenport, a veritable Aunt Edna of Kensington, whose own unhappy marital life parallels Alma's situation in some ways. The play contains one of Rattigan's most touching speeches on the necessity for understanding and beauty in life—perhaps Rattigan's farewell to the life that he loved so well.

His last three plays in one way or another are impassioned pleas for the honesty, fulfillment, and courage of flawed characters who insist above everything else on the ultimate right of every individual to tolerance and understanding. The painful conflicts experienced by the characters receive the fullest and most honest discussion offered by Rattigan. Indeed, the balance between social hypocrisies and personal needs is maintained throughout, resulting in the loss, perhaps, of the obliqueness and implicitness of earlier treatments. However, because characters articulate their ambivalences more clearly, they are much less the victims of themselves and society than they are vital participants in the drama of life.

The repressed needs of Rattigan's characters with their painful consequences are not unlike those dramatized in the new waves of experimentation that swept the English stage at the height of Rattigan's career. In particular, for example, the trio of characters in *The Deep Blue Sea* shares the frustrations of the trio in *Look Back in Anger*. Moreover, the emotionally dwarfed Sibyl Railton-Bell belongs to the wider traditions of Hedvig in Henrik Ibsen's *The Wild Duck* (1884) and Laura of Tennessee Williams's *The Glass Menagerie* (1944). Anne Shankland and John Malcolm in *Separate Tables* are British versions of Martha and George in Albee's *Who's Afraid of Virginia Woolf ?*. Even though not a participant in the experiments of the stage revolution, Rattigan in his adaptation of conventional dramatic techniques sustains the moods, attitudes, and experiences of playwrights such as Harold Pinter, John Osborne, and Joe Orton, combining in his own way something of the best of both worlds, the old and the new.

Interviews:

Barry Hyams, "A Chat with Terence Rattigan," *Theatre Arts*, 40 (November 1956): 20-22;

John Simon, "Rattigan Talks to John Simon," *Theatre Arts*, 46 (April 1963): 23-24, 73;

Ronald Hayman, "Life for Father," *Times*, 19 September 1970, p. 19;

J. W. Lambert, "Why Rattigan Must Struggle to See His Own Plays," *Sunday Times*, 3 July 1977, p. 5;

Philip Oakes, "Grace Before Going," *Sunday Times*, 4 December 1977, p. 35.

Biographies:

Michael Darlow and Gillian Hodson, *Terence Rattigan: The Man and His Work* (London: Quartet, 1979);

Susan Rusinko, *Terence Rattigan* (Boston: Twayne, 1983).

References:

Anthony Curtis, "Professional Man and Boy," *Plays and Players* (February 1978): 21-23;

Richard Foulkes, "Terence Rattigan's Variations on a Theme," *Modern Drama* (December 1979): 375-381;

Christopher Fry, "The Play of Ideas," *New Statesman and Nation* (22 April 1950): 458;

Martin Gottfried, "In Praise of Craftsmanship," *Stagebill* (John F. Kennedy Center for the Performing Arts), November 1974;

Holly Hill, "A Critical Analysis of the Plays of Terence Rattigan," Ph.D. dissertation, City University of New York, 1977;

Frederick Lumley, *New Trends in Twentieth Century Drama* (New York: Oxford University Press, 1967), pp. 306-310;

Sean O'Casey, "The Play of Ideas," *New Statesman and Nation* (8 April 1950): 397-398;

George Bernard Shaw, "The Play of Ideas," *New Statesman and Nation* (6 May 1950): 426-427;

Kay Nolte Smith, "Terence Rattigan," *Objectivist* (March 1971): 9-15;

John Russell Taylor, *The Rise and Fall of the Well Made Play* (New York: Hill & Wang, 1967);

T. C. Worsley, "The Expense of Spirit," *New Statesman and Nation* (15 March 1952): 301;

Worsley, "Rattigan and His Critics," *London Magazine* (September 1964): 60-72;

B. A. Young, *The Rattigan Version: The Theatre of Character* (London: Hamish Hamilton, 1988; New York: Atheneum, 1988).

Jean Rhys

(24 August 1890 - 14 May 1979)

This entry was written by Thomas F. Staley (University of Tulsa) for
DLB 36: British Novelists, 1890-1929: Modernists.

BOOKS: *The Left Bank* (London: Cape, 1927; New York: Harper, 1927);

Postures (London: Chatto & Windus, 1928); republished as *Quartet* (New York: Simon & Schuster, 1929);

After Leaving Mr Mackenzie (London: Cape, 1931; New York: Knopf, 1931);

Voyage in the Dark (London: Constable, 1934; New York: Morrow, 1935);

Good Morning, Midnight (London: Constable, 1939; New York: Harper & Row, 1970);

Wide Sargasso Sea (London: Deutsch, 1966; New York: Norton, 1967);

Tigers Are Better-Looking (London: Deutsch, 1968; New York: Harper & Row, 1974);

My Day (New York: Frank Hallman, 1975);

Sleep It Off, Lady (London: Deutsch, 1976; New York: Harper & Row, 1976);

Smile Please (London: Deutsch, 1979; New York: Harper & Row, 1980).

OTHER: Francis Carco, *Perversity*, translated by Rhys but erroneously attributed to Ford Madox Ford (Chicago: Covici, 1928).

Jean Rhys claimed to have been born in 1894, but it is more probable that she was born on 24 August 1890. The daughter of Rhys Williams, a doctor, and Minna Lockhart, Ella Gwen Rhys Williams was born in Roseau, Dominica, an island in the Lesser Antilles. Her father was Welsh and her mother a third-generation Dominican Creole, and this Creole heritage was a strong influence in Jean Rhys's life and in her writing. Also strongly influential were the religious training she received in a convent school and the firsthand knowledge of Negro culture that she gained from servants. Her imagination was further shaped by her deep attraction to the black culture—the warmth, the color, the music—and the racial mixture of the islands; but the cultural contrasts between colonial and native life, as the intensely private Rhys experienced them, also contributed to the restless uncertainty of her identity.

Jean Rhys left this island of lush vegetation and color and went to England around 1907. Her sense of cultural rift and displacement in the alien climate and society of England created a curious racial identification with blacks and gave her a lifelong affinity for the exile. She lived with her aunt, Clarice Rhys Williams, and attended for a time the Perse School in Cambridge. In 1908 she entered the Trees School (now the Royal Academy of Dramatic Arts). Their records show that she was eighteen when she entered the school, which further substantiates the 1890 birth date. Her father died soon after her arrival in England, and her mother came to England in poor health and soon died there.

After a term at the Royal Academy of Dramatic Arts, Jean began traveling with a musical-chorus troupe to the smaller provincial towns. Her experiences with the troupe were later transformed into art in her novel *Voyage in the Dark* (1934). After leaving the troupe, she took a variety of theatrical jobs, playing a chorus girl in light operas, such as Franz Lehár's *Count of Luxemburg* (1909). She also posed as an artist's model, and her face was once used for a Pear's Soap advertisement. Like Rhys herself, many of the young women with whom she associated at this time were pretty, uneducated, and poor, and many of them became prostitutes and mistresses. The ignominy of their common plight reinforced Rhys's preoccupation with the themes of financial dependence and male domination, of the helplessness and passivity of the female, which later ran through all her writing. Specific experiences of this sort of life are depicted in *Voyage in the Dark*.

It was during these early days in England that Rhys had her first real love affair, with a man whose name she never revealed. She was open and romantic; he was older, cautious, and soon tired of the relationship. At the end of the affair, Rhys began recording her experiences and feelings in a notebook which later became a

Jean Rhys and a friend (probably Germaine Richelot) in Paris

sourcebook for *Voyage in the Dark*. The man sent Rhys money until her marriage in 1919.

Near the end of World War I Rhys met Jean Lenglet, who later wrote under the pen name Edouard de Nève. Lenglet had led an adventurous life, serving in the French Foreign Legion in Africa, later fighting on the Western Front, serving in the Deuxième Bureau, and traveling on secret diplomatic missions for the French. Rhys and Lenglet were married in Holland in 1919 and moved to Paris. In the chaotic aftermath of the war, Lenglet worked for Japanese government officials who were representatives to the international mission charged with the administration of postwar Vienna. The couple moved constantly. A son, Owen, was born in 1919 but died three weeks after his birth. Feeling dislocated, fearful, and alone, Rhys exhibited in her despair an ironic sense of humor, which is reflected in her work, both relieving and deepening the bitter experiences of her heroines. The dark humor found in her novels has not received a great deal of attention from critics, but it adds an important

dimension to her themes. Rhys and Lenglet moved from Vienna to Budapest, to Prague, and then to Brussels, where their daughter, Maryvonne, was born in 1922. By this time Lenglet had left his post with the Allied Commission, and the couple soon returned to Paris. Some of the adventures of these years appear in Rhys's works, especially in the short story "Vienne."

Putting Maryvonne into the care of others first in Brussels, then in Paris, Rhys worked in a Paris dress shop and occasionally as a mannequin. Pearl Adam, the wife of the *Times* correspondent whom Jean had recently met, asked Rhys whether she ever wrote, and Rhys gave her some sketches, which Mrs. Adam fashioned into "Triple Sec," a loose collection of narrative scenes and stories. Pearl Adam tended to romanticize Rhys's material, and the writing project collapsed, but Mrs. Adam introduced Rhys to Ford Madox Ford in 1924. Around the time that Rhys met Ford, she and Lenglet were having acute financial problems, as usual, and Lenglet became in-

Front cover for the American edition of Rhys's first novel,
published in Great Britain as Postures

ates in these stories an entirely feminine world, a world where the feminine consciousness is not seen in the reflection of a masculine universe. The best of them—"Illusion," "Vienne," "La Grosse Fifi"—are harbingers of the more fully developed attitudes and characters that appear in her later novels. Rhys had a strong feeling for things French; and this affinity, with her straightforward style, her gift for understatement and directness, appealed to Ford's literary taste.

In addition to helping her with her writing, Ford began to take a more personal, physical interest in Jean Rhys (the name, she says, that he suggested she use as an author). Stella Bowen apparently assisted Ford in seducing Rhys, feeling that both she and Rhys were required to serve the stronger male, to be his servants and handmaidens. The curious psychological forces, the twists and turns of this relationship, were fictionalized by Rhys in her first novel, *Quartet* (first published by Chatto and Windus as *Postures*, 1928).

Although Rhys's work was never closely attuned to the technical innovations of modernism, it does share with the modernist movement the problem of moral ambiguity and the relativism of the post-Freudian world. Her style, as demonstrated in *Quartet,* is sparse, understated, and ironic, and the novel probes deeply the underlying relationships and conditions of the characters. *Quartet* also introduces the paradigmatic Rhys heroine, who with slight permutations and a more fully developed ironic humor appears in all of her fiction in the 1930s.

Marya Zelli in *Quartet* lives a precarious life in Paris with her husband, Stephan. When he is arrested and imprisoned, she is alone and broke. Enter the Heidlers, H. J. and Lois, the "good Samaritans" ironically referred to in the epigraph to the novel. Marya is helpless, passive, and Heidler gives her comfort, reassurance, and protection. A strange ménage à trois begins, with a variety of mixed motives and compromises. Lois thinks that a controlled affair under her aegis is a way to allow Heidler to stray only as far as her leash will permit. Marya's compromise has to do with a certain abandonment of her will. She sees herself as a victim; Lois sees her as a child, a toy that she and Heidler can use to amuse themselves. But despite Marya's aimlessness and passivity, she is also an adversary to Lois. Both women are in different ways subservient to the male, and both get what they want—Lois a position in the art world of Paris, recognition; and Marya a fundamental, if temporary, protection and security.

volved in the buying and selling of objets d'art, the ownership of which was uncertain. He was arrested and imprisoned (in his 1932 novel *Barred* the character is imprisoned from January until June 1925, and these are possibly the exact dates of Lenglet's incarceration).

With her husband in jail, Rhys was nearly desperate when she met Ford and Stella Bowen, the Australian painter with whom he was then living. Ford saw Rhys's potential and assisted her with her writing. He helped her refine and publish *The Left Bank* (1927), for which he wrote a long and somewhat self-serving preface. While the stories in this collection often lack subtlety or depth and are often merely fragments or impressions, they contain embryonic themes and ideas that dominate Rhys's later fiction. The Parisian world depicted in these stories is not that of the literary circle of Ernest Hemingway and his fellow American expatriates. Instead, Rhys deals with the underside of the bohemian existence. She cre-

Marya is ready to settle for the present—whatever its ultimate cost—if it obscures temporarily the unpleasant contours of life, but she realizes at the same time that she will soon be discarded. She characterizes herself as a "naive sinner" and in this way justifies her own seduction, her own willingness to play the game. Both she and Lois are victims, and they distrust, indeed hate, each other for this very reason. After a trip to the country and a quarrel, Marya allows Heidler to set her up in a hotel room. The narrative grows increasingly complex as it registers Marya's psychic descent through a series of interrelated images and extended metaphors, developing a structural rhythm that provides a special perspective on Marya's movements and reactions as events swarm around her. The realistic level of the earlier parts of the novel is blended with open-ended images and dreamlike flights that are, nevertheless, rigidly controlled by the direct, simple style. The imagery and rhythm of the second half of the novel render the dreamlike subtlety of Marya's consciousness, which breaks from the realistic strains of the narrative and marks the psychological dimensions of her entrapment. These passages reveal far more of Marya's subconscious motives and anxieties than she herself can realize, and thus they explore more profoundly the themes of the novel. On one level the force of the narrative seems to insist that Marya's inability to break away from those upon whom she is dependent is justified, but on a deeper level the consciousness revealed to the reader points to a broader framework of human culpability and to the underlying reasons for Marya's desperation, her flight from reality, and her amoral posturing.

Marya lies in her room, receives visits from Heidler, and goes to see Stephan in prison. Heidler has the money; Marya needs the money. She is torn between love and hate for Heidler, between loyalty to Stephan and despair at his situation. After his release and Marya's revelation that she has been Heidler's lover, Stephan violently flings her aside and leaves, ironically to be comforted by a stronger woman. The imagery which bears Marya's sense of her dilemma underscores her psychological vacillations and points to the inevitable consequences of her actions. The most persistent image in the novel is that of the caged animal, with predatory overtones and depiction of human confinement, and it accommodates the various forms of conflict within *Quartet*. In the novel's earlier stages, the metaphor is not

Jean Lenglet sent Rhys this photograph of himself and their daughter, Maryvonne, after the couple separated.

unpleasant—Marya thinks of herself "like some splendid caged animal," entrapped, but with resources for escape. Marya thus justifies the prospect of becoming Heidler's mistress as a chance for a new birth. The image, however, is transmuted as the complexity of the four-way relationship increases. Later, the sight of "a young fox in a cage" allows Marya again to entertain false hopes and justifications while at a deeper level intuiting the dire consequences of her actions.

This metaphor of entrapment is extended by the images accompanying the descriptions of the various hotel rooms in which Marya is "caged." Although the narrative voice on the realistic level exposes Marya's feelings, stylistic alterations between direct exposition and metaphoric language subtly probe and reveal underlying conflicts of which Marya is only partially aware. The cage imagery soon gives way to grotesque, Kafkaesque images of claustrophobia and vertigo, reflecting Marya's horror, fear, and desperation. As Marya seeks refuge in drink and then in fantasies, the style takes on a nightmare quality that pervades the surface realism.

All the characters in *Quartet* prove to be victims of their own moral blindness, hatreds, illusions, and self-pity. The two men are blind and un-caring, and the women are no better because in their desire for protection they become accomplices to their own self-destruction in a life-denying battle. The enclosed world in which they all live is an amoral one. Marya has been reduced to an object and thus reaches an emotional state in which the exclusive object of her psychic energy is the self. Although *Quartet* has been called a morbid work, the directness of style and Rhys's clear narrative focus and technique relieve the novel's intense subjectivity and offer a dramatic, human portrait of the female consciousness in the modern world.

As Rhys's affair with Ford drew to its inevitable end, Jean Lenglet was finally released from prison. Rhys's revelation to Lenglet of the nature of her relationship with Ford spelled the end of their marriage, but a deep and lasting bond was to exist between them for years—a bond that was not solely related to their daughter. Rhys's literary career in the late 1920s and early 1930s continued to show promise. Ford had gotten her the job of translating Francis Carco's *Perversity* (1928; erroneously attributed to Ford by the publisher), and *After Leaving Mr Mackenzie* and *Voyage in the Dark* were published in 1931 and 1934, respectively. Both novels received brief but favorable reviews; however, sales were disappointing. Rhys's technique and form were praised, but her subject matter—the down-and-out female on the fringe of society—did not draw readers, and both novels fell into obscurity.

Few writers before Jean Rhys in this century dealt sensitively with the unprotected woman in the contemporary world. The woman in the Rhys novel lives in a harsher, more naked, less sophisticated world than the women in the works of Virginia Woolf, Katherine Mansfield, or Dorothy Richardson. Rhys's women are without careers, ambitions, education, or particular talents. They move within a closed and essentially deterministic universe, and Rhys deals more directly with the sexual tensions and game playing that go on between a dominant male and a passive female. The subjects and themes of Rhys's fiction, however, were outside the mainstream of British fiction, and in her case originally did not lead to popular success.

After Leaving Mr Mackenzie and *Voyage in the Dark* amplify and enrich Rhys's vision of the feminine consciousness. *After Leaving Mr Mackenzie* deals with the Rhys woman long after youthful hopefulness and trust have vanished. The hero-

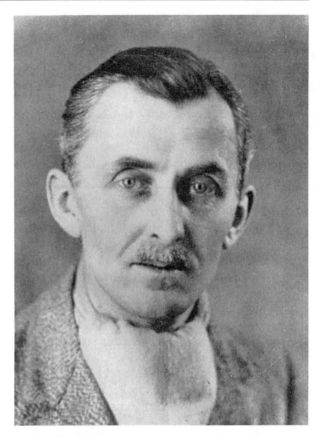

Rhys's second husband, Leslie Tilden Smith

ine, Julia Martin, is older, harder, more ravaged by the world than Anna Morgan of *Voyage in the Dark*. A precisely formed and structured novel, *After Leaving Mr Mackenzie* is compressed and relentless in its intimate portrayal of a woman fighting to delay her arrival at the nadir of her existence. Part one of the novel is set in Paris after Mr. Mackenzie has disposed of Julia; the second and longest section is set in London, where Julia visits her sister, tries to attend to her dying mother, develops an abortive relationship with Mr. Horsfield, and receives money from an old lover, who makes it clear that this is the last time she can expect to be helped by him; the brief final section covers Julia's return to Paris. While the novel traces Julia's search for money, it is, on a deeper level, concerned with her quest for some form of human engagement. The theme of failure is supported by images of ghostlike figures which emerge throughout, grim and foreboding, portents of a future where death is the only certainty.

Julia at the beginning of the novel inhabits the typically enclosed, restricted world of the Rhys heroine—in this case, the hotel room and strict schedule by which Julia has ordered her life, a controllable universe free from human intrusion, a world devoted exclusively to the self. It is a hiding place, a refuge created by Julia's defensive narcissism. Julia is bereft of those characteristics which give people identity—it is impossible to guess her age, nationality, or social background. She displays, however, a quality of self-respect, endurance, and inherent resiliency. She has also developed a carelessness and restlessness which become important defenses in the inevitable sexual power relationships that men impose upon her.

The narrative distance is better handled and controlled in this novel than in *Quartet*. In addition to her sure handling of the feminine consciousness, Rhys in this novel makes an entry into the male consciousness, which gives further dimension to the heroine as other characters interpret her. Julia sets out to confront Mr. Mackenzie, the man who has cast her off, and in so doing she confronts the whole social order. The scene between them is rendered from his point of view. Male motivation is revealed, and the external, social source of Julia's angst and the moral blindness of Mr. Mackenzie are also skillfully shown. His instinct for self-preservation underscores Julia's lack of a strong instinct of this kind. Ironically, the insincerity and cruelty of the Mackenzies of the world generate what little strength Julia has.

A more detailed and complicated analysis of male attitudes toward the female is presented in the character of Mr. Horsfield. The preliminary scenes and the early meetings with Julia are rendered from Horsfield's point of view. Rhys's skillful handling of point of view deepens the reader's sense of what might otherwise be seen as a prosaic, if not merely melodramatic, relationship between Horsfield and Julia. Their first meeting is rendered exclusively through Horsfield's motivations and intellectual juggling. His footwork is quite humorous at times as he bounces back and forth between caution and recklessness, attraction to and revulsion for Julia. But for their second meeting the narratorial focus moves back and forth between the two, revealing the byplay and parrying beyond the dialogue. The shift between the two consciousnesses is effective here as it was not in *Quartet*, where Heidler, for example, was not convincing as a character because the narrator could not free herself from Marya's point of view. This failure in *Quartet* nearly reduced the novel to melodrama, but the shifting point of view in *After Leaving Mr Mackenzie* not only accom-

Jean Rhys in Dominica, 1936, the only time she returned to the West Indies after her departure in about 1907

modates the unfolding of a relationship, it inaugurates and sustains the entire dramatic situation. When Julia finally acknowledges a need for him, Horsfield is able to indulge his sexual urges and at the same time maintain his self-image as the gallant protector. After sleeping with her, he silently leaves the room and feels an enormous "relief." He learns what Julia has learned but keeps forgetting—that self-protection is the rule of the jungle.

The third relationship depicted in this novel is that between Julia and her sister, Norah, who, while Julia (as Norah thinks) has been out living the high life, has been tied to the home, taking care of their sick mother. Norah has accepted lower-middle-class life in all its drabness; outwardly stoic, she is inwardly bitter and self-pitying. She is, as Julia says, "fierce"—with a fierceness created out of hatred and self-pity. Julia is vulnerable where Norah is hard; Julia has retained some capacity for feeling while Norah has only coldness and self-righteous moral superiority. Norah's indifference to her awakes a forceful if temporary determination in Julia to keep up the fight. Here, as in other Rhys novels, the heroine fares no better in her relationships with women than she does with men. In Rhys's novels, women are often betrayed by other women; and a natural feminine intimacy is no longer a part of the feminine consciousness.

After Leaving Mr Mackenzie is intimately concerned with the nature of human relationships at every level, the illusions and lies, self-deceptions, that exist for both sexes. The movement of the novel traces with shattering accuracy the desires and self-induced illusions of the male. It makes poignantly visible the male role in the sexual power struggle in which he must not only dominate but justify domination to himself. The results of this domination for the female are made very plain. The social and economic order is on the side of the male. As in *Quartet,* all four principals are victims to some extent. They are isolated; in each we see the impulse toward human companionship and, on the part of the men, the price they are unwilling to pay. The four are unwilling, incapable, or, in Julia's case, too broken down to find any meaningful human bond. Each is fixed, either by choice or circumstances, in a world whose highest value is protection, not love. And the metaphysical weight of the novel exposes the vacuity of this hierarchy.

After the publication of *After Leaving Mr Mackenzie,* Rhys turned to her notebooks and began writing *Voyage in the Dark,* which she originally titled "Two Tunes." The novel is highly autobiographical, dealing with a young woman's life in England as an actress in a traveling musical troupe. The experiences are based upon Rhys's own experiences, including her longing for the warmth and color of the Caribbean islands, her first love affair, and an abortion. Rhys is able to divorce the novel from events in her own life through her skillful use of first-person narration, without endangering the necessary aesthetic distance. The novel enriches one's understanding of the two novels that precede it as well as the two novels that follow it in the Rhys canon. It gives more shape to the earlier heroines, and its Caribbean background anticipates the fully developed exoticism of *Wide Sargasso Sea* (1966). The special intimacy of the "I" narrator allows for an important structural feature of the novel, Anna Morgan's memories of her childhood in the West Indies.

We have in *Voyage of the Dark,* because of Rhys's structuring technique, a triple level of observation: first, the experiencing self, Anna's life in the present; second, the narrative self that is distant from the events; and third, the self of Anna's memory who is recalled in dream or conscious recollecting and who experiences the events of childhood in the Caribbean. Without this element of memory and the dynamic resonance it creates, the novel would simply stand as a well-told but pathetic little tale of a young girl who through naiveté and lack of initiative falls into compromising circumstances. A series of beautifully constructed memory frames, however, blends into the narrative and sets up a cumulative and complex process of awareness, giving depth, richness, and moral focus to the novel. The contrast between the two worlds is wonderfully achieved; the deeper structures of civilization in the two cultures underscore their fundamental opposition, and Anna lives in both worlds. The style of the memory passages is clear and vibrant; the style of the England passages is often vague and dislocated. The development of these memory images gradually reveals a pattern and an accretive meaning. The narrative's dual focus on present and past invigorates the entire book as the two opposed worlds meet in Anna's experience, and the narrational self attempts to draw meaning from the personal struggle of the confrontation. It is in this matrix of both worlds that the deeper meaning of Anna's failure lies.

Anna seeks warmth, comfort, security. Her first lover, Walter, becomes for her a protector and comforter, a kind of surrogate father. She associates with him a kind of primal, noncarnal, human warmth. She is naive; he is skillful in seducing her. After her violation, the novel traces her downward path. The letter of dismissal inevitably arrives. Anna has been used and is now being disposed of when the male grows tired or fearful. She, in common with other Rhys heroines, has no real options; hers is a condition without recourse. Upon receiving the letter, Anna conflates in her mind images from the past and the present, an association of a prior rejection (by her uncle in the islands) with the present rejection. This fluctuation throughout the novel between Anna's childhood in the West Indies and her life in London is far more than a simple device to generate rhythms and set up contrasts. These earlier reflections by the "I" narrator create a fictional mode whereby the experiencing self of the novel is revealed beyond its contemporary context. Together, present and past create a kind of dual passage or voyage which has, for Anna, merged into a dreamlike world that has left her unable to define experience. This fictional strategy provides the thematic resolution of the novel as we see Anna's oscillation between the world of reflected experience and present circumstances.

After being cast off by her lover, Anna is at loose ends. Seeking her lost security, false though it proved to be, Anna drifts from one male to another. She becomes pregnant, seeks out an abortionist, and at the end of the novel she has been seen by a doctor who tries to stop her hemorrhaging. She thinks about starting over again, going back to her childhood, "about being new and fresh." Starting over again becomes a central concern for the Rhys heroine, young and old, but the phrase carries a bitter irony. The doctor, while Anna is thinking of starting over again, says the same thing to Anna's roommate, but his meaning is entirely different from Anna's. He means that she will be able to start the same dangerous cycle over again: the search for money, the going from one man to another, in short, prostitution. The juxtaposition of this phrase as it is thought and spoken by the two characters, Anna and the doctor, completes the bitter irony of the novel. Anna is suspended between her dreamworld and reality. Hope will keep her going, to be eventually replaced by the more natural, if less ennobling, instinct for survival. The will is gradually crushed, and survival, as she seeks the protection of another male, becomes a way of life. Anna represents the genesis of the Rhys heroine; most of the traits, including the tendency to drift into a netherworld of somnambulistic escape, are present in her in embryonic form.

The notices for *Voyage in the Dark* were favorable, but reviews continued to refer to the "dark subject matter" of Rhys's work, and the sales of both *Voyage in the Dark* and *After Leaving Mr Mackenzie* were disappointing. Since the early 1930s, after Rhys had separated from Lenglet, she had met Leslie Tilden Smith, a literary agent and publisher's reader. They began living together. Smith, associated as he was with the publishing industry, introduced Rhys to many of his literary acquaintances, but as with her life in Paris in the 1920s, she remained always on the fringes of the literary world, rather than anywhere near the inner circle. She found literary people "alarming," and her natural shyness predisposed her to be more reclusive than many other writers of the period. She did mention later in life that she had

met Rosamond Lehmann and others during the 1930s, but the acquaintances did not seem to develop into anything more substantial.

In the mid 1930s, Smith's father died, leaving Smith a substantial sum of money, and Smith and Rhys were married. Smith had been divorced from his wife earlier, but although he lived with Rhys, he had not remarried for fear of offending his father, a clergyman, and losing the inheritance. In 1936 Rhys and Smith made a trip to the West Indies, stopping for a time in Dominica, where, of course, Rhys's relatives and the quality of life on the island fell far short of her romantic memories. She tried to write on the island but was unable to get much accomplished. She never returned. Back in London she began to write *Good Morning, Midnight*. As Europe drew closer to war, Rhys's regular visits to the Continent were interrupted. Maryvonne, who lived with her father in the Netherlands, often visited her mother in England. The war also put an end to these visits, and during the war Maryvonne and her mother corresponded through friends in Portugal.

Good Morning, Midnight was published in 1939. In contrast with the socially conscious writings of others during this period, Rhys's writing seemed untouched by the military and political events of the day. Throughout the 1930s Rhys's heroines saw the world from the inside rather than the outside. Her aim was the perfection of rendering private consciousness through style, not the achievement of an enlarged vision of the contemporary world. *Good Morning, Midnight* advanced the major themes of her earlier work and deepened her portrait of women's emotional lives. Although it contains no specific mention of contemporary events, the novel comes at the end of the Depression and near the start of World War II, laying an enormous emphasis on how much things cost, how much money one needs, how much protection money affords. These things always concerned the Rhys heroine, however. Set in Paris, the novel brings Rhys's fiction full circle and confirms that her real literary affinities are French rather than English.

Sasha Jansen bears the cumulative burdens of Rhys's earlier heroines; she is Julia Martin grown a bit older, a bit more out of control, but for the present at least, less financially desperate. It takes more alcohol for her to keep things in place. Her attempts at self-control, the arrangement of her room, and her daily rituals have become substitutes for meaning in a life that seems

Dust jacket for Rhys's 1966 novel, which deals with the first marriage of Mr. Rochester,
a character in Charlotte Brontë's Jane Eyre

without purpose. Images of darkness, water, and drowning contrast with the heroine's tenuous, self-imposed hold on sanity, safety, and dryness. The references to drowning and water set up a psychological pattern of sexual violation and fear which gradually reveals the depth of the heroine's consciousness and the entire range of her personality and feeling. All of her actions and reactions seem attempts to master the threats that the world imposes. The obsessional consciousness that the novel will explore is introduced through these images.

Past and present collide in this novel as they do in earlier Rhys novels. The major portion of part one carefully develops Sasha's earlier memories of her Paris failures. She confronts in memory the manager of the dress shop where she once worked. The malignancy of the faceless and nameless oppressor is seen more clearly by Sasha than by any of Rhys's other heroines. With this combination of paranoia and insight, Sasha recognizes those forces in society which turn her into a weak and helpless figure who simply cannot get

on. We learn how her present attitudes and fears were formed, and this is important to our understanding of her later behavior.

Once again, such images as enclosing streets, threatening rows of houses, and small hotel rooms accommodate the consciousness of the heroine. Because, except for dialogue, *Good Morning, Midnight* is rendered entirely through Sasha's consciousness in first person narration, her psychological states are necessarily well controlled by the style, which not only reflects her various immediate states of mind, but, as it orders her consciousness in language, offers further clues to the deeper, inner self. Brutally understated, the novel's style gives penetrating focus to Sasha's dreams, and the imagery, with its sustained and continued tropes, amplifies and expands meaning beyond the immediate rendering of consciousness.

What proves to be the most significant encounter in the novel occurs near the close of part one, when Sasha meets a man on the street as she is leaving a bar. He is the poor gigolo René, charming, hopeful, and clever, and in spite of herself, Sasha is attracted to him as an underdog like herself. She believes she is invulnerable and can shut out the whole world. Ironically, in this novel René and two other impoverished male characters look to Sasha for comfort and protection because she has a bit more money than they do. After Sasha's meeting with the gigolo and others less fortunate than herself, the style of the novel becomes more open, the sentences longer, the images less grotesque, and Sasha's thought patterns less obsessive. The style softens as Sasha begins to look outside herself. She acquires a greater sympathy but still remains cynical and worldly in her ironic humor.

Again Sasha recalls the past and her marriage to Enno, who reminds us of Stephan Zelli in *Quartet*. They are young and hopeful, but their hopes are crushed, and Enno leaves her because "you're too passive, you're lazy, you bore me." It is out of this past that Sasha's present has been formed. As the novel reaches its dramatic close, we become increasingly aware that Sasha's is an almost archetypal journey of return. It begins as an attempt to face the past by revisiting it in a most cautious way, but despite the caution it floods up and nearly engulfs the present.

Agitated and increasingly excited by René, Sasha feels that she still has a grip on herself. The water and drowning imagery is evoked by her in a different manifestation as she thinks that "Underneath there is always stagnant water, calm, indifferent." Her indifference, however, has begun to evaporate. René brings Sasha out of herself; amid his gaiety and ebullience, she becomes witty, charming, clever, sarcastic—qualities she has always had but never had the opportunity to reveal. This transformation is one of the novel's most important elements, and it is executed with brilliant narrative skill. Even Sasha's memories are transformed as she exchanges recollections with René; they grow warm and humorous in contrast to her dark memories reported earlier in the novel. When René and Sasha discover a mutual link, however (they had known the same person and stayed in the same house), Sasha is again on her guard. As René questions her, she becomes increasingly defensive and finally almost hysterical as she admits her fear of men. She sees her illusion crushed by the whole image of her life, past and present. The most striking feature of this entire scene is its economy of detail and the precision with which Sasha's whole life comes before her. The style acts to modulate

every emotional phase that she goes through, and the reflexive quality of the images deepens our understanding of Sasha's despair. René persists, telling her that he wants to make love to her. The memory of vague, romantic yearnings from the past produces a profoundly complicated turmoil in Sasha in which her whole identity seems to give way. René is appealing to her sexual and romantic yearnings that have been long dormant.

The last section of the novel is a blur between dream and reality, hallucination and confrontation. The style never loses its sharp clarity, but in places it mounts to a lyric level as Sasha's mind absorbs a confusion between what she wants to believe and what is actually happening. With René in her room, she reaches an emotional pitch of joy and terror. She thinks of love, youth, spring, happiness, everything that she has lost, but suddenly the spell is broken, and she grows cold and wary. Even her physical body signals the riot of her conflicting feelings: "My mouth hurts, my breasts hurt, because it hurts, when you have been dead to come alive." She insults René by telling him to take the money and forget the lovemaking. He leaves, and Sasha does not know whether she is the passionate woman seeking but unable to accept even a fleeting moment of human passion, or the aging, lonely female who has narrowly survived the advances of a gigolo. She is in a schizophrenic state, not knowing which self is the true self—the self that wants to reach outward and love or the self that wants to withdraw and defend and protect. René, she discovers, has taken only a bit of money when he could have taken it all. Again, dreams of romance and love refuse to die and rise up within her as she imagines the gigolo returning. She lies in her bed waiting for him. Through the open door the man in the next room enters (a tension had been set up between him and Sasha throughout the novel); she reaches out to him, draws him down to her saying, "Yes—yes—yes," an ending with echoes of James Joyce's *Ulysses* (1922). It is a qualified affirmation, a hope for the possibility of union between man and woman in which each fulfills the other.

Theme and dramatic events have never been better wedded in Rhys's fiction than in *Good Morning, Midnight*, where they achieve artistic harmony and yield such telling insight into the consciousness of the heroine. Throughout the novel the reader is aware of the primary importance of style in all matters of form and expression. Its

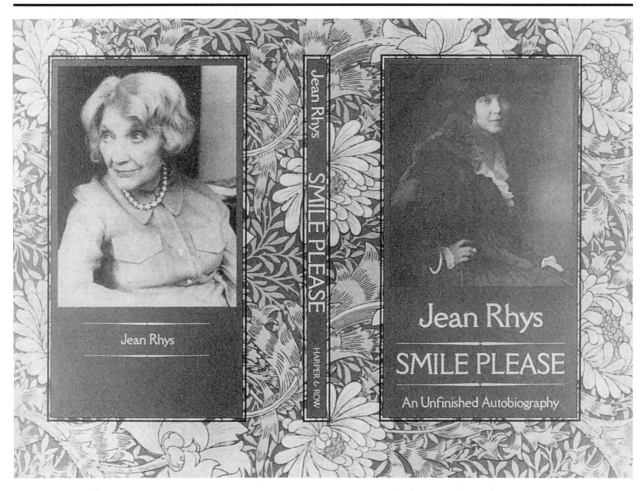

Dust jacket for the American edition of the book Rhys was at work on when she died. The photograph on the front of the jacket was taken in Vienna, circa 1920.

function here extends beyond the conventional expectations of prose. In the heroine's movements throughout the book and in her eventual illumination, the style seems to form a biaxial movement understating, modulating, and finally overcoming the heroine's plight. The language itself becomes a mediating element between the heroine and the outside world. The style seems to contest the development of the novel. The architectonics of *Good Morning, Midnight* emerge out of Sasha's obsessional preoccupations and the slender thread of events which take place during her brief visit to Paris, but it is the style which gives her the full configuration of this interplay between the private consciousness and the outside world. As the style carries us through the mediations between the inner and outer selves, the images found in memory, topography, and dream struggle for what seems another destiny that is finally released in the last words of the novel.

The "yes" at the end is no more a grand affir-

mation of life than Molly Bloom's. Sasha's acceptance is weighted with full ironic implications. For Sasha, "yes" is not necessarily an acceptance of life but a recognition of its force. Rhys also gives vision in this conclusion to the narrow choice a woman has in this work.

However we may interpret the complex reverberations at the close of *Good Morning, Midnight,* they give the book a cohesion and intricacy beyond that of Rhys's earlier novels. The loneliness of the modern experience has been drawn into the rich vortex of the feminine self and accommodated with a vitality and an understanding of human nature few novels dealing with the feminine consciousness have achieved. In Sasha there is strength that confronts the terror—a strength at once fragile and human, but no longer merely defensive. The synthesis in *Good Morning, Midnight* is realized through the character of Sasha. She is the most compelling and sympathetic of

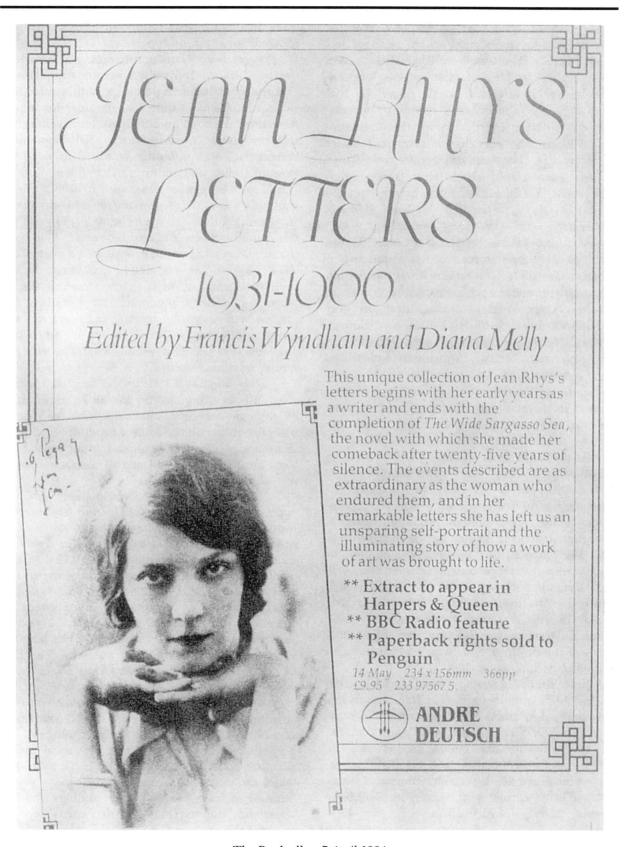

The Bookseller, *7 April 1984*

Rhys's heroines. Her bitter humor and sardonic wisdom provide us with abundant clues to her deeper nature. The women in Rhys's fiction have been crippled by life, but what we see— and nowhere more clearly than in this novel—is that there is a new consciousness forming, not one formed only from anger and despair, but one imbued with an awareness that women must share equally in life's promises and defeats, and if they do not, human life itself is lessened and even malformed. This revelation is nowhere better expressed in Rhys's fiction than in *Good Morning, Midnight.*

At the beginning of the war, Leslie Tilden Smith joined the air force. He was assigned to a radar station in Norfolk, where Rhys joined him temporarily, but she spent a great deal of time in London. Leslie died in Devon after the war ended, in October 1945. His cousin, Max Hamer, a family friend and solicitor, attended the funeral and soon became acquainted with Rhys. They were married two years later (1947) and lived in Beckenham, Kent. Rhys's writing career remained dormant during this time, and the few who had read and admired her work, which was now long out of print, believed she had died.

In 1949 the actress Selma Vaz Dias tried to find Rhys by putting an ad in the *New Statesman.* Rhys saw the ad, answered it, and this step became the first on the long road to a belated recognition of her novels and a certain measure of fame that had been denied her in her younger days. Vaz Dias sent Rhys a dramatic adaptation of *Good Morning, Midnight* and performed the work as a dramatic monologue at the Anglo-French Centre on 10 November 1949; it was later presented on BBC's Third Programme in 1957. Upon discovering that she and her works had not been totally forgotten, Rhys was encouraged to attempt writing again.

Rhys and Max Hamer visited London early in 1957 to have dinner with Vaz Dias, and at this time they talked about Rhys's ideas for *Wide Sargasso Sea.* Vaz Dias claimed ever after that the idea for the novel was born in her kitchen, and, obsessed with the idea that she and she alone had rediscovered Rhys, she laid claim to fees and royalties that Rhys earned at this time. In 1959 *Good Morning, Midnight* was broadcast in Bremen, Germany, while Rhys in England was saying that *Wide Sargasso Sea* just needed to be "pulled together." However, Rhys suffered a heart attack just before the novel was finished and was in poor health for years afterward. Publication was delayed for seven more years.

After *Good Morning, Midnight* was broadcast on the BBC in 1957, Rhys became friends with Francis Wyndham, a longtime admirer of her work, and Diana Athill, who became her editor at André Deutsch and helped her reenter the literary scene. A short story, "Till September Petronella," was published in the *London Magazine* in 1960, and another, "Let Them Call It Jazz," in the *London Magazine* in 1962. Movie rights to *Good Morning, Midnight* were discussed. In February 1966 part one of *Wide Sargasso Sea* was published in *Art and Literature.* The next month Max Hamer died, and in October 1966 *Wide Sargasso Sea* was finally published. It was well received, and Rhys finally achieved the acclaim she had long deserved. Photographers and interviewers visited her cottage in Devon; she was given awards by the Royal Society for Literature and received public attention when she received the W. H. Smith Award.

Wide Sargasso Sea differs in time and setting from Rhys's other novels, but in its exploration of the male-female relationship, it has an affinity with the earlier works. In this novel Rhys's characterization of Edward Rochester is the most complex and fully drawn of any of the male characters she had ever attempted.

The novel deals with the Rochester of Charlotte Brontë's *Jane Eyre* (1847) and his meeting with, marriage to, and early days with his first wife, Antoinette, who is known in *Jane Eyre* only as the madwoman in the attic. In the first section of the novel we learn of the child Antoinette and gain a view of the insular world in which she lived, both external and internal. As the reader understands the formation of the consciousness of Antoinette, he or she can understand her later behavior and her approaching madness. The first section provides a psychohistorical background for Antoinette's life. The setting is the West Indies after the emancipation of the slaves, a time bristling with resentment, hatred, and vindictiveness. Rhys concentrates on the psychological, the personal traumas which larger historical events produce upon the individual. We come to understand the vast cultural gap separating the young Antoinette from her own surroundings and the completely unbridgeable gap that exists between her and the Englishman Edward Rochester.

Early dramatic events have a profound impact upon Antoinette. When blacks burn down neighboring estates, her family has to escape; as they flee, a black girl she has thought of as her friend throws a stone at her. Her attraction to the black culture is disrupted by the rebellion, and a disjunction in her personality results. Her brother's death and her mother's madness (and domination by a former slave) confirm Antoinette's complete isolation and seal her fate in a private schizophrenic world between two times, two races, two cultures.

Part two, which takes up nearly two-thirds of the novel, is largely Edward's account of the events following his marriage to Antoinette, a marriage arranged along financial terms rather than for love. Here Rhys makes the Gothic mode an active element in the novel. This mode, of course, helps tie the novel to *Jane Eyre* and functions as a narrative idiom where the descriptions themselves, with their frequently elaborate portents, achieve a metaphysical relationship to the characters. Although part two is centered within Edward's intelligence, Rhys uses extensive dialogue between Edward and Antoinette. Her style in this section is triumphantly adapted to her narrative purpose. Its two qualities, which seem at first to conflict—an uncanny ability to describe an emotion completed and somehow resolved, and at the same time a rendering of feeling as much by implication as by statement—are fused by the close relationship she draws between the natural and psychological landscape.

Edward and Antoinette's honeymoon journey into the mountains is described in terms of the lush and exotic scenery through which they pass; it is an enclosed and intoxicating world, wild but menacing. The closeness and intimacy that Antoinette desires and needs is impossible for Edward, who is incapable of giving of himself. The whole exotic experience of the first few days at Granbois is a kind of initiation for Edward. There is a dominant sensual element— "too much blue, too much purple. . . . The flowers too red, etc."—he thinks. He finds this world at once seductive and hostile and goes on his guard after just a few short days and nights of abandon. Antoinette wants to draw him into her private world, to live passionately within the rhythms of the natural environment, but he is filled with deep foreboding. His thoughts and values have crystallized; he is egocentric, but not, perhaps, the conniving, malicious male he has been thought to be. He is blind rather than deliberately malicious, sad rather than vengeful.

The villainous Dan Cosway informs him that Antoinette has had other men before her mar-

riage to him. Edward, in typical Victorian fashion, is wounded and outraged. His inflated pride and imperious personality entrap him exclusively within himself, and any rapprochement with Antoinette becomes impossible. Two explicitly sexual scenes ensue. Antoinette, desperate to win him, asks the black Christophine for a potion. After drinking it, Edward indulges in the wildest sexual abandon. Antoinette has made the mistake of thinking that she can evoke and redeem his love through sexual passion. He, on the other hand, comes to hate her for causing him to lose control, to abandon his closely guarded self. Her attempt to bring them together through Obeah, a Caribbean form of voodoo, causes him to despise her forever. He will not allow himself to become exposed and vulnerable. Antoinette, like her surroundings, becomes something alien and hostile to him, but his pathetic sense of honor endures. He does, however, plan a deliberate act of revenge which symbolizes his hostility and need to dominate. He takes the black servant girl Amelie to bed just behind the thin partition that separates his room from Antoinette's to ensure that she hears them. He thus demonstrates to himself the power of his maleness and shows that he has the power to destroy Antoinette. Near the close of part two Christophine points out to Edward his real sin, "nobody is to have any pride but you." He has not been able to fathom the life of the passions; he fears it and retaliates in this way, thereby driving Antoinette a little further down the road to madness.

Part three of the novel is a coda which confirms Antoinette's wretched destiny. As she and Edward leave Granbois, we recall the exuberance and hope with which Antoinette arrived there. At the end of the novel the groundwork has been laid for Antoinette's fate in Edward's country house.

The characterization of Antoinette is the major flaw in the novel. There is something hollow in her that is not covered over by the exotic and mysterious qualities Rhys gives to her. She has little understanding and never advances beyond the world of childhood. Her limitations as a character enforce certain limitations upon the novel and upon her relationship with Edward. A mature union would have been impossible given her limited capacity for understanding. The novel, is, however, an extension of Rhys's basic themes; and Rhys's achievement is considerable, especially the way she captures with a lyrical intensity the rhythm between the physical and metaphysical worlds. *Wide Sargasso Sea* enriches one's rereading of *Jane Eyre*. However, whereas the nineteenth-century novel upon which it is based ends happily in matrimonial fulfillment, *Wide Sargasso Sea* is decidedly modern in that there is no fulfillment or reconciliation at the end.

After the publication of *Wide Sargasso Sea*, André Deutsch began republishing Rhys's earlier novels. *Good Morning, Midnight* and *Voyage in the Dark* were republished in 1967, and the other novels followed. Rhys published three books after *Wide Sargasso Sea*: *Tigers Are Better-Looking* (1968), *Sleep It Off, Lady* (1976), and the privately printed, autobiographical *My Day* (1975).

Tigers Are Better-Looking is a volume of short fiction, including nine stories from *The Left Bank*, a segment of the original introduction by Ford, and eight additional stories, all of which had appeared in various periodicals through the 1960s. It includes "Till September Petronella," which proves that Rhys's talent for dramatizing the polarization of the sexes did not diminish with age. She does in this story something she did not generally do in her fiction, and that is to tie the story to an exact historical date, in this case July 1914, just one month before the beginning of World War I, thus linking her war between the sexes to a grander, more violent war.

Sleep It Off, Lady contains previously unpublished stories, many of which predate in initial composition the eight new stories in *Tigers Are Better-Looking*. The majority of stories in this collection confirms the clarity of focus that always marked Rhys's work as well as that certainty of feeling within the narrow world she draws upon for her subject matter. She deals confidently with the very young and the very old in these stories, their vulnerability and their exclusion.

The publication of *Wide Sargasso Sea*, the new interest in Rhys, and the republication of all her earlier work had far-reaching effects upon Rhys's literary career and reputation. Her work became available to a whole new generation of readers. Her critical reputation has grown steadily. Critics have pointed primarily to her strong originality and her remarkable insight into the feminine psyche, and lying beneath most of the praise is the collective recognition that Rhys simply writes like nobody else; her talent and intelligence encompass dimensions not found elsewhere in the modern English novel. It is not only because readers are now more attuned to the feminine consciousness that Rhys has gained such wide attention, but, more significantly, it has come to be recognized that her work explores with compassion and a rare intelligence the panic and emptiness of modern life. The range of her subject matter is never wide, but her understanding of what it is to have been a woman in this century is comprehensive. Written in a style that brings form and content into a harmonious whole rarely equaled in modern fiction, her work reveals in its humor, sympathy, and understanding a fully realized and significant portrait of the female consciousness in the modern world.

Smile Please, her unfinished autobiography, published posthumously in the fall of 1979, is especially revealing in its treatment of Rhys's early childhood in Dominica. The later portions of the autobiography are less finished, but her commentaries on writing and the relationship of art to life are interesting aesthetic experiments in themselves. A selection of Rhys's letters was published in the spring of 1984.

In 1978 Jean Rhys was awarded a CBE for her services to literature. She died on 14 May 1979 in the Royal Devon and Exeter Hospital.

Letters:
Jean Rhys Letters 1931-1966, edited by Francis Wyndham and Diana Melly (London: Deutsch, 1984).

Bibliography:
Elgin W. Mellown, *Jean Rhys: A Descriptive and Annotated Bibliography of Works and Criticisms* (New York: Garland, 1984).

Biographies:
Arnold E. Davidson, *Jean Rhys* (New York: Ungar, 1985);
Carole Angler, *Jean Rhys: A Critical Biography*, volume 1 (Boston: Little, Brown, 1991).

References:
Alfred Alvarez, "The Best Living English Novelist," *New York Times Book Review*, 17 March 1974, pp. 6-8;
Diana Athill, "Jean Rhys, and the Writing of *Wide Sargasso Sea*," *Bookseller*, 3165 (20 August 1966): 1378-1379;
Hunter Davis, "Rip Van Rhys," *Sunday Times* (Atticus), 6 November 1966, p. 13;
Mary Lou Emery, *Jean Rhys at "World's End": Novels of Colonial and Sexual Exile* (Austin: University of Texas Press, 1990);

Judith Kegan Gardiner, *Rhys, Stead, Lessing, and the Politics of Empathy* (Bloomington: Indiana University Press, 1989);

Nancy Rebecca Harrison, *Jean Rhys and the Novel as Woman's Text* (Chapel Hill: University of North Carolina Press, 1988);

Louis James, "Unconquerable Spirit," in *Essays in West Indian Literature,* edited by James (London: Oxford University Press, 1968), pp. 11-23;

Paula Le Gallez, *The Rhys Woman: An Examination of Character in the Work of Jean Rhys* (New York: St. Martin's Press, 1990);

Elgin W. Mellown, "Character and Theme in the Novels of Jean Rhys," *Contemporary Literature,* 13 (1972): 458-472;

Rosalind Miles, *The Fiction of Sex* (New York: Barnes & Noble, 1974), pp. 96-106;

Arthur Mizener, *The Saddest Story: A Biography of Ford Madox Ford* (New York: World, 1971), pp. 346-350;

Ellen Moers, *Literary Women* (Garden City, N.Y.: Doubleday, 1976);

Teresa F. O'Connor, *Jean Rhys: The West Indian Novels* (New York: NYU Press, 1986);

Elaine Showalter, *A Literature of Their Own* (Princeton: Princeton University Press, 1977);

Thomas F. Staley, *Jean Rhys: A Critical Study* (London: Macmillan, 1979; Austin: University of Texas Press, 1979);

Michael Thorpe, " 'The Other Side': *Wide Sargasso Sea* and *Jane Eyre*," *Ariel,* 8 (July 1977): 99-110;

Selma Vaz Dias, "In Quest of a Missing Author," *Radio Times,* 3 May 1957, p. 25;

Peter Wolfe, *Jean Rhys* (Boston: Twayne, 1980);

Francis Wyndham, "Introduction to Jean Rhys," *London Magazine,* 7 (January 1960): 15-18.

Papers:
The largest collection of Rhys's papers is at the University of Tulsa.

Edith Sitwell

(7 September 1887 - 11 December 1964)

This entry was written by Robert K. Martin (Concordia University) for
DLB 20: British Poets, 1914-1945.

SELECTED BOOKS: *The Mother and Other Poems*
(Oxford: Blackwell, 1915);
Twentieth-Century Harlequinade and Other Poems, by
Edith Sitwell and Osbert Sitwell (Oxford:
Blackwell, 1916);
Clowns' Houses (Oxford: Blackwell, 1918);
The Wooden Pegasus (Oxford: Blackwell, 1920);
Façade (Kensington: Favil Press, 1922);
Bucolic Comedies (London: Duckworth, 1923);
The Sleeping Beauty (London: Duckworth, 1924;
New York: Knopf, 1924);
Troy Park (London: Duckworth, 1925; New York:
Knopf, 1925);
Poor Young People, by Edith Sitwell, Osbert Sitwell,
and Sacheverell Sitwell (London: Fleuron,
1925);
Poetry and Criticism (London: Hogarth Press,
1925; New York: Holt, 1926);
Elegy on Dead Fashion (London: Duckworth,
1926);
Rustic Elegies (London: Duckworth, 1927; New
York: Knopf, 1927);
Gold Coast Customs (London: Duckworth, 1929;
Boston & New York: Houghton Mifflin,
1929);
Alexander Pope (London: Faber & Faber, 1930;
New York: Cosmopolitan Book Company,
1930);
Collected Poems (London: Duckworth / Boston:
Houghton Mifflin, 1930);
Bath (London: Faber & Faber, 1932; New York:
Harrison Smith, 1932);
The English Eccentrics (London: Faber & Faber,
1933; Boston & New York: Houghton Mif-
flin, 1933; revised and enlarged edition,
New York: Vanguard, 1957; London: Dob-
son, 1958);
Five Variations on a Theme (London: Duckworth,
1933);
Aspects of Modern Poetry (London: Duckworth,
1934);
Victoria of England (London: Faber & Faber, 1936;
Boston: Houghton Mifflin, 1936);

Edith Sitwell

Selected Poems (London: Duckworth, 1936; Bos-
ton: Houghton Mifflin, 1937);
I Live Under a Black Sun (London: Gollancz,
1937; Garden City, N.Y.: Doubleday, Doran,
1938);
Poems New and Old (London: Faber & Faber,
1940);
Street Songs (London: Macmillan, 1942);
English Women (London: Collins, 1942);
A Poet's Notebook (London: Macmillan, 1943);
Green Song & Other Poems (London: Macmillan,
1944; New York: View Editions, 1946);
The Song of the Cold (London: Macmillan, 1945);

Fanfare for Elizabeth (New York: Macmillan, 1946; London: Macmillan, 1946);

The Shadow of Cain (London: Lehmann, 1947);

A Notebook on William Shakespeare (London: Macmillan, 1948; Boston: Beacon, 1961);

The Canticle of the Rose: Selected Poems 1920-1947 (London: Macmillan, 1949); republished as *The Canticle of the Rose: Poems 1917-49* (New York: Vanguard, 1949);

Poor Men's Music (London: Fore Publications, 1950; Denver: Swallow, 1950);

Façade and Other Poems, 1920-1935 (London: Duckworth, 1950);

A Poet's Notebook (Boston: Little, Brown, 1950)—contains most of *A Poet's Notebook* (1943) and *A Notebook on William Shakespeare* (1948);

Selected Poems (Harmondsworth, U.K.: Penguin, 1952);

Gardeners and Astronomers (London: Macmillan, 1953; abridged edition, New York: Vanguard, 1953);

Collected Poems (New York: Vanguard, 1954; enlarged edition, London: Macmillan, 1957);

The Outcasts (London: Macmillan, 1962); enlarged as *Music and Ceremonies* (New York: Vanguard, 1963);

The Queens of the Hive (London: Macmillan, 1962; Boston & Toronto: Little, Brown, 1962);

Taken Care Of (London: Hutchinson, 1965; New York: Atheneum, 1965);

Selected Poems of Edith Sitwell, edited by John Lehmann (London, Melbourne & Toronto: Macmillan, 1965).

OTHER: *Wheels*, edited by Sitwell (Oxford: Blackwell, 1916);

Wheels, Second Cycle, edited by Sitwell (Oxford: Blackwell, 1917);

Wheels, Third Cycle, edited by Sitwell (Oxford: Blackwell, 1919);

Wheels, Fourth Cycle, edited by Sitwell (Oxford: Blackwell, 1919);

Wheels, Fifth Cycle, edited by Sitwell (London: Parsons, 1920);

Wheels, Sixth Cycle, edited by Sitwell (London: Daniel, 1921);

The Pleasures of Poetry, First Series: Milton and the Augustan Age, edited by Sitwell (London: Duckworth, 1930; New York: Norton, 1934);

The Pleasures of Poetry, Second Series: The Romantic Revival, edited by Sitwell (London: Duckworth, 1931; New York: Norton, 1934);

The Pleasures of Poetry, Third Series: The Victorian Age, edited by Sitwell (London: Duckworth, 1932; New York: Norton, 1934);

The American Genius, edited by Sitwell (London: Lehmann, 1951).

Of all the modern poets who came of age during the second decade of the twentieth century, Edith Sitwell remains the least understood and least appreciated. The reasons for this apparent neglect include: sexual prejudice, reluctance to admit a woman to Parnassus; class prejudice, reluctance to accept as a serious poet the granddaughter of Albert Denison, Lord Londesborough; a belief in poetry as a private art, which made Edith Sitwell's public notoriety, as well as her performances of her poetry, suspect; and the mistaken idea, derived from a misreading of the early poems, that Sitwell was a poet without ideas. Edith Sitwell was born 7 September 1887 into an aristocratic country family. She was the daughter of Sir George Sitwell and his wife, Lady Ida Denison, daughter of Albert and Ursula Denison, Lord and Lady Londesborough. Her childhood was spent at her parents' home, Renishaw Hall in Derbyshire, and at her grandparents' home in Scarborough. The first child of an odd and unhappy marriage, Edith Sitwell had two younger brothers, Osbert, born in 1892, and Sacheverell, born in 1897. Renishaw gave Edith Sitwell a strong sense of family and history, and it was to play a large part in her poetic world. She was educated at home and began writing poetry when she was about twenty, but the major change in her life came when she moved to London in 1914 to share a flat with Helen Rootham, her former governess.

Although Sitwell had already produced a book of poems, *The Mother and Other Poems* (1915), she first came to public notice as the editor of *Wheels*, an anthology of contemporary verse published in six volumes, or "cycles," from 1916 to 1921. These anthologies were designed to provide an alternative to the poetry of the Georgians. Against the Georgians' rural, nostalgic values, the group that Edith and her brothers, Osbert and Sacheverell, gathered about them was developing the bright, hard, satiric style that came to be its trademark. The most significant contribution of *Wheels* to the history of modern poetry was the publication of seven poems by Wilfred Owen in the fourth cycle (1919). Like her brother Osbert, Edith Sitwell began her poetic career as an opponent of the monstrosity of

Edith and Osbert Sitwell

war and of the foolish self-satisfaction of Edwardian England. Later she would continue this concern and become the most distinguished poet of World War II with her poems "Still Falls the Rain," based on the air raids on England at the beginning of the war, and "Three Poems of the Atomic Age," based on the bombing of Hiroshima.

The Sitwells gave their first reading in December 1917 at an evening arranged by Lady Sybil Colefax, where they were joined by T. S. Eliot. Readings became important means for the establishment of Edith Sitwell's reputation, and much of her early poetry owes its character to the presumption that it would be read aloud. For it was Edith Sitwell more than anyone else who realized the importance of sound and texture in modern poetry and who introduced a poetry designed to take full advantage of the flexible rhythms of the spoken voice. Her interest in spoken poetry reached its fullest expression in the sequence of poems entitled *Façade*, first published in 1922.

The idea of declaiming poetry set to music was not invented by Sitwell, although her performances of *Façade* gave it its most distinguished form. Among the important precedents for the form were Arnold Schoenberg's *Pierrot Lunaire* (1912) and Erik Satie's *Parade* (1917). Sitwell's interest in modern art was considerable, and *Façade* should be considered an integral part of the international movement that embraced poetry, painting, and dance. Half of the poems that eventually found a place in *Façade* were composed earlier, while the others were written for music by William Walton. The poems were recited through a Sengerphone, a large megaphone with a mouthpiece. Since the Sengerphone and the speaker were concealed behind a curtain, the spoken voice achieved simultaneous clarity and impersonality. Sitwell considered the poems abstract: patterns in sound or virtuoso exercises. She saw them as explorations of the qualities of rhythm, in which meaning was secondary. There are obvious connections between this view of the poetry and the development of various schools of abstraction in painting. By allying herself with this forthright modernism, Sitwell was emphasizing her break with the Georgians. She was also exploring the possible application of the means of one medium to another. While this practice had already become frequent in the poetry of the French symbolists and their successors, nothing quite like it had been seen in English verse.

The poems were not sung but read, thereby emphasizing the inherently rhythmic quality of spoken verse. Sitwell explored the possibilities of rhyme, alliteration, assonance, and what she termed "colour." Her imagery was also startling, heightened by condensation. Sitwell linked her condensed imagery to Emanuel Swedenborg's theory of correspondences, which is given its most permanent poetic form in Charles-Pierre Baudelaire's poem of that name. The poems in *Façade* create striking synesthetic effects, as in these lines from "Waltz":

> Her hair seemed gold trees on the honey-cell sand
> When the thickest gold spangles, on deep water
>   seen,
> Were like twanging guitar and cold mandoline.

Many of the poems have titles linking them to popular dances ("Fox Trot," "Polka," "Mazurka"—this last poem not set to music by Walton), and the musical settings often enhance their parodic character. "I do like to be beside the Seaside" is set to a music-hall melody that underscores the poem's satire of romance and seduction. The comic feminine rhymes and lilting anapests contribute to the poem's jaunty effect:

> For the lady and her friend from Le Touquet
> In the very shady trees upon the sand
> Were plucking a white satin bouquet
> Of foam, while the sand's brassy band
> Blared in the wind.

The poems of *Façade* seem very much a part of the post–World War I decade. As Sitwell claimed, they show an extraordinary mastery of sound and rhythm, but they also reflect the sense of disillusionment and accelerated movement that characterized those years of social transformation. Drawing on Russian ballet as well as fairy tale and romance, Sitwell created a poetic world that vigorously asserted its modernity. The targets are many, ranging from the upper-middle class of "En Famille" to the lingering Calvinism of "Scotch Rhapsody" or Alfred, Lord Tennyson and his poetic imitators in "When Sir Beelze-

bub." The early poems and their public performances in 1923, 1926, and 1928 established Edith Sitwell as a leader in the movement of the Young Turks. It was she who consolidated the forces of revolution in modern poetry and brought them to public notice, and by so doing she confirmed the death of Victorianism.

Although published the year after *Façade*, the poems of *Bucolic Comedies* (1923) were for the most part written earlier. Nonetheless, there are similarities to the poems of *Façade*, despite Sitwell's statement that there are no technical experiments in *Bucolic Comedies*. The fairy-tale rhyming couplets of "Aubade" recall (or anticipate) some of the rhythms of *Façade*, and there is already considerable use of feminine rhymes (or partial rhymes) for comic effect: pollard/dullard, noodle/flopdoodle, affection/direction, Palestrina/leaner. The overall tone of the volume is far more serious and elegiac. Several of the poems introduce autobiographical elements, which became increasingly important in her work. The poems are based on memory of an enchanted world, but they also recognize the living death of that world which Sitwell associated with her childhood at Renishaw Hall and at Scarborough, the seat of the Londesboroughs. In "Winter," Osbert Sitwell is present as Dagobert, and Edith is five-year-old Anne in the frozen and strangely blighted world of the "Countess of L—." The final lines of the poem capture the sterility of her family's world and give an important indication of her development of the central images of gold and fire as symbols of creative energy:

> Can this be Eternity?—snow peach-cold,
> Sleeping and rising and growing old,
>
> While she lies embalmed in the fire's gold sheen,
> Like a cross wasp in a ripe nectarine,
>
> And the golden seed of the fire droops dead
> And ripens not in the heart or head!

In "The Man with the Green Patch," Sitwell's critique of her parents' world takes more specific form: although they provide access to a timeless and fairy-tale world, her parents are each blind in one eye and unable or unwilling to see

> The real world, terrible and old,
> Where seraphs in the mart are sold
> And fires from Bedlam's madness flare
> Like blue palm-trees in desert air;
> The prisons where the maimed men pined
> Because their mothers bore them blind.

Page from the manuscript for "At the Crossroads" (Elizabeth Salter, Edith Sitwell, *1979)*

Despite this strong indictment of the spiritual blindness of her family's class, Sitwell's attitude toward her past was always ambivalent, for her upbringing had also permitted her access to a timeless world of pure music:

> For there my youth passed like a sleep,
> Yet in my heart, still murmuring deep,
> The small green airs from Eternity,
> Murmuring softly, never die.

Troy Park (1925) is the major collection of poems dealing with her family and her relationship to the past. In "Colonel Fantock," probably

the most successful of the poems in this volume, Osbert, Sacheverell, and Edith Sitwell are present as "Dagobert, and Peregrine and I," and Colonel Fantock is a real person, a retired military man who had served as tutor to the Sitwells. Although parts of the poem are devoted to reminiscence, much of the poem is a meditation upon death. Colonel Fantock is seen as the comic character he apparently was, but he is also remembered for his magical qualities, his ability to transform reality into legend:

> For us he wandered over each old lie,
> Changing the flowering hawthorn, full of bees,

Into the silver helm of Hercules,
For us defended Troy from the top stair
Outside the nursery.

The mood is turned into grief, though, as Sitwell
recounts the day that Colonel Fantock overhears
a remark about his advancing age. On that day
the magic is broken, and awareness of death has
gained the "first citadel."

"The Little Ghost Who Died for Love" is narrated by Deborah Churchill (1678-1708), who
was hanged for shielding her lover in a duel. Sitwell drew upon historical material to evoke a romantic world that is doomed to destruction, and although the poem is cast as an elegy for the dead
woman, it is also a prophetic poem, warning of
the impending death of a society that has so punished love. The poem shifts from mourning lines
of great simplicity to evocation of spring and rebirth in bright lines of exuberant imagery, as if
to state its truth that good and evil, beauty and ugliness, are contained one within the other. In her
final words, Deborah proclaims her victory: "for
it is not I / But this old world, is sick and soon
must die!"

During the 1920s, the period of her greatest creative activity, Sitwell lived in a flat in
Bayswater, London, with Helen Rootham, her former governess, although she spent the summers
at Renishaw Hall. She participated with her brothers in the literary life of the capital and entertained on her own. Their friends included T. S.
Eliot and Aldous Huxley, although there was a
break with Huxley in 1922, following the publication of a story by him which included a very unkind portrait of Osbert. Edith was an admirer of
Eliot's work, but she was also concerned by the
fact that *The Waste Land* (1922) got far better reviews and far more critical attention than her
books. Although an acquaintance of Virginia
Woolf's, she was never more than on the fringes
of the Bloomsbury Group, which she thought of
as somewhat too "closely serried" for her rather independent tastes; nonetheless, there were affinities between the Sitwells and the Bloomsbury
Group, including their reaction against the Edwardian establishment and their strong opposition to war.

Throughout the 1920s Sitwell's poems displayed a mixture of elegiac memory with the
sense of a world lost through the recognition of
evil. Her long poem *The Sleeping Beauty* (1924)
evokes the enchanted fairy-tale world "of ghostly
flowers, all poignant with spring rain. / Smelling

of youth that will not come again." But this
world is clearly departed, and the poet recognizes her need to go beyond these memories, to
be reborn out of the timeless world of the dream
and into reality: "And now the brutish forests
close around / The beauty sleeping in enchanted
ground." The culmination of this development toward a position as a poet of social commentary occurred with the publication of the long poem
Gold Coast Customs (1929). Although many of the
poem's forms are obviously reminiscent of her earlier work (the elaborate use of both end rhymes
and internal rhymes, as well as strong rhythmic
patterns), the purpose to which these forms is
put is much more resolutely critical. Sitwell had
begun her move from the satiric and parodic to
the revolutionary and visionary.

Gold Coast Customs interweaves the funeral
customs of the Ashantee nation and contemporary society life of London. Sitwell's contemporary figure, Lady Bamburgher, is a symbol of the
moral and social corruption that lies beneath the
surface of fashionable life. The poem's strong
beat and clear voice give a striking portrayal of a
historical pattern of decay and betrayal. It concludes, however, with a vision of transformation
and salvation:

Yet the time will come
To the heart's dark slum
When the rich man's gold and the rich man's wheat
Will grow in the street, that the starved may eat,—
And the sea of the rich will give up its dead—
And the last blood and fire from my side will be
    shed.
For the fires of God go marching on.

As Jack Lindsay, a Marxist critic, has noted in his
important introduction to *Façade and Other Poems,
1920-1935* (1950), *Gold Coast Customs* represented
"the deepest—almost the only—political poetry"
of the age in England, but Sitwell was never to
be recognized as a political poet, perhaps because of her public reputation as a performer
and aesthete, perhaps because of her social position. It is even more likely that admiration for
Sitwell's political poetry was withheld because her
sense of injustice and impending revolution was almost always accompanied, as in this poem, with religious imagery of rebirth at a time when religious faith in poetry had become unpopular.
What was only a suggestion in *Gold Coast Customs*
would later become the keynote of her poetry.

Technically, *Gold Coast Customs* is a major accomplishment. It illustrates the almost complete

Edith, Sacheverell, and Osbert Sitwell (photograph by Baron)

abandonment of straightforward narrative line. Instead, the poem is structured around a series of contrasts, its effects cumulative rather than progressive. Geoffrey Singleton has linked Sitwell's practice to the film techniques of Sergey Eisenstein, showing her mastery of montage to accomplish rapid transitions back and forth among the levels (or tiers, as she called them) of the poem. Sitwell calls upon her reader to follow the action on various planes simultaneously by cutting from one to the other and hence by suggesting the interrelationships among the various periods or levels of civilization. The poem has also been said to have a polyphonic structure, bringing together several separate, although related, voice lines.

If the decade of the 1920s represented a period of great poetic advance and considerable public acclaim, the following decade was one of relative silence and personal loss. Sitwell devoted a large part of her energies to caring for Helen Rootham, who was seriously ill and would never recover. What writing Sitwell did was primarily in prose, which does, however, shed considerable

light on her interests as a poet. In 1930 she produced a biography, *Alexander Pope*, in which she indicated her sympathy for this lonely man with a misshapen body and with whom she identified herself repeatedly. That identification was not only personal, but, more important, poetic: she identified Pope as an important part of the English poetic tradition from which she sprang; the failure to appreciate Pope adequately thus indicated her own fate at the hands of the critics. She praised Pope above all for his "rhetoric and formalism" and his refusal to give in to the hopeful formulas of his day. He was also praised for his ability to join intellect and personal expression; as Sitwell put it, "a poem begins in the poet's head, and then grows in his blood." Her other major work of prose during these years was her novel, *I Live Under a Black Sun* (1937), based on the life of Jonathan Swift. Her structure is radical: a montage which shifts from the Middle Ages to World War I, moving Swift adroitly through time and place. Swift's acid satires and bleak vision of human folly were a perfect expression of her own state of mind. Her de-

spair at the madness of war broadened into a recognition of mankind's self-destructive nature and
was sustained by her own sense of personal loss.

Sitwell lived mostly in Paris with Helen
Rootham from 1932 until Rootham's death in
1938, and in Paris she made the acquaintance,
through Gertrude Stein, of the great love of her
life, the surrealist painter Pavel Tchelitchew.
Since Tchelitchew was homosexual, the love remained unfulfilled, and Sitwell often felt betrayed by him. Nonetheless, she remained a constant friend and supporter over many years and
attempted to find buyers for Tchelitchew's paintings. Since Osbert Sitwell was also homosexual, it
is certain that Edith Sitwell often moved in a homosexual milieu; most of her biographers believe,
however, that she preferred to ignore this fact.
The one poem which Sitwell wrote during the
1930s, "Romance," is a moving testimony to the
power of the love which she felt for Tchelitchew.
The poem is written largely in heroic couplets; Sitwell draws upon all her poetic resources to subtly
work within the iambic-pentameter line to create
a subtly rich harmony of sound and rhythm. The
imagery is lush and erotic:

> Green were the pomp and pleasure of the shade
> Wherein they dwelt; like country temples green
> The huge leaves bear a dark-mosaic's sheen
> Like gold on forest temples richly laid.
>
> In that smooth darkness, the gourds dark as caves
> Hold thick gold honey for their fountain waves,
> Figs, dark and wrinkled as Silenus, hold
> Rubies and garnets, and the melons cold
> Waves dancing . . .

The poem also recognizes the dominion of time
and loss, and finds strength out of suffering; although recognizing that winter must fall and that
"I must wake alone / With a void coffin of sad
flesh and bone," nonetheless the poet finds consolation in memory's "strange perfume."

Sitwell's other prose works during this period include a biography of Queen Victoria
(1936), a book about Bath (1932), and *The English Eccentrics* (1933), a celebration of the kind of
deliberate and outrageous nonconformity that
she was making her own hallmark. For Sitwell,
who had always suffered from a sense that she
was an inadequate woman because she was
not beautiful enough, learned to make of her
unusual appearance an element of theatrical
beauty, which is reflected in the portraits of her.
Cecil Beaton turned her into a gauzy romantic

Edith Sitwell, 1956 (photograph by Baron)

creature, Tchelitchew into a brooding Renaissance Madonna. Her own clothing was chosen to
reflect timelessness; heavy brocade dresses, tur-
bans, and enormous jewels gave her a dignity
and a kind of impersonality that were necessary
to complete her rebellion against the Edwardian
upper class.

The outbreak of World War II confirmed
Sitwell's sense of cultural despair and gave renewed impetus to her search for emblems of healing and renewal. "Still Falls the Rain" (in *Street
Songs*, 1942) is significantly subtitled "Night and
Dawn," a reference not only to the actual times
of the poem but to the hope for spiritual rebirth
out of agony. The form of the poem is loose; although the rhythms are largely iambic, the lines
are varied in length from two feet to seven feet.
The title phrase, with its extraordinary power and sonority, is repeated seven times. It
is rhymed, significantly, with "human brain,"
"pain," and "lain," and it acts as the organizing
principle for a series of repetitions based on paral-
lelism underscoring human failing and sin. The
sixth stanza offers a dramatic reversal, with a recognition of the Crucifixion and its offering of redemption, and the final stanza concludes with its

line ironically echoing the dominant chord, "Still do I love, still shed my innocent light, my Blood, for thee." Although the poem is described as a work about the air raids, it uses that rain of destruction as a representative of man's self-destruction, what Sitwell calls "the self-murdered heart, the wounds of the sad uncomprehending dark." Out of the agony of a nation, Sitwell turned to faith as the means for human recovery.

Other poems in *Street Songs* are equally powerful; the volume has been widely hailed as Sitwell's finest. Several, brilliantly blending Sitwell's personal feelings with cultural myths, are poems of age (Sitwell was in her fifties) and of hope, poems indicating that Sitwell has passed through her crises of the 1930s just as she believed mankind might pass through the crises of the war. Central to these poems is the symbolism of wheat, most often associated with gold. For Sitwell took as her principal persona in these poems a harvest goddess, offering birth from within herself. While a poem such as "Invocation" shows some relationship to Eliot's *The Waste Land* in its turn to myths of renewal and in its images of sterility ("the Lost Men / Who ask the city stones if they are bread / And the stones of the city weep"), it lacks the deep pessimism of Eliot's poem. "Invocation" sees in the goddess the hope that was lacking in the civilization of darkness that surrounded her. The poems in *Street Songs* gain power by their dramatic-monologue form, in which Sitwell speaks through the voice of the goddess. "Eurydice" is perhaps the finest of the series, melding personal love with the evocative power of myth. Although Eurydice has been touched by the freezing hand of Death, she finds recuperation within herself: "I cast the grandeur of Death away / And homeward came to the small things of Love, the building of the hearth, the kneading of daily bread." Led away from death by her lover (Orpheus or Adonis), she comes out of the tomb and into the light: "I turned to greet you— / And when I touched your mouth, it was the Sun."

Sitwell's great power as a love poet has been inadequately recognized. It is hard to think of another poet of the twentieth century, except perhaps her disciple Dylan Thomas, who has so powerfully written of the ecstasy of personal love and its power to transform. Sitwell's "Mary Stuart to James Boswell (Casket Letter No. II)" is an example of her love poetry at its finest. She is able to transform herself into the historic person and make her come alive. There is no better way of capturing the excess, and the grandeur, of love than these concluding lines in which Mary is transported by the vision of her love:

> But how should Pity stand between you and me!
> The Devil sunder us from our mates, and God
> Knit us together
> Until nor man nor devil could tell lover from lover
> In our heaven of damnation! Could these sunder
>   our clay,
> Or the seas of our blood? As well might they part
>   the fires
> That would burn to the bottom of Hell . . . . But
>   there is no Hell—
> We have kissed it away.

Sitwell had little sympathy for female poets—she singled out only Sappho, Christina Rossetti, and Emily Dickinson for partial exoneration from her general scorn of incompetence and flabbiness—but her own work depended upon a deep sense of affinity for women, such as Mary Stuart, destroyed for faith and love. And "Mary Stuart to James Boswell" does show a certain likeness to Dickinson's "I cannot live with you" despite obvious differences of poetic technique.

The end of the war brought the horror of the atom-bomb explosions in Japan and prompted *The Shadow of Cain* (1947), Sitwell's memorable poem of destruction and regeneration. Still echoing Eliot, Sitwell wrote of the alienation between men which had given rise to universal sterility. The poem is set in "that Spring when there were no flowers" and joins imagery of metal and darkness to convey the evil of man's murderous impulse: "And now the Earth lies flat beneath the shade of an iron wing." The gold which had been the alchemical symbol of perfection and the natural color of the wheat has been transformed into human greed, as men seek their own power and wealth and abandon their concern for their brothers. But in the midst of this horror, in the rain of destruction, there is also the potential for renewed fertility, as in the blood of Christ; there is new life for man. In the midst of destruction is renewed hope: "He walks upon the Seas of Blood, He comes in the terrible Rain."

In 1948 Edith and Osbert Sitwell undertook a lecture tour of the United States which lasted almost six months. It was highly successful and contributed greatly to her reputation in America. She made a new recording of *Façade*, and she was the guest of honor at a party given by the Gotham Book Mart, to which Marianne Moore,

Randall Jarrell, Elizabeth Bishop, Gore Vidal, Tennessee Williams, and W. H. Auden, among others, came. The success of this tour led to a second one in 1950, which included a visit to Hollywood, where she read from *Macbeth*. Her interest in Shakespeare had grown considerably over the past few years, and several of the plays, particularly *King Lear*, had a marked influence on her work. Her interest in the Elizabethan period included a fascination with Elizabeth I, which gave rise to her book *Fanfare for Elizabeth* (1946) and the ill-fated plans for a Hollywood film based on it, to be directed by George Cukor.

Largely unrecognized or scorned during her earlier years, Edith Sitwell was heaped with honors in her last years. In 1951 she received an honorary Litt.D. from Oxford (of which she was very proud, although she never forgave her father for a conventional girl's upbringing that had prevented her from obtaining a proper education and knowledge of Greek and Latin). Three years later, in 1954, she was made a Dame Commander of the Order of the British Empire. Her seventieth birthday was celebrated by a luncheon given by the *Sunday Times* and her seventy-fifth by a concert at the Royal Festival Hall, which included Benjamin Britten's setting of "Still Falls the Rain" as well as a performance of *Façade*. During these years she also worked hard on behalf of young artists whom she admired. She had always helped younger writers, beginning with Wilfred Owen and Dylan Thomas, and her new enthusiasms included Robert Lowell, Allen Ginsberg, and James Purdy.

In the meantime Sitwell's religious beliefs had intensified, and she decided to be accepted into the Roman Catholic church in 1955. She received instruction from Father Martin D'Arcy and was baptized at the Farm Street church in London. Evelyn Waugh and Roy Campbell were her godfathers. The church provided consolation for her during her last years of loneliness and ill health. She received the last rites of the church before her death in London on 11 December 1964.

Critical appraisal of her work has been mixed. Babette Deutsch praises the "luxurious beauty" of her poems but argues that sometimes they are hurt by an excess of richness, "an extravagance of imagery that sometimes almost overwhelms the poem." David Daiches, who sees her sources in the art and poetry of the seventeenth and eighteenth centuries, as well as in French symbolism, comments, "The deliberate confusion of the senses . . . the highly personal rococo images,

the painted artificiality, the playfulness alternating with a half-suppressed grimness, the dream quality hovering between farce and nightmare, the marshalling of bright and brittle phrases with deliberate disregard of their relation to each other, the carefully fantastic situations, the tom-tom rhythms, the preference for geometric rather than natural form, the clowning, the anarchy, the individuality—all these features of Edith Sitwell's poetry suggest a culture that has lost its roots and its normal function and as a result is being used as a quarry from which to dig up coloured counters that are tossed into the air with the skill of an expert conjuror yet in a mood of suppressed hysteria." Other poets have praised her extraordinary technical skills; Marianne Moore called her "a virtuoso of rhythm and accent" and "an expert of the condensed phrase."

Sitwell's reputation has always suffered from the exceptional success of *Façade*, which was often treated as if it were the only work she had ever written. Inadequate attention has been paid to her development as a social poet, as a religious poet, and as a visionary. Her career traces the development of English poetry from the immediate post-World War I period of brightness and jazzy rhythms through the political involvements of the 1930s and the return to spiritual values after World War II. Her technique evolved, and although she always remained a poet committed to the exploration of sound, she came to use sound patterns as an element in the construction of deep philosophic poems that reflect on her time and on man's condition. Edith Sitwell needs to be remembered not only as the bright young parodist of *Façade*, but as the angry chronicler of social injustice, as a poet who found forms adequate to the atomic age and its horrors, and as a foremost poet of love. Her work displays enormous range of subject and of form. With her contemporary Eliot she remains one of the most important voices of twentieth-century English poetry.

Bibliography:

Richard Fifoot, *A Bibliography of Edith, Osbert, and Sacheverell Sitwell*, revised edition (Hamden, Conn.: Archon, 1971).

Biographies:

John Lehmann, *A Nest of Tigers: The Sitwells in Their Times* (London: Macmillan, 1968);

John Pearson, *Façades: Edith, Osbert and Sacheverell Sitwell* (London: Macmillan, 1978); republished as *The Sitwells: A Family's Biography* (New York: Harcourt, Brace, Jovanovich, 1980);

Victoria Glendinning, *Edith Sitwell: A Unicorn Among Lions* (London: Weidenfeld & Nicolson, 1981; New York: Knopf, 1981);

G. A. Cevasco, *The Sitwells: Edith, Osbert, and Sacheverell* (Boston: Twayne, 1987).

References:

C. M. Bowra, *Edith Sitwell* (Monaco: Lyrebird, 1947);

James Brophy, *Edith Sitwell: The Symbolist Order* (Carbondale: Southern Illinois University Press, 1968);

David Daiches, *Poetry and the Modern World* (Chicago: University of Chicago Press, 1940), pp. 85-89;

Babette Deutsch, *Poetry in Our Times* (New York: Columbia University Press, 1956), pp. 220-228;

G. S. Fraser, *The Modern Writer and His World* (London: Deutsch, 1964), pp. 283-286;

Horace Gregory, "The 'Vita-Nuova' of Baroque Art in the Recent Poetry of Edith Sitwell," *Poetry*, 66 (June 1945): 148-156;

John Lehmann, Introduction to *Selected Poems of Edith Sitwell* (London: Macmillan, 1965);

Jack Lindsay, Introduction to *Façade and Other Poems, 1920-1935* (London: Duckworth, 1950);

Ralph J. Mills, *Edith Sitwell* (Grand Rapids, Mich.: Eerdmans, 1966);

Marianne Moore, "Edith Sitwell, Virtuoso" in her *A Marianne Moore Reader* (New York: Viking, 1965), pp. 210-215;

Vivian de Sola Pinto, *Crisis in English Poetry: 1880-1940* (London: Hutchinson, 1967), pp. 190-193, 205-208;

John Press, *A Map of Modern English Verse* (London: Oxford University Press, 1969), pp. 157-159;

Geoffrey Singleton, *Edith Sitwell: The Hymn to Life* (London: Fortune Press, 1960);

José Garcia Villa, ed., *A Celebration for Edith Sitwell* (New York: New Directions, 1948; republished, Freeport, N.Y.: Books for Libraries Press, 1972).

Papers:

Edith Sitwell's manuscripts are in the Harry Ransom Humanities Research Center at the University of Texas, Austin.

C. P. Snow

(15 October 1905 - 1 July 1980)

This entry was written by David Shusterman (Indiana University Southeast) for
DLB 15: British Novelists, 1930-1959: Part Two.

See also the Snow entry in DLB 77: British Mystery
Writers, 1920-1939.

SELECTED BOOKS: *Death Under Sail* (London:
    Heinemann, 1932);
New Lives for Old, anonymous (London: Gollancz,
    1933);
The Search (London: Gollancz, 1934; Indianapolis
    & New York: Bobbs-Merrill, 1935; revised
    edition, London: Macmillan, 1958; New
    York: Scribners, 1958);
Strangers and Brothers (London: Faber & Faber,
    1940; New York: Scribners, 1960); repub-
    lished as *George Passant* (New York: Scrib-
    ners, 1970);
The Light and the Dark (London: Faber & Faber,
    1947; New York: Macmillan, 1948);
Time of Hope (London: Faber & Faber, 1949; New
    York: Macmillan, 1950);
The Masters (London: Macmillan, 1951; New
    York: Macmillan, 1951);
The New Men (London: Macmillan, 1954; New
    York: Scribners, 1954);
Homecomings (London: Macmillan, 1956); repub-
    lished as *Homecoming* (New York: Scribners,
    1956);
The Conscience of the Rich (London: Macmillan,
    1958; New York: Scribners, 1958);
The Two Cultures and the Scientific Revolution (Lon-
    don & New York: Cambridge University
    Press, 1959); enlarged as *The Two Cultures
    and A Second Look* (London & New York:
    Cambridge University Press, 1964);
The Affair (London: Macmillan, 1960; New York:
    Scribners, 1960);
Science and Government (London: Oxford Univer-
    sity Press, 1961; Cambridge, Mass.: Harvard
    University Press, 1961);
Corridors of Power (London: Macmillan, 1964;
    New York: Scribners, 1964);
Variety of Men (London: Macmillan, 1967; New
    York: Scribners, 1967);
The Sleep of Reason (London: Macmillan, 1968;
    New York: Scribners, 1968);

C. P. Snow, 1950 (photograph by Paul Popper)

The State of Siege (London: Macmillan, 1969; New
    York: Scribners, 1969);
Last Things (London: Macmillan, 1970; New
    York: Scribners, 1970);
Public Affairs (London: Macmillan, 1971; New
    York: Scribners, 1971);
The Malcontents (London: Macmillan, 1972; New
    York: Scribners, 1972);
In Their Wisdom (London: Macmillan, 1974; New
    York: Scribners, 1974);
Trollope: His Life and Art (London: Macmillan,
    1975; New York: Scribners, 1975);
The Realists (London: Macmillan, 1978; New
    York: Scribners, 1978);

A Coat of Varnish (London: Macmillan, 1979; New York: Scribners, 1979).

C. P. Snow's place in twentieth-century letters is unusual; no other major writer in any creative literary genre established himself also in science and in the high ranks of governmental and public service. And in an age in which most leading literary figures prided themselves in being outside the establishment, Snow was almost from first to last securely within it; as such, he was frequently scorned and occasionally praised. But his position enabled him to understand what he called the "corridors of power" and to write perceptively of those who would seek to gain and use power. The main theme of his novels was the uses and abuses of power: power in government and outside—in science, in academe, in business, in personal relationships.

Charles Percy Snow was born in Leicester, England, on 15 October 1905 to William Edward and Ada Sophia Robinson Snow; his father worked in a shoe factory. Like most industrial families of the late nineteenth century, the Snows had faith in the importance of education as the chief means of enabling their progeny to rise above their working-class environment. C. P. Snow is a prime example of the success of this faith. Snow said more than once that, very early in life, he wanted to become a man of letters, but because his school in Leicester, Alderman Newton's Grammar School, did not have an area of specialization in the arts, he decided to specialize in science instead. He became remarkably adept in science and eventually became an important figure in that field. His knowledge of science and his lifelong association with leading scientists shaped his viewpoints on literature, man, and society. He won a scholarship to the University College of Leicester, graduating with a B.S. and receiving first-class honors in chemistry in 1927, and in 1928, after receiving a master's degree in physics from the same university, he was awarded another scholarship to Cambridge University to do research in physics. While still a student in Leicester he wrote his first novel, "Youth Searching" (an appropriate title), but destroyed every copy of the manuscript; it was never submitted to a publisher. At first his work in science was more successful; his first paper on the infrared investigation of molecular structure was published in 1929. In 1930 he was awarded a Ph.D. in physics and was elected a fellow in Christ's College, Cambridge, where he became associated with Lord Ernest Rutherford, who was England's greatest living physicist. During the 1920s and 1930s Cambridge became, according to Snow, "the metropolis of experimental physics for the entire world."

The young Snow became caught up in what he described as Rutherford's optimistic tone: "creatively confident, generous, argumentative, lavish, and full of hope." Rutherford had discovered the structure of the atom, and science was believed to be on the threshold of immense discoveries that would eventually reshape man's world. This attitude was in marked contrast to the tone of T. S. Eliot, F. R. Leavis, and most other leading literary people during the 1920s and 1930s, as well as during much of the rest of the twentieth century. If scientists have been optimistic, full of hope, literary people have tended to be pessimistic, not confident of man's abilities to solve the problems facing society. Undoubtedly, Snow's literary stance was molded by his early indoctrination in the prevailing optimistic tone of science.

While working in science, he continued writing. In 1932, when Snow was twenty-seven, he had his first success: *Death Under Sail*, a detective novel, was published. The next year an entirely different kind of novel, a science fantasy, *New Lives for Old*, was published anonymously. Though it has faults, it is better than a large portion of the novels in this genre, but even many years later Snow did not want this novel to be included among the works to which he would put his name. Since several characters make scathing comments about the stupidity and complacency of university dons, a few critics have suggested that the young Snow was fearful that the novel would detract from his chances of getting ahead in the university world. Because governmental leaders are depicted as corrupt incompetents, the older Snow, more balanced in his attitudes toward these leaders, may have regretted that he had ever indulged himself in such a negative attitude.

In 1934 *The Search* was published and drew some laudatory notices. With three novels in three years, Snow was well on his way, at age twenty-nine, to success in his literary career. "Publishers were bidding at me," Snow wrote later. *The Search* is about the struggles, disappointments, and success of a young scientist, a subject which Snow knew well. Success comes early to Arthur Miles at Cambridge; he delivers a paper before the Royal Society and is convinced that he is well on his way to greatness in science, but eventually, after a trip to the Continent and a lot of soul-searching, he decides to give up science and become a writer. Unlike Arthur, who has been ruthlessly honest in his scientific experiments, another scientist in the novel suppresses facts so that his experiments will be found successful. Arthur knows about this falsification, but he decides not to expose the dishonest scientist; his rationale is that eventually good scientists will expose the dishonest one. *The Search* is one of the better novels about science in our century though it has had its detractors.

Shortly after the publication of *The Search*, while on vacation in France, Snow conceived of the idea for a series of novels, and it was not long before he became engaged in writing the masterworks of his career later to be called, collectively, "Strangers and Brothers." During the time he was writing these works, he continued as a fellow, and then later became a tutor, at Christ's College, Cambridge; and for two years, 1938-1940, he edited *Discovery*, a journal of science. The first novel of the series, *Strangers and Brothers* (republished as *George Passant* in 1970), came out in 1940, the first full year of World War II. Snow had already been appointed, in autumn 1939, by the Royal Society to a subcommittee to organize scientists in behalf of the war effort, and in 1940 he officially joined the government in the Ministry of Labour to continue this work. In 1942 he took the job of director of technical personnel for the same ministry. In this position he was in charge of coordinating all the activities of Britain's scientists engaged in the war effort. During his six years in this service, Snow came to know the inner circles of government. Though there were other themes in the "Strangers and Brothers" series, it was the theme of men in the corridors of power that enhanced, more than any other, the later novels in the series, beginning with *The Light and the Dark* (1947).

The whole sequence of "Strangers and Brothers" is narrated by Lewis Eliot, who was born in 1905, the same year as Snow. Though dissimilarities exist between the author and his narrator—the main one being that Lewis Eliot is a lawyer—there are some striking similarities. The chief of these is that the narrator becomes a member of the Labour party and lives securely, for the most part, within the establishment. Though it may be unwise to assert that Eliot's reactions throughout the sequence are Snow's, many readers of the sequence have nevertheless made this assertion. Certainly there is not much evidence, except of the

most superficial kind, that the two are very different. In any case, though each of the eleven novels in the sequence tells a different story, many of the same characters appear and reappear, and all are observed by Lewis Eliot. His reactions to what occurred in English life during about fifty years of the twentieth century are the binding element of the entire sequence, the inner design, which Snow asserted "consists of a resonance between what Lewis Eliot sees and what he feels."

In *Strangers and Brothers*, Snow, not surprisingly, deals with a situation in a Midland town (similar to his hometown) from 1925 to 1933. In 1925 Eliot is twenty. Here, and throughout the series, the ages of the author and his narrator at a given time are the same or almost the same, another reason for the suspicion that Eliot is the alter ego for Snow. In *Strangers and Brothers* the main character is George Passant, who is a chief clerk in a law office and a part-time law instructor in the local college. He is probably the most dominant character in any of the novels of the sequence, having gathered around him a party of young people, like Eliot, whom he refers to as the "Group." Passant preaches a mild form of socialism, urging them not to be dominated by the restrictions of the older generation who have, they believe, made a mess of government. While Snow has been associated with the establishment, this novel (and perhaps a few other hints earlier) is probably evidence that, before he had left his hometown, he had flirted with an antagonism to the ruling groups of society. Snow, like many other writers, is interested in rebels; they are usually by far the most fascinating people for a creative mind to develop. George Passant is only the first of a group of rebels whom we find in Snow's "Strangers and Brothers" sequence.

Passant's rebelliousness is very mild. There were undoubtedly many like him in Europe and America in the period after World War I; the young people in that period had seen what had happened to others like them in the war and were determined that nothing like a great war would ever take place again. George preaches freedom for the young against the power structure and holds out the hope for his group that they can remake society and weaken the hold of the "damned lives" of the elderly. His one act of overt rebellion is the defense of Jack Cotery, a member of the group, who has, Passant believes, been unjustly deprived of a scholarship at the college where Passant teaches law. George defeats the college's administrators, but his victory is only a partial one because the administrators agree to grant Cotery a scholarship for only one more year.

Only part of *Strangers and Brothers* is about the incident of Cotery's scholarship, however. Most of the rest of the novel concerns the indictment of Cotery, Passant, and a young woman named Olive on the grounds of fraudulent conspiracy and the obtaining of money by false pretense. Lewis Eliot, meanwhile, having become a lawyer, has gone to London to practice his profession. But near the end of 1932 he goes back to his hometown to help defend Passant and the others. Being aware of the antagonism of the leading citizens of the town (whom Passant calls the "bellwethers," the term *establishment* not yet having been coined) toward young rebels, Eliot engages the services of an older attorney, Herbert Getliffe, to present the case to the jury. Getliffe makes a clever address to the jury, agreeing with their prejudices against the young, though at the same time insisting that the wasted lives of the young, like his defendants, have been brought about by defects in society. These young defendants are found innocent and are freed, but Passant's group is ruined. Passant himself is dismissed from his position at the college, and his chances of becoming a partner in a law firm are considerably diminished.

What may appear to be a curious ambiguity in Snow's method of narration for the series appears during this first novel, especially at the conclusion. The stories are presented entirely from Eliot's point of view—what he has seen directly and what he has learned indirectly from others, including documents that he has read—and everything is thus filtered through his mind; nevertheless, Snow makes an attempt to maintain an objective approach, which is generally easier to achieve by using the third-person method of narration. There are times, such as in the conclusion to *Strangers and Brothers,* when many readers become exasperated with Lewis Eliot for not committing himself and for, seemingly, withholding what may be important evidence from the eyes of the reader. Thus, the reader is, more often than is ordinary in a first-person narration, forced to make his own judgments about some matters. Many times Eliot unburdens himself and overwhelms the reader with everything that he sees and learns; at other times he is strangely reticent. Throughout the sequence of novels, the author, having committed himself to the limited first-person method of narration, often seems to have

wished that he had employed third-person narration, but he seems afraid to change in midstream. Near the end of this first book, Olive privately informs Eliot that Passant is indeed guilty of deception and fraud and has been freed because of Getliffe's clever approach to the jury. And in the conclusion, as Eliot and Passant walk together, Eliot imagines a voice saying in Passant's heart, "Your enemies are right. You've deceived yourself all this time." Yet Eliot not only tells of George's hope for the future but of his own commitment to George's hopes. In his heart he thus exonerates George for what he had done: "He could still warm himself and everyone round him with his own hope." In connection with this curiosity is a corollary: Eliot often refuses to make value judgments about some aspects of his story, though at other times he does not hesitate to do so. One is often left trying to understand just how Eliot—and Snow—would have one react to some important aspect of his subject. It is not clear whether the reader is supposed to appreciate Passant, to feel that he was a great person all along even though Snow definitely shows the grave weaknesses in his character. Of course, in defense of this method, certainly one of the themes of this novel sequence is the self-deception in the human heart, as shown by Eliot's study of himself. Nevertheless, readers have often felt that Snow sometimes carries his method of objectivity too far for a first-person story. Despite this fault, *Strangers and Brothers* is one of the best novels in the series.

During the war years the first overt recognition of Snow's work for the government came in his being made a Commander of the Order of the British Empire (C.B.E.) in 1943. In 1944 he became director of scientific personnel for the English Electric Company, a post he held in conjunction with his governmental duties. In 1945 Snow became civil service commissioner, a post he held until 1960, and in 1947 he became a member of the board of directors of the English Electric Company. In that year the second novel of the "Strangers and Brothers" sequence was published.

The events of *The Light and the Dark* take place from 1935 to 1943. One critic has called this book Snow's "black novel," since it reflects the tragedy not only of the leading character, Roy Calvert, but also the tragedy of England's drift toward the great conflagration of World War II. Lewis Eliot identifies himself more closely with Calvert than with anyone else in the series except with his first wife, Sheila. In *The Light and the Dark,* Snow abandons his attempt at an objective approach almost entirely; nowhere else in the sequence is the narration as subjective. The reason is, as Eliot says, that the friendship he had with Roy Calvert was the deepest of his life. (If a real person served as a model for Calvert, Snow never openly divulged his name.)

For the first time in the series Cambridge is the main setting. Roy is a don and at twenty-five should be happy: he is wealthy, has had successful love affairs, and has received the admiration of his colleagues for his work in languages. But he drinks heavily, is extremely melancholy, and wavers between the dark and light aspects of life. His melancholy derives from his discovery about the Manichees, a third-century Christian heretical group. Roy is the only scholar in the world to have deciphered a variety of Middle Persian known as Early Soghdian and has translated a liturgy of the Manichees. As he says, "The religion of the Manichees tried to give men peace against the flesh. In its cosmology, the whole of creation is a battle of the light against the dark. Man's spirit is part of the light, and his flesh of the dark. The battle sways from side to side. . . . The religion was the most subtle and complex representation of guilt."

Eliot watches over Calvert (one critic refers to Eliot's "mother hen complex") during much of the novel and several times is acutely disturbed when he sees Calvert's "manic-depressive behavior." Roy's wavering between light and dark during his time at Cambridge before the outbreak of World War II is sometimes comic but most often pathetic. Eliot asserts often that Roy has a many-sided nature and is a deep person, more complex than anyone he has ever known or would ever know. But to most of the other dons in the Cambridge college (and to many readers) he seems an immature and ridiculous figure, an arrested adolescent. He does not impinge on the reader's mind with as much effect as George Passant, and he is not as successfully drawn.

The most successful part of the book is in the latter half, when Calvert is in Germany flirting philosophically with the Nazis. In him and in Eliot are represented the ambiguities of Britain in the late 1930s: on the one hand, there is the desire to maintain peace at almost any price, and, on the other, there is intense dismay at the heinous Nazi policies. In the desperate months before the war breaks out, Roy goes to Berlin and adopts almost all of Adolf Hitler's beliefs except for the Nazi antagonism toward the Jews. Eliot's

friends at Cambridge are alarmed, though at the same time some of the more conservative dons feel much in tune with Roy and would like to follow his path. Roy asks Eliot to come to Berlin, hoping that he can convert Eliot to Nazism, while Eliot hopes he can show Roy the error of his ways. For the only time in Eliot's friendship with Roy, they clash. After meeting a minister in one of the Third Reich's departments, a Dr. Schäder, Eliot makes a crucial statement about people in power: "No one is fit to be trusted with power. . . . Any man who has lived at all knows the follies and wickedness he's capable of. If he does not know it, he is not fit to govern others." Fortunately for the friendship between Roy and Eliot, the war begins, and Roy rushes back to England to avoid being declared a traitor. Much to Eliot's surprise, Roy joins the air force to fight for the nation that, shortly before, he had thought of betraying. It is then that he tells Eliot he had never really been taken in by the Nazis. "It was a feeble simulacrum of his search for God," Eliot asserts. But Eliot's assertion is not entirely convincing.

Roy Calvert is an interesting portrait, though seldom does he come alive. He is killed while fighting for England, and the book ends with a quiet memorial service at the Cambridge college. As often happens in Snow's novels, the minor portraits are more successful. Among these is that of Arthur Brown, the historian who, much to Eliot's surprise, believes with the docility of the masses all of the government's official reports about the successes of the English air force. Eliot, who has moved from Cambridge into the inner sanctum of the government, knows that much of Brown's faith is misplaced. He remembers Dr. Schäder's assertion to him in Berlin that in time everybody becomes convinced by governmental propaganda, and he considers it a frightening prospect for a democratic society if a famous, professional historian can be so easily duped.

The third novel in the sequence, *Time of Hope* (1949), goes back to 1914 and deals with Eliot's life until 1933. In the previous novel small snatches of Eliot's disastrous marriage are described, but here the marriage is depicted directly. Eliot and Sheila Knight are an ill-matched pair. Sheila is undoubtedly Snow's most vivid portrait of a woman. One of their troubles is sexual: Eliot has the natural desire to be satisfied sexually, but Sheila is frigid and cannot satisfy Eliot or any other man. Her torment is that she knows her own shortcomings. In a later novel, *Homecom-*

1918, and despite all the problems of the next decade, hope for a better society to come buoyed up the young. Despite his unhappy marriage, Eliot shares this viewpoint with George Passant.

The year after the publication of *Time of Hope* was a memorable one for Snow. Not only did he marry Johnson, but his play, *View Over the Park,* was produced. In addition he was writing what would become his most celebrated, and to many his best, novel, *The Masters* (1951). In this novel Snow goes back to 1937. What happens in this book is, as Lionel Trilling says, a paradigm of political life in general. In narrowing his scope to a struggle for the position of master of one Cambridge college and in limiting his action to only one year, Snow managed to escape the diffuseness which often mars many of his other novels.

Roy Calvert is again a central character in the novel, and he and his friend Lewis Eliot are backing Paul Jago, a literary scholar, for the position of master. Jago seems to them preferable to Crawford, despite the fact that the latter is one of the world's great biologists, a leading figure in the Royal Society, and one who has brought more renown to the college than almost any other don in its history. Crawford, to Eliot and Calvert, seems cold, lacking in the humane qualities that they cherish, almost the very personification of scientific objectivity and indifference. On the other hand, Jago, despite occasional flights of temper and of pride, seems to them a man of humbleness, warmth, and a genuine feeling for humanity.

The whole novel is about the two sides among the dons that back either Crawford or Jago. What was not apparent to any great extent when *The Masters* was published is more apparent now: that Snow was beginning to consider the issues that became overt in his later nonfictional work *The Two Cultures and the Scientific Revolution* (1959)—the relationship between the traditional literary culture and the newer scientific culture. The novel is thus more than a paradigm of political life: it is what the author conceived as a paradigm of the relationship between the two cultures. The end result is, given Snow's temperament and intellectual interests, predictable: Crawford wins the fierce struggle. In a later novel, *Corridors of Power* (1964), Snow's readers learn that Eliot has changed his mind during the intervening years and has decided that Crawford was the best choice after all, that choosing Jago would have been wrong because he lacked the proper temperament to be an evenhanded and

Dust jacket for Snow's 1949 book, the third novel in the Strangers and Brothers *sequence*

ings (1956), when this unhappy marriage is terminated by Sheila's suicide, it is bruited about by some of Eliot's friends that Sheila's trouble was lesbianism; and in that later novel her father hints to Eliot that the rumor is true. Eliot's feelings about Sheila in *Time of Hope* range from masochism to sadism: he absorbs mental and emotional torture from his wife and usually keeps coming back for more; but a few times he treats her brutally, once even taking her sexually in a manner tantamount to rape. Before she married Snow in 1950, Pamela Hansford Johnson wrote that Snow's conception of Eliot and Sheila's marriage came directly out of Marcel Proust: Eliot and Sheila are Marcel and Albertine in English disguise.

The book's title means that, to those growing up and coming of age during the decade, the 1920s was a time of hope. The war had ended in

firm leader of the college's faculty. In *The Masters* the dons do not line up strictly according to their fields of scholarship. Calvert is a language scholar, and Eliot is a legal don; they are joined in support of Jago by Arthur Brown and Charles Percy Chrystal, both historians, and also by a young physicist, Luke. The leading supporter of Crawford is Francis Getliffe, also a scientist, who supports Crawford not because of his scientific achievements but because Crawford is a left-wing liberal while Jago is a right-wing conservative in politics. Jago is at first supported by Nightingale, a chemist, who eventually throws his support to Crawford not because of Crawford's ability but because Nightingale thinks that he will be able to rise more quickly in the hierarchy of the college under Crawford than under Jago. Nightingale is surely one of the most despicable of Snow's characters; a failure as a scientist, he is the complete opportunist. Chrystal also switches his support to Crawford at the last moment while the vote is being taken, but he is portrayed more sympathetically than Nightingale. The whole election process turns on many imponderables; like most election processes in a democratic society it is not clear-cut and is thus a paradigm of political life in general.

Though Crawford wins out because of Jago's deficiencies, it is difficult to say that while writing the book Snow's heart was mainly with the scientist and against the literary man. One defect in *The Masters* is an imbalance in the treatment of the two candidates, with Jago receiving more attention. This focus is not apparent at first reading. Snow may have found the figure of Jago so compelling, so much more interesting than Crawford, that he could not contain his zest for a more complete dissection of his literary man than of his scientist. Novels, after all, as George Eliot pointed out, often have a way of escaping from an author's conscious control. Jago is much more alive than Crawford; he is a fully developed character while the ultimate master, though not exactly a cipher, is not much more than one-dimensional.

In 1952 Snow's only son, Philip Hansford Snow, was born. It was probably around the time of his son's birth that Snow launched into the writing of *The New Men*, published in 1954. For this novel and for *The Masters*, Snow was awarded England's James Tait Black Memorial Prize in 1955.

As a scientist who had worked with many of the great nuclear physicists and who had directed the work of England's scientists during World War II, Snow, one would assume, was aware of the secret work on the development of the atomic bomb. While he could not write a nonfiction book about atomic research because of security considerations, he did write a novel about a group of scientists engaged in the development of the atom for the purposes of war. They are "the new men" in the sense that they are in the vanguard of scientists who are manipulating the new technological advances of mankind.

Unlike *The Masters*, *The New Men* has too many secondary themes and characters. Snow spends too much time on espionage and possessive brotherly love, and sometimes the reader loses sight of the relationship of the atomic scientists to the main subject, their work in developing the bomb. For the brotherly love theme Snow brings in Lewis Eliot's younger brother Martin, mentioned briefly in the earlier novels, who now, surprisingly, is a dominant figure among the atomic scientists. Lewis Eliot, though a lawyer, has a job in the government similar to Snow's: to recruit scientists for the war effort. Upon him falls the task of coordinating the atomic research establishment soon after the startling news arrives that the Germans are working on the bomb. Lewis recruits Martin and the other scientists for the project, which goes under the name of Mr. Toad. "I could hardly have had a more niggling job," Lewis states, and this may very well be exactly what Snow felt in the early years of the war. But gradually, as the work continues and as the governmental leaders keep pressing the scientists for immediate results, they are all caught up in the desperate efforts to beat the enemy to completion of the task. Many of them are, however, appalled when the startling announcement comes in those fateful days of August 1945 that the Americans have dropped the bombs on two Japanese cities: the new men finally realize, as all the world does, that they are now faced with war, man's oldest and worst enemy, on an entirely new and frightening scale—the threat of nuclear destruction.

Snow's next novel covers episodes in Lewis Eliot's life from 1938 to 1951. *Homecomings*, the original English title, is the appropriate one; the title of the American edition, *Homecoming*, is misleading because the book is shaped around two homecomings. The first has to do with Eliot's unhappy homecoming with his first wife, Sheila, and the second with a happy homecoming with his second wife, Margaret. Sheila is Snow's most interesting and most developed female character; Margaret is dull, underdeveloped. The short first part of this novel, which deals with Sheila, is one of the strongest sections in all of Snow's books. The harrowing marriage between Eliot and Sheila, dealt with in *Time of Hope*, is here continued. It is even more of a broken marriage than in the earlier novel, and it ends with Sheila's suicide from an overdose of sleeping tablets. The rest of the book not only has to do with Eliot's life with Margaret but also with Eliot's work in the government. George Passant returns to the series and becomes Eliot's assistant during a ten-year period from 1941 to 1951. As with the first section, which is enlivened by Sheila, it is Passant who mainly brings the last part alive. Passant does a good job during the war and shortly after, but in the concluding pages he is dismissed and sent back to his small town. He is unable to survive the inevitable retrenchment that comes with the transition from wartime to postwar government.

In 1957, when Snow was awarded a knighthood, he was writing one of his most unusual novels, *The Conscience of the Rich*, which was published in 1958. It was unusual because Snow, a Gentile, was writing about a Jewish family. He had known many Jews; some of them were among the scientists and people in government he had worked with over the years. His more recent novels had had as one of their themes the subject of possessive love, in marriage, as in *Time of Hope* and *Homecomings*, and among brothers, as in *The New Men*. Now he explored the subject of possessive parental love in *The Conscience of the Rich*. In a note preceding the beginning of this novel, Snow wrote that the inner design of his sequence of novels consisted of "a resonance between what Lewis Eliot sees and what he feels." In the ultra-rich and Jewish March family, Snow depicts the theme of possessive love through Eliot's observations of the relationship of Leonard March and his son, Charles. In Charles March, Eliot observes "both the love of power and the renunciation of power." Thus the themes of possessive love and power are combined into one narrative.

If this novel is a success—and opinions have differed—it is primarily because Eliot, as Snow presents him here, refrains, for the most part, from injecting his subjective attitudes into the telling of this difficult story; he is much more objective than anywhere else in the sequence of novels. Eliot, unlike Snow, has known only one Jew,

a little boy at his grammar school, before he meets Charles March, and he does not know that Charles is a Jew until Charles invites him to meet his family. Eliot learns that Charles is ashamed of being a Jew, but Eliot in his objectivity does not seem to comprehend fully the implications of what that means. Snow portrays the March family, particularly the father and the son, in the complexity of their humanity and not as stereotypical Jews. The charge of one critic should, of course, be considered: that Snow succeeds only because he does not dwell on their Jewishness but Anglicizes them, making them not essentially different from the Forsytes of John Galsworthy. However correct this critic may be, this Anglicized portrayal was no small achievement and essentially the right method to use. Furthermore, it is entirely consonant with Eliot's nature and background. *The Conscience of the Rich* is one of Snow's finer achievements, and a comparison to Galsworthy seems a fitting way of ultimately placing Snow in the history of the English novel.

During 1959 Snow became involved in the greatest controversy of his life, a controversy which made him, more than anything else in his career, a household word in the intellectual life of the English-speaking world. Though he was known before, he would become marked as an establishment figure and a symbol of that establishment to be attacked by many literary intellectuals. Among the many articles and book reviews that Snow wrote during the 1950s (about two hundred) was one called "The Two Cultures," written for the *New Statesman* in 1956, in which he propounded the same thesis that he would state in 1959: there is a separation in our society between scientists and literary people; "there is now precious little communication between them, little but different kinds of incomprehension and dislike." The literary culture, he maintained, is traditional and is "behaving like a state whose power is rapidly declining—standing on its precarious dignity, spending far too much energy on Alexandrine intricacies, occasionally letting fly in fits of aggressive pique quite beyond its means, too much on the defensive to show any generous imagination to the forces which must inevitably reshape it." The scientific culture, on the other hand, is "expansive, not restrictive, confident at the roots . . . certain that history is on its side, impatient, intolerant, creative rather than critical, good-natured and brash." Snow's intent undoubtedly was to bring about a reconciliation, and he was as critical of the one group as he was of the other, trying to be as evenhanded as possible.

When he was invited to deliver the Rede Lectures at Cambridge in May 1959, he expanded his earlier essay and called it *The Two Cultures and the Scientific Revolution*. In June and July *Encounter* magazine published the lectures, and later in the year they were published in book form. This time he cited the deficiencies, as he had done earlier, of both groups, but it was apparent that his tone was occasionally more strident against the literary culture, that his strongest strictures were aimed at it. It was this seemingly one-sided tone that aroused the animosity of his literary critics. For example, Snow compares Ernest Rutherford's "trumpeting: 'This is the heroic age of science! This is the Elizabethan age!'" to T. S. Eliot's "this is the way the world ends, not with a bang but a whimper," and, Snow concludes, it is hard "for the literary intellectuals to understand, imaginatively or intelligently... that [Rutherford] was absolutely right." Snow quotes, with seeming approval, one distinguished scientist's charge that William Butler Yeats, Ezra Pound, Wyndham Lewis, and "nine out of ten of those who have dominated literary sensibility in our time" are "not only politically silly, but politically wicked," and, the scientist asks, "Didn't the influence of all they represent bring Auschwitz that much nearer?"

What was called the "Great Debate of our age" broke out after *Encounter* published the Rede Lectures: for months proponents of both sides wrote to the magazine expressing their views. The controversy was just starting to wane when F. R. Leavis delivered the Richmond Lecture at Cambridge in 1962. This was the bitterest attack on Snow yet, and the "Great Debate" flared up again. If Snow's tone was somewhat one-sided and more scornful of the literary culture than of the scientific culture, the malevolence of Leavis's attack was unmistakable: he pulled no punches as he went after Snow, heaping invective not only on his views and his abilities as a novelist but on him personally. Leavis's lecture was published later in 1962 as *Two Cultures? The Significance of C. P. Snow*.

Leavis had been a don at Downing College, Cambridge, for many years and was the driving force of the critical periodical *Scrutiny*; he had written many books, among them *The Great Tradition* (1948) and *D. H. Lawrence, Novelist* (1956). Leavis had long regarded Lawrence as the greatest writer of the century and had developed a proprie-

tary interest in the writer, defending him against any who spoke or wrote ill of his work. Snow had been sniping away at Lawrence for years and in his *Two Cultures* had mentioned him as one of the natural Luddites among the literary intellectuals who had reacted in horror against industrialization, which, to Snow, "is the only hope of the poor." Among these Luddites who, Snow said, had "shuddered away" at the industrial world and had reacted with "screams of horror" were John Ruskin, William Morris, Henry David Thoreau, Ralph Waldo Emerson, and Lawrence. Now Leavis saw his chance to get back at Snow: "Snow is . . . portentously ignorant . . . he is intellectually as undistinguished as it is possible to be. . . . He is a portent in that, being himself negligible, he has become for a vast public on both sides of the Atlantic a mastermind and a sage." Moreover, Leavis asserted, Snow assumes that he is a novelist, but "He can't be said to know what a novel is. The nonentity is apparent on every page of his fictions. . . . I am trying to remember where I heard (can I have dreamed it?) that [Snow's novels] are composed for him by an electronic brain called Charlie, into which the instructions are fed in the form of chapter-headings. . . . Snow can't make his characters live for us." Leavis's whole lecture is compounded of such derogatory remarks, one of the most savage attacks by one writer upon another in our time.

Again, many writers took sides, and a reading of the various views makes an illuminating account of the fragmentation of the Western mind. This was one of the points that Snow made again in September 1964, when his *The Two Cultures and A Second Look* was published. Between the scientists and the literary intellectuals, wrote Snow, "there is little communication and, instead of fellow-feeling, something like hostility." It was a state of affairs, he asserted, "I passionately disliked. . . . Curiously enough, some commentators have assumed that I approved of it." The center of his whole argument in his original lecture, he maintained, was that the scientific revolution "is the only method by which most people can gain the primal things (years of life, freedom from hunger, survival for children). . . . To misunderstand this position is to misunderstand both the present and the future." In a time when "science is determining much of our destiny, that is whether we live or die, it is dangerous" to have two cultures which do not communicate.

There are at least two interesting footnotes to this "Great Debate." In the spring of 1962, when Snow was installed as rector of St. Andrew's University in Scotland, his inaugural address, later published, was entitled "On Magnanimity" and was a plea for the necessity of the magnanimous spirit in human affairs. Though Snow did not mention Leavis, it was obvious to almost everyone that the statement was aimed at the Downing College don. In 1970 Leavis resurrected the subject of his attitude toward Snow in a lecture entitled "Literarism versus Scientism: the Misconception and the Menace." Snow came back in the same year in an essay called "The Case of Leavis and the Serious Case." He charged that Leavis had not observed the most elemental ground rule of accuracy in quoting; Leavis had also made "wrong attributions, and incorrect biographical innuendoes." Consequently, there could not be, Snow maintained, any real debate between him and Leavis.

Meanwhile, Snow had become embroiled in another controversy, which was precipitated by his Godkin Lectures at Harvard University in December 1960. These were published in April 1961 as *Science and Government*. This book is constructed around Sir Henry Tizard and Frederick Alexander Lindemann, who later became Viscount Cherwell, "the right-hand man and grey eminence of Winston Churchill" during the war. Without Tizard's leadership, according to Snow, Britain would never have developed its radar chain in time for the Battle of Britain. But when Churchill became prime minister, Lindemann was installed as his scientific adviser, and Tizard was relegated to a minor role. The two men who had been friends for years became bitter enemies in 1936. Their enmity broke out again in 1942 over the subject of strategic bombing. Lindemann claimed that the bombing must be directed essentially against the German working-class homes in order to break the back of Germany. Tizard claimed that Lindemann's belief that fifty percent of Germany's housing would be destroyed was five times too high; a different strategy should, therefore, be developed. Lindemann won because he had the ear of Churchill, and his bombing strategy was put into action with the utmost effort of the nation's air power. To Snow, not only was the effort a failure, but Britain would have done better to have listened to Tizard, who stoutly maintained to the end of his life in 1959 that, had Britain followed his policy, the war might have ended earlier and at less cost. The moral of the whole story, for Snow, is that no democratic nation should listen to only one

man again. It is "dangerous to have a solitary scientific overlord." In an appendix to *Science and Government* in 1962, Snow charged that the Battle of the Atlantic, fought for control of the sea, could well have been lost because Churchill listened to Lindemann and diverted aircraft to the bombing offensive against Germany. It was only a miracle, said Snow, that the battle was not lost. Snow was criticized by a few followers of Churchill and Lindemann; he was called naive in believing that Churchill listened only to Lindemann and made his decisions without sufficient study of the problems involved. The controversy, however, was not as virulent as the one over the two cultures, because it lacked the acid pen of a Leavis, and also probably because it concerned the politics of an era that was past and a war that had been won. If the war had been lost, the controversy might have been greater. By the 1960s, despite the gratitude which Britons generally felt toward Churchill in leading them to victory, almost everyone was ready to admit that their wartime leader was not infallible.

Snow's prestige was at its height in the 1960s. Since 1959, when he was awarded an honorary Doctor of Laws by his hometown University of Leicester, he had been honored with degrees by many universities both in Britain and America. He crossed the Atlantic many times during the 1960s and 1970s, speaking, meeting people, and accepting honors. Leavis's attacks apparently did him little or no harm.

Meanwhile, his writing of the "Strangers and Brothers" novels continued. *The Affair* was published in 1960 but was overshadowed by the "two cultures" controversy. The story takes place in 1953 and 1954, and, like *The Search*, it concerns a scientific fraud. The offending scientist, Donald Howard, is a fellow in the same Cambridge college where several earlier novels in the series take place. Crawford is now well entrenched as master, and, surprisingly, Nightingale has become an efficient bursar, disproving Lewis Eliot's early belief that Crawford could never appoint Nightingale to an important position. Eliot's error of judgment was one of a growing set of clues indicating that Snow did not intend for his readers always to believe his narrator. Like all human beings, Eliot is often mistaken, but he is an honest man groping to the best of his considerable abilities through the darkness that surrounds our lives. Eliot is now nearing fifty, a highly placed government official, a trusted and admired member of the

a novel by
C. P. Snow
author of THE MASTERS · THE CONSCIENCE OF THE RICH

Dust jacket for the American edition of Snow's 1960 book, the eighth novel in the Strangers and Brothers *sequence*

establishment—for the first time that newly coined word is used by Snow in his novels. Donald Howard, a militant and somewhat obnoxious Marxist, is accused of scientific fraud and is dismissed from his post in the college. Martin Eliot, now a don, is one of Howard's leading defenders, and he is influential in bringing back his brother to defend Howard.

The issue is one of the most momentous in all Snow's novels. The novel's title comes from the case's supposed similarity to the Alfred Dreyfus Affair in France. The central question of the novel is whether justice should be accorded one whose views we violently dislike. Lewis Eliot charges that the view expressed by another don, G. S. Clark—that one's character and his opinions should be judged together—is dangerous nonsense. What Eliot is asserting is of paramount concern to a democratic society: justice should be administered impartially, should stand apart from political, religious, social, and emotional con-

cerns. The novel takes place at the same time as Sen. Joseph McCarthy's witch-hunt for Communists in America, and Snow may have had McCarthy, as well as the Dreyfus Affair, in mind when he wrote this novel. The final revelation of the well-wrought plot is that Nightingale again is the villain; a trusted adviser to Crawford, he has altered a scientific photograph in order to pin charges of fraud on the despised Howard. *The Affair* was dramatized and had a successful London run in 1961. *The New Men* was also dramatized and presented in 1962.

In 1964 Snow reentered the British government because of the victory of the Labour party; this time he served as parliamentary secretary in the Ministry of Technology, the post directly under the minister. Snow held this position for two years, leaving it in 1966. In August 1964 he was elevated to a life peerage as Baron Snow, of the city of Leicester. Appropriately, his novel *Corridors of Power* was published in that year. In an author's note Snow says that the title of this novel passed into circulation during the time the book was being written, a fact which caused him some consternation. He first used the phrase in *Homecomings*, and after critic Rayner Heppenstall adopted it as a title of an article about Snow's work, Snow reflected, "I console myself with the reflection that, if a man hasn't the right to his own cliché, who has?"

The action is set in the period from 1955 to 1958. The "corridors of power" are Parliament and the various governmental departments attached to it. The people in power are concerned with the future of nuclear weapons, and the book can be said to be a continuation of the subject of *The New Men*. The central question is again, to say the least, momentous: has the time come to call a halt to all the newer weapons of war, or should the arms race be escalated? Though Eliot is a socialist and a follower of the Labour party, he is chosen by Conservative Minister Roger Quaife as his closest political associate. This unlikely alliance, especially unlikely since Eliot's main job seems to be to act as hatchet man to help Quaife undermine his Labour party opponents, enables Snow to have Eliot know at close range the Conservative politicians and hangers-on whom he professes to despise. Snow could conceivably have had Eliot relate from the Labour party sidelines what was going on among the Conservatives, but this device would not have achieved the same sense of closeness to decision making that he felt he needed. Snow has written that the fault in Upton Sinclair's Lanny Budd novels is Lanny's "preposterous intimacy with the great." But, being a Lanny Budd admirer, he states he had a secret wish to be like Lanny. It is surprising that in the *Corridors of Power* he did not guard against the same fault.

Quaife brings about his own downfall as a minister because his idealistic belief that the arms race must be stopped is opposed by the other Conservatives. They are not idealists like Quaife but pragmatists in a tough world. The important subject is badly diluted by numerous peripheral matters, such as Quaife's adulterous love affair; the resurrection, for no apparent reason, of a minor character from one of the earlier novels, who turns out to be a homosexual; and much attention to Quaife's wife and her brother. On the other hand, there are some interesting vignettes, especially one concerned with Lord Gilbey, a Colonel Blimp type, who stirs the House of Lords by condemning those who would leave Britain defenseless in a world at arms. Snow's main technique by the time he came to write this novel was to immerse his readers sufficiently in the whole milieu of the period so that they could "see," as Lewis Eliot does, what is happening to society. This immersion is the chief method used by the realists and naturalists of the nineteenth and early twentieth centuries, and Snow is certainly of this school of novelistic technique. Unfortunately, Quaife seldom seems real and, primarily because of this lack of development, this novel of the dark corridors of power seems just a narrative study, a political essay, and not a strong novel. It is one of the weaker novels in the sequence.

In 1967, the year after Snow left his governmental post, *Variety of Men* was published. This book is made up of nine essays on Rutherford, Godfrey Harold Hardy, H. G. Wells, Albert Einstein, David Lloyd George, Winston Churchill, Robert Frost, Dag Hammarskjöld, and Joseph Stalin. In his preface Snow says that he had met all of them except Stalin, though he had met Churchill only at committee meetings. He says, without further explanation, that, as he states in his essay on Wells, a novelist ought not to write an autobiography "and I shall never do so." But throughout the essays are sprinklings of autobiographical comments, which help make most of the essays vivid and interesting. These were people who attracted his novelistic imagination.

The essay on Rutherford, which begins the book, not only shows Rutherford's immense optimism about man's scientific achievements and the

Dust jacket for the American edition of Snow's 1964 book, the ninth novel in the Strangers and Brothers *sequence*

promise for the future, but also reiterates Snow's view that of "the kinds of people I have lived among, the scientists were much the happiest." They "were buoyant at a time when other intellectuals could not keep away despair. . . . By the nature of their vocation and also by the nature of their own temperament, the scientists did not think constantly of the individual human predicament. Since they could not alter it, they let it alone. . . . So they gave their minds not to the individual condition but to the social one." Nevertheless, the portrait of Einstein that emerges from Snow's essay is of a brooding, introspective man who worried about the individual condition as well as man's social condition; he is not at all buoyant and optimistic; he has suffered and is now stoical. This portrait is probably the best in the book.

Since Snow had been highly critical of Churchill's judgment about the bombing during the war, and since they had always been in opposite political camps, the further strictures against Churchill in that essay are not unexpected: Churchill was egocentric; he could be petty in his dealings with others, especially subordinates; he was aristocratic by temperament. Anyone "used to drinking in London pubs and talking to service men before the 1945 election could not be surprised when he was thrown out of office. The soldiers had their heroes, such as Sir Bernard Law Montgomery, but Churchill was not one of them." Churchill's judgment was "seriously defective." Churchill had a very powerful mind, "but a romantic and unquantitative one. . . . That obsessive quality of his temperament drove him into his major errors, both in war and peace." Yet Snow concludes his essay with a remarkable tribute, stating that Churchill possessed deep insight, which with his aggressive egocentricity enabled him to lead the people to victory. "Whatever could be said against him, he had virtues, graces, style. Courage, magnanimity, loyalty, wit, gallantry. . . . He really had them . . . his existence had after all sweetened English life."

Snow's essay on Robert Frost is at its most interesting when he writes more generally about writers and expounds his views on their failures of character. In comparison to the scientific life, the occupational disease of the artistic life is envy because "a creative scientist usually has a reasonable certainty of the value of his work: most writers and painters haven't. . . . This uncertainty is responsible for a great deal of the misery, and some of the venom, of the artistic life . . . it wouldn't have occurred to Einstein to regard his opponents as the enemy. Of all professionals, I thought, seeing Frost in great age, still not serene, writers have the hardest job to make themselves good men." Frost was an extreme reactionary, according to Snow, but he was honest about it. Snow quotes Frost as saying that he would not have written about the poor "if I had thought anything was going to done about their poverty. I didn't do it to get rid of the poor." This is "a truer insight," Snow writes, "into the real core of political reaction than anything written by Lawrence, Eliot, Pound, Lewis. . . . They prettified or made apocalyptic or classicized their motives. Frost didn't, and to that extent is more respectworthy."

In 1968 *The Sleep of Reason* was published; this novel is a marked improvement over *Corridors of Power*. The title comes from Francisco Goya: "The sleep of reason brings forth monsters." One strand of the plot is a horrible murder which takes place in Lewis Eliot's hometown in the English Midlands. This murder is based upon the Moors Murders near Manchester, which attracted widespread attention. Snow and his wife, Pamela, attended the April 1966 trial in Chester of Ian Brady and Myra Hindley, who were charged with murdering three juveniles between 1963 and 1965 and burying the bodies on the moors near Manchester. Lady Snow had been asked by the *Sunday Telegraph* to write her impressions of the trial, but the effect of the trial on her was so great that she wrote a whole book about it, *On Iniquity*, published in 1967. To her, "the Moors Case . . . [is] a touchstone of what can go hideously wrong with two people." She was attempting to explore "whether there was not, in our increasingly permissive society, some compostheap of rottenness out of which some ugly weeds could flourish and grow lush." Again and again she blames permissive society, and she advocates that we "put the brake on the flow of sadomasochistic pornography," which, she believes, contributed to the development of the defendants' evil characters. She says that she had raised a storm by suggesting, in a letter to the *Guardian*, that Baron Richard von Krafft-Ebing's *Psychopathia Sexualis* (1886) not be made available in a cheap paperback.

The Moors trial and Lady Snow's strongly held views contributed much to the nature of *The Sleep of Reason*. It is difficult to assess the full extent his wife's influence had on Snow's novels, but it seems certain that her great interest in Proust, on whom she wrote a book, surely helped change the contents of the later novels in the sequence. More and more Snow brought back characters from the earlier novels and tried, like Proust, to show the past influencing the present. Some readers have charged that this relationship between the past and the present makes the reading of Snow's later novels more difficult. Historian A. J. P. Taylor, who had read only *The Masters* before reading *Corridors of Power*, complained that too many allusions to the past made *Corridors of Power* very difficult for him. Though probably this same charge can be made against *The Sleep of Reason*, to those who have read the whole sequence of novels the past's influence on the present becomes meaningful as they see George Passant's "resurrection" (for the last time). Lewis Eliot is drawn back to his hometown partly because of his association with Passant; one of the two women convicted of the murder of a small boy and sentenced, like the Moors murderers, to life imprisonment is Passant's niece. The trial of his niece proves profoundly shattering to Passant, who now realizes the hideous results of his permissive libertarian thinking. When Snow wrote the earlier novels in which Passant has a major part, he could not have been planning to end Passant's story in such a way. This change of direction is just one of the many clues that Snow revised his original conception of the entire sequence. In fact Snow may have had no more than a very vague idea of what he would actually do in his sequence of novels on that day in Marseilles when he claims to have had his initial conception. In *The Sleep of Reason* Snow tries to show that George's niece and her partner in crime were believers in Passant's libertarian view that one should enjoy one's instinctual desires without reference to the restraints of society. Now a man in his sixties, Passant still maintains his beliefs are correct, but even he is so shaken by the implications of his way of life that he decides to leave England rather than face up to what his life has become. If this is Snow's most Proustian novel, then probably Passant can be said to be an English version of the depraved Baron Charlus, though their sexual natures are quite different, Passant being a heterosexual. Though he is not religious, Eliot concludes openly what was only implicit in Lady Snow's *On Iniquity*, that though the faults of society have much to do with human depravity, the ultimate explanation is original sin. Earlier in *The Light and the Dark*, Eliot, when confronted with the nature of Roy Calvert, also stated original sin may be the ultimate answer to the depravity of man. Now, looking at his friend Passant, Eliot thinks that "without possessing a religious faith, I nevertheless—perhaps because I wasn't good myself—couldn't help believing in something like original sin."

The other strand of the plot in *The Sleep of Reason* has to do with the new university in the hometown. At the time dealt with in this novel, 1963-1964, Snow was rector of St. Andrew's University. Eliot returns to his hometown because, as a member of the governing board of the university, the elected representative of the students, he feels he should be there for an important meeting. Arnold Shaw, the vice-chancellor, the governing head of the university, is now threatened by a faculty revolt which is trying to unseat him. The students are also in opposition to Shaw, who is an extreme conservative in his educational views: to him the main function of a faculty is to teach, and that of the students is to learn. He

Dust jacket for Snow's 1968 book, the tenth novel in the Strangers and Brothers *sequence*

feels the students are not there for therapy, and if they cannot learn, then they ought to be dismissed: "This university ought to be half its size." Because the two young women convicted of murder are students in the university, the two parts of the plot are connected. Eliot at first is not in sympathy with Shaw's hard line on education, thinking it too authoritarian; but later, though the conclusion is somewhat ambiguous, Eliot seems drawn to Shaw's view that reason must prevail if man is ever to escape being prey to his deep and bestial instincts. How can an Auschwitz be prevented, Eliot thinks, if we allow reason to sleep? The educational process may well be one of man's main hopes, if not the most important hope, in preventing another such holocaust. In presenting Shaw as the chief spokesman for reason, Snow created one of his most vivid characters. Shaw is the direct antithesis of George Passant, Snow's outstanding creation.

Another important event in 1968 for Snow was his lecture delivered at Westminster College in Fulton, Missouri, as one of the John Findley Green Foundation Lectures. Snow's lecture was published in 1969 as *The State of Siege* and later incorporated, along with other public statements he had made since 1959, in *Public Affairs,* which came out in 1971. *The State of Siege,* which comments in part on the relationship of the Western democracies and the Soviet Union, evoked few denunciations. A mild one came from a Soviet academic who regretted that "a man who had tried his best according to his lights" should have become so fainthearted.

In making a brief reference to Churchill's phrase "the Iron Curtain" (a phrase Churchill coined during his own Green Lecture in March 1946), Snow maintains that the West is drawing inward, does not project outward: "We draw what in England we call the curtains, and we try to make an enclave of our own. . . . Enclave-making: that is one of the characteristic symptoms of our unease." The West is, in short, in a state of siege, and the complications of our Western society include unease about nuclear and biological weapons: "It goes without saying that to avoid major war, there has to be some sort of understanding between the U.S. and the U.S.S.R. . . . there has to be something more than an uneasy understanding, something more positive than coexistence, between the two great power centres of the world." Western democracies must also help the poor countries to revolutionize their food production and to reduce or stop their population increase. The West's future will depend on its relationship with these poor countries: "We have to make sure that people understand those ominous curves—the curve of population, the curve of food supply." The world must break out of this state of siege: "One hears young people asking for a cause. The cause is here. It is the biggest single cause in history: simply because history has never presented us with such a danger."

The tenor of this lecture is not hopeful about man's future. In an epilogue to *Public Affairs,* Snow states his belief that the danger of thermonuclear war between the superpowers has receded, but that the other two dangers have become more acute: "The gap between the rich and the poor countries hasn't lessened. It is becoming wider every year." Also, the menace of overpopulation hangs over all: "I don't believe that we shall destroy the species. . . . But it may very well find itself living in conditions which, to most

contemporary Americans or Englishmen, would seem intolerable." To avoid "a prolonged period of hardship, sporadic famine" will require "more foresight and will than men have shown themselves capable of up to now." If there is any source of hope it is in the educated young all over the West, who have discarded racial prejudices: "They are more genuinely international in spirit than any generation before them."

Snow's growing state of pessimism may have been partly engendered by his eye troubles; he had a displaced retina which required several operations. Several photos taken in the 1960s show him with a black patch over one eye. The last section of *The Sleep of Reason* deals with Lewis Eliot's eye defect, the same as Snow's, and his stay in a hospital where he had been operated on. The last chapter, entitled "The Dark and the Light," shows Eliot in "the claustrophobic dark," and in the last novel of the sequence, aptly titled *Last Things* (1970), Eliot requires a second operation during which his heart stops beating for a few seconds. (This happened to Snow also.) Eliot makes a dramatic recovery and is depicted as a man returned from the dead. Through several chapters Eliot indulges in an almost constant self-examination while he is lying quietly in a hospital bed with both eyes bandaged.

Eliot, now in his sixties, realizes that his personal relationships have not always been good; that he has sometimes been a bad husband, a bad son, and a bad friend. He regrets much that he has done in his life, though in the worldly sense he has been a success: an important figure in government, in the legal profession, and now as a writer. He finds himself no longer dominated by the urge to succeed in politics, in love, or in any other area where power is, or has seemed to be, a needed ingredient. This restrained mood, brought about by age, sickness, and the deaths of many of his old friends (Passant, for example, has died alone on the Continent), permeates the whole novel. The only semblance of a plot concerns the attempt of a few headstrong Cambridge students, among them Eliot's son, Charles, to steal an official document showing the university's collaboration with the military in research for germ warfare. This plan is aborted, being dealt with in only a few chapters, and the investigation of the students' activities is dropped quickly by the authorities because the son of a prominent Tory politician is in the group and also because national security has suffered no damage. Eliot then goes on to worry about Charles's involvement with a woman who has become his mistress, but this worry is quickly abated when Charles decides to leave her and go to the Middle East, where he hopes to become a journalist. The book closes in the quiet fashion of all Snow's novels as Lewis walks home thinking that though "in days soon to come" he may have other anxieties, he is at peace now and has the sense that (in the last sentence of the novel and of the sequence) "There would be other nights when I should go to sleep, looking forward to tomorrow." He is apprehensive about the younger generation, but only slightly: Charles and the other young people who were well educated in the universities will probably behave more responsibly than his own generation when they come to power. The note of indefiniteness, which had been growing in the later novels of the "Strangers and Brothers" sequence, hangs over the last novel, indicating that, if Eliot does have a feeling of assurance, it is a very uneasy one. The next-to-last sentence is "Who would dare to look in the mirror of his future?"

The last decade of Snow's life was as productive as the four which preceded it. Snow apparently never stopped writing despite the fact that he had been quoted as saying he found the act of writing tedious. At the age of sixty-six in 1972, he brought out another novel, *The Malcontents*, and one reviewer wrote that Snow had now been elevated from a phenomenon to an institution. The most surprising thing about his new novel was not that he continued writing after finishing the "Strangers and Brothers" sequence (some thought that Snow would conclude his novel writing with *Last Things*, apparently seduced into this view by the title), but that he used the third-person-omniscient point of view, which he had not used since the anonymously published *New Lives for Old* in 1933.

The Malcontents is another novel about the uses and abuses of power, but this time it is about the power wielded by the establishment over a group of seven young people who, calling themselves "the core," are in a conspiracy to expose a slum landlord who is also a prominent Tory politician. In essence it is a slight variation on the plot that Snow had aborted in *Last Things*. One of the seven, who turns out to be an informer, is given a dose of LSD in a drink, and he dies by falling out a window. Two members of the core are arrested for possession of drugs, and the authorities make an example of them by giving them prison sentences; the Tory politician

Dust jacket for Snow's 1970 book, the eleventh and final novel in the Strangers and Brothers *sequence*

and his friends in the establishment are thought to have instigated this treatment. The other four members of the core are allowed to go free. Under the ferocious onslaught of the establishment, the core disintegrates in the last part of the novel. In addition to the method of narration, *The Malcontents* featured two other departures for Snow: for the first time he abandoned chapter titles, which some of his critics had thought old-fashioned, and he used several well-known vulgar words. Since he was dealing primarily with young people, and they use these words freely, Snow, being a realist in fiction, thought he had to use their language to make the novel seem authentic. The young malcontents, who are from important upper-class families, finally realize that they cannot change society from the outside but must burrow from within—become part of the establishment. Whether this decision is a sellout, a convenient rationalization for the failure, or a good tactic is not stated. This book received a few favorable reviews, but most reviewers thought it too slow moving and that, though Snow wrote about the young, he was unable to capture their essential natures in effective characterizations. Christopher Porterfield wrote in *Time* that the discussions which took place among these young malcontents seemed to be very similar to the discussions of the men in committees in many of Snow's other novels.

Two years later another novel, *In Their Wisdom,* presented a subject closer to Snow's recent personal experience. As a member of the peerage, he had been attending the House of Lords, taking part in its debates and other activities. The scenes in the Bishops' bar and other places where the lords gather are probably presented authentically. Snow reveals groups of old, worn-out lords commiserating with one another over their sad plight in being forced to attend sessions of the body for the sake of the daily wage of £6 10s. The book is about money or the lack of it in modern Britain as a whole—the spectacle of a once great and mighty nation going downhill fast. These lords are supposed to be a paradigm of the whole nation obsessed with its dwindling material conditions. Snow presents this theme as a sort of prudery—not about sex because, unlike their Victorian predecessors, sexual matters do not bother the lords much—of the privileged classes in not wanting to face all the implications of their loss of money: "They didn't want to talk about it. They didn't want to face how much they cared and worried about it. They wished to present—to themselves as much as to others— that it affected them little. . . . They wanted to disguise their motives, because they would have liked loftier ones." It is not surprising that some reviewers asserted that Snow was too narrowly confined to the upper class and seemed to give little thought to the plight of ordinary people. Snow, however, was writing a realistic portrait of the type of people he was then living among; in his old age, a lord himself, he certainly knew this milieu better than almost any other. In this sense his presentation is probably not any less realistic than Anthony Trollope's—to whom Snow's has been compared—in his fine novels about Parliament.

Snow's interest in Trollope was great, and in early 1975 his *Trollope: His Life and Art* was published. It is a handsome book with many illustrations from Victorian periodicals. On the first page of chapter 1 Snow writes that Trollope was more loving than loved; that his fate was unfortu-

nate "like his short sight or his heavy lumbering physique," but that his fate probably endowed him with "the specific insight, the delicate fluid empathy, which made him the finest natural psychologist of all nineteenth-century novelists." Snow traces the events in Trollope's life and books with care and genuine affection. There are also two chapters on Trollope's writing in which Snow points out that critics, "in his own time and since, have never been comfortable with Trollope, and have tended to take refuge in a kind of patronizing unease." Snow approves of Henry James's comment that "Trollope will remain one of the most trustworthy, though not one of the most eloquent, of the writers who have helped the heart of mankind to know itself." To Snow, "There aren't many better statements about Trollope's percipience or the meaning of the realistic novel." Snow's is a strong defense of the Trollopian (and perhaps his own) kind of realistic novel. Trollope "was trying to suggest the present experience *as it might be considered later* [Snow's italics] and as it impinged upon future actions." There are limits in all art, Snow points out: "Some attempts to ignore the Trollopian limits have brought many novels to the condition of Alexandrian poetry. Such poetry can have its place, but its place is in the history of ingenious blind alleys, not in the revelation of human nature."

Three years later, in 1978, Snow brought out another nonfiction work, *The Realists,* presenting eight portraits of those he considered to be the greatest realistic novelists. There are a few surprises: Trollope is missing, as are Jane Austen, George Eliot, and Gustave Flaubert. The eight he chose are Stendahl (Marie Henri Beyle), Honoré de Balzac, Fyodor Dostoyevski, Lev Tolstoy, Benito Pérez Galdós, Henry James, Marcel Proust, and Charles Dickens. He tells us in his preface that he was sure the first seven are among the greatest realistic masters, but he hesitated over Dickens because "he is only realistic occasionally. . . . Still, with a little sleight of hand, one can bring some of his best work within the confines." He would like to have brought three other English novelists (Austen, Eliot, and Trollope) into the book, "But, against my own inclination, I can't pretend that any of them is of the same stature as the greatest realistic masters. Dickens is. . . ." There is only a perfunctory mention of Flaubert, whom many critics and scholars regard as the greatest of all realistic novelists. It seems idiosyncratic for Snow to omit Flaubert, and also

Lord Snow (photograph by Mark Gerson)

Austen and Eliot, from his pantheon while including Galdós, a nineteenth-century Spanish novelist. Snow's narratives of his subjects' lives are admirable, indicating once again his novelistic touch, but his analyses of their works fail, for the most part, to demonstrate what he tells in his preface he is trying to do: to show how the lives of these writers shaped their works. For example, he tells us much about the life of Stendahl, but his analysis of *The Red and the Black* (1831) is only two pages of generalities. Snow told his readers often that Proust was the novelist he most admired; yet other than stating in his chapter on Proust that *Remembrance of Things Past* (1913-1928) is the greatest literary work of our century, he has very little to say about it.

In his epilogue Snow draws a few conclusions. One is that these eight masters "were nearly all very short fat men, uncommonly bad at mathematics." Not one of these great writers

could be regarded as an exemplar for other human lives, he says, but it is probably more difficult for great writers to become moral exemplars: they have to live with the worst side of their natures. Finally, he asks whether it would be possible to write such realistic novels today. The chances seem to be against it; but such a literary art "is almost certain to rise again." He is quite certain that "the realistic novel is a wonderful form of art, and at its height has produced some of the richest literature so far known to man."

A year before his death, *A Coat of Varnish* (1979), Snow's second detective novel, appeared. It may not compare favorably with the better novels in the "Strangers and Brothers" series, but it is by no means below a few of them and is an improvement on *The Malcontents* and *In Their Wisdom*. In the early chapters Snow evokes a vivid portrait of the Belgravia area of London, a section that he knew well, having lived in it for some years. Being a realist, he takes the early chapters to introduce his readers to the characters before presenting the death of an old woman, and they are depicted in greater depth than in the usual detective story. One of the best scenes in *In Their Wisdom* is a realistic depiction of an operation. Here, the details of an autopsy are impeccable and realistically gruesome. There is a love affair which almost spoils the tension, but Snow is not writing the usual type of detective story but rather a novel in which there is a murder and detectives. He was probably trying to do something on the order of Dostoyevski's *Crime and Punishment* (1866), a novel which, Snow stated in *The Realists,* he admired and found "overpowering." *A Coat of Varnish* is, of course, not up to that masterpiece, but it is still fairly well done. Snow's two detective mysteries suggest that if he had turned his mind wholeheartedly to that genre, he might have become one of our modern masters in the field.

The title comes from a statement by Alec Luria, an American psychologist in the book, who says that "Civilization is hideously fragile. There's not much between us and the horrors underneath. Just a coat of varnish." This statement could have come out of *The Sleep of Reason* and probably indicates that this awful truth about human beings was much on Snow's mind in his last years. One suspects he was anything but sanguine at that point about the prospects for the human race.

Snow's last year was one of illness. However, he was planning a television dramatization of the "Strangers and Brothers" series. The *New York Times* obituary reported that, in a 1967 interview, the "portly, Buddhalike author" remarked: "All my novels are part of one complicated theme, which is power in the modern state. People are prudish about power when now they are not prudish about sex. And in writing about power I have been trying to show how it is really exerted in Britain, for its hidden ways are surely as elaborate as those of sex." This same obituary

stated that some likened him "to Proust for the sensitivity of his social observations." Others have compared Snow to Galsworthy; more often he has been compared to Trollope. One of Snow's friends, Herman Wouk, writing a month after Snow's death, called him "the Trollope of our time." Snow would have appreciated that statement.

Biographies:

William C. Cooper, *C. P. Snow* (London: Longmans, Green, 1959; revised edition, London: British Book Council, 1971);

Robert Gorham Davis, *C. P. Snow* (New York & London: Columbia University Press, 1965);

Jerome Thalé, *C. P. Snow* (New York: Scribners, 1965);

Philip Snow, *Stranger and Brother: A Portrait of C. P. Snow* (London: Macmillan, 1982);

John Halperin, *C. P. Snow: An Oral Biography Together with a Conversation with Lady Snow* (New York: St. Martin's Press, 1983).

References:

David K. Cornelius and Edwin St. Vincent, *Cultures in Conflict: Perspectives on the Snow-Leavis Controversy* (Chicago: Scott-Foresman, 1964);

Robert Greacan, *The World of C. P. Snow* (New York & London: House & Maxwell, 1962);

Frederick R. Karl, *C. P. Snow: The Politics of Conscience* (Carbondale: Southern Illinois University Press, 1963);

F. R. Leavis, *Two Cultures? The Significance of C. P. Snow* (London: Chatto & Windus, 1962);

Suguna Ramanathan, *The Novels of C. P. Snow: A Critical Introduction* (New York: Scribners, 1978);

David Shusterman, *C. P. Snow* (Boston: Twayne, 1975; revised, 1991);

Stanley Weintraub, *C. P. Snow: A Spectrum* (New York: Scribners, 1963).

Muriel Spark

(1 February 1918 -   )

This entry was updated by Margaret Moan Rowe (Purdue University) from her entry in
DLB 15: British Novelists, 1930-1959: Part Two.

BOOKS: *Child of Light: A Reassessment of Mary Shelley* (Hadleigh, Essex, U.K.: Tower Bridge, 1951; New York: Avon, 1974);

Emily Brontë: Her Life and Work, by Spark and Derek Stanford (London: Owen, 1953; New York: British Book Center, 1953);

John Masefield (London: Nevill, 1953; Philadelphia: West, 1973);

The Comforters (London: Macmillan, 1957; New York: Macmillan, 1957);

Robinson (London: Macmillan, 1958; Philadelphia: Lippincott, 1959);

The Go-Away Bird and Other Stories (London: Macmillan, 1958; Philadelphia: Lippincott, 1960);

Memento Mori (London: Macmillan, 1959; Philadelphia: Lippincott, 1959);

The Ballad of Peckham Rye (London: Macmillan, 1960; Philadelphia: Lippincott, 1960);

The Bachelors (London: Macmillan, 1960; New York: St. Martin's Press, 1960);

Voices at Play (London: Macmillan, 1961; New York: St. Martin's Press, 1961);

The Prime of Miss Jean Brodie (London: Macmillan, 1961; Philadelphia: Lippincott, 1962);

Doctors of Philosophy (London: Macmillan, 1963; New York: Knopf, 1966);

The Girls of Slender Means (London: Macmillan, 1963; New York: Knopf, 1963);

The Mandelbaum Gate (London: Macmillan, 1965; New York: Knopf, 1965);

Collected Stories I (London: Macmillan, 1967; New York: Knopf, 1968);

Collected Poems I (London: Macmillan, 1967; New York: Knopf, 1968);

The Public Image (London: Macmillan, 1968; New York: Knopf, 1968);

The Driver's Seat (London: Macmillan, 1970; New York: Knopf, 1970);

The French Window (London: Macmillan, 1970);

Not to Disturb (London: Macmillan, 1971; New York: Viking, 1971);

The Hothouse by the East River (London: Macmillan, 1973; New York: Viking, 1973);

Muriel Spark (photograph by Paul Popper)

The Abbess of Crewe (London: Macmillan, 1974; New York: Viking, 1974);

The Takeover (London: Macmillan, 1976; New York: Viking, 1976);

Territorial Rights (London: Macmillan, 1979; New York: Coward, McCann & Geoghegan, 1979);

Loitering With Intent (London: Bodley Head, 1981; New York: Coward, McCann & Geoghegan, 1981);

The Only Problem (London: Bodley Head, 1984; New York: Putnam's, 1984);

A Far Cry from Kensington (London: Constable, 1988; New York: Houghton Mifflin, 1988);

Symposium (London: Constable, 1990; New York: Houghton Mifflin, 1990).

OTHER: *My Best Mary: The Selected Letters of Mary Wollstonecraft Shelley*, edited by Spark and Derek Stanford (London: Wingate, 1953; New York: Roy, 1954);

The Brontë Letters, edited by Spark (London: Nevill, 1954);

Letters of John Henry Newman, edited by Spark and Stanford (London: Owen, 1957; Westminster, Md.: Newman, 1957).

Muriel Spark came to the novel after a variety of writing experiences. As a free-lance journalist after her intelligence work in World War II, Spark wrote for the *Argentor*, a jewelry trade magazine, and she had poetry published before she became general secretary of the Poetry Society in April 1947. That post led to her work as editor of the *Poetry Review*. In 1949 she left the Poetry Society and founded *Forum* (which lasted only two issues), wrote copy for a publicity agent, and edited *European Affairs*. At the same time, Spark began to write short stories, many of them based on her experiences in Africa, where she lived from 1936, after leaving Edinburgh, until the early war years. One such story, "The Seraph and the Zambesi," won the *Observer* Christmas story competition in 1951. Shortly thereafter, Spark, whose father was a Jew and whose mother was an English Presbyterian, became interested in Cardinal John Henry Newman and Catholicism. In "My Conversion" (1961) Spark maintained "that Newman helped me find a definite location." She was an Anglo-Catholic for about six months and then formally entered the Roman Church in 1954. Although accompanied by physical and psychological turmoil, her conversion, according to Spark, "provided my norm . . . something to measure from." In 1954, at the time of her conversion to Catholicism, she was asked to write a novel. In an interview she commented, "What happened was that Macmillans about that time had a new young man [Alan Maclean] whose job was to find promising new writers and he asked me to write a novel."

That promise was not immediately realized, however; though she was helped by financial support from Macmillan and from Graham Greene, Spark's first novel, *The Comforters*, was not published until 1957. One obstacle to the novel's completion was what Spark has identified as her own initial distaste for the form that would bring her fame; she told Frank Kermode that "I didn't think much of novels—I thought it was an inferior way of writing." Interestingly enough, the title *The Comforters*, which Derek Stanford, Peter Kemp, and others relate to Spark's interest in the Book of Job, suggests also the novice novelist's need for comforting as she sorted out the aesthetic, psychological, and religious turmoil in which she found herself. Much of *The Comforters* is concerned with the movement of its protagonist, Caroline Rose, from writing a study of the modern novel to deciding to write her own novel about "characters in a novel."

Between Caroline's work as critic and her work as creator, however, is her experience of the voices that come from beyond her wall and seem to be dictating a plot in which she herself is a character. Only after Caroline's decision to write a novel do the voices cease. Though never adequately accounted for in the novel, the voices point toward Spark's interest in the question of free will and characterization in fiction, an interest that flourishes in her work of the 1970s. For Spark, the author of fiction is akin to God, a belief underscored by Kermode, Spark's most supportive critic: "The suggestion is, in Mrs. Spark's novels, that a genuine relation exists between the forms of fiction and the forms of the world, between the novelist's creation and God's." Given Spark's Catholicism, such a relationship between fiction and reality leads to a tension between the demands of authorial providence—creative omniscience—and the demands of free will among her characters. When Spark comments on her style or technique, she often suggests something of an independent existence for her characters, as when she notes that a novel's dialogue "belongs to each character." Dealing with disembodied voices is only one of Caroline Rose's problems in *The Comforters*. Like Spark, Caroline is a Roman Catholic convert, and she faces psychological and emotional pressures because of that conversion.

Caroline's conversion causes major problems with her former lover, Laurence Manders, a lapsed Catholic and a member of a prominent Catholic family. Through Laurence, Caroline becomes involved with his grandmother Louisa Jepp, ringleader of a smuggling plot, and his mother, Helena Manders, a Roman Catholic convert. Ironically, it is through her association with Helena that Caroline first becomes involved with Catholicism, leading to the break in her sexual relationship with Laurence. (Spark's love of the intricate plot is clear even in her first novel.) Louisa Jepp is herself something of a creative personality in *The Comforters*, directing the movements of her small band of diamond smugglers who bring the gems into the country in religious statues. While Louisa characterizes her activity as sport, the activities of the hypocritical blackmailer Georgina Hogg, sometime servant in the Jepp and Manders households, are more serious.

On religious retreat, Caroline sees Mrs. Hogg and once more feels repelled by her: "Mrs. Hogg stuck in her mind like a lump of food on the chest which will move neither up nor down." Indeed, the character Mrs. Hogg is Spark's sharpest satire of the kind of Catholic whose existence delayed her own conversion; "I was put off a long time," Spark noted, "by individual Catholics, living ones, I mean. Good God, I used to think, if I become a Catholic, will I grow like them?" Beefy and pushy Georgina Hogg specializes in manipulating people, a specialty underscored at the end of the novel when Mrs. Hogg and Caroline, who have traveled to the countryside for different reasons, find themselves in a river; Caroline, a swimmer, instructs Mrs. Hogg to clasp her shoulder, "But the woman in her extremity was intent on Caroline's throat." Mrs. Hogg drowns while Caroline is rescued, a rescue which coincides with the silencing of her voices and the stilling of the anxieties that have kept her from completing her critical study. She finishes the study and goes on "a holiday of obligation" to begin her own novel.

The beginning of Caroline's first novel is, of course, the ending of Spark's first novel, a novel that suggests some of the ongoing concerns in Spark's work. Catholics, and particularly converts, in other novels will try to fit into secular society, while other fictional characters will strive for some autonomy from the will of the author. The world of *The Comforters*, dependent as it is on associations with the Manders family, is closely circumscribed—a characteristic of later novels also, as Spark turns her attention to the behaviors of small and select groups. Spark has admitted, "When I become interested in a subject, say old age, then the world is peopled for me—just peopled with them. And it is a small narrow world, but it's full of old people, full of whatever I'm studying." The later novels also demonstrate Spark's intense interest in the uses and abuses of moral and psychological power and her interest in the nature of the economies, or structures, established by individuals to exercise that power. *The Comforters*, therefore, offers insight into Spark's central preoccupations as a novelist, and in itself it is an interesting book. Despite the disembodied voices that call too much attention to them-

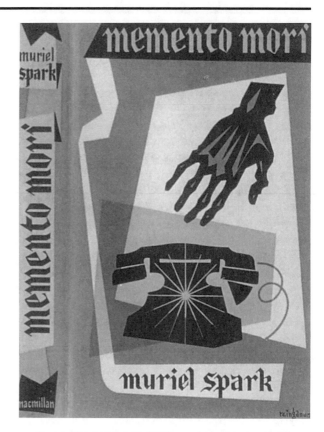

Dust jacket for Spark's 1959 novel about aging people experiencing moral and physical decline

selves as technique and end by becoming too precious, and despite a subplot about diabolism that is not important to the rest of the novel, *The Comforters* is a satisfying first novel that promised much for Spark.

Unfortunately, Spark's second novel, *Robinson* (1958), did not fulfill her promise. The setting is a small island in the Atlantic named for and controlled by a recluse called Robinson. Robinson's life on the island, solitary save for a native boy and a cat, is disrupted by a plane crash from which there are three survivors: Tom Wells, a salesman of lucky charms; Jimmie Waterford, a kinsman of Robinson's; and January Marlow, a journalist who has been converted to Roman Catholicism.

At Robinson's urging, January Marlow keeps an account of the two months and twenty-nine days on the island before her rescue by a pomegranate boat, thinking she "might later dress it up for a novel." But January does not "dress it up"; nor is the novel written by Spark sufficiently dressed up to win the reader. Spark's second novel is finally a rather tedious narrative that sets convert January against lapsed Catholic Robinson and, in January's journal, sets life and characters on the larger island, England, against life and characters on the smaller island. There is little in the narrative to win interest or enthusiasm. Spark tries to suggest the allegorical meaning of the island experience for January Marlow, for whom memory of the island seems to make "all things possible." But to suggest this meaning is not to show it, and, ultimately, the novel is not convincing. Critic Frank Baldanza is right in calling *Robinson* "a sharp decline" from *The Comforters*.

Spark's third novel, however, again displayed the literary talent promised by her first. *Memento Mori* (1959) is an account of men and women, most of whom are past seventy, in various states of physical—and in some cases, moral—decline. It is that common experience of decline and its end that links the older characters, who receive anonymous phone calls in which the caller, whose identity changes for each hearer, repeats the otherworldly warning: "Remember you must die." Many of the older characters are linked by the past as well. The novelist Charmian Piper is married to Godfrey Colston. Godfrey's sister, Mrs. Pettigrew, a manipulator and snoop on the order of Georgina Hogg in *The Comforters*, enters the Colston household. Pettigrew acts as a companion to Charmian, dominating her and trying to force her to be dependent. Charmian's former companion Jean Taylor, past lover of Alec Warner, the sociologist, is in the Maud Long Medical Ward. Jean captures the sadness of the aged in the ward and in the world of *Memento Mori* when she notes that "Being over seventy is like being engaged in a war. All our friends are going or gone and we survive amongst the dead and dying as on a battlefield."

But for Spark that engagement has its triumphs, and her emphasis is on the quality of the survival achieved by the characters reminded of death. Charmian Piper informs her anonymous caller that "for the past thirty years and more I have thought of [death] from time to time. My memory is failing in certain respects. I am gone eighty-six. But somehow I do not forget my death, whenever that will be," and she goes off to attain a small triumph over the domineering Mrs. Pettigrew by making her own tea. For Henry Mortimer, agnostic and retired inspector who investigates the calls and who himself receives a call, his own reminder links him more keenly to life: "If I had my life over again I should form the habit of nightly composing myself to thoughts of death. I would practice, as it

were, the remembrance of death. There is no other practice which so intensifies life. Death, when it approaches, ought not to take one by surprise. It should be part of the full expectancy of life." For Jean Taylor, too, the reminder is positive because for Taylor, Catholic convert and believer, that reminder puts her in touch with "the Four Last Things" and the possibility of heaven. But everyone is not sensitized by the call: Godfrey Colston continues his selfish obsession with his physical well-being. Too busy using Godfrey's sexual voyeurism to blackmail him, Pettigrew cannot see any kind of spiritual dimension; the complete materialist, she looks for her reward on earth. And reward she gets as she inherits money and lives out her life "jostling for a place by the door of the hotel lounge before the dinner gong sounds," surely a reward that would have pleased Dante.

Spark succeeds beautifully in bringing in a supernatural element—the memento provided by the mysterious phone calls—and making it plausible within the world of the novel; she chooses a commonplace convenience of the twentieth century for an uncommon message. Caroline Rose's voices in *The Comforters* are strained as that novel progresses. Not so the ringing telephones in *Memento Mori*; they call attention not to themselves as vehicles but to the tenor of their reminder. But then all of the natural and supernatural elements work in this very funny and very wise book.

The world of *Memento Mori* is miles away, geographically and socially, from the working-class world in Spark's fourth novel, *The Ballad of Peckham Rye* (1960). (Spark herself, according to Derek Stanford, lived in such a world on the South Bank of the Thames in the middle 1950s.) Indeed, the titles of Spark's third and fourth novels suggest the social change, as the formal and Latin title *Memento Mori* with its meditation on death among the middle class gives way to the populist and folksy title of *The Ballad of Peckham Rye* with its concern for life and death among the working class.

Into that world comes Dougal Douglas of Edinburgh and elsewhere. Hired by Meadows, Meade and Grindley, nylon-textile manufacturers, Dougal is commissioned "to bring vision into the lives of the workers," not too difficult a task for someone who describes himself as "one of the wicked spirits that wander through the world for the ruin of souls." Dougal offers that description to Humphrey Place, a fellow lodger at Miss

Dust jacket for Spark's 1960 novel set in a working-class neigh-borhood much like one on the South Bank of the Thames, where Spark lived in the mid 1950s

Frierne's rooming house. But Dougal cannot be categorized as a totally evil spirit and bringer of an evil vision; like his human identity (he calls himself Dougal Douglas on one side of the river and Douglas Dougal on the other), his spiritual identity is dualistic (a point well explored by Karl Malkoff in "Demonology and Dualism: The Supernatural in Isaac Singer and Muriel Spark" [1969]).

Whether his is a good or an evil visitation depends on the response people make to Dougal, who animates rather than dominates. He conducts his human research, preaching a doctrine of self-expression—a doctrine which proves attractive to some and threatening to others. For Merle Coverdale, head of the typing pool, Dougal's presence encourages self-assertion with Mr. Druce, who has used her sexually for years. Finally, Merle takes stock of what she terms "a rotten life"; but that stocktaking is a threat to Druce, manager of Meadows, Meade and

Grindley, who suspects Dougal of being a police-man or industrial spy and suspects Merle of helping him. So in one of his visitations, Druce "came towards her with a corkscrew and stabbed it into her long neck nine times, and killed her. Then he took his hat and went home to his wife."

Association with Dougal has a less dramatic outcome for Humphrey Place, who is temporarily freed from his life-denying relationship with Dixie Morse. The novel opens with Dixie's mother slamming the door in Humphrey's face after he has said no at the wedding ceremony. Dixie rightly sees Dougal's ideas standing in the way of her model bungalow and spin dryer—but not for long. Humphrey's freedom from Dixie and her grubby family is temporary, and *The Ballad of Peckham Rye* closes with the two, now newly-weds, driving off. Spark suggests that while Dixie remains her acquisitive self, Humphrey has been somewhat changed for the better by his association with Dougal, a change that the narrator underscores with Humphrey's vision at the end of the novel: "as he drove swiftly past the Rye, he saw the children playing there and the women coming home from work with their shopping-bags, the Rye for an instant looking like a cloud of green and gold, the people seeming to ride upon it, as you might say there was another world than this." But the vision seems an authorial afterthought to suggest Dougal's good influence, while nothing in Humphrey's characterization in the novel suggests that he has the willpower to act on his vision, the power to abandon Dixie and her grubby materialism. He is a man influenced by those around him, and he has married Dixie while Dougal has gone his pica-resque way. The moment of spiritual uplift at the end of *The Ballad of Peckham Rye* is actually at odds with the basically negative—and sometimes patronizing—presentation of the working-class world in Spark's fourth novel.

The world of *The Bachelors* (1960) lies across the river from the village of Peckham Rye, and Spark returns to the urban setting of *The Comforters* and *Memento Mori* to deal with another circumscribed society, middle- and upper-class bachelors "especially in Hampstead, especially in Kensington." And as she had in a more limited way in *The Comforters* in the activities of Willi Stock, suspected diabolist, and more pronouncedly in *Robinson* with the activities of Tom Wells, interpreter of occult signs, Spark turns to the occult in the person of Patrick Seton. Seton, chief medium of the Interior Spiral of the Wider Infin-

Dust jacket for Spark's 1960 novel about middle- and upper-class bachelors

ity, is, as Allan Massie has aptly put it, "a fake man but a genuine medium."

When not exercising his psychic powers, Seton spends his time avoiding Freda Flowers—an old widow whom he has bilked, forging letters and checks—and encouraging his young girl-friend, Alice, to abort their child. When she refuses, Seton plans Alice's murder by insulin over-dose. Seton's actions are at the center of *The Bachelors*, reflecting the worst quality, egocentric-ity, of many of the bachelors in the novel. Ewart Thornton, schoolmaster and member of Wider Infinity, uses his "mounds of homework" as an escape from the demands of human relationship. For Martin Bowles, barrister and only son, his aged mother and his housekeeper act as effective barriers to a permanent commitment to Isobel Billows, whose money Bowles is nonetheless happy to use. As Francis Eccles, one of the bachelors,

notes, "we are all fundamentally looking at each other and talking across the street from windows of different buildings which look similar from the outside. You don't know what my building is like inside and I don't know what yours is like." So-lipsism is the great temptation in this world, and only some of its inhabitants are capable of acts of love and courage that bring them out of intense isolation into connection with others.

Ronald Bridges, assistant curator of a small handwriting museum, is one bachelor who periodi-cally moves out of his isolation. As a handwriting expert, Bridges is brought into contact through the courts with Patrick Seton, who spends almost as much time forging as he does calling back spirits. But the connection between Seton and Bridges is more subtle than that relationship sug-gests because Spark sets them up as doubles. In so doing, she shapes two of the most fully re-alized characters in all of her work.

Both Seton with his trances and Bridges with his epileptic fits are physical exotics; they are also men who have considerable influence on those around them. But that influence comes from different sources. Seton's spiritualism en-courages his followers to forget themselves in a wash of emotion, giving the medium greater con-trol. Bridges's rather prickly Catholicism (he is a cradle Catholic rather than the usual Spark con-vert) forces on him the remembrance of self and responsibilities. Bridges might control people through his epilepsy, eliciting sympathy and pity, but he disciplines himself against this tendency, and "in latter years most of his fits occurred at home in his room . . . so that his friends came to believe that he suffered less frequently than he ac-tually did."

Both Seton and Bridges are also abstraction-ists who spend much energy on their own mental lives. Thus when the narrator enters Seton's mind, it is not surprising to find Seton and his own good view of himself at the center of it. More morally comforting to the reader is the con-flict in Bridges's mental life, a conflict that results from his inability to escape self-judgment. Recog-nizing his own willingness "to abstract his acquain-tance, in his mind's eye . . . to see the worst he could find in them," Bridges seeks through confes-sion to check his own excess.

Perhaps the best contrast between Seton and Bridges, though, is to be seen in their treat-ment of Alice and Elsie, waitresses in a coffee bar. For Patrick Seton, obsessed with himself, Alice becomes an inconvenience through her pregnancy, and he desires to be rid of her. Yet even in the midst of plotting her murder, he is able to justify his actions as being good for Alice: "And I will release her spirit from this gross body." In that and other scenes, Seton does not hear Alice's voice; his best conversation is always with and about himself. Self-interest, too, impels Bridges to visit Elsie, who has stolen Seton's forged letter, a letter to be used as evidence in the Flowers case. But he tells her directly that he is there for the letter "To save my own reputation," and all of this funny and poignant love scene involves Bridges talking and listening to Elsie (who says, "I have had sex without any relationships") as no man has before.

For Bridges there is a world outside of self; for Seton self is the world. Father Socket, Seton's rival as fraud and psychic, offers the best assessment when he argues, "What Patrick needs is *control*. Someone ought to control him." And control is the appropriate word to apply to Spark's admirable handling of technique and vision in *The Bachelors*.

Spark's sixth and finest novel, *The Prime of Miss Jean Brodie* (1961), is probably her best-known work, first serialized in the *New Yorker* and then produced as a book, a play, a movie, and a television series. The novel is certainly Spark's most critically acclaimed work; indeed, Mary Schneider speaks for most critics when she says, "*The Prime of Miss Jean Brodie* (1961) has long been recognized as a brilliantly woven novel, complex in its narrative techniques and themes." Once again, Spark focuses on a small group in an urban setting, but for the first and so far the only time in a novel, she uses her home city of Edinburgh in the 1930s and after as her setting. The Marcia Blaine School for Girls (much like James Gillespie's High School for Girls, which Spark attended) is the home ground of Jean Brodie and "the Brodie set": Monica Douglas, Rose Stanley, Eunice Gardner, Mary Macgregor, Jenny Gray, and Sandy Stranger.

Like Patrick Seton in *The Bachelors* and like the Fascist leaders she comes to admire during holidays on the Continent, Jean Brodie is a supreme egoist who dominates her girls and commits them to roles in her ongoing fiction about her elusive prime, the seemingly eternal apex of Brodie's physical and psychological power. But her fiction grows more complicated as the children in her care in the lower school become the young women of the upper school. For two of the group, Rose with her instinct and Sandy with

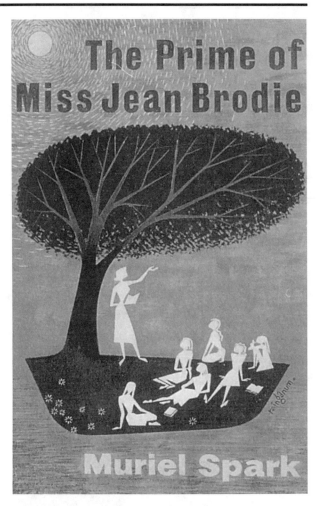

Dust jacket for Spark's 1961 novel, set in her home city of Edinburgh at a girls' school similar to the one she attended

her insight, Brodie shapes more complex roles; they are to realize her own passion for Teddy Lloyd, the art master: Rose as his lover and Sandy as Brodie's spy. Sandy, however, does some role changing. The most perceptive and deeply influenced of Brodie's girls, Sandy thwarts the plan: "it was Sandy who slept with Teddy Lloyd and Rose who carried back the information." Ultimately, Sandy also becomes Brodie's betrayer, supplying the political innuendo that leads to the teacher's dismissal.

No simple summation of central plot can capture the thematic and technical richness of Spark's novel. The best adjective to describe the technique that makes possible the thematic complexity is *economical*, a word used in the novel to describe Lloyd's artistic method. Nothing is wasted in the novel, which is so much about a waste of human energy. Spark's characterization works again through doubles, with Jean Brodie and

Sandy Stranger existing independently but acting as reflectors of one another. Economical, too, is the author's time frame: juxtaposing flash-forwards and flashbacks against the narrative line. Spark deftly counterpoints authorial omniscience with Brodie's attempts at omniscience; all that the author plans works, but not so with the plans of the title character.

Syntax also contributes to the novel's thematic complexity. For as David Lodge observes: "The novel echoes with [Brodie's] unqualified, declarative statements, which the girls tend to mimic in their speech, but against which the more subtle, syntactically complex passages of authorial comment or rendering of Sandy's consciousness are clearly contrasted." In fact, syntax economically underscores the primacy of Sandy's position in the novel, moving as she does from the child who suspiciously accepts Brodie's "unqualified, declarative statements," to the young woman who sees loyalty due to Brodie "Only up to a point," to the Roman Catholic convert and cloistered nun who in middle age becomes famous for "her odd psychological treatise on the nature of moral perception, called 'The Transfiguration of the Commonplace.'"

The description of the treatise, coming in a flash-forward early in the novel, acts as an ironic commentary on the actions of the novel, suggesting Sandy's imperfect progress to some measure of moral perception. The young girl is obsessed with psychological concerns; she is the sleuth seeking information "about the case of Brodie." Gradually that selfish preoccupation gives way to a growing moral concern that recognizes her obligation to others and compels her to stop Brodie's shaping of another set of girls. (That action, like all the actions of the novel, obviously springs from more than any single motive, and Spark suggests that Sandy's impulse is also tinged with jealousy.) But Sandy's moral recognition needs the leaven of charity, a leaven that comes with her recognition of her obligations to God.

Sandy's conversion and vocation make her less dogmatic in her judgments of others, in particular in her judgment of Jean Brodie. She comes to see Miss Brodie not as the monster she thought she saw at the Marcia Blaine School but as a fallible being "quite innocent in her way." (Spark has claimed, "My characters are not good and not bad.") There are many commonplaces transfigured in *The Prime of Miss Jean Brodie*, but certainly the most important is Sandy's movement from the easy task of forming an opinion

Dust jacket for Spark's 1963 novel, set in the 1940s at a club established "for the Pecuniary Convenience and Social Protection of Ladies of Slender Means. . . ."

(judgment) to her transformation into Sister Helena and the much more difficult work of knowing (perception). As with other Spark converts, Sandy Stranger's life is not eased by conversion; rather, her lot is much more complicated because of the prescriptions of her faith. Sandy is "not composed like the other nuns who sat, when they received their rare visitors [in their cloistered convent], well back in the darkness with folded hands. But Sandy always leaned forward and peered, clutching the bars with both hands. . . ."

Conversion does not make life easier either for Nicholas Farringdon in *The Girls of Slender Means* (1963), which first appeared in a condensed form in the *Saturday Evening Post* in December 1963. The novel opens with a flash-forward: news of Farringdon's death—"Martyred in Haiti"—a death that results from his having gone to Haiti as a missionary after his wartime conversion to Catholicism. As it had in *The Prime of Miss Jean Brodie*, Spark's narrative moves between past and present, but the narrative movement in *The Girls of Slender Means* is much more predictable and much less effective than in the novel that precedes it. London is the setting in both present and past time frames, but the book's primary focus is on the London of the early 1940s and, in particular, the May of Teck Club established "for the Pecuniary Convenience and Social Protection of Ladies of Slender Means below the age of Thirty Years. . . ." Its four floors house young women who work in London and three older women who have been there since before World War I; the novel places particular emphasis on the fourth floor, where "the most attractive, sophisticated and lively girls had their rooms."

One of the "lively girls," Jane Wright, brings Farringdon, then "known only as a poet of small talent and an anarchist of dubious loyalty," into the club. Farringdon quickly becomes a regular at the May of Teck, where he and Selena Redwood, a social climber, spend summer evenings sleeping on the roof. That same rooftop becomes the setting for events that lead to Nicholas Farringdon's conversion. As Farringdon watches from a nearby roof, an unexploded bomb goes off in the garden below, trapping fourteen women on the top floor with only the small window from lavatory to rooftop as means of escape.

The scene pits the values of Joanna Childe, a rector's daughter and elocution teacher, against those of Selena Redwood, who, because her devotion to her figure has made her slender, is able to get through the window. Selena goes through the window twice as other, less svelte girls hover in panic. Joanna tries to minimize the panic by reciting a psalm and calming the others; Selena gives herself over to rescuing the Schiaparelli dress she had so often borrowed from another of the "lively girls" and worn to social success, a success that seems even greater in the present as Selena is buffered by her "thousands of secretaries or whatever they are." No buffers exist for Joanna, shepherd of the frightened flock: "The house sank into its centre, a high heap of rubble, and Joanna went with it."

Nicholas realizes through witnessing the tragedy that "Nowhere's safe," especially for those who seem to be touched by grace. But that recognition and the conversion that leads him to death in Haiti are actually at odds with the tone of *The Girls of Slender Means*; the novel is a comedy of manners that works beautifully when directed toward satirizing the civilized savageries of the May of Teck Club. Spark is most successful with her

character types and the conflicts among them; she is much less successful when she tries to transfigure those same types and conflicts into allegorical matter. Powerful as it is, the scene in the lavatory and on the rooftop is ultimately all too neat, and Farringdon's subsequent association of Joanna's sacrifice with "The Wreck of the Deutschland" is too contrived. Perhaps the greatest problem in the novel is Farringdon's rather slender characterization; he is never as interesting and effective a character as he has to be to let the novel move from one level to another on the basis of his conversion.

Spark's interest in conversion surfaces again in *The Mandelbaum Gate* (1965), a novel that came out of the author's stay in Israel while covering the Adolf Eichmann trial in 1961 for British newspapers. Like Spark, Barbara Vaughan, the heroine, is a half-Jewish and half-Protestant Briton who has converted to Roman Catholicism. That conversion has happened before the novel's opening in Israel in 1961; as a result of her conversion, Barbara wants to make a pilgrimage to the Christian shrines in Israel and Jordan. She also wants to be near—though not too near—her lover, Harry Clegg, an archaeologist working on Dead Sea excavations in Jordan. She plans to marry Clegg if he can secure an annulment of a previous marriage; Barbara is very much the convert, and her faith seems sometimes too set.

Freddy Hamilton's conversion, however, is of a different kind. The novel opens and closes with Hamilton's walks from Jordanian Jerusalem through the Mandelbaum Gate—"a piece of street between Jerusalem and Jerusalem, flanked by two huts, and called by that name because a house at the other end once belonged to a Mr. Mandelbaum"—into Israeli Jerusalem. Between the walks that begin and end the novel, Hamilton, a middle-aged British consular official in Israel, is converted, at least temporarily, from observer and chronicler into man of action.

As the novel opens, Hamilton, who would have fit into the world of *The Bachelors*, is greatly concerned with the form his thank-you note to Joanna, "his hostess on the other side," will take. When not composing bread-and-butter notes, Hamilton spends a good deal of time shaping letters to be sent to his aged mother and her aged servant in England: he is a polite man. His concern with politesse is in ironic contrast to his presence in a divided and dangerous Jerusalem, where he disdainfully observes: "They dramatized everything." Soon enough Hamilton becomes part of

MARK GERSON

Spark

The Mandelbaum Gate

Muriel Spark

The Mandelbaum Gate

MACMILLAN

Dust jacket for Spark's 1965 novel, which grew from her trip to Israel to cover the Adolf Eichmann trial

the central drama, Barbara Vaughan's illegal entry into and journey through Jordan. Fittingly, however, Hamilton's active participation in that pilgrimage is caused by words.

In his first meeting with Barbara in Israel, Hamilton is politely and rightly annoyed by her smug way of quoting the Bible, particularly when those passages criticize his way of life. So when Barbara intones, "Being what thou art, luke-warm, neither cold nor hot, thou wilt make me vomit thee out of my mouth," Hamilton remains silent and then goes off to write a "bread-and-butter letter" to his hostess. But the condemnation stays in his mind, and he finds himself using similar words to describe his own and his friends' safe life-styles when he meets Barbara in Jordan. Those words prompt a dramatic change in Hamilton, a change that impels him to accompany Barbara on her dangerous pilgrimage. Hamilton also enlists the aid of Abdul and Suzi Ramdez, Palestinians who have learned that survival is the true faith in this setting of clashing faiths.

The danger of the pilgrimage liberates Barbara and Hamilton. He begins his adventure by putting letters he has written and letters he has received down a toilet: "Any correspondence

that's bloody boring, just pull the chain on it. That's my motto," he tells Barbara. And she, too, recognizes the significance of her own new beginning "and for the first time in this Holy Land, she felt all of a piece, a Gentile Jewess, a private-judging Catholic, a shy adventuress." But pilgrimages, and adventures, end, and for Hamilton breakthrough leads to both temporary breakdown (caused by sunstroke and the discovery of colleagues acting as spies for Egyptian president Gamal Abdel Nasser) and loss of memory after three exciting days in Jordan. Much of the narrative moves from recent past to present and back again as Hamilton struggles to remember.

Hamilton's memory returns, and so does much of the old Freddy, but not all: "Looking back at the experience in later years Freddy was amazed. It had seemed to transfigure his life, without any disastrous change in the appearance of things; pleasantly and essentially he came to feel it had made a free man of him where before he had been the subdued, obedient servant of a mere disorderly sensation, that of impersonal guilt. And whether this feeling of Freddy's subsequent years was justified or not, it did him good to harbour it." Barbara Vaughan is not transfigured by the experience, but she is united with Harry Clegg in an ending which is one of the most chaotic and least satisfying in Spark's fiction. Spark tries to pull together too many themes and too many characters in a conclusion that is at odds with the rest of the novel, and she has herself described the chief defect of *The Mandelbaum Gate*: "It's out of proportion: the beginning is slow, the end is very rapid."

Despite its many riches—the conversion of Freddy Hamilton, the characterization of the Ramdez family, the Forsterian depiction of the English abroad, and, above all, the felt power of Jerusalem—*The Mandelbaum Gate*, for which Spark won the James Tait Black Memorial Prize in 1966, is a disappointment. Anthony Burgess in *The Novel Now* (1967) and Warner Berthoff in "Fortunes of the Novel: Muriel Spark and Iris Murdoch" (1967) are among many critics who complain that Spark gambled on too expansive a form and lost. There is a noticeable lack of economy, and Spark's own comments about the book are most illuminating: "I got bored, because it was too long, so I decided never again to write a long book. Keep them very short."

In the books that follow, Spark adheres to her own guidelines. Peter Kemp sees these books as "stringently pared down to steely essentials." *The Public Image* (1968) is about half the length of *The Mandelbaum Gate*, and the many critics who responded negatively to *The Mandelbaum Gate* praised *The Public Image*. That praise is best summed up by Frederick P. W. McDowell, who calls it a "delightful if somewhat slight novel. . . . After her excursion into extended narrative in *The Mandelbaum Gate* (1965), Mrs. Spark has apparently returned to what she does best: the witty, ironic, and wry development in short compass, of an ethical issue of some importance and significance." (Between novels, in 1967, Spark's *Collected Poems I* and *Collected Stories I* were published.) Drawing on her experiences while she was writing press releases for celebrities and from her own celebrity, Spark distills setting and characterization in this fascinating novel and concentrates on "the expense of spirit" required to become and to continue as a public image.

The novel is set in Rome, the city to which Spark moved in 1967. (Perhaps the moves from Edinburgh to South Africa to Rhodesia to London to New York to Rome were what prompted Spark to refer to herself as "a born exile.") Annabel Christopher is a bit player transformed by Luigi Leopardi into "the English Lady-Tiger"

of the grade-B films in which she stars. The transformation, however, is as much the work of Annabel, who "was entirely aware of the image-making process in every phase," as it is of the Italian director. But that process is not acceptable to Frederick Christopher, Annabel's husband, part-time actor, and sometime writer of screenplays; by the time the novel opens, Frederick has written his most original and, ultimately, most successful script, though one that is to be played out in real life rather than on-screen: his suicide and her culpability.

Annabel's cinematic image involves a wedding of worldly wanton and faithful wife and mother, and Frederick's final script involves verifying the first part by annihilating the second part of her image. He jumps to his death in a church named for martyrs while an orgy he has arranged goes on in Annabel's apartment. He leaves letters to his dead mother, his errant wife, his infant son, and his best friend, knowing full well that the spicy notes soon will be devoured "in Italy, the Motherland of Sensation." Spark's depiction of the seamy side of celebrity, particularly the press's and the public's love of scandal, is masterful.

What Frederick does not reckon with is Annabel's will and imagination. Quickly rescued from Frederick's death and eerie letter, she starts living her own scenario; and in chillingly comic scenes, Annabel shapes a new image of bereaved wife, which she links to her existing image as devoted mother to her baby son. But more than image is at stake as she tells Leopardi, "I won't live up to a bad name." Annabel makes her stand because she begins to distinguish between "name," which has reference to a moral reality, and the banality of "image."

Once again, Spark presents a transfiguration of the commonplace but with none of the religious underpinnings of *The Prime of Miss Jean Brodie*. Like Freddy Hamilton's in *The Mandelbaum Gate*, Annabel's transfiguration is played out in a secular world; her breakthrough is psychological and moral, very much connected to the one part of her image which becomes real: her love for her son. Conceived to preserve the marriage and her public image, Annabel's baby takes on greater and greater significance in her life: "The baby, Carl, was the only reality of her life. His existence gave her a sense of being permanently secured to the world which she had not experienced since her own childhood had passed. . . . She felt a curious fear of display

Dust jacket for Spark's 1968 novel, a depiction of celebrity life in Rome, where Spark had moved in 1967

where the baby was concerned, as if this deep and complete satisfaction might be disfigured or melted away by some public image." Carl has such consequence in her life that she is able to pull back from the final immorality of "the image-making process," that of giving in to the blackmail of Billy O'Brien, her husband's friend and family hanger-on. She refuses to save her image in favor of saving herself.

Like Annabel Christopher, Lise, the central character in *The Driver's Seat* (1970), is greatly concerned with her public image. (*The Driver's Seat* appeared first in the *New Yorker* in May 1970 and was filmed in Italy in 1975.) But Lise's image-making is a reversal of the process in *The Public Image*, where the external image first imposed on Annabel threatens to subsume her internal life; Lise's public image is an external projection of an internal life gone awry. The novel opens with Lise's argument with a salesgirl who tries to sell her a dress "in the new stainless fabric," an attempt that Lise says she finds insulting. Instead she buys a stainable dress that fits her strange plan by making her conspicuous: "A lemon-yellow top with a skirt patterned in bright V's of

orange, mauve and blue."

The adjective *strange* applies to much in *The Driver's Seat*, where the action is not clearly located: planes that could be going anywhere and hotels that could be anywhere provide the minimal setting. In this novel, for the first time, Spark's narrative is principally in the present tense, with a few crucial flash-forwards carrying the reader into the gory future that awaits Lise. Perhaps one reason for the primacy of present tense in her tenth novel, several critics have suggested, is Spark's great interest in cinematic immediacy, which the present tense allows her to approximate in her narrative. Of greater importance, however, the present tense heightens Lise's seeming control of her own death.

She orchestrates her public image to draw attention to herself. Her garish clothing, loud chatter on a plane with a macrobiotic faddist, bizarre shopping trip with a stranger—all serve her plan as "she lays the trail, presently to be followed by Interpol and elaborated upon with due art by the journalists of Europe." That planning leads her to a newly released sex criminal, and to a chilling

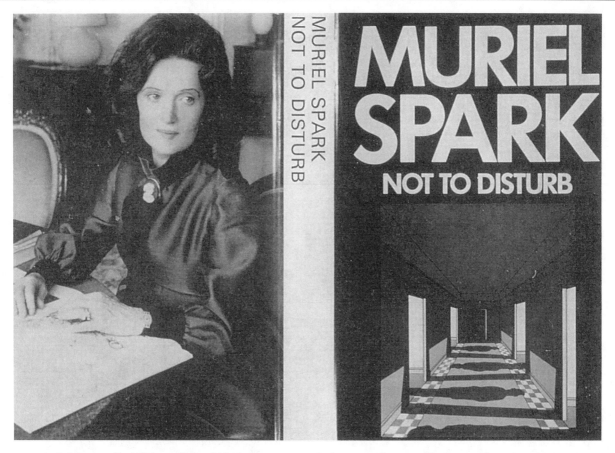

Dust jacket for Spark's 1971 novel, in which the servants at a Swiss estate plot to exploit their employers' suicidal rampage

scene in which she stage-manages her own murder. She controls almost everything; only her command to tie her ankles before the rape-murder goes unheeded. But even that slip is rectified as "He stands staring for a while and then, having started to turn away he hesitates as if he had forgotten something of bidding. Suddenly he wrenches off his necktie and bends to tie her ankles together with it." So at the end, Lise's plot has unfolded completely, and she remains in the driver's seat. In general, critical responses were cryptically favorable. For example, Phoebe Adams called the novel "a brilliant, backhanded cliffhanger," and Guy Davenport commented on "the wild pace." Some critics, however, found the novel unclear and suggested, as does Linda Kuehl, that Spark was only "interested in flexing novelistic method."

Not to Disturb (1971) is to some extent a continuation of Spark's interest in characters as collaborators in shaping plot. As in the novels before *The Driver's Seat*, Spark focuses on a special group and its behavior. The setting, a bit more substantial than that of *The Driver's Seat*, is the es-

tate of the Baron Klopstock in Switzerland, where the servants, dominated by Lister, the butler, seek to direct the activities of their employers' final night. The staff's direction is a good deal more indirect than Lise's; they endeavor not to disturb the baron, the baroness, and Victor Passerat, their secretary and lover, as that trio work out their jealous rage, a rage that will lead to murders and suicide in the morning. Obsessed with the passion for profit, the staff plans to exploit the scandal in press releases, articles, books, and films.

Spark captures the enormous ego involvement of the international staff, whose chief concern is with what their media images will be rather than with the grisly reality of the action in the library. The comic elements are vintage Spark; for example, Lister's preparation of a press handout about the murders relates his own biography with no mention of the Klopstocks, whose coming deaths make all of the planning and writing possible. Lister and his confederates have learned their amorality well, and the world of *Not to Disturb* is as far away from any moral con-

344

cerns as is the psychotic world of Lise in *The Driver's Seat*. Yet *Not to Disturb* has none of the compelling intensity of its predecessor, and what seems
clever at the outset in *Not to Disturb*—the servants
predestining the fate of the Klopstocks and their
secretary—grows stale by the end. Ultimately, *Not
to Disturb* is too little about too little. Critical response has been dramatially divided between
those who, like Patricia Meyer Spacks, see the
novel as "a Bergsonian comedy which maintains
a delicate poise" and those who, like Lawrence
Graves, maintain that the book's "philosophical
mysteries look suspiciously like pretenses."

   The Hothouse by the East River (1973) is an account of the madness of the Hazlett household in
an overheated, undercooled apartment by the
East River in New York City. Madness and its drastic dislocation dominate the city and its inhabitants: Elsa Hazlett casts her shadow in the wrong
direction; Poppy Xavier, Elsa's friend, conceals
"Under the protective folds of her breasts . . . a
precious new consignment of mulberry leaves
bearing numerous eggs of silk-worms"; and Peter
Pan is played by an actor in his sixties. But individuals locked in their private obsessions, an ongoing concern in Spark's work, are but part of a
larger picture of a civilization that is sick, a civilization in which "Sick is real." Indeed, the chief patient and character in the novel is New York itself (a love-hate tribute from Spark, who lived in
the city during the 1960s): "New York, home of
the vivisectors of the mind, and of the mentally
vivisected still to be reassembled, of those who
live intact, habitually wondering about their
states of sanity, and the home of those whose
minds have been dead, bearing the scars of resurrection: New York heaves outside the consultant's
office, agitating all around her about her ears."

   New York as setting—the most acutely deline-
ated place in Spark's fiction since the Jerusalem
of *The Mandelbaum Gate*—and as symbol is most effective, while the novel's attack on psychiatry is
on target and worthy of a writer who has questioned the existence of the unconscious. But
these virtues in *The Hothouse by the East River* are ultimately undercut by the allegorical confusion.
All the major characters in the present are dead
and are involved in what seems to be the dream
of Paul Hazlett, Elsa's husband, who is also dead;
but the very materiality of place is at odds with
the novel's allegorical thrust.

   For Paul, Elsa, Poppy, and a few others,
only the past is real, and the past brought in by
Paul's flashbacks is lived in a mysterious military

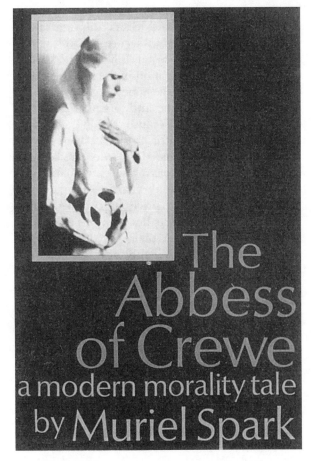

*Dust jacket for the American edition of Spark's 1974 novel
about an election at an English abbey*

installation called "The Compound" during the
summer of 1944; however, a V-2 bomb demol-
ishes a train carrying Paul, Elsa, Poppy, and others on leave. But life goes on in Paul's imagination, which transports people from the past into
a modern inferno in the 1970s. It is a journey
that the reader, trapped in the fictional hothouse, has difficulty making with any great interest.

   Perhaps an expiation for the complexities of
The Hothouse by the East River, Spark's next novel,
The Abbess of Crewe (1974), is set in the present
with a plot that is simplicity itself, particularly for
those who know anything of the Watergate scandal. The obvious connections are there with the
bugging devices, break-ins, and egomania of
Washington transferred to the election of an abbess in the Abbey of Crewe in England. And publicity about the novel and its film version, *Nasty
Habits* (1976), made much of that selling point.

   While the trappings are clearly of Watergate
vintage, the central issue in the novel—who shall

have dominion—is paramount in Spark's work. The successful candidate, Sister Alexandra, installs electronic devices to secure control and to rout her populist foe, Sister Felicity, who divides her time between fornication in the bushes and attempts to democratize the abbey. Against such opposition, the aristocratic and pragmatic Alexandra easily triumphs because she has, as Jean Brodie was wont to put it, "vision": "Here, in the Abbey of Crewe, we have discarded history. We have entered the sphere . . . of mythology. My nuns love it. Who doesn't yearn to be part of a myth at whatever the price in comfort?" Like Brodie, the abbess directs her energies toward realizing her will and her plans for others, and to that end she selects a band of loyal followers much like Brodie's crème de la crème. Unlike Brodie, however, the abbess has self-awareness as well as imagination, and that very self-awareness in the central character makes problems for the reader.

It is not clear what the narrator's view of the abbess is. If all of the plot elements are connected to a Watergate parallel, then the reader is tempted to side with the witless Felicity. No such temptation exists when the book is cut loose from that association. The abbess, with her love of Alexander Pope and John Milton and her grand style, overpowers Felicity, whose best lines come when she quotes the abbess: " 'Alexandra,' says Felicity, 'has actually said, "To hell with St. Francis of Assisi. I prefer Sextus Propertius who belongs to Assisi, a contemporary of Jesus and spiritual forerunner of Hamlet, Werther, Rousseau and Kierkegaard." ' " With no strong figure to offset the abbess, she dominates the action of the novel, and what is advertised as a satire of Watergate becomes a tribute to aristocratic egomania. Negative criticism of the novel, for example Michael Wood's review in the *New York Review of Books* and John Updike's review in the *New Yorker*, has been directed toward the Watergate apparatus, what Updike terms "the pull of topical actualities," in the novel.

Like the abbess of Crewe, Hubert Mallindaine in *The Takeover* (1976) has little time for history; he, too, seeks myth, but his is ready-made in the pages of Sir James Frazer's *The Golden Bough* (1890-1915). For Hubert sees himself as "the descendant of the Emperor of Rome [Caligula] and the Benevolent-Malign Diana of the Woods. . . ." And in an attempt to realize his kingly priesthood, he settles in a house at Nemi, Grove of Diana; more precisely, Hubert takes

over a house owned by Maggie Radcliffe, a rich American friend from whom he is alienated, and lives there with three young male secretaries. But Hubert's plans are soon upset when the young men go off to other pursuits and Maggie wants her property back.

Indeed, many personal plans and public certainties are upset by the discords of life in Italy in the 1970s, where the wealthy hire their own intruders to dupe real burglars. The country is faced with "the collapse of money" in 1974 because of rising oil prices, and with the threat to traditions posed by the Communist victory in 1975. These public "takeovers" find their place in Spark's novel alongside the sexual, social, and religious "takeovers" that result from the manipulations of the novel's characters. Greed is everywhere in this quick-paced and detailed book—Spark's densest book since *The Mandelbaum Gate*. Lawyers take fees and betray clients, friends defraud one another, and servants blackmail masters. And these microcosmic betrayals reflect the larger breakdowns in social and political orders that seem everywhere to be foundering.

In her review of *The Takeover*, Margaret Drabble rightly notes that Spark's "theme [is] . . . too large for the book" and then praises Spark for attempting so ambitious a theme. It is certainly a theme that allows Spark scope for her considerable satiric skill, particularly in the treatment of Hubert Mallindaine. Kinship with Diana leads Hubert to found his own church in the very shadow of Castelgondolfo, the pope's summer residence. Hubert's church is dedicated to immaterialism and its founder's material comforts, but his ecumenical, ecclesiastical plans—to syphon off some of the crowds who have come for the Holy Year—are ended by a riot during one of his meetings. Hubert bounces back and at the end of the novel prepares to aid some English Jesuits in a charismatic movement. That ending also finds Maggie Radcliffe taking over the role of terrorist to restore her fortune by having Coco de Renault, the financier who embezzled her fortune, abducted and held for ransom in the caves at Nemi.

It is in her disguise as criminal crone that Maggie meets Hubert for the first time in the course of the narrative (all their other contacts have been through letters and lawyers). They meet in the novel's final—and confusing—scene in the grove at Nemi. After raising all sorts of questions about the decay of Italy and Europe, Spark settles for an ending that has a strange, fairy-tale

Dust jacket for the American edition of Spark's 1976 novel about a man in Italy during the 1970s who regards himself as a descendant of Caligula

quality to it, with Hubert and Maggie restored to friendship and the narrator focusing on "the lush lakeside and, in the fields beyond, the kindly fruits of the earth." Spark provides a wishfully romantic close to a book that has rather exhilaratingly dealt with decrease and decline; the ending tries too hard to put the lid on things.

Territorial Rights (1979) is also set in Spark's adopted Italy, but its locale, Venice, is far from the grove at Nemi. Distant too is Spark's concern with the jet set and international finance. Yet the theme of betrayal, which is so prominent in *The Takeover* and in all of her other novels, is no less prominent in Spark's fifteenth novel. *Territorial Rights* focuses on a small group of people—mostly British—who find themselves in or close to the pensione Sofia, a small hotel in Venice. Robert Leaver, a young British art student who arrives at the pensione, has left Paris and his rich American lover, Mark Curran, to pursue Lina Pancev, a Bulgarian who has defected to get information about her father, Victor Pancev, last seen in Venice during World War II. Curran also comes to Venice, which "had been his territory

for the best part of his life," in pursuit of Robert. Curran stays at the Hotel Lord Byron, the same hotel to which Robert's father, Arnold Leaver, headmaster of Ambrose, comes with his mistress in pursuit of a holiday far from his wife, Anthea, in Birmingham. But Anthea gets into the action via phone calls from Grace Gregory, former matron at Ambrose, who follows her former lover, Arnold, to Venice. Anthea Leaver also hires investigators from "GESS (Global-Equip Security Services) Ltd." to track Arnold. The GESS agent in Venice is Violet de Winter, an old friend of Curran's. Curran, de Winter, and the sisters who own the Pensione Sofia had been accomplices in the murder and butchering of Victor Pancev during World War II. The complexities of the plot test the reader's willingness to suspend disbelief.

But the interconnections among the characters in the novel give Spark a wide range of human behavior to satirize. The bureaucrats of GESS, among them Mr. B., are actually well-organized blackmailers. Anthea Leaver's reading tastes run to realistic domestic fiction, but disliking realism in life, she willingly blinds herself to

Muriel Spark, circa 1981 (photograph by Jerry Bauer)

her son's malignant behavior. Lina Pancev's desire to be fairly treated in the West does not extend to her treatment of Jews, for after sleeping with Leo, Grace Gregory's companion, and discovering he is half-Jewish, she jumps into the canal to cleanse herself. These activities and others catch the eye of Spark's omniscient narrator, but, clearly, Robert Leaver's activities receive most of the narrative focus because Leaver—art history student, prostitute, kept man, author/blackmailer, and, finally, terrorist—is the link, though a weak link, among the characters.

Robert is the most startlingly amoral character in the novel: leaving Curran to pursue Lina, he expects the older man "to come and arrange things" in Venice, which Curran is all too willing to do. What Curran can not arrange, however, is

even a glimmering of moral responsibility in Robert, whom he had met when Robert "was a prostitute on the streets of Paris, posing as a student." Robert is a poser as a son and as a lover as well, so his dropping out of sight and contacting Curran and others in his new pose as author/blackmailer is not at all surprising, since all of his relationships have been parasitical. Robert's move from small-time hustling in Paris, to blackmailing in Venice, to terrorizing in Europe and beyond makes sense when one abstracts the action in *Territorial Rights*. But when one confronts the novel and, in particular, Robert's characterization, that movement is not so readily accepted. Like Nicholas Farringdon in *The Girls of Slender Means*, Robert Leaver is too ill-defined a character on whom to anchor the novel; Spark offers too little and asks the reader to fill in too much.

Perhaps because she is both narrator and central character, Fleur Talbot anchors *Loitering With Intent* (1981) quite nicely. Spark returns to a British setting, London shortly after World War II, and shapes a portrait of the artist as struggling writer and as female. The older, established Fleur Talbot who narrates the novel returns to a more straitened time in her life as she works on her first novel, *Warrender Chase*. The younger Fleur supports herself as a secretary/ghostwriter for the members of the Autobiographical Association, whose manipulative director, Sir Quentin Oliver, specializes in blackmail.

In the members of the Autobiographical Association, Spark is back to the superb deftness of description that characterizes the geriatric set in *Memento Mori* and the title characters in *The Bachelors*. The small coterie that forms the Autobiographical Association—among them Father Egbart Delaney, a defrocked priest; Sir Eric Findlay, a baronet with a nursery fixation; Miss Maisie Young, a preposterous pseudointellectual; and the pathetic Lady Bernice "Bucks" Gilbert, a socialite who commits suicide—provides the weaknesses that Sir Quentin plans to use against its members. What he does not take into account is the creative license that Fleur Talbot, one of Spark's more relaxed Catholics, exercises. Hired to transcribe autobiographical accounts, Fleur's imagination takes over, and the battle with Sir Quentin begins. Soon enough his machinations find their way into her own manuscript, *Warrender Chase*, and the wily Sir Quentin turns his considerable powers against Fleur. He enlists the support of Fleur's more rigid Catholic friend Dottie, whose husband, Leslie, has been Fleur's lover. Sir Quentin has Dottie remove the manuscript of *Warrender Chase* from Fleur's knitting bag. He also pressures Fleur's first publisher, Revisson Doe, to abandon plans to publish the novel.

What Sir Quentin does not reckon on is Fleur's enormous ego; her heroes are Cardinal Newman and Benvenuto Cellini. Nothing stands in the way of her becoming a writer. Sir Quentin also underestimates the power of love. His neglected mother, Lady Edwina, and Miss Beryl Tims, "the English Rose" who serves as his housekeeper, flower under Fleur's attention and kindness. Together, Fleur and Lady Edwina foil Sir Quentin's plans to play God with the lives of others. Fleur, however, plays God as author, has her first novel published, and—like her hero Cellini—goes on her way rejoicing.

The Only Problem (1984) displays too much intent and not enough loitering. Spark's novel is informed by the Book of Job, a linking that Anita Brookner praised in her *New York Times* review: "The Book of Job and the terrible reversals implied in the Biblical narrative . . . are a suitable subject for this fearless and fastidious writer and her thoughtful protagonist." Maybe so, but the results do not add up to a very engaging novel.

Harvey Gotham, separated from his wife, Effie, who has become an international terrorist, has retreated to Epinal, France, to write an exegesis on the Book of Job. In many ways the exegete turns into a modern Job, facing as Gotham does the trials brought on by a wife sought by the police; a sister-in-law, Ruth, who shows up with his wife's baby; and various unwanted visitors. At least that is the parallel the novel aims for as Spark pursues the question of God's benevolence and its relationship to human suffering.

What does not work in the novel, though, is Harvey's massive detachment from people and ordinary life. Spark is never able to center the reader's concern on Harvey, whose move from scholarly isolation to human caring is recorded in the book. The novel rests on convincing the reader that Harvey loves the wayward Effie, whose anarchist activities lead to her death in a shoot-out with the Paris police. But most readers would agree with Harvey's brother-in-law, Edward, who writes, "You can't have been so desperately in love with her. Quite honestly, when you were together, I never thought you were really crazy about her."

Leaving international problems behind her, Spark returns to a British setting during the 1950s in *A Far Cry from Kensington* (1988). She returns, too, to attachment rather than detachment in her narrative stance. Claire Tomalin's review of this book in the *Independent* is quoted on the Penguin paperback edition with good reason. Tomalin captures the spirit of the novel when she writes, "Love arises from the heart, says the narrator Mrs. Hawkins, and hate from principle. Her story is about principles, literary and other, though love makes a gentle entry too."

Mrs. Hawkins (Nancy) is both narrator and central character in the novel. The older Nancy returns to her days as an overweight, capable young war widow—called Mrs. Hawkins by almost everyone—who works in a postwar publishing world populated by frauds such as Hector Bartlett, who tries to destroy her because she terms him a "pisseur de copie." Bartlett enlists the aid of his patron, the successful novelist Emma Loy, against Mrs. Hawkins, but as she sheds pounds, Mrs. Hawkins acquires a more formidable status. Emma Loy attempts to enlist her aid in repairing Bartlett's reputation, which Mrs. Hawkins's phrase has harmed. In that attempt Nancy Hawkins learns of Bartlett's involvement with Wanda Podolak, a Polish refugee who lives in her boardinghouse in Kensington.

Wanda is part of a blackmail scheme that involves Bartlett, electronics, publishers, and political refugees. Bartlett has found a way to use Wanda's gullibility and guilt to put a curse on his detractor, Mrs. Hawkins. Wanda mistakes Mrs. Hawkins's weight loss as proof of the curse's power, and her guilt, occasioned by past political and religious experiences, intensifies and culminates in her suicide by drowning. Mrs. Hawkins can do little but grieve for Wanda, since written evidence that implicates Bartlett is stolen, and only later can she put all the pieces together. That grief itself, however, supports Tomalin's contention that "love makes a gentle entry" into *A Far Cry from Kensington*.

That love is best seen in the interactions in the boardinghouse run by Millie Sanders and populated by Mrs. Hawkins, Wanda, and others. Spark presents a community where people do the best they can to accommodate one another's eccentricities. The boardinghouse in Kensington is Spark's gentlest depiction of humankind. There, Mrs. Hawkins finds not only material for a narrative but also a friend in Millie Sanders and a lover and husband in William Todd, a medical student.

Not so gentle a scene is set in *Symposium* (1990). Spark dissects the relationships of the five couples at a dinner party given by the American artist Hurley Reed and the rich Australian widow Chris Donovan in contemporary London. The title echoes the Platonic dialogue in which Socrates questions the nature of love, but, as in *The Only Problem* with its echoes of the Book of Job, the parallel is more interesting to note than to read.

Through flash-forwards and flashbacks, Spark establishes a set of relationships that move from the genuine affection of the cousins Roland Sykes and Annabel Treece, to the civilized boredom of Ernst and Ella Untzinger, who share mutual passion for an American graduate student and part-time criminal, to the May-December mating of Lord Brian and Lady Helen Suzy, whose recent robbery is table talk and a foreshadowing of

the violence that will claim Hilda Damien, mother of William, a guest at the party. Indeed, much of the focus of the novel is on the identity of Margaret Damien, William's bride, whom he met when buying grapefruit. That question underscores one of the chief problems in the novel—two story lines that only artificially cohere.

On one level there is the dinner party and the social commentary that it invites from Spark, but somehow we have been on that terrain before, whether in the Italy of *The Takeover* or the Switzerland of *Not to Disturb*. There is the same sense of corruption (criminal servants, promiscuous employers, masses of things), although London is tame compared to Spark's depiction of the Continent. On the other level there is the past of Margaret Damien, née Murchie, of St. Andrews.

The Scottish story line is the more interesting one, particularly because of mad Magnus Murchie, a figure reminiscent of Dougal Douglas in *The Ballad of Peckham Rye*. Magnus acts as the family adviser. "Many families have at least one fairly mad member, whether in or out of an institution. But the families do not normally consult the mad people even if they have lucid periods; the families do not go to them for advice. The Murchies were different." Indeed, on one visit from the asylum, Magnus sets the scene for changing his mother's will, a scenario that leads to Mrs. Murchie's murder by an escaped inmate from the asylum. In a visit by Margaret to the asylum, her uncle advises her on choosing a husband, advice that leads to grapefruits and William. In between those visits, Margaret takes refuge in an Anglican convent run by leftist nuns—too easy a target for Spark. While Margaret is in the convent, a nun is murdered. The Murchies are a strange lot drawn from the Border Ballads that Spark loves; unfortunately, the other dinner guests are not as colorful.

Symposium is not vintage Spark, but less of Spark is better than more of most other contemporary writers. Her careful and controlled work in what she herself terms minor novels—particularly in *Memento Mori*, *The Bachelors*, *The Prime of Miss Jean Brodie*, *The Public Image*, *The Driver's Seat*, and *A Far Cry from Kensington*—has earned Spark a major reputation among British writers in the second half of the twentieth century.

Interviews:
"My Conversion," *Twentieth Century*, 170 (Autumn 1961): 58-63;

Frank Kermode, "The House of Fiction: Interviews with Seven English Novelists," *Partisan Review*, 30 (Spring 1963): 61-82;

"Keeping It Short—Muriel Spark Talks About Her Books to Ian Gillhan," *Listener*, 84 (1970): 411-413.

Bibliography:

Thomas A. Tominaga and Wilma Schneidermeyer, *Iris Murdoch and Muriel Spark: A Bibliography* (Metuchen, N.J.: Scarecrow Press, 1976).

Biography:

Derek Stanford, *Muriel Spark: A Biographical and Critical Study* (London: Centaur, 1963).

References:

Frank Baldanza, "Muriel Spark and the Occult," *Wisconsin Studies in Contemporary Literature*, 6 (Summer 1965): 190-203;

Warner Berthoff, "Fortunes of the Novel: Muriel Spark and Iris Murdoch," *Massachusetts Review*, 8 (Spring 1967): 301-332;

Malcolm Bradbury, "Muriel Spark's Fingernails," *Critical Quarterly*, 14 (Autumn 1972): 241-250;

Rodney Stenning Edgecombe, *Vocation and Identity in the Fiction of Muriel Spark* (Columbia: University of Missouri Press, 1990);

Peter Kemp, *Muriel Spark* (London: Elek, 1974);

Frank Kermode, *Modern Essays* (London: Collins, 1971);

Kermode, "The Prime of Miss Muriel Spark," *New Statesman*, 66 (27 September 1963): 397-398;

Judy Little, *Comedy and the Woman Writer: Woolf, Spark, and Feminism* (Lincoln: University of Nebraska Press, 1983);

David Lodge, *The Novelist at the Crossroads and Other Essays on Fiction and Criticism* (London: Routledge & Kegan Paul, 1971; Ithaca, N.Y.: Cornell University Press, 1971);

Karl Malkoff, "Demonology and Dualism: The Supernatural in Isaac Singer and Muriel Spark," in *Critical Views of Isaac Bashevis Singer*, edited by Irving Malin (New York: New York University Press, 1969), pp. 149-168;

Malkoff, *Muriel Spark* (New York & London: Columbia University Press, 1968);

Allan Massie, *Muriel Spark* (Edinburgh: Ramsay Head Press, 1979);

Jonathan Raban, "On Losing the Rabbit," *Encounter*, 40 (May 1973): 80-85;

Margaret Moan Rowe, "Muriel Spark and the Angel of the Body," *Critique: Studies in Modern Fiction*, 28 (1987): 167-176;

Patricia Stubbs, *Muriel Spark* (Harlow, U.K.: Longman, 1973; New York: British Book Center, 1974);

Dorothea Walker, *Muriel Spark* (Boston: Twayne, 1988);

Ruth Whittaker, *The Faith and Fiction of Muriel Spark* (London: Macmillan, 1982).

Stephen Spender

(28 February 1909 -   )

This entry was written by Doris L. Eder (University of New Haven) for
DLB 20: British Poets, 1914-1945.

SELECTED BOOKS: *Nine Experiments: Being Poems Written at the Age of Eighteen*, as S. H. S. (Hampstead, U.K.: Privately printed, 1928);

Twenty Poems (Oxford: Blackwell, 1930);

Poems (London: Faber & Faber, 1933; revised and enlarged, 1934; New York: Random House, 1934);

Vienna (London: Faber & Faber, 1934);

The Destructive Element: A Study of Modern Writers and Beliefs (London: Cape, 1935; Boston & New York: Houghton Mifflin, 1936);

The Burning Cactus (London: Faber & Faber, 1936; New York: Random House, 1936);

Forward from Liberalism (London: Gollancz, 1937; New York: Random House, 1937);

Trial of a Judge (London: Faber & Faber, 1938);

The Still Centre (London: Faber & Faber, 1939);

Selected Poems (London: Faber & Faber, 1940; New York: Random House, 1940);

The Backward Son (London: Hogarth Press, 1940);

Ruins and Visions (London: Faber & Faber, 1942; New York: Random House, 1942);

Life and the Poet (London: Secker & Warburg, 1942);

Citizens in War—And After (London, Toronto, Bombay & Sydney: Harrap, 1945);

European Witness (London: Hamilton, 1946; New York: Reynal & Hitchcock, 1946);

Poetry Since 1939 (London, New York & Toronto: Longmans, Green, 1946);

Poems of Dedication (London: Faber & Faber, 1947; New York: Random House, 1947);

The Edge of Being (London: Faber & Faber, 1949; New York: Random House, 1949);

World Within World (London: Hamilton, 1951; New York: Harcourt, Brace, 1951);

Shelley (London, New York & Toronto: Longmans, Green, 1952);

Learning Laughter (London: Weidenfeld & Nicolson, 1952; New York: Harcourt, Brace, 1953);

The Creative Element: A Study of Vision, Despair and Orthodoxy (London: Hamilton, 1953);

Stephen Spender, 1932 (photograph by Humphrey Spender)

Collected Poems, 1928-1953 (London: Faber & Faber, 1955; New York: Random House, 1955);

The Making of a Poem (London: Hamilton, 1955; New York: Norton, 1962);

Engaged in Writing and The Fool and the Princess (London: Hamilton, 1958; New York: Farrar, Straus & Cudahy, 1958);

The Imagination in the Modern World (Washington, D.C.: Library of Congress, 1962);

The Struggle of the Modern (London: Hamilton, 1963; Berkeley & Los Angeles: University of California Press, 1963);

Chaos and Control in Poetry (Washington, D.C.: Library of Congress, 1966);

The Year of the Young Rebels (London: Weidenfeld & Nicolson, 1969; New York: Random House, 1969);

The Generous Days (Boston: Godine, 1969; enlarged edition, London: Faber & Faber, 1971);

Love-Hate Relations: A Study of Anglo-American Sensibilities (London: Hamilton, 1974; New York: Random House, 1974);

Eliot (London: Fontana, 1975); republished as *T. S. Eliot* (New York: Viking, 1975);

The Thirties and After: Poetry, Politics, People, 1933-1970 (New York: Random House, 1978; London: Macmillan, 1978);

Henry Moore: Sculptures in Landscape (London: Studio Vista, 1979; New York: Potter, 1979);

The Oedipus Trilogy: A Version by Stephen Spender (London & Boston: Faber & Faber, 1985);

Journals, 1939-1983, edited by John Goldsmith (London & Boston: Faber & Faber, 1985);

Collected Poems, 1928-1985 (London & Boston: Faber & Faber, 1985);

In Irina's Garden, with Henry Moore's Sculpture (London & New York: Thames & Hudson, 1986);

The Temple (London & Boston: Faber & Faber, 1988).

OTHER: Richard Crossman, ed., *The God That Failed: Six Studies in Communism*, includes a chapter by Spender (New York: Harper, 1949);

The Writer's Dilemma: Essays First Published in the Times Literary Supplement Under the Heading "Limits of Control," introduction by Spender (London, New York & Toronto: Oxford University Press, 1961);

The Concise Encyclopedia of English and American Poets and Poetry, edited by Spender and Donald Hall (New York: Hawthorn Books, 1963);

Encounters: An Anthology from the First Ten Years of Encounter Magazine, edited by Spender, Irving Kristol, and Melvin J. Lasky (New York: Basic Books, 1963);

D. H. Lawrence, edited by Spender (New York, Evanston, San Francisco & London: Harper & Row, 1973);

W. H. Auden: A Tribute, edited by Spender (London: Weidenfeld & Nicolson, 1974; New York: Macmillan, 1975);

John Miller, ed., *Voices Against Tyranny: Writing of the Spanish Civil War*, introduction by Spender (New York: Scribners, 1986);

Don Bachardy, *Christopher Isherwood: Last Drawings*, text by Bachardy, John Russell, and Spender (London & Boston: Faber & Faber, 1990);

David Hockney, *Hockney's Alphabet*, edited by Spender (New York: Random House for the AIDS Crisis Trust, 1991).

TRANSLATIONS: Ranier Maria Rilke, *Duino Elegies*, translated by Spender and J. B. Leishman (London: Hogarth Press, 1939; New York: Norton, 1939);

Georg Büchner, *Danton's Death*, translated by Spender and Goronwy Rees (London: Faber & Faber, 1939);

Federico García Lorca, *Poems*, translated by Spender and J. L. Gili (London: Dolphin, 1939);

García Lorca, *Selected Poems*, translated by Spender and Gili (London: Hogarth Press, 1943);

Paul Eluard, *Le Dur Désir de Durer*, translated by Spender and Frances Cornford (Philadelphia: Grey Falcon Press, 1950);

Rilke, *The Life of the Virgin Mary*, translated, with an introduction, by Spender (London: Vision Press, 1951);

Frank Wedekind, *Five Tragedies of Sex*, translated by Spender and Frances Fawcett (New York: Theatre Arts Books, 1952);

Friedrich Schiller, *Schiller's Mary Stuart*, freely translated and adapted by Spender (London: Faber & Faber, 1959).

Stephen Spender is one of a group of poets—the Auden or Oxford Generation—which also includes Louis MacNeice and C. Day Lewis. They began having their poetry published in the early 1930s, a decade whose ever-worsening crises—Depression and massive unemployment, the rise of fascism, and the approach of World War II—increasingly turned their poetry toward political themes. A lyricist of considerable gifts, though overshadowed by the major talent of his mentor, W. H. Auden, Spender forced his poems of the 1930s into a political mold. At the end of that decade, he returned to a more personal poetic mode. He is remembered chiefly for poems he wrote in his twenties. From the 1950s through the 1970s Spender almost abandoned poetry for literary criticism and political journalism. As a critic, Spender, despite a broad comparative knowledge of the arts and plentiful ideas, is basically a nonanalytical, unsystematic thinker. His prose is clumsy and repetitive and has the quality of thinking out loud. As V. S. Pritchett observes, Spender's "insights are better than his arguments and he is best when he proceeds, as we would expect a poet to do, by vision." Stephen Spender is a visionary with an acute sense of his world and times, who has dedicated himself to the difficult integration of self with society.

Stephen Harold Spender was born 28 February 1909 in London. His father was the liberal political journalist Harold Spender. His mother, Hilda Spender, was an invalid, and both parents died while he was still an adolescent. Like most members of the 1930s generation, who grew up *entre deux guerres* and whose lives were lived in parentheses of crises "bracketed by war," Spender was acutely aware of the gulf separating generation from generation and English life before World War I from English life after that war. World War I, he said, "knocked the ballroom-floor from under middle-class English life." The Spender family was of mixed German and English origin. Stephen did not discover his Jewish ancestry until he was sixteen, and the discovery made a profound impact: "I began to realize that I had more in common with the sensitive, rather soft, inquisitive, interior Jewish boys than with the aloof, hard, external English. There was a vulnerability, a tendency to self-hatred and self-pity, an underlying perpetual mourning amounting at times to spiritual defeatism, about my own nature which, even to myself, in my English surroundings, seemed foreign . . . my feeling for the English was at times almost like being in love with an alien race." Spender's autobiography, *World Within World* (1951), indicates that he has felt himself an outsider much of his life and that he possesses an innate sympathy for outsiders and underdogs. He is also an ardent idealist. From his father he appears to have inherited not only an interest in politics and a craving for recognition but a strong Platonic strain, despite his rebellion against these traits. Spender views himself as having been brought up in a "puritan-decadent" tradition, against which he revolted in his teens. In his youth "the abstract conception of Work and Duties was constantly being thrust on me, so that I saw beyond tasks themselves to pure qualities of moral and intellectual existence, quite emptied of things," he says. Although he deplored his father's habit of turning everything into rhetorical abstraction, Spender is often

guilty of the same defect in his criticism; and his poetry sometimes evinces a disembodied Platonism that is also "quite emptied of things." Comparing himself with Auden, he observes that Auden could quote reams of poetry by heart while he prefers not to recall the words because "I wanted to remember not the words and the lines, but a line beyond the lines"—the essence of a poem, as it were. Spender, having been anatomized by Auden and Christopher Isherwood at Oxford, shrewdly diagnoses himself: "My problem was that of the idealist . . . [who] expects too much of himself and others. He is like an artist who cannot relate inspiration to form because the shift from vision to the discipline of form" is almost certain to diminish or dim vision.

Spender denies that the 1930s poets formed a group or movement, though he affirms Auden's preeminence, saying "a group of emergent artists existed in his mind, like a cabinet in the mind of a party leader." Thus, Auden introduced Isherwood to Spender as "the Novelist." Spender says "MacSpaunday" (MacNeice, Spender, Auden, and Day Lewis) "never met as a group, never referred to ourselves as a movement; curiously, the original three [Auden, Day Lewis, and Spender] didn't meet each other collectively until September 1949 in Venice." At Oxford in the late 1920s Spender felt isolated. He found Oxford divided into hearties and aesthetes, fell in love with one of the hearties ("Marston," who inspired some fine early lyrics), and did not really blossom on his own account until 1930, after Auden left. Spender thinks the atmosphere of Oxford in his day so strange that it would take Fyodor Dostoyevski to describe it adequately. It was so cloistered that he came to identify the town surrounding the colleges as the real world. The profound awareness of the subject/object dichotomy that informs Spender's thought and work was sharpened by his university education.

In the summer of 1930, before his senior year, Spender left Oxford without a degree and followed Isherwood to Germany. The attractions of Germany for young Englishmen during the *Weimardämmerung* were social, homosexual, and literary. Sexual liberation, literary and political ferment, and social unrest were rife, and the 1920s cult of hedonism was at its height. Both Spender and Isherwood have described sojourns in those modern Sodoms, Hamburg and Berlin, with unforgettable vividness. *World Within World* evokes the extraordinary mixture of "nihilism, sophistica-

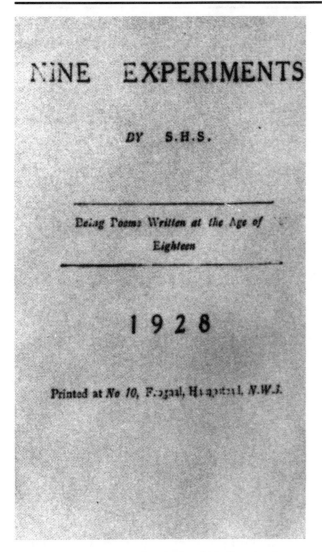

Title page for Spender's first book, which he printed on a small handpress

tion and primitive vitality" that was the zeitgeist of Germany in the late 1920s and early 1930s: "all this German youth . . . born into war, starved in the blockade, stripped in the inflation—and . . . now, with no money and no beliefs and an extraordinary anonymous beauty, sprang like a breed of dragon's teeth waiting for its leader, into the centre of Europe." Nude sun worshipers crowded the beaches, while storm troopers trained in nearby forests.

Spender's first important volume, *Poems*, appeared in 1933, the year in which Adolf Hitler assumed the chancellorship of the Third Reich. Like so many young English intellectuals, Spender was appalled at the rise of fascism. With Auden and Isherwood, he had a ringside seat in Berlin and Vienna. Spender's career exemplifies the

split between personal and political life felt by his generation. A world lurching from crisis to crisis under the threat of Fascist domination made luxuries of poetry and the private life. Spender and his colleagues felt obliged to write public, "committed," political, even polemical, verse. But they distrusted such literature even as they wrote it. Says Spender: "We were divided between our literary vocation and an urge to save the world from Fascism. We were the Divided Generation of Hamlets who found the world out of joint and failed to set it right." Like many of his generation, Spender briefly embraced communism—he had a party card but never attended a meeting—and went to Spain to promote anti-Fascist propaganda during the Spanish civil war. (The chairman of the British Communist party urged Spender to go to Spain and, preferably, to get killed, so as to give the Loyalist cause a Byron.) Katharine B. Hoskins in *Today the Struggle: Literature and Politics in England During the Spanish Civil War* (1969) remarks that Spender's "first and only act as a Communist was to write an article in the *Daily Worker* announcing his having joined but simultaneously attacking Party policy on all points at which he 'disagreed with it.' " Spender describes his experience of communism, and the Spanish civil war is in his contribution to Richard Crossman's *The God That Failed* (1949). Hoskins sketches Spender's political evolution: "He had come from a wealthy Liberal family with strong traditions of social responsibility, and he had trod the well-worn path from liberalism to socialism and then, because of the apparent failure of social democracy and the growing menace of fascism, to communism." Spender has said that embracing communism in the 1930s was less a matter of belief than of conscience: for a while it appeared the only viable alternative to fascism.

At the age of twenty-seven, Spender married Agnes (Inez) Pearn; she was an Oxford student, a scholar of Spanish, and a member of the Spanish Aid Committee. They had known each other only briefly when Spender, on impulse, proposed. He was on the rebound after the end of an affair with another woman in Austria and also after the end of a long, drawn-out, complex, and painful relationship with his secretary, T. A. R. Hyndman, who figures in his autobiography as "Jimmy Younger." In *World Within World* Spender is candid about being bisexual, as he is about everything else. He says he sought out men for intellectual and artistic comradeship—for relationships in which total identification was the aim—and women for a more sensual, mystical kind of union. In his own words, he became aware of an acute, irremediable "ambivalence in my attitude towards men and women. Love for a friend expressed a need for self-identification. Love for a woman, the need for a relationship with someone different, indeed opposite, to myself." Looking back from the perspective of mid-life, Spender declares in his autobiography that he finds his relationships with women to have been more satisfying and lasting than those with men. In an interview with John Gruen in *Vogue*, however, Spender reiterates the fear expressed in *World Within World* that intimacy with the opposite sex might rob him of his own identity. Spender also matter-of-factly observes that his mother was mad and expresses a fear of being controlled by women. The sharp dualism he discerns in male/female relations is likely traceable to his early childhood and was probably exacerbated by English methods of rearing and educating the sexes separately, since it appears symptomatic of many Englishmen of Spender's class and age. Spender's first marriage was childless and disintegrated in 1939, at which time he underwent a period of suffering and self-doubt so intense that he feared he might never write again. The poems of this period reflect his inner turmoil. For therapy Spender took up painting and underwent psychoanalysis.

In 1939 Spender and Cyril Connolly became coeditors of the magazine *Horizon*. In 1941 he married Natasha Litvin, a pianist, who bore him a son and a daughter. During the war Spender continued to live in London and served in the Auxiliary Fire Service, about which he writes engagingly in *World Within World*. This experience also inspired some vivid war poems. To the poets of the 1930s, who had watched the events of that "low dishonest decade" building to their cataclysmic climax, World War II had a profound and terrible significance. For Spender it signaled above all the end of individualism and of human control over destructive technology: "From now on, the fate of individuals was more and more controlled by a public fate which itself seemed beyond control. For control implies not merely putting a machinery into motion, but also being able to make it stop: modern war is a machine easy to make start, but it can only be stopped at the moment when it has destroyed or been destroyed by another war machine. Control means being able to relate a programme of action to the results of the action. . . . All this was

only leading to . . . plans for making atomic and hydrogen bombs to defend East against West or West against East in a meaningless struggle between potential ashes to gain a world of ashes."

Since World War II Spender has had little poetry published but has produced an increasing volume of prose works, including literary criticism, social and intellectual history, political and travel literature, translations, and reviews. In 1947 he made his first visit to the United States to see his old friends Auden and Isherwood. Spender and Auden frequently spent half the year in England, half abroad in an antithetical environment. During the 1950s and 1960s Spender divided his time about equally between England and the United States. During those years he held visiting professorships and lectureships at prestigious American and English universities, including the University of Cincinnati (1953), the University of California at Berkeley (1959), Northwestern University (1963), Cambridge University (1965-1966), the University of Connecticut (1968-1970), and University College, London (1969). He was consultant in poetry in English at the Library of Congress in 1965-1966, and from 1953 to 1967 he coedited *Encounter* magazine with Irving Kristol and Melvin J. Lasky. He had for some years been looking for a vehicle, transatlantic in scope, to publish work by the foremost literary talents of the contemporary world. Spender describes in *The Year of the Young Rebels* (1969) how neither he nor Frank Kermode (who succeeded him as British editor of *Encounter* when Spender became corresponding American editor) realized until late that the journal had received funds from the Central Intelligence Agency When Spender and Kermode discovered that such payments had been made, they resigned. From 1970 until his retirement in 1975, Spender occupied the Chair of English Literature at University College, London. He continues to be a literary-political spokesman and cultural ambassador for the transatlantic community, and in 1981 he was a visiting professor at the University of South Carolina.

The autobiographical impulse is obvious in Spender's poetry. He has said that all his work, whether verse or prose, constitutes fragments of an autobiography and that his poems "all attempt to record . . . truthfully . . . experience which, within reality, seemed to be poetry." The obsessive themes of the poetry are also those of his critical prose: how to connect outer and inner reality, the active and contemplative, the political and personal; how, in Wallace Stevens's words, to bring a "world quite round" in an age of unbelief. Spender's poetry has been a search for a valid, sustaining faith. He has not attained such a faith, remaining a skeptic conducting continuous forays from the inner into the outer world, seeking to transform external fact or reality into internal truth. Spender's poetry shows a lifelong, strenuous effort to objectify the subjective or to subjectivize the object. He has been strongly influenced by the Romantic poets in general and by Percy Bysshe Shelley in particular; indeed, he has been labeled the Shelley of the twentieth century, as well as the Rupert Brooke of the Depression. The former sobriquet is the more just one. Spender resembles Shelley in the nature of his lyrical gift, which is ethereal (F. R. Leavis calls it "glamorous-ineffable-vague"); in combining poetic with political interests; in his youthful idealism, now tempered; and in his somewhat feminine sensibility. Other influences have been Rainer Maria Rilke, T. S. Eliot, William Butler Yeats, D. H. Lawrence, and his contemporaries Auden and Isherwood.

Spender printed his first volume of poetry, *Nine Experiments: Being Poems Written at the Age of Eighteen* (1928), on his own handpress, on which he also printed Auden's *Poems* (1928). Spender later did not think well of this virgin enterprise and destroyed many copies. *Twenty Poems*, which appeared in 1930, comprises poems written between 1928 and 1930. Fourteen of these reappear in the volume that gained Spender recognition as a poet of the Auden Generation—*Poems*, published in 1933, with a revised, enlarged edition the following year. (The first edition of *Poems* contained thirty-three poems; the second, forty.) With this volume, Spender emerged as a mature poet at the age of twenty-four. His particular poetic characteristics are already in evidence. Horace Gregory said in the *Nation* that Spender showed promise of becoming the best lyric poet of his generation, a promise he cannot be said to have fulfilled, for Spender has always been overshadowed, like the other members of the Oxford Group, by the intellectual brilliance and technical virtuosity of Auden. In *Poems*, Spender's spontaneous lyric gift is constrained by a profoundly felt obligation to engage the ugliest, most recalcitrant features of the contemporary environment: the urban-industrial landscape, machinery and mechanization, unemployment, and fascism. (At the age of nineteen Spender had proclaimed, "Come let us praise the gasworks. . . .") "The Express" and

"The Pylons," both included in *Poems*, have for decades been seen as exemplifying the tenacious grasp of the Auden group on the contemporary scene, its celebration of "the quick perspective of the future." In such poems Spender fulfilled his declared aim of enveloping the brute phenomena of his day in the poetic spirit. "The Express" is rhythmic and more concrete than many of his poems, which sometimes dissipate in an impressionistic haze. There are poems, however, in which the poet unflinchingly confronts the miseries of his time, finding them beyond poetry's power to console, vindicate, or transcend. Thus, in "In Railway Halls, on Pavements Near the Traffic," the poet, watching long lines of the unemployed, says:

No, I shall wave no tracery of pen-ornament
To make them birds upon my singing-tree:
Time merely drives these lives which do not live
As tides push rotten stuff along the shore.
. . . .
Paint here no draped despairs, no saddening clouds
Where the soul rests, proclaims eternity.
But let the wrong cry out, as raw as wounds
This time forgets and never heals, far less
     transcends.

Spender's poems are plainspoken without their meaning necessarily being plain. He likes truncated, sonnetlike, but free-verse forms; as he developed, he used less rhyme or meter. The sound of his poems is distinctive. He is fully aware of the importance of sound, but he uses few seductive aural techniques, such as alliteration, assonance, full or near rhyme, or regular rhythms. The image is obviously of primary importance to this poet, but his images are often quite surreal, not easily visualized. The poetry, though painterly, often lacks concreteness. Some poems suffer from a Platonic blurring of the edges, similar to Shelley's; from first to last they are full of images of Shelleyan light, effulgence. Lyric and prosaic impulses are frequently at odds in his poetry. Spender's instinct for direct, lyric utterance is often betrayed by his predilection for the rhetorical, didactic, or homilectic, a weakness he attributes to the fatal attraction that platform speaking has for him. As a *Times Literary Supplement* reviewer said of *Collected Poems, 1928-1953* (1955), "The typical quality of his style, arising from this paradoxical combination of a desire to 'let himself go' and a fear of 'letting himself go' is a stumbling eloquence or a sweeping gesture suddenly arrested." The justly praised "Not Palaces, an Era's Crown" in *Poems* illustrates most of these traits. Apparently a strong-willed, forward-looking call for human equality, it is nevertheless full of latent nostalgia for an abjured, abandoned past evoked in "family pride," "beauty's filtered dusts," "gardens," and "singing feasts." The justly celebrated invocation—

> Eye, gazelle, delicate wanderer,
> Drinker of horizon's fluid line;
> Ear that suspends on a chord
> The spirit drinking timelessness—

exemplifies Spender's use of surrealistic images, here synesthetic and memorable, though difficult to visualize. (Spender is an amateur painter, as well informed about art history as poetry; he is also knowledgeable about music.) Though he loves nature and greatly admires the ability of a writer such as Lawrence to depict the outer world, Spender's own sensitive eye is inclined to be internal, a dilated pupil looking inward quite as much as it gazes on the outward scene. Thus, A. K. Weatherhead in *Stephen Spender and the Thirties* (1975) is right to say that Spender has written "no poetry that was not mediated through an analytic cerebration."

Vienna (1934) was written in 1934 while Spender was living half the year in Austria (as Auden did for many years). It is a long poem about the Engelbert Dollfuss regime's brutal suppression of the February 1934 socialist insurrection in Austria and the heroic death of Kaloman Wallisch, the socialist mayor of Bruck-an-der-Mur, who was executed by the Dollfuss regime. Interwoven with political events is the poet's personal life, enmeshed in guilt over his bisexuality. A four-part poem that shows the influence of the Eliot of "Gerontion" (1920) and of Auden, *Vienna* is full of clogged images, obscure and dated allusions, and prosy passages. Spender later repudiated it because it failed in its grand objective of fusing inner and outer worlds. In *World Within World*, Spender says of this nightmarish time, when he was observing at firsthand the brutalities of fascism, "in spite of everything, I did not plunge myself wholly in public affairs. Therefore a poetry which rejected private experience would have been untrue to me. Moreover, I dimly saw that the conflict between personal life and public causes must be carried forward into public life itself. . . . For our individualistic civilization to be reborn within the order of a new world, people must be complex as individuals, simple as social

forces." Spender's ambivalent admiration for men of action, compact figures of will and single unified identity, is always offset by his realization of the painful (and peculiarly modern) necessity of being passive, will-less, and multivalent, a realization expressed in his elliptical, Audenesque, early poem, "An 'I' can never be great man." In *Vienna* he cannot make his inner world cohere, let alone connect his life to the turbulent outer world.

Vienna looks forward to Spender's only excursion into drama, *Trial of a Judge* (1938), a verse tragedy in five acts written for Rupert Doone's Group Theatre, which premiered the play on 18 March 1938. Its protagonist is a liberal judge who, under a Fascist regime, convicts the brutal anti-Semitic murderers of an unarmed man and is then compelled (by new antigun legislation) also to convict a group of Communists who, in a scuffle with the Fascists, have accidentally wounded a policeman. *Trial of a Judge* enacts in strong verse the judge's struggle of conscience as he is finally brought to condemn both Fascists and Communists, the former for violating all principles of law and justice, the latter for travestying justice by creating and trying to enforce their own laws. The play is too monological to be dramatic, but it is highly charged poetry. MacNeice observed, "The intended moral of the play was that liberalism today was weak and wrong, communism was strong and right. But this moral was sabotaged by [Spender's] unconscious integrity." MacNeice describes how, at a meeting of comrades at the Group Theatre to discuss the play, an old man approached the youthful poet-playwright to say that he was sure he must be mistaken, but the play seemed to be advocating "Abstract Justice, a thing we know is non-existent." MacNeice records in *The Strings Are False: An Unfinished Autobiography* (1966) how Spender "deliberately towered into blasphemy. Abstract Justice, he said, of course he meant it; and what was more it existed." In *World Within World* Spender reveals his intense moralism. "My mind appeared to be a vehicle for a thought which existed independently of my own reasoning. This was that at some stage of our eternal and personal existence, we become aware of our significance in other lives, measured in terms of happiness and unhappiness, good and evil. . . . It was unbearable to me to think that people could do great good or great evil, without ever being completely aware, even for a moment . . . of what they had become as a result of what they had done."

Stephen Spender in his Auxiliary Fire Service uniform
(The British Council)

Spender has made several forays into fiction. Five short stories published under the title *The Burning Cactus* in 1936 are close in quality to his poetry, haunted, haunting, sometimes vivid, and reminiscent of Lawrence in their intense, suppressed emotionality and of Isherwood in their subject matter. The protagonists are hypersensitive, epicene, isolated, alienated, even solipsistic; interest is displaced from social to psychic contact and conflict. After World War II, Spender wrote two satirical sketches of postwar European life, which were published together as *Engaged in Writing and The Fool and the Princess* (1958). His full-length novel *The Backward Son* (1940) is a thinly disguised autobiographical account of English boarding-school life, which he hated.

The Still Centre (1939) is a key volume in Spender's poetic oeuvre because—although it contains many political poems, including some fine ones on the Spanish civil war—in the course of the book Spender turns from public and political verse back to the private and personal. He reiterates the need for the poet "to relate [his] small truth to the ... wider truth outside his experi-

ence," but he also remarks, "Poetry does not state truth, it states the conditions within which something felt is true." That is, poetry is not, like science, concerned with discovering facts, but with conveying the "felt truth" of reality. *The Still Centre* includes some longer poems, such as "Exiles from Their Land" and "The Uncreating Chaos," which, by the time they appeared in *Collected Poems, 1928-1953*, had been revised and abridged.

The poems growing out of Spender's experience in the Spanish civil war in 1937 show his powers of empathy and humanity and the influence of Wilfred Owen's poetry of World War I, as well as of Auden. Spender thought Owen the best of the World War I poets. Less involved and steeped in suffering than Owen's, Spender's poems are sympathetic without being sentimental, always focused on the individual pressed into inhuman activity, dwarfed in the huge, insensate violence of war. Their bittersweet, ironic spirit is reminiscent of Stephen Crane's "Do Not Weep, Maiden, for War is Kind" (1899). In "Two Armies" extraordinary effects are achieved through sudden, Audenesque shifts in perspective, from close up to far removed. The two armies, furiously pitted against each other by day, are seen by night as sharing a common suffering:

> Clean silence drops at night, when a little walk
> Divides the sleeping armies, each
> Huddled in linen woven by remote hands.
> When the machines are stilled, a common suffering
> Whitens the air with breath and makes both one
> As though these enemies slept in each other's
>   arms.

"Ultima Ratio Regum" explores the ultimate pity and waste of war. Somewhat facile opening lines— "The guns spell money's ultimate reason / In letters of lead on the Spring hillside"—lead to a brief lyric meditation on a dead boy lying under the olive trees, "a better target for a kiss" than a bullet. Again, the vast machinery and matériel of modern warfare are contrasted with the frail individual life, now extinguished. With wringing irony, the poet asks: "Was so much expenditure justified / On the death of one so young, and so silly / Lying under the olive trees ... ?"

A recurrent theme in the political and personal poems of *The Still Centre* is the search for "unity of being or an image of the integrated self," as Weatherhead observes in *Stephen Spender and the Thirties*. The most remarkable poem in this regard is the loose sestina "Darkness and

Stephen Spender, circa 1951

Light," which Spender also uses as an epigraph to his autobiography. Its imagery of light and darkness exemplifies the two poles between which Spender's universe is suspended. "To break out of the chaos of my darkness / Into a lucid day, is all my will," the poem begins. But, equally, "to avoid that lucid day / And to preserve my darkness, is all my will." This poem is Spender's most concentrated and masterful exposition of his conflict between subject and object, inner and outer, activity and passivity, center that is nowhere and circumference that is everywhere. The whole drive of the poem is to reconcile these opposites that have so bedeviled the poet's life: they are reconciled within the poem, but not in life. Weatherhead sees the "still centre" of Spender's title as "that residue of self . . . which, washed over by all tides of public occurrences, is finally untouched and lives independent of any conditioning whatsoever." Thus, this Manichaean conflict is also one between freedom and determinism.

Ruins and Visions (1942) is a revision of *The Still Centre*, with some new poems added. Spender's next volume, *Poems of Dedication*, which did not appear until 1947, contains "Elegy for Marga-

ret," a long poem in six parts written on the death of a beloved sister-in-law, the wife of Humphrey Spender. Despite some moving passages, this poem is flawed, falling far short of its aim. Reviewing this volume for the *New York Herald Tribune*, Babette Deutsch observed that Spender's "technical ability has not kept pace with the increase in scope and depth of his themes."

The Edge of Being (1949) is a slim volume, balanced between the longing for concrete existence and for abstract nonbeing, as Weatherhead observes. It contains some interesting new poems, such as "Rejoice in the Abyss," one of Spender's World War II poems, which, though not as directly apprehended as those written during the Spanish civil war, are impressive nonetheless. During World War II, Spender, serving in the Auxiliary Fire Service, experienced the fire and destruction of the London blitz. "Rejoice in the Abyss" is Blakean, striving for that strange fusion of cockney concreteness with gnomic abstractness that William Blake achieves in "London." The poem's theme is that espoused in Spender's critical works *The Destructive Element* (1935) and *The Creative Element* (1953), the Conradian "In the Destructive Element Immerse . . .":

> hollow is the skull, the vacuum
> In the gold ball under St. Paul's cross.
> Unless you will accept the emptiness
> Within the bells of fox-gloves and cathedrals,
> Each life must feed upon the deaths of others.

An almost surreal technique (roof slates jabbering, houses kneeling, the sky foaming with a Milky Way of saints ascending) is wedded to a long-cherished theme, but theme and technique are not fused at all points. The end, in particular, seems willed and didactic. This volume also contains a brief, deeply moving lyric on the Holocaust, "Memento."

Spender's *Selected Poems* appeared in the inauspicious year of 1940. Of the forty-six poems in the book, only a handful do not appear in *Collected Poems, 1928-1953*, published a decade and a half later. This later volume comprises 111 poems, only a few of which had not appeared in previous volumes. Most date from the 1930s, many from the original *Poems*. Louis Untermeyer has rightly characterized Spender's *Collected Poems* as "doggedly comprehensive." In his introduction, Spender describes the conscientious, painstaking method by which he put the volume together: "To collect and select these poems, I copied them out into a large note-book, then

360

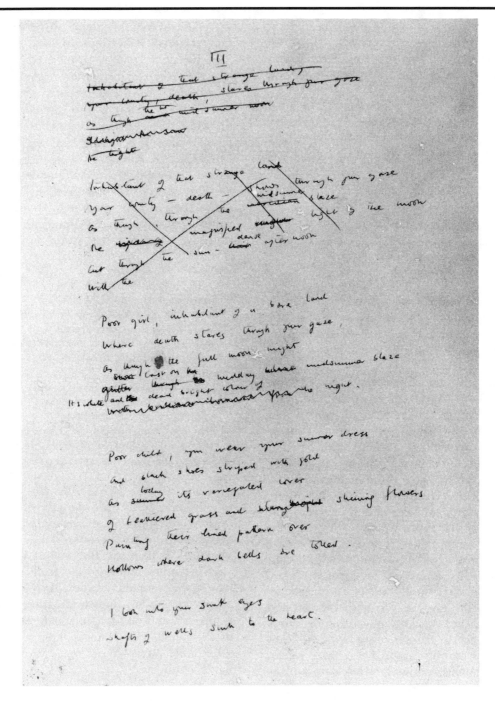

Page from Spender's notebook, in which he made revisions for Collected Poems, 1928-1953
(Harry Ransom Humanities Research Center, University of Texas, Austin)

typed them out and tried to consider how each poem would best take its place in a single volume. In this way, I have spent several months reconsidering and even re-experiencing poems I have written over the past twenty-five years ... my aim has been to retrieve as many past mistakes, and to make as many improvements, as possible, without 'cheating'.... Poetry is a game played with the reader according to rules, but it is also a truth game in which the truth is outside the rules." So Spender's revisions are technical, not thematic. He included poems of the 1930s that embarrassed him in the 1950s by their youthful ardor or awkwardness. His revisions are mostly for clarity or specificity, sometimes for metaphorical elaboration. Spender is no perfectionist like Yeats, Eliot, or Ezra Pound, and rarely wrestles sufficiently to arrive at *le mot juste*. He says so of his prose, but the same is true of his poetry. In the "Elegy for Margaret," to cite only one example, he amended

> Since, darling, there is never a night
> But the restored prime of your youth
> With all its flags does not float
> Upon my sleep like a boat.

to

> Since, Margaret, there is never a night
> But the beflagged pride of your youth
> In all its joy, does not float
> Upon my sleep, as on a boat.

The sought-for improvement is spoiled by the single word *as*, which undoes a fine image, for Margaret's youthful image *is* the vessel riding the flood of the poet's sleep; it is not, as it were, a passenger on a vessel.

Reading through Spender's *Collected Poems*, one is struck by a dozen or so poems that stand out as finely crafted, memorable, the poet's best. Most of these are early poems, written while he was still in his twenties and first published in *Poems* of 1933. Preeminent among them, flawlessly lyrical, is "I Think Continually of Those Who Were Truly Great." Here Spender allows his innate romanticism free rein: the poem is full of the nostalgia of William Wordsworth's "Ode: Intimations of Immortality from Recollections of Early Childhood" (1807), extolling the glory and the dream still "appareled in celestial light." Spender's characteristically Shelleyan imagery of light is beautifully integrated from first to last strophe. The rhythm is harmonious and hypnotic, and each word is chosen with extreme care. Streaming images of light, fire, spirit, voices, streams, mountains, winds, grasses, sun, and air flow into one another with an extraordinary élan to celebrate the devotees of life. The final two lines—"Born of the sun they traveled a short while towards the sun, / And left the vivid air signed with their honor"—poignantly convey Spender's simultaneous sense of the frailty and the grandeur of man, for he sets the spirit in its ephemeral perdurability against the immense background of time-space. The poem is one of the purest evocations of spirit imaginable, so that it seems severe of Weatherhead to complain of its impalpability and self-reflexiveness, or of its "delivering only the vaguest kind of intelligence."

The overriding theme of Spender's poems is the union of self with world. Bent as he is on fusing subject and object, on merging existence and being, there remains a thin integument separating the poet from the external world. In poems about art, as in war poems, Spender is aware of the transparent curtain dividing art from life, life from death. "The Living Values," like Auden's "*Musee des Beaux Arts*," concerns the relationships between art and life and life and death, as they are and as they are portrayed by the Old Masters. The curtain separating these realms of being is astonishingly thin; pierced in a moment, it leads to a looking-glass world:

> Alas for the sad standards
> In the eyes of the new-dead young
> Sprawled in the mud of battle.
> Stare back, stare back, with dust over glazed
> Eyes, their gaze at partridges,
> Their dreams of nudes, and their collected
> Hearts wound up with love, like little watch
>   springs.
> To ram them outside Time, violence
> Of wills that ride this cresting day
> Struck them with lead so swift
> They look at us through its glass trajectory
> And we, living, look back at them through glass,
> Their bodies now sunk inch-deep in gold frames.

Similarly, in "An Elementary School Classroom in a Slum," the poet sees the life of slum children as too removed from that depicted in schoolbooks, maps, travel posters of alpine valleys, and a bust of Shakespeare for any of these windows opening upon other worlds really to free them from their cramped, impoverished lives in the catacombs of modern industrial cities. Art is perpetrating a fraud on life. Unless, the poet proclaims in a final, Blakean stanza, these windows magically burst open to liberate these imprisoned minds and lives:

> Unless, governor, teacher, inspector, visitor,
> This map becomes their window and these windows
> That shut upon their lives like catacombs,
> Break O break open till they break the town
> And show the children to green fields, and make
>   their world
> Run azure on gold sands, and let their tongues
> Run naked into books, the white and green leaves
>   open
> History theirs whose language is the sun.

It seems unfair of Robert Graves to damn with faint praise what he calls Spender's "poor-little-rich-boy poems," full of pity for the poor. Though Spender's sympathy may be liberal and bookish, his entire work and life express a passion for social justice.

Spender has also written poems about the stealthy depredations of time, the gradual ruin of the flesh that is poignantly contrasted with the longing for perfection of the unquenchable spirit. His apprehension of time's power is profound, cosmic: "Time's ambition is all space, and hangs its flags / In night that never reaches us, years to which this world is dead." In poem number twelve in *Collected Poems*, about youth's great expectations, he writes:

> What I had not foreseen
> Was the gradual day
> Weakening the will
> Leaking the brightness away . . .
> . . . .
> Expecting always
> Some brightness to hold in trust,
> Some final innocence
> Exempt from dust,
> That, hanging solid,
> Would dangle through all,
> Like the created poem,
> Or faceted crystal.

If he has written few poems that achieve such crystalline perfection, Spender's is a true lyric gift, his voice one of deep and humane feeling.

The Generous Days (1969) shows a new leanness; Spender's free verse is becoming tauter, compressing more meaning into smaller compass. The American edition contains only ten poems, the English edition (1971), forty-seven. One is a sonnet to Auden on his sixtieth birthday. It is interesting to compare the late styles of these two poets, for, while Auden grew more colloquial, leisurely, and diffuse, Spender has become more disciplined, spare, and laconic. The most effective poems are those in which Spender so shapes inspiration within form as to attain the union of flesh and spirit, the two becoming one.

Criticism has become an increasingly important part of Spender's work, and his critical roles have had some effect on his own poetry. His first important critical work was *The Destructive Element*, published in England in 1935, in the United States the following year. He has described how "the idea for a book on [Henry] James gradually resolved itself . . . in my mind into that of a book about modern writers and beliefs, or unbeliefs; which turned again into a pic-

ture of writers grouped round the 'destructive element,' wondering whether or not to immerse themselves." Spender's definition of the destructive element is a world devoid of belief or shared values. He considers James's quintessential qualities to be as "his morality, his pity, his humanity, his feminine genius and feminine courage, his gift of profound understanding." He writes of James that his "morality is fogged and confused by the fact that a very great deal of his work is about nothing except that he is a New Englander who has spent his life trying to reconcile a Puritan New England code of morals with his idea of the European tradition."

Spender follows chapters on James with briefer assessments of Yeats, Eliot, and Lawrence. He complains that, compared with Eliot's, Yeats's poetry is deficient in magic. (Spender dislikes Yeats's supernaturalism, which he finds bogus, and Eliot's orthodoxy, which he finds constraining.) He finds the poetry and criticism of Eliot remarkable for their power of internalizing the external world. Like Eliot, Spender is obsessed by the modern dissociation of sensibility, the sundering of inner from outer reality. He views Eliot, Rilke, Marcel Proust, and Virginia Woolf as subjective artists with an extraordinary capacity for absorbing the outer into the inner self and transforming it, but he prefers Lawrence's respect, indeed reverence, for the external and tries to emulate the balance Lawrence strikes between inner and outer. Lawrence has profoundly influenced Spender. The outsider in Spender recognizes the outsider in Lawrence. He praises Lawrence for recognizing that "each person is outside everyone else and outside nature. It is on the basis of this separation of polarities that there is meeting. . . . Out of a fusion of opposites, a spark is struck." Spender also understands and explains well Lawrence's belief in the collective unconscious, for Spender has since childhood had a profound sense of the finitude and frailty of microcosmic human personality while sensing the expansiveness and durability of the macrocosmic consciousness contained within it.

The Creative Element (an adaptation of the Elliston lectures at the University of Cincinnati in 1953) is a companion volume or sequel to *The Destructive Element*. Whereas the first work is subtitled *A Study of Modern Writers and Beliefs*, the second has the subtitle *A Study of Vision, Despair and Orthodoxy*. Spender defines the creative element as "the individual vision of the writer who realizes in his work the decline of modern values

Louis MacNeice, Ted Hughes, T. S. Eliot, W. H. Auden, and Stephen Spender, 1960

while isolating his own individual values from the context of society. . . . The main impulse of the whole great 'modern movement' has been the individual vision," and therefore the emphasis in this book is on the great moderns as visionaries, with the center still the subjective consciousness of the artist, the circumference the circumambient external world.

The Creative Element is also concerned with the central problem of belief. Spender disagrees with Matthew Arnold that poetry can take the place of religion in the modern world, yet he proposes a role for poetry that is close to this. He sees poetry's task as "to restore the lost connection between man-made objects and inner life," to translate the life of the soul into the language of the modern city, and, through the rediscovery or reinvention of traditional symbols and the forging of new ones, to create provisional faiths.

Among his visionaries, Spender includes Rilke, Eliot, Lawrence, Yeats, E. M. Forster, and Arthur Rimbaud.

Like *The Destructive Element*, *The Struggle of the Modern* (1963) is clearly a product of the temporal context in which it was written. (This book comprises lectures given at the University of California at Berkeley in 1959 and at the Library of Congress in 1962.) Spender looks back at the modern from the perspective of the contemporary literary scene, finding the split between art and life (like that between the individual and society) ever widening, *Dichtung* (poetry) and *Wahrheit* (truth) drawing farther apart. He views as endemic to the modern movement the endeavor to heal this split, to see life as a whole. This endeavor necessitates, in Spender's view, confronting the present with the past. This technique of juxtaposing present and past is strikingly present in James Joyce,

Eliot, Yeats, Woolf, Lawrence, and others. He diagnoses nostalgia as the dominant emotion of modern art, because past has been amputated from present. Exploring and retrieving the past is the only way, as Eliot wrote of Joyce's mythic method in *Ulysses* (1922), of "controlling, of ordering, of giving a shape and significance to the immense panorama of futility and anarchy, which is contemporary history." Paradoxically, the vision of the whole to which the modernists aspire is achieved only through assembling fragments—"These fragments I have shored against my ruins," as Eliot wrote at the end of *The Waste Land* (1922).

Further, Spender observes that modernism was a movement in which all the arts cross-fertilized one another—poets, prose writers, painters, and musicians learned from one another. He traces the influence of painting on poetry and of poetry on prose, notably through impressionism and imagism, showing how concentration on modes of perceiving became itself an object of perception and how emphasis on the image gave the technique of stream-of-consciousness in Proust and Woolf and Joyce its living power.

The Making of a Poem was published in 1955, between *The Creative Element* and *The Struggle of the Modern*. Since it assembles reviews and occasional pieces, it is a more loosely organized, desultory collection of critical pieces than the other books and makes a less unified impression. Among the topics Spender discusses are Auden, Dylan Thomas, A. E. Housman, and Georgianism. The best essay is "Goethe and the English Mind," in which Spender compares Johann Wolfgang von Goethe with Shakespeare and the Goethean conception of *Dichtung* with the English conception of poetry. This essay, like the title essay, reveals a great deal about Spender and his own poems. He argues that English poetry springs from inhibition, guilt, and puritan repression. It is less an expression of public than of private life and conscience. It denies the dichotomy of form and content that Goethe could equably contemplate and exploit.

"The Making of a Poem" emphasizes poetry's dependence upon memory, establishing an equivalence of imagination and memory by remarking that we can imagine nothing we have not experienced in some way. He describes his own memory as self-centered, which is why his art is essentially autobiographical. He also confesses, "My mind is not clear, my will is weak, I suffer from excess of ideas and a weak sense of

Stephen Spender, 28 November 1968
(photograph by J. Jackson)

form," judgments the serious student of his poetry will corroborate.

Love-Hate Relations: A Study of Anglo-American Sensibilities (1974) is a recasting of the Clark Lectures that Spender delivered at Cambridge in 1965. It is concerned with Anglo-American literary relations during the preceding hundred years; with the West-East immigration of Pound, Eliot, and other American writers to Europe; and with the reverse East-West migration of Spender's friends and contemporaries—Aldous Huxley, Auden, Isherwood, and Lawrence. The subject is a fascinating one, about which Spender is well informed, but his study is vitiated by a diminished capacity for intellectual analysis.

The acme of Spender's achievement in prose is his autobiography, *World Within World*; by any standard a fine example of its genre, it was completed when the writer was in his early forties. The book corroborates and vindicates Spender's claim that all his art is essentially autobiographical: "what I write are fragments of autobiography: sometimes . . . poems, sometimes stories, and the longer passages may take the form of novels." The title is one of Spender's master metaphors or key symbols: that of microcosm with macrocosm, center within circumference, the individual contained within society and the universe. The personality revealed in the autobiography is intense, honest, and generous but also neurotic, ambivalent, and masochistic. Spender's candor is incandescent. At the age of twenty he noted in a journal, "I have no character or will power outside my work." He consistently judges himself objectively and dispassionately, even when such judgment shows him in an unfavorable light.

Spender's most important works, *The Destructive Element* and *The Struggle of the Modern*, contain some insights original at the time of publication, but on the whole Spender's criticism is repetitious and prolix, full of overgeneralizations and projective judgments. At its best, however, both Spender's poetry and his prose vividly fuse the concrete and the abstract, unifying flesh and the spirit, inner and outer existence.

Letters:

Letters to Christopher: Stephen Spender's Letters to Christopher Isherwood, 1920-1939, With "The Line of the Branch"—Two Thirties Journals, edited by Lee Bartlett (Santa Barbara: Black Sparrow, 1980).

Bibliography:

H. B. Kulkarni, *Stephen Spender: Works and Criticism. An Annotated Bibliography* (New York & London: Garland, 1976).

References:

J. J. Connors, *Poets and Politics: A Study of the Careers of C. Day Lewis, Stephen Spender and W. H. Auden in the 1930's* (New Haven: Yale University Press, 1967);

George S. Fraser, *Vision and Rhetoric* (London: Faber & Faber, 1959; New York: Barnes & Noble, 1960);

Katharine B. Hoskins, *Today the Struggle: Literature and Politics in England During the Spanish Civil War* (Austin & London: University of Texas Press, 1969);

Christopher Isherwood, *Christopher and His Kind, 1929-1939* (New York: Farrar, Straus & Giroux, 1976; London: Eyre Methuen, 1977);

Isherwood, *Lions and Shadows: An Education in the Twenties* (London: Hogarth Press, 1938; Norfolk, Conn.: New Directions, 1947);

H. B. Kulkarni, *Stephen Spender: Poet in Crisis* (Glasgow: Blackie, 1970);

D. E. S. Maxwell, *Poets of the Thirties* (London: Routledge & Kegan Paul, 1969; New York: Barnes & Noble, 1969);

Howard Nemerov, *Poetry and Fiction* (New Brunswick, N.J.: Rutgers University Press, 1963);

John Press, *A Map of Modern English Verse* (London & New York: Oxford University Press, 1969);

Francis Scarfe, *Auden and After: The Liberation of Poetry, 1930-1941* (London: Routledge, 1942);

Hugh Thomas, *The Spanish Civil War* (London: Eyre & Spottiswoode, 1961; New York: Harper & Row, 1961);

A. K. Weatherhead, *Stephen Spender and the Thirties* (Lewisburg, Pa.: Bucknell University Press / London: Associated University Presses, 1975).

Papers:

The principal repository of unpublished Spender papers is the Library of Northwestern University, Evanston, Illinois, which has a collection of 450 catalogued manuscripts and 131 letters, including considerable correspondence with Eliot. The Bancroft Library of the University of California at Berkeley has a collection of uncatalogued manuscripts, as well as notebooks containing drafts of poems, personal journals, and correspondence with Eliot, Pound, Forster, Huxley, Edith Sitwell, and others. Other libraries having Spender papers are the University of Notre Dame and the Harry Ransom Humanities Research Center at the University of Texas, Austin.

Dylan Thomas

(27 October 1914 - 9 November 1953)

This entry was updated by David E. Middleton (Nicholls State University) from his entry in
DLB 20: British Poets, 1914-1945.

See also the Thomas entry in DLB 13: British Dramatists Since World War II: Part Two.

SELECTED BOOKS: *18 Poems* (London: *Sunday Referee*/Parton Bookshop, 1934);
Twenty-Five Poems (London: Dent, 1936);
The Map of Love (London: Dent, 1939);
The World I Breathe (Norfolk, Conn.: New Directions, 1939);
Portrait of the Artist as a Young Dog (London: Dent, 1940; Norfolk, Conn.: New Directions, 1940);
New Poems (Norfolk, Conn.: New Directions, 1943);
Deaths and Entrances (London: Dent, 1946);
Selected Writings of Dylan Thomas (New York: New Directions, 1946);
In Country Sleep and Other Poems (New York: New Directions, 1952);
Collected Poems: 1934-1952 (London: Dent, 1952); republished as *The Collected Poems of Dylan Thomas* (New York: New Directions, 1953);
The Doctor and the Devils, adapted from Donald Taylor's story (London: Dent, 1953; Norfolk, Conn.: New Directions, 1953);
Under Milk Wood (London: Dent, 1954; New York: New Directions, 1954);
Quite Early One Morning (London: Dent, 1954; enlarged edition, New York: New Directions, 1954);
A Prospect of the Sea and Other Stories and Prose Writings, edited by Daniel Jones (London: Dent, 1955);
Adventures in the Skin Trade and Other Stories (New York: New Directions, 1955); republished as *Adventures in the Skin Trade* (London: Putnam's, 1955);
A Child's Christmas in Wales (Norfolk, Conn.: New Directions, 1955);
The Beach of Falesá, based on Robert Louis Stevenson's story (New York: Stein & Day, 1963; London: Cape, 1964);
Twenty Years A-Growing, adapted from Maurice O'Sullivan's story (London: Dent, 1964);

Rebecca's Daughters (London: Triton, 1965; Boston: Little, Brown, 1965);
Me and My Bike (New York: McGraw-Hill, 1965; London: Triton, 1965);
The Doctor and the Devils and Other Scripts (New York: New Directions, 1966);
The Notebooks of Dylan Thomas, edited by Ralph Maud (New York: New Directions, 1967); republished as *Poet in the Making* (London: Dent, 1968);
Dylan Thomas: Early Prose Writings (London: Dent, 1971; New York: New Directions, 1971);
The Poems of Dylan Thomas, edited by Jones (London: Dent, 1971; New York: New Directions, 1971);
Dylan Thomas: Selected Poems, edited by Walford Davies (London: Dent, 1974);
The Death of the King's Canary, by Thomas and John Davenport (London: Hutchinson, 1976);
Dylan Thomas: The Collected Stories (London: Dent, 1983; New York: New Directions, 1984);
A Visit to Grandpa's and Other Stories (London: Dent, 1984);
Collected Poems 1934-1953, edited by Davies and Maud (London: Dent, 1988);
The Notebook Poems 1930-1934, edited by Maud (London: Dent, 1989).

MOTION PICTURE: *Me and My Bike*, screenplay by Thomas, Gainsborough, 1948.

SELECTED PERIODICAL PUBLICATIONS—
UNCOLLECTED: "On Poetry: A Discussion," *Encounter*, 3 (November 1954): 23-26;
"Dylan Thomas On Reading His Poetry," *Mademoiselle*, 43 (July 1956): 34-37;
"Dylan Thomas on Edgar Lee Masters," *Harper's Bazaar*, 96 (June 1963): 68-69, 115;
"Poetry and the Film: A Symposium," *Film Culture*, 29 (Summer 1963): 55-63.

Dylan Thomas's life, work, and stature among twentieth-century poets are all matters of

Dylan Thomas, circa 1946

controversy and speculation. An essentially shy and modest man when sober, Thomas called himself the "captain of the second eleven" on the team of modern poets, an uneasy, pivotal ranking between the clearly major and the clearly minor poets. Others, too, such as John Crowe Ransom, have found difficulty in formulating a final opinion of Thomas: is he really only the best of the minor poets—those who achieve distinction within inherited modes and procedures—or is he the weak man, if that, among the major poets— those who absorb the tradition of ideas and forms which they then in some way radically change?

Until recently, Thomas's spectacular public life and personality, essentially distinct from the serious craftsman within, obscured the critical view of the body of work which the poet left behind. The burning ground of Thomas's four reading tours in America (1950-1953)—the endless drunkenness, the exhibitionist behavior, the masterful and deeply moving public readings, the early death from alcoholism at thirty-nine in New York—these events and more make Thomas's biography an interesting story in itself. Yet as

Thomas's closest childhood friend, Dr. Daniel Jones, said, Thomas's artistic sensibility was at war with his outer life. In Thomas's words, there was a traditional romantic conflict between the "interior world" of childhood fantasy, dream, poetic imagination and the "exterior, wrong world" of objective, adult reality, what Thomas fearfully called "the world-of-the-others."

Not only Thomas's life but even his poetry is dominated by the problem of the relation of inner and outer, of self and world. In a letter of 1933, written during the single greatest year of Thomas's poetic activity, the eighteen-year-old poet speculated about this troubling matter of "worlds": "Perhaps the greatest works of art are those that reconcile, perfectly, inner and outer." This problem remains the underlying theme of Thomas's poetry in its three major phases: the early juvenilia, the poems in the notebooks, and the post-notebook poems of 1934-1936; the middle-phase poetry of the late 1930s to mid 1940s; and the final poetry of the postwar years (1946-1953). Less centrally, the immediate themes of the poetry in the three periods evolve from an early obsession with a visionary, often demonic fusion of the processes of the body, especially intercourse and gestation, with the processes of nature and the cosmos; through a more directly personal encounter with the "exterior" challenges of marriage, fatherhood, and war; to a final period of imaginative recollection and dramatic evocation of a lost Wordsworthian childhood and a loving vision of nature and death as holy, sacramental, and good.

Dylan Marlais Thomas was born at home, No. 5 Cwmdonkin Drive, in the middle-class Uplands district of Swansea, Wales, on 27 October 1914. His father, D. J. Thomas, was a schoolmaster in English at the Swansea Grammar School, while his mother, Florence Williams Thomas, was a housewife who had previously given birth to a daughter, Nancy, nearly nine years older than Dylan. A bitter, disappointed man who thought his schoolmaster's job beneath his abilities, Thomas's father was rather cold, somewhat given to drink in his youth, an atheist who paradoxically cursed God for changes in the weather, yet a brilliant reader of Shakespeare to his class and to the preschool Dylan, and the owner of a surprisingly up-to-date library of modern and nineteenth-century poets, which his son absorbed. Dylan feared, respected, and deeply loved this rather terrifying father, and in some sense his life was an attempt to realize his father's frustrated dream of being a great poet. His mother, on the other hand, was a simple woman, loving and overly protective. She spoiled Dylan as a child and adolescent and even at the end of his life found no fault in his public behavior and drinking habits. Thomas's lifelong desire to remain in some way a child and to be free of adult responsibility probably resulted from his mother's overindulgence and from his own rebellion against his stricter, more demanding father.

Swansea and the Gower peninsula, No. 5 Cwmdonkin Drive, Cwmdonkin Park, Fernhill—these are the places which meant the most to Thomas in childhood and adolescence, from his earliest years until he moved to London for his first long stay in 1934. In Thomas's time, Swansea had around 100,000 residents. Built on hills curving around a bay (hills through which the River Tawe flows), Swansea was a middle-class, Anglicized seaport town, adjacent to the beautifully wild, heath-covered Gower peninsula. From his room at No. 5 Cwmdonkin Drive, the young poet could see the bay and also, across the street, Cwmdonkin Park, where he played as a child and which figures in poems such as "The Hunch-

back in the Park" as an Edenic place, visionary nature as seen by the poet as child. Fernhill was the farm near Llangain, owned by his uncle Jack Jones, husband of his mother's oldest sister, Annie, the subject of Thomas's poem "After the Funeral: in memory of Ann Jones." Here, Dylan spent many vacations as a child, as recounted in his best-known poem, "Fern Hill." Like Cwmdonkin Park, Fernhill (as it is normally spelled) became, in Thomas's later life, the focus of nostalgic yearnings for the lost world of the romantic child.

Schooling proved to be no real threat to such childhood happiness as Thomas grew into adolescence. In 1925 he entered the Swansea Grammar School, where he stayed until 1931. Under headmaster Trevor Owen, the school was run in a relaxed, liberal atmosphere, one in which the studious boys were encouraged and the lazy ones, including Dylan, left pretty much alone.

As Thomas later said, his real education came from the freedom to read anything in his father's library and more. He absorbed a bewildering array of works and authors: "Sir Thomas Browne, Robert W. Service, de Quincey, Henry Newbolt, Blake, Baroness Orczy, Marlowe, *Chums*, the Imagists, the Bible, the *Magnet*, Poe, Grimm, Keats, Lawrence, Austin Dobson and Dostoievski, Anon and Shakespeare." The Bible and Shakespeare were particularly important sources of Thomas's imagery, rhythms, and poetic syntax. John Keats was for Thomas a conscious model and measuring rod to whom he frequently compared himself. Of William Blake, Thomas once said, "I am in the path of Blake, but so far behind him that only the wings of his heels are in sight."

During his stay at the grammar school, Thomas edited, almost single-handedly, the *Swansea Grammar School Magazine*. Here he published his juvenilia—comic and wittily imitative poems that do not reveal Thomas's private struggle to achieve a serious, profoundly original voice. That struggle was occurring, in utmost privacy, in the notebooks (1930-1934), of which four survive. These notebooks chart Thomas's gradual development of his well-known early style. That a young boy, sixteen to nineteen years old, in a Welsh sea town should create such original poetry at first seems amazing, but Thomas's precocious essay "Modern Poetry" (1929) shows Thomas to be aware of many modern poets: Thomas Hardy, Robert Bridges, Gerard Manley Hopkins, Edith Sitwell, William Butler Yeats, the World War I

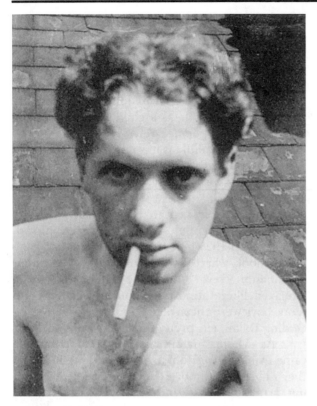

Dylan Thomas in Kensington, 1935

poets, D. H. Lawrence, and Ezra Pound.

Another important influence on the young poet was his friendship with Dan Jones, later Dr. Daniel Jones, musical composer and editor of *The Poems of Dylan Thomas* (1971). At Dan's house, called Warmley, Thomas found many books on modern poetry. The two young artists composed poems together, and they created, like the Brontë children, a vast fantasy world of poets, musicians, and others whose works were "broadcast" through jerry-built loudspeakers over the Warmley Broadcasting System. The word games and poetic exercises were part of Thomas's deliberate but essentially private development from school wit to serious young poet in the notebooks. When Thomas left school for good in July 1931, he entered into the most productive three-year period of his life. From mid 1931 until he moved to London in late 1934, Thomas lived an intense poetic life, which he recorded in the notebooks.

In the Swansea of the Depression year 1931, Thomas was lucky to land a job, probably with D. J. Thomas's help, as copyreader and then reporter for the *South Wales Evening Post*. Thomas held this job for nearly a year and a half, leaving at Christmas 1932 by mutual agreement. From

all accounts, he was a terrible news reporter: he got facts wrong, and he failed to show up to cover events, preferring instead the pool hall or coffee at the local artistic hangout, the Kardomah Cafe. Thomas's most significant journalism from this period is a series of articles for the *Herald of Wales* (weekend complement to the *Post*) on "The Poets of Swansea." The most intriguing of these critical essays is the one on Llewelyn Prichard, a fiery nineteenth-century figure whose personality and fate forecast in eerie fashion Thomas's own: "No one can deny that the most attractive figures in literature are always those around whom a world of lies and legends have been woven, those half mythical artists whose real characters become cloaked for ever under a veil of the bizarre. They become known not as creatures of flesh and blood, living day by day as prosaically as the rest of us, but as men stepping on clouds, snaring a world of beauty from the trees and sky, half wild, half human." Thomas also wrote about his reporter days in his poignant BBC reminiscence of prewar Swansea, "Return Journey," in which an old reporter and two young reporters discuss the long-gone young Thomas. The narrator, too, recalls Thomas the young poet and reporter: "He'd be about seventeen or eighteen . . . and above medium height. Above medium height for Wales, I mean, he's five foot six and a half. Thick blubber lips; snub nose; curly mouse-brown hair; one front tooth broken after playing a game called Cats and Dogs, in the Mermaid, Mumbles; speaks rather fancy; truculent; plausible; a bit of a shower-off; plus-fours and no breakfast, you know; used to have poems printed in the *Herald of Wales* . . . a bombastic adolescent provincial Bohemian with a thick-knotted artist's tie made out of his sister's scarf, she never knew where it had gone, and a cricket-shirt dyed bottle-green; a gabbing, ambitious, mock-tough, pretentious young man; and mole-y, too."

As a self-affectedly bohemian poseur, Thomas began acquiring his reputation as a great drinker, the "conscious Woodbine" cigarette dangling from his lips. He began to develop a public persona as jokester and storyteller, which became his trademark later on in the London years. Thomas's first visit to London seems to have occurred in August 1933. Only one poem, "And Death Shall Have No Dominion," had appeared in a London publication before this first trip, and that was in A. R. Orage's *New English Weekly* (May 1933). Contacts made in August 1933 and on later trips led to the publication of early poems in the *Adelphi*, the *Listener, New Verse,* and T. S. Eliot's *Criterion*. Although Eliot subsequently declined Thomas's poems for Faber and Faber, he wrote to Thomas's biographer Constantine FitzGibbon that "I certainly regarded him always as a poet of considerable importance." In 1933, however, it was the unlikely figure of Victor Neuburg, a strange poet who was once under the influence of the occultist Aleister Crowley, who discovered and widely promoted Thomas's work. Neuburg edited the "Poets' Corner" in Mark Goulden's newspaper, the *Sunday Referee*. Between 1933 and 1935, Neuburg published seven poems by Thomas in the "Poets' Corner." In March 1934 Thomas followed Pamela Hansford Johnson in receiving the second "Poets' Corner" Prize: the publication of a first book of poems. David Archer, owner of the Parton Bookshop, shared printing costs with the *Referee,* and *18 Poems* by Dylan Thomas was published on 18 December 1934. Earlier, in 1933, Johnson had written Thomas a letter in admiration of the poem "That Sanity Be Kept" (*Sunday Referee,* 3 September 1933). From this letter developed Thomas's most extensive correspondence on the ideas embodied in his early poetry. Although in love with Thomas, Johnson sensed that his irregular life and especially his drinking would not do, and the relationship was eventually broken off.

In his letters to Johnson, Thomas clearly stated his defiantly Romantic view of poetry: "There is no necessity for the artist to do anything. There is no necessity. He is a law unto himself, and his greatness or smallness rises or falls by that. He has only one limitation, and that is the widest of all: the limitation of form. Poetry finds its own form; form should never be superimposed; the structure should rise out of the words and the expression of them. I do not want to express only what other people have felt; I want to rip something away and show what they have never seen." In another letter, Thomas described his characteristic method in the early poems of linking cosmic and bodily processes: "All thoughts and actions emanate from the body. Therefore the description of a thought or action—however abstruse it may be—can be beaten home by bringing it onto a physical level. Every idea, intuitive or intellectual, can be imaged and translated in terms of the body, its flesh, skin, blood, sinews, veins, glands, organs, cells, or senses. Through my small, bone-bound island I have learnt all I know, experienced all, and sensed all.

All I write is inseparable from the island. As much as possible, therefore, I employ the scenery of the island to describe the scenery of my thoughts, the earthquake of the body to describe the earthquake of the heart." For Thomas, the poet is the great healer and unifier, for whom words are living things and living things are words. To Johnson, too, he said what he would often repeat, that poets either work *toward* words or *out of* words. He himself worked *out of* words, trying to release from words, like a shaman, their magical powers that would unite all opposites of human experience. Such a procedure often led to obscurity, as Thomas confessed to Johnson in a May 1934 letter, in which he called himself "a freak *user* of words, not a poet."

In October 1934, on the eve of his departure for London, Thomas discussed his poetic goals more affirmatively in answers to a *New Verse* questionnaire. There he defined poetry as "the rhythmic, inevitably narrative, movement from an overclothed blindness to a naked vision.... My poetry is, or should be, useful to me for one reason: it is the record of my individual struggle from darkness towards some measure of light." He also accepted Sigmund Freud and revolution. Shortly after his arrival in London, Thomas wrote to Swansea friend Charles Fisher about "my theory of poetry." Slightly altering his quotation from Blake, Thomas pronounced: "I like things that are difficult to write and difficult to understand; I like 'redeeming the contraries' with secretive images; I like contradicting my images, saying two things at once in one word, four in two and one in six.... Poetry ... should be as orgiastic and organic as copulation, dividing and unifying, personal but not private, propagating the individual in the mass and the mass in the individual." This statement is matched by his famous response to Henry Treece about his imagistic method of composition. A poem of his begins, he said, with a "host of images," one image breeding another, often its opposite, a "dialectical method" that begins with the "central seed" and proceeds through a series of "creations, recreations, destructions, contradictions" to reach "that momentary peace which is a poem."

The years 1935-1937 brought to a close the first phase of Dylan Thomas's life and art. In these years he reworked most of the best of the remaining notebook poems and wrote new long poems that led up to the ten sonnets of the "Altarwise by Owl-light" sequence. This time period also found Thomas plunging into the art world and bohemian quarters of London, establishing a reputation as poet, pub crawler, character, storyteller, and "damned soul," in the nineteenth-century French tradition, the demonically destructive angel-child whom many acquaintances wished to mother and protect.

Thomas lived first at No. 5 Redcliffe Street, near Earl's Court in South Kensington. He shared rooms with Swansea artist friends Fred Janes, Mervyn Levy, and William Scott. Soon, however, he was living in one place and then another, as girls or friends came and went, making do with beer and cake or an apple for breakfast, no pajamas, and only a mattress on the floor at Janes's flat, when he was there at all. His squalid domestic and hygienic habits earned him the nicknames "Ditch" and "The Ugly Suckling," among others. Relishing the image of the poet-in-the-gutter, Thomas loved to be sung to sleep by Levy with a song whose line "For I am waiting and watching, an outlaw defiant" the poet loved best.

In public, Thomas lived up to this image of the artist as "an outlaw defiant" in his often outrageous, sometimes hilarious, at other times disgusting behavior. He made up strange fantasies about "Night Custard," or a universe in which all things are made from oil (an "oily verse"), about the delectability of a sandwich of dried eyes. Most of Thomas's pub stories and jokes are lost, and the fragments still recalled by listeners usually pale without Thomas's presence, delivery, and the beer; nevertheless, countless reports seem to confirm that before getting too drunk for wit, Thomas was one of the great conversationalists of his day. In June 1936 he fit right in at the famous international Surrealist Exhibition at the Burlington Galleries, London, where he carried around a cup of boiled string, asking, "Weak or strong?" At a poetry recitation there, he read a postcard. Apparently, too, he caught a social disease from a girl at this time and went home to Wales to recuperate. In fact, from 1934 on, Thomas established a lifelong pattern of travel between London and some rural retreat, usually in Wales. London meant drink, possibly employment by the BBC, and no work on poems. Wales and elsewhere meant work on poems, somewhat less to drink, but no employment, eventual boredom, and the inevitable return to London for dissipation.

Thomas's second book, *Twenty-Five Poems*, was published in 1936 by J. M. Dent (second only to Faber and Faber as a poetry press) through the offices of Lascelles Abercrombie, who knew

an editor at Dent, Richard Church. Church accepted *Twenty-Five Poems* in spite of his fear that the poems were too obscure and fashionably surrealistic. Although Thomas denied the charge and Dent published the volume, his poetry was becoming more and more obscure and continued to be so until World War II. In a letter to Vernon Watkins, Thomas admitted his fears: "now, I'm almost afraid of all the once-necessary artifices and obscurities, and can't, for the life or the death of me, get any real liberation, any diffusion or dilution or anything, into the churning bulk of the words." Thomas's own fears were echoed in the mixed reviews of *Twenty-Five Poems*, although sales were high, with four printings of more than three thousand copies by October 1944.

Thomas first met Caitlin Macnamara in the Wheatsheaf, a London pub, in 1936. She was accompanied by the painter Augustus John, with whom she was intimate. Blue-eyed, yellow-haired, once called a true poet's girl, Caitlin Macnamara was a fair-skinned Irish beauty, strong-willed, violently emotional and argumentative at times, and a truer bohemian than the essentially middle-class Thomas. A good writer and a superb freestyle dancer, she had a brief career in Paris and London before becoming Thomas's wife.

Thomas fell in love with Caitlin at first sight. They had an affair at the Eiffel Tower Hotel on John's tab but were afterward separated when Thomas went to Cornwall. In July 1936 Thomas met her again at Richard Hughes's house in Laugharne, where she and John were staying. A fight ensued between Thomas and the much older John, with John knocking Thomas down and driving off with Caitlin. However, by 11 July 1937 Thomas and Caitlin were married in Cornwall, and the first phase of Thomas's short life came to an end.

The critical reception of Dylan Thomas's poetry may be divided into four phases. First, there was a generally polemical reception of the various volumes of poetry from *18 Poems* (1934) through *Collected Poems: 1934-1952* (1952). This critical debate occurred mainly in the review columns and editorial pages of the important English and Welsh newspapers and poetry journals of the day. Second, with the exception of Henry Treece's *Dylan Thomas* (1949), the 1950s and 1960s saw the appearance of the first book-length critical studies of Thomas's poems. Most of these studies were general surveys of Thomas's work emphasizing the immediate problem of explicating difficult texts for the general reader. Third, in the mid 1960s and the 1970s, academic studies shifted to an interest in placing Thomas in one of several contexts such as Jungian psychology, Gnosticism, Christianity, Nietzschean Dionysianism, or the Welsh bardic tradition. Each of the studies in this third phase sought to give unity to Thomas's poetry by defining his poetic development in terms of one of these contexts. Fourth, in the 1980s there was a period of consolidation in Thomas studies. The appearance of the collected letters, the collected stories, the re-edited notebook poems, and a new edition of the collected poems with more than one hundred pages of explanatory notes made virtually all of Thomas's work available and accessible both to scholars and to students. Caitlin Thomas finally told her own story of the years of her marriage to Dylan in *Caitlin: A Warring Absence* (1986); Rob Gittins added more details to our knowledge of Thomas's final American tour in *The Last Days of Dylan Thomas* (1986); and in *Dylan Thomas and Vernon Watkins: Portrait of a Friendship* (1983), Watkins's widow, Gwen, described one of Thomas's most rewarding personal and poetic relationships. All in all, the 1980s saw Dylan Thomas firmly in place as an important poet in the Welsh, Romantic, and modern literary traditions.

Thomas's first book, *18 Poems*, appeared in a poetic decade usually characterized as one in which the poet's political responsibility and awareness were paramount in influencing the kind of poetry he wrote. Yet the poets of the 1930s are not as homogeneous a group as might first be thought. In his 1952 *Spectator* review of Thomas's *Collected Poems: 1934-1952*, Stephen Spender looked back on Thomas as having purposefully rebelled against the conscious intellectualism, wit, and political emphasis of "Macspaunday" (his name for Louis MacNeice, himself, W. H. Auden, and C. Day Lewis, often called the Auden Generation). The Romantic personalism of the poetry of Edith Sitwell and the blossoming of the British variety of surrealism in the 1930s gave that decade a more complex character than is sometimes acknowledged. Certainly the reviewers of the period saw Thomas in a Romantic context. The subjective, expressionistic nature of his poetry was emphasized as well as its struggle to articulate a new mode of consciousness. Some critics condemned him for being a surrealist or for not being more politically aware. By the end of the decade, however, Thomas himself was

Dylan and Caitlin Thomas at Sea View, Laugharne, circa 1938 (photograph by Nora Summers)

adopted as the patron saint of a group of British poets known as the Apocalypse, whose most important members, Henry Treece and J. F. Hendry, were advocates of a new Romantic poetry, surrealistic and antimechanistic in style.

Although Dylan Thomas said that he preferred "what I think about verse to be *in* the verse," he left numerous letters, essays, broadcasts, and lecture notes that include important statements of his views on the nature of poetry. Like the letters to Pamela Hansford Johnson, Thomas's other prose statements are a rich source of evidence in support of the proposition that the problem of *self* and *world*, of subject-object relations, as inherited from the Romantic tradition, is a central concern of Thomas as a poet. Thomas often expresses this theme in terms of the Romantic myth, that is, the Romantic displacement of the Creation, Fall, and Redemption phases of the Christian version of history into a secular, psychological context. In the Romantic scheme, Creation is the sense of unity of being present most clearly in childhood, a sense of oneness with nature and a unity among the faculties of the mind. The Fall is the decline of the child into adulthood and attendant self-consciousness, a sense of isolation, estrangement, division. Redemption, then, becomes the self-generated effort of the Romantic to achieve reintegration by exercising the poetic imagination in such a way as to release a healing love into the world. Keeping the theme of self and world as embodied in the Romantic myth in mind as the key to Thomas's poetry, one may list important secondary traits that emanate from that central concern. These include the importance of the imagination as an image-making power; the epiphanic moment; poetry as the expression of intense emotion; the poet as the hero of his own poems, an exile from society; the organic nature of the image and the poetic process; the desire of the poet to remove the ontological barrier between word and thing; the inner quest for psychic unity; the problem of self-consciousness; the child as a figure of unity of being; the displacement of religious values into psychological and poetic terms; the importance of the relation of man and nature; and the poetic significance of the power of love.

The most authoritative comments on the question of Thomas's periods of poetic development are two made by Thomas himself. In a conversation in a New York bar with the critic William York Tindall, Thomas agreed with Tindall's division of the poetry into three phases: a "womb-tomb" period that included the poems in *18 Poems* and *Twenty-Five Poems*; a troubled middle period about marriage and war in *The Map of Love* (1939) and *Deaths and Entrances* (1946); and a final "period of humanity" or acceptance of the tragedy of the human condition in some of the later poems in *Deaths and Entrances* and in the poems of *In Country Sleep* (1952). However much overlapping there might be among the volumes of these three periods, there seems to be little doubt among critics that Thomas brought to fruition two major strains of poetry. The first strain is that of the early poems, originating mostly from the notebooks, written in a packed stanza of intense, obscure imagery, making use of assonantal and consonantal rhyme, and concerned with the development of an assertive Romantic self, a development that culminates in the spiritual and poetic autobiography, "Altarwise by Owl-light," the quest-romance that closes *Twenty-Five Poems* and which Thomas himself came to

see as the ultimate development of the tendencies in his first major period of creativity.

The second strain of major achievement begins with poems in *Deaths and Entrances*—"Poem in October," "A Winter's Tale," and the final poem of the volume, "Fern Hill"—and ends with three finished sections of the projected poem "In Country Heaven" ("In Country Sleep," "Over Sir John's Hill," and "In the White Giant's Thigh"), the final birthday poem entitled "Poem on his Birthday," and the "Author's Prologue" to *Collected Poems*. This second period of major poetry is one in which the Romantic self finds its true place in the role of priestly interpreter of nature and purveyor of the forces of imaginative perception and of love which redeem humanity from isolating self-consciousness and destructive rationality by revealing nature as a place of holiness.

Between these early poems of the assertive Romantic self and the later poems of regenerative landscapes falls what some call a separate period, often designated as Thomas's "dark," "troubled," or "transitional" phase. The poems in this middle period are the "marriage" poems and the "war" poems in *The Map of Love* and in *Deaths and Entrances*. What the marriage and the war poems have in common is that both represent serious incursions of what Thomas called the "exterior" world of the "others" into the "interior" world of the youthful Swansea poet. The central question posed by the problem of marriage and of armed conflict was whether the Romantic self's claim that it could govern its relation to the outer world was valid. In seeking a way out of this dilemma, Thomas discovered the Romantic self's true task in the fostering of love and in the praise of the spiritualized landscape in face of the threats to humanity and the natural world posed by the atomic bomb. This final task of the self, then, becomes the subject of the later poems.

One difficulty with any examination of Thomas's poems is what may be called the problem of chronology. Because he wrote so slowly, Thomas reworked poems from the notebooks for inclusion in his second and third volumes, *Twenty-Five Poems* and *The Map of Love*. Most of the poems in his first volume, *18 Poems*, come from the last notebook, begun in August 1933. Thus, many of Thomas's poems written before those in *18 Poems* were first published in book form in the two volumes that followed *18 Poems*. The most helpful way to see Thomas's poetic development clearly in the early period is to examine the poems as they appear in the four extant notebooks first, and then, if necessary, to examine radical revisions of notebook poems when these revisions result in the virtual creation of a new poem.

Although written concurrently with some unimportant schoolboy verses, the private notebook poems represent a more intensely serious effort at poetic composition. Headed "Mainly Free Verse Poems," the poems in the 1930 notebook show the obvious influence of certain poets and poetic schools, including Yeats, Pound, the Imagists, and Keats. The first group includes poems that deal with the tendency of the self to transform or to absorb the world, usually by way of the process of poetic creation. In poem eleven, for instance, the poet takes two growing plants—a cornstalk and a blue flower—and speculates on how his imagination must operate to "free" the corn and flower from the restrictions of rational perception, of the laws of growth and decay in the fallen world. A second group of poems examines the relation of the self and world in terms of the self's desire for, or fear of, absorption into the external world. Poem twenty-seven is spoken by a bird, a favorite image of Thomas's, in this case to be identified with the poet in the act of poetic creation. Poem eighteen seems heavily indebted to Keats's "Ode to a Nightingale." The poet experiences a Romantic moment of the loss of self-consciousness: "So I sink myself in the moment, / I let the fiery stream run." He becomes a garden in which the bird sits and sings, bringing such intense joy that the poet is "all but cut by the scent's arc," as in Keats's poem.

The idea of a perfect woman who wavers between the status of nature and art is the subject of poem thirty-three. The poet addresses a real woman who has been transformed into an ideal by the poet's imagination. Thus he says, "I bought you for a thought," and calls his mind "your panopticon," or distorting mirror, that makes the woman over to suit his desires.

Other poems compare the poet to the natural world. Sometimes Thomas sees nature as a place of vitalistic, primitive energy, where human self-consciousness does not disturb the harmony. For instance, poem eight, a Lawrentian beast poem, expresses a desire to be like the lion who is "balanced," has a "clean" mind without superfluous vanity, and who is a "vital, dominant creature," unlike the "unbalanced," "frail" poet. More often, nature is seen as an object for imaginative

redemption or as a desirable object for union with the isolated self. As an object for redemption, nature in its fallen form is released by imagination in the poem on the endlessly growing cornstalk and blue flowers (poem eleven), or in the poem on the similarly unlimited expansion of sacramental trees (poem twelve).

Several of these poems on nature link the virtues of the natural world with the poet's quest for a love to bring release from self-consciousness. In the 1930 notebook, love appears as pure sensuality or mundane human love; as the poet's anima or its dark reverse, the femme fatale; or as an agent of redemption. Three poems—poems twenty-one, thirty-nine, and forty-two—include the figure of the female dancer who unites art and nature, spirit and body, pattern and embodiment in one. Poem thirteen apparently invites an Egyptian goddess ("Oh, eagle-mouthed") into the poet's inner world, while poem twenty invites an angel, a seraph, to enter a cavernous Jordan of the imagination. Poems ten and thirty-eight take opposite attitudes toward the union of the poet's lover or anima with natural powers, poem ten seeing the lover-anima as drawing strength from nature, and poem thirty-eight bemoaning Artemis's degradation from myth into the material world.

All the themes of the 1930 notebook continue in the 1930-1932 notebook. Somewhere in the middle of this notebook emerges Thomas's most characteristic early style, comprising a dense, packed line that is heavily rhythmical, a catalogue of arcane images which often seek to become polysemous metaphors for three simultaneously presented creative processes: nature, sex, and poetry. Besides this emergence of a more sophisticated style, what distinguishes the 1930-1932 notebook from its predecessor is the poet's increasing awareness of the necessity and yet supreme difficulty of exercising the imagination in poetic composition in order to govern the external world on terms congenial to the self. A growing sense of deathliness in nature as well as a sense of the multiple faces of love—sexuality, necrophilia, the ideal woman or anima—and the experience of the relative failure of these forms in redeeming the self from isolation are also major themes of the second extant notebook.

Poem two ("To-day, this hour I breathe") addresses the problem of the artist whose imagination, operating according to the same organic laws that govern nature, encounters recalcitrant objects that violate its own laws. In an epiphanic moment, the poet and nature are linked by the Romantic metaphor of the correspondent breeze by which internal symbol and external object are made one: "To-day, this hour I breathe / In symbols, be they so light, of tongue and air."

A poem whose subjects are nature, imagination, and love is poem eighty, the 1932 version of "The Hunchback in the Park." Though alone in nature, "a solitary mister," the hunchback is not isolated from nature; rather, nature lends support to the hunchback, "propped between trees and water." From the degraded perspective of modern urban dwellers, the hunchback is a madman, "going daft," while his physical deformity brings on the cruel laughter of children. They call him only "mister" as if to deny him identity, yet with some irony it is they who tease him and run into the oblivion beyond the park, the limit of the hunchback's perception: "Past lake and rockery / On out of sight." At night, when the park is emptied of all but the Yeatsian "three veteran swans," the hunchback assumes his true identity as Romantic poet by creating in the mind a figure of ideal feminine beauty, which he then transposes from the inner self to the outer landscape. He makes

> A figure without fault
> And sees it on the gravel paths
> Or walking on the water.

The feminine ideal brings unity of being and may be a nature spirit, for she is "frozen all the winter" and appears only in the summer. That the hunchback is a poet exercising imagination we know directly: "It is a poem and it is a woman figure." She calls to him from the water of the lake, and while he responded angrily to the taunting children, he now smiles at the woman who has left his imagination to live in the park.

A similar poem in Thomas's emerging early style is poem twenty-one ("High on a Hill"), which attempts to create a polysemous metaphor for the self's relation to nature, sex, and poetic creation. The poet seems to be riding a hill like a bucking bronco, yet this hill is surprisingly female—"straddle her wrinkled knees"—just as the adder, snake, and shell-bursting bird are creatures of nature but also representative of the penis. The poetic dimension of the imagery is made explicit in the exclamation "Christ, let me write from the heart," which makes the "carnal stem" not only flower stalk and penis but also the poet's phallic fountain pen which deflowers the

virgin paper, a frequent metaphor in Thomas's letters. As he writes from the "heart," the "blood's ebb" is of the detumescent penis and the receding moment of poetic inspiration.

The 1930-1932 notebook also marks the emergence of Thomas's brooding over the endless cycles of creation and decay in the universe, an imprisoning cycle from which he seeks escape by trying to invoke the power of poetic creation to reverse or end the cycle. Poem twenty-five is an obscure meditation on two impulses toward poetic creation—death and love—both of which relieve the poet of his burden of self-consciousness. Even as the poet writes, death's promise comes nearer in the passing of time: "I have a friend in death, / Daywise, the grave's inertia."

Ralph Maud designates the February 1933 notebook and the surviving poems from the lost 1932-1933 notebook as the beginning of Thomas's "inlooking" poems, phantasmagoric evocations of "process" in the body and in the natural world to which the body is linked. Actually, Thomas's Romantic concern with self and world and the links between the two (sex, death, imagination) begins with his earliest poetry. The real changes in successive notebooks or published volumes are Thomas's increasing mastery of poetic technique and the periodic risings and fallings of his faith in the ability of imagination to heal the gap between subject and object.

One of the most despairing in this group of poems on poetry and nature is "Especially When the November Wind," a 1932-1933 version of the well-known "Especially When the October Wind," from which it radically differs. One month further into the cold than its later version, the 1932-1933 poem has as its theme the paradox that the more intensely the poet writes in order to find a way to link himself to the outer world, the more self-conscious he becomes of his isolation, which is seemingly made worse by the very self-consciousness of the act of poetic creation itself. An evil version of the Romantic metaphor of the correspondent breeze, the "November wind / With frosty fingers, punishes my hair" as the poet's fingers respond to the creative breezes of inspiration. The poet seems to face two unpleasant choices: to expend his animal youth in a nature that is killing him even as he enjoys the release from the burdens of human thought, or else to compose an aesthetic poetry that cannot create unity of being for the fully human poet in a fully natural world. Thus, the "raw / Spirits of words" and "arid syllables" op-

PROLOGUE

This day winding down now
At God speeded summer's end
In the torrent salmon sun,
In my seashaken house
On a breakneck of rocks,
Tangled with chirrup and grass,
Flute, apple, ~~seal~~, fin and quill
At a wood's dancing hoof,
By scummed, starfish sands
With their fishwife cross
Gulls, pipers, cockles, and sails,
Out there, ~~yonder~~ birdlike, man
Tackled with clouds, who kneel
To the sunset nets,
Geese nearly in heaven, boys
Stabbing, and herons, and shells
That speak seven seas,
Eternal waters away
From the cities of nine
Days' night whose towers will catch
In the religious wind
Like stalks of tall, dry straw,
At poor peace I sing
To you, strangers, (though song
Is a burning and crested act,
The fire of birds in
The world's turning wood,
For my sawn, splay sounds),
Out of these seathumbed leaves
That will fly and fall
Like leaves of trees and as soon
Crumble and undie
Into the dogdayed night.
Seaward the salmon, sucked sun slips,
And the dumb swans drub blue
My dabbed bay's dusk, as I hack
This rumpus of shapes
For you to know
How I, a spinning man,
Glory also this star, bird
Roared, sea born, man torn, blood blest.
Hark: I trumpet the place,
From fish to jumping hill! Look:
I build my bellowing ark
To the best of my love
As the flood begins,
Out of the fountain head
Of fear, rage red, manalive,
Molten and mountainous to stream
Over the wound asleep
Sheep white hollow farms

Page from a late draft for Thomas's "Author's Prologue" to Collected Poems: 1934–1952
(Houghton Library, Harvard University)

press brain and heart. Being caught in the "chain of words" and "shut in a tower of words," the poet envies animals, children, or unself-conscious men, who in their primitive "language" or in silence find the unity with nature that escapes the poet.

A nearly complete version of "Ears in the Turrets Hear" dramatizes the isolation of the poet from the outer world. The poet is both an island and a tower (imagination) to which ships and their sailors come to make threatening noises. A masterpiece of sound and rhythm in an essentially trimeter line with appropriate trochaic and anapestic substitutions, the poem imagines intrusive sounds being made outside the tower door by surrealistically disordered pieces of the human anatomy (both his own and the intruders'):

> Ears in the turrets hear
> Hands grumble on the door,
> Eyes in the gables see
> The fingers at the locks.

The tower is surrounded by "a thin sea of flesh / And a bone coast" beyond which lies the unreal outer world: "The land lies out of sound / And the hills out of mind." But fiery winds and anchoring ships entice the poet either to death or to salvation in the outer world:

> Shall I run to the ships,
> With the wind in my hair
> Or stay to the day I die,
> And welcome no sailor?
> Hands, hold you poison or grapes?

Is the poet lured on by a correspondent breeze in sea and hair? He certainly comes to know that his isolation from the world is no final solution.

As equally self-divided as Thomas's attitudes toward nature in the February 1933 notebook are his attitudes therein toward love. Poem eighteen ("Make Me a Mask") calls for a mask to repel the outer world, where the poet perceives "Others betraying the inner love" that motivates him. The degradation of love is sometimes associated with Eliotic cityscapes as in the typescript poem thirty-three, where we are sardonically told of "a girl whose single bed held two / To make ends meet," or in poem twenty-four, whose hero-quester sees in the dark nighttime city women's faces "with serpents' mouths and scalecophidian voids." Other corruptions of love include reli-

gious prudery, in poem fifty-three, and onanism, in poem forty-three.

That the August 1933 notebook marks Thomas's substantial arrival as an important poet seems undeniable. From the forty-odd poems in this notebook, Thomas chose thirteen for *18 Poems* as well as five for *Twenty-Five Poems*. Poems in the August notebook mark the emergence of the endless "process" of birth and death as an obsessive theme. Even more important, however, the many poems that address the central Romantic problem of the relation of self and world begin to fall clearly into the three phases of the Romantic myth—Creation, Fall, Redemption. Undoubtedly, the awareness of "process," the natural cycle of birth and death, led Thomas first to identify himself with the cycles but second to hope for some final end to these cycles in a vision of unfallen nature, some final religious apocalypse, or the poet's own exercising of imagination in the world.

Several poems key on the creation phase of the myth. A unified sensibility may be associated with a sacramental nature, the experience of one's own birth, an awakening apprehension of the unity between the evolving individual consciousness and the evolving outer world, or else a feeling of identity between God's creating Word and the poet's creating words.

With a natural bias toward the inner world, Thomas could write poems that attempt to describe simultaneously inner and outer processes, the goal of the polysemous metaphor. Two well-known examples of this process are the August 1933 notebook versions of "Light Breaks Where No Sun Shines" (poem thirty) and "In the Beginning" (poem forty). The first of these begins mysteriously:

> Light breaks where no sun shines;
> Where no sea runs, the waters of the heart
> Push in their tides;
> And, broken ghosts with glowworms in their heads,
> The things of light
> File through the flesh where no flesh decks the bones.

These opening lines may be read as an evocation of the dawn of consciousness, the physical act of conception, and the first creation of the cosmos.

The action of "In the Beginning" is obviously a creation, primarily, one assumes, of the universe; but it is also clear that Thomas is attempting to identify the poet's words and creative imagination with the creation of the cosmos and of the child, these two creations being the objects of simultaneous presentation in the five stanzas of the poem. Thus, in stanza one:

> In the beginning was the three-pointed star,
> One smile of light across the empty face;
> One bough of bone across the rooting air,
> The substance spread that marrowed the first sun;
> And, burning ciphers on the round of space,
> Heaven and hell mixed as they spun.

Several important poems in the August 1933 notebook emphasize the fall of man. This fall is not the result of moral transgression but the inevitable consequence of birth, the agonies of self-consciousness and isolation being overcome in the twin extremes of prenatal existence and death, or else in a moment when nature's unfallen form is revealed to the poet.

Poem seven ("Before I Knocked") differs from the version in *18 Poems* only by the presence of two stanzas later cut and two words later changed. The central issue of the poem is the identification of the speaking "I," who has been called a sperm cell, an unreleased female egg, the unborn Christ, the unborn poet, or the spirit of the child entering its body at conception:

> Before I knocked and flesh let enter,
> With liquid hands tapped on the womb,
> I who was shapeless as the water
> That shaped the Jordan near my home,
> Was brother to Mnetha's daughter
> And sister to the fathering worm.

The images describe the conception, gestation, birth, brief life, and crucifixion-death of a speaker who is essentially a composite of the poet and Christ. The true subject of the images that evoke pictures of these actions is the psychological experience of a fall from unity into division and, in this poem, not redemption but death. The biblical pattern of creation-fall-redemption is thus internalized in two senses: the images describe the inner processes of gestation, and this imaged process of an action of the body figures forth the psychic experience of a fall into self-consciousness.

A final group of poems in the August 1933 notebook, dealing with the relation of self and world, includes the well-known "process" poems: poem twenty-three ("The Force That Through the Green Fuse Drives the Flower") and poem thirty-five ("A Process in the Weather of the Heart"). Many readers have noted that "The Force That Through the Green Fuse Drives the Flower" has as an important theme: the idea that the process of growth and decay existing in the external world also exists in the inner world of the poet's body. Each of the first three five-line stanzas presents one and a half lines devoted to the process of inner and outer growth, one and half lines devoted to the process of inner and outer decay, and two refrainlike lines that are the poet's commentary on the first three lines:

> The hand that whirls the water in the pool
> Stirs the quicksand; that ropes the blowing wind
> Hauls my shroud sail.
> And I am dumb to tell the hanging man
> How of my clay is made the hangman's lime.

The final two lines of each stanza hold the key to the most crucial theme of the poem, for instance, in stanza one: "And I am dumb to tell the crooked rose / My youth is bent with the same wintry fever." Far from rejoicing in his unity with nature, the poet is all too aware that this oneness is a oneness of death; furthermore, as a poet, he is unable in this poem to use his poet's language as a means of establishing a deeper communion with nature (the rose), his own body (the veins), or another human being (the hanging man). In other words, this poem is really about the limits of poetic language, the poet's feeling of self-consciousness that estranges him intellectually from the world.

One of the most striking features of the August 1933 notebook in comparison to the February 1933 notebook is the revival of the idea of love as a healing power. A good example of this theme is in poem forty-one ("If I was Tickled by the Rub of Love"). Although it is probably just chance that this poem ends the fourth of the extraordinary notebooks that document a young poet's emergence as a significant talent, "If I was Tickled by the Rub of Love" is distinguished by being the only one of several autobiographical notebook poems that combines the form of the spiritual autobiography of the poet-as-poet with the theme of love as a redemptive agent.

In the poem the proposition "If I was tickled by the rub of love" is counterbalanced in stanzas one through four by a description of the poet's progress through his own love autobiography: conception by his parents, gestation and birth, childhood and adolescence, and manhood and old age. In each stanza the poet is saying that if love could be shown to be a restorative power, he would not fear any of its attendant drawbacks or downright evils.

Throughout the four notebooks, Thomas's line of development has been consistent with the statements in his letters that the reconciliation of inner and outer worlds by the imaginative identification of microcosmic man and macrocosmic universe to form something like Blake's Universal Man is his ultimate goal. But Thomas-the-Christ, whose "wordy wounds" are a Romantic displacement of Christ's sacrificial blood into a secular variety of redemptive love, never averted his face from the realities of death, time, narcissism, evil, and the limitations of love itself. Still, it is the "rub of love" that must fuse man with the cosmos. Thomas's great attempt to embody that action is the sonnet sequence "Altarwise by Owl-light," written in 1935-1936.

"Altarwise by Owl-light" is in the Romantic tradition of the internalized quest-romance and the spiritual autobiography of the poet-as-poet. In sonnet ten, the last, Thomas takes upon himself a part of the role and power of Christ and achieves a reintegration of all opposites in the image of Eden rising up from the drowned waters. This is the Romantic variation on directional movement toward redemption, from the Christian idea of heaven as "up there" to the Romantic concept of an inner heaven of psychic unity and undivided, visionary perception "down there" in the deeper regions of the human mind and in nature.

In sonnet one the birth of the poet and the death of Christ are presented simultaneously by polysemous metaphors. Christ, having risen from the tomb, visits the poet in the poet's cradle just as the Magi visited Christ; Christ addresses the infant poet and reveals His nature to him. In Romantic terms, the poet is describing his sense of estrangement from the world and the arising from the subconscious ("that night of time") of his own Blakean Christhood that promises inner and outer unity. Having received this vision of his own greater poetic self, the poet describes in sonnets two through ten the long quest to realize in himself that Christhood which he only sees in a vision in sonnet one.

Undoubtedly, sonnet two may be said to be a continuation of the autobiography of the poet which began in the first sonnet's description of the poet's conception and birth. The poet's early infancy is discussed, and his future "fall" into self-division and estrangement from nature is outlined. As in sonnet one, the figure of Christ

Dylan Thomas in London, circa 1939
(photograph by Bill Brandt)

weaves in and out of the narrative, now fusing and now separating from that of the poet, but always providing the final model of achieved power over opposites and over fallen nature that the growing poet wishes to take for his own.

Sonnet three seeks out the origins of the "fall" into division and thereby defines the role of the Christ-poet composite in overcoming that division. Adam's fall from paradise necessitated Christ's sacrificial entrance into history and/or the poet's childhood unity with nature gave way to a sense of deathliness in nature and dark sexual process. As a result, in both cases, Christ and the poet as incarnate powers are engaged in battle with the forces of decay. By the theory of progression through opposites, they are able to link natural regeneration (spring) to the more permanent springs of Christian salvation and/or the Romantic apocalypse of imagination.

The primary concern of sonnet four is the growth of the poet into a later phase of childhood, where his incessant questioning indicates a precocious facility for language that will later blossom into mature poetry. Having become increasingly aware of his tool of imagination, the creative word, and love, the young poet turns, in the zany and obscure sonnet five, to a scrutiny of his inherited answer to all questions: orthodox Christianity.

In sonnet five the young poet rejects orthodoxy and embarks on a quest through the uncharted waters of world and mind. Institutionalized Christianity has become a self-serving body which perverts Christ's true nature and cheats its members with false dogma; thus, the poet has left the church to search for his own version of Adam's paradise, but what he has found initially was that he was cast forth on a phantasmagoric quest in a weird, natural-supernatural landscape, an exile in the sea of his own experience with no inherited cosmology to order his perceptions. This sonnet's final line seems a conjuration of the Romantic poet's creative faculty, the anima, counterbalanced by the opposing figure of the fatal sirens, the voyaging poet's double-natured source of his own power as he goes forth to forge his own relation to the world and to his own mental faculties.

Still churning about in the fantastic seas of sonnet five, the young poet comes to see in sonnet six the integrated processes of poetic and sexual creation as the avenues by which his own self-redeeming Christhood may be obtained. Beginning in the womb or his sea-cliff room at No. 5 Cwmdonkin Drive, the poet begins the process of poetic creation and the breaking down of the barrier between word and thing. By doing so, the poet discovers that the power of love is released into the world, thus purifying his own perceptions and rendering harmless to him all embodiments of the male and female principles which are integrated in poetry and love. Finally, the young poet begins to write his early poems—the poems of the notebooks—which are predominantly poems about the fall into self-division but which also develop the concurrent theme, fully realized in "Altarwise by Owl-light" itself, of the poet as his own Christ.

The Christlike nature of the poet's self-sacrificing, expressionist act having been established, Thomas proceeds in sonnet seven to examine the young poet's first attempts to write poems that unite language and nature as sacrament. In sonnet eight the poet achieves his own Christhood. Christian myth and Romantic poetics are fused in this climactic sonnet of the sequence. A lucid, simultaneous presentation of Christ's Crucifixion on Golgotha and the poet's "self-immolation in the agonies of the imagination," sonnet eight describes the ultimate Romantic epiphany, in which the poet's imagination unites it-

self with a redeemed external world to which it is linked by a love that, for once, transcends the cycles of sex.

In sonnet nine desert burial is a symbol of the tribulations of the poet's poem of redemption: publishers, critics, and the ravages of time. Abruptly switching from Christian to Egyptian myth, Thomas explores the ill fate of the orthodox "version" of Christ and the fate of his own poems in the hands of critics. Finally, in sonnet ten the poet comes to an understanding of the nature of his poetry, his quest, and his fate. The poet commands his own usurpation of the role of the orthodox Christ and prophesies a final restoration of nature and the self to their Edenic states by the reconciliation of all opposites: let the poet who has displaced Christian myth into a secular, poetic context thus unite the creative word to nature, which that word redeems by using and shaping any myth to suit its own purposes. Let Simon Peter, first pope and founder of the orthodox church, lean out from heaven to ask Christ or Aphrodite what phallic poet this is who has caused Eden to rise out of the waters of nature and of mind. Whatever its own nature, may that garden with its two trees rise up forever on Judgment Day, its central tree (phallus, cross, world tree) a whole made up of various opposites: good and evil, male and female, fruition and decay, the self (phallus) and the world (the world tree), and others.

With all its awkwardnesses, obscurities, and even grotesqueries, "Altarwise by Owl-light," written by a poet of twenty-one, is a heroic attempt to create a powerful Romantic self whose imaginative powers might bring about the realization of the redemption phase of the Romantic myth. A history of the young poet's inner world as well as a history of the poetic self's relation to the external world which it hopes to redeem, "Altarwise by Owl-light" marks the final fruition of the early poetry.

The second phase of Thomas's life and art extends from 1937, the year of his marriage, to 1945, the year of the conclusion of World War II and of the composition of "Fern Hill." This poem marks the end of Thomas's successful transition from his early obscure, subjective, "cosmic" style to his later clear, objective, odelike style, with its prelapsarian vision of a sacramental landscape, perceived and experienced by the child, celebrated by the death-conscious adult poet. Marriage, fatherhood, and war—the three resistantly objective, outer experiences which form the poet's biography in these years—were also stimuli to the development, in this transitional middle phase, of the later, clearer style.

The Thomases spent part of the summer of 1937 in Swansea, then moved on to Caitlin Thomas's mother's house in Hampshire for the winter and spring of 1937-1938. Dylan's sole new poem of 1937 was "I Make This in a Warring Absence," a marriage poem whose subject—a spat—is inappropriately embodied in the clotted imagery of the early style. In the spring of 1938, Thomas's radical revision of "After the Funeral" from the notebooks marks the first real movement toward clarity, the poem emerging as a more sympathetic elegy for his aunt. *The Map of Love* (1939), Thomas's third volume, is a mix of sixteen poems and seven short stories. *Portrait of the Artist as a Young Dog* (1940) comprises objectively realistic stories of his childhood and adolescence in Swansea.

Thomas's marriage satisfied him deeply, but it also created problems that would aggravate his personal flaws and lead him down the road to America and death. In the 1938-1940 period, the Thomases moved back and forth between his parents and her mother, London and Laugharne, where they lived in houses called Eros and Sea View. Caitlin Thomas was pregnant in 1938 and gave birth to the couple's first child, a son, Llewelyn, on 30 January 1939. Turned down for a grant from the Royal Literary Fund, Thomas obtained a little money from doing book reviews, from writing begging letters to friends, and from the Blumenthal Poetry Prize, which brought him $100. He tried to start his own literary fund, "Thomas Flotation Limited," but with no luck. On 18 October 1938 he did his second stint for BBC Radio, appearing on the program "The Modern Muse" with Auden, Spender, Day Lewis, and MacNeice.

One source of income that failed was a projected collection of early stories to be called "The Burning Baby." Both Dent and Europa Press in Paris backed out, for they feared that obscenity charges might arise. In addition, *The Map of Love* and *Portrait of the Artist as a Young Dog* did not sell too well, probably because of the change of mood caused by the outbreak of war in Europe in 1939. However, Thomas's earlier negotiations with his first American publisher, James Laughlin of New Directions, climaxed with the publication of selections from his work in *The World I Breathe* (December 1939). There also survive from this period a few episodes from his un-

finished novel about a young provincial poet's initiation into London, *Adventures in the Skin Trade* (1955), and a comic novel written in collaboration, first with Charles Fisher and later with John Davenport, *The Death of the King's Canary* (1976), a wild detective story whose suspects are caricatures of famous poets and other writers of the day.

Thomas's reaction to the war was complex. Superficially, his only concern was to avoid conscription, to which end he tried sponsoring a writers' antiwar petition and considered declaring himself a conscientious objector on religious grounds. Thomas's letters on this matter are unseemly and narrowly selfish at best. In any case, he need not have worried, for he failed his medical exam, though the reason he did so remains unclear—possibly asthma or weak lungs.

Thomas's deeper response to the war is contained in his moving elegies "Ceremony After A Fire-Raid" and "A Refusal to Mourn the Death, by Fire, of a Child in London." Here, the holiness and the horror of human suffering in war are captured in what may well be the two greatest poems in English written about World War II. The successive experiences of marriage, fatherhood, and war also led to the emergence, in the poems of 1941-1945, of an intense nostalgia for the world of the Romantic child, the world of vision in which pantheistic nature is sacred and all things appear in imagination's eye. Thomas's desire to recapture the lost world of the visionary child of Romantic tradition was made more intense as the war continued from 1940 to 1945.

Thomas's life during the war years centered around the necessity of avoiding the London bombing yet the need for traveling to London to work with Ivan Moffatt and Donald Taylor for Strand Films, Taylor's company, which was then involved in making war documentaries for the Ministry of Information. Here Thomas earned eight pounds to ten pounds weekly for the duration of the war. Still, Thomas was always short of money and ill-advisedly sold the rights to *18 Poems* for fifteen pounds. In a more complicated move, he sold his notebooks to the Lockwood Memorial Library of the State University of New York at Buffalo in the spring of 1941. At the time he spoke of having to "burn your boats" and of his lifelong sense of competition with Keats. Keats died at twenty-six, and Thomas was twenty-six when he sold the notebooks. The young bohemian poet was dead, and Thomas resolved not to keep going back to the notebooks

The Boat House, Laugharne, Thomas's home from 1949 until his death

for more poems. After a dry period as poet (1941-1943), Thomas emerged at the war's end as the poet of "Poem in October" and "Fern Hill," writing of lost childhoods in odes of great clarity and wide feeling.

The movements of the Thomases during the war years are complex. Spending Christmas of 1939 with Caitlin Thomas's mother, the Thomases moved on, in the summer of 1940, to Marshfield, the country home of the gregarious poet and critic John Davenport. A man of means, Davenport decided to entertain friends lavishly that summer as the war entered its darkest phase. Davenport and Thomas worked on their comic detective novel, *The Death of the King's Canary*, and caroused, while Caitlin Thomas played Mozart on the gramophone and danced. In late 1940 and throughout 1941, the Thomases wandered from one place to another, looking for safety for Caitlin and Llewelyn Thomas: Bishopston, Talsarn in Cardiganshire, and Laugharne Castle. In 1942 they returned to London, where

they lived in two bare studios: first, Sir Alan Herbert's in Hammersmith, and later, No. 3, Wentworth Studios, off the Manresa Road in Chelsea. Caitlin Thomas was pregnant again and gave birth to a daughter, Aeron, in March of 1943.

Caitlin Thomas disapproved of Thomas's work on Taylor's films, and, near the end of the war, of his work for the BBC as broadcaster of various prose reminiscences of his Swansea youth. These activities, along with the increasing dominance of the clowning, drunken, "public" Thomas over the introspective, "private" Thomas who wrote the poems, disturbed her greatly. After leaving No. 5 Cwmdonkin Drive, Thomas always did his best work in Wales in rural isolation. In 1944 and 1945, in fact, he enjoyed a second flowering as a poet in these surroundings, producing poems such as "A Winter's Tale," "A Refusal to Mourn the Death, by Fire, of a Child in London," and "Fern Hill." The widening split between Thomas's roaring London life and persona and his poetic life in Wales became critical by the end of the war, so that the pattern of London partying followed by recuperation and work in Wales was "writ large" as America, especially New York, displaced London in this deadly scheme.

Of Thomas's wartime and postwar filmscripts and broadcasts, little need be said. Most of the scripts were hackwork, written as part of Thomas's job. More relevant to Thomas's postwar poetry of childhood in nature are the prose reminiscences written during the last decade of his life. These are collected in the volume *Quite Early One Morning* (1954). The first, "Reminiscences of Childhood" (1943), is a camera's-eye view of the poet's Swansea childhood, Cwmdonkin Park being his "world within the world"— its hunchback, celebrated in "The Hunchback in the Park," the centerpiece of the broadcast—and ending with Thomas the child flying in fancy over the town now lost in time: "The memories of childhood have no order and no end." The talk "Quite Early One Morning" is a humorous account of a Welsh seaport (New Quay) waking up—a study for his play for voices concerning a whole day in such a town, *Under Milk Wood* (1954). "Memories of Christmas" and the famous "A Child's Christmas in Wales"—the latter a rival still today to Charles Dickens's classic *A Christmas Carol* (1843)—also appeared as broadcasts. "A Child's Christmas in Wales" is a masterful and fantastically detailed recollection of Christmas—its weather, sights, sounds, its food, presents, and its melancholy close—as perceived by the happy child Thomas apparently was. Matching these evocations of Thomas's childhood is the later broadcast "Return Journey" (1947). Here Thomas returns to Swansea—whose town center was gutted by German air raids during the war—in search of his old haunts as adolescent poet and reporter. The narrator inquires after the young Thomas, but the boy, like the pubs and stores and friends he knew, is lost. The narrator's quest comes to an end in Cwmdonkin Park, where the old park keeper answers the question of young Thomas's fate: "Dead . . . Dead . . . Dead . . . Dead . . . Dead . . . Dead."

In addition to these broadcasts about his early life, Thomas often read his own and others' poetry for BBC Radio and took part in dramatic readings. A few BBC talks on poets and poetry also survive as well as prose introductions to his own poetry readings in America. The scripts and talks of the 1940s and the 1950s were essentially done for money or diversion from the poetry, and their importance extends little beyond whatever light they shed on the poetry.

The "Altarwise by Owl-light" sequence represented what Thomas recognized as a carrying of "certain features to their logical conclusion," a task that "had . . . to be done" even though the result be "mad parody." The remainder of Thomas's poetry may be viewed as a second phase (1936-1953) or as two phases: a transitional "middle" phase that consists of the poems on marriage and war (1936-1945), and a final phase, emerging only slightly later than the middle phase (1946-1953), but becoming increasingly dominant in its depiction of the particular sacramental landscapes of childhood. The dominant feature of these later poems is the transformation of the assertive, apocalypse-fostering Romantic self as Christ whose testament is "Altarwise by Owl-light" into a less domineering self—a self as priest, functionary, agent, and medium of the divine power in nature whose interpreter the poet is. This shift implies that Thomas came more and more to realize the resistant otherness of the external world, too easily absorbed into the self in many of the earlier poems by the cosmic analogy, and that subsequently he relinquished his claims to contain all necessary power to transform the outer world. Relying on visionary memory to evoke the spiritualized landscapes of his childhood, Thomas came to find in a vision of sacramental love infusing the landscape the final answer to the problem of the recalcitrant *other* that

baffled him in most of the marriage poems and that posed an almost insurmountable threat in the war poems. The poet's final task was, through imaginative action, to release that power of love into the world.

Many poems on the poetic process from this period register Thomas's struggle to realize the substantial otherness of the external world while at the same time fostering a relationship between self and world based on love. One of these, "Once It was the Colour of Saying," deals with the poet's fears that his early, florid style (a synesthetic "*colour* of *saying*"—italics added) was only a way of drowning external reality, not of achieving any valid relationship with it. Now viewing his earlier verse as a sort of aesthetic indulgence, he calls for a chastening of style that gives the outer world its due as a separate entity. Lines 1-6 describe the earlier verse that "soaked my table" or created a "capsized field" (that is a field that is both overturned and the size of a cap—a field that fits the poet's head) or "seaslides of saying." These colorful words enlivened the outer world, yet now he fears that his imaginative coloring of the external world was an illusion that he must "undo" so that "the charmingly drowned" innundated by the magical charm of the imagination may "arise" in their separateness to live and die as themselves. In a basic change, Thomas is announcing that his future poems of love will seek not to transform the outer world radically to the heart's desire, but rather to honor the integrity and otherness of the object even as he still hopes that a single spirit of love may unite the two.

One of Thomas's most beautiful lyrics, "In My Craft or Sullen Art," affirms that his poetic audience is common humanity. As Thomas says, he writes his poems not for the proud and the great

> But for the lovers, their arms
> Round the griefs of the ages,
> Who pay no praise or wages
> Nor heed my craft or art.

These lines also exhibit Thomas's newly won clarity of expression, so often absent in the earlier poems.

Unlike the poems on poetics—most of which are successful definitions of Thomas's own views on the relation of imagination, nature, and love—ten poems, spread over a decade, that deal with Thomas's own fiery marriage to Caitlin and his subsequent fatherhood have been almost universally condemned. Rushworth Kidder sees in these poems evidence of "reintegrated disintegration," a patchwork of fragments, a "whipped mixture of oil and water" remaining in "unstable union." Trying to discover cosmic implications in a lovers' quarrel or ecstatic union or reunion, Thomas somehow failed in the majority of these poems.

A representative example of the marriage poems is "Into Her Lying Down Head," the immediate occasion for which seems to have been a marriage argument resulting from the poet's sexual jealousy and fears. The specific complaint of the poet is that in sleep Caitlin Thomas dreams of imaginary male lovers who exclude the poet from the crucial consummation of physical love. Egocentrically conceived, this poem seems to argue that the poet's particular needs in his inspiring mate dominate her own needs for an ideal mental lover, a lover that Thomas applauded as a good thing for the poet in poems such as "The Hunchback in the Park" and "Love in the Asylum." Apparently, Thomas is saying that unity of being within himself, between the lovers, and between the lovers and nature depends upon a union of the imagined and the real. Thus, section one may be paraphrased as follows: through orifices of maidenhead, eye, and ear, a woman's imaginary lovers enter her body; the erotic power of nature and the unconscious rise mightily to take her, her conjured images of that power ranging from kings and queens to famous lovers of those betrayed in love or attractive persons passed on the street or stair; behind all these images a single young "blade" scythes the hayfield of her thighs; all England seems her love, the giant Albion, who brought her the new sleep of lost innocence and pregnancy. In section two the poet, meditating on the consequences of the woman's betrayal of him in her dreams, finds that their sacramental love has been turned into a satanic sacrament instead. Then, elaborating largely on how betrayal of human love leads directly to similar betrayals in nature, the poet takes us through analogies between the human lovers and two sand grains, a she bird, grass blade, and stone, lamenting at the end his exclusion from the woman's dream because only his union with her could reverse the similar process of betrayal in nature.

The poem ends with the poet's final lament over his absence from the ceremony of sacramental love. He is "torn up" and mourning in the "sole night" where she is also "alone and still" though unconscious of her betrayal or the poet's

loss. What she sought to do with "the incestuous secret brother," her dream lover, is what only lovemaking with her human lover could accomplish: "to perpetuate the stars" (have children). The imaginary lovers, by separating two human lovers, myriad natural lovers (bird, stone), and the divine from the material in all, deserve their final name—"the severers"—who "bury their dead" of imaginary, infertile sperm in the woman's sleep. In an earlier version, the poem's final lines clearly associate human love and reproduction, divinity in woman, and the sustaining of an external nature informed by goodness:

> Will his lovely hands let run the daughters and sons
>   of the blood?
> Will he rest his pulse in the built breast of impossi-
>   ble great god?
> Over the world uncoupling the moon rises up to no
>   good.

Symbol of love, nature, and imagination, the moon, by her betrayal, turns evil, and nature itself is torn apart like the human lovers—"the world uncoupling."

If the first threat to Thomas's early poetry's obsessive theme of the imaginative identification of poet and cosmos was his experience of marriage and fatherhood, the second, and in many ways more powerful, threat was his experience of the blitz in wartime London. The war was a "pressure of reality" that had to be balanced by a "pressure of imagination," but as tragic subject it had to be handled with the greatest delicacy yet also without flinching before the human suffering of the "others" who had died. Of the handful of poems written on the war, Thomas composed at least two extremely fine poems—"A Refusal to Mourn the Death, by Fire, of a Child in London" and "Ceremony After a Fire-Raid"—that, unlike many war poems, have completely survived their original occasions and contexts.

"A Refusal to Mourn the Death, by Fire, of a Child in London" explains its occasion in its title. Written in four stanzas rhyming *abcabc* with lines 2 and 4 of each stanza being short lines of five syllables and, with the first thirteen lines of the poem forming a single, syntactically grandiloquent sentence, the poem achieves an oracular, stately tone that is appropriate to its grave, weird, and awesome subject: an elegy without mourning for a young girl killed in an air raid in wartime London.

Thomas quite consciously and deliberately embeds within his elegiac statements about the child, himself, and the child's future existence as a part of nature language that makes the psychic and the physical life of all creation and of the single human being correspond to significant stages in the Christian myth: creation (stanza one), Old Testament Judaism (stanza two), New Testament Christianity (stanza three), and, in a significant historical addition, Romantic pantheism (stanza four), which is also a return to the Genesis and creation of stanza one.

In a series of compound adjectives modifying the noun *darkness*, with the hyphens left out for ambiguity, Thomas, in stanza one, magnificently recapitulates the arising of natural creation out of the void and begins to tell us the only conditions (the impending end of all things in an apocalypse of dark stillness) under which he would mourn the child's death:

> Never until the mankind making
> Bird beast and flower
> Fathering and all humbling darkness
> Tells with silence the last light breaking
> And the still hour
> Is come of the sea tumbling in harness.

If stanza one reveals the single human life and the history of nature as parallel to Christian creation, stanza two takes us into the Old Testament for sacramental images of the self's final fusion with nature:

> And I must enter again the round
> Zion of the water bead
> And the synagogue of the ear of corn.

Moving farther along in the Christian myth as analogue, Thomas, in stanza three, describes the girl's death as a merely physical crucifixion ("the mankind of her going"). He refuses to utter the "grave truth" of the Anglican burial service nor will he "blaspheme" down his own "stations of the breath" by speaking of the self-evident youthfulness of the child. Having developed his feelings about the child and pantheism by displacing Genesis, Judaism, and Christianity into Romantic personalism, Thomas completes the cycle in stanza four by touching briefly on Genesis again before moving, without any further analogy to the Christian myth, into direct statements about the union of self and nature according to Romantic doctrine. Although she is "London's daughter," the child is not associated with a single image from the modern cityscape. Instead, she escapes the city, the war, and adulthood's estrang-

ing self-consciousness to join "the first dead," Adam and Eve, as well as the Londoners first killed in the air raids:

> Deep with the first dead lies London's daughter,
> Robed in the long friends,
> The grains beyond age, the dark veins of her
>   mother,
> Secret by the unmourning water
> Of the riding Thames.
> After the first death, there is no other.

The stateliness of the "riding Thames" brings to mind Sir Edmund Spenser's "Sweet Thames, run softly till I end my song" in *Prothalamion*, a not inappropriate association to make, for Thomas's unmourning antielegy celebrates the child's marriage to nature and nature's ongoing fertile power of renewal.

"Poem in October" and "Fern Hill" in *Deaths and Entrances*, two odelike poems whose subjects are the poet's imaginative recollection of his childhood in nature, forecast the dominant pastoral concerns of his final volume of new poems, *In Country Sleep* (1952). "Poem in October" is listed by Vernon Watkins as among those poems that Thomas wrote in 1944-1945 after the horror of living through wartime London "compelled his imagination forward . . . to the beautiful poems evoking childhood." What is significant about "Poem in October" is that it is Thomas's first acknowledged "place poem," a poem set in a particularized landscape. "Poem in October" is set both in the seaside village of Laugharne and on Sir John's Hill, whose green-wooded shouldering cliffs protrude into the neighboring estuary on which Thomas's seaside house was situated.

Beginning in the town (stanzas one and two), the poet climbs Sir John's Hill (stanzas three and four), and there he undergoes a transformation, as he regains his childhood sense of wonder in nature (stanzas five through seven). Identifying the occasion as his thirtieth birthday, Thomas sets the poem in a definite time (1944) as well as in a definite place, thus making "Poem in October" a striking example of a greater Romantic lyric. Beginning with a description of the landscape in the present by the poet as an adult (stanzas one through five), he then vividly recalls the same landscape as he saw it so differently as a child (stanzas five and six and stanza seven, lines 1-4), and he ends by returning to his adult self in the present landscape (stanza seven, lines 5-10), where his exclamation of hope for the fu-

Dylan Thomas in Laugharne graveyard a few months after his father's death in December 1952 (photograph by John Deakin for Condé Nast Publications)

ture represents the rejuvenating power of visionary memory.

Leaving Laugharne on his thirtieth birthday, the poet climbs Sir John's Hill among all the sights and sounds of nature. Then, in a long evocative description, the adult regains his childhood's spontaneous apprehension of nature as ordered, benevolent, and divine. Moving from adult "fancy" to childhood "imagination," Thomas quite clearly indicates the differences in intensity of perception. The merely "blithe country" perceived by the adult is left behind to *turn* down "the other air" and "the blue altered sky" of imaginative perception. Not merely a marvel, now it is a "wonder of summer" with its apples, pears, and currants, and the poet is possessed by familiar sights seen by the imagination:

> And I saw in the turning so clearly a child's
> Forgotten mornings when he walked with his
>   mother
>   Through the parables
>   Of sun light
> And the legends of the green chapels.

In a spot of time or moment of epiphany, the adult poet perceives nature once more as fully divine, its own decipherable language. The poet now possesses completely his own childhood, called "the twice told fields of infancy" because once lived and a second time recollected, and, in one of Thomas's simplest and most moving lines, the poet says of his recovered childhood self: "his tears burned my cheek and his heart moved in mine."

A greater Romantic lyric concludes with an anticipation of the future. Thus, in the short third section of Thomas's poem (stanza seven, lines 5-10), the poet ends the long vision of childhood simply and briefly:

> O may my heart's truth
>   Still be sung
> On this high hill in a year's turning.

Though the "town below lay leaved in October blood" of reddened, fallen leaves, the poet "stood there then in the summer noon" of hilltop and childhood, knowing he must again descend to the town. It was on this high hill of the joyful Romantic child and his heightened consciousness that Thomas wished to stay. "Poem in October," however, stands almost alone in its nearly unadulterated joy and affirmation—possibly the reason it reflects more than any other of his poems the exact form of the greater Romantic lyric.

"Fern Hill," the final poem in *Deaths and Entrances*, represents a peak in Thomas's development, just as "Altarwise by Owl-light" was the culmination of the tendencies in the earlier poems. "Fern Hill" superimposes the adult's less visionary view of nature on top of the child's by various devices, from irony and ambiguity to direct statement, progressive clusters of images, and several parallel syntactical structures that contain these images. "Fern Hill" is an example of the Romantic concern with the growth of a poet's mind, for we see the "fall" of the child's spontaneous perception of visionary nature, the growing into adolescence with its sexual awakening, and adulthood with its consciousness of estrangement, death, and time. Against this dismal flow, however, emerges implicitly a faith in imagination and memory, the faculties of mind that are able to recover, embody, and thus evoke forever the lost childhood vision.

Composed in lines strictly syllabic and with assonantal rhyme, stanza one is the first of three which describe the cycle of a single day at Fernhill from night to day to night. Following the pattern of creation in Genesis, these three stanzas present all the child's days at Fernhill as one holy day, enclosed by a night that only completes the day and is unthreatening. Narrated by the poet as an adult, the poem includes from the very first line a contrast of the Wordsworthian "two consciousnesses" (child and adult) and the twin landscapes they perceive; but though present, the adult's view lurks more often only in certain disturbing ambiguities than in direct statement. In stanza two, the child's joy in nature builds to a climax:

> Time let me play and be
>   Golden in the mercy of his means,
> And green and golden I was huntsman and herds-
>   man, the calves
> Sang to my horn, the foxes on the hills barked clear
>   and cold,
>   And the sabbath rang slowly
>   In the pebbles of the holy streams.

In stanzas three and four, the child sleeps and wakes in utmost security, although hints about death, sad wisdom, and nascent adolescent sexuality foreshadow the inevitable end of the child's world. Stanza four ends with a vision of creation that is stunning in effect:

> So it must have been after the birth of the simple
>   light
> In the first, spinning place, the spellbound horses
>   walking warm
>   Out of the whinnying green stable
>   On to the fields of praise.

The last two stanzas are more completely dominated by the adult poet's understanding of the child's lost world. The poem ends with a full recognition both of the true joy of the child's world and the ineluctable fact of its loss:

> Nothing I cared, in the lamb white days, that time
>   would take me
> Up to the swallow thronged loft by the shadow of
>   my hand,
>   In the moon that is always rising,
>   Nor that riding to sleep
>   I should hear him fly with the high fields
> And wake to the farm forever fled from the child-
>   less land.

> Oh as I was young and easy in the mercy of his
>   means,
>   Time held me green and dying
> Though I sang in my chains like the sea.

Thus, in "Fern Hill," as in "Poem in October," Thomas imaginatively reenters his own childhood consciousness, savoring it, knowing it, and finally recapturing it, but not out of a corrupting nostalgia; for the adult consciousness is also fully developed as a dramatic counterweight to the lost childhood vision.

The last years of Thomas's life (1946-1953) may be divided into two periods: the immediate postwar struggle to find a job and money in England (1946-1949), and the period of the famous reading tours in America (1950-1953).

In 1946-1949 Thomas spent most of his time looking for steady employment in the film industry and at the BBC, and for publishers from whom he sought and sometimes received advances on books that he often did not deliver. Both his actual drinking and his reputation for drinking meant that a permanent job with the BBC was out of the question, although he made frequent broadcasts over radio until the end of his life. In 1948 he signed a contract with Gainsborough Films to produce three scripts during the year, which he did, but his scriptwriting career ended there, and only one of the films was produced.

As early as 1945 Thomas was writing to Oscar Williams about a possible job at Harvard University or *Time* magazine, should he decide to emigrate. James Laughlin, his American publisher, was also approached, in 1946, about Thomas's moving to the United States. These inquiries were fruitless, however, and the Thomases were soon moving again from place to place, with no money. In 1945 Thomas left New Quay for London and spent Christmas of 1945 with A. J. P. Taylor and his wife, Margaret, in Oxford. Margaret Taylor let the Thomases stay in a summerhouse on the grounds for some months, until The Authors' Society granted Thomas £150 from its Travelling Scholarship Fund for an Italian holiday. The Thomases spent time in Rapallo, Florence, and Elba during their vacation, which lasted from April to August 1947. The heat, the language barrier, and the intelligentsia they met in Florence (near which the Thomases had rented a villa) all exasperated Thomas, who drank a great deal of wine and completed his poem "In Country Sleep," a section of his long, unfinished "In Country Heaven."

Thomas was now more and more in demand for public appearances. He did readings in London, often performing brilliantly if he was not too drunk. His failure to show up for an address to the Swansea chapter of the British Medical Association in 1949 was atypical. When it came to public readings, Thomas was unusually reliable. In March of 1949 he even attended a conference in Prague, celebrating the beginning of the Czechoslovak Writers' Union. Politically naive, Thomas did little there besides party and make a vague speech about the international brotherhood of writers.

In May of 1949 the Thomases moved to another house bought for them by Margaret Taylor. This was the now well-known Boat House, in Laugharne, a picturesque seaside village in Wales whose inhabitants are lovingly caricatured in *Under Milk Wood*. Set up on stilts high on a cliff overlooking an estuary into which three small rivers flow, with Sir John's Hill to one side, and surrounded by the gulls and herons that inhabit the poems written during his time there, the Boat House, with its nearby shed (Thomas's workroom), is as romantic in appearance as it must have been uncomfortable to live in. Except for the inevitable, lethal sprees in London and later in America, Thomas lived in Laugharne for most of the rest of his life. The Boat House is now a shrine for tourists.

The Thomas some of these tourists seek is not Thomas the poet, but Thomas-the-Poet, the roaring public image of the Romantic bard which Thomas had cultivated since adolescence. The final exaggerated, grotesque, and deadly version of this persona found the ideal stage for its bloody fifth act when Thomas received an invitation that May from John Malcolm Brinnin, a young American poet and newly appointed director of the YM-YWHA Poetry Center in New York. Thomas asked Brinnin to arrange readings, both in New York and at universities all across America, and suggested January or February 1950 as a convenient time for him to come. From May 1949 until February 1950, Thomas was able to work on poetry again, and on 21 February 1950 he arrived at Idlewild Airport in New York, where Brinnin was waiting for him.

Thomas's first tour of America, which lasted until 1 June 1950 set the pattern for the next three. Beginning with a series of parties and readings in or near New York, Thomas moved on to read at numerous universities, recording his poetry for the Lamont Library at Harvard and for the Library of Congress. Most of the stories about Thomas's wild behavior are collected in Brinnin's *Dylan Thomas in America* (1955). In retrospect, many of the incidents seem merely boorish or boyish, but in the America of the early 1950s, Thomas managed briefly to maintain a reputation as the Dionysian minstrel.

Most of the Thomas stories concern his drinking, awkward sexual advances, petty thievery (especially of shirts), witty remarks, and yet his admittedly miraculous ability to recover from dishevelment to perform stunning readings of his own and others' poetry. He was, he said—in parody of Eliot's self-designation as classicist, royalist, and Anglican—a drunkard, a Welshman, and a lover of women. He had come to America "to continue my lifelong search for naked women in wet mackintoshes." During one party, he lifted Katherine Anne Porter (age fifty-nine) up to the ceiling; at another, an explicit four-letter word descriptive of the sexual theme of his "Ballad of the Long-Legged Bait" silenced conversation. Women babied him, and some slept with him. Academics, whom Thomas—as a dropout—always feared, did not know how to put him at ease. One party with Yale professors was especially uncomfortable.

From the point of view of money, the tour should have been a success—but it was not. Thomas spent most of what he earned on the spot. Brinnin, in fact, secretly placed eight-hundred dollars in a handbag (a gift for Caitlin Thomas) to insure that the poet's wife saw at least that much of Thomas's earnings. Thomas saw Robert Lowell in Iowa City, and in New York City he was introduced to Theodore Roethke, the one American poet he especially wanted to meet. In California, he fell in love with San Francisco and spent an evening with a childhood idol, Charlie Chaplin. Back in New York, Thomas survived a series of farewell parties, began a liaison with a woman whom Paul Ferris and Constantine FitzGibbon call "Sarah," and sailed home on the Queen Elizabeth on 1 June.

The next eighteen months of Thomas's life were spent in England, with one exception. That was a brief trip to Iran in January 1951 to do a documentary film for the Anglo-Iranian Oil Company. Prior to the trip, in the previous September, Caitlin Thomas had caught her husband renewing his affair with Sarah, who was in England. Thomas's marriage was severely strained in 1950-1951, and Caitlin was suspicious thereafter. Throughout the spring and summer of 1951, Thomas strove to repair his marriage and enjoyed his last brief flowering as a lyric poet. He wrote "Lament," "Do Not Go Gentle Into That Good Night," and "Poem on His Birthday," and worked on *Under Milk Wood,* as well as the verse prologue to his forthcoming *Collected Poems: 1934-1952,* "Author's Prologue."

Thomas's second American tour (20 January - 16 May 1952) was much like the first, except that this time Caitlin went along, so even more money was spent, and partygoers were treated to the Thomases' publicly enacted spats. New Directions published his *In Country Sleep,* the six poems written since *Deaths and Entrances,* in February, and the young founders of Caedmon Records persuaded Thomas to record his poetry for their label, an event that would eventually produce a great deal of money, though Thomas would not live to see it. As at the end of the first tour, Thomas again left America totally exhausted and with little profit.

Back in Laugharne, Thomas spent the summer of 1952 working on *Under Milk Wood.* "Author's Prologue" was completed, and on 10 November 1952, Thomas's *Collected Poems: 1934-1952* appeared. The collection was prefaced by an author's note in which Thomas said that his poems were written "for the love of man and in praise of God." In the 102-line "Author's Prologue," Thomas addresses the readers, the "strangers," in the guise of a modern Noah who would save the creatures of the natural world in his ark of art from the molten flood of nuclear holocaust. Looking over this body of early and recent work, most critics granted Thomas the status of major poet. Philip Toynbee called Thomas "the greatest living poet" writing in English. Many were charmed by the pastoral poems, such as "Poem in October," "A Winter's Tale," "In Country Sleep," and the instant favorite, "Fern Hill." Thomas received £250 for winning the Foyle's Poetry Prize for *Collected Poems.*

Thomas's third tour of America was somewhat shorter than the first two, lasting from 21 April to 3 June 1953. This tour saw the premiere of Thomas's play for voices, *Under Milk Wood,* on which Thomas had been meditating and working since the late 1930s. Earlier entitled "The Town That Was Mad" and "Llareggub: A Piece for Radio Perhaps," *Under Milk Wood* borrows the daylong structure of James Joyce's *Ulysses* (1922) as Thomas takes the listener through a typical day

in the lives of a host of inhabitants of a small Welsh sea town. The geography of the village, from Milk Wood to Coronation Street and down to Cockle Row and the sea, is reminiscent of that of New Quay, but the flavor of the work, the caricatured citizens with their Dickensian eccentricities, reflects Thomas's years in Laugharne.

Under Milk Wood celebrates the town, what the First Voice calls "this place of love," and the play becomes a comic variant of the happy pastoral world of the late poems. Love in all its forms and guises flourishes in the forgiving presence of Captain Cat. As the play begins and ends at night, the brief day of love and sun that the inhabitants enjoy seems more poignant than the superficially playful tone of the piece might suggest. When Captain Cat, for instance, converses with the image of his long-dead Rosie, she fades away at last with these lines:

Remember her.
She is forgetting.
The earth which filled her mouth
Is vanishing from her.
Remember me.
I have forgotten you.
I am going into the darkness of the darkness forever.
I have forgotten that I was ever born.

Like much great comedy, *Under Milk Wood* holds within itself a tragic sense of the brevity and the preciousness of human love and life.

Under Milk Wood had its premiere at the Fogg Museum, Harvard, on 3 May 1953, in an unfinished state with Thomas reading all the parts. On 14 May the first full-cast reading occurred at the YM-YWHA Poetry Center in New York with Thomas reading the parts of First Voice, Reverend Eli Jenkins, and the Second and Fifth Drowned. This production, as well as the second one done two weeks later, was a great success with the audience. During this time also, Thomas eagerly agreed to write the libretto for a proposed opera with Igor Stravinsky. The subject was intriguing and reflected Thomas's deepest feelings about language and innocence: after a nuclear holocaust, a new Adam would recreate for his Eve a new language in which there would be no abstractions. The words would blow from a new Tree of Knowledge, each of whose leaves would be imprinted with one letter of the alphabet. It would be a world of physical perception only—people, things, and words referring to things. (Thomas was about to fly to meet Stravin-

To E P

Twenty Three.

The force that through the green fuse drives the flower
Drives my green age ; that blasts the roots of trees
Is my destroyer.
And I am dumb to tell the eaten rose
How at my sheet goes the same crooked worm,
And dumb to holla thunder to the skies
How at my cloths flies the same central
storm

The force that through the green fuse drives the flower
Drives my green age, that blasts the roots of trees
Is my destroyer.
And I am dumb to tell the crooked rose
My youth is bent by the same wintry fever.

The force that drives the water through the rocks
Drives my red blood ; that dries the mouthing
stream
Turns mine to wax.

Page from the manuscript for "The Force That Through the Green Fuse Drives the Flower" (Lockwood Memorial Library, State University of New York at Buffalo)

sky in California to begin work on this opera when he died.) On 3 June, Coronation Day, when he flew back to London, he seemed on the verge of becoming as successful as a writer of more dramatic, public works—like the radio play and the proposed opera—as he had been as a successful lyric poet for the last twenty years.

Between June and October 1953 Thomas was in Britain. He covered the International Eisteddfod in Wales that July, worked on the "Elegy" for his father and, over Caitlin's strong objections, resolved to go back to America that year. Alcoholism and the chronic inability to take charge of his life so as to solve the problem of money and regular employment made another trip to America seem the only escape from an impossible situation.

Thomas's fourth and final American tour began on 19 October 1953 and ended with his death on 9 November at St. Vincent's Hospital in New York City. On 24 and 25 October, Thomas read First Voice in the third and fourth productions of *Under Milk Wood* at the YM-YWHA. He participated in a "Poetry and the Film" discussion, organized by Cinema 16, on 28 October. A New York doctor, Milton Feltenstein, who had treated him on his third visit, was called in to give Thomas an injection of ACTH to relieve the effects of incessant drinking. Thomas must have known the end was near. To one person he said: "I've seen the gates of hell tonight," and to his intimate friend Liz Reitell he said he wished to die and "to go into the garden of Eden." Waking up during the night of 3 November Thomas left his room at the Chelsea Hotel and returned in an hour or so, saying "I've had eighteen straight whiskeys. I think that's the record." The next night, 4 November, he fell into unconsciousness and was rushed to St. Vincent's. He lingered in an irreversible coma, caused by a lifetime of alcoholic poisoning, but probably aggravated by Feltenstein's ill-advised injections (possibly of morphine) earlier in the day on 4 November. Caitlin arrived before he died, went into hysterics and was temporarily straitjacketed and placed in a Long Island clinic. After his death on 9 November, Thomas was buried in the churchyard in Laugharne, where a simple white cross marks his grave. He was thirty-nine.

Between 1946 and his death in 1953 Thomas composed only nine poems, two of which are fragments, in addition to several BBC broadcasts on childhood and the play *Under Milk Wood*. Six of the nine poems appeared in the volume *In Country Sleep* (1952): "In Country Sleep," "Over Sir John's Hill," "In the White Giant's Thigh," "Poem on His Birthday," "Lament," and "Do Not Go Gentle Into That Good Night." In addition to these poems, Thomas wrote "Author's Prologue," the long verse preface to *Collected Poems*. "Elegy," left unfinished at the poet's death, was, after "Do Not Go Gentle Into That Good Night," Thomas's second poem on his father's death. "In Country Heaven," the framing poem of the ambitious unfinished sequence by the same name, exists in several drafts.

In the final poems, the poet still appears as an intermediary figure—father, Aesop, lapidary, local historian, Noah, sea voyager—but one who is less an active agent than a more deeply satisfied, happily resigned observer, spectator, describer, witness, and perceiver of a spiritualized landscape whose mysteries now seem more fathomable. The great evils of both the early and the middle poems, time and death, are finally worked into the poet's vision of nature as holy; in fact, all of the last nine poems deal with death in some fashion. Finally, Thomas tried to create poems in which what he understood as "God" and "man," "heaven" and "earth," becomes clear. In trying to come to terms with death and God, the natural and the supernatural, Thomas begins but does not complete a reintroduction of the "cosmic" perspective of the earlier poems as a background to poems that still continue to be set in a localized landscape.

The most ambitious of these poems of his last years is the unfinished "In Country Heaven." In a long prose synopsis of the epic action of this poem and in an extant fragment of a framing poem, "In Country Heaven," Thomas tells us that the earth has destroyed itself in an atomic war. Learning of the death of earth, God weeps, and his pastoral retainers, "heavenly hedgerow-men," recall what they can of their lives on earth. The three poem sections that Thomas completed for the overall poem are "In Country Sleep," "Over Sir John's Hill," and "In the White Giant's Thigh."

Like its predecessors, "Poem in October" and "Fern Hill," "In Country Sleep" deals with the problem of the perception of nature by the child and by the adult. Unlike the earlier poems, however, "In Country Sleep" greatly lessens, in fact almost entirely abolishes, the sense of a great divide between child and adult in the perception of nature as holy. Although the poet, speaking the poem to his sleeping infant daughter, identifies a mysterious figure called the "thief" who will visit the child, this thief, a development of the similar figure of "Time" in "Fern Hill," robs the child of its visionary perception of nature only in order to perpetuate a higher unity and greater good after adulthood's separation from continuous vision: that greater good is the assumption of the grown-up child into Country Heaven, where it shall enjoy an eternal, deepened apprehension of nature as vision. Significantly, it is the father in the poem who describes, in a long chain of epiphanies, the revelation of Country Heaven *within* the landscape. Unlike "Poem in October" and "Fern Hill," in which the perception of holy nature was carefully ascribed to the child, here that distinction is pointedly omitted. In fact, the child remains asleep throughout the entire poem, and the poet, who addresses her directly in section one, moves to the more objective third-person perspective in section two, in order to show that these epiphanies are his as well as hers. Only the father's adult knowledge that the thief must come and his less intense response to nature separate him from his daughter.

Unlike "In Country Sleep" with its sweeping landscape, the second of the three poem sections, "Over Sir John's Hill," is almost a case history or outdoor laboratory experiment seeking answers to two questions: how can particular acts of killing in nature be justified, and how can the poet possibly write poems about visionary landscapes that keep collapsing into scenes of death?

"Over Sir John's Hill" is written in a complicated stanza of twelve lines of various lengths, carefully patterned with syllabics and end rhymes that may be full or assonantal, and with a free use of sprung rhythm. The general action of the poem's five stanzas is as follows: above Sir John's Hill, a hawk waits to kill sparrows and other small birds, while below a heron and the poet observe. While the sparrows answer the hawk's call for their deaths, the poet praises both hawk and sparrows for the parts they play in the natural, holy cycle. Described as a saint or priest, the heron seems as conscious as the poet of the mystery of death, and his mournful singing is transcribed by the lapidary-poet onto a stone by the shore. God is asked to have mercy on the sparrows and to save their souls.

Observing the slaughter, the poet is a priest reading from the psalter, nature's priest who interprets her actions, as well as being an Aesop, whose animal tales ended with moral statements drawn from the action of the tales. Also, in creat-ing his own poems, the poet makes the poem a critique of nature: nature is a book the poet reads, and his poem is his analysis of that book. By re-creating the landscape in his poem, entwining within that re-creation his own sympathies and thematic interpretation of the outer landscape, the poet is completing the process of understanding nature by linking outer landscape to inner, subjective response in a single imaginative act.

The birds that engaged in child's play were innocent and are now guilty, that were living are now dead, that received justice are now candidates for mercy. These opposites are significant to an understanding of the poet's call on God to "have mercy" on the birds "For their souls' song." God exists not independently but as an immanence in nature ("God in his whirlwind silence save"). There is even a hint that the birds are a part of God, his voice, like the hymning heron and the fabling poet, without all of whom God cannot speak or sing. The final completed poem section of "In Country Heaven" is "In the White Giant's Thigh." Like the paternal and Aesopian roles of the previous two poems, the poet's role here as what Walford Davies calls "the sad historian of a Welsh pastoral community" is one that places him at some distance from the landscape but in a position of teacher, interpreter, chronicler, and commemorator of the events, past and present, that make up the history of the landscape. Walking on a hillside, the poet dreams of women long dead, who once met and made love to their lovers there. Though the women and their lovers are now turned to dust, the poet longs to know their undying love: "Teach me the love that is evergreen." The poem becomes a great celebration of the physical joys of love in a rustic setting.

Another moving poem on love and death is the villanelle Thomas addressed to his dying father, "Do Not Go Gentle Into That Good Night." The point of the poem is contained in its double refrain: "Do not go gentle into that good night. / Rage, rage against the dying of the light." Thomas examines different ways to meet death—that of wise men, good men, wild men, and grave men (such as philosophers, moralists, hedonists, everyman)—and finds all ways of meeting death inadequate. The only solution is to live each moment of life with a burning intensity, yet also recognizing inevitable death as "good," a part of the scheme of things. "Do Not Go Gentle Into That Good Night," in its powerful simplicity and genuine sympathy for the dying father, is one of the best villanelles in English. Equally moving is an elegy to his father, the unfinished poem in terza rima, "Elegy," found among Thomas's papers after his death.

Two final poems that draw on the landscape of Laugharne to assert the poet's faith in life and sacramental nature are "Poem on His Birthday" and "Author's Prologue." In the birthday poem, Thomas affirms ambiguously his faith in "fabulous, dear God" and in "Heaven that never was / Nor will be ever" yet which nonetheless is "always true." Like the seaside world of fish and fowl, the poet rejoices in life and resolves to praise life even as he approaches his own end:

> That the closer I move
> To death, one man through his sundered hulks,
> The louder the sun blooms
> And the tusked, ramshackling sea exults;
> And every wave of the way
> And gale I tackle, the whole world then,
> With more triumphant faith
> That ever was since the world was said,
> Spins its morning of praise.

Thomas's last finished poem, and one of his best, is "Author's Prologue" to *Collected Poems: 1934-1952*. Set in the Laugharne estuary, with the poet at work in his cliffside hut, the poem divides into two parts. The first half is in four sections: an opening description of the seaside below Thomas's workshop window in Laugharne; a contrasting description of the great cities of the world that the poet imagines will be gutted by nuclear firestorms; a meditation on the nature of poetic creation in light of these two descriptions; and finally, a description of a terrible molten flood that is flowing westward from London toward Wales, where the poet as Noah is building his ark-poems against the coming flood. Nature is holy, but the poet is deeply disturbed. Nuclear war threatens to annihilate the world, which it is his task to praise. Building his ark-poems out of love, the poet symbolically serves the members of creation by releasing a saving love into the world of the Cold War. The second half of the poem, in fact, is a long call to the animals to come into the poet's wordy ark and ride out the molten flood in safety. At the end of the poem, in Shelleyan fashion, love transforms hatred and destruction:

> We will ride out alone, and then,
> Under the stars of Wales,

> Cry, Multitudes of arks! Across
> The water lidded lands,
> Manned with their loves they'll move,
> Like wooden islands, hill to hill,
> Huloo, my proud dove with a flute!
> Ahoy, old, sea-legged fox,
> Tom tit and Dai mouse!
> My ark sings in the sun
> At God speeded summer's end
> And the flood flowers now.

The sun shines over the ark into the stilled flood water, transforming the rage and fear of humanity into flowers. The fire and water images that first signaled natural order and then man-made deathliness now again coalesce fruitfully and peacefully in the poem's consummate flowering flood. The sailing arks are flowers on the flood because they are also seeds of windblown puffballs. The flowering flood, too, is all of the poems in *Collected Poems*. Poetry, nature, and love—the flood is inseminated by the beams of the sun and "flowers" into a new creation of life on earth. Finally, the rainbow, symbol of divine covenant with an earlier Noah, is also the flower of the flood.

A complete integration of Thomas's Romantic concerns, "Author's Prologue" presents a landscape in whose events we can see the projection of Thomas's complete inner poetic life: the endless struggle of the self to find its place in the landscape without being annihilated by absorption into it; the linkage of inner poetic process and events in the external, natural world; the linkage of word and thing both in nature and man as not ontologically dissimilar; the fostering of love by imaginative action as the poet's way of deeply communing with all that is outside the self; the poet's assumption of the role of Christlike savior, first of himself, and, in his latest poems, of the natural world threatened by the dark products of scientific rationalism and the antinatural "cities of nine / Days' night"; and even that most difficult of Romantic concerns, the integration of poetic creation with revolutionary political action.

During the last years of his life and just after his death, Dylan Thomas may well have been the most popular major poet since Byron. Unlike Byron, whose life and poetry enhanced and illuminated one another, Thomas lived a life at odds with his deepest poetic instincts. Thomas wrote his best poems in Wales and about Wales—about his childhood and experience of nature there as a child. He worked best in comfortable, utterly middle-class surroundings, whether in his room at No. 5 Cwmdonkin Drive or in one of

John Malcolm Brinnin and Dylan Thomas

the many places in rural Wales and England that Caitlin Thomas made into a home for him. In London or in New York, little truly creative work was done, and Thomas's public image and attendant drunkenness eventually created an unbridgeable split in his nature. Like Arthur Rimbaud, Paul Verlaine, Hart Crane, and others, Thomas became ultimately self-destructive.

Dylan Thomas the legend now seems sadly dated, and the hour of his public fame has passed as other suicidally Dionysian figures in art and the entertainment world fill his place, but Thomas the man remains fascinating, pitiable, yet tragically heroic as well; for in spite of the dark side of his nature, he did produce a substantial body of poems, modern in technique and Romantic in theme, the best of which seem able to stand the test of time and the shifts in poetic fashion that it brings. Criticism of Thomas's poetry has, of course, been severe. It has been called narrow in emotional and intellectual range, hopelessly obscure in the earlier years, narcissistic, nostalgic, lacking in nuance and subtlety, and incurably adolescent in sensibility. Yet T. S. Eliot, W. H. Auden, Stephen Spender, Edith Sitwell, Kathleen Raine, and many other poets have praised Thomas's best work.

If, as Yvor Winters once said, a great poet is a poet who has written at least one great poem, then Thomas may well be just inside the circle of major poets in the twentieth century. Cer-

tainly on the basis of such poems as "Altarwise by Owl-light," "The Hunchback in the Park," "A Refusal to Mourn the Death, by Fire, of a Child in London," "Ceremony After A Fire-Raid," "A Winter's Tale," "Poem in October," "Fern Hill," and "Do Not Go Gentle Into That Good Night," Thomas is, at the very least, one of the greatest lyricists in the ongoing Romantic tradition.

Letters:

Letters to Vernon Watkins, edited by Vernon Watkins (London: Dent & Faber, 1957; New York: New Directions, 1957);

"Love Letters From a Poet to his Wife," *McCall's*, 93 (February 1966): 78, 173;

Selected Letters of Dylan Thomas, edited by Constantine FitzGibbon (London: Dent, 1966; New York: New Directions, 1967);

Twelve More Letters (Stoke Ferry, Norfolk, U.K.: Turret Books, 1969);

The Collected Letters of Dylan Thomas, edited by Paul Ferris (London: Dent, 1985; New York: Macmillan, 1985).

Bibliographies:

J. Alexander Rolph, *Dylan Thomas: A Bibliography* (London: Dent, 1956; New York: New Directions, 1956);

Ralph Maud, *Dylan Thomas in Print: A Bibliographical History* (Pittsburgh: University of Pittsburgh Press, 1970).

Biographies:

John Malcolm Brinnin, *Dylan Thomas in America* (Boston: Atlantic/Little, Brown, 1955);

Caitlin Thomas, *Leftover Life to Kill* (London: Putnam's, 1957; Boston: Atlantic/Little, Brown, 1957);

Bill Read, *The Days of Dylan Thomas* (London: Weidenfeld & Nicolson, 1964; New York: McGraw-Hill, 1964);

Constantine FitzGibbon, *The Life of Dylan Thomas* (London: Dent, 1965; Boston: Atlantic/Little, Brown, 1965);

Nicolette Devas, *Two Flamboyant Fathers* (London: Collins, 1966);

Andrew Sinclair, *Dylan Thomas: No Man More Magical* (New York: Holt, Rinehart & Winston, 1975);

Paul Ferris, *Dylan Thomas* (London: Hodder & Stoughton, 1977; New York: Dial Press, 1977);

Daniel Jones, *My Friend Dylan Thomas* (London: Dent, 1977);

Rollie McKenna, *Portrait of Dylan: A Photographer's Memoir*, introduction by Brinnin (Owings Mills, Md.: Stemmer House, 1982);

Gwen Watkins, *Dylan Thomas and Vernon Watkins: Portrait of a Friendship* (Seattle: University of Washington Press, 1983);

Rob Gittins, *The Last Days of Dylan Thomas* (London: Macdonald, 1986);

Caitlin Thomas, with George Tremlett, *Caitlin: A Warring Absence* (London: Secker & Warburg, 1986).

References:

John Ackerman, *Dylan Thomas: His Life and Work* (London: Oxford University Press, 1964);

Sam Adams, ed., *Poetry Wales: A Dylan Thomas Number*, 9 (Autumn 1973);

John Bayley, *The Romantic Survival* (London: Constable, 1957);

John Malcolm Brinnin, ed., *A Casebook on Dylan Thomas* (New York: Crowell, 1960);

Robert K. Burdette, *The Saga of Prayer: The Poetry of Dylan Thomas* (The Hague: Mouton, 1972);

Richard Burns, *Ceri Richards and Dylan Thomas: Keys to Transformation* (London: Enitharmon, 1981);

C. B. Cox, ed., *Dylan Thomas: A Collection of Critical Essays* (Englewood Cliffs, N.J.: Prentice-Hall, 1966);

Aneirin Talfan Davies, *Dylan: Druid of the Broken Body* (London: Dent, 1964);

Walford Davies, *Dylan Thomas* (Cardiff: University of Wales Press, 1972);

Davies, *Dylan Thomas* (Portsmouth, U.K.: Open University Press, 1976);

Davies, Introduction and notes in *Dylan Thomas: Selected Poems* (London: Dent, 1974);

Davies, ed., *Dylan Thomas: New Critical Essays* (London: Dent, 1972);

Clark Emery, *The World of Dylan Thomas* (Coral Gables: University of Miami Press, 1962; London: Dent, 1971);

J. M. and M. G. Farringdon, *A Concordance and Word Lists to the Poems of Dylan Thomas* (Swansea, U.K.: Ariel House, 1980);

G. S. Fraser, *Dylan Thomas* (London: Longmans, Green, 1957; revised, 1972);

Georg Gaston, *Dylan Thomas: A Reference Guide* (Boston: G. K. Hall, 1987);

Gaston, ed., *Critical Essays on Dylan Thomas* (Boston: G. K. Hall, 1989);

Margaret Hardesty, *That Momentary Peace: The Poem* (Washington: D.C.: University Press of America, 1982);

David Holbrook, *Dylan Thomas: The Code of Night* (London: Athlone, 1972);

Holbrook, *Llareggub Revisited: Dylan Thomas and the State of Modern Poetry* (London: Bowes & Bowes, 1962);

T. H. Jones, *Dylan Thomas* (Edinburgh: Oliver & Boyd, 1963);

R. B. Kershner, *Dylan Thomas: The Poet and His Critics* (Chicago: American Library Association, 1976);

Rushworth Kidder, *Dylan Thomas: The Country of the Spirit* (Princeton: Princeton University Press, 1973);

H. H. Kleinman, *The Religious Sonnets of Dylan Thomas* (Berkeley & Los Angeles: University of California Press, 1963);

Jacob Korg, *Dylan Thomas* (New York: Twayne, 1965);

Gary Lane, *A Concordance to the Poems of Dylan Thomas* (Metuchen, N.J.: Scarecrow Press, 1976);

Min Lewis, *Laugharne and Dylan Thomas* (London: Dobson, 1967);

Ralph Maud, *Entrances to Dylan Thomas' Poetry* (Pittsburgh: University of Pittsburgh Press, 1963);

J. Hillis Miller, *Poets of Reality* (Cambridge, Mass.: Harvard University Press, 1966);

William Moynihan, *The Craft and Art of Dylan Thomas* (Ithaca, N.Y.: Cornell University Press, 1966);

Louise Murdy, *Sound and Sense in Dylan Thomas's Poetry* (The Hague: Mouton, 1966);

H. R. Neuville, *The Major Poems of Dylan Thomas* (New York: Monarch, 1965);

Elder Olson, *The Poetry of Dylan Thomas* (Chicago: University of Chicago Press, 1954);

Annis Pratt, *Dylan Thomas's Early Prose: A Study in Creative Mythology* (Pittsburgh: University of Pittsburgh Press, 1970);

A. M. Reddington, *Dylan Thomas: A Journey from Darkness to Light* (New York: Paulist Press, 1968);

Tryntje Seymour, *Dylan Thomas' New York* (Owings Mills, Md.: Stemmer House, 1978);

Don Sinnock, *The Dylan Thomas Landscape* (Swansea, U.K.: Celtic Educational Services, 1975);

Derek Stanford, *Dylan Thomas: A Literary Study* (London: Spearman, 1954; revised, 1964);

E. W. Tedlock, ed., *Dylan Thomas: The Legend and*

the Poet (London: Heinemann, 1960);

William York Tindall, *A Reader's Guide to Dylan Thomas* (New York: Farrar, Straus, 1962);

Henry Treece, *Dylan Thomas* (London: Drummond, 1949; revised edition, London: Benn, 1956);

Robert C. Williams, *A Concordance to the Collected Poems of Dylan Thomas* (Lincoln: University of Nebraska Press, 1967).

Papers:

Thomas's notebooks are located in the Lockwood Memorial Library of the State University of New York at Buffalo. The Harry Ransom Humanities Research Center at the University of Texas, Austin, has a large miscellaneous collection. Other material exists in the BBC Archives, the British Library, at M.I.T., and at Harvard University.

Index to Volume 7

Index

This index includes proper names: people, places, and works mentioned in the texts of entries for Volume 7. The primary checklists, which appear at the beginning of each entry, are not included in this index. Also omitted are the names London and Dublin, because they appear so frequently. Volume 8 of the *Concise Dictionary of British Literary Biography* includes a cumulative proper-name index to the entire series.

Cumulative Index of Author Entries for
Concise Dictionary of British Literary Biography

Cumulative Index
of Author Entries

ISBN 0-8103-7987-2